What people are sa

Conversations with So

Dr. Neal Grossman's book, *Conversations with Socrates and Plato,* takes the reader from a beginning understanding of afterlife research to a much broader and more in-depth view of the implications of these findings.

Is it Neal, or is it Plato? I am not sure where to draw that line. What I am sure of is that all of the quotes in the book come from some of the most brilliant people who ever lived. I include Neal in that group.

Allan Botkin, PsyD, author, *Induced After Death Communication: A Miraculous Therapy for Grief and Loss*

What happens when Plato and Socrates have an extended chat with a contemporary philosopher about things that matter – the nature of our mind, sexuality, child-rearing, life and death, the hereafter, and dozens of other issues that perplex all of us? I know of nothing comparable to philosopher Neal Grossman's remarkable book. *Conversations with Socrates and Plato* is spiced with wisdom, wit and humor on every page. It presents a perspective of life and social conduct in which consciousness is fundamental, not derived from the atoms and molecules of our physical brain, and in which a deep unity and connectedness between people are factual. To see why these majestic views are valid, and what difference they can make in your life, buckle up and jump in!

Larry Dossey, MD, author of *One Mind: How Our Individual Mind Is Part of a Greater Consciousness and Why It Matters*

A fascinating dialog about a possible future in which "all together seek the common advantage of all." Neal Grossman, a professional philosopher uniquely qualified for such a task, lays out in detail how

our future children must be educated for this vision to be realized. The book is a feast of well-written, lively discussion of many of the subjects that thoughtful people wonder about. Neal's rich and original insights about the nature and origin of beauty, in particular music, and what we should expect at death especially delighted me. And the final pages will be treasured.
Prof. Stafford Betty, PhD, author and academic

Conversations with Socrates and Plato by Neal Grossman is original in style and substance. Grossman has authored a book-length dialogue between himself and Socrates, Plato, Spinoza, and William James. With this cast of characters, we are taken through spirited discussions of basic aspects of social reality: reason, language, emotion, love, friendship, sexuality, beauty, inspiration, all this culminating in a fresh and daring consideration of old age and death. The key to the importance and great value of this book lies in the subtitle. A social order that is "post-materialist" must also be post-consumerist, post-capitalist, and post-militarist. So this is a book about a necessary revolution of consciousness, and deserves to be widely read.
Michael Grosso, PhD, author of *The Final Choice: Death or Transcendence?*

Through a fantastic (double entendre) conversation with four now-disembodied philosophical giants, Grossman takes readers on a playful joyride through the highlights of Western philosophy, all in pursuit of very serious subjects: the nature of human existence and of the social order that would enable humanity to proceed from its currently precarious future on earth to a future characterized by dynamic yet secure sustainability. Previous knowledge of philosophy helpful but not required to join and enjoy the ride!
Janice Holden, EdD, LPC-S, NCC, ACMHP, Chair Professor, University of North Texas

This is one of the most innovative, meaningful, and historically important books I have ever read. Dr. Neal Grossman, Associate Professor Emeritus of Philosophy from the University of Illinois in Chicago, has spent years engaging in conversations – in his head – with four of the greatest minds in human history. Sub-titled "A Post-Materialist Social Order," the timing of this book is propitious: its publication occurs during the founding of the Academy for the Advancement of Postmaterialist Sciences (www.AAPSglobal.com). Grossman's book provides a philosophical grounding and vision for this profound evolution in human consciousness and understanding. Are these dialogues fictional, or are they real? The conclusion from contemporary postmaterialist science is that we should not only thank Dr. Grossman for writing this seminal book, but we should express our deepest gratitude to Socrates, Plato, Spinoza, and William James for their continuing wisdom and caring as well.
Prof. Gary E. Schwartz, The University of Arizona, author of *The Afterlife Experiments* and *Super Synchronicity*

Conversations with Socrates and Plato

How a Post-Materialist Social Order Can Solve the Challenges of Modern Life and Insure Our Survival

Conversations with Socrates and Plato

How a Post-Materialist Social Order Can Solve the Challenges of Modern Life and Insure Our Survival

Neal Grossman

Winchester, UK
Washington, USA

JOHN HUNT PUBLISHING

First published by iff Books, 2019
iff Books is an imprint of John Hunt Publishing Ltd., No. 3 East Street, Alresford, Hampshire SO24 9EE, UK
office@jhpbooks.com
www.johnhuntpublishing.com
www.iff-books.com

For distributor details and how to order please visit the 'Ordering' section on our website.

ISBN: 978 1 78904 143 9
978 1 78904 144 6 (ebook)
Library of Congress Control Number: 2018943172

A CIP catalogue record for this book is available from the British Library.

Design: Stuart Davies

UK: Printed and bound by CPI Group (UK) Ltd, Croydon, CR0 4YY
US: Printed and bound by Thomson-Shore, 7300 West Joy Road, Dexter, MI 48130

Contents

Foreword

by Eben Alexander

Cultures tend to follow the lead of their more profound thinkers in shaping the world-view adopted by society at large. Hence, humanity over the last century or so has tended to follow the lead of scientific thought. That conventional public version of science can be broadly labeled as reductive materialism, highlighting the assumption that all that exists is the material world (also known as physicalism, the notion that all that exists is physical matter).

Of course, such a scientific stance demands that the brain must *create* mind or consciousness, since nothing exists but the physical world perceived with the physical senses. A profound implication is that humans do not have free will. Assuming that thoughts and perceptions are nothing more than the confusing result of chemical reactions and electron fluxes in the substance of the brain, what would be the agent or source to inject "free will" to influence the course of those molecular reactions and larger scale events in human lives?

The scientific revolution has been ongoing for the last four centuries or so, and the most recent 100 years mark the culmination of such thought. It has converged on this notion of physicalism, because that is what many of those scientists have studied — the physical world. Crucially, they've missed one important fact — that what humans witness is phenomenal conscious experience, but never the direct "physical" reality presumed to underlie it.

According to modern neuroscience, all such experience, perception and thought depend on the activity of the brain's neurons. And yet those neurons are not operating like balls on billiard tables with Newtonian determinism applied to all the relevant particles. Each neuron is absolutely functioning in the realm of Heisenberg's Uncertainty Principle, where tight spatial confinement of ions in ion channels opens wide the momentum vector. Thus, the very action of neuronal firing at the fundament of all thought and perception is directly due to quantum effects. To those who muse over the confusing aspects of consciousness and quantum physics, it becomes obvious that they are two sides of the same coin.

Recent advances in psychology (especially parapsychology, with all of the associated evidence of non-local consciousness) and quantum physics are converging towards a shocking, yet liberating, realization — that the universe is mental, and that the objective physical universe is but a projection from the more primordial organizing forces of the collective mind. As these extraordinary features of reality are illuminated, mysterious but empirically refined over many decades, a new world-view is emerging. It is one that supports the foundational reality of metaphysical (or ontological) idealism — that is, that all of physical reality is projected out of consciousness.

A physical mechanism for mind-over-matter, and for the explication of our witnessing of an apparent mental universe, are the extraordinary gifts of this arrangement. The physics community, operating from a fundamental disdain for the nonphysical, or spiritual, thus broadly assumes that, for example, Hugh Everett's Many-Worlds Interpretation of infinite parallel universes emerging from every subatomic observation is sufficient to explain the measurement paradox in quantum physics. The emerging scientific consensus suggests we would be wise to follow the lead of the founding fathers of the field (i.e. Max Planck, Wolfgang Pauli, Erwin Schrödinger and others) who all suggested that consciousness is fundamental in the universe, and that the physical is projected from the mental, not the other way around.

As the scientific community begins to make sense of the implications of this fundamental shift in world-view, it is crucial to realize the erroneous basis of so many assumptions about the nature of reality, originating in the falsehoods of materialism and its associated illusion of separation. And as a consequence, we must now modify our social fabric and larger aspects of human behavior to reflect this radical new unified reality.

Scientific models of consciousness, informed through increasingly-refined experiments in quantum physics, not only allow for, but in many ways *demand* the notion that we are spiritual beings in a spiritual universe. This shift in world-view energizes a seismic shift in our understanding of who we are, where we came from, and where this is all going, both for individuals, and for human society at large.

Arguably, many worsening problems in modern society, such as the opioid crisis, rising rates of depression and suicide, multiple theaters of modern warfare and violent conflict, destabilizing economic polarization, cataclysmic ecological damage, etc., are the result of the false sense of separation inherent in physicalist thought. Combined with the egotistical self-focus of our modern society, and a general lack of responsibility for one's decisions towards the higher good, this spiritual vacuum in our modern world contributes to the decline of our entire civilization.

How can we most effectively benefit humanity given this radical new world-view? Enter Neal Grossman, an emeritus associate professor of philosophy at the University of Illinois at Chicago whose academic career began with the study of quantum physics at the Massachusetts Institute of Technology (MIT). Throughout his career, he harbored a profound interest in the works of Plato, Socrates, Benedict Spinoza and William James.

Neal calls these great thinkers to task in re-imagining the possibilities for our current world. They examine how we might transform as a result of the radical shift in understanding that the nonphysical realms are real, that we seem to be sharing one mind, while also offering solutions to many of the world's current problems. Reading this grand work impresses one with the extraordinary wisdom and insight that one would expect from such great minds – all with the sage *knowing* and playfulness inherent in such outstanding genius, and with insight to Truth that spans the eons.

Idealism has always been a "pie-in-the-sky" philosophical position suggesting that the loftiest goals of human existence, our grandest dreams and aspirations, are attainable. Many will thus find it not only affirming, but quite comforting, that the leading edges of quantum physics and psychology (informed by all aspects of human consciousness, both the mundane and the exotic) point to the concrete existence of idealism as the rule of the universe. The grand potential for humanity to consciously and mindfully manage our unfolding reality suggests that together we can create peace, prosperity, and harmony for all beings in our currently conflicted world.

Neal's fantastic work consolidates the great wisdom of some of the most extraordinary minds ever to exist. Thus, it becomes a practical guide and roadmap towards something far grander as a realistic possible future for humanity. Although one might bicker with the details of this vision, it is clear that the overall alternative is the end of human civilization. *Conversations with Socrates and Plato* is a vital gift to humanity at this critical time in our history, one for which I believe Socrates, Plato, Benedict Spinoza and William James all would be (or *are*) proud!

Eben Alexander III, MD
Neurosurgeon and author of *Living in a Mindful Universe* and *Proof of Heaven*
Charlottesville, Virginia
June 14, 2018

Chapter I

Introduction

(I'm waiting for an opening sentence. Usually, in the weeks and even months before beginning a writing project, many themes and ideas float through my awareness. I then wait patiently for an opening sentence to come – a sentence that just "feels right" – and then the material seems to flow. It's as if the arrival of the opening sentence signals that the melody of themes and ideas that have been floating through my awareness is now sufficiently "baked" and ready for manifestation in the temporal order. So I'm sitting here, in front of my computer screen, feeling a readiness to begin, and waiting for the opening sentence to come –)

1) The Form of Social Justice

Socrates: Well, patience is a virtue, as they say, but even though you will live into old age, you do not have the time to wait for the usual opening sentence.

Neal: What? Are you saying that even if I wait another 20 years the opening sentence will still elude me? But even if that "perfect" first sentence never comes, every piece of writing must logically begin with a first sentence.

Plato: *(smiling)* Calm down, my friend. There's a joke hidden in what Socrates said; his statement does not literally mean what you think it means.

Neal: You guys seem to enjoy beginning our conversations by getting me confused right away… will I have to wait until the end to get the punch line of this joke?

Socrates: No, I'll give you a big hint momentarily. But first I want to acknowledge what has not escaped your notice: that you are beginning this undertaking at the physical age of my own death.

Benedict Spinoza: – Just like you were the age at which I died (44) when we began our writing project together.

Plato: And, although we won't be superstitious about such things, there is some general truth to these symbolisms and synchronicities, so it is always good to acknowledge them when they occur.

Neal: Yes, I find these synchronicities somewhat curious, but don't know what to make of them.

Socrates: No need to make anything of them; *(with humor)* after all, maybe it's just a coincidence. Well, at any rate, here's that little hint I promised you:

Neal: I'm listening.

Socrates: OK. Not only do **you** not have enough time to wait for the opening sentence, but also **we** do not have enough time to wait for it either.

Neal: But that's ridiculous. You guys live in the eternal order, in which all time is contained, so how could you possibly **not** have enough time? Wait, hmmm, I think I see something, but it still doesn't make sense to me.

Plato: What do you see?

Neal: Well, suppose there existed something whose true home was the eternal order – say *(to Plato)* one of those forms of yours – such a form could never appear in the temporal order, no matter how long one were to wait. Neither I, nor you, would have "enough time" for, say, the form of beauty, or the number three, to appear in the temporal order, since neither the form of beauty nor the number three have anything to do with time at all. But even so, an opening sentence is not itself an eternal object, but rather, is the beginning of a temporal manifestation of something, like perhaps, an instantiation of a form – like a physical thing that is beautiful, or a representation of the number three.

Plato: Not bad – you are suggesting that Socrates' statement contains some allusion to a distinction and relationship between the Real – the eternal order – and the so-called physical world – the temporal order. The Form of Social Justice is an eternal object, and as such, can never manifest itself as a temporal object, although efforts to participate in this Form – to create a just society in the temporal order – can certainly manifest. But there is a further, less metaphysical, reason why there can be no opening statement here, even in this temporal representation.

Neal: I've got it! It's the difference between linear and circular motions. If one is walking along a finite line, there is a beginning and an end to the line. But if one is walking around a circle, there is no beginning point. One has to just jump in and start walking.

Socrates: … Or writing, as the case may be.

Plato: One might compare this situation to a large symphony orchestra playing beautiful music, rich in harmony and counterpoint. Our task is to describe the music to someone who cannot hear it. How might you "begin" describing the music?

Neal: Well, assuming the person has some background in music, I would describe the notes that each instrument in the orchestra is playing, and hope that the person might get some sense of the music's nature and beauty from such descriptions.

Plato: Then it wouldn't matter, I suppose, which instruments you described first, which second, and so on.

Neal: No. The instruments all play their parts simultaneously, and to get a sense of the music as a whole, our hearing-impaired friend must strive to keep in mind all the parts "at once". The various parts must be described repeatedly, but not necessarily in any order – the violins are doing this, while at the same time the winds are doing that, and the percussion is playing such and such rhythm, etc., etc.

Plato: The description is likely to be lengthy, is it not?

Neal: Yes. A person who cannot hear would have to study the score in depth, so to speak, and this can be a lengthy process. A person with hearing, by contrast, can simply listen to the music, and hear all the parts "at once".

Socrates: And, for someone who cannot hear, is it guaranteed that studying the score will give that person a sense of what the music actually sounds like?

Neal: No, of course not. Obviously, a trained musician who has become deaf, like Beethoven, will easily be able to construct in his mind the sound of the music by reading the score. But someone with no training, or who is tone-deaf, will never be able to get a sense of the harmony by studying the individual components.

Plato: So, to make the analogy explicit, the Form of Social Justice is a Reality that the soul, unencumbered by a body, can envisage all at once, as a single whole. Taking on a body causes the soul to forget its prior vision. But reading descriptions of the vision, as reported by some mystics and Near-Death Experiencers, may trigger a recollection of the vision. Whether, in any individual case, reading a description successfully triggers a recollection depends on how much philosophical training the soul has undergone, both during past and present lives, and in between lives. For it is not given to everyone to understand such things, and most embodied souls, that is, most human beings, are so spiritually tone-deaf that they cannot hear the (spiritual) harmony no matter how much they study the score.

Let me add that I am using the words "philosophy" and "philosophical" in the way I originally used it, *not* as people who call themselves by those names currently use that term. But this will become clear as we proceed.

Neal: Understood.

Plato: Yet many are the souls who, prior to taking on a human form, have caught a good sight of the Form of Justice, and although not explicitly recollecting the vision, are driven by the effects of that vision to do what they can to actualize on Earth the model of social justice that they have seen beforehand.

Neal: There is no other way, I think, to explain the difference between a human being who is motivated primarily by greed, and hence dedicates himself to the pursuit of wealth and reputation, and a human being who is genuinely motivated by the desire to help others. But, Plato, is this even possible? The forces of greed and separation are everywhere rampant, and the idealism of my youth is gone. It seems that the human race is now heading for self-destruction. Why should I believe that Justice can be realized "on Earth, as it is in Heaven"?

Plato: The short answer to your question is that the Form of Justice is worthy of study and verbal articulation regardless of whether it can be actualized "on Earth". I think I can convince you of this. But more practically, the survival of the human race depends on whether, and to what extent, Humanity collectively strives to realize this Form of Justice. It need not, and cannot, manifest the Form in its completeness, but it can regard the form as a model, to which it continuously looks to shape and structure its institutions and social norms, which are now structured by greed.

Benedict: *(to me)* I'm wondering whether you now agree with me, that greed is a kind of madness.

Neal: *(smiling)* Yes, most assuredly. But in the past it was not easy for me to come to this conclusion, since greed for wealth and reputation is a social norm, in which I participated. But now, it is difficult not to come to this conclusion, as it is everywhere obvious that the greed of those who seek wealth and status is destroying the planet.

Benedict: And any motivation that leads directly to suicide, whether individual or collective, must be recognized as insane. But words like "madness" and "insanity", although not inaccurate, carry emotional connotations, and it might be better to state the case more logically.

Neal: More logically?

Benedict: Yes. Would you agree to the following premise: human beings are inherently social, and hence must live together?

Neal: Yes, of course.

Benedict: Then, given that humans must live together, the only further question is whether humans must also live together discordantly, as is presently the case, or, can humans find a way to live together harmoniously?

Neal: Our survival depends on the latter being the case, so let's assume that it is.

Benedict: Good. And would you agree that, in order for humans to find a way to live harmoniously, they must first desire to live this way.

Neal: That's obvious.

Benedict: Then tell me: is greed – the desire to have more wealth and reputation than others – compatible or incompatible with the desire to live harmoniously?

Neal: Clearly incompatible. OK, I see the logic here.

Benedict: Lay it out.

Neal: Our first premise is: (i) if the human race is to survive, it must find a way to live harmoniously. The second premise is (ii) if a way of harmonious living is to be found, it must be sincerely desired by humans. Third, we have (iii), greed is inconsistent with the desire to live harmoniously. In fact, I think we can say more. Not only is greed inconsistent with the desire to live harmoniously with others, but is the exact opposite. That is, I believe that subsequent discussion will show that greed can be defined as the desire to live inharmoniously with others. So the "logic" is quite clear: it is not logically possible both to live harmoniously with others and to not live harmoniously with others.

Benedict: We hasten to add, of course, that it *is* logically possible for humans to have simultaneous incompatible desires. But with respect to the desire to live harmoniously with others, greed, or the desire to "have more" wealth and reputation than others, goes off in the opposite direction. For the desires to "have more" than others or to be "thought better" than others are really desires to live in competition with others, would you not agree?

Neal: Yes, of course.

Benedict: Thus the desire of greed necessarily causes people to live inharmoniously with others, and is hence formally inconsistent with our present desire to describe a harmonious society.

Neal: I see your point. If a harmonious society were ever to come into existence, then the presence of greed in the psychological makeup of any given individual would be a threat to that society, since greed must necessarily destroy social harmony. Thus greed must be regarded as a serious mental illness.

Plato: – Very serious, indeed. We can easily make the case, which should be quite obvious now in your present culture, that the person who is predominantly motivated by greed and ambition is criminally insane.

Neal: Isn't that a rather harsh judgment?

Plato: – Not at all. It seems harsh to you only because you are living in a culture that idolizes greed and ambition; so it doesn't seem that unusual. But is it not insane to believe that one's worth and value depend on wealth and the opinions of others? And is it not by now obvious to you and everyone in your culture that those who are motivated by greed have entirely corrupted your economic and political process in order to amass and preserve their wealth?

Neal: Yes, it is quite obvious to anyone who (i) is not greedy, and/or (ii) has not been brainwashed by those who are greedy, that the greed of the wealthy is the only cause of this country's current economic mess. But what do you think of the objection – made by most philosophers, psychologists, and sociologists – that human beings are competitive and greedy by nature (not nurture), so that the best that humans can do is to manage excessive greed?

Socrates: *(laughing)* I think it is a ridiculous objection made by people who are themselves greedy. How will people who are themselves greedy "manage" the excessive greed of others?

Plato: Look at it this way: in previous conversations we spoke about (i) the "way up" and (ii) the "way down". What we called the way up is a movement within consciousness that may equivalently be described as a movement towards union with the Divine Being, or a movement towards the experiential knowledge of one's essential nature, or towards the recollection of one's true self, or in a word, towards self-knowledge. What we called the way down is a movement within consciousness towards separation, towards the forgetting of one's essential nature, towards establishing the ego (the seat of the lower desires) as ruler of one's mind.

Neal: And I assume that what we said before still stands: that the mind of any human contains simultaneous desires that go in both directions.

Socrates: Yes, and we emphasize that it is not "wrong" to have desires towards separation; it is partially definitive of what it is to be human.

Plato: But only partially definitive, since desires towards wholeness are also partially definitive of the human condition. And this is what your culture and its so-called scholars have completely missed. They have assumed that the human being is constituted only by desires towards separation.

Neal: Yes, the "selfish gene", and all that Behaviorist and Freudian nonsense that seeks to give an account of the human condition in terms of egoic greed alone. They are blind to the fact that altruism and compassion are as easily observed among humans as are greed, competition, and selfishness. They "see" only what their preconceived materialist beliefs allow them to see. But compassionate behavior can be observed in many animals, as well as in human beings.

Plato: Yes, but we are not going to waste much time here arguing with such people. For they are generally immune both to empirical evidence and to reasoned argumentation.

Neal: *(with humor)* So I take it we will not be inviting the likes of Thrasymachus or Callicles to join our discussion.

Plato: *(laughing)* No indeed! But I must confess to a sort of perverse delight I had with them in my dialogues.

Neal: And you kept them "in character" throughout, that is, they never become convinced of the truth even after you (or Socrates) establish the truth beyond a reasonable doubt.

Plato: Yes, it would be contrary to their personality types if they had the ability to become convinced of a gentler, kinder approach to life than the "might makes right" (Thrasymachus) approach or the "greed is good" approach (Callicles). But they don't have that ability. And, incidentally, neither do those hyper-skeptical pseudo-critics of current parapsychological research. But you see, neither in my time nor in yours were such people motivated by the desire to discover what is true and good, and that is why we shall not invite them to participate in our discussions.

Benedict: *(smiling)* But of course, you can still require your students to read what these people have to say, but more as an exercise in fallacious reasoning than as a possible perspective that might be true. It is appropriate for 19-year-old students to sharpen their wits about such things, but when 40 or 50 year olds still attempt to justify and defend the lusts for fame and riches, well, this is simply a refusal to mature and "grow up".

(To Plato) And yes, I know you have qualms about exposing young people to philosophical arguments at all. But I'm sure we will discuss this in more detail later.

Neal: So, if I may summarize, we shall assume as a premise that the human being is constituted by many desires, some of which move towards Separation (greed, ambition) and pit humans one against the other, and others of which move towards Union (the desire to know, to help, to love). And ideally, as you have said, the latter desires should rule over the former, which is rarely the case.

Socrates: Forgive me for correcting your wording, but could we replace "which is rarely the case" with "which has rarely been the case until now"? *(With a mischievous glance towards Spinoza)* We must not suppose that the future will be the same as the past with respect to this, especially since there is not likely to be a future for humans if greed and ambition continue to rule.

2) Three Perspectives

Neal: Correction accepted. And may I assume that we will be discussing things from our usual two perspectives?

Plato: No. In addition to our usual "two perspectives", yours and mine, so to speak, we shall add a third perspective.

Neal: A third perspective? What could that be?

Plato: *(playfully)* I suppose one could say it is a perspective intermediate between yours and mine.

Neal: *(also playfully)* And I suppose you're going to make me guess?

Plato: But you already know what it is. You talk about it with your students when you teach, ahem, me. Think about the thematic material in books two and three of the old version.

Neal: Oh, of course. Yes, this will be very important. My goodness, this third perspective is so crucial to any account of an ideal, or just, society.

Benedict: *(I felt Benedict getting restless and wanting to break in)* Can we define our terms, please? Before we go off talking about "perspectives" or whatever, (i) let's state clearly what we mean by the term "perspective", and (ii) let's give clear definitions of the three perspectives we have been alluding to.

Neal: Good idea. By "perspective" we mean a center of conscious experience. One perspective is (i) the human perspective, or the perspective of consciousness that has become embodied in human form. In this perspective, consciousness experiences itself as if it were a body. Then there is (ii) the nonhuman perspective, or the perspective of consciousness as it is in itself, unattached to form. And the third perspective that Plato refers to here concerns itself with the experiences of consciousness as it leaves perspective (ii) in order to enter into perspective (i).

Plato: Or in other words, the third perspective is that of the infant, baby, toddler, child, and adolescent. And this is of crucial importance. It is quite pointless to talk about an ideal society without also talking about the process by which a soul leaves Home and, through a lengthy process, becomes a member of that society. One aim of such a society is to make it possible for every member without exception to develop his or her full potential – to activate, one might say, the purpose of embodiment for that soul – and this requires that we take very seriously this third perspective, or the experiences of the soul as it passes through the stages of childhood.

Neal: While I of course agree with what you have just said, this might pose a difficulty for our discussions, because, unlike the case with the first two perspectives, we cannot bring a living representative of the third perspective into our discussions. We cannot just ask an infant or toddler how she feels about things.

Plato: True enough. But still, there are several ways of finding out about a child's subjective experience: (i) it is possible for a medium or psychic to get information about an infant's conscious experience by communicating with the soul of the infant. (ii) It is also possible, for some people, to retrieve early childhood memories through hypnosis. But we do not really need to use these methods, as (iii) the collective findings of child psychologists over the years, together with basic common sense, will be sufficient for our needs.

Benedict: Good. And we must recognize that, although there are common properties that pertain to each of our three perspectives, there is endless variety within each perspective. The human experience, for example, may be characterized generally as identification with a body, since such identification is common to all human experiences, but there are as many different individual human perspectives as there are human beings. And when it comes to the perspective of souls who are not embodied, there are limitless infinities of such perspectives.

Neal: But now, we must acknowledge that these three "perspectives", as we are calling these modes of conscious functioning, are not all on the same level, in that the perspective of embodied consciousness is contained within the perspective of non-embodied consciousness.

Plato: Ontologically this is true, in the same sense that one might say that the dream consciousness is included in the consciousness of the waking person. Just as the waking perspective becomes the dream perspective in sleep, so the non-embodied perspective – the soul, if you will – becomes the personality while still retaining its identity as soul. But ontology aside, the actual experiences are quite different, and it is not clear whether it is correct to say that the experiences of the personality are included, in any straightforward sense, in the experiences of the soul.

Neal: What? If the personality is included within the soul, how is it possible that the experiences of the former are not also included in the latter?

Plato: Let's not go into this too much right now. But consider this: fear is an experience of the human personality, is it not?

Neal: Yes, of course.

Plato: But does the soul itself experience fear?

Neal: Oh, no.

Plato: So the soul does not experience fear, even though it contains within itself many "lives" or "personalities" that do experience fear. So what we are calling "perspectives", or "points of consciousness" or…

Benedict: … Or "modes of thinking"…

Plato: … are all interconnected with one another and with the whole they collectively constitute; but we will not here attempt to depict all these interconnections, as they are vastly complex, and probably not capable of exact description in words.

Neal: Not "probably", but rather "most definitely" incapable of verbal description.

Socrates: *(laughing, to me)* Hah! And since when have you become taskmaster for exactness of linguistic expression?

Neal: *(smiling)* Well, you guys are having some influence on me.

Socrates: Glad you've finally noticed.

Neal: Well, but speaking of the interconnection of all things, this makes it difficult to isolate portions of the Whole, and to talk about them as if they were independent, or quasi-independent, as language compels us to do.

Plato: Don't worry, we will be giving constant reminders about the uses and limits of language. Recall our previous metaphor: Reality is like a chord of rich harmony, played by a large symphony orchestra. For those of us who are presently non-embodied, we hear the chord, with all its elements, all at once. For those of us who are presently embodied, we, or rather *(smiling at me)* you, are constrained to hearing the chord one element at a time, and then relying on your discursive intellect to put all the elements together into a single coherent system.

So, deep within the Many Mansions of the Divine Being, there is a "place" where the vision of social justice that I once called

"The Republic" fully exists. We "see" it the way Mozart "saw" his compositions: all at once, with all details fully elaborated. And just as Mozart was able to write down what he "saw" in terms of separate parts for each instrument, which when played together approximate what he "saw", we will do the same for the vision of social justice that pervades our new World Order.

(It has been about a year since my previous writing for this conversation. During that time, William James participated in another conversation ["Conversations from Café 21: William James Corrects Some Errors"]. I do not know whether William will appear in this present conversation. Indeed, there were times during the past year when I was not certain that I myself would continue with this conversation, as, when I would reflect on it, I was, and am, quite clueless as to how to proceed. Moreover, it seemed to me at times pretentious and arrogant to think that Plato's The Republic, *perhaps the greatest book ever written, can be or ought to be "reworked".)*

William: Let me immediately address the question of whether I shall appear in this conversation: yes, here I am, and I wouldn't miss it for anything. But I can see why you might wonder whether I would be interested in this conversation, since, unlike these two *(gesturing towards Benedict and Plato)*, there is nothing in my writings that indicates a concern for forms of social and political organization.

Neal: Yes, that is what I was thinking.

William: However, as a psychologist, I am keenly interested in thoughts and emotions, both conscious and subconscious. And I will have some things to say about the interface between the two, the "margins", as I called it, as well as the role of the brain as a receiver, not a producer, of consciousness. So there is much that I am interested in here. As for your own uncertainty with regard to continuing with this project, part of your concern is, hmm, that you do not now have the whole picture in your mind. But you have to remember our musical metaphor, and allow that concern to drop away. You will be hearing the notes one at a time, and as you well know, worrying about whether the notes all hang together interferes with the process, *our* process you might say, of communicating the notes to you. All you have to do is show up, and lead with the notes you're hearing right now.

3) Two Concerns

Neal: Well, right now I'm hearing two discordant chords that threaten to undermine this project even as it is just beginning.

William: Excellent. What are they?

Neal: *(with a little humor)* I want to preface what I am about to say with, "This is just between you and me, William," but I know that Plato and Benedict are listening.

William: *(smiling)* … And what is it you sort of wish they wouldn't hear?

Neal: Yeah, well I don't know how they're going to get along here.

(Benedict and Plato are chuckling in the background; Socrates gestures towards William to continue questioning me.)

William: And why wouldn't they get along?

Neal: Their respective approaches to Philosophy are in diametric opposition to one another. Both have the same overall World-View, yet in describing that World-View they utilize very different, perhaps even incompatible, words and concepts.

William: How about an example?

Neal: Yes, well I can well-imagine Benedict here wincing in logical pain whenever Plato launches into one of his allegories or myths, and I can also imagine Plato rolling his eyes at Benedict's insistence in clear literal definitions regarding things that are beyond the physical.

Socrates: No problem. By the god, I will compel them to sign an oath, wherein they pledge to behave themselves and refrain from coming to blows over this. Do you, Benedict, promise that you will not wince in logical pain at Plato's myths and metaphors…

Benedict: *(laughing)* Yes, I promise. At the very least, my wincing will not be noticeable.

Socrates: … and you, Plato, do you promise not to roll your eyes at Benedict's efforts to use literal language to depict that which lies beyond linguistic form?

Plato: Most assuredly, I do. But if my eyes occasionally appear to be rolling around a little, it will be merely because I'm gazing at the scenery.

Socrates: *(to me)* Now, ye of little faith, did it not occur to you that there could be a resolution of their methodological differences? Or do you think it is merely a coincidence that two of the major mystical philosophers in Western History used radically different methods in characterizing their Philosophy.

Neal: Huh?

Socrates: OK. So, on the one hand, we have Benedict here, with his almost neurotically rigorous logical and literal use of language…

Plato: *(with humor)* … to describe in words that which cannot be described by words.

Benedict: *(also, with humor)* … And just what do you mean by "neurotically rigorous"? It is hardly neurotic to want to be as clear and precise as one can in one's use of terms and concepts.

Plato: … As "clear and precise as one can", yes, but not clearer than one can, as you tried to do.

Socrates: Now stop it, you two. We don't want to give our friend here further grounds for concern about this. As I was saying, we have Benedict here, with his efforts to use words and concepts rigorously, logically, and literally, and on the other hand, we have Plato with his more poetic, playful, and allegorical use of language. Yet it is clear that their writings both express the same perennial philosophy.

Neal: Yes, it is clear that both are expressing the same underlying Philosophy, although their use of words and concepts are greatly different.

William: Ah, but this is the point. It is "clear" to you, Neal, and it is "clear" to anyone who has recognized the perennial philosophy. But it is not "clear" to the overwhelming majority of scholars.

Neal: No, it isn't.

William: Because one must first recognize that the Perennial Philosophy is distinct from the words and concepts that may be used to articulate that philosophy, and scholars as a group tend to be unable to see the philosophical forest because of their obsession with the verbal and conceptual trees.

Socrates: So is it not reasonable to believe that the god – in his effort to instruct humans on the difference between True Philosophy, on the one hand, and the words and concepts that articulate that philosophy, on the other hand – would send, as his two emissaries of this Philosophy *(with a nod to Plato and Benedict)*, individuals who differ greatly in their use of words and concepts?

Neal: I suppose it makes some sense, although I fear Benedict must be showing great restraint by not wincing at your use of language here…

Benedict: I've already bitten through my lower lip, trying to conceal my wincing at what Socrates just said. But seriously, I would express Socrates' point by stating that, in the first place, everything is caused, so there is a cause of the fact that Plato and I appear on the scene 2,000 years apart, using different conceptual schemes to express the same philosophy. The cause of this fact – that our minds and personalities were so constituted as to utilize language and concepts in the ways that we did – lies in the eternal order, and hence involves a mind or intelligence greater than the human personality. And I suppose it is not too big a stretch to refer to this greater intelligence as "the god".

Plato: Here's another way to look at it. If the symbol "6" were the only way available to humans for referring to the number six, it would be easy to confuse the symbol with what the symbol refers to. But when we use multiple symbols, "6", "six", "VI", all of which refer to the same thing, then it is easier for the student to distinguish between the symbol and the thing referred to. So also, we can think of all the words used in my writings, and all the words used in Benedict's writings, as different symbols that refer to the same underlying Philosophy. But you know this.

Neal: Well yes, I'm familiar with the idea that there can be different linguistic and conceptual representations of the perennial philosophy, but what intrigues me is the suggestion that there is intelligence behind the fact that you and Benedict appear on the scene 2,000 years apart.

Plato: Do we not believe that there is intelligence behind everything?

Neal: Yes.

Plato: So it is not according to some random coincidence that souls make their entrances into the theater of Earthly incarnations.

Benedict: And even though we need not conceive of the intelligence that structures these incarnations theistically, after the fashion of Western Religion, it is intelligence nevertheless.

Plato: And if I may use the term "World Soul" to refer to the intelligence that, among other things, both structures and contains within itself the reincarnation series, it is clear that the whole temporal order is included within the World Soul.

Neal: Hence, from the perspective of the World Soul, neither space nor time exist, or exist "all-at-once". So two events may be widely separated in space and time – such as your respective appearances 2,000 years apart – and still be internally connected to each other.

Benedict: Or connected in essence, as the jargon of my times compelled me to express the point. But today people use the expression "non-local" to refer to connections that occur behind the veil of space and time.

William: OK, well this is not the time to get metaphysical.

Plato: According to you, William, there is never a time to get metaphysical.

William: I detect a pun in what you just said, which I'll ignore for now. But now I want Neal to state the other "discordant chord" that he mentioned above.

Neal: Alright. Plato, in your Republic, the political/economical unit is the Greek city-state. As you initially conceived it, the Republic is a city-state amongst many other city-states, hence the need for a military and readiness for war. What is the political/economic unit for the social order that we are now constructing?

Plato: Well, the unit clearly can no longer be the Greek city-state, since that no longer exists. Nor can it be the nation-states, or countries, that have defined your world until now. No, for the economies of the countries are now so entangled, and communication instantaneous, that the proper unit is the planet as a whole. For if the human race is to continue to exist, the nations must indeed beat their swords into plows, and Humanity must study war no more. In my original *Republic,* I considered how a state governed by spiritual Wisdom might hold its own against neighboring states that were not so governed. But is it not now obvious to everybody that, unless the planet as a whole is governed by Wisdom – that is, by individuals who are themselves spiritually enlightened, and who, because of that, do not suffer from greed and ambition, which we must now regard as mental illness – unless, I say, the whole planet is governed by Wisdom, the Human Race cannot continue to exist, for the simple reason that, blindly motivated by the insanity of greed and ambition, Humans will destroy the Earth's ability to sustain human life.

Neal: The human race seems to be in a very precarious situation at this time, and our survival as a species is by no means guaranteed. So it seems important to ask, if the human species is to survive, how must society change?

Plato: It is equally important to ask: if the human species is to survive, how must individuals change? In a way, they are the same question, for the psychological qualities of large numbers of individuals constitute a society, which in turn produce the very individuals that constitute it. This is why the same concept of justice applies to both the individual and the collective. Now, there is an interesting application of my analogy – I think it is really more than just an analogy – between the individual and the collective that perhaps gives some insight into the present human predicament.

Neal: What is it?

Plato: Consider a human being at the earliest stages of her life: there is nothing, absolutely nothing, that an infant can do that could threaten her survival. She can cry however much she wishes, she can defecate whenever and wherever she wishes, can vomit whatever she is unable to digest, and she can flail her arms and legs as hard as she wishes. None of these behaviors will jeopardize her continued existence, even if her flailing arms and legs were to strike someone. The same is more or less true for a toddler; a temper tantrum in the local supermarket might have consequences for her (no treats at dinner), but these consequences will not be life threatening. One toddler may even hit or kick another toddler, and even though there may be consequences for such behavior, these consequences will not threaten the continued survival of the child. But as the child gets older, these very same behaviors will have consequences that may threaten the child's continued existence. A 12- or 13-year-old child, and for certain a 16- or 17-year-old child, who cannot control his or her bodily motions, especially the motions of arms and legs, and/or who throws temper tantrums when she doesn't get her way, cannot function in society, and would need to be institutionalized in one way or another.

Now, something similar is true for the human race considered as a whole. For in our infancy – I'm thinking of small hunter-gatherer extended family units – there was absolutely nothing we could do that could threaten our survival.

Neal: May I interject something here?

Socrates: *(with humor)* Yes, please do. He's *(referring to Plato)* warming up to some major speech making, unless we find a way to derail him.

Neal: But I don't want to derail him. I want to hear what he has to say; this is important.

Socrates: Oh? *(Looking at me quizzically)* So you think whether or not the human race continues to exist is something important?

Plato: *(laughing softly)* Don't mind him *(referring to Socrates)*, although it is perhaps useful to be reminded that in the grand scheme of things, the human experiment may very well not be that important.

William: Well, whether or not it is "that" important, it is important for humans and for the behind-the-scenes entities that are concerned with the human experiment.

Neal: "Behind-the-scene entities"?

Plato: We'll get to that later. For now, interject what is on your mind, so that I may return to my *(glancing at Socrates)*, ahem, little speech.

Neal: OK. You stated that, in its infancy, neither a human individual nor a human collective has the ability to behave in a way that could threaten its continued survival. I agree, and just wanted to make explicit the conditions upon which continued survival depends. For the individual, survival of the infant depends upon the parents (or other adults) continuing to feed and nurture the child, and there is nothing the infant or toddler could do that could cause her parents to cease caring for her. This becomes less true as the child ages, and becomes doubtful as the child enters puberty. In the case of the collective, survival depends on the Earth's ability to sustain life, and there was nothing our hunter-gatherer ancestors could do that could in any way threaten the planet's ability to sustain human life.

Plato: Good. Then, as the units of social organization become larger and more complex – we can conceive of the human collective as moving through the toddler years (perhaps the city-states of my time) then childhood (nation-states) – there was still little that humans could do that would threaten the Earth's ability to feed and nurture them. But things are different now. The human race experienced a rather traumatic puberty (the 20th century), and as it is now entering adolescence, the Earth's continued ability to support human life is under severe threat. The human race is presently having a collective temper tantrum, which may indeed lead to its own demise.

Benedict: And the phrase "temper tantrum" is quite appropriate here, because it identifies, as the cause of the planet's inability to support human life, the inability of humans to control their emotions, either individually or collectively. And the emotions that specifically need to be controlled are our old friends, greed and ambition. Indeed, even the two year old throwing a tantrum at the supermarket does so because he cannot control his greed for something his mother will not allow him to have.

Now, using this developmental model, I suppose one could say that I lived in the early childhood of the human race. There was certainly plenty of greed then. There were individuals who desired only to "have" whatever they could, as well as nation-states that were greedy for their neighbors' land and resources. But there was always room for other human motivations, like honor, patriotism, courage, duty. Until now, or rather, a hundred years ago, there did not exist human collectives whose sole and only purpose was the unmitigated exercise of greed. I'm referring to what you call corporations. And I'd like to use Plato's analogy between the individual and the collective to point out how insane humanity has become to allow such monstrosities even to come into existence.

Neal: OK.

4) The Insanity of Greed

Benedict: Now, it is very rare to find an individual human being who is motivated only by greed. Even the greediest of humans might still care about things other than money. But a corporation is a group of greedy individuals who, insofar as they constitute the corporation, exclude all motivations except for greed. A corporation seeks only to maximize profits. Hence corporations are necessarily sociopathic organizations, as they inflict harm and suffering on human beings without any pangs of conscience. Any individual who wishes to "succeed" as a member of an organization dedicated only to maximize profits must himself either be or become a sociopath. To care about the environment, to care about the suffering of people harmed by corporate greed, is to have motivations other than greed, which cannot be allowed in an organization dedicated to greed unmitigated by anything else.

Plato: At the level of the individual, the greedy person clearly satisfies any definition of insanity, since his mind is absorbed exclusively with thoughts of money and profit, and anyone whose mind is focused on one thing to the exclusion of everything else suffers from obsessive-compulsive disorder. So at a minimum, the greedy person is mentally unbalanced in this sense. But the extraordinarily harmful consequences of greed are more easily seen in the collective, in groups of people who come together and organize (I believe "incorporate" is the word they use) for the purpose of being able to exercise their greed without limit. Now if one person is insane in such a way that he harms others, he is called criminally insane. The same appellation should be used to describe organizations that harm others while pursuing insane desires. No greater harm can be done to human beings than destroying the Earth's ability to sustain human life. Hence it is fair to conclude that corporations are criminally insane organizations, which if allowed to continue to flourish will, like a cancer, destroy the Human Race.

William: *(smiling bemusedly)* Strong words, and I never would have agreed when I was embodied. We, the whole culture, believed that the profit motive was necessary for progress, and people would not be motivated to do anything were it not for the profit motive.

Neal: And even now, even with undeniable evidence that corporations, powered by greed, are destroying the planet's ability to support human life, even now, our universities are filled with people who believe that greed is good and necessary. They "reason" along the lines of Adam Smith, who held that people should be as greedy as possible. Then, as if by magic, there will be an "Invisible Hand" that funnels and channels individual greed into social progress, or something like that.

William: *(chuckling)* Please don't remind me. I really thought there was something to those arguments at the time. But this doctrine of Adam Smith, and anyone who thinks that greed is necessary for society to flourish, is simply a grand rationalization of the lowest of human motivations. Why should society be based on the lowest of human motivations?

Plato: And now, to continue with our analogy, that the human race is entering its adolescence, not all human motivations have survival value, and in particular, the motivations of greed and ambition, when magnified in the collective, have negative survival value.

Socrates: The Earth used to be your Mother, but now it is your Father.

Neal: Huh?

Socrates: Well, forgive me for using stereotypical gender roles. While Mother accepts all motivations and behaviors of infant, toddler, and child, Father's acceptance is contingent upon socially responsible behaviors. Father Earth will not accept a child who defecates wherever she pleases, as corporations do (in the form of pollution). Nor will Father Earth accept a teenager who throws temper tantrums (war) whenever he doesn't get his way.

Benedict: Or, in less metaphorical terms, continued corporate defecation will destroy the Earth's ability to support human life. One can speak of "Father Earth" rejecting the teenager, but it is really a case of the teenager destroying the Father – destroying that upon which his continued existence depends. Similarly with war.

Neal: I understand. And to drive your point home, however one defines the terms "sane" and "insane", it is prima facie obvious to everyone that "destroying that upon which [one's] continued existence depends" must exemplify insanity.

Benedict: And it is good to note that we have not yet given definitions of the terms "sane" and "insane". We will in due time, but we must attempt to capture the sense in which many spiritual teachers refer to the ego itself as insane. This "sense" is different from the sense in which a given individual, whose thoughts and behaviors are different from what is considered "normal", is called insane.

William: *(smiling wistfully)* Ah, it was much simpler in my times, when everyone believed that our culture was the flowering of mankind's noblest potentials, and that competition brought out what was best in people. So it was quite easy to define "sanity" with respect to adaptation to culture. But it never occurred to people then that a whole culture might be insane, in which case, adapting to it would by no means render the individual "sane". For to "adapt" to what my culture has now become, that is, to be "successful" in the eyes of this present culture, one must foster the motivations of greed and ambition as much as possible; that is, one must foster in oneself the very insanity that is destroying Earth's ability to support human life. I would like to hear more about what Benedict mentioned above, about the sense in which the ego, or the human condition, is itself insane.

Plato: Good, you will. We have been emphasizing, indeed, dramatizing, the extremely negative consequences of greed and ambition. We want you, and those listening in, to agree, without doubt, that Benedict here was by no means exaggerating when he wrote that "greed and ambition are species of madness" – madness that is not recognized as such because the whole culture participates in it. If there is to be a future for humanity – speaking of dramatizing – then these emotions will be recognized as such and guarded against. A child who fantasizes about having more money or status than others will be watched as a potential danger to society, in the same way as a child who today fantasizes about killing others would be carefully observed and either helped or removed from society. And in actual fact – to dramatize a little more – the desire to "have" or "be" more than others is even more dangerous to society than the budding mass-murderer, because, as our friend Tolstoy analyzed over a century ago, the wealthy, in exercising their greed, have murdered countless millions of people, "legally" of course, since they own the politicians who make the laws. But much has been written about this, and we need not go into the details… Well, OK, Neal, I see that there is one little detail you wish to mention. Go ahead.

Neal: Most people reading this are not going to believe that corporate executives are worse than mass murderers. Indeed, I sometimes have trouble believing it myself.

Socrates: *(with humor)* That's because you are blinded by the expensive Italian suits that they wear. If they were as ugly on the outside as they are on the inside, there would be no difficulty seeing them for what they are… but continue with what you were saying.

Neal: Yes, so here's a case that Tolstoy actually wrote about, and that fully justifies identifying corporate executives with mass murderers. I'm certain that you, William, must have heard about it; you were around when it happened.

William: Yes, I was, but what's the case?

Neal: An elevated train here in Chicago fell off its tracks, landing on the ground below, killing and injuring many people. What Tolstoy wrote is that the executives of the railway knew in advance that there were problems with safety. But, before the accident happened, they calculated that it would be much cheaper to pay off the families of victims, should there be an "accident", than it would cost to fix the safety issues. So from the point of view of maximizing profits, which is the only point that corporate executives view, it makes no sense to fix the safety problems, as it is much more cost-effective to pay off the families of victims. So the cause of the death of the victims is the greed of corporate executives, and since they knew in advance that people would die to serve their "profit motive", they are no different, in terms of valuing human life, from the mass-murderer. And they do much more harm, since their power enables them to kill many more people than the crazed mass-murderer. Just think of the tobacco industry. Millions of people died to satisfy the greed of tobacco company executives. So it is quite right to refer to them all as a bunch of sociopathic mass-murderers, and the failure of most people to see this is because most people are also afflicted with, that is, have internalized, the values of greed and ambition.

Plato: I think we have sufficiently dramatized the human condition, and from your perspective, it is not a pretty picture. But to arrive at a deeper understanding of these matters, we must now shift to a different perspective. For the statement that the ego is insane – that the human condition is one of insanity – cannot be fully understood from within the human perspective. We must attempt to convey some sense of how these things look from within *our* perspective – that is, from within the perspective of conscious beings who are not embodied.

Benedict: And notice that Plato said "some" sense, not "complete" sense or even "adequate" sense. For to grasp the complete sense of how things look from within the non-embodied perspective, you will have to become non-embodied yourself.

Neal: *(smiling)* I get the point, and I am not now in any hurry to grasp the "complete sense". But a little hint at what it might be like would be useful.

Plato: And *(glancing at Benedict)* "what it might be like" is the best that words can do. *(To me)* Recall, a few conversations ago, that we analyzed the human condition as a sort of hiding from God, or, hiding from full knowledge of what one is.

Neal: Yes, I remember.

Plato: The soul, in order to become human, that is, in order to incarnate as a human being, must forget its own real identity, which includes not only knowledge of its identity with God, but also knowledge of its interconnectedness with all sentient beings. This knowledge is part of our conscious experience as non-embodied souls, but it is not part of your current experience as an embodied soul. Because of this forgetting, souls that are embodied, that are having a human experience, look a little different *(to we who are not embodied)* than the normal soul.

Neal: The "normal" soul? What does that mean?

Socrates: *(laughing)* See, I'm not the only one who can have a little fun at your expense. Plato is calling your attention to the fact that the normal or usual condition of the soul is to be unembodied.

Neal: *(also laughing)* So I'm abnormal just because I'm human? Well I've always suspected something wasn't quite right with me –

Plato: You jest, but that's the point exactly. Every embodied soul, that is, every human being, carries with her some sense that something isn't quite right. And this sense is a direct consequence of the separation from the Divine Being.

Benedict: Plato is speaking loosely here, because nothing can "really" be separate from God.

Plato: Thank you, Benedict. *(To me)* Do you see how graciously I accept Benedict's correction?

Neal: *(laughing)* Yes, my fears that you might not get along appear to be groundless.

Plato: So, in order to fully enter into the illusion of embodied experience – it is an illusion to the soul, but not to the embodied personality – the soul must "forget" that it is really connected to God. A consequence of this forgetting is a constant low-level restlessness, or anxiety, in the human psyche, perhaps analogous to the low-level background radiation left over from the Big Bang. Now, the only thing that will completely ease this restlessness is the recovery of this "lost" knowledge. But humans don't know this, so they seek relief by looking outside themselves.

Benedict: And the first thing they notice when they look outside themselves is other people, and they come to believe that the cure for what ails them lies in imitating the behaviors that they believe make other people happy. And so the child or young adult sees most people chasing after wealth, status, and pleasure, and hence cannot help but come to believe that this is what he must do too, if he is to be happy.

5) The "Way Up" and the "Way Down"

Plato: Now, from our metaphysical perspective, we have previously discussed what we called the "way up" and the "way down". What we call a "human being" is the result of the soul's desire to experience itself as separate from its eternal Source. Following this desire, the "way down", the soul becomes human. But the nexus of desires and motivations that constitute the way down do not disappear when the soul becomes human; it continues to function so as to more deeply attach the embodied soul to its physical circumstances, causing the soul to increasingly identify with its body. Now, once the soul has become human, another set of desires and motivations begins to function, and we refer to this as the "way up". So humans experience simultaneous motivations (i) to regain lost knowledge, and (ii) to sink ever more deeply into forgetfulness. In any given human being, one set of desires usually dominates.

Neal: We have stated that greed and ambition are the desires and motivations that constitute the downward path. Shall we state the desires and motivations that constitute the way up?

Plato: Yes, of course. Go ahead.

Neal: I think that the desires and motivations that constitute the upward path fall under three headings: (i) compassion, or the desire to help others, (ii) curiosity, or the desire to know, and (iii) the desire to develop one's talents and abilities as best one can.

William: To avoid any ambiguity, let us note that the word "ambition" is sometimes used to describe an individual who falls under the third heading above – who desires and is ambitious to develop his abilities as best he can. Perhaps this usage was more common in my time.

Neal: Yes. My dictionary defines "ambition" as "eager or inordinate desire, as for power, wealth, or distinction", and this is the meaning I intend.

Benedict: In fact, we can distinguish the two meanings of the word with a simple example: suppose a person has a specific talent, say for acting, or for sports, or for mathematics. If the person forms a desire to develop his respective talents as best he can, then his desire falls under (iii) above, and is part of the way up. But if, instead, he desires to become the *best* actor, the *best* athlete, or the *best* mathematician, then his desire constitutes an ambition – he seeks status and wants to be thought better than others, and so his desire forms part of the way down.

Plato: And let us note that there is nothing wrong or immoral or bad about the way down. There would be no world without it. So we are being descriptive, not judgmental. And let us also note that the majority of humans experience both kinds of desires simultaneously. It is just as rare for an individual human being to be motivated exclusively by greed as it is for one to be motivated exclusively by the desire to help others.

William: It not infrequently happens that an individual who desires to "do good" joins an organization dedicated to helping others. After a while, the person finds his motivations shifting, from wanting to help others to seeking status within the organization he has joined. Or a person, motivated by curiosity, wants to learn as much as he can about his subject of interest, goes to the university, studies hard, earns his PhD, becomes a professor, and finds that he has become more interested in his status within the university than in his original subject matter.

Neal: *(smiling sadly)* Yes, I certainly have observed this. Sometimes I fantasize how wonderful it would be if curiosity were the only motivator allowed in academia.

Socrates: And while you're at it, you may also fantasize how wonderful it would be if politicians were motivated only by the desire to help and care for their fellow citizens, or if people in the Health Industry were motivated only by the desire to keep people as healthy as possible, or if preachers and clergy were motivated only by the desire to help people become kinder and more compassionate, or…

Neal: *(laughing)* OK, you and your endless examples, I get the point. Nevertheless, if we assume that humans come with both sets of desires, then why is it the case that our social/political/economic/educational institutions seem to select primarily for those motivations that follow the downward path?

Socrates: *(playfully)* That's because, how do you put it, the wheel that squeaks gets the grease.

(Everyone laughs. I think I get the point, but am not sure.)

Benedict: If Socrates does not object, I think we can give a more nuanced response to Neal's question.

Socrates: *(glancing at Benedict)* You don't like squeaky wheels? Well, go ahead.

Benedict: First let's rephrase the question. If it is the case, as we have been assuming, that humans experience simultaneous desires to follow the way up **and** the way down (curious metaphor, as if "up" and "down" have anything to do with this), then one might expect that both sets of motivations be equally represented in large-scale social institutions. But this is so rarely the case that one might well wonder whether our assumption is true. The first thing to note, however, is that these desires – (i) to further separate from Source and (ii) to return to Source – are not equally present in all humans. We might think of the distribution of these desires as following some sort of Bell Curve.

William: And of course, the desire to further separate from Source necessarily involves many secondary desires to separate from other human beings, because in Source, all beings are intrinsically connected. Conversely, the desire to return to source necessarily involves secondary desires to connect with one's fellow humans.

Benedict: Yes, and the most effective way to separate oneself from other human beings is to play competitive games; whereas the most effective way to join with others is to practice compassion and forgiveness.

Plato: So those at the tail end of the bell curve, in whom the desire to separate from Source is most prominent, seek most ardently to play competitive games, whereby they can use wealth and status as a measure to mark themselves off from society as a whole. That's why such individuals are drawn, like moths to a light, to opportunities to compete: for status, for power, for money. And that is why professions that involve such things (politics, finances, being CEO of some organization, etc.) naturally attract those in whom the desire to separate is strongest.

Well, I've certainly labored over this point before. Those at the other end of the bell curve, in whom compassion reigns, and who, because of that, are most qualified to lead, are so disgusted by what they see in public life that they turn to some quieter way of expressing themselves.

Socrates: *(to me)* Yours is an upside down world, and you have heard this before. If humans are ranked in terms of spiritual awareness, then your world is ruled by the worst among you, especially in the economic sphere. If it is ever to become "on Earth as it is in Heaven", then this must be reversed.

Plato: But now let us return to the point that started this discussion.

How does the lower end of the bell curve – the "one percent", I'm tempted to say – how does this look from our non-embodied perspective?

Socrates: And keep in mind that "our" perspective is beyond even the upper end of that bell curve.

Neal: OK, well like all humans, they experience the anxiety/fear/loneliness of separation from Source, but oh my goodness, they seek to alleviate their suffering through activities that create further separation, activities that increase their suffering enormously. The pattern here is identical to drug addiction. Initially the drug is used to ease suffering; but the individual quickly needs increasing amounts of the drug to relieve the suffering. So the person who seeks to alleviate the suffering intrinsic to the human condition through wealth or status needs ever-increasing amounts of wealth and status to feel good about himself. So from your perspective, those who seek wealth/power/status do so out of desperation, and are to be pitied and helped, rather than blamed and denigrated. Is that what you mean?

All: Yes.

Neal: I'm supposed to feel compassion for the very ones whose greed is destroying the planet I happen to be living on right now?

Socrates: *(smiling)* Yes. After all, are they anything other than poor souls who have lost their way?

Neal: No, I suppose not. The only other alternative would be that they are intrinsically evil, or have become possessed by Satan.

(Everyone laughs.)

Benedict: But of course, this is not an alternative that is open to those of us who know and believe that all individual souls and minds are like thoughts in a single "One Mind".

Plato: *(to Benedict)* I think you mean this literally, in which case the word "like" should be deleted.

Benedict: Yes, yes, of course. *(To me)* You see how graciously I accept his criticism?

Neal: *(smiling)* Yes, I do.

Benedict: But I must confess that hanging out with this guy *(gesturing towards Plato)* has opened my mind to the value of non-literal use of language.

Plato: Yet it is sometimes right to use language literally, even with respect to matters metaphysical. The statement that all individual minds are included within a single One Mind is a statement of the philosophy that guides our discussions, and no poetic license is intended here; just the literal truth.

Socrates: Let's return to our "lost souls". Our general principles teach us that there is no such thing as an "evil" soul, and that it is impossible for a given soul to separate itself from the One Mind to which it belongs.

Neal: I agree.

Socrates: And do we not also accept the teachings of *A Course in Miracles* that state that every human behavior is either an expression of Love or a cry for Love?

Neal: What? Are you saying that the behavior of bankers, corporate executives, and the politicians who serve them – and you can throw in the right-wing religious nuts – are just cries for love?

Socrates: Is there really any alternative? Or do you perhaps think they should be separated off from the Whole and sent to the lower regions of Hades for all eternity?

Neal: No, I know that's a metaphysical impossibility, but they are so cruel, so obnoxious…

Socrates: *(with humor)* … that you would really prefer not to be a part of the same One Mind with them.

Benedict: Socrates is calling your attention to the fact that, like all human beings, you have the tendency to want to separate yourself from those you believe to be "bad" or "evil", just like those "right-wing religious nuts" you referred to a while back. And this tendency belongs to the nexus of desires and motivations that constitute what we have been calling "the way down".

Plato: *(to me)* And before you use Benedict's remarks to judge negatively against yourself, bring to mind our two perspectives: (i) from within the human perspective, the human drama is dramatic indeed, and every drama needs good villains, and those who are playing the role of villains in your present culture are doing so with remarkable consistency and intensity. These are the people you so love to hate. And from within your perspective, such hatred is not uncalled for. But (ii) from within our perspective, your so-called villains are just as much a part of the One Mind as you and I, no matter how "lost" and desperate they seem to be.

Benedict: And to use our developmental model, although the human race as a whole is struggling with its adolescence, not all humans are at the same stage. Some humans are already spiritually mature, the sign of which is that they have the power to live according to the Moral Law (Golden Rule) in all aspects of their lives. But some humans are still in the toddler stage, or "terrible twos" as it has been called. And like two year olds, they know nothing of the Moral Law, and hence are either oblivious to, or unable to care about, the great harm that they do.

William: So when you have a two-year-old brain running an adult body, what you get is a true sociopath. And this is the case for your corporate executives and their political stooges. But I'd like to follow up on Benedict's "terrible twos" remark.

Neal: Go ahead.

6) A Toddler's Temper Tantrum

William: This will be an analogy. Let us suppose that a two-year-old child is throwing a rather robust temper tantrum at the local supermarket. And let's examine this situation from two different perspectives. The first perspective will be the usual one; everyone is upset with the child's behavior and the child, most of all, the embarrassed mother.

Neal: *(smiling)* Yes, it's bad enough having to be around when someone else's child is throwing a tantrum, but even worse when it's your own kid. Is the second perspective the non-embodied perspective?

Benedict: No, for then it would not be just an analogy. The second perspective is that of an experienced, compassionate child psychologist.

Neal: Oh, I get it. Wow! Although the psychologist might be as irritated by the child's behavior as everyone else, most of her attention will be focused on the child's inner mental state, rather than on his outward behavior.

William: Good. For the therapist has been trained to bracket the obnoxious behavior of the child and instead focus her attention on the inner psychological state of the child that generates the difficult behavior.

Neal: Yes.

William: And when the child psychologist turns her attention away from the outer behavior and towards the psychological state of the child, what is she likely to experience, in terms of her own thoughts and feelings?

Neal: Compassion, for she sees that the child must be suffering internally in order to behave as he does. And the seeing into the suffering of another constitutes compassion. But –

William: – This does not mean that the behavior is condoned. We must be pragmatic here: the child must be stopped from knocking things off the shelves, and even physically removed from the store. But taking pragmatic action is not incompatible with feeling compassion; one need not "hate" the child in order to keep him from doing further harm to both himself and the store.

Neal: OK, I get the analogy. So, when you non-embodied beings look at those individuals whose collective greed-induced temper tantrums are destroying the store of Planet Earth, you, like the child psychologist, focus more on their inner states of consciousness than on their outer behavior. You see their pain, their anguish, and their horrible inner suffering that leads them to the competitive and addictive behaviors that are destroying the planet.

William: And, to pursue the analogy, wouldn't your child psychologists be in general agreement that children who "act out" the most – who lie, steal, cheat, bully – do so because they are in inner torment? They want others to feel their own pain, and so their behavior, as *A Course in Miracles* states, is a desperate cry for help.

Neal: Yes.

William: And is it any different for your Wall Street bankers and corporate CEOs?

Benedict: And psychologically, they *are* children, never having matured beyond puberty, as their complete lack of conscience indicates. A mature adult has a sense of social responsibility – this is what makes an adult "mature" – and this is completely lacking in those who rule your economies. Like a toddler, immediate gratification is the only desire of which they are capable. Yet their stilted development causes them enormous suffering, because none of their conscious desires – for more money, power, etc. – will bring them the happiness they really want, and yet the only thing they know how to do is to continue being as greedy and ambitious as they can, which adds to their suffering.

Neal: It does seem a bit strange to say that those who are causing the most harm are doing so because they are suffering the most inside, and hence need our love and compassion.

Plato: *(laughing)* Well, yes, from your perspective it does seem a bit odd. But suppose you saw someone attempting to relieve his headache by banging his head against the wall. Aside from the foolishness involved, wouldn't you feel some sympathy for him?

Neal: Yes, because his behavior is increasing the pain of his headache.

Plato: And then, if he were to notice that his headache was not going away and thought that it would go away if only he could bang his head against the wall harder or faster…?

Neal: He's caught in a pattern of delusional thinking.

William: And if he has an exceptionally hard head, he might actually damage the wall, or cause the building to collapse. So the best outcome is to physically remove him from the wall, so that he cannot continue to damage both himself and the building, and then send him off to therapy.

Plato: And in a way, this is the major challenge facing the world today. The temper-tantrum throwing toddler must be physically removed from the store, after which his emotional needs are addressed. Among the more entertaining scenes, from our perspective, is that of a parent trying to reason with his toddler while the latter is in the midst of a temper tantrum.

Benedict: *(to me, laughing)* And you entertained us in just that way, more than once.

Neal: *(also laughing)* Spare me the memories, if you don't mind. But how is this the "major challenge facing the world today"?

William: Let's look at Plato's analogy again, and let us add two things: (i) the wall against which the man is banging his head is part of what holds up the building; (ii) a crowd of people have gathered and are watching the man banging his head against the wall.

Neal: OK.

Plato: So the "challenge" facing this crowd of people is to physically, or forcefully, stop the man from banging his head against the wall. Or will they just stand around doing nothing, until the wall collapses and brings the whole building down upon them?

Neal: Oh my. The people in the crowd who do nothing to stop the crazed man are just as crazy as the man who seeks to relieve his headache by banging it against the wall.

Socrates: And wouldn't you agree that this is, or is a consequence of, the general insanity that pervades the human condition?

Neal: Yes, I see. So we cannot reason with Wall Street bankers or corporate CEOs. Emotionally, they are no different from two year olds in the midst of a sustained temper tantrum. Will the rest of humanity understand this in time to remove them, forcefully if necessary, from their positions of economic power – and after which, of course, send them off to compassionate therapy, where their childhood wounds may be cared for – or will humanity just sit around and do nothing, until the temper tantrums of the very rich destroy the planet's ability to sustain human life? This is a huge challenge, because the rest of humanity is afflicted with the same mental disorder as the wealthy, just not as intensely, believing that the cure for whatever ails them is more money, more status, more whatever.

William: And this, despite the fact that psychologists know that happiness does not lie in pursuing addictive behaviors. In any kind of sane society, scientific knowledge would be widely distributed, and public officials would base policies on fact, instead of believing in, and living according to, make-believe fantasies, as many of our fellow countrymen are now doing, especially those who think of themselves as "religious". And the biggest make-believe fantasy of your time (mine too) is that competition is both good and necessary. This, I'm afraid, is the central fantasy that is destroying our planet. This fantasy is promulgated mostly by individuals who are at the lower end of our bell curve, and in whom the desire to separate from Source and from other humans is strongest.

Plato: Now, the human condition, as we have said, is the result of the World Soul separating from Source, not a "real" separation, to be sure, but a separation that nevertheless feels real to the souls that undertake the process. From within the human situation, there are motivations to reconnect with Source, and motivations to further separate from Source. And we have noted that the political and economic "leaders" of your world are those in whom the desire to separate greatly dominates – not in every case of course, but on the whole. And we have explained why this is so: the measure of separation is wealth and status, which are naturally pursued by those in whom the desire to separate is greatest. And although there is a perspective from which the human condition is itself illusory, from within the human perspective it is fair to say that the desires to return to Source are "more real than" the desires to continue to separate, which take one more deeply into fear and illusion.

Benedict: And both sets of desires have a natural and inevitable culmination: the upward path culminates in the consciousness awareness of the union between the human mind and the Divine Mind; the downward path leads to the destruction of the Earth's ability to support human life, that is to say, it is inherently suicidal.

And just like cancer cells do not have the power to cease from reproducing in order to save the life of both its host and itself, those at the lower end of that bell curve, those who are now holding economic and political power, do not have the personal power to cease pursuing wealth and status, even though such pursuit is destroying both themselves and their host (the Earth). Like drug addicts, they are incapable of thinking about anything other than their next "fix".

William: And because their thinking has been completely taken over by their addiction, they are truly insane.

Plato: There is, of course, a sense in which the human condition is itself insane. Why, after all, would any Soul in its right mind desire to separate from Source in the first place?

Neal: A question I've often asked myself.

Plato: But these individuals, whose whole mental focus is only on their next fix (profit, "deal", promotion, etc.) are insane even by ordinary human standards. Your psychologists and psychiatrists know this – they know that the super-rich live in a fantasy bubble, that they are psychologically immature, having not developed emotionally beyond their adolescence. For we insist, do we not, that by ordinary psychological standards a mature human being is one who has a conscience and cares for the social order. This is what it means to be a mature human being. The super-rich, the people running your world today, demonstrate by their collective behavior that they have no conscience, and no ability to care for anything other than immediate self-gratification. So their emotional development has been seriously truncated. Yet these sick, emotionally immature individuals are now running your world…

Neal: This is getting depressing. Not only is the human condition characterized by what you've called the background insanity stemming from the soul's decision to separate from Source, but it seems that a consequence of this general insanity is that we have allowed ourselves to be governed by those who are the worst among us, by those whose insanity is obvious even from within the human perspective. And what we know about addictive behaviors – what even our psychiatrists and psychologists know – is that they are far more likely to "lead" the world to its own demise than they are to recover their sanity and cease from their insane behaviors.

Benedict: Now, in referring to the wealthy as "the worst among us", you are of course making a judgment. But a judgment requires some principle with respect to which the judgment is made.

Neal: My "principle", with respect to which I judge the wealthy to be "the worst among us", is the desire to return to Source. Since that desire is absent in the very rich, they are truly the worst of all humans.

Socrates: But suppose that such a person were to say to you something like this: "You are to be commended, perhaps, for your desire to return to Source. However, the point of corporeal existence is not to stay connected to Source, but rather to separate from It, to create a realm of being where knowledge of Source is absent. This is the very purpose of embodiment, and with respect to this purpose, we are the very best, not the worst." How might you respond?

Neal: I would point out the "natural and inevitable culmination" that Benedict observed a few paragraphs ago. It is not merely the case that with respect to *my* motivations the wealthy are bad and with respect to *their* motivations their behaviors are good. The Earth simply can no longer support the desires and cravings of the rich. Oh, OK, so the "standard" here is the desire that consciousness continue to express itself in human form on this planet – that human life continues to exist on Earth.

Benedict: So the judgment, that the very rich are "the worst among us", is relative to the desire that the Earth continue to support human life. But we must note that it would not be "bad", in any absolute sense, if the Earth loses its ability to support human life.

Neal: What? Are you saying it would not be bad were the human race to cease to exist?

Benedict: Yes. It would be neither good nor bad.

Socrates: *(smiling)* Species come and go, planets come and go, so do stars, and so do galaxies. Who knows? Maybe it's time for the human experiment to come to an end, just like there was a time for dinosaurs to be kicked off the planet, and the super-rich are to be praised for hastening humanity's demise.

Neal: *(slightly sarcastic)* Well thanks for the reality check, but at least the dinosaurs didn't destroy the planet, and other life forms were able to emerge.

Socrates: Yes, but the wealthy cannot destroy the planet; they can destroy only the planet's ability to sustain human life. And again, who knows? Perhaps, just like how it was with the dinosaurs, after humans are removed from the Earth, new life forms will emerge that are as much superior to the human as the human is to the dinosaur.

William: The "big picture" here that Socrates is reminding us of is worth keeping in mind, although I would have resisted it while alive. For man is not the final measure of all things, and your judgment – that it would be "bad" were the human race to cease to exist – is a judgment made from within a perspective that desires the human experiment to continue. After all, is it not the case that many Near-Death Experiencers move so deeply into the Being of Light that they lose all thought of their previous human life?

Socrates: And in the grand scheme of things, just how important can human life be, if so many NDErs are upset and angry with those who have resuscitated them, forcing them back into the human condition?

Neal: But I want the human race to continue.

Socrates: *(quizzically)* ... And this "I" that desires the continuation of the human race, is this the "I" of ego or the "I" of Source?

Neal: *(explicative deleted)*

(Everyone laughs, and as usual, their laughter is contagious, and I find myself laughing too. But I really got angry. How could they joke about something so important? How could they insinuate that my desire that the human race continue to exist is merely "my" desire? It was one thing for them to refrain from judging against those who are destroying the Earth's ability to sustain human life; it is another thing to suggest that

the continuation of life on Earth may not be all that important in the larger scheme of things.)

Socrates: *(playfully)* I sense that Plato here is conjuring up one of his stories, for our edification. But let us suppose that the worst, according to you, actually happens, and humans get kicked off the Earth, or what is the same thing, consciousness can no longer express itself in human form. Suppose that happens. How would that affect me?

Neal: *(sudden indescribable insight)* Oh my! It wouldn't affect you at all.

Socrates: ... And what about Benedict? How would it affect him?

Neal: Not at all.

Socrates: ... And Plato?

Neal: Again, not at all.

Socrates: And William?

William: I'll answer for myself. I think it would have some effect on me.

Socrates: *(laughing)* But that's only because you are still somewhat addicted to all the drama down there. It's like a big soap opera for you, and you love watching all the plots and subplots evolve. Whatever would you do with all your spare time, so to speak, if you were deprived of your favorite soap opera?

William: *(bristling slightly, but with good humor)* Well, I'd probably go into withdrawal for a few eons, then find another soap opera to watch, or even better, create one in which I participate again.

Socrates: *(to me)* So you see, if we were to put the matter to a vote among ourselves, it would be three and a half to one and a half (counting William's as a split vote) in terms of who would be affected by humanity's ceasing to exist. But I think Plato has his story ready for us.

7) Plato Tells a Story

Plato: Yes, but before we begin, a few disclaimers are in order. This will be a story, not a literal account of anything. And the purpose of telling a story here is to give some sense, to the human imagination, of how things might be like, not of how things are in themselves. For the latter cannot, in principle, be conveyed by words.

Neal: Agreed.

Benedict: Good. So when Plato uses temporal language to characterize a process that occurs in the eternal order, where time does not exist, that should immediately signal a non-literal use of language.

Plato: So if I begin my story in the usual way – "once upon a time" – we are not referring to real events that happened a long time ago, for the events to be described, like all events in the eternal order, are happening in the eternal Now. We are merely providing, for the human imagination, some sense of what it all might be like.

Neal: Understood.

Plato: Once upon a time there was a large cluster of many souls that desired to experience something different from the usual ecstatic union with the Divine Being that it had been experiencing for many eternities.

Neal: Wait a minute. What do you mean by a "cluster of many souls"?

Plato: Let us compare souls with stars. Now stars do not come to exist all by themselves, nor are they created "one at a time", but are created in larger structures, called galaxies, in which they live and have their being, so to speak. The same process that created the star around which the Earth circles also created every other star in your galaxy. Thus, by analogy, individual souls do not come to exist by themselves, nor are they created "one at a time", but rather are created in larger mental structures, in which they live and have their being. Now we may call this larger mental structure a "World Soul", but we must keep in mind that there are as many World Souls as there are Worlds, that is to say, infinitely many. The same process that created the soul of which your personality is an aspect also created the souls of all others who are now having a human experience. And, we might add, just as galaxies can group together to form clusters and super-clusters of galaxies, so too can World Souls organize themselves into various mental groupings, so that the whole process is indefinitely complex and beyond description.

And just as a galaxy contains within itself tens of billions of stars, so also a soul-cluster, or World Soul, contains within itself tens of billions of individual souls. Now it happened one day that a particular soul-cluster formed a desire to experience itself as separate from its interconnections with all other soul-clusters. So it went about creating a realm of experience in which the knowledge of its interconnections with the Whole was lost. Not really, of course, but apparently. This is what we have been referring to as "the way down". But simultaneous with creating a "way down", the World Soul also created a "way back", for no soul, individual or group, can ever be truly lost, although it can wander about and appear that way for quite some time.

Now it should be noted that from the perspective of the World Soul, the way down and the way back are like opposite sides of the same coin. But from the point of view of an individual soul, or a personality within an individual soul, the way down and the way back are quite different, especially with regard to the difficulties involved. To give an example, it is much easier to jump into a pool of quicksand (the way down) than it is to extricate oneself from it (the way up). It is, generally speaking, much easier for a soul to drink from the River of Forgetfulness than it is for the soul to recover its memory, which from the perspective of the individual soul often involves a lengthy and arduous process. However, we must note that no matter how lengthy and arduous the process of extrication, a soul or group of souls can always extricate itself from whatever situation it has gotten itself into.

Neal: But why?

Plato: Why what?

Neal: Why would a soul-cluster want to separate itself from the knowledge of its interconnections with all things?

Socrates: Now, now, you certainly do not expect a literal answer to that question?

Neal: I guess not.

Socrates: Good, then it's sort of like this: say you are strolling down the street, and you find yourself having a passing thought that expresses some fleeting desire. Perhaps the fleeting desire is to see a movie, to travel somewhere, to call so and so, to bake cookies, to have sex with someone, etc.

Neal: Yes, that happens.

Socrates: But unlike you, the World Soul is so powerful that whatever it desires, even a fleeting desire, is instantaneously manifested. So we can imagine the World Soul strolling along among the galaxies, richly enjoying its interconnectedness with all other World Souls, as well as with the Source of all World Souls, when it suddenly has the fleeting thought: I wonder what things would be like if I were not so lovingly interconnected with All-That-Is. And that fleeting thought creates what you call the whole physical world, into which the World Soul, fragmented into individual souls, can project themselves and hide from the knowledge of what it really is.

Neal: We humans are just the result a fleeting thought? *(Everyone laughs.)* Well, OK, Plato, continue with your story.

Plato: Thank you. Now I forgot to mention that the World Soul is itself too vast to successfully "hide" in the physical reality it has, as we are imagining it, just created. So in order to have the experience of "getting lost" it fragments itself into individual souls, each of which further fragments itself into what you call "personalities", or "lives" or individual human beings. Then the souls and their personalities jump onto the stage of physicality, where they successfully lose the knowledge of what they are. *(To William)* How do you like my little story so far, my "over-beliefs", as you once put it?

William: *(smiling)* A rather far cry from my admittedly meager "Something More". As a scientist, I did not want to speculate even one iota beyond what the data suggested. But now, as a philosopher, I see that there is a view from above, as well as a view from below. Proceed.

Plato: We also must add that the general rules of the theater apply to our story.

Neal: Huh?

Plato: Sure. When you see a good play, not everyone concerned with the play appears on the stage, right?

Neal: Yes, of course. There are many more people behind the scenes than on stage – the lighting, props, scenery, costumes, etc., require many people working together. And with something like opera, even more people are required behind the scenes. Perhaps ten to one.

Plato: And the ten to one ratio applies only at some instant, at a temporal cross section of the whole process.

Neal: What? Oh yes, if one includes the full temporal history of the performance of any opera, not just a single performance, that history must include many, many more people who never appear on stage, such as the people who train and coach the singers/actors, the people who design, make, transport the costumes, the individuals who make the lights, arrange for the staging – the list goes on and on.

Plato: Good. So let's say the ratio is about a hundred to one. For every soul who is embodied, who is experiencing the memory loss called "human life", there are a hundred, perhaps even a thousand, that remain in the wings, assisting with the drama of embodiment in various ways, or perhaps just watching it. A good drama needs an audience, after all.

Now, it was foreseen by the World Soul that a crisis would develop midway through the drama, and extraordinary measures were put into place to "manage" the crisis.

Neal: What crisis? What do you mean?

Plato: Now, now, it's only a story. The "crisis" is analogous to the following. Imagine that the script called for a fire to be lit on-stage. The actors were taught how to start the fire, but it was foreseen that they might not know how to manage the fire once it got started. But if the fire got out of control, it could burn down the props, scenery, and even the stage itself, before the last act was finished.

All flammable material must be gotten out of the way. The problem is that, while onstage, the actors have forgotten their knowledge of what is flammable and what is not. So extraordinary measures had to be taken to remind the actors of this knowledge, for only the knowledge of the on-stage actors, acting together, could avert the disaster. Thus it was decided to put two small exemplars on-stage: one would be of something completely inflammable, the other would be of something that ignites very easily. By "small" I mean that the example of the flammable substance would not be sufficient to burn down the theater.

And so it came to pass that the World Soul asked for volunteer souls that would incarnate in order to provide the great majority of souls with the exemplars. Now many were the souls who volunteered to be exemplars for the inflammable – they take on embodiment almost immune to the flames of greed and ambition. And even though many such souls may suffer while embodied, in that they have no stomach for the competitive games that are required down there, when they are finally released from their bodies they return Home without delay, and with no difficulty. But only the bravest of souls came forth to volunteer to play the role of the flammable, for they knew in advance that the process of cleaning off the mud of corporeality for which they were volunteering would be subjectively very difficult. To accomplish their mission they would be required to drink so deeply from the River of Forgetfulness that they would become insane, true sociopaths, with no conscience that might restrain them from harming others in their mad quest to satisfy their greed and ambition. They would then become role models of greed and ambition, and hence the "average" soul, by noticing the extremes, and noticing where the extremes lead, would choose not to burn down the theater, but instead burn off the greed and ambition within themselves. It is as if those brave souls that chose to exemplify the flammable are saying to the others: "Look at me. Because of greed and ambition, not only am I a miserable wretch of a human being on the inside, but also I am so out of control that my behavior is destroying the planet. Look at me, but don't follow me; learn from my negative example, and destroy that in you that would have you follow along my path."

Now, among those poor brave souls who drank so deeply from the River of Forgetfulness, some became bullies and criminals of various kinds; others became little tyrants in their personal lives. But those who drank the most, the "worst" among them, so to speak, became politicians and heads of corporations. And to clarify, we are not talking about corporations that make or do something useful. We are talking about (i) corporations whose sole purpose is to gamble with other people's money: insurance companies, financial institutions, etc., and (ii) corporations that make something with regard only to profit, regardless of whether what they make is harmful to people or the planet (drug companies, tobacco companies, oil companies, etc.). They were veritable exemplars of the "way down", of the lust to separate themselves off from humanity as a whole, in order to judge themselves and think of themselves as "better than" the multitude. But it was not easy for the multitude to see the exemplars of evil for what they were.

Neal: Why is that?

Benedict: *(who had been restraining himself for some time)* Wait a minute, hold on, you can't just throw in a word like "evil" without defining it properly.

Plato: Quite right, especially since we hold the view that evil does not exist in Reality.

William: But it does appear to exist, and we can define the term relatively, with respect to values or human ideals. And perhaps the chief value for our purposes, as we have said, is that the human race continue to exist. With respect to that value we may call "good", those human emotions and behaviors that are in harmony with that value; and "bad" or "evil", those emotions and behaviors that are not. Unmitigated greed and ambition are bad because those who are possessed exclusively by such desires are presently destroying the Earth's ability to sustain human life.

Benedict: So it is not, in any absolute sense, "wrong" or "bad" or "evil" to find oneself at the tail end of this bell curve we have been talking about. Neither is it "wrong" or "bad", in any absolute sense, to destroy the whole planet. But relative to the desire that the planet continue to be able to support human life, we may continue to use those terms, and call "bad" or "evil" those motivations and behaviors that are now destroying the planet.

William: And actually this is close to common usage of these terms. Those whose lack of conscience allows them to harm others are usually called "bad" people, and those with social conscience, who are led primarily by desires that recognize the interconnectedness of all beings, are generally called "good" people. But I think we will be returning to this later.

Neal: Yes, later is fine. Right now I want to know why it was difficult for the multitude to see the exemplars of evil for what they were.

Socrates: There is a reason why, don't you think, that when a culture personifies the pure desire to separate from Source – the "devil" or "Satan" or whatever – this imaginary being is often portrayed as a gentleman, well-dressed, refined, cultured. This depiction, although quite silly from any literal perspective, nevertheless captures the difficulty most people have in recognizing evil for what it is.

Neal: Ah yes, I understand. Those Wall Street bankers and insurance company executives look good in their fancy Italian suits, don't they?

Plato: And there is a big difference, as I repeatedly emphasized in my writings, between "what looks good" or "what seems good" and "what is good", is there not?

Neal: Yes.

Plato: So, to get back to my story, we could talk about fancy Italian suits, but the real reason that the majority of humans have difficulty recognizing the exemplars of evil for what they are is the simple fact that they – the people – were themselves largely constituted by desires and motivations that characterize the "way down". So they were mostly envious and jealous of the exemplars of separation and competition, greatly envying their wealth and status, and actively opposed the exemplars of lovingkindness that the World Soul also manifested in equal numbers. The point of this was, as I said, so that the so-called average human, in whom the desires to compete and cooperate are mixed, could see (i) very clear examples of each set of desires, (ii) could learn to discern what *seems* good from what *is* good and (iii) could clearly see that the Earth can no longer support the downward path. And once they became conscious of (ii) and (iii), the people would also see (iv) that the personal inner life of those who have followed the downward path exclusively – the bankers, corporate executives, etc. – is absolutely wretched and miserable. Instead of being envied they would instead be pitied, and human consciousness would collectively evolve to a higher frequency of vibration. That was the plan.

Neal: Did it work?

Plato: Yes it did, barely. Human consciousness was able to shift into a higher level of functioning, and the planet was saved. But our story is not complete until we describe the journey of those souls who volunteered to be the exemplars of evil. Now of course, it goes without saying that they all made their way back to the knowledge of, or union with, the World Soul. But from their perspective it was a lengthy and very difficult journey.

Neal: I think I'm beginning to understand.

Plato: Yes, for as soon as they left the body, they began to suffer immensely. I will describe their suffering in a moment, but you see, they knew prior to incarnating that they would have to undergo this suffering, which is why I referred to them as "brave souls".

Benedict: May I gently interject a reminder that this is just a story. In eternity there is no "before" or "after", so there is no such thing, literally, as "prior to incarnating".

Plato: Yes, of course. After all, from the perspective of the World Soul, the whole affair happens in the Eternal Now. But that is not the perspective of humans, nor is it the perspective of souls that are newly freed from their bodies. So, Neal, you know how it goes. It is a Law that each soul, after quitting a body, must experience the full consequences of everything that was said, thought, done, and felt while human – the Life Review. And this is in detail, not in general. So, to consider an example, an insurance company executive whose salary and bonuses come from denying medical coverage to sick people, or a tobacco company executive whose salary and status are earned by making a product that kills tens of thousands of humans, will experience the pain and suffering of each and every person they have harmed, including family members. For most of these executives, the numbers are in the millions and tens of millions, because all things are interconnected. So their life reviews are lengthy and very painful, and they knew they would have to experience this before they signed up for their mission. But they don't usually remember this right away, because souls don't recollect their true nature until after the Life Review. Many such souls did everything they could to avoid the pain of their Life Review, and ended up as earth-bound spirits for quite some time, neither here nor there. Others were so ashamed of what they had done that they could not go into the Light (where their true memories were stored) and tried instead to invent punishments for themselves, including lifetimes of unnecessary suffering. They felt deeply unworthy and refused the help and assistance that were being offered to them to find their way back.

But, since all our stories have happy endings, with much help from everyone else, they eventually found their way Home to the Light, recovered their memories, and were welcomed as true heroes.

(As Plato was finishing his story, they were all kind of staring at me, wondering whether I had understood the point of it. I understood it perfectly well, of course, yet there was a portion of me that wished I did not understand it, if that makes any sense.)

Socrates: It might help to recollect that this – so-called physical reality – is not Real. It is a collective dream, illusory, and those damn snakes you so love to hate, to use a previous metaphor, will turn into harmless ropes as soon as you awaken. The point of Plato's little story, aside from conveying some slight sense of how it might be like

– is to encourage you to turn your hatred (of what is evil) into love right now. After all, why wait until you quit the body to let go of all negativity.

William: Aw, but that would spoil the fun. A good drama needs good villains, and those Wall Street bankers are as good as it is possible to get.

Neal: Good? Oh, you mean good at being bad?

Benedict: Almost. They are good at playing the role of evil, for a soul cannot be bad, do we not agree?

Neal: Yes, we must agree upon that, for otherwise we would have to think that "evil" is something real in itself, whereas we hold that what is called "evil" is merely an absence of the Good.

Socrates: But since, in Reality, the Good is never absent, we are forced to conclude that the Good can appear absent only in an illusion or a dream, which is what you are experiencing right now. For if in Reality the Good cannot be absent, then, should goodness appear to be absent, one is not in Reality. But I really don't wish to spoil the fun that you, and to a lesser extent William, have by rooting against the bad guys…

William: *(to me)* I assure you, you can still have fun with it, even with the understanding that the souls of the "bad" guys are just as much an expression of the Divine Being as are the souls of you and me. You just have to recall that you can see a movie or a play, which is 100% unreal, a copy of a copy, as Plato might put it, and still feel all the relevant emotions, just as if it were real.

Plato: Good analogy, William. Think of a play or opera with a good villain. The audience is of course emotionally manipulated to hate the villain, but after the play is over the actor playing the role of the villain takes his bow alongside the hero, and the cast goes out to party in friendship and camaraderie. So William's hatred of the bankers is like the hatred you might have towards the villain in a play. You can continue to enjoy the drama of the play, hating the villains and loving the good guys, but in the knowledge that in Reality, it's all just a play.

Neal: Yeah, well I know you're right; my emotions tend to lag behind my understanding.

Plato: And also, remind yourself of what you said you believed, that all human behavior is either an expression of love or a cry for love.

Neal: *(laughing)* Yes, and those bankers are crying mightily for Love. OK, I get it now. They are the two year olds throwing a temper tantrum in the supermarket – unpleasant, destructive, obnoxious, but clearly, a cry for love.

Socrates: *(also laughing)* And is there such a thing as a two year old who is too unpleasant, too destructive, or too obnoxious to be loved?

Neal: Well, it certainly seems that way. But the answer to your question has to be no, especially since their terrible behavior is actually a desperate cry for love.

William: And we must keep in mind their important function as exemplars for the rest of humanity. Will humanity continue to envy the wealthy and strive to emulate them? Or will they take pity on the wealthy, and strive to educate and love them and prevent them from further harming themselves?

Plato: And it is a pitiful sight indeed, from our perspective, to watch the wealthy strive to fill the hole at the center of their being with expensive toys and material acquisition, only to become increasingly miserable in the process. But we have been telling our stories because we want you to see the so-called "Big Picture", and not be angry with them when they cry out for love so obnoxiously, but instead, respond to their cry with lovingkindness in your heart. For it is never the case that there is any reason to have less than loving feelings for any and every aspect of Creation.

Neal: I agree.

8) First Principles?

Benedict: At this point I think it will be useful to succinctly summarize the metaphysical principles that underlie our discussion.

Neal: Good. Let's do it.

Benedict: Perhaps the most fundamental of our principles is that what we are calling the separation from Source and the return to Source "happen" in the eternal order. The eternal order contains the temporal, so in Reality, there is no temporal distance between the separation and the return. Thus, if time is to be mentioned, we must say that the separation and the return are occurring simultaneously.

Neal: And what we are calling "separation" is simply a desire, or nexus of desires, on the part of consciousness, to experience itself as separate from its Source. And similarly for what we are calling the "return". For souls that have become human, these two sets of desires and motivations occur simultaneously.

William: But the distribution and strength of such desires are not the same in all humans. Those in whom the desires to separate are predominant will seek to play competitive games, so that they can feel themselves separate from others, and judge themselves better than others in terms of wealth, status, and other forms of "winning". But notice, even those who lose at such games still get to feel separate from the ones who win. So, win or lose, those who play competitive games get to feel separate, and that is the point of all such games. On the other hand, those in whom the desires to return predominate will seek to play cooperative games, to recognize that we are our brothers' keeper, and seek to live in peace and harmony with one another. So on balance, humans seek to compete with some and to join with others.

Plato: And at the extremes are (i) those whose souls have little or no desire to separate. These are your "saints" or positive role models, many of whom have been persecuted and murdered by (ii) those whose souls have little or no desire to return. These latter are your negative role models.

Benedict: And we have also noted that, as Socrates so charmingly put it, Mother Earth has become Father Earth, and will no longer continue to support the behaviors of the negative role models. If we desire that the Earth continue to be a stage upon which individual souls may incarnate, then we must also desire that the Earth be ruled by those in (i) above, and that those in (ii) be removed from positions where they continue to harm themselves and the planet. Thus, with respect to the desire that the Earth continue to support human life, we may use the word "good" to describe whatever is useful to that end, and "bad" or "evil" to describe whatever is a hindrance to that end. So we will continue to use those terms, "good" and "bad", but we are using them in this relative sense only.

Plato: And this is the reason we are not inviting the likes of Callicles and Thrasymachus into our discussion. For if those who are ruled only by the desire to separate have any say at all in the matter, Father Earth will no longer allow souls to incarnate here.

Neal: 2,400 years ago, you said that spiritual wisdom and political power must coalesce in the same persons for people to be happy. Now we must add that this must happen if people are to survive, let alone be happy.

Plato: Yes, the issue is being forced, so to speak. We will talk about this later, but for now, *(smiling mischievously)* let's continue with Benedict's desire to succinctly list our metaphysical principles.

Socrates: Yes, I agree, even though I fear the succinctness Benedict desires may ultimately elude us.

Neal: Why do you say that?

Socrates: Think back to the analogy that began our present conversation.

Neal: Oh yes, the analogy with a symphony orchestra. One who can hear, hears the notes succinctly, all at once; but one who cannot hear, has to read the score note by note, and then try to construct in his mind what the music would sound like. And this note-by-note construction can by no means be done "succinctly".

Socrates: Yes, and we must also question, when we talk about "metaphysical first principles", what we mean when we use the term "metaphysical".

Neal: Well, the word is usually used to refer to abstract things like soul and God that are beyond the physical.

Socrates: *(smiling)* Are you calling me an "abstraction"?

Neal: From the human perspective, anything that is not a concrete sense experience is abstract, so the concept of non-embodied consciousness is an abstraction.

Socrates: But what about me? Am I just a concept?

Neal: No, of course not. Thank you for reminding me of our "two perspectives"; what is perhaps just a concept from the human perspective is a concrete reality from the perspective of non-embodied consciousness. So our list of principles (I'll omit the qualifier) should begin with this:

1) Consciousness, or mind, or soul exists in itself, independent of body.

Socrates: Oh? Is this really the "first" principle?

Neal: It isn't?

Socrates: Those three words, "consciousness", "mind", and "soul", can be used abstractly, or they can be used concretely. Instead of talking about consciousness per se, consider it concretely: the particular consciousness that you are now experiencing yourself as being. So if the particular consciousness that you are now experiencing yourself as being is not produced by the body, and does not produce itself, then it must be produced by a greater consciousness.

Neal: Necessarily.

Socrates: Then is not this "greater" consciousness, which produces the lesser consciousness that you are now experiencing yourself as being, more fundamental than the latter?

Neal: That would have to be the case.

Socrates: Then should not this be the "first" principle: the particular consciousness that you and other humans experience yourselves as being is produced by a greater consciousness?

Plato: Or do you think that there might perhaps be an even greater consciousness that is producing the consciousness that is producing the "you" that you are now experiencing yourselves as being?

Neal: I think I see your point. From a human intellectual perspective, there are many ways of slicing the pie and we should not worry about lining up our principles in any order. What do you think, Benedict?

Benedict: *(laughing)* Well, one must have a sense of humor about

any attempt to describe these things in human language. I certainly thought I was laying it all out clearly and logically, with "first principles" and all that, but given how very few so-called philosophers have understood what I have written, I have many times called into question the efficacy of my efforts to approach the matter with logical rigor. And of course, hanging out with this guy *(gesturing towards Socrates)* has caused me to become much more playful, and has cured me of any belief that these things can be explained by words, however logically arranged.

But, if I may digress a little, the decades after my death were very interesting to me, in terms of seeing the effect of my writings on others. I thought, when alive, that my writing was clear, straightforward, and even obvious. The faculty of reason is the same in all people, whether "enlightened" or not. The reasoning skills required for my writings are no more advanced or difficult than the mathematical reasoning required to understand that the number of even numbers is the same as the number of even and odd numbers taken together. But when I observed that people very skilled in reasoning completely missed the point of my writings, I began to think that something besides the ability to reason was needed in order to understand my writings. And this point was further impressed on me when it became clear that some 19th century poets understood my writings quite well, even though they could not follow all the reasoning.

If there is one thing that can be stated succinctly, it is that it is difficult for reason to function in the presence of strong emotional desires and attachments that involve the subject matter of what one is reasoning about. For example, in the case of Leibniz and Kant, they were both strongly attached, that is *emotionally* attached, to their belief in Theism. They wanted it to be the case that the personal God of the Bible is the "true" god, and they were unable to call into question their personal desires about these things. So, as all therapists know, in the presence of strong emotional attachment, the ability to reason deteriorates into mere cleverness, and is thence used only to justify what one already believes. Thus, with boundless complexity, the two aforementioned philosophers were able to "justify" in clever ways that which they already believed. But the overall pattern is now very clear to everyone: in the presence of strong emotional attachment, human beings are unable to reason at all. But they *are* able to use words, to arrange them in clever ways, so as to justify to themselves their antecedent beliefs. We will call this "cleverness". The so-called "deniers" of your time are very clever, but they are unable to reason.

Neal: Yes, from the point of view of mere logical consistency, any belief may be held on to come what may, that is, irrespective of any evidence to the contrary, if one makes adjustments elsewhere in one's belief system. The general principle, that one can always do this, is perhaps interesting, but particular applications of it are not.

William: *(laughing)* Tell me about it. Whenever I would attempt to tell my colleagues about *(the medium)* Mrs. Piper, I was amazed at the bizarre "theories" they would concoct to explain away her incredible accuracy, rather than call into question their own limiting *(materialist)* beliefs about such matters. But they were very confused about what they were doing. They thought they were reasoning, but they were just being clever. They were simply using words to justify to themselves what they already happened to believe.

But this does raise an important psychological question that we shall have to address. How is an honest seeker of truth to know when she is using her reason, and when she is merely being clever, that is, merely using words to justify what she already believes?

Plato: *(clears throat conspicuously)* We agreed that reason cannot function well, if at all, in the presence of emotional attachment to the subject matter one is attempting to reason about. Enter mathematics! No human being can be said to be emotionally attached to mathematical theorems, to whether the number of odds and evens together is the same as the number of odds, or whether there are the same number of fractions as there are whole numbers, or whether the square of a hypotenuse is or is not equal to the sums of the squares of the sides. That is why mathematics, aside from being intrinsically interesting, is so essential for education. For with respect to mathematics, reason functions purely, and everyone can learn for herself what it is like for reason to function in and of itself, without any admixture of cleverness.

Neal: And I suppose, then, that mathematics will continue to be an educational requirement in our New World Order?

Plato: You suppose correctly. For mathematics gives the human mind a clear example of what it is like to use mental powers without emotional attachment to the subject one is thinking about. Or in other words, mathematics gives the human mind a clear example of the exercise of reason. Only then can Benedict's "hard problem" be faced.

Neal: "Hard problem"?

Benedict: How, and to what extent, can reason be applied to subjects about which one *does* have emotional attachment; one's personal life, for example. It is by no means as easy as I had thought. But we shall delve into these matters later. For now, let's turn our attention to one of Plato's favorite subjects: the education of children.

Plato: And by the word "education", we are referring not merely to a formal process of attending school, but rather to the entire temporal process that begins with a newborn infant and ends when that infant has matured into a young adult member of the society, which we may arbitrarily take to be about 20 years of age.

Chapter II

The Infant or Newly Embodied Soul

1) Original Purpose

(In the past several days, I have been thinking about this topic, and noticed that there are several different ways we could proceed. I was/am indecisive about how to begin.)

Socrates: *(smiling)* That's because there is no beginning. A child cannot begin to exist unless a society is already in place; a society cannot come into existence, or continue to exist, unless children grow up.

Neal: Then, in describing the upbringing of children, we shall assume that a society is already in place.

Socrates: Yes. And although the main features of our New World Order will be described in due time, we will say this much about it now: the New Society must be approved of by Father Earth; otherwise there will be no society at all.

Neal: Understood.

Socrates: And whereas Mother Earth was very tolerant regarding all sorts of ways humans might organize themselves into various societies, Father Earth is not so tolerant. In fact, he is not tolerant at all. Now, the first rule that Father Earth lays down is that human beings must conduct themselves in such a manner that he is able to give to them what they need in order to continue to exist as a species.

Neal: *(laughing)* That seems more of a tautology than a rule.

Socrates: *(also laughing)* Perhaps it is not a bad idea to begin a philosophical discussion with a tautology, or something so obvious that one would need to be insane to reject it.

Plato: And our second rule, which is really a consequence of the first rule, is this: in order to live in harmony with Father Earth, human beings must live in harmony with one another; that is, they must organize themselves cooperatively, not competitively. Society must organize itself in such a way as to reflect the fact – you may call it a "metaphysical" fact if you wish, but it is a fact nonetheless – that the souls of human beings collectively constitute the Soul of a Single Being, that is to say, each human mind is a part of the same larger mind.

Benedict: And this is the deeper meaning of the phrase "on Earth, as in Heaven"; in Heaven, the souls know of their mutual interconnectedness, and this knowledge must now be brought to Earth and activated.

Neal: And so we shall assume that our newborn infant is being raised in a society wherein this knowledge has been activated.

William: But there is another approach to this subject (the education of children) that has occurred to you. Why not state it now?

Neal: OK. Let's suppose we were not acquainted with Father Earth and his rules for a New Society. Let us suppose, even, that we have no idea at all about the form of our future society.

William: Continue.

Neal: So all we know about the infant is that we have before us a newly embodied soul, who *(glancing at Plato)* bravely crossed the River of Forgetfulness in order to incarnate here on Earth. Suppose we knew something about the specific purpose or intent of the given soul regarding its mission on Earth. Let's call this the "original purpose" that the soul had prior to incarnating. After all, nothing happens for no reason, and souls do not incarnate haphazardly, without reason or purpose or intent. So if we accept this, we can ask: what form of human society will best facilitate the soul's original purpose in incarnating?

Plato: We can certainly approach our problem from this point of view. Now, what is your hunch?

Neal: My hunch is that approaching the question of social organization from the constraint of honoring the original intent of the soul, that is now manifesting as an infant, will give us the same result as would approaching the question from the constraint of living in harmony with Father Earth.

Plato: Interesting. Why do you think that?

Neal: If it is the case that the physical world, including the Earth, was created in order that individual souls may experience themselves as "separate" from the Divine Being, then it should be possible for souls to have this experience without destroying the Earth. Something like that is what I have in mind. Or to use an analogy from several conversations ago, it should be possible for souls to go to the theater of forgetfulness, and enjoy the show without destroying the theater.

Socrates: *(smiling mischievously)* All right, but how do you know that the script, the so-called "original purpose", does not call for the destruction of the theater?

Neal: I don't. *(To Socrates)* I know you're trying to get me to lighten up about this, about whether or not the human drama will continue into our future, or whether this is now the time for the whole thing to come to an end. But even if I were as indifferent to the outcome as you are, it is not unreasonable to assume that we humans **will** continue to exist, and then ask: what must be the case for this assumption to be true?

Socrates: Good. We will henceforth make that assumption, and playfully draw forth the consequences.

Neal: Playfully? Well OK, yes. So, to continue, we have before us a newborn infant, and the soul that has now manifested as this infant has some specific purpose in mind that it wishes to fulfill through this manifestation. But the newborn infant is not yet the personality the soul wishes to manifest. For the desired personality to come into place, the infant needs 18–20 years of nurturing and support from its environment, without which it cannot flourish.

Plato: Hold on. Let's back up a bit, and let's consider a specific example. The process – Benedict might use the word "cause" instead of "process" – according to which a non-embodied soul becomes embodied into a particular life or personality is enormously complex, and will never be grasped literally by human language. So we shall be using language playfully, as Socrates has just suggested. As you recall, I once described the process as a mixture of Fate, Choice,

Knowledge, and Luck – not very helpful, to be sure, but by using incompatible metaphors, I tried to remove any attempt to think of it in literal terms.

Neal: Yes, I recall.

Plato: So let's consider a specific example, perhaps a soul who, enamored of celestial music, desires to manifest that music in Earthly terms, or in other words, desires to become a musician. This non-embodied soul must now shop around for a suitable body, for not all bodies are suitable for making music.

Neal: I understand. The body should not be tone-deaf, if the soul wishes to express music.

Plato: So the soul must choose (i) a body that is genetically well-disposed towards music, and (ii) environmental conditions that will convert the genetic material – the fertilized egg – into a 20-year-old adult who is a proficient musician. Now in the past, this presented a major problem for the about-to-incarnate soul.

Neal: What do you mean?

Plato: What I am calling the two choices of the non-embodied soul – its heredity and its environment – are, or rather, were, conflated into one choice. For in choosing its genetic makeup, it also automatically chose its environment and its upbringing. Often it would happen that a soul would select a body with an excellent genetic disposition for music, only to find that the parents of that body had no liking for music, and never exposed the child to music of any kind.

Neal: Then the soul's intent would be thwarted, because it is not possible to become a musician without childhood exposure and encouragement. No one becomes a pianist without taking piano lessons as a child.

Plato: So our poor soul leads a frustrating life, never bringing forth the music that was in his soul. When he dies, or rather, when the personality dies, the soul examines in great detail what had gone wrong, and next time selects parents who are not only ardent music lovers, but have the means to send him to the finest music schools. But, alas, it turns out that his music-loving parents did not have the right genetic combinations for producing a body with a talent for music-making.

Neal: *(laughing)* This happens all the time, with Mom and Dad schlepping their untalented kid to music lessons, much to the frustration of the poor music teacher, who can't get the kid to carry a tune. So I suppose that the next time around it will be more careful, and select for both (i) genetics and (ii) upbringing. But as long as (i) and (ii) are not independent choices, it will be very difficult for the soul to find a "just right" combination.

Plato: Yes it will, unless it decides to wait for our New World Order, which will separate (i) from (ii).

Neal: My goodness, how will it do that?

Plato: We will address that question momentarily. Recall that we raised the question: what is the Society, or, what is the form of social organization, that will allow humans to live in harmony with Father Earth. Humans will never be able to live in harmony with Father Earth until they learn to live in harmony with one another. If we were to follow this track – which we will later on – we would talk about the Moral Law, or the Golden Rule, and how to raise children such that this Law is written into their (human) psyche.

Neal: Agreed.

Plato: But then you suggested that the New World Order might perhaps be realized by asking what is the original purpose that a non-embodied soul has for incarnating, and what kind of Social Order best suits that purpose. This is the track we are now following. The original purpose of the soul is greatly facilitated by separating (i) and (ii) above. For the ability to bear children is not also the ability to raise children. In our Society, the primary responsibility for raising our children lies with Society as a whole, not with individual parents. More specifically, since "society as a whole" is sort of an abstraction, the responsibility for raising a given child lies in the child's local community. Whether or not a given child shall receive music lessons is a decision made by the child's local community, and is based on the child's talents and proclivities, not on the parents' desires.

Neal: I doubt that anyone could seriously argue with this, since we have so many negative examples of parents who mistreat and abuse their children.

William: And we also know now – we didn't know this in my time – that environmental influences begin much earlier than physical birth.

Plato: Yes, so prenatal conditions are of utmost importance, both physiological and emotional. Physiologically, the embryo requires oxygen and various nutrients that the mother's body must be capable of delivering. But the embryo also feels the mother's emotions, so a woman who is chronically depressed, or who is angry much of the time, should not be allowed to pass those emotions on to her fetus, any more than she would be allowed to pass on a communicable disease, if it could be prevented.

Neal: Plato, you're going to have problems with this, same as before. People believe strongly that they have a right to have children, and that the children they have belong to them.

Plato: People used to believe that they had a right to own slaves. In my own time, slavery was the norm, and to suggest otherwise in that society would invite the same outrage and ridicule as to suggest, in your culture, that children are not the property of their biological parents, and hence, should not necessarily be raised by them.

Neal: So are you saying that newborn children should be regarded as citizens of our New Society, and the task of raising them falls on Society as a whole?

Plato: Yes and no. Every human being, no matter what age, is the "property of" his/her very own soul, so to speak. They belong to the soul of which they are an expression, and do not belong either to their biological parents or to the larger society in which they will be raised. Do we agree on this point?

Neal: Yes, of course.

Plato: Then this has a consequence that most biological parents cannot grasp.

Neal: What do you mean?

Plato: There is no correlation between the physical age of the body, and the maturity of the soul of which the infant is an expression.

Benedict: Hold on again. We have to get clear about the meaning of the expression "maturity of the soul".

William: Yes, for with regard to bodies, maturity is measured by time, so that the older a body is, the more mature it is said to be. But the soul is not a temporal object, so if we wish to introduce a concept according to which some souls may be more or less mature than others, we should state what we mean by that.

Plato: Do you think such things can be stated with any precision using human language?

Socrates: Perhaps at this point, instead of trying to get clear on the concept of "mature" or "immature" souls without using temporal language, it would be better to rely on what I used to call "old wives' tales".

Neal: What tales?

Socrates: *(smiling)* I'm glad you asked.

Neal: I fell for that one, didn't I?

Socrates: *(laughing)* Yes you did. Well, I didn't mean very much by the expression "old wives' tales" – just the general story, passed down in the various esoteric texts, that some souls have lived very many lives on Earth, and others are relatively new to the Earth experience. So when you look around at a sampling of humans, the souls of which they are manifestations are not all the same with respect to the number of such human manifestations pertaining to a given soul.

Plato: And in fact, such stories can be used in the same way that you are fond of using my River of Forgetfulness story.

Neal: Yes, I understand. If a given human is, say, deeply fearful and anxious, and concerned more with her body than her soul, we can say either: (i) this is a young soul, inexperienced with Earth conditions, hence fearful, or (ii) this soul has consumed too much from the River of Forgetfulness, which has caused her to lose all memory of her connection with Source, and as a result she is fearful.

Plato: But unlike the River, which is pure metaphor, there is some literal truth to the idea that not all souls are at the same level of maturity, with what you call "enlightenment" being the natural condition of the mature soul. Perhaps we will develop this idea later on. For now it is sufficient to realize that, when one gazes into the eyes of a newborn infant, the soul of which that infant is a manifestation may very well be significantly more mature than the souls of the parents. And so the infant must be treated with the dignity and respect that befits a soul, and most assuredly must not be treated as the property of others. For procreation creates only the opportunity for a non-embodied soul to become embodied. It does not create the soul itself, hence the ensuing personality does not belong to the parents.

William: And this is easily seen in a humorous way by observing that parents who regard their children as "belonging" to them do not also regard themselves in turn as belonging to their parents.

Neal: *(laughing)* Yes, I remember that at the time I thought my children were "mine", I was most decidedly certain that I was not the property of my own parents, God forbid, an inconsistency that eluded me at the time. So where are we? The infant belongs neither to its biological parents, nor to Society as a Whole. Yet it must be raised, nurtured, and cared for. By whom, and how?

2) A New Social Contract

Plato: Children will be "raised, nurtured and cared for" by those (in our World Society, which we assume to be in place) who are most fit to do so. No role in our Society will be more honored than the role of raising children; those who are to receive this honor must demonstrate an innate love for children, and have extensive psychological training in how to best care for children. So let's now consider our newly born infant and ask: what is Society's contract to this infant, such that this infant will receive everything (s)he needs in order to transform into a 20-year-old adult, fully equipped to manifest the original purpose of his soul. This will be the new "Social Contract", according to which our new World Order is obligated to every child to provide the material and emotional support needed to manifest the soul's original intent.

Socrates: Actually, the only way to provide "equal opportunity for all", a motto advertised by your culture, is to raise every child the same way, and to guarantee that the physical and emotional needs of every child are satisfied.

Neal: Yes, so being born into poverty will not disadvantage the infant, and being born into great wealth will not be an advantage to any child.

Plato: In the new Order, there will be neither poverty nor (private) wealth.

Neal: Hmmm – perhaps you will say a little more about that.

Plato: Certainly. We agree, do we not, that our World Society exists for the purpose of facilitating the original purpose of the soul as it manifests as a specific human personality?

Neal: Yes. In fact, our science has shown that consciousness is the fundamental existent, and that purpose or intent are fundamental properties of consciousness, so souls must have purpose and intent prior to incarnating as human.

Plato: But now, consider a specific soul – and we will have to use temporal language here – and conceive if you will that this soul has a desire to express itself as human.

Socrates: – If I may interject, realize that a soul rarely desires to become human just for the sake of becoming human. *(Laughing)* The process (of becoming human) is much too difficult for a soul to undertake just for the fun of it.

Neal: I understand. The soul has some intention in mind, and then chooses a body based on what it desires to learn or accomplish by becoming human.

Plato: So the intention of the soul, what we are calling "original purpose", cannot involve the body, since the former occurs to the soul prior to the body, which itself is chosen as a means to fulfill the original purpose.

Neal: I can agree with that. The body is an instrument chosen by the soul in order to best manifest some specific intent on the part of the soul.

Plato: And so, would acquiring material riches ever be part of a soul's original purpose in incarnating?

Neal: Oh my, no, that could not be possible. Prior to incarnating, the soul sees and understands that what is called physical reality is fundamentally unreal, a play of shadows, as you described it. It could not possibly think that it could in any way benefit itself by chasing after shadows.

Benedict: And hence the desire for riches and reputation – which I called a "species of madness" – is *never* desired by souls as they are in themselves, but only by souls who have become deranged through association with the body. The true purposes of the soul have to do only with those things it will take with it after leaving the body – Love and Knowledge.

William: Which means, if I may spell it out, that every human desire that does not pertain to Love and Knowledge, that is, all desires for money and fame on the part of an embodied soul, indicates how far the given soul, in its human manifestation, has deviated from its original purpose and become insane.

Socrates: *(to me)* So all those villains you so love to hate – the bankers, CEOs, politicians, and so forth – are not following their soul's original purpose, simply because we know that original purpose can have nothing to do with chasing after wealth and reputation, but on the contrary, chasing after wealth and influence is a symptom of the soul's insanity. And surely, my friend, you can have a little compassion for those who have become insane through embodiment.

Neal: *(laughing)* Well all right, I suppose so. But these villains are not just insane, they are criminally insane, in that their "insanity" is causing incredible harm to others and indeed to the whole planet.

Plato: Ah, not so fast. We agree, do we not, that one who while embodied harms another, harms himself much more.

Neal: Yes, we agree.

Plato: Then the embodied soul who brings harm to others brings much more harm to himself. Hence the "criminal" aspect of his behavior is a further demonstration of his insanity, for it is truly insane for a soul to manifest a personality that in turn causes harm to the soul. So again, compassion is what is called for.

Neal: I guess I need constant reminders.

Socrates: ... As do all humans, because forgetfulness of one's interconnection with all beings is a hallmark of the human condition.

Benedict: But let's come back to the main point here: the soul, in and of itself, is magnificently Real, and enjoys being independent of corporeal shadows, to use Plato's language. Unlike the personality, which is what the soul becomes through association with the body, the soul, when not associated with a body – as in the circumstances we are now envisioning – can form no desire to aggrandize the as yet nonexistent body and personality. To do so would be *like* – and watch me now as I philosophize like Plato here – ahem, to do so would be like an actor, who, after putting on her costume for the play, becomes so enamored of the costume that she forgets her lines. And instead of playing the part she had studied and rehearsed, her mind is filled with thoughts only about her costume and the costumes of others.

Plato: *(smiling)* Ah Benedict, there's hope for you yet. A most excellent metaphor. So instead of playing her part, she becomes obsessed over her costume, is upset that other actors seem to have finer costumes, is fearful that other actors are getting more attention, and plots incessantly to "beg, borrow, and steal", until she has the finest costume on the stage.

Benedict: Now of course in a real play, it would be clear to everyone – cast and audience alike – that the actress has become insane, and she would be forcibly removed from the stage. But in Earthly life, things are not that clear because humans are conditioned to believe that the costumes are real. The purpose of education – and Plato will really like how I am philosophizing now, since I am almost quoting what he had written – is to turn the embodied soul around, from gazing mindlessly at mere costumes, to recognizing its true condition as embodied soul.

Neal: So, the desire for fame and riches is not a desire that a soul can have insofar as it is itself; thus the presence of such desires in a soul that has become embodied is a sign that the soul has become insane – that embodiment has caused the soul to become insane.

William: Now, as we have said, it's quite complicated to describe this in words because, you see, a touch of insanity is necessary to bring about the human condition. But the human condition by no means requires the amount of insanity present today, which must be greatly reduced if the human race is to survive.

Plato: And we might note the old truth: no one, on his deathbed, has ever regretted not spending more time at the office. The regrets are all with respect to either personal relations or undeveloped talents. This is because, as the body dies, memory begins to return to the still-embodied soul, and it is relieved of the illusion that its own happiness and well-being could ever be found in acquiring either riches or reputation. And so it is, my friend, that in our New World Order, there will be no wealthy people. There will be wealth, to be sure, but wealth will be used for one purpose only: to maximize the likelihood that every newly embodied soul has the physical and psychological means to fulfill her original purpose in becoming embodied. This is our New Social Contract. And it is worth noting that, *because* no one will be rich, no one will be poor either.

William: To quote Theresa again: "Oh! If human beings might only agree together to regard it (money) as so much useless mud, what harmony would then reign in the world! With what friendship we would all treat each other if our interest in honor (reputation) and in money could but disappear from earth! – it would be a remedy for all our ills."

Socrates: And St. Theresa's prayer will be fully granted in our New Society.

Benedict: And so, in our New Society, greed and ambition will be listed as among the more serious forms of mental illness, and children who exhibit such proclivities will be cared for, loved, and corrected at a very early age. This will be relatively rare, for as Plato has said, children learn mostly by imitation, and in our Society there will be no adult role models for greed and ambition, and lots of role models for curiosity, kindness, and compassion. The so-called "profit motive" will disappear from the face of the Earth, for in our Society, no one will desire material gain at the expense of other human beings.

Neal: Or perhaps we could say that the false profit motive, which is concerned with material aggrandizement, will morph into the true profit motive, which is concerned only with what truly profits the soul.

3) Needs of the Infant

Plato: Let us now return to our infant – actually I would prefer to replace the word "infant" with the phrase "newly embodied soul", because the latter phrase reminds us that this is what an infant is. We are talking about a soul. And when we speak of the "upbringing" or the "raising" or the "educating" of a child, we are referring to a process that transforms an infant – actually, a fertilized egg – into a 20-year-old adult, fully able to fulfill the original purpose set forth by the soul. By separating bearing children from raising them, the soul, prior to embodiment, concerns itself only with the choice of genetic materials for its new human experience, and need have no concern about how it will be raised. The New Social Contract guarantees that each embodied soul will have everything it needs to manifest its original purpose.

Neal: I think I see a problem with what you are trying to do here.

Plato: I haven't quite stated what I'm trying to do, and you already see a problem? OK, what is it?

Neal: The problem I have is whether separating bearing children from raising them is compatible with the child's psychological needs. Now way back you suggested that infants should be separated from their biological parents, so that all children will be raised in the same way, and that parents could not favor their biological children over other children, since they would not even know the identity of their biological children.

Plato: And do you think this suggestion would work for our New Society?

Neal: I'm not sure. We do want a society in which parents do not use their children to compete with one another. We want a society in which no parent regards his biological children as in any way "better than" or "more deserving than" any other child. But perhaps there is another way of accomplishing this than removing children from their biological parents.

Plato: Or to put it a bit differently, we wish a Society in which no parent regards his child as an extension of his or her egoic self. But as you say, perhaps there might be more than one way to bring this about. And so, to put this in historical perspective, let's see if this can be accomplished by arranging things as I initially suggested way back when, so that parents do not know who their biological offspring are. Thus each adult will regard anyone 25 years or so younger than themselves as potentially their child, and by the same token, children will regard everyone 25 or so years older than themselves as potentially their parent. In this way the "Family of Man" (pardon the sexist language) will come into being, or rather, will be perpetuated once it has come into being. Now, what is the problem that you see?

Neal: There will of course be no problem meeting the child's physical needs, but I am concerned about whether such an arrangement could meet the child's psychological needs. A child needs to bond psychologically. It cannot bond with an abstraction such as "society as a whole", nor can it bond with a steady stream of child-care workers marching in and out of its life. Rather, the child can bond only with a relatively small number of other humans, who must be constantly and continuously present in the child's life. Do we agree?

Plato: Yes, we agree. Continue…

Neal: So, in the past, this need to bond was provided by the family, and the extended family. The parents, siblings, uncles and aunts, cousins, and grandparents of the given infant constitute the "relatively small number of other humans" who are "constantly and continuously present" in the child's life. Whatever replaces this system in our New Society will have to be sufficiently like it, if bonding is to occur, so that the same or similar difficulties will arise. Two difficulties, actually: (i) whoever (plural) raises the child, that is, whoever is constantly and continuously present in the child's life from infancy to age 20, will be regarded by the child as "special", as having raised him, and so, as an adult, will naturally seek advantage for those people, just as he would in the old family system; and (ii) whichever adults are included in the "small number of humans", with whom the infant is to bond, will themselves bond with the child, in the same way that biological parents bond with their children. So they will still regard the children they raised as "theirs", in the same way that adoptive parents do, and so they will regard them as special, and seek for their advantage over other children.

Plato: *(smiling)* And if this objection is not sufficient in blocking this path to our Society in which no one seeks advantage for their biological progeny, there is a further objection that has already occurred to you that will be decisive. But at this point I must confess – and now I am finding myself a case in point with respect to what we discussed with William in a previous conversation, that an author, once departed from the body, can no longer alter what he had written, even though his views may have changed – that I did not adequately consider the psychological needs of the child for its first two years of embodiment. In fact, I sort of ignored what I said about the beginning of the child-raising process being so important, and (in books 2 and 3 of *The Republic*) discussed the education of the preschool child, age 2–5, which is not really the "beginning".

William: *(laughing)* Now, don't be too hard on yourself for that. After all, in both our cultures we men had almost no contact at all with infants or babies. How could we have had any idea what their psychological needs might be?

Socrates: Well, you could have consulted with the experts of your culture.

William: The experts? Who do you mean?

Socrates: *(laughing)* I mean the mothers, grandmothers and wet nurses.

William: *(also laughing)* Will there be no end to my learning just how much of my culture's sexism I had internalized?

Plato: Don't be too hard on yourself, William. After all, even I, the only philosopher to get it right *(glancing at Benedict)* regarding the equality of men and women with respect to social roles, never thought to consult a wet nurse about an infant's psychological needs. I'm not sure I was even aware that the infant *has* psychological needs – in particular, the need to bond with a small group of other humans who are constantly and continuously present for him. My former educational program for the child begins at about age two, when the child is old enough to express itself verbally, and to respond to music and stories. But that was then and this is now, and now we are considering the needs of the embodied soul from birth, from conception actually, to adulthood.

Neal: We have so much more knowledge today about the needs of the infant than was available in your time. There is that famous, or infamous, case from about a century ago. It occurred in an understaffed orphanage. The physical needs of the infants and babies were well met; they were all fed, bathed, and changed, but they weren't held or caressed. All of them died.

Socrates: Hey, that's putting it too negatively.

Neal: What do you mean?

Socrates: Instead of saying "all of them died", you might try to express what happened from the perspective of the babies themselves.

Neal: What? Oh! *(Laughing)* From their perspective, it might be something like, "Well, what's the point in hanging around if no one wants me?" and so they just quit their bodies and went back to Source.

Socrates: Exactly. No point overdramatizing the situation. From the human perspective, it's quite the tragedy. Poor helpless infants, so unloved and uncared for that they all died. From the perspective of the souls who *were* those infants, you might say that they took a little peek into your dimension, did not like what they saw, and returned

Home.

Neal: OK, so it turns out that for the newly embodied soul to want to remain embodied, it needs some encouragement to stay, which encouragement is given in the form of touch, caresses, soothing voices, playfulness. In fact, science can trace in some detail how touching the skin of an infant affects the development of the infant's brain and nervous system. Without considerable touching and caressing, the infant's brain does not develop properly.

William: It still amazes me, how yin and yang could have gotten so separated. We males did not know anything about an infant's and baby's inner life. We would probably even have denied that they had an inner life until they reached the age where they could verbally report their feelings. The women knew. The mothers, grandmothers and wet nurses knew that most of the time a baby cried, it cried because it needed to be held and touched. But we men didn't know that until we got "scientific studies" that related touching to brain development. How out of touch can one be?

Plato: A large part of male disassociation (from their own intuitive knowing) has to do with being bred and raised for competitive social games, so that many males, having been thus raised, are uncomfortable with the very idea of touching and nurturing, which they then dismiss as "women's work". But we are creating a different world, and it will be useful to separate two themes, which are often conflated. (i) How must Society be organized so that every embodied soul will realize its original purpose in incarnating? And (ii) how can society transition from its present (2013) dysfunctional and Earth-destroying condition to the one envisioned in (i)? These are very different subjects, and our present focus is on (i). We will have some things to say about (ii) later on.

Now, to recapitulate the argument thus far: we first suggested separating genetics from upbringing, so as to ensure the soul maximum opportunity for realizing its original purpose. We explored whether a viable way to accomplish this was to ensure that biological parents did not know who were their offspring, so that they would treat all children as potentially their own, and would not be able to play competitive games through their children. Then you pointed out that the newly embodied soul – the infant and baby and toddler – needs a relatively small number of people who are constantly and continuously in its life, otherwise it cannot bond. Thus for each child there will be people who are special to him, and for each caregiver of children, there will be children – the ones he has cared for – that will be special to him. But this is not the only reason why the program I outlined 2,500 years ago will not work today. (Mind you, I do not concede that it could not have worked back then.)

Neal: Yes, and here's a further reason why it won't work now: we are constructing our Society on the basis of what the newly embodied soul needs in order to accomplish its original purpose for incarnating. And we are agreed that we will use the findings of science to ascertain the needs of the newly embodied soul, not only the needs that must be satisfied if it is to survive, but also the needs that must be satisfied if the baby is to thrive. Now, as it turns out, not only is human milk the best food for any infant, but more importantly, there is some evidence that the biological mother fine-tunes her production of milk to fit the particular physiological needs of the infant. So the birth mother produces the best milk for the infant she birthed.

Socrates: *(smiling)* There is no human experience more intimate than being carried in someone's womb for nine months. Not only do they interact physiologically, but psychologically as well.

Neal: Yes. In fact, newborn infants can recognize their mother's voice, so some psychological bonding already occurs in the womb. So does this mean we're back to the nuclear family?

Plato: Not quite. But first, one further reason why separating babies from birth mothers won't work is that our New World Order will not tolerate lies and deceits of any kind. All facts will be available to everyone, and this includes all facts about one's birth and upbringing. People will be able to trace their biological ancestry all the back, if they wish. The caveat here is that in our New Society, people will not be identifying very much with their biological ancestry.

Neal: But now, it would seem, we are back to the proverbial drawing boards. How will we prevent parents from trying to give their biological children every possible advantage?

Socrates: *(smiling mischievously)* On the contrary, my friend, we will encourage parents to give their children every possible advantage.

Neal: What!? I thought we were building a society in which no child or adult has any advantage over any other.

Socrates: *(very mischievously)* Ah, but what you are missing is that it is to every child's advantage not to have any advantage over any other child.

Neal: Huh?

Benedict: Socrates is equivocating over the word "advantage". Recall that old saying

For what shall it profit a man,
If he shall gain the whole world
And lose his soul?

And although the question is rhetorical, the answer is "Not at all", and this principle will be among the "obvious truths" of our New Society. It would never occur to a parent that wealth or social status – the very things that parents today believe are "advantages" for their children – would be advantages at all. The true "advantage" to the child is to assist in every way possible the child's efforts to realize the original purpose of the soul. And notice, unlike material advantage (wealth, status), "spiritual advantage" is something a parent can desire, not only for his biological children, but also for *all* children. For what truly profits the man is what profits the soul of which he is a part, and it is never the case, I repeat, *never the case*, that the soul profits when the man gets lost chasing after wealth and status.

William: And this is why, in these current times, the greedy and the ambitious are the lost souls, so far have they deviated from their souls' original purpose.

Neal: You guys never lose an opportunity to impress this on me.

You want me to convert my disgust and anger towards the wealthy – who are mindlessly destroying the planet, *my* planet, mind you – into compassion and lovingkindness.

Socrates: *(laughing)* Ah, my friend, and here we thought we were being subtle, but you see right through us. Nevertheless, we are succeeding, a little bit at a time. It's really just a matter of perspective.

Neal: Perspective?

Plato: Yes. Just remind yourself how it looks from our perspective, that is, from the perspective of non-embodied souls. Consider one of your villains, say a Wall Street banker, or corporate executive. We who are not embodied can "see" the soul of that banker, we can "see" the original purpose of that soul in manifesting as the human who becomes the banker, and we can "see" how far that banker has strayed from his soul's original purpose in creating him. And we can "see" him, after his body dies, returning to his soul empty-handed, a miserable failure. And so yes, we do feel the compassion and lovingkindness we are urging you to feel too.

Benedict: Or, to return to an analogy we have used before, imagine an actor preparing for a performance. He studiously rehearses his lines, both by himself and with others. But when the time comes to go on stage, instead of sticking with the script, he becomes enamored with the props, and spends his entire time on stage thinking only about the costumes and props, how to acquire them, how to acquire **more** of them than the other actors, and so forth.

Neal: *(smiling)* We might say that it is never the case that an actor profits by chasing after costumes and props. Yeah, I get it. Money and status are just the costumes and props of this physical world.

Plato: Exactly. And this will be among the common principles of our New Society. Our parents will seek the true advantage of their own children, which has nothing to do with wealth or status.

Neal: All right. So our newly embodied soul comes into a world that has been designed to provide every advantage for realizing his or her original purpose. I want to ask you how those entrusted with raising the child will come to know what is the original purpose of the child. But first, can you elaborate on what you said earlier when I asked if we are back to the nuclear family?

Plato: Yes, I said "not quite". In our New Society, there will be complete freedom to experiment with different forms of social and communal organization. This will not be a "one-size-fits-all" type of society. The traditional arrangement of two adults cohabitating will be one option, but with the divorce rate at 50% in your present society, there is considerable evidence that this option does not work for most people. So people will be free to experiment, individually and collectively. Some will prefer to live alone, some will prefer to live with one other person, and some will prefer to live with several other people at the same time. Whatever the choice, there will be no judgment, and sexual jealousy will become a thing of the past. The only constraints will be if one desires to have and raise children. For this purpose, some living arrangements will be better suited than others, but even so, there will be much variety.

Neal: Yes, well I can see how, if someone wants to live alone on some mountaintop, or if someone wants to live in such a way as to maximize her number of sexual partners, that neither of these living arrangements would be beneficial for raising children. But then, it is doubtful that someone who desired such living arrangements would also desire children. But how will sexual jealousy be eliminated?

Plato: We'll discuss that a little later. For now, it suffices to say that our New Society will be constructed in harmony with – rather than opposed to – the natural biology of the human body. But let's look at your other question: how will those entrusted with raising a given child come to know what is the original purpose of that particular child?

Benedict: Let us tighten up the question, for it is the soul, not the child, who has an "original purpose". The child or baby is a consequence of the soul's original purpose. Or in other words, the soul, in and of itself, intentionally manifests as this or that child in order to accomplish a specific purpose or desire that is internal to itself. We may speak loosely of the child's "original purpose", as long as we understand that the latter is what it is because of the soul.

Socrates: And, as a brief aside, Benedict, may I comment on your words "or in other words" that you just used above.

Benedict: Of course. *(To me)* As if saying "no" would have any effect on him.

Socrates: *(to Benedict, playfully)* I heard that. I can keep quiet if that would please you.

Benedict: No, no, speak your mind. After all, what could you or anyone possibly have to say about an innocuous phrase totally devoid of philosophical content? Having aroused our curiosity, you will be compelled to speak.

Socrates: Then speak I will. And I will also convince you, I think, that the phrase is not totally devoid of philosophical content – "mostly" devoid, perhaps, but not totally.

Benedict: I'm listening.

Socrates: Recall when Neal was talking with someone the other day about reading your writings and those of Plato. He cannot read the languages in which you guys wrote, so in order not to be influenced by any idiosyncrasies of a particular translator, he will often read several different translations simultaneously, especially for passages that are somewhat obscure.

Benedict: *(playfully, with pretend indignation)* Me obscure? Plato maybe, with all his myths and metaphors and similes that wander all over the place. Who knows what they all mean? But I defined all my terms and rigorously deduced everything from first principles.

Plato: *(with pretend sarcasm)* Oh yes, your writing was so clear and your meaning so transparent that you had to wait until Neal here came along so that, with him, you could rework your ideas into a form that someone not trained in obscure 17th century philosophical jargon could understand.

Socrates: *(with humor)* OK, you two, knock it off. Now, as we all know, there are words in one language that have no exact equivalent in another. For such terms, the best that a non-linguist can do is to consult many translations, and the different English words that render the same passage in Latin or Greek greatly assist the reader in approximating the meaning of the original. Thus, when reading a translation from a language one does not understand, "other words", that is, other translations, are very useful.

Neal: I think I see your point. The Form of Social Justice, of which our New Society is an expression, is, one might say, written in a language that humans do not understand. So when one is attempting to grasp these things through language, as we are here attempting to do, it is always useful to use "other words", that is, to use (i) different linguistic expressions to express the same truth, and (ii) to use language itself in different ways, from very literal to very figurative. But now, Plato, let's continue the train of thought we were following before Socrates sidetracked us with his "other words".

Plato: Good. How will those entrusted with raising a given child discover what is the original purpose of that child? And to incorporate Benedict's point, when we use expressions such as "the original purpose of the child", we mean to refer to the original purpose of the soul in manifesting as that particular child.

Neal: Understood.

Plato: And do we also understand that the body and its personality are not the original purpose of the soul, but are instruments for accomplishing that purpose?

Neal: Agreed.

Plato: And then, since the body is just a means to the soul's ends, those "ends" – the original purpose – can never have anything to do with the body and its accoutrements per se.

Neal: Also agreed. We may lay it down as a principle that no soul ever incarnates for the purpose of accumulating more material toys than others, chasing after money and reputation, or harming the corporeal manifestations of other souls. But now, having ruled out the conscious desires of most humans as candidates for the soul's original purpose in incarnating, the question still remains.

Plato: It is important to know where not to look for that purpose, which is why we have been stressing the negative a bit. OK, I can think of three basic ways. There may be more that will occur to me, or us, later. So (i) the first way that will enable caretakers to know the original purpose of (the soul of) the child they are now raising is the one I originally suggested. The child will be carefully observed while at play, for the free and playful behaviors of the child indicate the proclivities of the soul. (ii) The second way will be to consult with mediums. For the veil between our worlds will be considerably thinner than it is at present, and mediumship will be a socially acceptable way of communicating between our worlds, as it was in my time. But perhaps most important, (iii) children will be taught meditation at as early an age as possible, so that lines of communication between the soul and its embodied manifestation (the child) will be kept more or less open.

4) Thinning the Veil

Benedict: Now, when we speak of the "veil" between our worlds, this is just a manner of speaking. There is, of course, no literal veil, for all is Consciousness. But to create what is called "the human condition", or the "human experience", Consciousness closes off a part of itself to the fullness of what it is, creating an illusion of separation. But it is useful to speak of a "veil", and we may continue to do so.

William: Psychologically, in terms of the human psyche, the "veil" occurs in the form of what I called the "margin" between the conscious and unconscious mind.

Neal: Yes, now of course the term "unconscious mind" is a bit of an oxymoron, and I greatly prefer the term "subliminal mind" that was used in your time. But I sense we will be discussing this later in our conversation.

William: Correct. Right now I wanted to say that I am extremely curious to observe this process, to see how thin the margin can become without rupturing altogether. And the margin begins to form in the age period we are now concerned with, from birth to about two years old.

Neal: What do you mean? – Wait, I see, if the margin ruptures, the soul cannot continue to have a human experience, because the margin is what separates the conscious mind from the knowledge of its Source. So for the human experience to continue, some forgetfulness is necessary, but not nearly as much as at present.

William: Yes, and to use the analogy of a membrane, we want the veil generally to become more porous than it has been, so that information might flow more readily across the boundaries of our worlds. So how thin can the veil become without rupturing? And what influences, coming from the child's physical environment, might contribute to thinning the veil?

Neal: What do you mean?

William: Well, as Benedict might put, some external influences, as they act on the infant's body, increase the overall health and well-being of the body; others decrease the body's power, and still others have no effect. Some external influences will have the same effect on all infants, others will be specific to the individual. For each stage of child development, there will be child-care experts who have studied the matter empirically, and the best knowledge of the time period will be applied to the process of child development.

Neal: I'm not sure I understand your meaning completely. Could you give some examples?

William: Certainly. The general principle is this: the healthier and happier the child, the thinner will be the veil. The more the child thrives and flourishes, the thinner the membrane that seems to separate the child from its Source. Your present science already knows much about this – about what is conducive to the child's flourishing – but future science will discover much more, as the physiological correlates to thriving and flourishing are discovered and explored. OK, you wanted some examples. Touching and caressing a baby are external influences that assist every child to thrive. So does being talked to and sung to. Same with food. But in this case, the influences might vary with the child. As we have said, mother's milk is good for all babies, but the benefits of other foods might depend on the baby's specific physiology. And I suppose that cyanide would be an example of an external influence that is harmful for all babies, along with the so-called "American diet", consisting mostly of salt, fat, and sugar.

I'm particularly interested in examining the effect of music, and combinations of sound, on the developing brain.

Neal: Yes, I very much agreed with you when you wrote that music has "ontological messages". So if it turns out, as has been suggested, that Mozart's music has a beneficial effect on the developing brain, then babies in our New Society will be listening to Mozart's music.

Plato: And if it turns out some other combinations of sound have a deleterious effect on the developing brain, then our babies and children will be protected from that.

Neal: *(to Plato, smiling)* You've gotten a bum rap for this over the years – you had the audacity to suggest that the guardians of Society must censor the forms of "art" that children are exposed to.

Plato: *(smiling)* Yes, especially from those with a "democratic" temperament, unable to discern that not all pleasures are equal.

Neal: But you know, I think I've found a very simple explanation for people's extraordinary resistance to what is a simple, and in many ways, obvious idea.

Plato: I'm listening.

Neal: It's sexism, plain and simple! Look, every decent parent does the best he or she can to protect her child from negative environmental influences. So censoring environmental influences is the job of every parent. But until recently, (i) no men were involved with parenting, and (ii) only men were reading your writings. So the people criticizing you on this point were those who had no experience with raising children. But now women are reading your writings, men are becoming involved with child-rearing, and they will see for themselves the difference in their babies' responses to gentle music and loud, discordant sounds. If, or rather, when, it can be demonstrated that Mozart has a positive effect on infant brain development, whereas other forms of so-called music, like "rap" and "heavy metal", have a negative effect on infant brain development, then I assure you that even your loudest critics will be censoring what their children are exposed to.

Plato: *(with humor)* Then perhaps they will also be consistent in their treatment of their children and their treatment of me. That is, hopefully they will recognize that they are applying my ideas to how they are raising their children.

Neal: *(laughing)* I suppose it is not beyond human inconstancy for a so-called Plato scholar to robustly censor his child's environment while equally robustly criticizing you for making that suggestion.

Benedict: That should be the worst of human inconstancies. But now, while agreeing with what has been said, there is an assumption lurking in our discussion that ought to be recognized.

Neal: What assumption?

Benedict: William began this discussion talking about the veil, or margin, that separates human consciousness from nonhuman consciousness. Can this margin be made thinner without rupturing? The conversation then shifted to environmental influences on the child, some of which contribute to the flourishing of the child, others of which do not. All well and good. But the implicit assumption here is that what assists the child in thriving and flourishing also helps keep the margin thin. Although I'm strongly inclined to agree with this assumption, I think we need to discuss it.

Socrates: Good. And I will play the role of Devil's Advocate by suggesting that the very opposite of our assumption might be true.

Neal: What do you mean?

Socrates: Recall that case involving infants that you alluded to earlier –

Neal: Yes, the one where they all died for lack of nurturing.

Socrates: The one where they all returned Home because they felt unwelcomed in your dimension. *(Smiling)* You see the importance of using "other words", that is, of describing this from different perspectives. From your perspective, the human perspective, yes, they all died. But from my perspective, they were never really in your world at all. That is to say, in their case, the "margin" or "membrane" that William is fond of, did not begin to form. They did not identify with their bodies, and thus, from their perspective, they did not become human.

Neal: Huh? I think you need to elaborate on this.

William: Socrates is quite correct. We agree that the soul, in order to have a human experience, must separate off a portion of itself from the full knowledge of what it is.

Neal: Oh yes, so in the case that appears "unfortunate" from my perspective, the souls involved did not reach the stage of separating off a portion of themselves from the knowledge of what it is.

William: And to reach this stage of forming a margin (it does not matter whether we call it a "margin" or "veil" or "membrane" or "boundary"), that is to say, of becoming human, the soul must be enticed to identify with a body.

Socrates: And this "enticement" takes the form of nurturing the infant, caressing it, singing to it, playing with it, etc. *(With humor)* It's really a sort of trickery, don't you think?

Neal: What?

Socrates: Well, when the mother is nurturing what she perceives as an infant, what is she really saying to the soul that is manifesting itself as that infant?

Neal: *(laughing)* She's saying something like "come on in, the water's fine", or "see how much fun you can have in this body?" or "it's safe for you to identify with this body", or "you can still feel Love when you enter this body".

Socrates: – And so the soul gets tricked, more or less, into identifying with the body. Of course, from the soul's perspective, it desires to be tricked in this way, but it needs the assistance of a welcoming environment for the trick to work.

Now, to continue with my role of "devil's advocate", if the environment is 100% unwelcoming, the "trick" will not work, the margin will not be formed, and the soul will not have a human experience, at least, not with that particular body. But what might happen if the environment were, say, only 50% or 60% unwelcoming?

Neal: Well, one possibility is that a margin begins to form, but only partially, since the soul might have mixed feelings about identifying with a body under such conditions. So it might want to keep the door partially open, so to speak, to exiting and returning Home.

Socrates: And keeping the door open means, using William's metaphor, the margin does not form properly or completely, but rather, remains somewhat porous. And because the margin has not formed properly, influences from our world, the non-embodied world, can seep through the pores of the margin and affect the conscious thinking of the human. So to make my argument, it would seem that contrary to our assumption above, that what keeps the margins thin is a less-than-supportive environment.

Neal: *(to Socrates, with some humor)* You get off on this, don't you?

Socrates: *(innocently)* Whatever do you mean?

Neal: You know exactly what I mean. You take something obvious, something that everyone agrees with, turn it upside down, leaving it to the rest of us to straighten it out again, if it can be straightened out. Well, I see that honesty compels me to even strengthen your argument for you.

Socrates: Oh?

Neal: It seems that there is empirical evidence that you are correct. I take it that we all agree that mediums – those who can communicate directly with non-embodied minds – are examples of humans who have porous margins. Communications from spirits flow through holes in their margins to reach their conscious minds.

William: Yes, that is certainly how I conceived of the matter. Mediums are examples of humans with relatively thin margins, allowing communications from the subliminal mind to impress itself upon the conscious mind. But what "empirical evidence" are you referring to?

Neal: Some studies appear to show that mediums, as a sample of the population, suffer more abuse as children than the population as a whole. When, as children, they are being beaten or raped, many just detach from their bodies at the time. "Disassociation" is the clinical term. So physical abuse causes the child to disassociate from its body, and by doing that repeatedly as children, their margins are more porous than most other children, so that when they become adults, they retain the ability to "disassociate" and communicate with spirit. So it would seem that Socrates' "devil's advocate" argument has some empirical support. But I really do not like this conclusion.

William: *(smiling)* Neither do I. And we would certainly be in a fine mess if it turned out that the only way to keep the lines of communication open was to abuse our children. Fortunately, this will not be the case.

Neal: I certainly hope not. But before we investigate this, I want to mention some cases that provide additional support for Socrates' "devil's advocate" argument.

Socrates: *(winking at me)* Now who's getting off on playing devil's advocate?

Neal: Yes, yes, I know. Well here it is: there are lots of cases involving children with verified memories of "past lives". Now usually our so-called "past lives" are on the other side of the veil, and because of that, we humans do not have access to them. So for a child to have the actual memories of a past-life personality, the veil would have to be somewhat porous.

Socrates: And in order to make the veil porous, are these children with the memories abused?

Neal: No. A different mechanism, if I may use that term, seems to apply. It turns out that almost all of these remembered past lives ended rather badly, usually with a sudden and violent death, often an accident of some sort. I don't know of a single case in which the past life personality died of old age. So it appears that a sudden, violent death in one life increases the odds of having a porous margin in the next.

Socrates: Now, now, to say that these remembered lives "ended rather badly" involves a judgment of some sort. In truth, all lives end in perfect harmony with the script according to which the entrances and exits of all souls to and from the theater of embodiment is determined. Death, as I urged in my little public speech, is never a bad thing.

Neal: What little speech?

Socrates: The one I gave in Athens some 2,400 years ago.

Neal: *(blushing)* Yes, I know it well. But now, how shall we respond to our "devil's advocate" argument? I want to show that the best way to keep the veil thin is through love and nurturing, not abuse and violence.

William: This will not be too difficult, I think. First of all, let us note that there is a difference between a veil or margin that is thin, and one that is shot full of holes. Indeed, there are many circumstances under which a margin does not form properly, having tears and ruptures that do not allow for a coherent human experience. Mental illnesses such as psychoses and schizophrenia are examples of what can happen with a margin shot full of holes, so to speak.

Benedict: And we should also note that abuse does not invariably lead to mediumship, but more often, leads to mental illnesses of various kinds and degrees. So abuse is not a sufficient condition for producing a medium.

Neal: And neither is it a necessary condition, since there are many mediums who were not abused in childhood.

Benedict: And if something is neither a necessary nor sufficient condition for the production of something else, then the two cannot be causally related. Do we agree?

Neal: Yes. We can agree that early childhood abuse may indeed affect the veil in the developing human being, and that although this "affect" may in some circumstances lead to mediumship or other psychic or creative abilities, it will more often lead to mental illness, or what Plato once characterized "mortal maladies".

Plato: Yes, I remember. For although both "divine madness" (inspiration from the gods) and "mortal madness" (schizophrenia, psychosis) involve porous margins, they are not "porous" in the same way. So we want to examine early childhood influences that thin out William's margins in a way that leads to inspiration, not insanity. But before we do that, I want to say a word or two about the reincarnation cases.

Neal: Go ahead.

Plato: There are many factors that influence, in a given case, the thickness or thinness of a margin, and whether and to what extent it may be "shot full of holes", to use William's phrase. Some of these factors are on our side of the veil, some are on your side, and we are primarily interested in the latter, such as early childhood education. In the reincarnational cases, the primary influence is what you call the past-life personality, whose sudden departure sometimes leaves it with "unfinished business". Of course, its business really is "finished" with its death, but it doesn't initially realize this, so it seeks further expression through another human expression of its own soul, the so-called "present personality". This desire to continue expressing itself as itself on the part of the past personality affects the development of the veil of the present personality, so as to allow incursions from the past personality into the conscious awareness of the present personality. But after a while, several years usually, the past personality ceases its activities and goes about its proper business on our side of the veil, and the present personality develops normally. In almost every such case, both personalities belong to the same soul, and it is at that level that things get resolved. So these cases are not really of concern to us now, except to add that the present personality is a small child who, in order to come to terms with the "intrusions" from his past-life personality, will need acceptance, understanding, and love.

Neal: I agree. "Acceptance, understanding, and love" are needed by every "small child", not just those who have may have issues with past-life personalities.

Socrates: And it will be good to remind ourselves that our New Social Contract requires that we organize our New World Order in such a way that the needs of every child are met.

William: And that will do the trick nicely!

Neal: Huh? What trick?

William: *(smiling)* The "trick" of thinning out the margins without rupturing them. Now, we are using the concepts of "margins" and "veils" as analogies. Our concern is that the newly embodied soul – the infant, baby, and toddler – retain in its psychological nature the original purpose(s) for which it has incarnated in the first place. And we are asking: what are the psychological factors that, from the human side of the veil, help or hinder the human consciousness to remember its original purpose.

Plato: And this "remembering" need not be fully conscious. So if the original purpose be, say, a life as a musician, then it will suffice if the embodied soul be conscious of its desires to make music, even though it is not conscious of its full connection with its Soul. This is the thinning of the veil we wanted: not so thin that the soul cannot have a human experience, which requires a certain amount of forgetfulness, but thin enough so that influences from the Soul, in the form of subtle thoughts and desires, may yet enter into the human consciousness, so that the human desires for herself the very same thing that the Soul desires.

Neal: OK, so we must now investigate what it is that causes the developing human personality to lose sight of its original purpose, or in other words, what causes a human consciousness to become so "hardened" that it is unable to receive influences from its own soul. And let's consider an example discussed earlier, where we concluded that it is never the case that a soul incarnates in order to accumulate lots of money. What has gone wrong, may we ask, in the case of a soul whose original purpose was to be a musician, but who now finds himself a money-making banker?

William: The culprit, in this case and every case, is the presence of fear. As the baby becomes self-conscious, it becomes conscious that it is a self separate from other such selves. This is the human condition, and fear is a necessary consequence of separation. If the amount of fear is beyond a certain point, the developing human will shift its energies away from its original purpose, and towards sustaining and securing its embodied form.

Plato: Now as we have said, all humans must experience this

existential fear; it goes with the territory so to speak, and is a necessary consequence of the separation. But this fear (or loneliness, or anxiety) can be greatly influenced by environmental conditions. A child raised under very loving conditions will be less fearful than a child raised under harsh conditions that exacerbate the original existential fear.

Benedict: And now, here's where things get interesting.

William: *(with humor)* Have we been boring you up until now?

Benedict: *(laughing)* No, no, not at all. I just got a little excited about applying some of my own philosophical ideas to our present situation.

William: *(more seriously)* You know, Benedict, I like most others who approach your written works come away with a sense of it as high level, rarified abstractions. I will greatly welcome the opportunity to understand how it can be relevant in addressing the issue of fear in infants and babies…

Neal: *(to William)* And I will insist, on Benedict's behalf, that one has not fully understood those "high level rarified abstractions" until one understands how it is relevant in addressing the issue of fear in babies.

William: And I'm quite willing to be convinced of the relevancy. Proceed, Benedict.

5) Existential Angst

Benedict: There are two basic concepts in my written philosophy (by which I mean to refer to my *Ethics*) that are relevant to our present discussion: I'll mention one and use the other. Every individual endeavors or strives to flourish in its own being. ("Flourish" or even "unfold" is a much better English word than either "persevere" or "maintains".) The flourishing, when applied to an infant, is greatly impeded by fear. In fact, the presence of fear in an infant decreases its power-of-action, and prevents the natural unfolding and flourishing of its own nature. Whatever environmental factors reduce fear will also increase the infant's striving to flourish, which striving constitutes the very essence of the infant, and originates from our side of the margin. So reducing the fear makes the margins more permeable.

But in order to satisfy William's request that my "rarified abstractions" become more practically applicable, we need to know when and to what extent a given infant or baby is feeling the emotion of fear. The baby, as we have noted, cannot just tell us what he is feeling. But there are specific correlations between emotions and physiology, many correlations of which have already been established, and many more of which will be established in the near future. Now it is quite obvious that a baby who is crying is in emotional distress; and it is perhaps just as obvious that there are clear physiological indicators of this stress. Crying is itself such an indicator, and the near future will bring more subtle measurements of, say, brain activity, cellular communication, blood flow, etc. Science will show, if it has not already shown, that all physiological correlates of the emotion called fear are harmful to the overall health and development of the body.

William: I think I see how this could be very useful. We could... *(William was about to describe some possible experiments that might establish more subtle correlations, when Socrates interrupted.)*

Socrates: Hold on, Will. Before we discuss some of the subtle correlations between a baby's inner life and outward behavior, we must fully absorb what Benedict has said about one important not-so-subtle correlation.

William: What did he say?

Benedict: *(to Socrates)* Indeed, what did I say?

Socrates: *(smiling)* You said that a baby's crying is itself a physiological indicator of its emotional state of mind. The world has not yet fully understood this fact.

(As the meaning of Socrates' words unfolds in my mind, a sadness descends upon me; tears flow freely, I don't know why.)

Socrates: *(to me)* You understand now, do you not?

Neal: Yes, I think so. I will need time to absorb this.

Socrates: *(smiling)* No, you don't need more time. You have been "absorbing" this lesson all your life. The emotions you are now feeling indicate to you that learning this lesson has been one of your purposes in incarnating. This present moment is merely a recognition of what has been learned. Incidentally, you might want to prevent your tears from dripping into your computer.

Neal: *(laughing)* Thanks for the warning.

Socrates: Don't mention it. And now, we, or rather you, must tell the others what has just happened.

William: Yes, please tell us.

Benedict: We could see a wave of emotion moving through you, and being released; but what is the connection between those emotions and Socrates' obvious statement that a baby's crying is a physiological indicator of its emotional distress? So go get yourself another cup of coffee, then come back and tell us what happened.

Neal: Ah, yes, coffee is so good. Well, those emotions were as intense as they were unexpected. This got triggered when Socrates said, "The world has not yet fully understood this fact." My immediate reaction was something like, "What does he mean by that? Everyone understands that a baby cries when it is in distress."

William: And what is it about that simple statement that, according to Socrates, the world has not fully understood?

Neal: The world tends to think that a baby's distress must be physiological. When it shows its distress behaviorally, by crying, we assume that it is crying for some physical reason; it is hungry, or wet, or having indigestion. It does not usually occur to us that a baby can cry for raw, existential reasons that have nothing to do with bodily functions. The thought came to me suddenly, after Socrates said what he said, that most of the times a baby cries it is not so much for the needs of its body, but rather an expression of angst at finding itself embodied. A baby's cry expresses the suffering inherent in the human experience: separation from the Source of Unconditional Love, and the subsequent fear. So perhaps we can say that the main reason a baby cries is because it feels fear, and the best way to help a baby is holding and caressing. The effect of caressing a baby can be measured physiologically, and we can state categorically that the best way of responding to a baby's fear is through holding, caressing, and gentle and soothing sounds.

Socrates: So we can say that the primary cause of a baby's distress is embodiment per se; being hungry, wet, etc. are merely additional details.

Plato: And we can buttress this conclusion by noting a relevant feature of the Near-Death Experience.

Neal: Which feature?

Plato: On the whole, people who have an NDE do not wish to return to embodied life, and when they are told they can't stay, or when they just find themselves back in their body, they are often very upset. They feel, so to speak, like they have been thrown out of Heaven, and are sometimes quite angry with the poor doctors who resuscitated them.

Socrates: This is what a baby experiences every day.

Neal: *(some of the sadness I had experienced before begins to return, as I become more aware of the full horror of the human condition)* Every day.

Plato: Yes, every day. For you have heard it said that until roughly two years old, when language controls the brain, the consciousness of the baby is not rigidly attached to its body, so it can return Home at times, hang out with friends, and bathe in Unconditional Love. Then, after being immersed in the waters of Unconditional Love, when it finds itself stuck in a body, seemingly cut off from Love, it responds in the only rational way one could respond to such a situation. It cries, sometimes unconsolably.

Neal: And so, what the world still needs to learn, is that a baby's crying is akin to how a Near-Death Experiencer feels upon finding herself back in the body, separated from the Source of Love. It is very painful psychologically, and a baby feels this pain every day. To the soul, there is no greater distress than that of feeling separated from Love.

Socrates: Yes. Now, to return briefly to the emotional release you recently experienced, these thoughts were all in your mind, but they were instantaneously applied to what I referred to as one of your "lessons" for this life. The emotional release accompanied this application.

Benedict: What "lesson" is he talking about?

Neal: The lesson, as if you didn't know, is to release all feelings of righteous indignation towards my favorite villains. In that moment, instead of seeing those bankers and CEOs as obnoxious two year olds throwing a temper tantrum, I saw them as two-month-old babies, crying because of loneliness, because of fear, because of profound grief over the loss of their connection to the Source of Love. In that moment, my anger towards them completely dissipated, and tears of compassion flowed freely.

(Several months have passed since my last writing session. During that time, the insight described above seems to have held firm. Subtle and not-so-subtle feelings of "superiority" and "righteous indignation" with regard to the very wealthy, whose collective greed is destroying the planet's ability to sustain human life, are being transformed into kinder and more compassionate feelings. And when those old "righteous indignation" feelings return, I find that William's suggestion to think of it as a play is very useful. I can still root against the "bad" guys, but with the understanding that they are playing an essential role in this human drama of ours, that I am not really any "better than" they, that the various "roles" assigned to humans by Central Casting, so to speak, does not make one human being better or worse than another, and that we are all expressions of the same "One Mind". On occasion, in spite of myself, I have even felt compassion towards some of these "villains", when I have been able to see past their fancy Italian suits into their suffering. For to derive one's sense of self-worth from money or status alone is, in reality, to have no sense of self-worth at all.)

Plato: Good. This is not an easy lesson to learn, and, as we discussed in a previous conversation, while embodied, I was never quite able to forgive the Athenians for dispatching Socrates the way they did. And any inability to forgive is really an egoic clinging to a sense of superiority.

Neal: I understand. There is something quite delicious about those feelings of righteous indignation, because they allow one to feel superior to others. But from the perspective of the One Mind, we are all in this together, and the fact that we are all expressions of the same One Mind must become the Source of self-worth for all humans, regardless of the role we are currently playing. In our New World Order, we must find a way to raise children so they do not become encumbered with feelings of superiority or inferiority with regard to their fellow human beings.

Plato: Yes, but this must be done, or attempted, in full knowledge of the difficulties involved. As Benedict wrote, the human body is physiologically hardwired to produce feelings of envy with regard to other humans. We will address this in some detail a little later. For now, let's return to what we were talking about just before Socrates' word triggered that shift in your own consciousness.

Neal: OK. We were discussing how to raise a baby so that his felt connection between the realm from which he is emerging (the non-embodied) and the realm into which he is emerging (the embodied) is not completely obliterated. Or in William's terms, we want the veil or margin between the two to be as thin as possible, without rupturing.

Benedict: Yes, and Socrates' little remark that triggered your own insight is also very important with regard to raising infants and babies. An infant never cries for "no reason", and the main reason involves existential angst with regard to embodiment per se. The remedy is touching, caressing, and nurturing in every way possible.

Neal: So those so-called child-rearing methods, according to which a crying baby should be left by itself, will come to be seen as barbaric.

Benedict: Well, perhaps "barbaric" is too strong; "ignorant" is a better word. The cure for ignorance is knowledge, and scientists have already accumulated quite a bit of knowledge on these matters.

William: Yes, for example, the physiological effect of crying on the development of the infant's brain can be studied and measured. The further effect of caressing on the nervous system of a baby can be measured.

Benedict: And as the body goes, so goes the mind. The physiological indicators of a thriving infant and baby are already somewhat known, and much more will be discovered in the years to come. With respect to a model of physiological health, it will be discovered that allowing an infant to cry unattended is not physiologically healthy, and that picking up, holding, caressing, etc. a crying baby greatly reduces the harm engendered by the crying. Touching and caressing are necessary for the baby's nervous system to develop properly. And, we might also mention, so is proper nutrition.

William: And future science will be able to tailor nutrition to the specific needs of a given baby. During infancy, of course, the best nutrition will be milk from the infant's biological mother. But later, when the baby starts eating solid foods, it is not necessarily the case that the same diet will be equally beneficial for all babies. The effects of various kinds of food (meat, grains, dairy, fruits, vegetables, etc., etc.) on the developing body can and will be ascertained on an individual level, and this information will then be used to discover what kind of diet is best for the individual baby.

Neal: *(smiling)* I suppose there will be no such thing as "fast foods" in our New Society.

William: No indeed. For the word "food" will be used only with reference to what is truly nutritious to the body, and as everyone knows, the so-called "fast foods" of your culture not only have no nutritional value for any body, but they are quite harmful for every body.

Neal: So to summarize, whatever assists the baby's body to grow, develop, and thrive will be provided to that baby by our New Society. Is there anything more to be said regarding this first stage of the soul's adventure into human form?

Benedict: Only this: the process of embodiment begins at conception, and the nine months spent in the womb are just as important as the subsequent two years after birth. The thriving of the developing fetus depends very much on the mother's overall sense of well-being, as well as diet and level of exercise.

Neal: You mean that the fetus can sense and is affected by its mother's emotions?

Benedict: Well yes, you could put it that way, but instead of saying that the fetus is affected by the mother's emotions, it might be better to express this in physiological terms.

Neal: I get it. The mother's emotions have physiological correlates. There are physiological correlates to so-called negative emotions like depression, anger, anxiety, as well as to positive emotions like joy and love, and future science will no doubt establish that the physiological correlates of the negative emotions hinder the optimal development of the fetus, while those of the positive emotions assist the development of the fetus.

Benedict: Exactly. So everything possible will be done to assist the mother to overcome all negative emotions during pregnancy, and to enjoy, that is, to feel joyful, throughout her whole pregnancy.

Socrates: Participating in the process by which a soul becomes embodied will be regarded as a sacred and joyful responsibility, not only for the mother, but also for society as a whole. We emphasize "joyful", because as Benedict has said, joy is the human emotion, the physiological correlate of which is most conducive to the thriving of the fetus.

Chapter III

Linguistic Consciousness

1) Lying

Plato: So I think, with these remarks, we are ready to move on to the next stage of child development. Of course, it goes without saying that talking about "stages" here is just for conceptual purposes. In reality all stages are present at all times.

Neal: What do you mean?

Plato: Nothing deep. For example, in discussing the infancy stage, we stressed the importance of nurturing touch for proper brain development. But a human being never outgrows her need to be touched, and even in advanced old age, touch is highly beneficial for both physical and psychological health. Another example: in the next stage, toddler/early childhood, we will be discussing, among other things, the effect of language and music on the developing brain. But the child's body is affected by music and language in utero, and continues to be affected throughout her whole life.

Neal: I understand. Besides language and music, what are some other issues that are important in the toddler stage? What kind of stories will we tell our children?

William: Not so fast. We must go slowly here. From my present perspective I can see there are difficulties both with language acquisition and sense experience. Now, when I use the word "difficulties", I mean with respect to our desire of keeping the margins porous, so that the child is able to receive messages and influences from Spirit even as language takes over.

Neal: What do you mean when you refer to language taking over?

William: When language "takes over", it is no longer possible to be aware of a thought without also having the words one would use to express that thought to another. The person then confuses his own consciousness with words and becomes identified or trapped within his language. Language adds quite a bit to the thickness of our margins, so we must investigate whether, and how, children may learn language effectively, but in such a way that language acquisition does not by itself block non-linguistic forms of communication.

Plato: And we agree, do we not, that non-linguistic forms of communication are superior to linguistic forms.

Neal: Yes. After all, non-embodied souls communicate without language. But for embodied souls, that is, for human beings, it seems that language is the basic mode of communication.

Benedict: *(smiling)* Yes, but only for a culture that values lying. We must guard against the naturalist fallacy, and not assume that, because language is the basic mode of communication in your present culture, language must be the basic mode of communication in any culture.

Plato: You see, when a child learns language, she has, for the first time, the ability to conceal her inner reality – her thoughts and feelings – from those around her. One could make the case that this ability is your culture's highest value, as no one can be successful in business or politics, and most other professions as well, without the ability to use language to conceal one's inner reality from others.

Socrates: The soul, as we have been saying, is hiding in a body, but the embodied soul continues and extends its hiding when it uses language to conceal its inner reality from others, that is to say, when it lies.

Neal: So, presumably, children of our New World Order will learn language, but not also learn how to use language to lie?

Plato: Yes, more or less, but we must review the argument a little to see why this must be so. Our most fundamental purpose here is the construction of a social order that will allow humans to live harmoniously with Father Earth. Otherwise, as we have said, souls will no longer be permitted to have a human experience. So the only social order possible is one in which humans live in harmony with the planet, and humans cannot live in harmony with the planet until they learn to live in harmony with one another.

Benedict: And since, of all possible human motivations, greed is the one that is now destroying the planet, it follows that greed must be eliminated from human consciousness if humans are to survive. Since lying is almost always in the service of greed, it follows that lying can have no place in our future society.

Plato: And then you, Neal, suggested that we could get some insight into the structure of this New Social Order by conceiving it as maximally supportive of the soul's original purpose in having a human experience. This is the line of argumentation we have been following.

William: Yes, the reason we want a thinner, rather than a thicker, margin, is that it is in the soul's best interest that its developing personality feel connected with its source, the soul.

Plato: So we ask the simple questions: (i) is it ever the case that it is in the soul's best interest that its developing personality be lied to? – And (ii) is it ever in the soul's best interest that its developing personality lie to others? By "developing personality" I mean the child at whatever developmental stage we are considering.

Neal: The second question is easy. Every time a person or child attempts to conceal its thoughts and feelings from others, that is, every time it lies, it adds a layer to the margin that separates the personality from its soul. So with respect to our desire that the personality be maximally in touch with its soul, lying is never in the soul's best interest.

Plato: And why do you think the first question may not also be easy?

Neal: *(smiling)* Because children are notorious for being able to ask questions that cannot be answered in terms that the child could understand?

Socrates: *(laughing)* And do you think grown-ups are any different? You so-called grown-ups are always asking the same absurd questions, like: "Why is there something rather than nothing?" "Why does God allow so much suffering?" ... or to get personal, "Why is your soul presently manifesting as the personality called Neal?" ... or even more personal: "Why does the Divine Being love you so much?"

Neal: Hah! You almost hooked me with that last question, as I almost found myself wanting to challenge its premise – that the Divine Being does in fact love me. But you have taught me well.

Socrates: Good. But the philosophical point here is to notice that language can be used to ask questions that cannot be answered in terms of language. But these questions, nevertheless, do have answers.

Neal: Yes. The NDE literature is filled with accounts of people bringing these questions, and others like them, to the Being of Light.

Socrates: *(playfully)* And how does this Being of Light answer these questions?

Neal: As if you didn't know. What people report is that their questions dissolve in the loving presence of the Being of Light. But alas, we cannot induce a Near-Death Experience in every child or grown-up who asks a question to which language cannot literally respond.

Plato: Hence *(glancing at Benedict)* the need, or usefulness, of using language non-literally. Now, many are the spiritual teachers, e.g. the Buddha, who simply refused to address such questions; instead, they focused on guiding their disciples to the Experience in which their questions were dissolved. But children are not monks, and neither will be the majority of grown-ups in our new society. So language must be used, but used non-literally, and explicitly so.

Neal: What do you mean?

Plato: Earlier you asked the question, "What kind of stories will we tell our children?"

Neal: Yes.

Plato: The most important thing about the stories we tell our children is that they be clearly labeled as "stories". Much suffering is caused by the failure of society to do so.

Neal: Please explain.

Plato: I fully intend to. There are two forms of suffering imposed upon the human condition that can be traced to society's failure to label the stories it tells its children as stories. The child, as I noted several thousand years ago, cannot distinguish what is literal from what is metaphorical, and hence tends to believe whatever grown-ups are telling him as literal truth. But we hold that language can be used literally only with reference to the physical world, so when language is used to talk about the spiritual reality from which the physical world emanates, then language is necessarily being used metaphorically or allegorically.

Benedict: I more or less agree with your last statement, but I think we should note that it is not absolute. There are cases in which the literal use of language fails, even with respect to the physical world, and cases in which language can be used literally with respect to spiritual reality.

Neal: I was thinking along the same lines. No words can literally describe the processes that, according to quantum theory, occur at the subatomic level. And statements like "consciousness is not produced by the brain", "consciousness continues after the body dies", and William's favorite, "there is a 'Something More' than the merely physical", seem to be statements that are literally true.

William: Yes, but if the stories we tell our children are confined to what can be said literally, our stories will be very short indeed.

Socrates: *(with humor)* ... And hardly suitable as bedtime stories. It is one thing for a spiritual teacher like the Buddha to silence his monks' metaphysical questions by pointing out the limitations of literal language and redirecting their attention to inner experience. But a child will not be so easily silenced, and will nag his parents relentlessly until they tell some story about what this Something More is like.

William: And anything that is said of this "Something More", other than the mere fact that it is, will involve a non-literal use of language that the child will tend to take literally. But I am curious to know, Plato, how this leads to two kinds of suffering?

Plato: The first form of suffering is obvious. Religious wars are the direct consequence of the inability of human beings to discern the difference between the literal and metaphorical use of language.

So children of a given religious, cultural, and ethnic background are told stories that they take as literally true. They then, as adults, happily murder those who, as children, were told and believed different stories. Historically there is perhaps no greater single cause for human suffering than organized religion – at least, those religions that insist their stories are literally true.

William: Indeed, organized religions are organized around words that are believed to be literally descriptive of Spiritual Reality – that is, of that which in principle cannot be captured by words. So the whole enterprise appears to be misguided from the very beginning. And what is the other kind of suffering?

Plato: It is more subtle than the first, but more insidious and psychologically damaging. Your psychologists have discovered that a two-year-old child has no understanding of the concept of lying, but a four-year-old child does. A four- or five-year-old child knows that it is possible to use language (i) to conceal his true feelings from others, and (ii) to misrepresent his actual behavior to others. No one of course explicitly teaches the child that he can or should use language to lie about what he feels or what he has done, and he does not know this at ages two and three, so lying is not innate.

Socrates: Indeed, the child has recently arrived from a Place where lying is not even conceivable.

Neal: *(laughing)* I know of no NDE account where an experiencer has tried to deceive the Being of Light, or fake his Life Review. One cannot lie in the presence of God.

Benedict: *(smiling, to me)* And to follow that train of thought to its logical conclusion, since there is no such thing as the "absence of God", it would seem to be the case that one cannot lie period.

Socrates: *(laughing)* A much too hasty conclusion, even if true. But it should serve as a reminder that embodied experience is inherently illusory.

Neal: So, Plato, if the ability to lie is neither innate nor explicitly taught, how does the child learn to lie?

Plato: – By observing adults and older children, that is, by imitation.

Benedict: Can we find another word for the term "observing", since that word suggests considerably more emotional detachment from the situation than the child has?

Plato: I see you have taken up Socrates' injunction to use "other words". Yes, you are right, the child is certainly not an unemotional observer; in fact, the emotions involved are often deeply traumatic, as they were for you, Neal.

Neal: Huh? What do you mean?

Plato: Let's consider a simple example, common in your culture. Every child is told the story of Santa Claus – a jovial, corpulent fellow who lives at the North Pole, and once a year brings presents to children with the help of a team of flying reindeer. Every two-year-old child who hears this story believes that it is literally true.

Neal: Yes.

Plato: But at age four or five, the child knows the story is not literally true.

Neal: Yes.

Plato: And what is the psychological effect of this experience on the child? By "this experience" I mean the experience of having been told something by one's parents and relatives, of believing that it was literally true, and then subsequently discovering that is not, and was not, true?

Neal: The child learns that his parents can lie.

Plato: Now, from the parents' perspective, it is a small thing. But from the child's perspective, nothing could be more devastating, psychologically. He has learned that his parents, his Earthly source of love, indeed of survival itself in physical form, can lie, and not just about little things, but about things that, like Santa Claus, are of vital importance to the three-year-old child. And of course, adults lie to children not only about "big things", like God and Santa Claus, but also about little things, usually to get the child to stop asking questions. But in either case, the psychological trauma that the child experiences upon first learning that adults lie is profound and permanent. Do you understand what I mean by using the word "permanent" here?

Neal: *(sadly)* Yes, I think so. Shall I state it using those "other words" that Socrates is so fond of?

Socrates: *(laughing)* Yes, exactly. *(Looking at me, addressing the sadness that has just come over me)* It is a sorry tale indeed, when told from the perspective of the developing child, which is what we are now attempting to do. But as you tell the tale, keep in mind that this is a sort of play or illusion, and that much if not most of the suffering within the illusion is caused by the ability of humans to lie: to use language in a way that conceals their feelings, thoughts, and behaviors from others. In order to create our New World Order, which will be our response to the prayer "on Earth, as in Heaven", we must examine in some detail the psychological process by which a soul, fresh from Heaven where deceit is both unknown and impossible, becomes a human being for whom lying and deceit are habitual, and even defining of your present social order.

Benedict: So allow the sadness you feel with regard to the experiences of the child as it becomes a member of your present social order to be mixed with joy at realizing that lying and deceit will play no role in our New Society.

Neal: All right. There are two major traumas that face the soul upon human embodiment. The first trauma is embodiment per se, which is unavoidable if the soul is to have a human experience. We have discussed this previously, and have laid down some guidelines for minimizing the effect of this trauma on the soul. The second trauma is the child's realization that grown-ups lie. Because there is no template (or "Form") for lying in the spirit world, the child has no understanding of lying and deceit when she first encounters it. So she is initially deeply confused. However, she has no choice except to internalize her new "reality": unlike the Place from which she has come, here on Earth the very source of her love and nurturing cannot be trusted to always be truthful. This insight is deeply traumatic, and the trauma, because it has no place else to go, forms another layer on

William's margins.

William: ... And a rather thick layer at that. Let me add that most of the lying that parents do with regard to their children is, from the perspective of the parent, trivial and inconsequential. For example, a child may ask for, or nag for, some candy. The parent, to stop the child from nagging, says the candy is all gone. Later the child discovers where the parents have hidden the candy. No parent thinks twice about telling their children such little "white lies", because they themselves have internalized the culture's paramount value of using language to hide, conceal and deceive. But from the child's perspective, the effect is devastating.

Neal: So parents teach lying to their children by lying to their children, and are completely unaware that this is what they are doing.

Benedict: And the only mechanism for changing this pattern is to bring awareness to the whole process, which is what we are now doing.

Neal: So the trauma becomes permanent in the sense that it adds a layer to the margins that separate the human world from the spirit world, and the personality develops with that margin in place. In a very real sense, all humans in our present culture suffer from post-traumatic stress disorder – the stress incurred from being lied to by those who are his source of nurturing and love.

Plato: You said above that there are two major sources of trauma that face the soul upon embodiment. Actually, there is a third, which we shall discuss later. Now the first source of trauma, embodiment per se, is a necessary condition for the soul to have a human experience. But the second source of trauma, lying, is not a necessary condition for embodiment, and hence, is avoidable. And since we are constructing our social order with a view to what is truly advantageous to the newly embodied soul, or child, we raised the question of whether it is ever advantageous to the soul for the child either to lie or to be lied to. Our analysis appears to have led us to the conclusion that it is never beneficial to the soul for the developing personality either to lie or to be lied to.

Socrates: In a sense, even the first trauma involves a lie: the lie that it is possible both to be and to be separated from Source. But this lie – the Big Lie of Forgetfulness, if you will – is necessary for the soul to have a human experience, and we assert without argument that having a human experience is of some benefit to the soul. *Lying* continues the soul's downward journey by (i) further separating the soul from the knowledge of its source, adding to the thickness of the margins, and (ii) separating the embodied soul from its connections with other humans. But the "way down", as we have called it, can go only so far before it self-destructs and burns down the theater in which the human drama plays itself out.

2) A Social Order Without Lying

Neal: So whether we consider the matter from the perspective of what is best for the soul or from the perspective of our desire that the human experience continue into the future, lying, and a social order predicated upon lying, must come to an end. But some people will protest that a social order without lying is not possible.

William: *(with humor)* And those who protest the loudest are undoubtedly society's biggest liars, who falsely believe they can gain advantage over others by lying and concealing.

Benedict: *(smiling)* Watch out for the naturalist fallacy here! Just because there may have been no past social order that was free from lying and deceit, that does not mean that no such social order is possible. To establish that latter claim, one would have to demonstrate that there is a necessary connection between (i) being human, (ii) living together with other humans and (iii) lying, such that the first two entail the third. But there is no such connection; there is no gene for lying.

Plato: So with unabashed optimism we assert that a social order in which humans do not lie, ever, is possible. More than just possible, it is necessary for such an order to come into being if the human race is to survive. We will have much more to say regarding the general features of our New Social Order. For now, it suffices to say that it will be a Society in which people do not lie, and because of that, children do not learn lying by imitating adults.

Neal: But, Plato, it is still the case that we must tell stories that are not literally true to children who, as you have said, cannot distinguish what is literal from what is allegorical. Are they not still liable to feeling that they were lied to, when they discover that a story they took literally – because they take all stories literally – was not literally true?

Plato: Well then, it appears that we must tell a fuller story about telling stories. The main story we have been telling is that the soul becomes human in order to experience itself as separate from God, or what is the same thing, to experience itself as separate from the Knowledge of what it is. So embodiment is a sort of Hiding from this Knowledge. The embodied soul, or human being, continues the downward path by (i) playing competitive games with one another and (ii) lying, that is to say, using words to hide from others her thoughts, feelings, and behaviors. We could even argue that (i) and (ii) are closely related, in that one must lie in order to play competitive games.

William: Indeed, those who are most successful at playing competitive games – the very rich – have lied so much, that is, have put so much effort into concealing their thoughts, feelings, and behaviors from others, that they have very little awareness of their own inner life.

Neal: I agree. They become truncated human beings. Not only are they, like all humans, unaware of their connection with the Divine, but also, they are unaware of that which is human within themselves.

William: But we must now notice that there is considerable variation in the extent to which humans lie. There is even some variation in the extent to which humans become embodied.

Neal: What do you mean? A soul is either embodied or it is not.

William:. Yes, but we could say that a soul that drinks deeply from Plato's River of Forgetfulness is more deeply embodied than a soul who drinks only a little. Or in Socrates' "other words" such a soul identifies more completely with its bodily form, which identification adds to the thickness of its margins.

Plato: Let us insert here a reminder that there are no literal rivers or margins. And this reminder also serves as a partial response, Neal, to your question above. We can insert reminders like this into the stories we tell our children. We can say to our children, while telling the story, things like: "We can picture that reindeer can fly, but we know that really they cannot," "We can imagine that animals talk in words, but really they do not." We can ask them to imagine other things that they know are not true.

Benedict: I like your last little exercise, for by teaching children to distinguish what they can imagine from what they know is true or false, we teach them the beginnings of reasoning, about which we will have much to say a little later.

Neal: I'm sure we will. But, William, what was your point in calling our attention to the variation in the degree to which humans lie.

William: It was to make the point, already made, that lying is not innate to the human condition. Those who have only the gambler's talent, the ability to lie with a straight face, will argue that everyone are liars just like them, except they are better at it than most. But the truth is that not all humans are liars just like them. And although it is the rare human who, like Socrates, is the "same man in public as he is in private", there are many who are as authentic to their inner thoughts and feelings as they can possibly be.

Neal: Well if such truth-telling humans exist, and they do, then all we need to do to get our New Society off the ground is to put them in charge of things.

Plato: Ah, but the only way that truth-telling humans will be put in charge of things is if the majority of humans become truth-telling themselves. A society such as your present society, in which all children are raised to be liars, could never tolerate being led by one who speaks only the truth. Now, William, you are right to point out that, in this present society, not all humans lie to the same extent.

There are many who strive to be as truthful "as they can possibly be". But how truthful is it possible to be in your society? Aside from the fact that many professions require lying (e.g. advertising, law, politics, business, etc.), a whole class of lies is explicitly sanctioned by your society, namely, so-called harmless little "white lies". But these white lies, which every child learns by imitating adults, are the very foundation of the big lies of Corporate America. Without a thorough training in the fine art of "white lying", children would not be able to master the kind of advanced lying required to be a successful con artist, which is what those corporate executives really are.

But I think we shall examine this later, when we consider how we might transition from your current society to our New Society. Right now we are describing this New Society, from the perspective of the needs and optimal development of the newly embodied soul. And since it is never a part of the needs of the soul to either lie or be lied to, and since children learn by imitation, lying cannot play any role in the social environment into which the soul manifests, or equivalently, into which the child is born.

Benedict: Even though we shall be discussing this later in more detail, I would like to mention a few things concerning your present society, and to expand on Plato's observation that little white lies are the foundation of corporate Big Lies. For people in your culture have so deeply internalized the values of lying that they hardly recognize their lies as lies. We define a lie to be any statement a person makes while knowing or believing that what is stated is not true. So little white lies, so beloved of your culture, are lies nevertheless, even though the person making the false statement does not intend to harm another. The two kinds of things that people are trained to lie about the most are (i) their own behavior, and (ii) their inner thoughts and feelings. Here are a few examples of how children are trained to lie: (i) little Johnny has taken a cookie without his parents' permission. If he admits it and tells the truth, he knows he will be punished; so to avoid punishment, he lies. (ii) Big Sister has snatched a toy from Little Sister. Mommy makes Big Sister return the toy and apologize to

Little Sister. When Big Sister utters the words "I'm sorry," she knows it is not true; she is not sorry at all, and regrets only getting caught by Mom. So Mom has forced her daughter to lie. When these scenarios, and many others like them, happen many, many times, the child grows up believing that such lies are normal and appropriate. These are the seeds of which the lies of your corporate CEOs and other con artists are the flowering.

Socrates: And we should perhaps emphasize that this process of conditioning is highly stressful to the newly embodied soul, as lying is not natural to the soul and hence induces further separation of the soul from its developing personality. By "adapting" to a culture in which lying is the norm, the child adds further layers to the "margins".

Plato: *(smiling)* It's almost as if the soul has been compelled to drink from the River of Forgetfulness not just once, but twice.

Neal: How so?

Plato: The first time is to become embodied. But then, as if embodiment per se were not sufficient, the soul, after a few years of being embodied, is compelled to return to the River and drink even more, adding additional layers to the margins. Not only must they suffer the trauma of realizing that grown-ups lie, they are forced to suffer the further trauma of becoming liars themselves. In our New Society souls will not be compelled to return to the River once they have become embodied.

Neal: If, in our New Society, we are forbidden from sending newly embodied souls back to the River a second time, then our methods of child-rearing will have to be quite different from what they are at present.

Socrates: Now, now, my friend, don't strain yourself trying to figure it all out right now. Suffice to say, the general principles of dog training will apply.

Neal: What?

William: *(laughing)* Socrates is not being as inscrutable as he seems. All dog owners know that to train a dog properly, one must never hit the dog, yell at it, or punish it. Patience, consistency, positive reinforcement, no deception, and lots of love and affection, are the ways of the dog trainer. Now dogs are predisposed to love and play with whoever loves and plays with them, and it is this predisposition to love and be affectionate that causes the dog to want to please her trainer. But humans come into the world with the same predisposition to love and play that dogs have.

Neal: So if dogs can be trained to be obedient without suffering violence to their bodies or their souls, then so can children. But actually this is a profound statement, and quite contrary to what is currently believed, which is that the human being is a "blank slate" at birth, or if not a blank slate, then a mere body filled with animal desires that must be "civilized" out of them. But our metaphysics tells us that the child comes from Love, or what is the same thing, from the knowledge of its interconnections with all things, hence its predisposition to love.

William: And it is a predisposition that must be "civilized" out of the child if he is to become a conscienceless sociopathic corporate CEO. Now, learning language itself adds a layer or two to the thickness of the margins, but teaching the child to use language to lie and deceive adds many more such layers.

Neal: How does language by itself add to the thickness of the margins?

William: Do we agree that before a child has learned language it is conscious and has a rich inner life?

Neal: Well, to play devil's advocate, the "blank slate" folks would argue that the child is not fully conscious until after it has learned language. And they might support this belief by pointing out that people usually cannot remember anything that happened prior to learning language. But, on our principles, a newly embodied soul must be conscious, since it is still connected with Source, which is Consciousness Itself.

William: So then, the process of learning language funnels and truncates this spark of Divine Consciousness, so that it experiences the world in terms of the language it has learned. It is very difficult for conditioned adults to be able to think a thought without also thinking of the words that would be used to verbally express the thought. So consciousness has become entrapped by language.

3) Non-Linguistic Modalities

Neal: So we can say that embodiment per se imprisons the soul into a body, language further limits the (now embodied) soul by compelling it to experience itself only in terms of what can be expressed in language, and teaching children to use language to lie and deceive further alienates the soul from its own inner knowing. But what might be some examples of conscious experience that is independent of language?

Socrates: *(looking at me quizzically)* Surely you are not asking us to use words to describe conscious experience that cannot be put into words…?

Neal: *(laughing)* Well, no, but…

Plato: But nevertheless, we remind ourselves that what we may call "linguistic consciousness" – consciousness that experiences itself as mediated through the forms of language and words – the dominant form of consciousness on the planet today, constitutes by far the smallest portion of the soul's experiences and adventures.

Socrates: *(playfully)* So small, in fact, that it hardly exists at all.

Neal: *(also playfully)* I'll ignore your insult of my present condition.

Socrates: What condition are you talking about?

Neal: The human condition.

Socrates: *(with humor)* Ah yes, a rather delicate condition for any soul to find itself in. But not to worry, I expect the patient to make a full recovery from its present condition, after which we shall playfully discuss whether and to what extent it was real.

Neal: Thank you, doctor. But I get the point. Language plays no role whatsoever in the experiences and communications of the soul when it is not embodied, which is the soul's true reality. Then, after two or three years of embodiment, most of what it experiences as its identity is in linguistic form, and it experiences both the world and itself in terms of words and concepts. Can we raise our children in such a way that linguistic consciousness does not become the whole of what it experiences itself as being?

Plato: Yes, of course. Although it is certainly necessary that the newly embodied soul learn language, it is not necessary that the totality of the newly embodied soul's experiences be confined only to linguistic form. So what, you have asked, might these other forms of consciousness be – consciousness that is (i) embodied but (ii) non-linguistic? It is part of the pathology of your culture – that is, part of the reason your culture is unable to live in harmony with Father Earth – to believe that linguistic consciousness is the only form of consciousness, or, if other forms do exist, they are vastly inferior to linguistic consciousness. The irony here is that non-linguistic forms of consciousness are well known to all, but are not reinforced by the child's environment, except in special cases.

Neal: Such as…?

Plato: I'll mention a few right now, but then I want to say a few more things about what we are calling linguistic consciousness. A few examples of non-linguistic modes of human conscious experience are: music, gymnastics, art, dance, and the development of skills (techne). We may also include the kind of conscious awareness associated with emotional intelligence and the ability to empathize with the emotions of others. Moreover, psychic and mediumship abilities, of which all children are capable before language has captured the brain, will be encouraged instead of repressed. So the children of our New Society will grow up spending lots of time in non-linguistic forms of consciousness, and hence it is much less likely that they will become trapped into the illusion that linguistic consciousness is the only, or the best, or "highest" form of consciousness.

William: And of course, *The Varieties of Religious Experience* must be included in the list of non-linguistic forms of conscious experience of which the embodied soul is capable. No doubt shamanic rituals of various kinds – which give humans direct experience of non-linguistic forms of consciousness – will be an important part of every child's upbringing.

Neal: But many shamanic rituals involve using psychoactive plants to induce altered states of consciousness.

William: Exactly! For by the word "altered" you cannot mean anything other than "different from what humans usually experience", or equivalently, "different from linguistic consciousness". Do you see how your comment reflects your culture's bias that non-linguistic forms of consciousness are somehow suspect?

Benedict: *(with a little humor)* And don't you think that, instead of commenting on obscure ancient texts written in obscure ancient languages, it would be better if 13-year-old boys – and girls too, now – were given a direct experience of their intrinsic connection with all beings?

Neal: I suppose so. But before we go into this I want to hear what Plato has to say about linguistic consciousness.

Plato: The overall function of language is to allow humans to communicate with one another about events in the physical world. Language has no power to depict the spiritual reality from which all souls emanate, which is why all mystics and Near-Death Experiencers – well *(glancing at Benedict)* most of them anyway – utter frequent caveats about the inability of language to describe their conscious experiences. But language has far less ability to describe even embodied experience than is generally supposed.

William: *(with humor)* "Generally supposed", especially by those whose brains have become excessively encrusted by linguistic form. *(To me)* I'm referring to our colleagues, of course.

Neal: Of course.

Plato: *(smiling)* And our children will be prevented from succumbing to the grand illusion about language that has befallen your colleagues.

Neal: What is this "grand illusion"?

Plato: I'm glad you asked. It is the illusion that words have meaning. *People* have meaning, and sometimes use words to express meaning, but the words, independent of the minds that use them, have no meaning. Your colleagues, who may be taken as extreme examples of humans in whom linguistic consciousness reigns supreme, are unable to think without also having in their consciousness the words they would use to convey their thought to others. So when there is something they wish to express to another, they automatically become aware of the words, and then falsely come to believe it is the words, not they themselves, that carry the meaning. But actually, this is known even to your colleagues. Psychologists who study human communication know that only a relatively small portion of any communication between humans is carried by words – most is carried by tone of voice, facial expression, and gesture.

William: I think this is very important. The most meaningful experience reported by human beings is the experience of being absorbed into the Light, where language is completely absent. Separating *meaning*, which pertains only to consciousness, from *words* that might be used to partially communicate meaning, is essential to prevent human consciousness from devolving into exclusively linguistic forms. So children, as they learn language, will also learn non-linguistic forms of communication.

Plato: Yes, and Socrates' "other words" will be useful here too.

William: What do you mean?

Plato: Suppose a child has two or three languages at his disposal. Then, if he wishes to communicate something, he will not be limited to only one way of expressing his meanings and feelings linguistically. He will have several such ways, and this will render him much less likely to be bound by the words and concepts of any one language.

Neal: So our children will be bilingual?

Plato: Or trilingual. The point is that our children grow up with a sense of their inner subjectivity as something over and above language and concepts. For language can become a tyrant, sucking the whole of the consciousness associated with the body into itself, so that almost the totality of the person's inner experiences consists of words. This is what has happened in your culture. But with several languages at his disposal, the child will be less likely to confuse the mental reality that is his self with words used to express that reality.

Benedict: And children will thus learn the difference between a thing and the symbolic representation of the thing. The "thing" here is the child's inner mental state, although, *(glancing at Plato)* it could also be mathematical objects. But in addition to learning more than one language – actually a child does not "learn" a language so much as effortlessly absorb the languages spoken in her environment – our children will be exposed to the many forms of non-linguistic consciousness mentioned above: music, meditation, gymnastics, etc.

Now we have already discussed that language acquisition creates the possibility of lying and deception, a possibility that did not previously exist. A nine-month-old baby cannot lie or deceive. A culture like yours that is ruled by people who have become mad with greed and ambition must necessarily use language to deceive, since their insane desires for more and more cannot otherwise be satisfied. But I would like to point out that language makes possible a second kind of deception that is perhaps even more harmful than the first.

Neal: Before you expand on this second kind of deception made possible by language, let us remind ourselves that the word "harmful" is being used not in any absolute sense, but with respect to our desire to keep the margins semi-porous, so that influences from the realm of Spirit, which includes the non-embodied soul, can reach the embodied soul or personality.

Benedict: Thank you. Reminders are always useful. And the way you just put this is also useful, for consider: these "influences from the realm of Spirit" that we over here are always sending to those of you still embodied – are these influences likely to be in the form of human language?

Neal: I think I see where you're going with this. No, it is hardly likely that the so-called "language of the soul" is human language. So if human consciousness is entirely absorbed into human language, it will be less likely to be able to receive the messages from the spirit world. But why do you call this a "deception" of language, rather than just say that the language-encrusted human mind cannot receive communications from its own soul.

Benedict: Well, that in itself is a sort of deception, as the mind has been tricked into thinking that no communications are being sent. But that is not what I had in mind. The point can be expressed in many different ways. Here's one such way: language confuses the mind into believing that something other than the present moment exists. The human mind can arrange words so that they seem to refer to abstractions called "the past", "the future", and "fantasy" or states of affairs that are contrary to fact. In reality, all thoughts that refer to the past, future and fantasy are occurring in the Now, but a human who is lost in such thoughts is deceived into believing that such thoughts are real or are about something that is real. And so language seduces the human into believing that time is something real, whereas all spiritual teachers teach the opposite.

Neal: I see. So because (i) language gives humans the ability to arrange words so that they seem to refer to nonexistent "realities", and because (ii) when language captures the consciousness of the human mind, (iii) the human mind then experiences itself in terms of language (words, concepts, etc.) and (iv) comes to believe that what it experiences (the words etc. pertaining to the future, etc.) are real. So to counter this tendency of language to create the illusion of time, our children will be taught to experience non-linguistic consciousness.

William: Well, they don't really have to be taught to experience non-linguistic consciousness, since that is what they already are. The inner life of a six-month-old child does not consist of words. We want the child to be allowed to retain her sense of herself as non-linguistic consciousness, even as language is being acquired. This will not be easy. In fact, it will be a most interesting research project for the next generation. You see, following Benedict's ideas, it will be possible to measure in great detail the effect on the developing brain of language acquisition. In particular, how does language acquisition reduce the brain's ability to receive non-linguistic communications? Are there external stimuli that, when applied to the brain, allow it to retain its non-linguistic experience of itself while it is learning language?

Or maybe, au contraire, it is the absence of external stimuli, as in meditation, that will allow humans to learn language without losing themselves in all the words?

Benedict: We could put the matter as follows: The language centers of the brain develop in response to auditory vibrations in the child's environment. Are there other auditory vibrations which, if added to the linguistic vibrations, could prevent the consciousness from being entirely sucked into language. Music is an obvious candidate. For example, what happens to the brain if, while learning language, it is also exposed to Mozart's music for 15 minutes a day?

William: And here's another experiment we could do. I'm so excited about this one that I'm actually thinking about incarnating again to become the scientist who does this experiment.

Socrates: *(rolls his eyes at the thought of anyone becoming excited about taking on human form)* Well now, what is this "experiment" that would tempt you to leave our exalted company?

William: OK, OK, so I'm still a little addicted to the human drama. The experiment would involve examining the brains of mediums while they are receiving communications from our side of the fence, so to speak. Now, among humans, mediums are especially receptive to our communications, and their special talent is that they are receptive to communications in linguistic form. Can this brain state be induced through sound waves? Can it be induced in children? Or are the brains of small children already in this state of receptivity? If so, can sound waves – I'm thinking of the sorts of things they do at the Monroe Institute – be designed to help sustain this state of receptivity even as the brain is being modified by language acquisition?

Benedict: Not only sound waves, but light waves too, or rather, electromagnetic waves across the full spectrum. After all, the visual channels from eye to brain are much wider than the auditory channels from ear to brain – that is, many more neurons are involved in visual perception than in auditory perception. So perhaps it might be possible to use light, in addition to sound, to moderate the developing brain's tendency to favor language over other areas of possible expression.

Neal: I'm not sure I fully understand –

Plato: Look at it this way: most of the influences from our realm to yours come in the form of hunches, "lucky guesses", inspiration, assurances, creative impulses, and so forth. Yet some among you, mediums, are able to receive communications in linguistic form. But are there cases in which, say, Grandma comes not only as a voice in someone's head, but also as a three-dimensional body that is perceived just as real as any other physical body?

Neal: Oh yes. Some mediums report receiving communications in visual form. And also, a number of people who report what is called "after-death communications" – ADCs for short – report actually seeing the deceased. And perhaps more important for our present discussion, two year olds often have what psychologists call "imaginary playmates".

William: And what a delightfully question-begging phrase that is! The question is, can children have visual experiences of realities that adults can no longer have, except under very exceptional circumstances? And if so, is it because the structures in the brain that facilitate language prevent other structures in the brain from developing or developing properly, so that by the time language has fully set in, at three or four, the child is no longer able to perceive non-embodied spirits?

Plato: Well, William, these are certainly most interesting questions, and I can see why you are tempted to jump into it again. But we must be a bit careful in how we describe things. We must be careful about assuming that there are structures in the brain that are specific to the perception of spirits, which structures become blocked or fail to develop once language is acquired. After all, *(with humor)* you and I have no brains at all, yet we have no difficulty perceiving spirits.

Neal: *(laughing)* Good point. I'm the only one here who has a brain, and I'm also the only one here who cannot perceive (non-embodied) spirits.

Socrates: *(to me)* And if you could perceive spirits with the same ease that we can, you would not be having a human experience.

Neal: Yes, I think I understand. To have a human experience, the soul must close off direct connection with spirit, or with the knowledge of what it is. So it is not a question of discovering new pathways in the brain that might facilitate communications with spirit.

William: And there is evidence already at hand that shows, or at least strongly suggests, that communications between our worlds involve, not additional neural pathways, but a reduction of and synchronization of brain activity, as in meditation, entheogens, and mediumship. And as Socrates reminds us, our purpose here is to reduce the thickness of the margins between our worlds, not eliminate them entirely. So although the acquisition of language adds to the thickness of the margin, such addition is necessary if the soul is to have a human experience. But to have a human experience, it is not necessary that the margins be as thick as they presently are. We want a Social Order in which the majority of adults are not lost in thought, that is, lost in linguistic forms and concepts, so that at least they can have direct, honest relationships with one another. Thus, by studying the effects of language acquisition on the developing brain, we will be able to see more clearly how it is that language tends to suck the whole of embodied consciousness into itself, so that the adult consciousness is no longer able to experience anything that is not mediated by linguistic form. *(To me)* And this pathological consequence of language acquisition is most strongly manifested in our colleagues, who are unable to conceive that anything could exist that cannot be represented by language.

Neal: And so it will be important that our children's environment actively reinforce the reality and importance of non-linguistic conscious experience, even while language is being acquired. Now, Benedict, you were saying something a while back about language and time, before we got a bit sidetracked by William's research project, so to speak. Could you expand on that? Were you saying that language is involved with time, or the sense of time?

4) Language and the Illusions of "Past" and "Future"

Benedict: Let's put it as follows: language is involved in the appearance to humans of a temporal order. Human beings are structures within the field of Consciousness to whom time appears real. To the soul, prior to incarnating, time has no reality and no meaning. At some point after incarnating, only time and temporal events have reality and meaning. It is quite an amazing process, when you think about it a little. How does it come about?

Plato: And we will see, soon enough, that it could not come about without language, which engenders the illusion that "past" and "future" are something real, and that time somehow "flows" from one to another. But before we get into the role of language in engendering the illusion of time, perhaps we should say a few words about why we are saying that time is an illusion.

Neal: *(with humor)* Well, we are saying it because it is true.

Plato: Very funny, and it is good to joke about things. OK, the temporal order that humans experience as real is an illusion. But underlying this illusion is Unchanging Reality, which I, and Benedict here, have called the eternal order.

William: When I was human, I had great difficulty with the concept that there is something beyond the temporal, even though, I suppose, my vague sense of a "Something More" did not suppose that this "Something More" was subject to the vicissitudes of time. *Now* of course I know there is something over and above the temporal order, because that's where I'm now hanging out. But let's say a few things that might be helpful to a human who has difficulty conceiving of anything beyond the temporal. Perhaps you should say them, Neal, since you have no difficulty with the concept of an eternal order even though, unlike the rest of us, you are not hanging out in the eternal order.

Neal: *(laughing)* I have no difficulty as long as I don't think about it. But now you want me to think about it.

Socrates: What you just said is more profound than you realize; but it will wait until a little later.

Neal: OK. First of all, the great spiritual teachings and teachers of the world's religions teach that there is a Changeless Reality beyond the temporal order. Second, many people report direct experience of this Reality; people return from the Near-Death Experience saying things like "past, present and future were equally there" or "there is no time in Heaven", and so forth. And third, intellectual efforts by scientists and mathematicians to understand the nature of time have come to the conclusion that time, and space too, are not fundamental entities, but depend on something that is nontemporal. And as Benedict and I have discussed, if one formulates a concept of a "something" that causes the Big Bang, it is not difficult to show that this "something" must be outside of the temporal order. There are perhaps other reasons, but these three, from Authority, from direct experience, and from theoretical physics, should be sufficient for us to follow this line of thought, according to which the temporal order is an illusion.

Now, Plato, when you defined time as "the moving image of eternity" you could not have known that a few thousand years later there would actually be examples of "moving images" that emanate from unchanging objects. These examples constitute a wonderful analogy in terms of which your definition may be more easily pictured.

Plato: Continue.

Neal: OK. So, playing a movie is a temporal unfolding of information contained in a disc, or DVD. The disc is analogous to an eternal object. The whole movie is there, all at once, and the disc does not change as the events on the screen, analogous to the temporal order, unfold. This is a good way to understand the idea that something that changes – the action on the screen – may emanate from something – the disc – that does not change.

Plato: *(smiling)* Nice. And we can add a bit to the analogy by noting that the disc by itself does not produce the action on the screen.

Neal: What do you mean?

Plato: You need a device of some sort, like a player and a screen, to extract the information contained in the disc, and present it in a linear or temporal sequence.

Neal: Yes, so…?

Plato: So, according to our analogy, where the disc is analogous to the eternal order and the "moving pictures" on the screen is analogous to the temporal order, what is analogous to the device that plays the disc?

Neal: Oh, the human body.

William: And what a marvelous device is this human body, receiving transmissions from the eternal soul, constricting and limiting those transmissions into the finite, three-dimensional temporal order experienced by human beings.

Neal: But wait, there appears to be a problem. In our analogy, the device that plays the DVD belongs to the same "order" (the three-dimensional physical order) as does the disc; whereas the action on the screen belongs to a different order (two-dimensional images). The device that plays the disc is not itself an image on the screen, but is as real as the disc itself. But the human body belongs to the temporal order, not the eternal order. So how can the body – the "device" that "plays" the information contained in the eternal soul – be located in an "order" that comes into existence only after, or as, the information is "played"?

Plato: And you are right to use the word "appears", because from your perspective – the embodied perspective, so to speak – there appears to be a problem. We must first of all remind ourselves that no analogy is perfect; if it were, it wouldn't be an analogy. But pointing out the limitations of an analogy, as you have done above, is always useful, as it serves as a reminder to embodied consciousness that conceptual thinking cannot, in principle, comprehend how it all works. But I think Benedict has something to say.

Benedict: Yes I do. Recall in a previous conversation we asked you to consider how we who are not embodied experience you, who are embodied.

Neal: Yes, sort of.

Benedict: Since we are not in the temporal order, we do not experience time, and because we have no experience of time, we do not experience your body as a temporal object. But you do experience your body as a temporal object. Now "ego" or "personality" is what we are calling that part of your soul that does experience the body as a temporal object. Hence it is the result, or effect, of the "device" being applied to the soul. Your body, as you experience it, cannot be the "device" that projects your soul, or aspects of it, into the temporal order, as you have pointed out. You, as you are now experiencing yourself, do not experience the "device", but we do. In my writings, I referred to this "device" as the essence of the body, which essence belongs to the eternal order.

Neal: *(smiling)* Oy, I think I'm getting a headache. So my body as I experience it is part of the flow of images on the screen, but my body as you experience it is in the eternal order, along with the "disc" that contains all the information pertaining to the movie that is my life.

Benedict: Good enough for now. Later perhaps we will expand on some of these metaphysical issues.

Socrates: *(playfully)* Yes, we could have a whole section entitled "On inducing headaches in human minds", or something like that.

Benedict: *(laughing)* Yeah, something like that. *(More seriously)* Yet the *effort* to understand conceptually that which cannot in principle be conceptually understood can lead, like a Zen Koan, to more than just headaches, especially if the limitations of conceptual understanding are understood at the outset. *(Laughing again, to me)* And I suppose I should apologize to you, my friend, for giving you so many headaches in the past.

Neal: Apologies accepted. But now I think we should continue with our discussion about the role of language in generating the human experience of time.

Plato: Good. The soul, prior to embodiment, experiences itself as vast and unlimited. But its inner life does not contain thoughts that pertain to "past" or "future". It is in the eternal Now, always present to itself. After becoming embodied but before it has acquired language, it experiences itself as more limited, but still, its inner life does not contain thoughts that pertain to past or a future. Are we agreed on this point?

Neal: Hold on a moment. Simple Pavlovian conditioning has been shown to occur in babies, even in infants. So given some stimulus, their behavior shows that they are expecting a certain response. Does this not show that a baby has some sense of the future?

Plato: It shows that two ideas, or two kinds of event, have become connected in the mind of the baby, so that given one, the other is expected. We could say that expecting an event is not the same as thinking about it. Or, if expecting is regarded as a kind of thinking about a future event, then we note that the baby has such thoughts only when the stimulus has been applied, but otherwise, unlike adults, the baby is not thinking about the future. Most of the inner life of an adult in your culture consists of thoughts that either reference the past or future, or are altogether fictitious. A baby does not have such thoughts.

Neal: Agreed.

Plato: The inner mental life of a typical adult consists mostly in the flow of words, or equivalently, in the flow of thoughts in the form of words.

Neal: But surely there is a difference between thoughts on the one hand, and words that are used to express the thought?

Plato: Yes, but the human condition is such that the consciousness has become so deeply embedded in the words that it only rarely has any sense of itself independent of words. For it is hardly possible for you to become aware of any thought without also becoming aware of the words you would use to express that thought to another.

Neal: Yes, that is so.

Benedict: If I may interrupt, I think a few definitions might be useful now. One problem, as I see it, is that human language, which we are constrained to use in this conversation, is OK as a tool to communicate about the physical world, but is considerably impoverished with regard to describing inner mental experience.

Moreover, words that purportedly reference inner experience – idea, thought, consciousness, mind, awareness, experience – have not been used consistently by past philosophers and spiritual teachers, and so mean different things to different people.

William: Yes, I struggled with this. The state of a physical object, including one's body, can be described (in words) in ever greater detail, but there can be no such thing as a complete description of one's inner mental state.

Benedict: Yes, but even though your "stream of consciousness" forever eludes exact verbal description, if we're going to talk about it at all, which we are, then I want to make an attempt to define some terms, even if such definitions should ultimately prove futile.

William: OK, give it a try.

Benedict: Prior to incarnating into a body, and also after the body has died, the inner life of the soul, although indescribable in words, is rich, vast, unfathomable by humans. This non-embodied state of conscious experience does not involve language or words. This is the state of consciousness experienced in the so-called "Near-Death Experience".

Socrates: And this nonverbal state of consciousness is the "normal" state of consciousness of the soul.

Neal: *(jokingly)* Are you calling me abnormal?

Socrates: ... If the shoe fits...

Benedict: *(laughing)* Stop it, you two; I'm trying to be a bit serious here. But yes actually, the inner life of a soul that has become human is highly abnormal, because its inner life consists mostly of words, which words have made the soul a prisoner of time. Of course, this usage of the term "normal" is with respect to the entirety of the soul's experiences, of which the human component is but a very small part. But it is the human component that we are here discussing, and we are noting that the inner mental life of humans consists in the flow of words, and little else.

Neal: I agree, although I have a feeling that the "little else" will become important later on.

Benedict: Now, whatever may be the soul's experiences prior to embodiment, the soul, after becoming embodied but prior to learning language, say six months or a year old, has an inner life, has experiences of which she is conscious. And without attempting an exhaustive description of a baby's preverbal experiences, everyone can see that a baby perceives things in her environment, and experiences feelings and emotions. It also experiences desires. These aspects of a baby's inner conscious experience are easily inferred by observing its behavior. So a baby experiences these three states of consciousness – perception, emotion, and desire – independently of language, since language has not yet been acquired.

Neal: Yes.

Benedict: But once language has been acquired, then the inner life of the soul consists mostly of words. Perception, for example, which formerly was independent of words, is no longer independent of language. As even your philosophers have observed, sense perception is "laden" with the concepts one has that pertain to the object one is perceiving, so all perception by adults is mediated by language and the concepts inherent in language.

William: The "doors of perception" become clouded by language, and can be partially cleansed, temporarily, by the use of entheogens. It is interesting to note, in this regard, that the effect of such substances on the body is to reduce the activity of the so-called "language centers" of the brain. But I digress.

Benedict: So, I'm looking for a word that will name the kind of conscious experience that the soul has after language has taken hold. I suggest that we use the word "thinking" in this regard. The inner mental life of the typical adult human being consists mostly of "thinking", which in turn consists of a flow of words. Now I am aware that this word "thinking" has been used in many different ways, and that my suggested usage has the perhaps absurd consequence that *(with humor)* Socrates here is not thinking, but –

Socrates: *(laughing)* I'm much too busy *being* to bother with thinking.

Plato: *(to me, with humor)* So you see, *being* is the normal state of the soul; *thinking* is an abnormal, but temporary, state of the soul, brought about by its identification with a body.

Neal: OK, I get the point. Now, Benedict, how does language make the soul a prisoner of time?

Benedict: Well, perhaps that's an inexact locution, as it implies that there is a "something", called "time", that has the power to imprison a soul. The soul is imprisoned by language, and it is language that enables the soul to generate both the illusion of time and the illusion that something other than "what is" could exist. Let's examine the latter first.

Neal: Yes, it seems obvious that what is entirely fictitious depends entirely on words and images. To have the thought of, say, Santa Claus, is to think the words "Santa Claus", along with associated images induced by those words. To think that a given thing could be other than what it is involves becoming conscious of words that would be used to describe the thing's being other than what it is. And conversely – ah, I think this is the point – because of language, the mind can arrange words so that they appear to describe something that is fictitious, and hence, the mind is seduced into believing that what words purport to describe might actually be the case. So the basis for believing that a given thing "really" could be other than what it is, is that words can be arranged in certain ways, to seem to describe things that are contrary to fact.

Benedict: So that, although the facts can never be contrary to what they are, the words that are used to describe the facts can be rearranged so as to describe something contrary to fact, and because consciousness has devolved into mere thinking – the ability to arrange words and symbols in various ways – it thinks that its thinking is indicative of reality, and so comes to believe that what is fictitious could have been real. Now, the mind's ability to arrange and rearrange words, which is what we are calling thinking, deceives the mind into believing that what it is thinking about has some reality over and above the thinking. So, without language it would be impossible to formulate any concept of something other than "what is". And similarly with regard to what is called "past" and "future". Indeed, all conscious experience occurs in the eternal Now. When a human thinks about the past or future, those thoughts always occur in the Now. When the future comes it is always experienced as Now.

Neal: But, Benedict, not to quibble over the use of words, you yourself, in your writings, used the words "thought" and "thinking" quite differently, attributing thinking even to God.

Benedict: Words, words, words. How much better off we'd be if we did not have to use them. But use them we must. In my time it was not uncommon to use terms like "thought" and "idea" to refer to mental experience generally, in a way similar to how the word "thing" is used to refer to any physical object. But today, these words no longer carry the essential connotation of what it is to be mind. Words like "awareness", "consciousness", or "inner experience" are better than the words "thought" or "idea". So now I would say something like this: the Divine Being expresses Itself in infinitely many ways, and is consciously aware of each such way. This "conscious awareness" of a given dimension of the Divine Being, of which the physical universe is one such dimension, I referred to with words something like "God's Idea of the physical"; and the totality of God's ideas of each of the dimensions of His Being, I called the "Attribute of Thought".

And as much as possible, we should use words in the same sense that they have when being used by ordinary people. Despite my incessant warnings not to confuse ideas with "dumb pictures" on a blackboard that would hence require a "mind" to observe them, people continue to read my writings oblivious to my meaning. Had I used words like "awareness" or "consciousness", instead of "idea" and "thought", there would perhaps be less confusion. At any rate, that was then (speaking of time) and this is now, and using the word "thinking" to refer to mental experience that essentially involves words is more in accordance with general usage.

Neal: I agree, especially when we wish to contrast mental experiences that essentially involve words with mental experiences that do not involve words. However, one would be hard-pressed to find adult human experiences that are not "laden" with words and the concepts that words represent.

Benedict: That is correct, but to be explicit, we should note that by "experiences", we mean conscious experience. There is much that the brain does that does not involve language, such as breathing, digesting food, circulating blood, producing white corpuscles to fend off disease, and so forth.

Neal: Yes, but the mind is not conscious of such activities.

Benedict: That's the point, exactly. The mind's conscious experiences are almost entirely mediated by language. It is extremely rare for the adult mind to perceive any object or feel any emotion without language being involved.

William: And to invoke your "parallelism", Benedict, this shows up physiologically, in that the language centers of the adult brain are always active when the human is conscious. But this is not the case for the brain of a preverbal child.

Neal: Yes, it is obvious that a preverbal child, say around a year old, perceives. But it does not perceive in the same way that an adult human is said to perceive, because the language center of the brain, which has not yet formed in the child, is always active whenever an adult perceives.

William: Except…

Neal: Except when the activities of the language center are shut down or diminished by cultivating non-linguistic modes of consciousness, such as meditation, dance, music, sports, or by ingesting peyote and other substances that have this function.

Socrates: Go ahead and share the story.

Neal: Huh? What story?

Socrates: The memory that just flashed across your mind.

Neal: But…

Socrates: But you think that would sidetrack our discussion.

Neal: Well yes, sort of…

Socrates: *(smiling)* And just when you're thinking you can see your way clear through the next few pages – you see, I'm not sidetracking our discussion, only your expectation that it go one way or another.

(Usually when I sit down to write, I do not know what words will come. I do not write from any outline. Occasionally I can see a few paragraphs ahead, and infrequently, I can sense we'll be on a certain topic for several pages. This latter sense gives me, or my so-called ego, some security, as if I now know what I'm doing. Of course, I don't, and Socrates' intervention has brought that point home to me, although I was slightly irritated with him, as I wanted to continue in the direction I thought we were going.)

Neal: Well OK, so much for expectations. Many years ago, when my daughter was a preverbal child, I took some peyote and spent the whole afternoon crawling around on the floor with her. Now, prior to this experience, I had noticed that while crawling around, she would often stop and look intently at something insignificant – like a speck on the carpet, paint on the wall, a toy – and I would wonder what she sees that absorbs her attention so profoundly. Under peyote, I could see what she saw, and recall saying repeatedly, now I know what she sees. The richness, the depth of color, the profound beauty, of even a little pattern in the carpet! In that experience I understood that the doors of human perception were all muddied up by language and conceptual thinking.

Socrates: Thank you. And you can see the truth behind the injunctions of various spiritual teachings to become innocent like a child – innocent of language, that is.

Plato: For a preverbal child can literally "see a world in a grain of sand and heaven in a wild flower". It can "hold infinity in the palm of (its) hand, and eternity in an hour". This is the baby's inner experience. For an adult to have this experience, he must either be a mystic like Blake, or ingest a substance that reduces the activities of the brain's language center.

Neal: Is it possible, then, for a child to learn language without completely losing "heaven", "infinity" and "eternity"?

Benedict: The operative word here is "completely". Forgetfulness, as Plato has put it, is a necessary condition for the soul to have a human experience. But a little less forgetfulness, even a very little less, will render the human experience much more enjoyable. The human race is currently in utter darkness, so even the tiniest amounts of spiritual light will make a very big difference. We shall have to leave the empirical findings to William's future research project.

Neal: Empirical findings…?

William: Yes, it is after all an empirical question whether language can be learned in such a way that the "doors of perception" – or, to be absolutely clear – the doors of *spiritual* perception will not become permanently closed as a result. The brain, especially the perceptual centers, will be closely monitored, before, during, and after language acquisition. We will discover, among many other things, what it is about language – the physiology of language, so to speak – that causes the language center of the brain, once developed, to override and control the perceptual center.

Neal: So we will tinker with the process of language learning, to see if the soul can drink a little less from Plato's River of Forgetfulness on its second return. Now that our child has learned language – hopefully in a way that hasn't completely obliterated her spiritual memory – I suppose we will be telling her many more stories.

Plato: You suppose correctly.

5) Teaching the Moral Law

Neal: We have talked a little about the form, or manner, that our stories shall be told. That is, as much as possible, our stories will be labeled as stories, not as literal truth. But we have not said anything about the content of our stories. What shall our stories be about?

Plato: Do you recall…?

Neal: Yes I do. Many years ago, a spiritual teacher (Maharishi Mahesh Yogi) was asked the same question. His answer has stayed with me over the years. He said that children should be told that (i) all things, physical and mental, have an "inside", and that (ii) the insides are more powerful than the outside. The body is "more" than what it appears to be through visual perception. The mind is "more" than what it experiences itself as being while in human form. In the case of the body, the "more" involves the cells, organs, blood, and so forth. In the case of the mind, the "more" involves aspects of itself that are beyond the range of its conscious experience. The child can be taught, through stories, that just as there is more to the body than appears to his senses, so also, there is more to his mind than he is conscious of at any one time. This "something more", as William puts it, begins with his own subconscious mind, involves its connectedness with all other minds, and culminates in the Kingdom of Heaven, which (I suppose) is the deepest thing within a human being.

Plato: Yes, and a consequence of this, of the interconnectedness of all things, is that many of our stories will make the point that two things may appear very different on the outside, yet be internally connected. The interconnectedness of all minds is the basis of the Moral Law, which is really the only thing a child need know to fit into our Society, but the knowledge must be so deeply ingrained that his very bones form around it.

Neal: But, Plato, how will we teach the Moral Law? All religions preach the Golden Rule, yet the attempt to teach this to humans, over several thousand years, has resulted in utter failure.

Socrates: *(laughing)* That's because bones don't form in Sunday School.

Neal: Huh?

William: *(smiling)* Socrates is correct, on several points. In the first place, being "preached to" or "lectured at" is the least effective way to learn anything. Second, religions, insofar as they are constituted by human beings, rarely practice what they preach, and children learn by imitation, not by abstract concepts. But most important for our purposes, by the time a child is old enough to go to Sunday School, his bones have already formed, and it is too late for the kind of learning we will require for members of our New Social Order.

Plato: Perhaps it is not so much a matter of learning the Moral Law as it is of recollecting it. Every soul, prior to embodiment, already knows the Moral Law. I will state it succinctly: (i) All individual souls are fragments of a single World Soul. Hence (ii) all souls are interconnected, and because of this, (iii) it is never possible for a soul to benefit by harming another soul. So to harm another is to harm oneself. The Moral Law is the highest expression of one's true self-interest.

Neal: Wait a minute. By the time a child is old enough to follow your reasoning here, his bones will have been formed for many, many years.

Plato: But it is not through reason that the child will be taught.

Neal: Well that was my question. If not through reason, how?

Plato: – Through the child's natural ability to empathize. I think Benedict wants to fill in some of the details.

Benedict: Yes, thank you. So developmentally, we are speaking of a child after language has been learned, but before formal schooling has started, say between two and five years old. Now, do we agree with the following statement: when a child sees another child expressing an emotion, there is a tendency for the first child to feel that same emotion.

Neal: Yes. As you argued a few centuries ago, the very perception of, say, sadness in another involves the brain and body of the perceiver in such a way as to recreate in oneself the sadness of the other. And this is very easily observed, as children can cry just because another child is crying, and a child can desire something for no reason other than another child desires it. Emotions, we might say, are contagious, especially in children.

Benedict: And because of this fact, that emotions are contagious, the very perception of a child experiencing an emotion engenders the same emotion in the perceiver, the Moral Law will be easy to teach. Actually *(nodding to Plato)*, the Moral Law does not need to be "taught", since it is innate in all humans. Your present society, by emphasizing greed and status-seeking, teaches children to forget the Moral Law; our new world order will endeavor to keep the memory of the Moral Law alive.

Neal: But is not the Moral Law what the soul must forget if it is to have a human experience? Is it not precisely the interconnectedness of all human minds that the soul "forgets" by drinking from Plato's River?

Plato: *(smiling)* Yes, but one might say that forgetfulness comes in degrees.

Neal: Huh?

Benedict: Good. Yes, as I wrote, humans are not born into the state of consciousness I called "Blessedness" or "Salvation". So this state of consciousness – the Knowledge consciousness has when it experiences itself as the Mind of God – gets left behind at the river, so to speak. But there is what we might call a residual memory that does not need to be eradicated in order that the soul have a human experience.

Neal: Say more about what you are calling residual memory.

Benedict: Certainly. Every child knows that it feels good when another child is kind to her, and feels bad when another is mean to her. But the converse is equally true. It feels good to help another, and feels bad to harm another. If we call the former "generosity" or "kindness" and the latter "selfishness" or "cruelty", children will be taught that kindness feels better than cruelty.

Plato: Actually, not so much taught as reinforced. OK, how, you ask?

Neal: Yes, exactly.

Plato: But isn't it obvious? Through play. As children play, they sometimes harm another and they sometimes help another. Under adult supervision, and/or the supervision of older children, our young children will be encouraged to express, share, and discuss their emotions and behaviors in small groups. Through this process, which shall always be non-judgmental, children will learn to identify and accept both their own emotions and the emotions of other children. So we might imagine a scenario something like – alright, Benedict, what's so funny?

(Socrates had whispered something into Benedict's ear, after which he started giggling.)

Benedict: He *(gesturing towards Socrates)* suggested that I could have saved myself the trouble of writing down my philosophy had I realized that I had a better chance of being understood by a three-year-old child than by an "educated" grown-up. *(Everyone laughs.)*

Socrates: And really, it – the ultimate truth of things – is that simple. A child can understand it easily, but not an adult whose mind has been warped by a social order rendered mad by greed and ambition. But now, Plato, please continue with your scenario.

Plato: OK. So imagine a scenario in which six or seven children are playing together. Within a short period of time, the following four kinds of interactions will have occurred: (i) a child is harmed by another (physically or emotionally), (ii) a child harms another, (iii) a child is helped or assisted by another, and (iv) a child helps or assists another. Since every child has herself experienced all four situations, they know what each situation feels like. Hence it will not be difficult for adults to encourage the children to express how they feel under each situation, and to share and discuss this with the other children.

Benedict: We stress that the adults involved will have no judgment about which behaviors are better. The child who harms another will under no circumstances be blamed; the child who helps another will under no circumstances be praised.

William: I get it! Wow. This is as brilliant as it is counterintuitive.

Benedict: Counterintuitive?

Socrates: Counterintuitive to a Western educated gentleman perhaps *(pointing to William)*, but not to a three-year-old child.

William: *(laughing)* OK, I'll own it. To this, ahem, "Western educated gentleman" then, it would appear that children learn when adults encourage positive behavior (iv above), and discourage negative behaviors (ii). But in that case, the child's subsequent behaviors are a response to the adults' judgments about what is good and what is bad, rather than arising from the child's direct knowledge of the emotions themselves.

Benedict: Exactly. One reason, perhaps the main reason, your present culture is so dysfunctional is that children are taught to repress and lie about their real emotions – so that by the time they reach adulthood it may require considerable therapy *(glancing at me)* for an individual to be able even to identify their emotions. But our children will not be taught to lie, nor will they be taught that some behaviors or emotions are "better than" others. And, through expressing, sharing, and discussing, they will come to know by direct experience that some behaviors feel better than others.

Neal: So our children will realize rather quickly that of the four possible situations above, the behavior that engenders the most joyful feelings in oneself is (iv), helping or assisting another; and conversely, they will realize that the kinds of behaviors that engender the most sorrowful feelings in oneself fall under (ii). Because every child has experienced all four situations, and because no one situation will be singled out by adults as "good" or "bad", our children will understand that selfish behavior *feels* bad (not *is* bad) and altruistic behavior *feels* good (not *is* good). In this way children, by seeking what feels good, will generally seek opportunities for behaviors that help others while shunning opportunities for behaviors that harm others. But perhaps I am being too quick to assume that (iv) feels the best. I can imagine someone arguing that it feels best to "win" in a competition with others, which necessarily involves harming the feelings of those who did not "win".

William: Perhaps a "Western educated gentleman" might argue in this way, but not the present company. Our children will know better. They are raised in an environment where it is the norm to express, share, and discuss emotions. Every child has been in a situation where he/she has hurt the feelings of another child. They will be encouraged to share in detail how they felt while they were harming the other, and how they felt after. Because the adults will have no judgment, the children will not be encouraged to conceal their feelings so as to please the adults.

Neal: So little Suzie will share and discuss how she was feeling as she snatched the toy away from Johnny, and also how she felt right afterwards. She will then share and discuss how she was feeling as she helped Mary zip up her jacket and gave Timothy a piece of her cookie. And of course, Johnny, Mary, and Timothy will also share and discuss how things felt from their side.

Benedict: Thus, if our children practice this emotional hygiene on a daily basis, starting as soon as they can express themselves in language, then the "residual memory" that I referred to earlier will remain in place as the children mature, and the Moral Law will have been written into their very bones. It will no more occur to them to harm another human being than it would to eat something that tastes putrid or deliberately go about getting infected with some illness.

Neal: So what we are calling a "residual memory" involves the ability to live according to the Golden Rule – that one must never treat another human being as a means to one's ends. Although the child will have lost the experiential knowledge of its interconnectedness with all minds, and with the larger Whole that all minds constitute, it will still retain some memory that will allow it to recognize that helping others feels better than harming others, and live its life accordingly.

Yet, although I agree with all this – especially the statement that children can learn to recognize that helping another feels better than harming another, I fear that we have not said enough to address the concerns of our "Western educated gentleman". I can almost hear him protesting in the background.

6) A "Western Educated Gentleman" Objects

Socrates: Well then, by all means invite him to join us for a while. But you and William will have to give him a voice, since you two know best what it is like to be a "Western educated gentleman".

Neal: OK, I'll give it a try if William helps me.

William: Go for it. I'll chime in when I feel inspired to do so.

Neal: Here goes: There are so many things to disagree with here that it is difficult to know where to begin. Most important is your assumption that it does in fact "feel better" to help someone than to hurt someone. What if this isn't empirically true? How do you know that Johnny will feel better by sharing his toy with Suzie than he would feel by snatching a toy away from Suzie? Isn't this the reason why children are often mean and unkind to one another – that it boosts their egos to put another kid down, physically and verbally. All this talk about "feelings". Children must learn to develop a thick skin and stuff their feelings. Otherwise how will they compete in the real world?

William: And don't we know from Darwin's explorations that only the fit survive, and that the cream always rises to the top. So those at the top of any hierarchy are there because they have beaten all their competitors and hence deserve to be at the top. If the "feelings" of the competitors have been harmed, so be it. It is but a small price to pay for the evolution of humanity; it is the process of evolution itself that drives men to compete one against the other, so that the best come to dominate. Thus children, if they are to be successful in this world, must be encouraged to compete against one another, and to enjoy and seek those delicious feelings that arise from winning.

Neal: And this is so even though we acknowledge that the "delicious feelings" that the winner enjoys necessarily involve hurtful feelings on the part of the losers. But why care about the losers anyway? Evolution is passing them by, and so should we. After all, we might say it is too bad that the zebra's feelings are hurt when it is being eaten by a lion, but in an eat or be eaten reality, nature does not seem to care much about the feelings of those who are eaten, whether physically, in the case of the zebra, or economically and emotionally, in the case of humans playing competitive games against one another.

William: And we might add that what we are calling "competitive games" are simply the creative forces of evolution operating through the human species; and the winners of such games, in whatever sphere of human activity, are riding the crest of evolution's wave.

Socrates: *(playfully)* Well, that was quite a torrent. I thought we were not going to invite Callicles to join us, but it appears he has snuck in through the back door and forced you two to utter those terrible words on his behalf.

William: *(also playfully)* We had no need of Callicles' assistance, as we were both raised in a culture that embraces his world-view. So we know it intimately, alas. Yikes, I did not realize how easy it would be to recreate the mind-set that gave rise to those horrid thoughts just expressed. But how shall we reply?

Socrates: There are several components to our collective reply. The first is simply to agree with our "Western educated gentleman" friend.

William: Agree with him!?!?

Socrates: Why yes. He thinks we are raising our children to fit into the only kind of society with which he is familiar, the kind of society in which, not cream, but greed and ambition rise to the top. With respect to the goal of raising children so that they will fit into a society based on what is lowest in a human being – greed and ambition – then we have no quarrel with him. But our goal is different. Our reply, at this level, is that we are raising our children, not to fit into a society based on the lower human motivations, but rather, to fit into a new society that is predicated on living in harmony with Father Earth. We would point out to our friend, if he is willing to hear it, that a social order based on winning competitive games – capitalism, in a word – (i) necessarily leads to the eventual destruction of the Earth's ability to support human life and also (ii) maximizes the amount of suffering among humans, both for those who "lose" and those who "win".

Plato: And our New Social Order is in harmony, not only with Father Earth, but also, with our underlying metaphysics, which explains with great clarity why it is the case that it feels better to help another than to harm another. This was not some random statement we happened to make that we merely hoped would receive empirical support from the children, but is a logical consequence of our metaphysical world-view applied to the human condition. Shall we review this?

Neal: Yes.

Plato: Let us begin, then, with our concept of a "One Mind", or, as I referred to it, "The World Soul". The World Soul, Itself vast, unlimited, eternal, is a Unity that contains within itself all individual souls, each of which partakes in that same vast, limitless, eternal order. Now, for reasons that cannot be expressed in human language, some individual souls form a desire to experience themselves as something they are not.

Benedict: What in the world do you mean, "as something they are not"?

Plato: Patience, my friend. In Reality of course, Consciousness cannot possibly experience Itself as something it is not.

Socrates: And this is why we tend to regard the human experience – which is the direct consequence of the soul's desire to experience itself as what it is not – as not fundamentally Real. But continue the story.

Plato: And so the individual soul along with many other individual souls get together and plan and execute what we call "the Grand Experiment" and what you call "the human experience". In this "human experience" the soul does indeed experience itself as something it is not, that is, as a body that is born, lives, and dies in time. Are we OK, Benedict?

Benedict: *(laughing gently)* Well I suppose we could argue a bit about the ontological status of "physical reality" or "embodied existence", with me giving it a little more status than you are inclined to do.

Neal: Actually, Benedict, I think you give it – the human experience – considerably less status than is generally supposed. For you say, do you not, that even though memory and the personality do not survive the death of the body, yet what does not survive is "of no consequence" compared with what does survive, at least in the case of one who is enlightened.

Benedict: Yes, yes, I did write that.

Neal: And surely that which is "of no consequence" to the soul cannot partake of the same order of reality as that which is of great consequence to the soul.

Plato: The reason why the individual soul, upon the death of its body, immediately recognizes that its previous so-called "life" is "of no consequence" compared to what it now, free from embodiment, experiences itself as being, is that it sees that it had been experiencing itself as what it is not. And what it is not, a body, is "of no consequence" compared with what it is, a soul. Now at some point we will enter into a more detailed discussion of the joys and sorrows, pleasures and pains, available to the soul while it is having a human experience. Needless to say, our children will be taught from the earliest ages to discern what *is* good from what merely *feels* good, and as much as possible align the latter with the former. But we can now address the concerns raised above by Callicles through his able, albeit temporary, spokespersons *(glancing playfully at William and me)*.

William: And I think we can put the matter very directly as follows: it feels good to win competitive games. That's why people compete: whether in sports, in one's career, in Wall Street, in politics, it feels good to win. This is an empirical fact, a fact that stands independent of its usual justifications in terms of Darwinian "survival of the fittest" or Freudian competition for mating privileges. What we now wish to show is that this "good feeling" that arises from winning a competition is inferior to the good feeling that arises from helping another.

Socrates: I suspect we can show more than that.

William: What do you mean?

Socrates: I think we can show that the "good feeling" that arises out of winning a competition actually harms the soul, whereas the "good feeling" that arises from helping another benefits the soul.

Benedict: Wait a minute. If we are going to use terms like "harms the soul" and "benefits the soul", then we need to be clear about what those terms mean. After all, do we not hold the opinion that a soul cannot really be harmed? Didn't you say that at your trial?

Socrates: I said that a good person cannot be harmed by a bad person.

Benedict: From which it follows that a good person cannot be harmed period, since only a bad person would attempt to harm another, whether that other be "good" or "bad". Now it is clear, or at least, clear to me, that the body can be helped or harmed, and also that the associated embodied mind can likewise be assisted or restrained in its efforts to flourish. But what does it mean to say of a non-embodied soul that it can be harmed or benefited? Surely these terms are not being used in any absolute sense.

Socrates: Ah, Benedict, you wish to rein in my poetic use, or misuse as the case may be, of language. Well, I agree that from an absolute perspective, no soul can be harmed, period. From an absolute perspective, God's in his Heaven, all's right with the world, and everything is, how do you put it, peachy fine and hunky dory. But that's from an absolute perspective, or, from the perspective of the World Soul Itself. This is not necessarily the perspective of either an individual soul or an individual soul that has become embodied.

Plato: We spoke earlier of Parmenides' metaphor of the "Way Down" and the "Way Up". From the absolute perspective, the Way Up and the Way Down are occurring simultaneously. But from the relative perspective of an individual soul, this is not the case. For as soon as an individual soul loses the knowledge of its connection with its Source, the World Soul, it immediately forms a desire to regain that lost knowledge. From the Absolute Perspective, the soul's desire to return to Source and the soul's desire to separate from Source are opposite sides of the same coin. But from the perspective of an individual soul, they are very distinct processes. Thus we may state that, with respect to a given soul's desire to return to Source, some things will assist that desire and some things will thwart that desire.

Benedict: And so we may say that those things that thwart the soul's desire to regain the knowledge of what it is are harmful to the soul, whereas those things that assist the soul's desire to return to Source are beneficial to the soul.

Socrates: But now, we should state, what are the things, or kinds of things, that can either harm or benefit a soul?

Benedict: What do you mean?

Socrates: Did you not say, or make me say, that a soul cannot be harmed by another soul?

Benedict: Yes.

Socrates: And of course we agree that a body cannot harm a soul, any more than that which is dreamed can harm the dreamer.

Benedict: Yes, we agree on that point.

Socrates: Yet we stated that a given soul can be harmed in the sense that its desire to return to Source can be thwarted.

Benedict: Yes.

Socrates: So if a soul can be harmed, but not by another soul or body, then it follows, does it not, that the only thing that can harm an individual soul is that individual soul itself?

Benedict: Yes, that appears to be the case.

Socrates: Then how does a soul harm or benefit itself?

Benedict: *(smiling)* Very nice.

Socrates: What's "very nice"?

Benedict: Well the argument has only one conclusion: that the soul harms itself the most which, while embodied, deviates the most from the Moral Law.

Plato: Yes, for the Moral Law is really just an expression of the Knowledge that is forgotten upon embodiment, namely, the Knowledge that all individual souls are so interconnected as to constitute a Unity, the World Soul. Thus when an embodied soul – which is still a soul even though it has become human – helps another embodied soul, this in turn strengthens the Unity, which in turn assists the given soul. Conversely, when a given embodied soul harms another embodied soul, which it does by limiting and/or interfering with its expression through the given body, this weakens the Unity (or that with which the individual soul is necessarily connected), and hence weakens the individual soul itself. What do you think, Benedict?

Benedict: *(with humor)* Well aside from the minor point that it is absolutely absurd to think that the Unity of Souls can in any way be harmed or benefited by human behavior, nevertheless, what you say does convey some sense of what things might be like.

William: But there's more than metaphor here. If we consider the matter now from the perspective of the embodied soul, the human perspective, it becomes clear why the joy that a human experiences through helping another is greatly superior to the "joy" that is experienced through winning competitive games, which necessarily involve harming others. For the Golden Rule expresses in human terms the knowledge that all souls are interconnected. Even though this knowledge is not consciously retained, every time one human helps another, she is both expressing this knowledge and strengthening the knowledge within herself. And conversely, every time one human harms another, she is expressing the ignorance of separation and reinforcing that ignorance within herself.

Benedict: And we can add that the joy that arises through helping another is pure, whereas the "joy" that arises through harming another is always mixed with some sorrow. For there cannot be "winners" unless there are "losers", and so the joy that is experienced by winning comes at the expense of the sorrow of the losers. And in most competitive games, the collective sorrow of those who "lose" is much greater than the "joy" of the one who wins. So winning a competition generally creates much more sorrow than joy, whereas helping another creates only joy. The "winner" must find a way to hide from himself the knowledge of the suffering that his "winning" has caused in others.

Neal: But even if he can hide this knowledge from himself, or hide himself from this knowledge, as in the case of the sociopath, the very endeavor to hide truncates his experience of himself, as his sense of self now excludes the other, and he becomes less; whereas the one who helps another enlarges his experience of himself by including the other, and becomes more.

Plato: And so the pleasure that arises from winning competitive games is akin to those pleasures that feel good in the moment, but are actually harmful to the embodied soul – harmful with respect to the original purpose of the soul prior to incarnating. No soul incarnates with the intent to harm itself or another, and winning competitive games necessarily harms others; thus no soul incarnates with the intent to win competitions, which latter intent is really a seeking for status and reputation.

7) An Ounce of Prevention

Neal: I am satisfied that we have adequately addressed the complaints of our "Western educated gentleman", but how are we going to explain all this to our children?

Socrates: On the contrary, my friend, it will be much easier to explain this to our children than to Callicles in the form of our "Western educated gentleman". For unlike the latter, our children will not have been conditioned by the values of greed and ambition. Actually, children in your present society are taught the values of greed and ambition largely through playing competitive games with one another, competing for grades, competing in sports, competing for the teachers' recognition and approval, and even competing to be "popular" with other children. They are taught that "winning" is everything, and they are taught to ignore the feelings of the many more who do not "win". So, Neal, when you get a 19- or 20-year-old student whose sense of identity is wrapped up in winning competitive games, his mind is likely to be so fogged up that he will have considerable difficulty following our simple arguments. As I jokingly remarked to Benedict here, we'll have a much better chance with the three year olds than with the adults.

Plato: And of course, we will not be "explaining" all this to our children conceptually, as we have done for ourselves. Furthermore, conceptual understanding is not really necessary in order to produce a functioning citizen of our New Society.

Neal: What do you mean?

Plato: A person can follow health maxims for caring for the body without understanding, the way a physician understands, the conceptual details of why and how following a given maxim engenders good health. For example, moderate exercise is good for the body. A physician understands this conceptually; she knows all the whys and wherefores of how exercise strengthens the body. But certainly one need not have this conceptual understanding in order to exercise and enjoy the consequent good health. Similarly, our citizens will have internalized the Golden Rule, and this Rule will be operative in everything they do. So a conceptual understanding of the Golden Rule, understanding why it leads to maximum happiness both individually and collectively, will not be necessary for everyone.

William: I'm wondering if we could now apply these ideas to our children, whom we left several pages back. We were, as I recall, in the process of teaching them that helping another feels better than harming another, even though the latter can feel good in the moment. We were then challenged to show that we were not merely brainwashing our children to believe in the Golden Rule, but rather, teaching them to observe that it really does feel better to help another than to hurt another. I think we need to say more about this process, especially since it does not involve conceptual teaching.

Benedict: *(with humor)* Well, I seemed to have just learned that one has to be careful about allowing this guy *(gesturing towards Socrates)* to whisper anything into one's ears.

Socrates: *(innocently)* Why, Benedict, whatever do you mean? It was just a little joke.

Benedict: Ever since your little joke I have been unable to stop thinking about how, if charged with the task, I would go about teaching my system of philosophy to a bunch of three-year-old children.

Socrates: Well then, consider yourself charged with the task.

Benedict: I'll do my best, although these ideas are still new to me. Well, the goal of my system of thought was – perhaps I should say "is" – to produce a human being who is free from dysfunctional human emotions, and because of that, has the power to live according to the guidance of reason, that is, according to the Moral Law. But as everyone knows, it is very difficult to remove a dysfunctional emotion once it has set in and taken hold of the personality. To be specific, let's consider an especially insidious human emotion, the lust for vengeance, which is to be contrasted with its opposite, the desire to forgive. Now, in your society, and mine too, males are raised to place primary importance on this emotion. One is not considered to be "manly" if one does not strive to get back at those who he perceives have harmed him. Although possible, it is very difficult to remove this emotion from someone into whose mind this emotion has grooved deep pathways. Not the least of the difficulties is that those whose minds have been warped with thoughts of vengeance do not want to exchange those thoughts for thoughts of forgiveness. But prevention is much more effective than cure, and so we wish to raise our children in such a way that whenever they feel harmed by another, their minds automatically turn to thoughts of forgiveness rather than thoughts of revenge.

Neal: We want our children to experience that thoughts of forgiveness *feel* better than thoughts of vengeance. There is an old saying that holding a grudge against someone is like drinking poison and expecting the other to die. Now someone raised in my culture who finds himself holding a grudge against someone generally nurses the grudge, and does not experience the grudge itself as poison, as harmful to himself. So he does not, again generally, seek to remove the grudge and replace it with forgiveness. And even if one who holds a grudge does desire to replace it with forgiveness, this is usually very difficult to do, and requires considerable effort and alertness. So it makes sense to ask if we can raise our children such that they do not hold grudges, or if they do, are able to replace the grudge with forgiveness as soon as they become aware of the grudge within themselves. Can we train them so that they themselves will experience a grudge as "poison", and thence seek to remove it, rather than hold on to it?

Benedict: I suspect the answer will be "yes, to some extent". But before getting into this, that is, before we discuss emotions and desires that arise out of the children's interactions with one another, it might be easier for them to learn Plato's Principle as it relates to their own bodies, rather than to one another.

Neal: And by "Plato's Principle" I suppose you mean something like "not everything that feels good *is* good"; and conversely, "not everything that feels bad *is* bad." For example, it appears that the human body is wired such that it likes foods that are sweet, and excessive sweets are harmful to the body. So the "food environment" of our children will be carefully controlled, since they do not have the power to control their taste buds, unless –

Benedict: Unless they do have that power. This is the question: can a child's subjective sense of taste be aligned with foods that are good for the body? Your American "diet" of sugar, salt and fat is the cause of most of the illnesses that plague your society. If children could be taught to align their sense of taste with what is good for the body, then they would be healthier and happier both as children and as adults.

William: Let us assume that this is possible, that a child's subjective sense of taste is not hardwired, but is to some extent malleable and can be aligned with what is healthy for the body. The evidence for this assumption is that children born and raised in different parts of the world almost always adapt to the foods and diet common in their environments. So children's taste buds are at least partially cultured by their environment.

Neal: And the food environment that our New Society will provide for its children will consist only of foods that are healthy for the body. But this is not really a limitation, since there are very many foods that are healthy, and although children's taste buds may differ, each child will be able to find plenty of healthy foods that are to its liking.

William: I will go so far as to speculate that a child that is exposed only to healthy foods for her first three or four years will experience as distasteful the fat, sugar, and salt of the American diet.

Neal: Yes, I see it now. I have been eating mostly healthy foods now for many years, and as a result, foods that are excessively salty, sweet, or fatty taste repulsive to me. And if an adult like me can retrain his sense of what tastes good to align with what is good for the body, how much easier it will be for a child who will not have to "undo" any misalignment of taste with health.

Plato: *(with great humor)* What's this? You're going to put the "Pastry Chef" out of business!

(In the dialogue "Gorgias", Plato compares a spiritual teacher with a nutritionist. The former advocates for the long-term health of the mind, whereas the nutritionist advocates for the long-term health of the body. Plato then asks us to imagine what might happen if a nutritionist has to debate with a pastry chef in front of an audience of children. The former argues that children should care for the overall health of the body, whereas the latter argues that the children should care only for what tastes sweet in the moment. The pastry chef would win the debate every time, since children cannot reason and hence cannot think beyond what tastes sweet in the moment. And similarly, adults whose thinking is not much more advanced than children will ignore the spiritual teacher in favor of the "sweetness" that arises from following greed and ambition.)

Neal: At least your pastry chef used only natural ingredients. Our "pastry chefs" – the hawkers of fast foods, sugary drinks, and candies, all marketed to children – use chemicals, poisons, psychological manipulation of children's minds – whatever they can, so as to cause the children to become addicted to their products.

Plato: This is perhaps a good time to remind ourselves that the so-called "profit motive", the economic basis of your society, will have disappeared from the face of the Earth. Greed and ambition will be regarded as forms of insanity that lead to violent and criminal behavior.

Neal: Isn't that overstating the case a bit?

Benedict: Not at all. In your culture, a company or corporation that markets unhealthy "foods" to children makes their profit by making children sick and/or weakening their immune systems so that they are much more liable to sickness when they get older. Think about it. The executives of these companies, and there are many, make their money by harming children. Is this not criminal? And is it not insane for a society to monetarily reward those criminals who seek to profit by harming the children?

Neal: Yes, I agree. It is insane for anyone to want to harm children, and only a society that is collectively insane would allow their children to be so harmed. The "right" of the rich to profit by harming children is, in my society, more important than the right of the children to be protected from harm.

Plato: But, not to worry, there will still be a role for our pastry chef in our New Society, but he will not be allowed to advertise his products to children. The first order of business of any sane society is to protect and nurture the children, who will become the next generation. Thus, because greed and ambition will have no role in our New Society, there will not be anyone who seeks to profit by harming our children.

Neal: OK. So the physical needs of our children are well cared for. These needs revolve around nutrition and exercise, and we will see to what extent it is possible to train our children's sense of taste so that "what tastes good to the tongue" and "what is good for the body" will be as closely aligned as possible. Let us now return to our discussion of our children's emotions. What are the emotional needs of children? And, as we were previously discussing, can children be taught to recognize that helping another feels better than harming another?

William: Good. Assuming that the physical needs of our children have been taken care of, we now turn to their emotional needs. But let us remember that we are not talking about the emotional needs of children insofar as they are striving to adapt to your current insane society. For the effort to adjust to an insane culture engenders insanity in the child, and the emotional needs of a child that has been thus damaged are without end. On the contrary, we are constructing our Society based on what is maximally advantageous to our children. And conceived in this way, I will venture to state that a child has only one emotional need, and every child has the same need.

Neal: Just one need? Can it really be that simple?

Socrates: Yes, it really is that simple. Things become "complicated" for humans only when there is a deviation from Truth.

Benedict: Yes, and here's a readily understandable example: the truth about the movement of planets is that they move in ellipses. But if one is attached to preconceived ideas, and believes that planets "must" move only in perfect circles, then one has the endless complexity of adding endless "epicycles" to the descriptions of the planets' motions. So if one has the preconceived idea that children must adapt to a dysfunctional society, then their needs will not be simple. But if instead we are constructing our society so as to fulfill the needs of our children, not the other way around, then things become simple.

Socrates: And the Truth here is that a child is an embodied soul. What does this embodied soul need in order to flourish, that is, in order to manifest and fulfill the soul's original purpose in incarnating? Physically, the embodied soul needs nutrition and exercise. Mentally, or psychologically the embodied soul needs –

Neal: Oh my, I've got it. Previously we talked about the case of babies in an orphanage, whose physical needs were cared for yet all of whom died. They died because their emotional needs were ignored. They were not touched, or held, or played with, or sung to. So emotionally, the baby needs to feel wanted, welcomed, and included. And an older child has this same need, to feel included and liked by those around him.

William: And even adults have this same need, to feel included, to feel that they belong to something larger than themselves.

Socrates: If the emotional needs of our children are to be met, then they must "study war no more".

Neal: What do you mean? Children, even in my greed-based dysfunctional society, do not study war.

Socrates: Oh really? What do you think a child learns by being taught to play competitive games? Every time a child plays a competitive game, he is studying war. Our children will not be taught to compete one against the other, but instead will be taught cooperative games.

Neal: But, but…

William: *(smiling, to me)* This is a difficult one for us, is it not, having been brainwashed by our culture to believe that competition is good, that it brings out the best in children, and that it builds character. But none of this is true. Competition brings out the worst in children, not the best, and the "character" it builds is one that is fitted for a society based on greed and ambition, which is definitely *not* the kind of character that we want for our New Society.

Plato: It is of course true that the games children play are essential to developing character. The question is: what kind of character do we wish to develop, or encourage? Is it the character of one whose sense of self-worth involves being kind, compassionate, and helpful in his relationships with others, or is it the kind of character who is self-centered, and whose sense of self-worth revolves around feeling that he is "better than" others? Competitive games tend to produce the latter kind of personality, cooperative games the former. Later on we shall discuss how competitive games may be rendered cooperative, but for now, competitive games are your culture's training grounds for competitive and sociopathic adults.

Neal: Hmm. I'm beginning to see the point. A competitive game is one in which, by definition, there are "winners" and "losers". As in war, one child, or one group of children, is pitted against another. All the children may enjoy playing the game, but when it is over, the "winners" feel good and the "losers" feel bad. The winners feel that by winning, they are "better than" the losers, who feel that by losing, they are worse than the winners. But what they are really learning is that in life there are winners and losers, and that it feels better to win than to lose. Moreover, those who win, in order to enjoy the "high" that comes from winning, must shield themselves from the pain of those who lose, and thereby learn to cut themselves off from other human beings. Oh my, this is why the wealthy in our present society have no compassion for the poor, and need to construct ideologies for themselves according to which the poor deserve to be poor and they deserve to be rich. For they could not fully enjoy their wealth unless they hide from their awareness the fact that their very wealth is the cause of the poverty of the poor.

Plato: And so our children will be taught only cooperative games, games in which there are no winners and no losers. In fact, the words "win" and "lose" will be absent from their vocabulary.

Neal: But suppose someone were to argue that competing motivates children to try harder, to do their best. This, or something like it, is the rationale for making our children compete with one another.

Socrates: Let's back up a moment. What is it that motivates a soul to incarnate?

Neal: Well, that probably differs from one soul to another.

Socrates: Alright, but is it ever the case that a given soul incarnates in order to compete with other souls?

Neal: No, of course not.

Socrates: No indeed, for the soul, prior to incarnating, knows and experiences its interconnections with other souls, and knows that it is impossible to gain advantage for itself by "competing" against other souls. Cooperation, not competition, is the motivation among souls.

Benedict: And so, if we are to bring Heaven to Earth, our New Society must be such that souls that have become embodied are able to have the same motivations as they had prior to becoming embodied. And these motivations *never* include competing with other souls, whether embodied or not.

Chapter IV

Emotional Intelligence

1) Emotional Hygiene

Neal: Well then, what are the true motivations of the soul, embodied or not?

Benedict: This is very difficult to describe in words. Plato, how would you put it?

Plato: *(laughing)* It is difficult to put into words only if one insists that words have an exact meaning.

Benedict: *(also laughing)* Well then, it is sort of like this: the soul incarnates as part of the endless, infinite, and eternal Creativity of the Divine Being. Its intent, insofar as it can be said that the soul intends, is to express Divinity in a realm, the so-called physical, where Divinity seems not to be. There are two interconnected ways in which the embodied soul attempts to express Divinity: (i) by developing and expressing talents and abilities, and (ii) by contributing to the common good. The greatest feelings of happiness and joy come to those who follow (i) and (ii), not to those who seek to "win" at various competitive games. This latter statement is an empirical fact, which your psychologists know very well, yet are loath to state publicly because it contradicts the values of your current social order.

William: This is an interesting point, as it shows that the wealthy must alienate themselves, not only from other human beings who have "less" status than themselves, but also from their own inner feelings. For a life dedicated to the pursuit of wealth and status cannot in principle be a happy life, yet they have convinced themselves that they are happier than others, although they would not be able to convince a clinical psychologist.

Plato: And so one who pursues such a life is necessarily alienated from his own inner feelings, and becomes less as a result. And by the same necessity, one whose life revolves around developing talents and abilities, and/or helping others, lives in harmony with his inner feelings, and becomes more as a result. I think we may state that the most important part of a child's education is to make certain that our children never become alienated from their inner life, that is, from their emotions and desires. We want our children to know what they are feeling, to behave harmoniously with their feelings, and to develop the vocabulary to express what they are feeling to others.

Neal: This requires that the children experience no judgment with regard to their emotions. That is, the adults and other children in the child's environment must never project a judgment that some emotions are better than others. For the child will then internalize that judgment, and block those of his emotions that are not in accord with the judgment of parents and others. All the child's emotions will be accepted and encouraged, not just those emotions approved of by parents.

William: That way we won't have a society of miserable people walking around with an artificial smile frozen on their faces. I can see that our teaching philosophy, if I may call it that, will be one of drawing forth what is within the child, rather than filling up with facts a mind thought to be "blank". My goodness, what harm and violence we have been doing to our children, by causing them to become alienated from their inner life.

Neal: I agree. A three-year-old child knows what it is feeling. It doesn't need to be taught this. But if it is to retain this knowledge into adulthood, then its environment must be such as to encourage verbal expression of what it feels.

Socrates: And we cannot stress this enough. The part of the embodied soul that *feels* is deeper, closer to Source, than the part that thinks. And human happiness, we might say, is directly proportional to closeness to Source.

Benedict: Not only does a three-year-old child know what it is feeling, but also, it knows the emotions of other children. A child can become sad and cry for no other reason than it perceives another child who is sad. And this is another big difference between our new

Social Order and your present society. Your present society, in its educational process, selects for cleverness – the ability to manipulate symbols. This is the only thing your various "tests" test for. Our New Society will select for emotional intelligence, especially during the child's early years.

Neal: And I can see two ways in which we may select for emotional intelligence. The first, as we have discussed, is to be sure the child's environment is absolutely non-judgmental with respect to emotions. A child's emotions are not "good or bad"; they simply are. Second, we will begin a practice of emotional hygiene. This will involve (i) the child expressing her emotions to both adults and other children, and (ii) listening to and receiving the emotions of other children. This could be done daily at home and/or in school. The most important thing is for the child to develop a non-judgmental awareness of her inner life, her emotions. And for this to happen, it is essential that there be no judgments coming from her external environment. If she feels or intuits that parents, teachers, or other children prefer some emotions over others, then it is likely she will censor, and hence lose awareness of, those of her emotions that are not acceptable, or are less acceptable, to others. This is how we have created the current emotional dysfunctional society, by denying our children their right to be emotionally authentic.

Plato: So it would seem that the first order of business in educating our children is what we might call emotional integrity. Our children will not be taught to *lie* about their emotions, which constitute their inner lives. A child, even a three year old, will tend to adjust what she says to what she thinks is expected of her. Let's consider a typical example: suppose one child, say A, has shoved another, say B, or snatched a toy away. The teacher or parent observes this and makes A apologize to B. So A says the words "I'm sorry" to B, but is not really feeling sorry at all. Meanwhile, B says the words expected by the teacher, "That's OK," but it is not really OK with B. In this way, and in many similar ways, children are taught to lie about their inner life – what they are actually thinking and feeling – in order to "please" the teacher. When this process continues into adulthood, the finished product is a person who is alienated from his emotional life. This is why people in your society, especially men, chronically lie about many things, and why those that are most alienated, the very wealthy, and their politicians, are able to lie with an expressionless face.

Neal: And hence it is so vitally important that the child's environment be such that he feels absolutely safe to express any and every emotion he feels.

Socrates: *(playfully, to me)* Remember when you chided me for reprimanding Crito's misuse of language?

Neal: Yes. As you were drinking the hemlock he asked you how he should bury you, and you replied that he should not speak of burying Socrates, but rather, of burying the body of Socrates. I must admit that when I first read that passage I thought you were being callous and indifferent to your friend's grief, focusing on points of grammar rather than on Crito's imminent loss.

Socrates: And now what do you think?

Neal: I think it was the kindest thing you could have said to him, reminding him that Socrates cannot die, only his body. And by extension, Crito too cannot die, and he should hold that inspired thought throughout his life. This, I think, was your gift to him.

Socrates: *(smiling)* And for you too, my friend.

Neal: It is a gift for all who read that passage. For I too, along with Crito and the others, found myself in tears while reading that passage. And your words served as a powerful reminder that you were not being harmed in any way.

Socrates: And indeed, in our New Social Order, death will be seen for what it is – a transition, not an ending – and the language used in talking about death and dying will be metaphysically appropriate.

Benedict: And similarly, we will teach our children to use language in ways that are always metaphysically appropriate.

Neal: Wait a minute. Children can't learn metaphysics. Or do you think that children can be taught the difference between "burying

Socrates" and "burying Socrates' body"?

Benedict: Well, by "metaphysics" I was not referring to anything that I, or Plato here, wrote. Nor was I referring to the difference between a body and a soul, although children can, I think, grasp that distinction if taught in the right way. We are raising our children so that throughout their lives they remain aware and cognizant of their feelings, because feelings, emotions and desires are closer to, indeed, expressions of, the very essence of a person. A person's conscious thoughts and/or beliefs are much further removed from the inner reality of who he is. Thus one who is cut off from his own feelings and desires is cut off from the deeper part of himself. But for children to remain cognizant of their inner life as they mature, they must be taught, or rather, encouraged, to introspect and to verbally report what they are feeling. And this requires that language be used and used appropriately.

Neal: Well then, are you going to tell us how our children will use language in describing their inner life?

Benedict: You bet I will. Ever since Socrates whispered into my ear, I've been unable to think about anything other than applying my philosophy to three year olds. For it is one thing for an adult, raised in an emotionally dysfunctional society, to then endeavor to remove his afflictive emotions – envy, anger, greed, depression, ambition, pride, etc. It is quite another thing to ask whether children can be raised in such a way that their afflictive emotions are substantially reduced, so that as an adult they are not controlled by them.

Neal: I think I can see where you're going with this.

Benedict: Then let's develop these ideas together, as we did in our book.

Neal: Good. First of all, our children will be taught to experience their emotions as occurring within themselves. Perhaps the most egregious misuse of language in this context – the context of verbally reporting an emotion – involves confusing an emotion with a judgment.

William: Could you give an example?

Neal: I was about to. Johnny shoves Suzie. Suzie is asked: "How did you feel when Johnny pushed you?" She replies, "I feel that Johnny should not have shoved me." The latter is clearly a judgment, not a feeling. Linguistically, the word "that" signals that a proposition, expressing a belief or judgment, is about to come. So the two words "feel" and "that" must never occur together.

Benedict: So we will gently correct Suzie's use of language by telling her, "You think that Johnny should not have shoved you, and you believe that Johnny should not have shoved you, but your feelings are located in your own body. Go inside your own body and see if you can find the feeling you had when you were shoved."

Neal: And if Suzie then says, "I felt angry," we will go further with her and encourage her to find and feel the emotion within her body. Does she feel tightness in the throat, or queasiness in the stomach, or constriction in the chest?

Benedict: And of course, the diagnosis is also the cure, as all therapists know. For as soon as the light of conscious awareness shines on an emotion directly, as it is occurring in the body, the emotion begins to dissipate. The constriction felt in the chest begins to dissipate as soon as she becomes consciously aware of it.

Neal: And again, as all therapists know, the best way to process an emotion, especially a difficult emotion, is to experience it deeply. This is very difficult for adults in our emotionally dysfunctional society, but I suspect with a little encouragement and role modeling, our children can be taught to process their emotions without much difficulty.

Benedict: Yes, for adults in your society carry an incredible amount of "baggage" in the form of half-repressed and fully repressed guilts and anxieties, coupled with many beliefs and judgments of which they are only partially aware. But the steps we are now taking with our children will greatly counter any tendency to accumulate such baggage. When a child is emotionally upset, she will be trained to become aware of that "upsetness" as something occurring in her body. And when with her conscious mind she feels the emotion in her body, and holds that feeling in her awareness for half a minute or so, the feeling itself will begin to lessen. Thus our children will have the tools they need to process their emotions as they are occurring.

Neal: Now, Benedict, I can certainly see how this process that we are teaching our children is therapeutically appropriate, but what did you mean when you said it was metaphysically appropriate?

Benedict: Oh, nothing profound. I was thinking along the following lines: children, at some point early in their developmental process, distinguish between what is inside of them and what is outside of them. What is inside of them are their thoughts and their emotions. What is outside of them is everything else. This was the "metaphysical" distinction I had in mind. And we want our language not to confuse the child about what is within and what is without.

Neal: OK, I get it. An emotion is necessarily within the person who has the emotion. So whatever words follow the expression "I feel…" must refer to something within the body/mind of the person. But the word "that" always signals reference to some state of affairs outside the mind/body of the person. Thus the statement "I feel that Johnny should not have shoved me" is linguistically or metaphysically inappropriate, in that the statement "Johnny should not have shoved me" refers to events outside of Suzie, but the word "feel" necessarily refers to events within Suzie.

Socrates: And so shall we declare this the first law of language: the word "that" must never follow the word "feel" in any spoken utterance.

Neal: *(with a little humor)* No, this will be the second law of language. The first law belongs to you. When someone dies, it will be forbidden to say (or write, or in any way imply) that we are burying the person who has died. Rather, we shall say that we are burying only a body, for which the person no longer has any use.

Socrates: *(jokingly)* Then perhaps we should also ban the use of the word "die", since no one ever really dies.

Neal: Perhaps. I suppose if we wanted to be rigorously metaphysically appropriate, we would have to ban the word, since death is a metaphysical impossibility. But in time and with consistent usage, the word "death" could come to have a meaning similar to "transition" or "going home" or "quitting the body" or something like that. But I think we have a bit more to say about using language to express emotion.

William: Yes, we do. Our educational system will be very different from the one currently in place. The current educational system, with a few notable exceptions, conceives of the child as an empty mind that needs to be filled with facts and concepts. The child's inner life is ignored. But our new educational system will be mostly oriented to the child's inner life, her emotions and desires, especially at the beginning, the 3–5 year olds. For the child's inner life is what is closest to its soul's original purpose in manifesting as that child, and our Society will do everything possible to assist the soul in its original purpose. If the child's life is to remain aligned with its soul's purpose in manifesting as that child, it is essential that the child **never** lose touch with its inner life. The child's environment must be such as to encourage free uncensored expression of its inner life. And so we must lay it down as a rule or set of rules that: (i) a child's emotions shall not be ignored, (ii) children will express and process emotions together, with the help of adults and older children, and (iii) the child's environment will not select for specific emotions.

Neal: I want to emphasize your third rule; I think it is very important. It is of course quite natural for adults to want children to experience only, or mostly, happy emotions. This desire on the part of the adults is something children readily pick up on, and they will modify what they say to please the needs of the adults. So the adults who we trust to care for our children must take care not to project their desires onto the children, or better, to eliminate those desires from their own minds. The child must believe that it is just as acceptable to experience the emotion of, say, envy, as it is to experience compassion. For if the adults in the child's environment believe that the emotion of compassion is "better than" the emotion of envy, then the child will learn to repress the latter. And this would begin the process whereby the child becomes alienated from his own inner life. So we will be teaching our children what might be called "non-judgmental awareness" of their own inner lives.

Benedict: Good. By providing our children with a non-judgmental environment for feeling and expressing emotions, we will not be teaching them that some emotions are better than others. This will give them permission to experience their own emotions deeply and authentically, and through their own direct experience they will come to know which emotions feel better. For we do not deny that the emotion of compassion feels better than the emotion of envy or anger. But our children must discover this for themselves, and discover it in a way that does not cause them to repress the difficult emotions when they occur.

But now, thanks to Socrates, I can see another way to apply my therapeutic "remedies" to our children, which will lead to our third rule of language.

Neal: And I think I can see what you are seeing. Our children will be taught to separate an emotion from their thoughts about what caused it.

Benedict: Exactly. Metaphysically speaking, it is never the case that a person's inner feelings are caused by another person's behavior. For we all believe, do we not, that a person's inner happiness and well-being is independent of external events, and perhaps the major goal of all therapy worthy of the name is to help the individual understand that his happiness is not contingent upon outer events.

Neal: If our children can learn that, they will certainly not need therapy when they become adults.

Benedict: *(smiling)* Well I suppose one could say that the goal of any therapist is to become unnecessary for their patients' well-being. But let's consider a concrete example. Suppose Johnny is upset and believes that he is upset because Mary has teased him or insulted him. As long as he believes that Mary is the cause of his hurt feelings, he will continue to feel upset. So we will assist him, if we can, to detach his feeling of being upset from Mary's behavior.

Neal: Yes we can. In our present society, when a teacher notices that a child is upset she will likely ask the child, "Why are you upset?" And this question, which seems so natural, is the wrong question, for it invites the child to seek an external cause for his feelings. The child then says, "I'm upset because Mary teased me," or something like that.

Benedict: And what's the right question, may I ask?

Neal: *(smiling)* I'm glad you asked. The right question is: "Where in your body are you feeling upset?" and the teacher will make sure that Johnny has all the time he needs to place his awareness inside of his body and feel the hurt that he is feeling. It is only the light of Johnny's own consciousness that can dissipate the hurt feelings.

Benedict: So we will train our adults to refrain from asking children for the causes of their emotions, since this encourages the children to direct their attention away from their emotions and onto outer events. And language will be used appropriately. Our children will not say things like, "I'm angry because Mary teased me," but rather, "I felt anger when Mary teased me." The latter locution recognizes that the child experiences a correlation between his inner feelings and someone else's behavior, but does not express the correlation as cause and effect.

William: I certainly agree with everything that has been said, yet I have a concern. To the child it really does seem that his inner feelings are caused by the other person's behavior. How can we get him, a three year old, to see that this isn't so?

Benedict: I suspect it will be easier to get a three year old to see this than a 30 year old who is convinced that his happiness depends entirely on the outer circumstances of his life. But, Neal, you have a nice example that you use in your teaching that beautifully illustrates the point we are making. I'll suggest you state the example, and then we'll tinker with it to see if we can get it into a form suitable for three year olds.

2) Inner Awareness and Outer Events

Neal: All right. Conceive, if you will, the following two scenarios: (i) a man, say Paul, is a guest at some social event. Another guest, say Peter, walks up to Paul and insults and curses Paul, using profane language. What emotions will Paul likely feel? (ii) Paul is a guest at the same event. But as soon as Paul arrives, the host of the event takes him aside and explains to him that there is another guest present, named Peter, who suffers from Tourette's Syndrome, which affects the language centers of his brain, causing him to utter unpremeditated profanities. Shortly after that, Peter walks up to Paul and says exactly the same words as under the first scenario. Now what emotions will Paul likely feel?

William: *(smiling)* Yes, good example. In the first case, Paul will be afflicted with a range of possible emotions, from hurt feelings, a sense of outrage and indignation, anger towards Peter, etc. In the second case, hmmm, well it is never pleasant to be on the receiving end of a barrage of profanities, but Paul could not possibly be angry with Peter. If anything, Paul might feel compassion for Peter, because Paul now knows that Peter's diseased brain caused him to utter the profanities.

Benedict: This example illustrates that there is no direct connection between outer events and a person's emotional response to those events. For Peter's behavior is exactly the same in both scenarios, yet Paul's emotional response to that identical behavior is very different. Hence Paul's emotional response to Peter's behavior cannot be explicated in terms of Peter's behavior, but only by Paul's mind, which in the second scenario, but not the first, contains knowledge about the illness affecting Peter's brain. Peter's obnoxious behavior (the behavior is still obnoxious, even though we now understand the cause) gets filtered through Paul's knowledge of Peter's illness, resulting in feelings of compassion rather than feelings of hurt and anger.

Neal: And I'm sure that we, or our children's teachers, will be able to discover many examples that will convince our children of this general point, that their emotional well-being is not necessarily dependent on the behavior of others.

Socrates: Wait a minute. There's more that we can learn from the example you gave above.

Neal: What do you mean?

Socrates: Well, the example can be generalized.

Neal: Generalized?

Socrates: Generalized to cover almost all human interactions.

Neal: *(smiling)* There's that sparkle in your eyes again, so I know you're onto something. OK, I'll play with you. How can that example be generalized? After all, certainly not all obnoxious human behaviors can be explained in terms of Tourette's Syndrome.

Socrates: Ah, my astute friend, although it is certainly true that not all humans have Tourette's Syndrome, it is just as certainly true that all humans do have a brain. Would you not agree?

(I could feel Socrates' delight in playing with me – that he was leading me to some insight, beginning as usual with some innocuous statements that were obviously true, and ending – well, we'll see where this goes soon enough.)

Neal: Yes, of course I agree. No one could deny that all humans have a brain.

Socrates: Hah! I heard that parenthetical remark above. And actually, you are right. Leading people to insights about themselves was among my greatest delights while embodied. I was only occasionally successful in that past, but I know, and so do you, that I shall be successful right now. *(With humor)* Thank you for agreeing to my first innocuous statement.

Neal: You are most welcome. What's your second?

Socrates: Not so fast. What is it, in your example, about Paul that mitigates his initial emotional response to Peter's verbal behavior.

Neal: Paul learns that Peter's words are caused by Peter's brain that is afflicted with illness. And because Peter's words are caused by his abnormal brain, Peter cannot be held responsible for them, and Paul's anger turns into compassion.

Socrates: And is it not the case that anything spoken by anyone is caused by the brain of that person?

Neal: Yes, of course. One can see this physiologically. A column of air passes from an individual's lungs through the voice box and out the mouth. This column of air is modulated by the voice box, which in turn is controlled by muscles that cause the voice box to expand and contract. The muscles are controlled by nerves that ultimately connect to the brain. One might say that a brain suffering from Tourette's Syndrome sends the wrong signals to the nerves that control the muscles that control the voice box.

Socrates: And the physiology is the same for any word that is spoken, regardless of whether the brain in question suffers from Tourette's?

Neal: Yes, of course.

Socrates: Good, and so this is my second innocuous statement, that the cause of any spoken word arises in the brain of the speaker. Now you stated above: "Peter's words are caused by an abnormal brain." The use of the word "abnormal" implies, perhaps, that there is such a thing as a "normal" brain, and that we have some understanding of what the word "normal" means in this context. Shall we examine whether this is true?

Neal: Oh, I think I understand. The term "normal" cannot have an absolute, or "normative" meaning, but refers only to what is usual and customary in the culture in which the given brain was raised. So the brain of someone who, say, sincerely believes that the best way for him to get to heaven is by killing people is not "normal" with respect to my present culture, but it is "normal" with respect to the culture, or subculture in which that individual was raised. But of course, I cannot state that my culture is "normal", or that his is "abnormal" in any absolute sense.

William: Now of course from a medical perspective one can make some distinction between a medically normal and a medically abnormal brain. A brain suffering from cancer is medically abnormal, regardless of the culture that produced that brain. But the mere absence of some specific medical condition cannot be the definition of a "normal" brain, since brains differ markedly from one culture to the next.

Socrates: And a culture that is dysfunctional in a certain respect will most likely produce brains that are dysfunctional in that same respect?

Neal: Yes, this is how cultures perpetuate themselves.

Socrates: And in your world today, is there such a thing as a culture that is not dysfunctional?

Neal: Maybe somewhere deep inside the Amazon jungles?

Socrates: Ah, you romantic. But even there you will find some dysfunctionality, although not nearly in the extreme proportions that one finds in your present culture. And so my third statement, perhaps not quite as innocuous as the preceding two, is that all brains are raised or "cultured" to reflect and perpetuate the dysfunction inherent in the society that raises them.

Benedict: May I interject something here? I notice, Socrates, that instead of saying "all people are raised or 'cultured' to reflect etc., etc.," you said, "all brains are raised or 'cultured' to reflect etc., etc." I applaud your use of language, because it draws attention to the physical, which is what words are. And a person, after all, cannot be blamed for having a dysfunctional brain, any more than a person can be blamed for having Tourette's Syndrome.

Socrates: Yes. And so the words that come out of anyone's mouth are caused in exactly the same way as the words spoken by one who suffers from Tourette's Syndrome. If one agrees that one who suffers from Tourette's Syndrome is not responsible for the words that come out of his mouth because it is caused by a dysfunctional brain, and hence we should not be angry with him, by the same reasoning we conclude that the words that come out of anyone's mouth is likewise caused by a brain rendered dysfunctional by its upbringing, and neither should we be angry at him.

Benedict: And so our children will be taught that there never is any reason to feel hurt or angry because of what another has said.

Negative behavior, verbal or bodily, on the part of one child will not be able to afflict the minds of other children with harmful emotions, because our children will be taught, through their own experience, that negative behavior is caused by a brain that has been afflicted with illness, permanent illness in the case a brain afflicted with Tourette's Syndrome, temporary illness in the case of a brain afflicted with envy, anger, anxiety, or any other of the numerous afflictive emotions.

Neal: So the basic idea here is that every case in which one person uses language to harm the emotions of another is structurally the same as in Tourette's Syndrome. Well, Socrates, it seems that once again you have managed to turn everything upside down.

Socrates: What do you mean?

Neal: Just this. In our present society, when one child harms another, with verbal or bodily behavior, the child that is harmed gets all the attention, and the child that harms gets a time-out, or is punished in some other way. But now we understand that the child who harms is the one most in need of attention, because his brain has been temporarily afflicted with envy, greed, anger, or some other form of insanity. A brain afflicted with anger is temporarily insane, and is no more responsible for what it does than a brain afflicted with Tourette's Syndrome.

Plato: You seem a bit surprised at our conclusion, but yet, do we not agree with *A Course in Miracles* when it says that all human behavior is either an expression of love or a cry for love?

Neal: Yes, we have mentioned this before.

Plato: *(with a little humor)* And this remains true no matter how obnoxious the cry for love? Whether it's the corporate CEO, the schoolyard bully, or our two-year-old child throwing a temper tantrum in the supermarket – these are all cries for love, for affection, for inclusion.

Neal: Yes. And I suppose we must extend this to include even the most egregious cases of dysfunctional human behavior, such as murder, rape, war crimes, and so forth. All bodily behavior is caused by a brain, and dysfunctional behavior is caused by a brain that has been rendered dysfunctional through upbringing.

Benedict: And our children will learn this, first experientially, then later, perhaps much later, conceptually.

Neal: Yes, I see. So in a typical scenario where Suzie uses language to hurt Johnny's feelings, Suzie's feelings are just as important as Johnny's. Of course, Johnny will receive whatever comfort he needs from parents, teachers, and other children, but Suzie also will be comforted, not blamed or punished. Suzie will be encouraged to express the emotions she was feeling while she was saying hurtful words to Johnny. And since our children's emotional environment will be non-judgmental, Suzie will feel "safe" to express her real emotions. Perhaps she was feeling upset in some way, in need of attention, insecure. As she expresses her emotions, with the assistance of adults and older children, the other children will recognize that they too have felt this way often, so they will be naturally compassionate to Suzie in her distress. This will constitute the loving attention that her behavior cried out for, and even Johnny's hurt feelings will dissipate in the compassion being generated for Suzie.

Benedict: And one can easily conceive that the children, if led in the right way, will be able to come up with alternative solutions to such problems and conflicts. The children will discuss among themselves what they might do if one of them feels anger towards another, or feels excluded from the group in some way. It is the latter feelings of exclusion that lead to the most dysfunctional behaviors, so our children (and the adults) will be taught to notice both (i) when she herself feels left out, and (ii) when another child feels she is not included.

Plato: And we have identified this, the need to feel included, as the most important psychological need of our children, indeed, of adults too.

Socrates: We should relate this need to the peculiar metaphysical condition of the consciousness that constitutes the human condition.

Neal: "Peculiar"?

Socrates: Why, yes. Look, when one surveys the vast, limitless domains of consciousness at play in the infinite One Mind, and one sees that all forms of particular consciousness, from the individual soul to clusters of individual souls, to the souls of galaxies and beyond – one finds enjoyment of infinite delight, feeling always the interconnectedness of all things, and feeling the Love, as thick as pea soup, that structures all things, then yes, the human condition, compared to all that, is indeed peculiar. For it is a condition of consciousness in which Love seems to be absent, and in which the individual embodied soul feels itself unconnected with its Source.

Neal: *(laughing)* Pea soup? That's a new one; I doubt that anyone has compared God's Love with pea soup before.

Socrates: *(also laughing)* Well, from my present perspective, Divine Love is so thick, so omnipresent, that the only way one could miss it would be not to exist.

Neal: *(with humor)* I'll ignore the implications of that last remark.

Plato: This is why the embodied soul's first order of business, so to speak, is to seek inclusion in some group. That seeking is an expression of the soul's longing to return Home to the knowledge of its inclusion in the One Mind. Eventually of course, our children will learn that the inclusion for which they are really seeking can be found only deep within themselves. And this is why our children's inner life – their emotions and desires – are so important, and why the child's environment, at home, in school, with playmates, will be structured so as to maximally facilitate the children's awareness of their inner lives, as well as the inner lives of other children.

(At this point I sensed that both William and Benedict had something important to say, and I was not sure who to let speak first.)

William: Let me speak first, since what I have to say will not be as lengthy as what Benedict wants to say.

Benedict: *(jokingly)* And since when is brevity of expression a reason for expressing first? But by all means, go ahead.

William: A most magnanimous gesture. Well, you all know of my interest in mediums. Earlier we discussed the possibility that mediums might be used to assist the embodied soul to stay connected with the original intent of the soul prior to manifesting as a body. But I find myself now wondering whether mediums could also be useful in this stage of our children's development.

Benedict: OK, you've got my attention. Proceed with your wondering.

William: The goal of education, as Plato once put it, is to turn the embodied soul around, away from its tendency to become absorbed by what is external, and towards what is deep within itself. So teaching and encouraging our children to know their emotions and desires is part of teaching the children to look within. But within a child, there is more than emotion and desire.

Benedict: What do you mean?

William: Some of our children are able to perceive non-embodied spirits. And some have memories from a previous life. Psychologists refer to the former as "imaginary playmates" – a question-begging phrase if ever there was one. We shall encourage our children to express and share such experiences, and mediums might be very useful for this purpose. Perhaps a medium, gifted at working with children, can assist the children in staying connected with non-embodied spirits, even as they grow up. And, my goodness, Benedict, just as your philosophy might be better understood by three year olds, perhaps mediumship-development classes should likewise be taught to our three year olds, so that they will feel themselves connected with and in communication with spirits, even as they mature.

Benedict: And no doubt, speaking of brains, that the scientists of our New Society will be closely monitoring the brains of our children.

William: Yes, good. We expect that the neurophysiology of children who can communicate with spirits will be a little different from that of children who cannot communicate. We will explore whether and to what extent the desired brain state, which allows for such communication, can be induced in our children, perhaps through some meditative practice, or through manipulation of sounds in their environment.

Neal: And this connects with what we discussed earlier, the

question of whether a brain can acquire language without closing off its receptivity to such communication. Our neuroscientists will have lots to do with raising our children.

William: And so will our nutritionists, psychologists, physical fitness teachers, massage therapists, and meditation teachers. In our present society, the so-called helping professions "help" mostly adults whose problems arise from a dysfunctional upbringing. But in our New Society, the collective knowledge and wisdom of these professions will be applied at the earliest developmental stages.

Neal: You mentioned "massage therapists". I suspect that learning to give and receive massage will be an important part of our children's education. In the orphanage case that we discussed, all the infants died because they were not held and touched. So touching is necessary for physical embodiment. There already are plenty of studies that show the effect of touching and massage on brain development, and many more such studies will be forthcoming. I believe that it will be seen from these studies that many instances of negative behavior on the part of children are caused by a deficiency in touch. The physical sensations of being touched and massaged calms the brain of its restlessness and anxieties. Perhaps it will be possible to teach Suzie, who is about to say unkind words to Johnny, to recognize that she is feeling anxious or excluded and needs to be touched. So instead of swearing at Johnny, she might simply request that someone massage her back or shoulders for five or ten minutes.

William: Indeed, one of the reasons for physical violence is that hitting is, after all, a form of touching. So the child who hits is really craving some form of physical contact. Teaching our three year olds to give and receive massage – to touch one another in ways that benefit their developing brains – will prevent most of the dysfunctional violence that occurs later in life, and will be an essential component of our children's education. But now, Benedict, I am eager to hear what you have to say.

3) Envy and Compassion

Benedict: Let me begin by making a statement for which I shall then attempt to argue. The statement is: as a child begins to interact with other children, its brain is hardwired to produce emotions of both envy and compassion. In raising the child we shall attempt to tip the scales toward compassion, but envy, or at least the tendency to be envious, is innate to the human condition.

William: But don't you think that the negative emotions can be mastered?

Benedict: Yes, but not by a three year old.

Neal: Well then, explain what you mean.

Benedict: We know that the body both limits and structures the experiences of the mind insofar as it is embodied.

Neal: Yes.

Benedict: And by knowing something of the nature of the body, it is possible to say some general things about *how* the body limits and structures the soul's experiences. For example, we know that the body's optical system responds only to electromagnetic radiation that is between .00004 and .00008 centimeters wavelength. The body is hardwired so that it cannot receive information and communications that occur outside of this narrow region. So the visual appearance of things to an embodied soul is determined and limited by this fact about the body's optical system.

Neal: Agreed.

Benedict: It is not difficult to see that human sensory experiences are structured by the body, but it is perhaps slightly more difficult to see that the same is true for emotions.

Neal: Oh, I don't know if it will be more difficult to show this. After all, both sensory experience and emotional experience are possible only insofar as consciousness has become embodied.

Socrates: *(smiling)* Unless one counts the experience of infinite, eternal, continuous BLISS to be an emotion.

Benedict: *(laughing)* No, for present purposes we will not be counting the natural state of the soul as an emotion. Now, everyone knows that children tend to imitate the emotions and behaviors of other children. As we have noted, a child may cry for no other reason than he perceives that another child is sad or crying. This is the root of compassion. Similarly, a child can want to play with a toy for no reason other than he sees another child playing with the toy. This is the root of envy. Everyone has observed this, but let us examine why this is the case. We shall consider compassion first, and our explanation will be solely in terms of physiology.

William: I'm intrigued. Usually compassion is conceived as a higher-order feeling, involving consciousness, etc.

Benedict: But, William, there is no need for compassion in the non-embodied state of pure consciousness, since in that state of consciousness, one cannot perceive suffering of any kind, either in oneself or in another. So there is nothing to feel compassionate about, except while embodied.

William: OK, I get it. While embodied, our explanations will be physiological.

Benedict: Exactly. So here's our scenario: for whatever reason, three-year-old Mary is sad and crying. Peter sees Mary crying, and begins to cry himself. What we need to explain are the tears in Peter's eyes. It is certainly not the case that Peter goes through any mental process about Mary and then "decides" to cry.

William: I agree. Peter simply looks at Mary and experiences that his eyes are welling up with tears. And I suppose the cause of Peter's tears is ultimately Peter's brain. For in order for his eyes to produce tears, the brain must send the proper signals along the nerves that stimulate the tear ducts to produce tears, or whatever the physiological details may be.

Benedict: And so, just by looking at Mary, Peter's brain has been put into a state whereby it sends the signals along the nerves to the tear ducts. How does the very perception of Mary's crying put Peter's brain into a state whereby it sets in motion a causal chain leading to the production of tears in Peter's eyes?

Neal: If we were to speak in the manner that is usual and customary, we would say that Peter has identified with Mary's sadness, which identification has made Peter himself sad.

Benedict: We may begin with this, but we must quickly point out two errors in this way of describing the situation.

Neal: Yes, I think one error is that the level of description is mental, whereas we are looking for a physical or physiological description.

Benedict: Correct. But even as a mental, or psychological description, it begs the question of whether Peter consciously identifies with Mary's sadness, or simply discovers that he has tears in his eyes. We are seeking a physical description that produces in Peter a brain state that causes tears. This talk about "identifying" is for the child psychologists, not for the children.

Neal: Let's trace the steps physically. Light, or electromagnetic radiation, reflects off the body of crying Mary, and into the eyes of Peter. Peter's retina responds to only a very narrow band of the incident light, sending electrochemical signals along the optic nerve to his brain. These signals, when they reach Peter's brain, put it in a state of readiness to produce tears.

Benedict: You've left out the most important step, for our purposes.

Neal: What? Oh yes. When the signals propagating along the optic nerve reach the brain, they interact with the brain itself, and it is the result of this interaction, between incoming signals and the present state of the brain, that engenders the brain's readiness to produce tears.

William: So we must say something about this "present state of the brain", such that, when the signals from the optic nerve reach it, it produces tears.

Neal: Yes, for we note that were Suzie to cry in front of an eight-month-old child, or in front of a 12 year old or an adult, it is unlikely that tears would be the result. So there is something that pertains to the brain of a three year old that causes it to produce tears when it interacts with the signals propagating up the optic nerve. I take it that it is this "something" that we're trying to get a hold of now.

Benedict: Yes. Now, if we were to utilize the common way of

speaking about such things, we might say that an eight-month-old baby is not able to identify with the emotions of a three year old. And moreover, neither can a 12 year old or an adult. To be sure, the latter two perceive that the three year old is in distress, and may take steps to comfort the child, but they do not identify with the child in that they do not experience the child's emotions as their own. But Peter does experience Suzie's emotions as his own. And this is what we shall mean when we use the phrase "imitation of the emotions". Hence the brain of a three year old must differ from that of the eight month old and the 12 year old in this respect.

We might put the matter as follows: imagine a situation where an eight month old, a three year old, and a 12 year old see Suzie crying. The same electromagnetic radiation falls on the retinas of all three; the same electrochemical signals travel up the optic nerves of all three. Yet only the three year old cries. Why?

Neal: Well, I can't describe what goes on in the brain, but I can say that the 12 year old knows and understands that whatever Suzie is crying about is no big deal, that children often cry, or that crying children are a part of life. This knowledge that the 12 year old has (but the three year old does not) must be correlated with the brain itself, so there will be some physiological difference between a brain that has this knowledge and one that doesn't. This is speaking very loosely.

William: Why do you say it is speaking loosely?

Neal: Because knowledge pertains to minds, or consciousness, not brains.

Benedict: Good. So Peter's perception of Suzie crying is physiologically correlated with Peter's brain, which now is in a state of readiness to produce tears. This brain state is in part caused by electromagnetic radiation reflected from Suzie's body that enters Peter's body through his eyes, and in part caused by the original state of the brain itself. For neither the 12-year-old brain nor the three-month-old brain produces tears under the same circumstances.

Neal: We also want to emphasize that when Peter cries, he is crying for himself, not for Suzie; for the light that reflects off Suzie's body and into his eyes, when it reaches his brain, is the physiological correlate of the sadness he is now feeling. If he should then come to Suzie's assistance, it would be to alleviate his own feelings of sadness.

Benedict: And this, then, is the basis of those emotions we call "compassion" and "empathy".

William: My goodness, this is the exact opposite of what we were all taught.

Neal: What do you mean?

William: Well, do not our psychologists and theologians assure us that emotions like compassion and empathy, and the capacity for what is called altruistic behavior, are advanced, higher-order feelings that only a small percentage of highly evolved humans are capable of manifesting?

Neal: Yes, that's what we have been told by various "theories" of moral development. The ability to genuinely care for the well-being of others is for the saints among us, not ordinary people.

William: And yet our analysis, if correct, has shown that the ability for compassionate behavior is hardwired into the brains of every three-year-old child.

Plato: Yes, and then the process of adapting to your insane culture causes the original tendency for compassion, hardwired in the three-year-old brain's ability to generate the emotions of others in itself, to become overlaid with so much nonsense that it loses its former ability. And by "nonsense" I mean the physiological correlates of your culture's beliefs and values: that competition is good, that it is good to be thought better than others, that it is good to "have more" toys than others, that one's reputation and wealth make one "better than" others. A three year old has not yet internalized these values, and so is able to feel the emotions of others.

Benedict: But when two 6 year olds play a competitive game, the winner, in order to fully enjoy the "high" that comes from winning, must of necessity conceal from himself the knowledge of how bad the other feels, or rather, train himself to actually feel good because the other feels bad. So he must disassociate from the brain's innate tendencies towards compassion – which is to produce tears when another cries – so that in some sense he actually enjoys the misery of others.

Neal: So our present culture causes children to lose their innate tendencies towards compassionate behavior, although those innate tendencies are still there. Thus adults, in adapting to our dysfunctional society, become cut off from what is natural and innate in themselves.

William: And then, having become alienated from themselves, some try to find their way back through theology or psychology, and struggle to overcome the egoic beliefs that they had internalized.

Neal: So those theologians and philosophers, who like Kant, state that compassion and moral development depend on overcoming the ego's desire for self-aggrandizement, have gotten things upside down. To be sure, the child's little ego does desire self-aggrandizement, as I believe Benedict will explain to us shortly. But also, and equally, it identifies with and empathizes with the emotions of others, which engenders compassionate thoughts and behaviors. It is this latter ability that our culture causes to atrophy in an individual, mainly through forcing our children to play competitive games, one against the other. But our New Society will encourage compassionate feelings and behavior, by teaching children cooperative games, and of course, creating social environments in which they are encouraged to share and express emotions.

William: So our children will not have to struggle against their lower emotions in order to feel kindly towards one another.

Benedict: Perhaps we should say that they will not need to struggle nearly as much as they do now, but some "struggle", or whatever word we wish to use, may still be necessary.

Neal: But why? Why would it, or should it, be a struggle for one person to feel compassion for another.

Socrates: *(laughing)* Because we are not going to blow up Plato's Cave.

Neal: What?

Plato: Socrates is right. We have shown that the brain of a three year old is hardwired to produce feelings of sadness when another child is sad. This is the root of what is called "compassion". And we may assume as true what Benedict will soon show, namely, that the brain is also hardwired to produce feelings of envy. Just as your culture reinforces mostly the latter, our new culture will reinforce the former, but yet, the latter feelings of envy will not be completely unavoidable.

Socrates: Nor can they be, if the soul is to have a human experience.

Neal: But what did you mean about blowing up the Cave?

Socrates: We have certainly used this metaphor of a theater before. "The World is a stage" etc. So imagine, if you will, a bunch of people at the theater, watching a play or a movie. The audience identifies with the characters on the screen. Now, if the emotions get too difficult for the audience to handle, one solution might be to blow up the walls surrounding the theater. Then the full light of the Sun could enter, and that would end all the dysfunctional emotions associated with the play.

Plato: *(laughing)* But then of course, the play comes to an end. So with respect to this human drama of ours, or rather, *(to me)* of yours, the only way not to experience any afflictive emotions would be to blow up my Cave, destroying the Theater of time and corporeality, and allowing the Light of Divine Understanding to wash all negativity away.

Neal: Hmm, it is difficult to find myself opposed to "allowing the Light of Divine Understanding to wash all negativity away". But I can see that if that were to happen, then souls could no longer have a human experience. So we will keep the light of day from shining into our theater.

Benedict: And the best way, the only way, to do that is to ensure that the human condition necessarily involves some afflictive emotions, or dysfunctionality. So, just like a tendency for compassion is built into the structure of the body, so also is the tendency for selfish and egoic emotions and behaviors. Shall we examine this now?

Neal: Yes, by all means.

Benedict: There is, of course, more than a grain of truth in your psychologists' developmental models according to which small children cannot think beyond immediate gratification. Indeed, our analysis of the biological root of compassion holds that the child who cries in sympathy with the sorrow of another child is really concerned about alleviating his own sorrow, and his efforts to assist the other is really an effort to remove the sadness from his own mind. So it is certainly not the case that a three year old has the same capacity for compassion as a saint – because the "compassion" of a saint, if we can call it that, does not involve any sadness on the part of the saint. The sense in which the Buddha is said to be "compassionate" is a very different sense of the word than the sense in which a three-year-old child feels compassion. Nevertheless, the human body is hardwired to resonate with the emotions of other humans, a fact that we will lovingly use in raising and guiding our children. But the human body is also hardwired for a little mischief.

Neal: "Mischief" you call it?! Don't you mean the kind of dysfunctionality that is now destroying my planet?

Socrates: Now, now, calm down, my friend. But there is a perspective, not the human perspective to be sure, from which it does appear that the souls who have gotten stuck in the quicksand of corporeality are like children who are creating a lot of mischief that the more mature souls will have to clean up. This is a bad analogy, of course, but yes, mischief is what happens when souls separate themselves from the Knowledge of Source. But, Benedict, you were about to tell us what it is about the body that guarantees that embodied souls will get into mischief even in our New World Order.

Plato: And we add that there would be no World Order at all if souls did not get into mischief. Then all souls would retain the knowledge of their connection with God, and there would be no desire to have a human experience, that is, an experience of themselves as apart from God. So, Benedict, what is it about the human body that virtually guarantees that the souls that occupy it will get into mischief?

Benedict: Perhaps I should preface my remarks by commenting on the word "mischief". First of all, Socrates is correct in that, from our perspective, every difficulty that humans get themselves into amounts to nothing more than a little mischief, easily correctible in the grand scheme of things. And this is so regardless of whether the mischief is war, murder, stealing, lying, or cheating. All souls find their way back to Source, from which Perspective the human experience is an illusion. That said, Father Earth can no longer sustain the kind of mischief that leads to war, economic crimes, and crimes against the environment. So some, but not all, forms of mischief will have to be eliminated if humans are to survive as a species.

Neal: Well, I can certainly understand that the human motivations that cause war, cause the destruction of the environment, etc., will need to be eliminated if our species is to survive. But then, what are the remaining forms of mischief that will be allowed?

Benedict: Perhaps we can use Shakespeare as an analogy. The kind of mischief that goes on in his tragedies (murder, war, violence…) will cease, but the kind of mischief that goes on in his comedies will continue. For example, there will always be situations in which, say, A is in love with B who is in love with C who is in love with A. Of course, such situations will be handled quite differently than they are today, and will be utilized as opportunities for spiritual growth, rather than as opportunities to wallow around in jealousy and frustration.

Plato: If I may interject something here, we should perhaps use the expression "in lust with" rather than "in love with". This is an area that, as Socrates might point out, the misuse of language – using the word "love" to describe a mere sexual attraction – has led to enormous confusion. Our children, when they become teenagers, will use language correctly, and will not be confused between feelings of love and feelings of lust. But for now, let us wait until our children become teenagers, and then we will discuss these things at some length. Proceed, Benedict.

Benedict: We have considered the imitation of the emotions

with respect to the emotion of sorrow. A child, A, can cry for no reason other than he perceives another child, B, crying. B's sorrow is contagious and has infected A who may attempt to remove this infection by assisting B, or by redirecting his attention so that he is no longer aware of B. But now, what if B is joyful instead of sorrowful? Is joy just as contagious as sorrow?

Neal: I think we have to affirm that this is the case. We said before that the very perception of B's sadness by A is a physiological event in A's body, an event that causes A's body to be in a state similar to B, so that A feels a sadness akin to B. But the same analysis should apply if B is feeling happy. The perception of B's joy by A is a physiological event in A's body, and should recreate in A a joy akin to B's.

Benedict: Good. As we have said, when A feels the sadness induced via his perception of B, the consequent desire in A is to remove or diminish the sadness in himself. One way to remove the sadness he feels is to assist B, and this, we have said, is the biological basis for compassionate behavior. Now, what happens to A when he feels the joy induced by his perception of B, who we assume is now manifesting joy instead of sadness?

Neal: A would want to preserve or augment the joy induced by his perception of joy in another.

Benedict: And what kind of behavior might A engage in that will preserve the joy induced by his perception of B's joy?

Neal: He will want for himself whatever he perceives is the cause of B's happiness. If B is happily playing games with other children, A will want to join in. If B is happy playing with a toy, A will want that toy for himself, believing that the toy is the cause of B's happiness.

Benedict: This, then, is the root of envy, which necessarily pertains to the human condition.

Plato: Now we emphasize that our children will receive lots of guidance and support as they begin to socialize. By the time a child has reached the age of three, she will have experienced all four situations described above: (i) feeling sad, (ii) feeling the sadness of another child, (iii) feeling joy, and (iv) feeling envy towards a child who is feeling joy. With the assistance of adults and older children, our children will be taught to recognize those emotions in themselves, and to openly discuss them with other children. It will not be uncommon for little Johnny to go to a teacher and say, "I'm feeling jealous because Suzie is playing with a toy that I want to play with too." In our new society, no teacher will ever say to Johnny, "You shouldn't be jealous," but instead will accept and honor the reality of Johnny's emotions. What does one do, then, with feelings of envy and jealousy? I'll bet our children will be able to come up with many healthy responses to this question, once they are given full permission to feel, express, and discuss all emotions.

William: So the first order of business, with regard to educating our children, is emotional intelligence. And this really does not have to be taught, since a three year old already knows what she is feeling and also knows what other children are feeling. She needs only an environment that does not teach her to repress her emotions, as our current environment does, but instead, allows and encourages the full expression of emotions, and gives her some tools for handling the more difficult emotions. After all – and this is a point that you, Benedict, will want to make –

Benedict: You make it for me.

William: – Yes, we shall respect the child's mind in the same way we respect her body. If Suzie experiences bodily pain, say she scrapes her knees or twists an ankle or jams a finger, preschool comes to a stop and everyone pays attention to Suzie's body. But for our children, in addition to treating bodily pain, we will also treat mental or psychological pain. If Suzie is in distress because, say, another child is playing with a toy that she wants, preschool will also come to a stop, and her emotional distress will be treated with the same care and attention that is given to scraped knees. This will become a "teaching opportunity", as Suzie is encouraged to share her emotions with the other children, who I might add will understand them perfectly as they have each experienced the same thing on different occasions.

Plato: Good, and I would like to emphasize that although emotional intelligence is the "first" order of business for our young children, it is also the second and third and fourth, etc., orders of business. For our children even into adulthood will feel, discuss, and process emotions, individually and in groups. Emotional hygiene, like washing one's hands, is an ongoing process for the lifetime of the individual.

Socrates: And speaking as a "physician of the soul", as Plato here once characterized me, is it not obvious that emotional or psychological hygiene is every bit as important, if not more so, as physical hygiene? Emotions are contagious, just like germs, and a principal cause of the ills of your present society is that the people running it, especially in the economic sphere, are emotionally sick. Just as hand-washing, nutrition, rest, and moderate exercise are essential for a healthy body, so expressing emotion, sharing feelings with others, meditating, and reflecting often on one's inner experiences are just some of the regular practices that will be helpful in maintaining emotional health – practices, I might add, that will be put in place as soon as the child begins to socialize. But, Neal, you have a few questions.

4) Three Possible Responses to the Suffering of Others

Neal: Well yes, but it might involve shifting the topic a bit, and I wasn't sure if this is the right time to bring up my concerns.

Socrates: Right time? *(With humor)* You're the only one wearing a watch here. As for myself, any time is the "right time".

Plato: And also, recall the analogy with which we began this conversation.

Neal: The analogy to a symphony orchestra, where those who cannot hear the music all at once are constrained to reading the score note by note?

Plato: Yes. So if we have been discussing what the flutes are doing, and now you want to talk about what the trombones are doing, it might seem like an abrupt change of subject. But we remind ourselves that although the flutes and trombones are doing different things, they are doing them simultaneously. In the case of an orchestra playing a symphony, there is indeed a literal "pre-established harmony" in which all the instruments participate and co-create. Why not assume that there is a sort of "pre-established harmony" involved in our discussions, so it is not just some random haphazard thought that has come to you, but rather, a thought that might be a necessary component of the harmony we are attempting to describe?

Neal: Well, when you put it that way…

Benedict: *(with a little humor)* But really, is there any other way to put it that is consistent with our world-view?

Neal: *(smiling)* OK, I get the point. Here are my questions: (i) When one child perceives another child in emotional distress, we agreed that the very perception of distress on the part of the first child engenders or is concurrent with an emotional distress similar to that of the second child. The nervous system, so to speak, of the percipient becomes aligned with that of the perceived. The biological basis for compassionate behavior is that the first child assists the second in an effort to lessen his or her own distress at perceiving distress in another. But we did not say that compassionate behavior is the only response that could lessen the child's discomfort. If other responses are possible, we should state what they are, and also state whether and how we shall guide our children to follow the compassionate path, rather than the other possibilities.

Benedict: *(with humor)* Well this question should keep us busy for a while. Dare I ask what is your other question?

Neal: It is this: (ii) While it is certainly the case that insofar as a soul is embodied, what we are calling "compassionate behavior" – behavior that aims to reduce the distress of another – has a profound biological basis. But surely it also has an equally profound non-biological, or spiritual, basis as well. After all, a three-year-old child is still somewhat "fresh from Heaven", and perhaps still has residual memories of the interconnectedness of all souls. So a child's compassionate behavior could perhaps be motivated by a vague recollection of this interconnection, in addition to (being motivated by) the effort to remove from herself the discomfort induced through perceiving another in distress.

William: If I were still embodied I might say something like, "Let's all take a deep breath and consider how we will respond to these questions." In my time, as well as in yours, the feeling of concern for the well-being of another was considered to be a "higher order emotion". But our three year old is concerned with his own well-being.

Socrates: Yes, but contrary to your culture's beliefs, the only way to be genuinely concerned with one's own true well-being is to be concerned with the well-being of others. We *are* our brothers' keeper, and happiness, individual or social, is not possible without this understanding. Nevertheless, there is considerable semantic confusion with respect to words like "compassion" and "love", about which, not to worry, I'm sure Benedict will offer a few clarifying definitions.

Benedict: *(smiling)* Alright, I will take on the role of semantic police for now, but I must say that that I've lost some of my prior concerns about linguistic exactness. These words, "compassion", "love", and I might add "God", are used and misused by your culture without any clear meaning in mind. You will notice that in the above discussion I used the term "compassionate behavior" instead of the term "compassion", and that this behavior involves assisting another who is suffering in some way. But there is of course a big difference between (i) compassionate behavior that is motivated by a desire to lessen or remove the discomfort in oneself that the other's suffering engenders, and (ii) compassionate behavior that is motivated by the experiential knowledge of the interconnectedness of all minds. The sense in which one speaks of the compassionate Buddha and the sense in which a three-year-old child exhibits compassionate behavior are very different.

Neal: But if we define "compassionate behavior" as any behavior that seeks to alleviate the distress of another, then it would seem that both the Buddha and a three-year-old child are capable of such behavior.

Benedict: Yes, the outer behavior may be the same in any specific case, but the inner feelings, the inner states of consciousness are quite different, so the same word should not be used to refer to both.

Neal: Yes, for the three year old, the perception of sorrow in another child engenders sorrow in himself. Compassionate behavior is a possible response – we will be examining other possible responses soon enough – but it is an effort to remove the engendered sorrow of the perceiver. But the Buddha, or any enlightened human, does not feel sorrow at the sufferings of others. And because, as NDErs testify, they experience themselves as identical with all other souls, compassionate behavior is their only possible response to the distress of another.

Benedict: But even here, or especially here, we must be careful with language, because strictly speaking, in the enlightened state of consciousness, there is no "other" towards whom one could feel compassion.

Plato: And really, from the perspective of an enlightened consciousness that experiences continuously its identity with the World Soul, and hence with all individuated souls, an embodied soul who appears to be suffering is akin to a human having a bad dream.

Neal: Hey there, sometimes we have nice dreams too.

Plato: Whether your dreams are nice or nasty, they are still dreams, are they not?

Neal: Yes, of course. And it is probably more difficult to awaken from a "nice" dream than from a "nasty" dream?

Plato: You better believe it, which explains why a given soul, eager to wake up, might take on a nasty dream, with lots of suffering, in the hope that it will wake up more quickly.

Benedict: So we might state something like this: the compassionate behavior of a three year old, and of all humans who are not enlightened, is motivated primarily by a desire to alleviate one's own distress triggered by perceiving another in distress. It is a desire to make the other's dream become a happy dream. But the behavior of an enlightened human is motivated by the desire to help the soul wake up, rather than a desire to change the soul's dream – its human experience – from relatively nasty to relatively nice.

Socrates: *(with great humor)* And let me assure you that it is far easier to wake up a dreaming human than it is to wake up a dreaming soul. For one thing *(laughing)* a dreaming human is not likely to kill you for shaking him awake.

Neal: You mean not "kill you" but rather "kill your body".

Socrates: *(looking pleased)* Of course. But you know I think we need to loosen up with all this exactness around using words with precise meanings. I know I started it with my remarks to Crito, but I suggest that now we just allow the words to flow however they come to you, and we can always edit and explain possible semantic ambiguities as they arise.

Neal: OK, but first I want to say a few words about the meaning of the word "love". I think its misuse in my present culture causes at least as much harm to the soul as did Crito's saying that he was going to bury you.

William: I suspect we will be talking about this in depth when our children are 13 years old. But I think we can state your meaning briefly now: if by the word "love" one means a genuine, deep caring for the well-being of another, without regard for how that "other" is treating oneself, then humans are not capable of such feelings, except sporadically, and are under great illusion in believing that they are.

Plato: Yes, and this is why I explicitly defined the word "love" as a desire for something one doesn't yet have, and why Benedict here defined it as sort of a feeling of affection towards another that one believes has made his dream a bit less nasty than it was before. Nothing high-minded here; just ordinary everyday human emotions. And to briefly anticipate how we shall not be using the word "love", let us flash forward about ten years in our development process. When 13-year-old Johnny becomes sexually aroused by gazing at 13-year-old Suzie's developing body, we shall say, and teach our children to say, *not* "I am in love with you," but rather, "I am in lust with you." That way neither Johnny nor Suzie will become confused about what is going on. But now, back to our three year olds and the two questions you raised.

William: Let's look at your second question first, although they are very much interrelated. Our three-year-old children, because of how we have raised them, will have thinner margins so to speak, and hence will have a greater recollection of the Unity of all minds than do your present three year olds. This "greater recollection", I believe, will be decisive in guiding our children to respond to the suffering of others with compassionate behavior, rather than the possible alternatives.

Neal: Now we must state what these other alternatives might be.

Plato: That's obvious.

Neal: What do you mean?

Plato: Nothing deep. The "other alternatives" are the ones that have been taken by your present society, greatly augmenting the overall level of misery. There are three logically possible emotional responses to the suffering of another. The first response, which we have been discussing, is to feel sorrow at another's suffering, and to address the sorrow by endeavoring to alleviate the other's suffering. A second response is to be emotionally indifferent to the suffering of others, and a third response is to feel joy because another is suffering.

Benedict: But I insist that only the first response is a natural and immediate consequence of the child's physiology. The other two responses have to be taught through cultural conditioning, and are unnatural to the embodied soul. They require hiding more deeply from the knowledge of the interconnection of all minds. But you are right in that this is how people are raised in your culture, and it is why people are for the most part so horribly alienated from their own inner knowing.

William: I just want to interject that we are doing a "Platonic" thing here – *(to Plato)* if I may use your name in that way – shifting back and forth from the individual to the collective.

Plato: By all means.

William: Then it seems that most people in our present society are raised to ignore the sufferings of others. Otherwise, homelessness would not exist, and no one would starve in the presence of abundance. But the very rich are much more alienated, for they have been raised to exult in the sufferings of others. For them, it is a good thing that there are poor, hungry, and homeless people, because this is the reason for their wealth in the first place. If there were no people who were materially suffering, then the wealthy could not feel that their wealth makes them better than others.

Neal: And in some sense the wealthy must enjoy the material suffering of others, since it is their wealth, and their endless seeking after more wealth, that is the cause of material suffering in the first place. But the source of such dysfunctional emotional behavior must lie in how we are raising our children.

Plato: Well, this might be a "chicken or the egg" sort of issue. After all, your children, that is, children raised by your current society, are raised to become members of that society. They are raised to embody the values of the society that raises them. Sometimes these patterns – the possible emotional responses to the suffering of another – are easier to see in the collective, sometimes in the individual. But the origin of any pattern in the psychology of an individual originates in early childhood conditioning, which is why we are spending so much time on our children when they are at the very initial stages of socializing with others. This is the most crucial phase of the educational process, especially if we are to create a society that is sustainable. So returning now to our children, let us inquire how our second and third responses to the discomfort of another child might arise in a given child.

Neal: Well, the third case is easily observed by anyone who has raised more than one child. We call it "sibling rivalry". If Peter and Paul, say, are close in age and have a history of fighting and competing with one another, then it will not be unusual for one to rejoice at the misfortunes of the other.

Benedict: *(smiling, to me)* And if I might point out to you – to you who are still in some denial about wisdom to be found in the traditions of our ancestors – the story of Cain and Abel highlights this tendency.

Neal: Yes, OK, I can see it. As Benedict has said, envy is just as natural a biological response as compassion, and in the case of siblings, these two possible responses interact and often the former wins out. But we are dealing with two and three year olds, and envy can be addressed through understanding the causes of envy. I think the children of our new society will experience much less envy and sibling rivalry than the children of my present society.

William: Why do you say that?

Neal: Well, as Benedict has said, when one child perceives happiness in a second child, that perception induces a momentary happiness in himself that he desires to hold onto by acquiring whatever he believes is causing happiness in the second child. I can think of two possible causes: (i) the second child is happy playing with a specific toy that the first child now wants. But probably more important, and more subtle, is (ii) the second child is happy because he is getting attention from other children and/or adults, and the first child now desires such attention for himself.

William: And how will these "two causes" be remedied in our new society?

Neal: There will be enough toys and attention to go around.

William: – With attention being the more important, by far. From my present perspective, one of the saddest things to observe – well, sadness is quite impossible in my present state of consciousness, but if it were possible, I would be tempted to feel sad watching what happens when a child is denied the attention she needs and craves. If you were here with me (and in a sense you are) you would see how layers upon layers get added to the margins when the newly embodied soul lacks for attention.

Plato: Yes, you see the child's craving for attention is the soul's desire to recollect its prior experience of feeling connected with the

World Soul. Feeling connected to other humans is, one might say, the consolation prize for becoming embodied. If even that is denied to our poor embodied soul, it will either return Home quickly (as in the case of the orphaned infants) or, if it stays embodied, will become mad, as has happened to most people in your present society. This is why a two- or three-year-old child can become so envious and distraught when another child is the center of attention. But our children will never lack for sufficient attention.

Benedict: And moreover, as soon as they are old enough, say four or five, they will be able to intelligently discuss their emotions that get triggered by such situations, which will quickly turn into opportunities for learning. For example, Suzie sings some little song, and the other kids applaud; the teacher notices that Mary can barely bring herself to applaud. The teacher now gives attention to Mary, who, we might say, has scraped her psychological knees with all the attention Suzie has received, and asks Mary to describe how she is feeling. And, I repeat, because developing emotional intelligence is the first and *only* order of business with respect to our young children, and because our children have been raised to believe that *all* emotions are welcome and appropriate, Mary will have no difficulty in stating what she is feeling. Other children will weigh in with what they are feeling, and since every child will have experienced at some point in their lives what Mary is now experiencing, they will deeply understand her emotions.

Neal: Although we have mentioned this before, it is worth repeating: an ounce of prevention is worth a pound of cure. Many adults in our present society go to therapy in an effort to heal from childhood traumas, to reconnect with their inner emotions, and to reprogram dysfunctional patterns of emotions and behaviors. But if we bring all the resources of our therapists to bear on our developing children, we can prevent most of the dysfunctional patterns from ever taking hold in the individual.

William: Yes, but we will need not only the presence of our therapists and child psychologists, but also the absence of all cultural influences that tend to conflict with and negate the healthy influences of our teachers on our children. After all, if we wish our children to align their taste buds with what is nutritious for their bodies, we must not only surround them with healthy foods, but we must not also, at the same time, expose them to substances that are harmful, like sugar, salt, and fat, lest Plato's pastry chef win the argument once again.

Neal: OK, we will certainly surround our children with lots of healthy psychological food, that will nourish their minds, help them connect caringly with others, process difficult emotions as they arise, and so forth. But what is the psychological "sugar, salt, and fat" that we must be careful not to expose our children to, especially when they are young and impressionable?

William: This might be difficult for people to see, because just like the harmful physical "sugar, salt, and fat" exist everywhere in the so-called American diet, so also the harmful psychological "sugar, salt, and fat" are everywhere in our culture, and our poor children are exposed to this as soon as they begin to socialize. Then, just like with unhealthy foods, children become accustomed to it and addicted to it, and seek it out for themselves. I speak of the great harm that is done to our children when we teach them to play competitive games, games in which one person or team "wins", and another person or team "loses".

Neal: You are certainly right to say that this will be difficult to see because it is so pervasive in our culture. From the very beginning children are taught that winning is good, that competition builds character and brings out the best in people.

Plato: And the consequence of this teaching is your current dysfunctional society, well on its path to self-destruction. Among the major causes of this dysfunction is the teaching of competitive games to your children. Now, we are not going to be canceling the Olympics, but we will be canceling the competitive games our children are forced to play, as if they were training for the Olympics. We must understand the great psychological harm that playing competitive games does to our children. Competitive games are the mechanism by which your culture teaches children to override their natural biological response to the suffering of others (compassionate caring) in favor of the unnatural response of indifference and rejoicing. Shall we take a closer look at this?

Neal: Yes, by all means.

5) What Children Learn By Playing Competitive Games

Plato: Then let us ask, what does a three- or four-year-old child learn by being taught to play competitive games, games in which there are "winners" and "losers"?

Socrates: And as we address this question, let us recall the question we raised when we talked about the kinds of stories we should tell our children. In particular we asked, what does the story of Santa Claus teach our children? And we answered that the story of Santa Claus teaches our children that grown-ups can lie, and can lie about the most important things. This realization traumatizes every child. How, we are asking, are children traumatized and otherwise psychologically damaged by being forced to compete with one another, and, insult to injury, by being taught that such damage is good for them. And what is it that a child "wins" when she wins some competitive game?

Neal: I think what the child "wins" is attention from the other children and adults, and the feeling that he/she is better than another, or others, with respect to whatever competition the child has "won". Whether the competition is for the fastest runner, the prettiest hairstyle, the best grades, the best dancer, having the most "friends", the "winners" get attention.

Plato: And the losers?

Neal: The losers feel like losers.

Plato: And is this an appropriate way to raise children, to make most of them feel like losers? After all, it must be remembered that in any competitive game involving more than two people, there will necessarily be more losers than winners.

Benedict: Moreover, to see the stark cruelty and illogic of forcing children to compete with one another, imagine the following two descriptions of the same activity: a teacher says to her class, "Let's play some games to see (i) who can run the fastest, (ii) who has the neatest desk, and (iii) who is best at math." This is one level of description. The second is: a teacher says to her class, "We are going to engage in some activity. The outcome of this activity is that one of you will feel happy and everyone else will feel sad." Now the second level of description describes accurately the effect that playing competitive games has on the children (and adults) who play them. The winner feels happy and the losers feel sad. From an emotional perspective, it is at best a zero-sum – is that the right expression? – activity. The joy of the winner comes at the expense of the sorrow of the loser. But since there are usually many more losers than winners, playing competitive games creates more sadness than joy.

Plato: And is it not both illogical and cruel to compel children to participate in a process that creates more suffering than joy?

Neal: It is insane, but *(with a little sarcasm)* necessary so that children will grow up to become well-adjusted to our insane society.

Benedict: *(with a little humor)* Well, *we* don't have to worry about raising children in a way that is contrary to their biological and spiritual nature.

Neal: What do you mean by "biological" nature? You know that many of our biologists would argue in the opposite direction.

Benedict: What do you mean?

Neal: Oh, survival of the fittest stuff. By teaching our children to compete against one another, we are teaching them to survive in a dog-eat-dog world.

William: But this, of course, is just culturally self-serving nonsense. Dogs don't eat dogs, and cooperation is by far more readily observed in nature than is competition. So your, rather our, biologists have deeply internalized their culture's values, which they then project onto nature itself.

Benedict: Yes. So when I used the expression "biological and spiritual nature" above, I meant something like this: the spiritual nature of a child contains traces of memory of its state of consciousness prior to embodiment. This will be much more so for *our* children, since we have taken care to keep their margins clean and lean during their infancy. The biological nature of a child includes the tendency of the child to produce tears upon perceiving another child in distress. Teaching very young children to compete against one another teaches them to override both their spiritual and biological nature.

Neal: Well, the spiritual part is obvious, since there are no winners or losers in the non-embodied realm from which all humans come, and competition is totally foreign. But how does competition teach children to override their biological nature?

Benedict: What must the "winner" of a competitive game do in order to fully enjoy winning?

Neal: He must learn to ignore the feelings of the loser.

Benedict: Exactly. He must be taught that it is good to ignore the feelings of the children who lost. And this is completely contrary to what we are teaching *our* children: to be maximally aware and honestly expressive of their own emotions, and to be aware and empathetic to the emotions of other children. Actually, the last phrase is redundant, because to be aware of another's emotions is to biologically resonate with them, and hence empathize with them. It is this natural empathy that atrophies through the process of playing competitive games.

William: The winner, in order to enjoy winning, must override his own biology, which still wants to produce tears at the sadness of another. So he learns to ignore those tendencies in himself towards identifying with and feeling the sufferings of others, and after participating in many competitive activities over many years, he learns to enjoy the sufferings of others. Life, for him, consists of winners and losers, and he rejoices when others are feeling badly for losing, since his "happy" feelings are purchased at the expense of much sadness on the part of others.

Benedict: It is psychologically, perhaps even logically, impossible for one person to genuinely wish another well when both are competing for a prize that only one can win. So the "winners" learn to ignore the feelings of the "losers", or to put it more accurately, they learn to ignore the effect on their own psyche that the perception of sadness in another causes, thereby becoming less. For when the "winner" of any contest perceives the sadness in the loser, that very perception still, as before, engenders the physiological readiness to produce tears – a sort of emotional resonance with the other. But culturally induced beliefs about the value of winning, or rather, the physiological correlate of those beliefs, are so powerful that they easily override the natural tendencies towards empathic resonance. But the "losers" are also harmed in a way that goes far beyond their initial sadness at losing a competition.

Neal: How so?

Benedict: Consider the following scenario: Johnny has just lost some competition, say, he finished last in a race. His self-esteem is momentarily lowered, and in his sorrow, he turns to his teacher for help. What will the teacher say?

Neal: Yeah, well the teachers in my present dysfunctional society will likely tell little Johnny that he shouldn't feel so bad, that it was just a game, and that winning or losing was not important.

Benedict: And what does the child learn when an adult tells him that he "should" not be feeling what he in fact is feeling?

Neal: Yikes! The full horror of the situation – what we are doing to our children in my present society – is becoming manifest. The child learns two things: (i) the child learns that he cannot trust his own inner feelings, since it is a respected adult who has told him he should not be feeling what he is feeling, and (ii) he will be careful to align what he says to the adult with what the adult has told him is the "right" way to feel. So he learns to lie about his inner feelings.

Benedict: And this is the beginning of all lying, is it not? It is the beginning of inauthenticity, which begins when the words used to describe one's inner feelings are designed to be acceptable to the hearer of those words, rather than accurately and simply express the inner feelings themselves. So the words that poor Johnny will use to describe his feelings after losing will now be arranged to harmonize with the values of the adults around him, since above all else, he needs the support and approval of those adults.

William: Yes, so the loser must report his feelings, if he now bothers to report them at all, in such a way as to conform to the teachers' belief that it was all "just a game". Winning or losing may not be that important to the teachers, but it certainly is for the children who compete. So to please the teacher, he will put a plastic smile on his face and either lie about how he is feeling, or repress his feelings altogether. In this way he becomes less, that is, cut off from his own inner life, which process adds more than a few layers to the margins.

Neal: So, win or lose, the effect of teaching children to compete against one another is harmful to the child. Specifically, the harm consists in causing the children to become shut off, or alienated, from the deeper aspects of their own being. Yet it was said a while ago that we shall not be ending the Olympics, so presumably, there is some sense in which competition can be beneficial.

Plato: Yes, but not for three-year-old children. When our children are a little older and more mature, they will have deeply internalized the Moral Law (or the Golden Rule). Through playing cooperative games, they will have learned that by working and playing harmoniously together, they can accomplish much and have much more fun. They will all feel sufficient self-worth and self-esteem – this is the job of education for the first several years, say 3–7. But their self-esteem will in no way be associated with winning, but rather, with being authentically who they are. Then, with this solidly in place, older children may gradually be exposed to games that at some level involve competition, but always in such a way that they are playing not to "win", but to develop their skills.

Socrates: After all, there are many activities that are fine for adults but not for children. If one is to become any good at playing chess, to take an example, one must lose many games to players who are better than oneself. By the time our children are old enough to learn such games, they will understand that even though they are trying to win, they are really developing their abilities, so they will not feel bad upon losing. We shall protect our three year olds from the harmful effects of competition in the same way that we protect them from the harmful effects of alcohol.

But there is another issue that I think we should address at this time.

Neal: Yes?

Socrates: Using our analogy with a symphony orchestra, we are now going to look in on another instrument. Our children, that is, our newly embodied souls, come with innate talents and abilities that seek expression in the physical realm. Do we agree with this statement?

Neal: Yes, of course. It is a major premise of our argument.

Socrates: And our New Society, unlike the old one, will be such as to maximize the ability of each soul to manifest and express all talents?

Neal: Yes.

Socrates: And our children will have different talents?

Neal: Yes, of course. Some will be musically inclined, some will have healing abilities, others will be good at organizing things, some will be good at math, and so on and on and on.

Socrates: So we must raise our children in such a way that they will never become envious of the talents of another, but always rest content to develop their own specific talents, while deeply appreciating the talent in another that they do not possess. Using our analogy, we might say that the violist shall not envy the flutist, as all members of the orchestra contribute essentially to the total harmony. Our children will understand this. So as Benedict has explained, the biological tendencies towards envy must be openly acknowledged, deeply accepted and understood, and finally overcome and transcended, so our children will rejoice in the talents and happiness of other children, rather than being encouraged to feel the envy that then generates competitive behavior.

Neal: Perhaps the best opportunity for teaching our children how to handle feelings of envy is around birthday parties.

Socrates: What do you mean?

Neal: First of all, there is complete equality in the distribution of birthdays; every child has exactly one birthday every year, where they are the center of attention. Birthday parties will not only be a time for celebrating and gift giving, but also a time for the other children to share and process what they are feeling while someone else is the center of attention. And while it may seem odd to turn birthday parties into group therapy sessions…

Plato: Ah, but it is "odd" only with respect to your present culture which celebrates children's birthdays by poisoning them with junk food. *(With humor)* In your culture birthday parties are an opportunity for the pastry chef to once again defeat the nutritionist. But I assure you, by the time our children are three, four, five years old they will have had more experience with group therapy than most of your adults receive in a whole lifetime. They will enjoy the process, and look forward to it. Their attitude will be something like this: what is the point of us all coming together if we don't talk about our inner life, our feelings? So the child whose birthday is being celebrated and who is now the center of attention will share how he is feeling with the others, and the others will share how they are feeling with regard to not being the center of attention themselves, but instead, are giving their attention to another.

Socrates: Ah yes, the gift of giving one's attention to another. You know, when I hung around the markets of Athens, this is what I did, and in a sense, it is the only thing I did. I gave the people I questioned my undivided attention. And many were very uncomfortable being the center of my attention, so to speak, as it compelled them in turn to pay attention to aspects of their lives that they would rather not pay attention to.

Neal: Like pursuing money and reputation. I guess it is fair to say that everyone who pursues these things knows, at some level, that they are not following the path of their soul's intent. When you forced them to pay attention to this, they got angry, and their anger protected them from their conscience, that is, from their own inner knowing that they were pursuing false gods. My goodness, what a hopeless task you set for yourself.

Socrates: Now, now, I could say the same about you, especially since you really do understand that my task was not hopeless, not at all.

Neal: What do you mean?

Socrates: Well, when you wrote that book with Benedict, why were you writing it? Was it not a rather thankless task, as you knew that none of your colleagues would bother to read it. And similarly about this present writing. People could say, "My goodness, what a hopeless task you set for yourself." But are you experiencing this as a hopeless task? I know you do not get up every morning and think to yourself: now I will spend a few hours at my writing desk engaged in this "hopeless task". And if it is not hopeless, what are you hoping for?

(I must confess I am somewhat taken aback with Socrates' abrupt change of subject, or so it seems to me. We had been discussing what children feel when they give and receive attention from others. And now I'm not sure what we are talking about, with Socrates drawing attention to the process of writing itself.)

William: *(to me)* Let me help you a little. Whatever it is that you are hoping for, you have certainly outgrown, as have I, any expectations or "hope" that our colleagues will either read or understand what you wrote with Benedict or what you, or rather, we, are writing now.

Neal: That is true.

William: Also, you are not hoping that you will gain fame or reputation through this writing project.

Neal: Certainly not. When I was younger, perhaps I would have wanted that, but now, at my age, and my proclivity for solitude, fame would be more of a burden than anything else.

William: So given that the usual outcomes that authors hope for do not pertain to you, any more than they applied to Socrates in Athens, what are you hoping for?

Socrates: Hint: What was it that made you feel that the book you wrote with Benedict was worth the effort?

Neal: Oh, that's easy. When someone told me that reading the book helped them in their personal lives, that's when I felt it was all worthwhile. It feels to me that it is a blessing to have had the opportunity to do something that genuinely helps another.

Plato: So if only one person is benefited by the writings of another, that is sufficient to make it all worthwhile.

Socrates: *(to Plato, radiating joy)* And for me, dear friend, you were that "one person" who understood my teachings and transmitted them to the world. But we must bear in mind that, although the "hope" involves a desire that others, at least one, benefit from what we are doing, this cannot be our motivation for doing it.

Neal: Yeah, well for me, there is nothing else I would rather be doing.

Socrates: And that's how it was for me in Athens. There was nothing else I would rather be doing. And is this not what we desire for our children? That whatever they do, it is not for external effect, but rather, simply an authentic expression of who they are in that moment.

William: So our children will be encouraged, as much as possible, to be self-motivated. And this will create a kind of human being that is very different from one whose actions are motivated primarily by desires for approval and/or recognition from others.

Plato: And the reason why our children will become self-motivated is that the causes of *non*-self-motivated behavior will have been addressed. For the causes of ***non***-self-motivated behavior, or rather, the emotions that generate such behavior, are always the child's feeling that he is not good enough as he is, that he will not be accepted for who he is, and so he gradually "learns" to adjust his behaviors and motivations to what will gain him approval. But our children will be raised to believe and feel that who they are is sufficient. Approval by the social order, like God's unconditional love, is guaranteed.

Benedict: This is really the problem of envy, is it not? For what children most envy with regard to other children is receiving attention and recognition from others. The reason children want to be "popular" and are envious of those who are "popular" has to do with being the center of attention. Receiving attention and approval from others is absolutely necessary for the psychological health of humans, and the failure to receive attention and recognition can lead even to death, as was the case with our infants in the orphanage. This is why children are "hardwired", so to speak, to seek attention. Children will tend to be envious of skills, behaviors, and characteristics that generate attention for other children. Our goal is to raise Johnny in such a way that he can listen to Suzie singing her song, feel the joy Suzie feels from the applause, without feeling any lack within himself. He already feels accepted and approved of, nor will he be tempted to think that he must grasp Suzie's specific happiness for himself by imitating her singing. He will rest comfortable in the knowledge that he, like all other children, has unique skills and abilities. And because he will not envy Suzie, he will be able to share in her joy.

6) A Symphonic Analogy

Neal: I think there is a nice analogy we can make with our symphony orchestra.

Benedict: Yes?

Neal: The score of a symphony calls for many instruments that play their parts simultaneously. The overall effect depends on each instrument playing its own specific part as best it can. Suppose now that the strings notice how loud the trumpets and trombones can play, and begin to feel envious of the brass who can play much louder than they can. Or suppose the trombone players envy the soulfulness of the oboe? Or the violas and bassoons, whose individual voices rarely stand out, were to become envious of the flutes and violins, saying to themselves, "Those guys always carry the melody; why can't we?" Or when the music reaches a climax with loud bangs from the percussion, the audience applauds wildly, and the other musicians are envious of all the attention the percussion gets.

William: *(laughing)* We would then have complete chaos in the orchestra, with every musician striving to imitate whatever other musicians are getting attention for, and no one is content to be playing their own part. In fact, one can carry this example to absurdity, with the musicians scrambling so much to imitate each other that their "parts" – the sheets of music on their stands – go flying all over the place, so that they no longer even know what their parts are.

Neal: Your image of the parts flying all over the place as the musicians scramble to imitate other musicians is hilarious, and worthy of a Marx Brothers movie. But it saddens me a bit, as it seems to be too appropriate an image for our present society. The margins have become so thick that people rarely know what part they are supposed to be playing individually, as they scramble to play whatever "role" they think will get them the most attention or recognition.

Socrates: Oh, you, lighten up.

Neal: Huh, me?

Socrates: Yes, you. You said it "saddens" you. Did not Dante refer to the human condition as the divine comedy?

Neal: Yes.

Socrates: *(mischievously)* Then rest assured that some of us over here are experiencing this human drama of yours *as* a comedy, just as if it really were a Marx Brothers movie. I know I do not yet convince you of this, but laughter is a sane response to the human condition and the silly things that souls do when they become human. Imagine a violinist in an orchestra, in the middle of a performance, putting his own instrument down, running over to the brass section, and grabbing a trombone from the hands of a brass player. Of course, he quickly discovers he doesn't know how to get a sound out of the trombone, but by this time it no longer matters as he hears the climax approaching and rushes over to the percussion section in an effort to get credit for the big bangs that the audience loves so much. But now he no longer remembers where he left his violin, or where he was sitting in the first place. This is really funny, and is not an inaccurate parody of the human condition as it has manifested in your culture.

Neal: Well I suppose we will have a good laugh together when I share your perspective. But still, that kind of behavior on the part of an orchestra, while good material for the Marx Brothers, nevertheless causes so much suffering for humans.

Socrates: No doubt about that. And there's also no doubt that such behavior on the part of real musicians would bring about the collapse of the orchestra, as the music intended by the composer could no longer become manifest. And this, in part at least, is the cause of the collapse of your present society. No one rests content with who they are, but rather everyone is intent on rushing around trying to imitate those who are getting the most attention in your society; and usually, I might add, the attention is for negative behavior, that is, behavior that benefits neither oneself nor society as a whole.

Neal: But…

Socrates: But keep in mind, when I state that there is a perspective from which the human catastrophe, as we might call it, is humorous, this is also a perspective from which the human drama is perceived as not real. The embodied souls cannot die: in fact, they cannot even really suffer, any more than the Marx Brothers "suffered" or caused suffering as they wreaked havoc on the stage of Verdi's opera.

Neal: So to perceive the human condition as a comedy…

Socrates: Which I often do.

Neal: … one must also perceive it as Divine.

Socrates: … Which I always do.

Neal: I think I understand. But I have a further question about this analogy.

Socrates: What is it?

Neal: OK, so let's suppose we have convinced our musicians to settle down and cease from competing one against the other. We have convinced them that the music sounds best when each musician plays his or her own part as best she can, and follows the lead of the conductor. Now in the case of the orchestra, the music originates in a coherent vision on the part of the composer. Although the many different instruments play different parts, the coherence of the orchestra as a whole is guaranteed by the vision of the composer, and it is the conductor's role to explicate that vision as best she can. In the human experience, what plays the role of the composer or score, which guarantees that each musician playing his part will produce a coherent effect, and what plays the role of the conductor?

Plato: Let's respond to your first question, leaving the second for later. It suggests a very important item for our lesson plans, as we educate our children and they grow a little older and become capable of conceptual thought. They will be taught that insofar as they are a body, (i) they have parts that require care and nourishment, and also (ii) they themselves are "parts" of a larger physical "body", called their ecosystem, which also requires care and nourishment. They will know where their food comes from, and the importance of quality air, water, and soil. Our children will know that it is the height of insanity to poison and destroy those aspects of planet Earth on which their continued existence as a body depends. So the concept of a larger physical whole, which has produced his physical body and to which his body belongs, will be inculcated in our children over many years with many examples.

Benedict: And then, having become familiarized with the concept of Wholism with respect to their body, a child will be taught Wholism with respect to his mind. He will be taught that, like his body, the very consciousness that he now experiences himself as being also belongs to a larger whole. And just as the "larger physical whole" – the Earth as a Whole, so to speak – that has produced and includes his own body, has also produced and includes all other bodies, likewise, the larger mental whole that has produced his consciousness, or mind, has also produced and includes within itself all other minds.

Plato: And this larger mental whole is what I referred to as the World Soul, and what Benedict, using the strange terminology of his times, might have referred to as a mediate infinite mode of God, or the mind thereof. But it doesn't matter what we call it. In terms of the analogy, the World Soul plays the role of the composer, who has both created the human drama *and* has manifested Herself as the various human souls with their constituent personalities that experience the drama as real. It is as if Beethoven not only writes his *Ninth Symphony*, but also manifests as all the musicians who play it, as well as the audience who hears it.

Neal: *(with humor)* My goodness, that's a lot of manifesting.

Plato: But not to worry, because the World Soul has infinite time in which to manifest whatever she wants, or perhaps more accurately, She is not bound by time, so perceives Her symphonies, or Creations, instantaneously. And so did Mozart, incidentally.

Neal: OK, but I think there is something missing in our analysis.

Plato: What do you think is missing?

Neal: It is certainly true that there will be chaos in the orchestra if the musicians try to imitate the parts of other musicians. But it would be incorrect to conclude that each musician should be aware only of his own role in creating the music. The best musicians, while focusing on their part, nevertheless sustain some awareness of the music as a whole, and how their part contributes to and fits in with the design of the composer. So they must listen to and appreciate, without attempting to imitate, what the other musicians are doing.

Plato: Good. So our children will not only be busy developing their own skills and abilities, they will be taught to appreciate the skills and abilities of other children, without becoming envious of them. They will be taught that every child plays an essential role in creating the overall harmony of our New Society.

Socrates: And for this we will need a conductor, or many conductors.

Neal: Yes, so what is the role of the conductor, and what is the analogue of the conductor in our society?

Socrates: In your present dysfunctional society, there is, alas, no analogue for the role of the conductor, which is one of the main reasons your society is so dysfunctional. But in our New Society, there will be a very important analogue.

William: This will be interesting, for we note first of all that the conductor plays no instrument, and hence does not contribute to the sounds produced by the musicians.

Benedict: *(with humor)* Yes, and the musicians of our dysfunctional orchestra, who have been competing with one another so much that they have completely lost sight of the music – of the composer's vision – will have no use for a conductor, who, they will think, makes no contribution to the music but merely stands and waves a stick in the air. But by the word "music" they no longer understand sounds that constitute a coherent whole, but rather are just a bunch of individuals blowing, scraping, and banging on their instruments in whatever way will get them the most attention in the moment.

Plato: So the conductor, free from having to focus his attention on any single part of the music, focuses his attention on the music as a whole. The conductor embodies the design of the composer, and it is his job to manifest this grand design through the contributions of the individual musicians. The music as a whole – the vision of the Whole, so to speak – is continuously in the consciousness of the conductor, and it is with respect to this vision that she directs, guides, and prods the individual musicians. Do you now understand who will be the "conductors" in our New Society?

Neal: I think so. This analogy is really the same as an analogy you have used before – the analogy of the ship of state. A ship cannot function without a captain who knows something about navigation, an orchestra cannot function without a conductor who is continuously conscious of the music as a whole, and a society cannot function without individuals who have experienced and internalized a vision of the Form of Social Justice. And something else is required, I might add: it is that the respective sailors, musicians, and citizens recognize and understand their need for a conductor.

Plato: Yes, and the last thing you said is important, because insofar as our sailors, musicians, and citizens are caught up in their little egoic desires, which they mistake for understanding, they will be oblivious to those around them who do have understanding. But perhaps the expression "vision of the Form of Social Justice" is a bit archaic.

Neal: Well I suppose if we wish to modernize our language about these things, we could use the language associated with descriptions of the Near-Death Experience. In that context, people talk about experiencing and Knowing the interconnection of all things and all beings, that once one has experienced this directly one Knows that it is impossible to gain advantage through harming others, and that the Golden Rule, or Moral Law, is the only way to live one's life that is in harmony with the vision of the Unity of all souls.

Plato: And so our New Society must be led by, or guided by, individuals who have experienced this Knowledge directly. Not only must society as a whole be guided or "conducted" by such individuals, but also, every aspect of society must be guided by those individuals who, through spiritual training and achievement, desire nothing for themselves that they do not also desire for everyone else, because, in their vision, they have "seen" that they in fact *are* everyone else. Well, we will come back to this later at greater length, but now, *(laughing)* where did we leave our children?

Neal: I think we left them at a birthday party or something. But to conclude our orchestra analogy, may we state that the music sounds best when (i) each musician focuses mainly on his own part, and (ii) is able, while playing his part, to hear with appreciation and without envy the parts of the other musicians, and (iii) always has one eye on the conductor, from whom he receives a sense of the music as a whole, that is, a sense of his own part in the context of the music as a whole. So our children, as they mature, will be taught that their lives will be happiest and best when they (i) focus on developing their own talents and abilities while (ii) being aware and appreciating without envy the talents and abilities of all other children, and (iii) developing a sense of a "Whole" that is greater than the sum of all the parts. And for (iii) I suppose that direct experience of the Whole is best, but what you called "true belief" will be sufficient.

Plato: Well, the whole society will be permeated by true belief, so everyone will have it. But while not everyone will emerge from my Cave – if that were so there would be no need for anyone to go back into the Cave, and the realm of space-time would come to an end – nevertheless, many more will have done so than ever before. And because of medical technology, many will have caught a little peek of the Sun through what you call the Near-Death Experience. So every aspect of our New Society, every profession, every social role will have people who have caught a glimpse of what I called the form of social justice. It is only direct experience, not true belief, that fixes the Knowledge of the interconnectedness of all beings in the consciousness of the individual, as a consequence of which it is impossible, psychologically impossible, for the individual to desire for herself anything that she would not also desire for others. These are the individuals who will be our conductors. Now, shall we get back to that birthday party?

7) Giving and Receiving Attention

Neal: By all means. I think we were discussing what children feel when they give attention to others and when they receive attention from others.

William: And I think we need to understand more deeply what it means to give attention to another and to receive attention from another. This must be something very basic and essential to understand, since your, or rather, our, culture has become mad with so many people desperate to be the center of attention. This must be a deep human need.

Plato: The felt need and desperation to be the center of attention reflects a deep longing for the "attention" – the continuous attention – the soul feels when it feels itself a part of the One Being. It reflects a longing for what has been lost when the soul took on human form.

Socrates: And so we must ask: what is it that a human – a child in this case – receives when he receives attention from others? What is it that a child gives when he gives attention to others? What is this thing we are calling "attention"?

Neal: It is awareness.

Socrates: And what is this thing you call "awareness"?

Neal: Well to be aware of something is to be conscious of it. Oh yes, it is consciousness itself, in the form of a human being. Oh my!?

William: "Oh my" indeed! The one thing people of our culture have the most difficulty with is paying attention, or in a word, being conscious and present to what they are doing and feeling in the moment. But even so, there has been a regression from my time to yours, in that people were more conscious and better able to pay attention in my time than in yours. In a sense, although it may seem strange to say, there is somewhat less consciousness associated with an embodied soul now than there was in my time.

Neal: And people become desperate to regain lost consciousness, but seek it in ways that are guaranteed to fail. Multitasking, so common in my culture but largely absent in yours, is simply a way to lower the overall level of consciousness available to the individual.

William: Yes, and all the frantic running around that people do, desperate to get attention from others yet unable to give their own attention to others – because they don't know how to pay attention to one thing at a time – this running around is really a running away from their own consciousness, from their own inner light.

Plato: But our children will be trained to pay attention. Well actually, they already know how to pay attention, so we won't have to teach this, since paying attention pertains to the nature of consciousness itself. But we will no longer prevent them from maximally using this ability. So the event of a child's birthday is a natural opportunity for him or her to be the center of attention, that is, to receive consciousness from others, and to generate more consciousness within herself.

Neal: But if that is to be the case, then the birthday parties in our New Society will have to be quite different from how they are at present, which is centered around playing games, getting presents, and being poisoned by unhealthy foods.

Benedict: We will keep the first, jettison the third, and modify the second. Playing games is an important aspect of every child's development. But our children will not be taught competitive games. There will be no "winners" or "losers". Instead, the games we teach our children will be for the purpose of developing and expressing skills and talents, for developing a sense of social cohesion, and for the sheer joy of physical exuberance.

Plato: And of course, in addition to the structured games we teach our children, there will be plenty of time for spontaneous unstructured play, so that children can invent their own games and structures. As I wrote several thousand years ago, children best manifest their inborn talents when they are at play, and so they must have the freedom to play on their own. But they will still be supervised.

Benedict: As for the third, our semantic police will strike again. For the word "food" shall be used only in connection with substances that are beneficial to the human body. Nothing that is not useful to the body, and especially, nothing that actually harms the body, will be called "food". So those things that are currently referred to as "junk food" will be more accurately labeled by the word "poison".

Neal: If it were not so pathetic, it would be humorous to reflect that we teach our children to refer to what harms and poisons their bodies as "treats". But now, Benedict, what about giving and receiving presents? How will that be modified?

Benedict: That's easy. What is the most important thing that one human being can give to another?

Neal: Their attention, or consciousness.

Benedict: Exactly. So a child's birthday party will be an occasion for the child to celebrate the unique expression of embodied consciousness that she is, and to receive as a gift undivided conscious attention from the other children and adults. This way our children will learn that nothing they buy or have is as valuable or important as the consciousness that they already are. So, you ask or are about to ask, how does a three- or four-year-old child give conscious attention to another?

Neal: Yes, but I think I know the answer.

Benedict: What is it?

Neal: It involves what Socrates whispered in your ear a while back. For most of the therapy techniques now applied to adults who seek help for having adapted to an insane society can be applied to children, with obvious appropriate modifications. An ounce of prevention, as they say, is worth a pound of cure.

Benedict: I was thinking the same thing.

Neal: So here's a little exercise, one that I did years ago with adults, and which, although powerful and effective with adults, will be much more so with children. The birthday boy sits in the center of a circle, with the other children comprising the circle around him. The birthday boy faces each child, one at a time, and listens attentively, as each of the other children states what it is about the birthday boy – talents, abilities, behaviors, quirks, personality – that they like and enjoy about him. The birthday boy receives this in silence, saying only "thank you" after each child has spoken. Then the children are guided to process this experience, saying how it felt to receive attention, and how it felt to give attention. And *(smiling)* I suspect these exercises will be easier for our children than they were for the adults when I did them. The adults generally enjoyed, really enjoyed, giving positive attention, but most had enormous difficulty with receiving positive attention from others.

Benedict: That's only because adults, having adapted to your insane society, have been taught to think of themselves as "sinful", or if not religious, as certainly not "good enough", and not worthy of the very attention they so desperately crave. So when they get it, as in your groups, it is so contrary to all that they have internalized through adapting, that they don't know how to handle it and become quickly befuddled.

Neal: I'll admit to becoming befuddled by this myself, years back.

Benedict: But our children will not be taught that there is anything sinful or deficient in them; instead they will be taught that they are unconditionally loved and accepted by the Divine Being, of Whom they themselves are expressions. So it will not seem unusual to them to know that they are liked, and liked in specific ways, by other children, who after all are themselves not separate from the Divine Being. Exercises like this also train children to focus attention, that is, to augment the amount of conscious energy available to them.

Plato: And they will also learn that the gift of conscious attention is far more valuable than anything material. Toys and gadgets are all well and good, but hardly worthy of being given to another on an occasion as important as a child's birthday.

Neal: Whereas in my present society, by receiving material gifts on their birthdays, children learn that material possessions are the most important thing to acquire.

Benedict: Yes. It is important to understand – well, let me put it this way – it is important for people in your present society to understand that children in and of themselves do not lust after toys or material possessions, but are trained to do so by adults. What little children do lust over, so to speak, is whatever they see other children enjoyably doing. So if Paul observes Peter happily playing with a toy or happily playing with other children or happily eating an apple, it is true that Paul will want those things. But what Paul really wants is the **happiness** that he perceives Peter enjoying, and believes that it is the toy, the other children, or the apple, that is causing Peter's happiness.

William: Do you think that this can be taught to young children? Can Paul come to understand that it is Peter's happiness that he wants, not necessarily the particular toy Peter is playing with?

Benedict: I am hopeful. For such understanding, permeating our whole Society, is the Divine Spark that will bring Heaven to Earth and gloriously instantiate the Form of Social Justice.

Plato: *(smiling)* That was rather poetic for you, my friend.

Benedict: *(laughing)* Well, pardon me, I guess I did get a bit carried away. But the possibility of dramatically reducing the amount of social envy, even if not eliminating it altogether, is quite profound. No one has previously raised the question of whether the tendency towards envy can be addressed through early childhood education.

Neal: *(with a little humor)* But wait a minute. Before you go off and celebrate the arrival of Heaven on Earth, do you not believe that the tendency towards envy, as well as towards compassion, is hardwired in the human body? Oh, but you also say these tendencies can be overcome.

Benedict: Yes, my "Man of Reason", as well as Plato's "Philosopher", describes the individual who has overcome the afflictive emotions. But very few adults are able to do this. What excites me now is the prospect that our children will be given the tools to overcome these tendencies before they even reach first grade.

Plato: Perhaps you can say a bit more about what these tools are, and also how removing the tendency to envy constitutes the "Divine Spark" referred to above, in your moment of poetic indulgence.

Benedict: The elements are all in front of us, and have already been discussed. But you want me to state this in my more usual manner?

Neal: Yes, exactly. And I suspect doing so will also constitute a summary and review of what has already been discussed.

Benedict: Very well. The tendencies toward both envy and compassion are biologically hardwired. What I mean by this is that the nervous system of Paul, while he perceives Peter as happy or sad, recreates those emotions in Paul. The very perception of joy or sorrow in another engenders those same emotions in oneself. This is easily seen in small children, as we have discussed, but it, the imitation of emotions, is also the principle behind all theater, opera, and movies.

Neal: Yes, and we have described how the perception of sorrow in another engenders sorrow in oneself, and that compassionate behavior is the best way for children to remove their own sorrow. But now, with envy, it seems to begin as a joy but then quickly becomes a sorrow.

Benedict: It becomes a sorrow, called "envy", because the child wants what he believes causes happiness in the other. Initially, we maintain, a child feels the joy of the other, but is unable to rest content in that feeling and strives to acquire what he believes to be the cause of the other's joy. The challenge for us is to see if we can teach our children to rest content with, and to actually enjoy, the joy of another.

Neal: Yes, yes, I see it is possible. The phenomenon of movies and theater provide the empirical evidence that it is possible to enjoy the joy of another, without envy. For the whole audience rejoices without envy when the hero overcomes whatever difficulties the plot imposes upon him. Now we said a while ago that what Paul really desires, when he perceives Peter playing with a toy, playing with other children, or getting attention, is Peter's happiness – the happiness itself – and desires the toy, playmates, attention only because he believes it will bring him the same happiness that he perceives Peter experiencing. But our children have been taught, are being taught, and will always be taught, that the cause of happiness lies not in outer things, but deeply within oneself.

Socrates: Ah yes! For we must never forget that consciousness itself is an intrinsically joyful affair. The intrinsic nature of consciousness, of that which constitutes the essence of All, is Being, Bliss, and Understanding, as our Hindu friends have characterized the situation. Through stories our children will be taught that there is a reservoir of joy deep within themselves, and that there is hence never any need to envy the external situation of anyone else.

William: And we could use some basic conditioning techniques here, and train our children to associate the joy of another with the joy in themselves. That is, the perception of joy in another could become a "trigger" or "reminder" for the child to look for the joy that already exists within him. *(To Benedict)* I believe this is one of your "remedies".

Benedict: Yes, but we are now considering this conditioning process, not as a "remedy" for afflictive emotions, but as a "prevention" from allowing such emotions to take hold of the personality in the first place. OK, so here's the little review you wanted: and let's review sorrow as well as joy. We can enumerate the process as follows:

(1) Paul perceives Peter's joy or sorrow. (2) That very perception – your scientists now talk of "mirror neurons" – constitutes a joy or sorrow in Paul's body/mind. (3) Paul now desires to remove or diminish his sorrow and retain or increase his joy. (4) In the case of

sorrow, there are three possible responses to the sorrow that Paul now feels within himself: (a) compassion – he can strive to reduce or remove what he believes is the cause of Peter's sorrow, or (b) he can strive to ignore it by literally diverting his eyes (as many people do when they encounter homeless people), or (c) they can remove their sorrow by replacing it with an ideology according to which those who suffer "deserve" their suffering (this is what the wealthy do – this is what the wealthy *must* do if they are to enjoy their wealth – indeed, in the case of many rich people, the ideology has so debilitated their minds that they actually rejoice when they perceive the sufferings of others). Needless to say, our children will be taught to follow the path of compassion. But (5) in the case of joy, the perception by Paul of joy in Peter constitutes an emotion of joy in Paul's body/mind. There are two possible responses to this momentary joy that Paul is now feeling. One response is the usual one, where Paul grasps at whatever he believes is causing happiness in Peter's body/mind, so that he may "have" Peter's joy for himself. The other possible response is for Paul to utilize this feeling of joy that has arisen from perceiving joy in Peter, as a "trigger" to go more deeply within himself so that he may experience something of the joy, or as I put it, the very Blessedness that is within his own mind.

Neal: But…

Socrates: Of course this is possible. Look, how do you think a so-called enlightened person experiences the happiness of another human being? It merely tickles his own inner happiness, and feelings of envy are completely out of the question.

Neal: I think I understand. But I also think that maybe we do not need to look at the example of enlightened individuals for a non-grasping, non-envious response to the happiness of others.

Socrates: Who then are we to look to for such an example?

Neal: To the parents of children, who exult in their children's joys, without wanting to snatch the toys for themselves.

William: Yes, but can children be trained to react that way with regard to other children? Parents of course can feel the joy of their children, and hopefully of all children, without giving way to envy. And older children can feel without envy the joy of younger children. But can children react in this way to other children of the same age?

Neal: I think so, but only if we train our children to look within, so that they can access the joy within – I was going to say "the joy that is their birthright", as the expression goes, but the joy of which we now speak has nothing do to with one's entrance into the physical dimension, but is an intrinsic aspect of consciousness itself.

Socrates: One might say, not their "birthright", but rather their "existence right".

Plato: We must be careful here, for the path we are treading is very delicate.

Neal: What do you mean?

Plato: Suppose, just hypothetically, that it would be possible to raise children in such a way that they never lose contact with Source, and remain what you call "enlightened" from childhood through adulthood. Perhaps William here will return, as he playfully suggested he might do, and invent some electronic gadgets that will prevent the margins from ever forming in the first place. Suppose that were possible. What then?

Neal: Hmm. Well if the margins don't form, so that embodied souls are always in contact with their Source, well, that's the same as saying that the souls will no longer have to drink from the River of Forgetfulness, and so they would retain from birth the Knowledge of the Divine throughout their lives.

Socrates: And this seems to be a good thing, does it not? Then humans would be spared the trouble of so much aimless wandering around, and the mud of corporeal experience would be transformed into Heavenly Light. Hey, William, pack your bags, we're sending you down there again.

William: *(laughing)* Not so fast. As you stated previously, we are not going to blow up the whole theater. *(To me)* You get the point?

Neal: Yes, I think so. If no margins are allowed to form, if souls are not required to drink from the River of Forgetfulness as they enter into embodiment, then they cannot have a *human* experience.

Plato: And the analogy with a theater is a good one. For if humans want to go to the movies, or to a play, they must first enter into the darkness of the theater. Without that darkness, the images would not show up on the screen. Without the darkness, the audience would not be able to fully enter into the drama of the theater, which drama, although a fiction and an illusion, is what theater-goers have paid good money to experience. So the walls of the theater, which keep the light of day away, are necessary if one is to fully experience the emotional reality of the play.

Benedict: I think we can further use this analogy to get at what we are attempting to do. So yes, souls will still have to drink a little from the River of Forgetfulness, so that the margins form properly, and the full Light of Source appears to be walled off from human experience. Yet there is an important difference between (i) a soul having a human experience, and (ii) a human having a theater experience. Suppose we go into the theater, and approach a human who is having a theater experience. She has appropriately identified with the protagonist, whose emotions she feels as her own. Let us further suppose something "bad" has happened to the protagonist, and our human theater-goer is in tears. As he or she experiences the sorrow, we ask her if she is aware that this is only a movie and she can in fact leave the theater anytime she wishes.

Neal: She is likely to snap at you, saying of course she knows it's only a movie, and tells you to go away so that she can continue to have a good cry.

Benedict: Good. *(With humor)* Now suppose that a given soul is having a human experience, and has appropriately identified with the protagonist – her body, in this case – and experiences the protagonist's (her body's) ups and downs, its emotions, as her own. And let us further suppose that, while experiencing a particularly difficult emotion, we ask her the same question we asked our movie-going human: "Are you aware that this is only a movie and you can return Home anytime?"

Neal: Ah, I see your point. There is no corresponding awareness. The embodied soul having a human experience, unlike the human in the theater, will believe completely in the reality of what she or he is experiencing. She will lack the – what shall we call it – subconscious background knowledge that all movie-goers have, to the effect that it is only a movie, and not fundamentally real.

William: But in our New Society, there *will* be the corresponding awareness. The whole society will be everywhere permeated by true belief. In the same way that the movie-goer's experience is permeated by the true belief that what he is watching is not fundamentally real, and that his true identity awaits him outside the theater, so, in our New Society, the experiences of the embodied soul will be permeated by the true belief that what he is experiencing is not fundamentally real, and that his true identity awaits him outside the theater of space and time. We emphasize that this is a "background awareness" only, for if such awareness were constantly the center of personal attention, the soul would not be having a human experience, any more than a human could have a theater experience if his consciousness were focused on his real life outside the theater.

Plato: So you see, our task is indeed a delicate one. On the one hand, we really do want to teach our children to look for joy and happiness within, that such joy and happiness is their "existence right", and that the source of their well-being is not external to themselves. On the other hand, if they were all to find the Divine Light within, then, because that Light shines so brightly, no one would be able to "see" the images on the wall of my Cave, which like the movies require darkness in order to be seen, and they would then no longer be having a human experience.

Neal: But, Plato, this need not be an "all or nothing" affair.

Plato: What do you mean?

Neal: With your permission, I'd like to explain my meaning in terms of your Cave allegory.

Plato: *(smiling)* Permission granted, of course.

Neal: OK. Let's first consider the two extremes: (i) in the allegory as you originally presented it, which accurately describes my present society, the attention of the prisoners is so glued to the images appearing on the wall of the Cave that they have no sense that there is anything else. They fully believe that they are their body and that they will surely perish when their body dies, and that the only purpose to life is to grasp at the shadows passing in front of them. (ii) *All* the prisoners find their way out of the Cave. Perhaps the meditation techniques we have taught to our children are so successful that they all become enlightened by the time they are four years old. In that case they are all out of the Cave basking in the radiant joy of the Divine Sun. There would be no point in any of them going back into the Cave, since there are no prisoners left to be rescued. So the second alternative leads to the end of the Cave, that is, the end of souls experiencing themselves as bodies in space-time. But the first alternative, the one currently operative, also leads to the end of the Cave, since the misery and suffering of the prisoners is now so great that, collectively, they are destroying the planet's ability to sustain human life, as we have said before.

Plato: And so we must find something intermediate between these two extremes. Can you see it?

Neal: Yes, I think so. Between these two forms of consciousness, the human embedded in space-time and the enlightened embedded in the Divine Light, are many intermediary forms. In terms of your Cave allegory, we could perhaps train our prisoners, especially if we have access to them while they are small children, to turn their heads ever so slightly away from the images on the wall of the Cave so that, without leaving the Cave, they can behold the fire whose light casts the shadows they are perceiving. Perhaps they might even catch a glimpse of the objects whose shadows they are seeing. That kind of experience – an experience of a "Something More", as William put it – although short of enlightenment, is nevertheless sufficient to loosen somewhat the shackles of the prisoners.

William: *(with humor)* So they will be taught to experience a "Something More", but not an "Everything More". We should say a few things about what this "something more" will involve for our children.

Benedict: First let's be clear about what we mean by the expression "something more". We mean simply, something more than ordinary sense-experience. But notice: we have been teaching our children to (i) become emotionally intelligent – to have the ability to express their emotions and to recognize the emotions, the inner life, of other children, and (ii) to experience the giving and receiving of conscious attention. Both of these pertain to inner life, not to outer experience, and so they constitute a "something more" than mere physical experience.

Plato: Children in your present society, well in fairness perhaps I should say, children in every society except for the one now under construction, are taught to focus on outer things only, on their bodies and outer experiences. So when they talk among themselves, they talk primarily about outer, physical things. But *our* children, when they talk among themselves, will not be afraid to talk about their inner experiences. They will discover that they have many experiences that fall under the rubric of "psychic", and through which experiences they know that they are intrinsically connected with a wider field of consciousness than they are experiencing as mere bodies.

William: We could call this "experiences beyond the margin that all children routinely have but are negatively reinforced by adults". We might begin with the phenomenon that is called "imaginary playmates".

Neal: I assume we shall take the view that small children are in fact able to perceive non-embodied beings that adults are not able to perceive. Of course, not every child has such an experience, but many more do than is reported because children quickly learn not to discuss things with adults. But our children will be encouraged to discuss such experiences with others, which discussion will trigger and reinforce similar experiences in other children. In addition, many children experience memories from past lives.

William: And our children will be encouraged to discuss such memories, not only with the psychiatrists who study them, but more importantly, with other children, creating an environment in which it is fully acceptable to talk about all inner experience. And another kind of inner experience that all children have is dreaming.

Neal: Yes, many therapies stress the importance of discussing dreams, of keeping a dream journal, and analyzing dreams as if to get information from the subconscious mind.

William: I don't much care for the phrase "subconscious mind". All mind is conscious.

Neal: I know you prefer the phrase "subliminal mind". Me too. But the former phrase may be understood as referring to an aspect of mind of which the present ego consciousness or personality is unaware.

William: Agreed. So our children, as soon as they are able to write, will be encouraged to write down their dreams. And even before they can write, they will be encouraged to share their dreams with others.

Neal: And do we accept that theory of dreams that I once heard, as Socrates might put it, from wise men and women of old?

Socrates: *(laughing)* Referring to "wise men and women of old" was just a way of saying that I, or Plato as he was writing it down, could not remember where he first heard the story. But go ahead and state the theory.

Neal: OK. What humans lump together and call "dreams" really involve three very different kinds of nocturnal experience. (i) Some of what is recollected as "dreams" involves a processing of emotions from daily life. (ii) Some of what is recollected as "dreams" involves a processing of emotions unresolved from childhood. But the consciousness we experience as our "self" leaves the body every night for a brief return to Source, which experience it is unable to remember upon waking. This is called "deep sleep". But while out of the body it will have adventures in the astral plane or whatever, which adventures it will attempt to translate into concepts familiar to the human personality. So (iii) some of what is recollected as "dreams" are symbolic representations to the human of experiences that are outside space and time. What do you think?

Plato: I think we can accept this as a most likely story. So by encouraging our children to talk about their dreams, we shall be encouraging them to remain open to inner experience, and to reinforce the idea that sometimes messages from beyond the margin will come to them, through dreams or through non-embodied spirits. Incidentally, some of our children's dreams will be precognitive in nature, and this will be openly discussed too.

Neal: I have a hunch that just about every kind of psychic experience that exceptional adults report are had routinely by children. Such experiences are beaten out of them in my present society, but will be strongly reinforced by our New Society.

William: And speaking of "hunches", our children will be encouraged to share and discuss their various "hunches" and "intuitions" about things. For hunches and intuitions come from beyond the margins and are the source of all human creativity. Merely discussing this among themselves will reinforce and widen the channels along which the hunches flow.

8) Instilling Good Habits

Benedict: So we have taught our children that they are not identical to their body and its personality, that they originate from beyond the physical, and that they may still communicate with and receive messages from the nonphysical. But now we want them to learn that their true happiness is within, so that they may live their lives without envy.

Neal: In a sense they are already learning this, since there is great joy associated with honest discussion about and sharing of one's inner life. The process of sharing deepens the children's sense of connection with their inner life, and hence necessarily brings more joy into their consciousness.

Benedict: This is true. But we shall also teach our children meditation, which will enable them to look within, and find happiness and peace of mind.

Neal: But do you think that meditation can be taught to small children who can't sit still for a minute?

Socrates: Believe me, it will be much easier for our children to learn meditation than it is for your adults.

William: And we are not speaking of sitting for 20 or 30 minutes at a time. 20 or 30 seconds will be sufficient for our three- or four-year-old children.

Plato: Hold it a minute. Let us first expand on Socrates' remark, then on William's, although the order doesn't really matter.

Socrates: Well then, go ahead and expand.

Plato: We have alluded to the fact that there has been a de-evolution of consciousness over the years, especially from William's times to Neal's. But we will now be a bit more precise *(nodding to Benedict)* about what this means. Invoking Benedict's way of putting it, but without using his more precise language, we might say that every physical thing or body has associated with it a consciousness, which constitutes the mind of the given thing. But to put it crudely, the amount of consciousness associated with each thing varies enormously from one thing to another. The "mind" of a rock, say, holds less consciousness than the mind of a bacterium, which holds less than the mind of a cat, which holds less than the mind of a human, which holds less than the mind of the Earth. *(To Benedict)* Are you OK with how I'm putting this?

Benedict: Yes, it will do.

Plato: Good. Then we must also notice that the amount of consciousness –

Benedict: But of course this is quite crude indeed, to speak of consciousness in "amounts", as if consciousness were something that could be quantified. But if we are to speak of such things, it cannot be without some crudity, since as Rumi put it "language is a tailor shop where nothing fits", or something like that. But please continue…

Plato: As I was saying, the amount of consciousness fluctuates from one human body to another, and for a given human body, it fluctuates from one moment to the next. Now, all spiritual teaching worthy of the name teach that the portal from your world to ours lies in the present moment. But never before in the history of Humanity has the human mind had *less* ability to focus on the present moment. Indeed, the constant and continuous distractions of your culture are designed to prevent humans from becoming as conscious as they might be. Until William's time, the average human mind could pay attention to one thing at a time. When a human paid attention to one thing at a time – whether it was a task at hand, writing a letter to a friend, whatever – the whole mind was focused on what was happening in the present moment. But in your culture this rarely happens, as attention is dispersed over many things at the same time, and so there is less overall awareness. A person ostensibly doing one thing, such as conversing with another human, is simultaneously thinking about many other things pertaining to the past and/or future, so that one's 100% attention is rarely focused on only one thing. But meditation is a process by which the mind focuses on only one thing, which is why it is so difficult for adults in your culture to meditate. Having been raised in a culture where background noise and so-called multitasking is common, they grow uneasy and restless when called upon to sit still.

Benedict: But in our New Society there will be no constant background noise to distract our children, so they will be comfortable with the outer silence that is conducive to focusing attention, and to explore and to be present to their inner worlds. And this is why it will be easier, as Socrates said, for our children to look within than it is for your adults.

Neal: *(with a little humor)* Well, as the only one here who is a product of this present society, I agree. I sometimes feel great inner resistance to being focused in the present moment. Sometimes, say, when I'm reading I'll turn music on, and I'm beginning to sense that I do that in order to prevent my mind from being focused in the present moment. But if I can push through the resistance –

Socrates: – you become content with what is, and lack for nothing.

Neal: Well, yes, sort of.

Socrates: Recall in one of our previous conversations we discussed your resistance to the process of this writing?

Neal: Yes, and so part of that resistance involves simply being in the present moment, since I cannot focus in on you guys if my attention is diluted with background music or anything else.

Socrates: *(with humor)* And once you stop dancing around your desk to avoid focusing attention in the present moment so that you can be with us, what happens?

Neal: I become still, curious, and content.

Socrates: And I know you have observed that your restlessness and resistance has become noticeably less over the years. Just imagine if it had never been there from the beginning.

Neal: I see. So we are raising our children to be comfortable being fully in the present moment, and the ability of the mind to be focused in the present moment is a prerequisite, perhaps the only prerequisite, for looking within. But now I have a question. We stated that one of the reasons we want to teach our children to look within, or to meditate, is to short-circuit the tendency toward envy. Peter, we stated, upon seeing Paul happily playing with a toy, thinks he wants the toy for himself. But really what he wants is Paul's happiness, which happiness, we said, he can find if he looks within. Consciousness, as Socrates reminded us, is an intrinsically joyous affair, but…

Socrates: "Blissful", actually, but "joyous" will do.

Neal: But why should we believe that a three- or four-year-old child will find bliss by meditating for 20 or 30 seconds?

Socrates: *(mischievously)* Actually, our children will not be allowed to experience Bliss.

Neal: What do you mean?

Socrates: If they do, they might not come back.

Plato: Bliss is the experience of pure consciousness insofar as it is in itself. But insofar as consciousness is encumbered by a body, it will be temporarily satisfied with something less than total "bliss". Joy, peace of mind, and contentment with what is are available to our children when they look within. And most emphatically, the joy that Peter experiences from getting a new toy – *that* level of joy will be easily experienced by Paul when he looks within. But now let's examine William's point, that 20 seconds or so will be sufficient for our children.

Benedict: Yes, and we should remember that insofar as consciousness is associated with a body, there will be observable physiological correlates to all conscious experiences. And we should also remember that we have already taught our children to look within.

Neal: What?

Benedict: Sure. We have taught our children to be emotionally intelligent. This means (i) they can describe what they are feeling, (ii) they can express what they feel, and (iii) they can locate their emotions within their body. And of course (iv) they will be aware of and comfortable with the emotions of others. But (iii) is what gets them to look within.

William: So when Suzie tells us she is feeling sad, or fearful, or envious, we will ask her where in her body she is having that feeling. If she does not know, we will assist her with questions that direct her attention to specific parts of her body. (Is it in the stomach? The chest? The throat?)

Neal: This is a standard therapeutic technique, and actually one of your "remedies",. Benedict. But no one has thought they could be applied to children.

Benedict: That's because until now, no one ever thought to raise children in the best way possible *for the children*. Adults, themselves insane from having adapted to an insane society, raise their children so as to fit into an insane society, and the best way to create an insane society is to prevent children from coming to understand, or even to feel, their emotions, and so they grow up feeling alienated from who they really are. No one really cared about what children were feeling, as witnessed by the old saying, "Children should be seen but not heard."

William: So Suzie, in order to locate emotions in her body,

must focus her attention. And the focusing of attention is in itself a meditative practice, is it not?

Plato: We need not be precise in our definition of what constitutes a meditative practice, especially when it concerns little children. Anything that gets them to look within for a sustained 20 or 30 seconds could be counted as a meditative practice for three- or four-year-old children. But let's stay with our example, in which one child, Paul, sees another child, Peter, happily playing with a toy. We want Peter's happiness to rub off on Paul. We agree with Benedict that Paul momentarily feels Peter's happiness, but that it quickly turns to the sorrow called "envy" as Paul realizes he lacks what he believes is making Peter happy. We have told Paul that the happiness that he thinks Peter feels is within himself, and now we must teach him *how* to find and experience that happiness.

Benedict: And our instructions to Paul are so simple that any child can follow them. *(Jokingly)* Adults are another matter. First, we will tell Paul, focus your attention. Second, with focused attention scan your body until you find and feel the physical sensations that constitute the emotion of envy. Third, breathe slowly and deeply into those sensations, and watch as the sensations begin to dissolve. The sensations may dissolve immediately, or it may take a little time.

Socrates: *(with humor)* You are tricking our children.

Benedict: What do you mean?

Socrates: Two things: first of all, only the first step is necessary, as focused attention is itself the cure to whatever ails you. However, the other two steps are quite useful, in that they are aids to focusing attention. If Paul could do a simple breath meditation for a few minutes, the emotion of envy would likely dissipate by itself. But perhaps the more important "trick" is that through this process our children will learn that focusing attention in itself feels good, regardless of whether one is focusing attention for a specific purpose.

Neal: And so we shall establish for our children a regular, daily meditative practice – perhaps a breath meditation is simplest. We will tell them that everyone does this, which will be true in our New

Society, and that it is a form of mental hygiene, just as washing one's hands regularly is a form of physical hygiene. We can begin with half a minute or so, then gradually increase the time as the children mature.

William: And the philosophical idea to which we have already alluded, and which will be explained to our children, is that their emotions are like ripples on a pond that prevent them from seeing the happiness at the bottom of the pond. I'm sure many more such metaphors can be discovered. The way to access the happiness at the bottom of the pond is to calm the ripples on the surface. And the way to calm the ripples on the surface is to quiet one's mind. And the way to quiet one's mind is by focusing attention.

Benedict: Through this simple meditative practice, our children will have the tools they need ready at hand to dispel most of the ripples as they arise.

Plato: And so it is that our children will reach school age, say five or six, with good habits already well established. In particular, we note that with envy greatly reduced, if not altogether eliminated, there will be little standing in the way of our children's accomplishing their soul's original purpose in becoming human.

Neal: Before we move on *(although I do not know where we might be moving on to)*, let's have a brief review of these "good habits".

Plato: Certainly. You start, and we'll chime in.

Neal: We are raising our children so that, as adults, they will remain cognizant of their soul's original purpose in manifesting as human. Only this, we maintain, can save our planet from the destruction now impinging upon it because humans have allowed themselves to become insane through greed and ambition. But if a child is to become cognizant of her original purpose, she must always feel free to fully express her inner feelings and desires, which constitute her very essence as it unfolds in time. So there will be no judgments on the part of adults that some emotions are "better than" others, or that some desires are better than others. And in an environment free from such judgments, our children will not be compelled to lie about their inner life, which is how children, and the adults they become, get to be so alienated from themselves. For after years of such training, humans lose the ability even to know what they truly feel and want, and wander about like robots, truncated versions of what they might be.

Benedict: And so, with no incentive for lying, it will never occur to our children to use words to conceal their inner life, or rather, their state of consciousness. And because they will not use words to conceal their inner lives, neither will they use words to misrepresent any outer experience. So we have a society in which there is no lying.

Plato: Yes, but we were going to list the "good habits" we have instilled into our children.

Neal: Well, the "good habit" here is that children will regularly discuss and explore their inner lives with adults and with one another. They will talk about, and listen to other children talking about, their emotions, their dreams, their "imaginary playmates", and their "fantasies". Children will use words, not to conceal what is within, but to express it. They will not learn that their own inner subjectivity is less real than the physical world around them. On the contrary.

Plato: So good habit #1: children shall regularly practice using words to describe, express, and explore their own inner experiences. What's good habit #2?

Benedict: *(to Plato)* I appreciate your conciseness here. *(To me)* We have already discussed the reasons for these habits.

Neal: Yes, I know.

Benedict: *(smiling)* Yet you feel that the "habit" should be listed as a logical conclusion to an argument, and you want to be sure we have all of the premises before us.

Neal: Yeah, I guess. Well, Plato warned at the beginning that this would be repetitive.

Plato: Yes, alright, but make the premises as concise as possible. What are the premises leading to good habit #2?

Neal: The soul is not an island, but is deeply interconnected with all other souls. It loses the experiential knowledge of these interconnections upon embodiment, and this loss is a source of deep and chronic anxiety. This anxiety and fear is itself the source of much that is dysfunctional about my present society – such as the debilitating madness of greed – and so we shall develop habits and practices that minimize the formation of such anxiety. We cannot eliminate it altogether, for in that case the soul could not become human, but we can greatly reduce it.

Plato: I'm waiting.

Neal: We know that an infant will die if it is not touched and caressed. We know that the brain development of babies and children is greatly enhanced through nurturing touch. And we also know, or are about to find out, that the adult brain and other health indicators respond positively to touch. The human body never outgrows its need to be touched, and so *(to Plato)* here it is, good habit #2: our children will be taught, from the earliest ages, to touch one another in ways that are nurturing and pleasurable. "A massage a day," we might tell our children, "keeps the doctor away."

William: *(with humor)* Later in life it will also keep away the psychiatrists and therapists. But Plato wants to keep this moving, so no need to go into all of the many ways lack of nurturing touch is the root cause of the violence that is epidemic in the culture today. So moving right along, it is not only the body that needs to be touched, but the mind as well. For the mind that has become human has disassociated itself, one might say, from its connections, or rather from its knowledge of its interconnections, with all other minds. As human, it hungers after these connections, but usually in ways that bring the opposite of what it seeks.

Neal: Yes. Humans seek the attention from other humans; this is how one feels connected, when others are giving their attention to you. And so we have produced a truly insane society, where everyone is seeking attention from everyone else, willing to do whatever it takes to gain reputation, approval, and fame.

William: And when a human, as a child or adult, is so desperate, so needy for attention that he will do "whatever it takes" to get it, then he has become quite alienated from the original purpose of his soul. But Plato here is twiddling his thumbs, waiting for us to quickly lay down the premises for good habit #3: our children will regularly practice giving and receiving attention, not just on their birthdays.

Plato: Yes, and it is through the giving and receiving of undivided attention that humans may recapture, to some small extent, the sense of interconnectedness that was lost upon embodiment.

Benedict: And it goes without saying that all the various techniques that your therapists have come up with, such as "active listening", will be employed with our children. It will then become second nature for a child to listen attentively to – or in other words, receive the consciousness of – another. Then, as adults, they will not be needy for approval, since they will have had approval from day one, so to speak. Since they are not hungry for approval, they cannot be manipulated into doing "whatever it takes" to get it.

Neal: Then I think we can quickly add the remaining two habits: good habit #4. I think we referred to this as a sort of emotional hygiene. Every day, each child will give some attention to his or her emotions and inner life. This can be done in various ways, or in some combination of various ways: (i) by keeping a journal, (ii) by keeping a dream journal, (iii) by locating emotions within his or her body, and/or (iv) by verbally expressing emotions and other inner experiences to others. And underlying this is good habit #5: meditation. Each child will be taught daily meditative techniques that are appropriate to its age and personality.

Socrates: Well, this about sums it up, as far as early childhood education is concerned. But I think we might need to add one more little habit to our list.

Neal: What is it?

Socrates: It is this: *(Playfully)* Good Habit #6: our children shall not become slaves to habits.

Neal: Huh?

Socrates: We want our children to be creative, do we not?

Neal: Yes of course. And since creativity comes from beyond the margins, so to speak, our children will be creative because our five habits will keep the margins from thickening beyond the point where creative impulses can penetrate.

Socrates: Yes, but creativity must be practiced. Children must have plenty of free time to receive impulses and communications from beyond the margins. I guess you would call this "spontaneous play" or something like that. As Plato remarked some time ago, it is mostly during times of unstructured spontaneous play that children's talents and abilities are manifested. We must allow them all the time they need to play, and refrain from structuring every minute of their time with activities.

William: Good. Adults call what children do "play". Another term for it would be "spontaneous expressions of creativity".

Benedict: And with this definition, even adults in our New Society will regard what they do as "play". Future psychologists will study this question: How may a child's sense of spontaneous creative playfulness remain intact as the child matures?

Neal: What a question! Our most creative scientists, musicians, writers, and artists often, if not usually, have a sense of themselves as child-like. Isaac Newton said he felt like a child picking up pebbles on the beach, while the vast shores of the eternal lay unexplored before him, or something like that. So our children will be given lots of time for unstructured play. They will invent their own games and make their own rules. And I can envisage, as they mature, that the children will be able to discuss the games they invented. What worked, and why? What didn't work, and why? Well, I sense we will be coming back to this a little later. For now, we can state that we shall separate spontaneous play from any subsequent analysis of it.

Socrates: "For the play's the thing wherein we'll catch the conscience of the King", as well as his creativity. How's that for a mangled quote?

Neal: What do you mean? What does conscience have to do with spontaneous play?

Socrates: Oh, just looking ahead a bit. By observing children at play, and the games they invent, adults can begin to trace the moral development of our children. Do some children cheat? Bully others? Throw a fit when they don't get their way? Or, at the other end of the scale, are some children especially caring about the well-being of others? In your present dystopia, these issues are never addressed, so children grow up to become adults who cheat, bully, and throw temper tantrums. This is the "quality" of those individuals who become politicians and CEOs. But these and other issues can be nipped in the bud, so to speak, and will be in our New Society. But for now, I think I can see a need for one more habit.

Neal: What is it?

Socrates: Actually, it is not really a habit, more of an "unhabit", like the need for spontaneous play.

Neal: Yes?

Socrates: And it is really more of a rule for the adults who care for our children, than it is for the children themselves. The children are already experts at this, and don't need to be taught.

Neal: You're leading me on. Out with it!

Socrates: *(laughing)* Well, don't be upset with me, this is just a little habit of mine, speaking of habits. Here it is: *Day*dreaming is just as important as *night*dreaming, and adults will do nothing to discourage, or infringe upon, our children's daydreaming. For what is called "daydreaming" is the child's spontaneous internal play, while in a state of deep receptivity to impulses from beyond the margin.

William: A statement that no doubt will be substantiated by future scientists. They will explore the physiological correlates to the state of consciousness called "daydreaming", and will discover many advantages.

Benedict: Indeed. And future psychologists – and I'm almost tempted to join you, William, and become one of them – will no doubt recommend daydreaming, as they now do meditation, for health. "A daydream a day keeps the doctor away." Actually, more than one. Many more.

Plato: Indeed, it is no more possible not to daydream than it is possible not to nightdream. Children could be encouraged to keep a daydream journal, as well as a nightdream journal. But your culture values only what is external, so it has missed the importance of daydreaming to both physiological and psychological health and well-being.

Neal: Yes, my culture regards daydreaming as a waste of time.

William: As it regards everything that enhances playfulness and creativity. Now, Plato just mentioned journaling. The point of keeping a nightdream journal is to bring into physical consciousness, by putting into words, insights and impulses that originate beyond the margins. But transmarginal impulses also arise through daydreaming, and so a daydream journal could be a further way of keeping the transmarginal pathways more open.

Neal: Yes. Now as Socrates said, children do not need to be taught how to daydream, since, like nightdreaming, it is physiologically hardwired. And he is also right that adults need to be taught not to interfere or discourage daydreaming. But perhaps we could acknowledge the importance of daydreaming by including it in our curriculum, so to speak, along with meditation.

William: What do you have in mind?

Neal: We have already introduced a brief meditation practice. Perhaps the teacher could say to the children something like, "For the past two minutes we have attempted to focus our minds on our breathing. When, during that time, we noticed that our mind was wandering, we brought it back to our breathing. Now we are going to do the exact opposite. We will close our eyes for two minutes, but this time we shall not attempt to control where our mind wanders; we shall allow it to go wherever it will." Of course, our children will daydream many times throughout the day, but by including it within a little structure, it emphasizes the importance of the experience to both the children and the adults.

Plato: And we will do even more with this little exercise later on. For now, however, there is one more thing our children need for this stage of their education to be complete.

Neal: It seems that there is always "one more thing".

Plato: *(laughing)* Yes, and to you humans this is necessarily the case. Now earlier we stressed the importance of the children having unstructured time for spontaneous play. But we want them to make friends not only with other children, but also with themselves. So some of their unstructured time – that is, time not structured for them by adults – will involve playing alone by themselves. And it is during unstructured alone time that children will most likely manifest their inborn desires and talents, as they will naturally gravitate towards what interests them the most. But now I wonder whether we all agree that, with our six "good habits", and a just right balance between free time and structured time, alone time and social time, we have laid the proper foundation for our children to become members of our New World Order. If so, then our children are ready to begin more formal schooling. Or does anyone think we may have missed something?

William: No, I think we are ready to continue with our children's education. Yet there is one more point that we should make explicit.

9) Guarding Against the Usual Suspects

Plato: What is that?

William: It is the caveat that we are not laying down an absolute blueprint for our children's education, but only a general outline. Our approach is always empirical, which means that future psychologists, teachers, and caregivers will necessarily encounter situations that we cannot now foresee, and our methods must also be amenable to future discoveries regarding the best way to raise our children.

Plato: I accept what you say, with the additional caveat that by the phrase "the best way to raise our children", you mean to use the word "best" with regard to maximizing the potential for the soul to express its original purpose(s) in manifesting as human. There is no doubt that future neuroscientists and psychologists will discover many things that are useful for that purpose, and anything we have here laid down that upon practice turns out to be less than maximally useful will be revisited and revised.

William: Then we are agreed. But how shall we continue? Our children are now about six years old, and ready to begin a more formal learning. What is the next stage of education? What subjects shall be covered and how?

Plato: And what do you mean by "a more formal education"?

William: Just the usual. Reading, writing, arithmetic.

Plato: Well of course our children will learn these things, and much more, but the way in which they learn these things may not be by "formal" education – in the sense of a traditional classroom. This – how the children will learn and be taught in the best way – will be determined by future educators, with deep understanding of neurology and psychology. Also, at this point, individual differences among children may require that different children be taught in different ways.

Benedict: Yet future educators must never forget that children must be internally motivated to learn, and that the best motivation is always their innate curiosity. So everything must be done to enliven and inspire their curiosity, rather than deaden it, as your present system appears to be doing.

Neal: Yes, I believe it was Einstein who spoke about the "holy flower" of curiosity that is as fragile as it is holy. So great care will be taken never to teach children in ways that dampen their curiosity. We want our children to remain curious throughout the whole educational process, and indeed, throughout their entire lives. As William once wrote somewhere, there can be no final accounting of the human experience until the last human has lived his or her life. Curiosity, an openness to new situations and experiences, will be greatly encouraged, and our future educators will no doubt devise the best means to do so. And of course, this will most probably not be a "one size fits all" situation, as our children arise from different souls, and have different brains, and hence learn in different ways. But now, I have a question.

Plato: Yes?

Neal: Well, people in my present culture are likely to complain that all the attention we are giving to our children requires vast resources, so that a large portion, a very large portion, of the world's resources will be involved in educating our children. I can hear our critics asking: but who will pay for all this?

(Everyone laughs, and I think I understand why.)

Plato: Yes, you get it. This question could only arise from someone raised in a culture that, like yours, greatly values greed and ambition over the welfare and upbringing of children.

Benedict: And it is so easy to see how in your culture, the predominance of greed and ambition has led society to abandon its obligation to educate and raise children properly, as most of the resources of your culture are dedicated to placating those who have become insane through greed and ambition. It is they who will ask, "Who will pay for this?" while refusing to share the wealth they have accumulated only for themselves. The raising and educating of children is the means by which a society extends itself temporally into the next generation. Nothing can be more important than this, because otherwise a culture cannot survive, but self-destructs from within. Can anything be more insane than a culture that refuses to allot sufficient resources for raising children in the best possible way?

Neal: I think not.

Plato: So if our New Society is to be viable and able to extend itself into future generations, then nothing, absolutely nothing, is as important as the education of our children, and the first priority of our culture must be to devote whatever resources are necessary to our children. I suppose we might add that we are conceiving that the educational process is not just for small children. In a real sense, education is a lifelong process, of which a peaceful, inspired and noble death is the outcome.

Socrates: Hey there, Plato, rephrase that last sentence.

Plato: *(laughing)* Quite right. Speaking of education, this fellow *(gesturing towards Socrates)* never misses an opportunity to educate me. You see, the word "death" has rather negative connotations in your present culture. But from our perspective, death is the return of the soul to Itself, no longer dragged down by a body. It is a glorious experience, and the cause of much celebration here, as we welcome back old friends who seem to have fallen asleep for a little while.

Neal: Yes, I understand. Someone once remarked that when a baby is born, everyone is happy except the baby; and when a person dies, everyone is sad except the person who dies. Something is not quite right with this picture.

Plato: But in our culture, people will be educated to rejoice when someone dear to them makes his transition, especially if he has led a good life. Well, we shall be talking about death, ah, I mean transitions, at some length later on. Shall we return to our children now, or should we say a few more things about how our Society will be able to afford raising them in this way?

Neal: Well, I for one would like to hear a little about the latter.

Plato: The "how" is really quite simple. What is the experience that vaccinates a human being, so to speak, against any temptation towards greed and/or ambition?

Neal: That's easy. Humans who have an NDE or any other kind of spiritually transformative experience are indeed transformed in such a way that they are incapable of harming others.

Plato: And this is because they have caught sight of the Unity of all souls, which constitutes the form of social justice. They know from direct experience that it is not possible to harm another without also harming themselves. These are the individuals who will govern, not just politically, but economically as well.

Neal: So those holding economic power and who make all the financial decisions regarding the allocation of wealth will be the best of us, not the worst as is presently the case.

Plato: Moreover, not only will spiritual wisdom rule at the highest levels, but we envisage a Social Order in which those who preside over the various institutions of our Society – businesses, universities, hospitals, agriculture, transportation (the list goes on and on) will also be, if not enlightened by direct experience, at least spiritually mature. Worldly power and spiritual wisdom must coalesce in the same individuals if the human race is to survive.

William: But there's no need to worry about finding such individuals, as modern medical technology is reviving many patients who come back transformed. In fact, there may already be on the planet a sufficient number of such individuals to run things –

Neal: Yes, well good luck with that thought – first you would need to convince those who now have such power that they are unfit to wield it, and should hand it over to the NDErs, who do not want it.

Plato: *(laughing)* Well, we shall see how it all unfolds soon enough. But do I convince you that if the leaders – conductors is perhaps the better term – of our Society have all directly experienced the interconnection of all things, then there will be no problem for our Society to prioritize the raising of its children above all things, allocating whatever resources necessary.

Neal: Yes, I agree. And I would add that, not only is this a sufficient condition for the proper raising of our children, but a necessary condition as well.

Plato: So running the world's economy, the allocation of resources, etc., will be in the hands of those who are spiritually enlightened, or at the very least, have caught a glimpse of the Form of Social Justice. Many people, not just the leaders, will have had some such experience, because of which their individual goals will be in harmony with the requirements of Justice. We need not bother with details, much of which cannot be foreseen in advance. But the general rule will be that the wealth of the Earth shall be distributed evenly among the population. Remember, the way we are raising our children will effectively prevent the insane desires of greed and ambition from arising, so no one who is not mentally ill will have any desire or motivation either to accumulate private wealth or to chase after reputation and status. As things stand now in your present society, the inmates are indeed running the asylum, since control over the resources is in the hands of those who have become insane through greed and status-seeking. So any question about allocation of resources – will there be enough resources to educate our children in the manner we are describing? – is predicated upon the false assumption that most of society's resources will continue to be allocated to satisfy the insane desires of the very rich. But no culture can both educate its children wisely and tolerate the presence of those who have siphoned off for private use the wealth of society. Your so-called "profit motive", deemed so essential by your economists, will be regarded as a thing of the past, like honor killings, slavery, bigotry, and starting fires with sticks. So our New Society will not lack for resources sufficient to raise our children in the best way.

Benedict: As a reminder, when we use the word "best", we are using it to mean with respect to our purpose of maximizing the opportunities for the soul to achieve its original purpose in manifesting as human. And we observed earlier that this original purpose never includes greed and/or status-seeking. So by banning greed and the profit motive that greed gives rise to, we are actually doing a big favor for those souls who might otherwise not be strong enough to resist such temptation.

William: Now of course we are not simply going to legislate against greed and status-seeking, as if that would do any good…

Plato: *(laughing)* Sorry to interrupt, but there is nothing more comical, both in my time and in yours, than watching greedy legislatures trying to pass laws to limit their own greed. The loopholes are always so big that one could drive a chariot through them.

William: *(also laughing)* You mean a truck. So our goal is to prevent the formation of greed and ambition in the psyche of our children.

Socrates: There is no doubt that the way we have raised our children thus far goes a long way towards preventing these dysfunctional desires from taking root in the psyches of our children; yet our Society must constantly and continuously be on guard against such desires, in the same way that physicians guard against harmful physical illnesses.

Benedict: *(mischievously, to Socrates)* Perhaps I can return the favor?

Socrates: What favor?

Benedict: Well, you sort of playfully hinted that maybe I had wasted my time trying to teach adults when children are better learners.

Socrates: And not only are children better learners, especially with regard to emotional intelligence, but what is learned as a child inoculates them against much dysfunctional emotions in the future. But how will you return the favor?

Benedict: Well, maybe you too wasted your time, wandering around Athens trying to persuade greedy men to abandon their greed. A most thankless task, for once greed has taken possession of the psyche, it is like a cancer, spreading everywhere and most difficult to eradicate. But as a physician of the soul, instead of hanging around the marketplace, you might have had better luck hanging around the playgrounds talking with small children. They would have understood you much better than the adults.

William: *(with humor)* Well said, Benedict. I think this is exactly where we should put this fellow *(gesturing towards Socrates)*, in the playground or wherever children hang out. There he could observe the children carefully, and by questioning them in his usual manner as they go down the slides, guard against the formation of greed and ambition in their psyches and then, should any problem arise, we can nip it in the bud.

Neal: And we might add that at least the children would not have you put to death for trying to awaken them.

Socrates: *(to me, with humor)* I still do not persuade you that being put to death was rather a blessing than a misfortune? *(Smiling)* Well no matter, I assure you that when death comes for you, you will experience it as the greatest of blessings, and you will feel only gratitude towards whatever might be the material cause of your body's death. But actually, I do know that you and the others were just joking and teasing me, and it was perhaps inappropriate of me to respond to your banter so seriously.

Plato: But underlying the banter is something important, perhaps several things that we must articulate.

Neal: Yes, I think I can see them, or at least one of them.

Plato: What do you see?

Neal: Well, we were all joking a little with Socrates, about him being a "physician of the soul" and that he might have had better luck guiding children than adults. I think we need to develop this analogy, between a physician of the *body* and a physician of the *soul*. The aim of both kinds of physicians will be preventative rather than curative – the one to guard against physical illness, the other to guard against mental illness – and even though our educational process has already prevented many dysfunctional emotions from arising, perhaps we need to say more about preventative mental health as our children begin their more formal education. And finally, it seems there will always be a need for physicians of the body, as unforeseen illnesses can always arise, to say nothing of fixing broken bones and the usual injuries that typically befall humans. But will there always be a need for a physician of the soul, or is it possible that our method of raising children will inoculate them against mental illness?

Socrates: *(with great humor)* Or in other words, will I still have a job in this new world order of ours?

(Everyone laughs.)

Plato: Not to worry, old friend, for not only will you still have a job, but a most important job, equal in importance to the job of those we were calling "Leaders" or "Conductors". For you, and those like you, shall assume the role of Guardians of the World Order.

Socrates: *(to Plato)* Do you have a job description for this role, in case I wish to apply?

Plato: *(to Socrates)* Now it is you who uses humor to derail my effort to get a little serious. Well, OK, I admit that perhaps the phrase "Guardians of the World Order" is a bit too fancy sounding. But I want to say something about my previous use of the term "guardian", especially for those who are familiar with how the term is used in *The Republic.*

Neal: In *The Republic*, the "Guardians" were the Rulers and leaders. And now?

Plato: Let me back up a little. In my previous work, I described a city-state run by spiritually enlightened Rulers. The rulers had to protect the city from its enemies both from without and from within. For the former, a military was necessary, and the Leaders of the city were chosen from the military…

Neal: … But with considerably more education than mere military leaders.

Plato: Yes, but our New Society is a World Society, and there will be no enemies from without. But the enemies from within, then and now, are by far the more formidable, and we must continuously guard against them.

Neal: So we will have no need for military forces?

Plato: No. Police, yes, but no military. Hence the word "guard" or "guardian", as we shall here use it, will have no military connotations.

Neal: If there are no enemies from without, what are the enemies from within that we need to guard against? The usual suspects, I presume?

Benedict: Yes. Here's one way to look at it. If it is true that the Kingdom of Heaven is within, then it is also true that the barriers to experiencing the Kingdom of Heaven are also within.

Neal: Agreed.

Benedict: But these "barriers" are nothing but the "margins" we have discussed earlier.

Neal: Yes, and some barriers are necessary for the soul to have a human experience, but if the barriers of margins become thickly encrusted, the world self-destructs, as is happening now. So as we have repeatedly said, the margins must be thinned out, if the world is to survive.

Plato: And hence our Society must guard against those forces that add to the thickness of the margins. These forces are the enemy from within, and they take the form of our "usual suspects" of greed, ambition, cruelty of any kind, holding grievances against others, and a host of dysfunctional emotions, such as envy, jealousy, depression, pride, low self-esteem, and any emotion or desire that arises from one person comparing himself with another person and judging himself and/or the other "better" or "worse".

Neal: So our "Guardians" are really spiritual psychologists and therapists.

Plato: Yes. But you can drop the qualifier, since all of our psychologists and therapists will be spiritually attuned. For "psychology" will be properly defined in the way that William originally defined the term – as the study of the human psyche, and the human psyche is simply consciousness insofar as it expresses itself as human. It is they who will guard against those emotions and desires that seek, not to express the soul's intent, but to tightly bind the soul to its body, so that it confuses itself with the body through which it experiences the world, and every bodily experience is then like a nail that further rivets the soul to the body.

Neal: Hmm, this will really be a different educational system than any that has previously been on the planet, and many will argue that the "usual suspects" mentioned above are actually definitive of the human condition and cannot possibly be guarded against.

William: The only thing humans are "by nature" is mortal. So-called "human nature" is infinitely malleable, and the judgment that the usual suspects cannot be rounded up and dealt with comes from those who were raised within a society that encourages those dysfunctional emotions. No one has ever observed or conceived what might be possible when humans are raised in a society that honors the soul's original purpose in manifesting. But *(nodding to Benedict)* I think you have something to say.

Benedict: Yes, thank you. Let us notice that most, but not all, of our usual suspects – I like this way of referring to dysfunctional emotions – arise because a person has compared himself with others. The tendency to compare oneself with others is absent in infants, babies and toddlers, but arises when our children reach the ages of three or four. At this age, children begin to notice other children. And they notice that different children have different talents and abilities. Because your present culture, but not our New Society, values some talents and abilities over others, envy and jealousy begin to arise. Recall the analogy we made earlier about a dysfunctional symphony orchestra?

Neal: Yes, an orchestra in which the violas notice that the violins carry the melody more often and become envious; where the violins notice how much louder the trombones and trumpets can play, and become envious; where the trombones notice the sweetness of the flute, and become envious; and where everyone envies the bass drum who gives the audience a rousing bang at the end.

Benedict: *(laughing)* Well said.

Neal: And we also said that in a functional symphony orchestra, each musician has some sense of the music as a whole, and understands that his own part makes an essential contribution to the whole, and hence is able to appreciate without envy the abilities of other musicians.

Benedict: Good. Now our children, say around five years old, will notice differences in talents and abilities in other children. A few examples: some children can run faster than others, some have sweeter voices than others, some can solve math problems faster than others, some are more extroverted than others, some are better readers than others – the list goes on and on. So our question is: how can children appreciate the talents of other children without any trace of envy?

William: And also, around this age, we will be introducing our children to some competitive games. Can this be done without this present culture's emphasis on "winning", which engenders envy and does some harm to the soul.

Neal: But I thought we were not going to allow our children to compete one against the other.

Plato: Hold on, hold on, we are not presently in the eternal order, and hence must necessarily restrict our discussion to one thing at a time. We shall discuss the role of competition later, but for now we may remind ourselves that no one becomes any good at chess without losing many games to better players. So competition is not an intrinsically negative affair, but must be conducted in full harmony with our spiritual values. Now let's focus on Benedict's question: can children learn to appreciate the talents and abilities of other children without feeling envious.

Socrates: Yes, and although Benedict's question is a good one, his answer is even better.

Benedict: My answer? What are you talking about?

Socrates: *(smiling)* Why I'm talking about you, Benedict, and I think you may have answered your question before you asked it.

Benedict: My goodness, and here I thought with Plato that I was in the temporal order, where questions usually precede their answers.

Socrates: Here is what you said: "Because your present culture, but not our New Society, values some talents and abilities over others, envy and jealousy begin to arise." This suggests that the emotions of envy and jealousy come into play, not so much because some children are more talented than others, but because society places more value on some talents than on others.

Neal: Ah yes, I see your point. A society that values, say, a fast runner over a slow runner will give more attention to the former than the latter. So the slower runners envy the faster runners, not because the latter can run faster, but because they get more attention by winning.

Socrates: So they are really more envious of the attention, than of the skill or talent of the winner, except insofar as the latter gets them attention. And this, Benedict, is how you, wisely in my opinion, defined ambition, as the desire to do whatever it takes to get attention and approval from others.

Benedict: Shall we review what we have said about ambition, and then investigate whether our method of raising children has effectively inoculated them against that particular form of mental illness?

Neal: Yes, but first we should remind ourselves of the two senses, or meanings, of the word "ambition". In the positive sense: a person is called "ambitious" if she is internally motivated to develop her talents as best she can. In the negative sense: a person is called "ambitious" because she is needy and hungry for approval, status, and reputation, and will do whatever it takes to satisfy her needs.

Benedict: And it is easy to see, is it not, that the person who is ambitious in the second sense has departed from her soul's original purpose in manifesting as human, since she is now concerned only with what she imagines will be pleasing to others, and has no inner sense of direction. So from now on, let's use the word "ambition" in this second sense, for it is by no means madness to strive to express one's latent abilities. The madness, against which we must guard, is to allow oneself to be motivated by the desire to win approval from others, through status, reputation, and wealth.

William: We note that our children have been trained, since they were toddlers, to give and receive attention from others. Moreover, this giving and receiving of attention is unconditional. We did not teach our children that receiving attention from others depends upon behaving in ways that are approved of by others. We give our children all the attention they need, not because of what they do, but rather because of what they are.

Socrates: And we remind ourselves that, what children *are*, are newly embodied souls, who have just left a condition in which they experience continuous connectedness with their spiritual environment. Then suddenly they find themselves embodied and their former sense of connectedness seems to have been terminated. This loss of the sense of connectedness is painful to the embodied soul, which it seeks to recapture by getting attention from others. This is the spiritual cause, if you will, of ambition in human beings. This is why, in many humans, from children to adults, the overriding motivation is to do whatever it takes to gain approval, recognition, and status, from others.

Benedict: And of course we must remind ourselves that this cannot ever work, that is, the loss of connectedness that the soul experiences upon becoming human can never be compensated for by ambition – by the seeking of approval from others. And so the more one strives to compensate for the loss of connectedness in this way, the further one descends from Source, and the more alienated one feels. And then they try even harder to achieve recognition, which only further alienates them from their spiritual Source.

Neal: It is rather sad, as well as absurd, to see how humans try to fill the hole at the center of their being – the emptiness that derives from the loss of connectedness – by doing things that actually increase the size of the hole.

William: Yes, or putting it in terms of our "margins" metaphor, the ambitious feel deeply the pain of separation and seek to alleviate that pain in ways that only increase their suffering. Everything they do adds to the thickness of their margins, cutting them off even more deeply from their own inner knowing. As you have said, it is both sad and insane.

Socrates*: (to me)* And if you focus on the part that's sad, can you not feel some compassion for these poor miserable souls who have so lost their way?

Neal: Of course. Why wouldn't I feel compassion for those who suffer the most? Wait. Oh my.

Socrates: *(mischievously)* Yes?

Neal: You guys have been setting me up for this all along.

Socrates: *(innocently)* Setting you up for what?

Neal: *(with a little humor)* Well it is one thing to invite me to feel compassion for "poor souls who have so lost their way", and I was prepared to do so until I realized that you were describing those villains I so love to hate. *(Everyone laughs, especially me)* It is weird for me to think of the bankers, CEOs, politicians – the villains who contribute the most to the destruction of my planet – as spiritually sensitive souls who feel so deeply the apparent loss of interconnection with all souls that in their great suffering they spare no effort to regain that lost sense of connection and…

10) The Spiritual Source of Greed and Ambition

Benedict: Hold it right there. "In their great suffering they spare no effort to regain that lost sense of connection." Everything they do is an "effort to regain that lost sense of connection", even if their efforts are seriously misplaced. Of course, we grant that they have become insane, and that the efforts they make – through competing against one another for attention, reputation, wealth – serve only to increase their sense of loss. But they are struggling mightily to recapture that lost sense of connection, are they not?

Neal: Yes.

Socrates: And don't you now agree that their struggle is nothing other than a cry for love?

Neal: I suppose so.

Socrates: And the fact that they are all struggling in ways that only increase their sense of loss is simply an error, is it not?

Neal: Yes, and I suppose you're going to suggest that they deserve double compassion from us.

Socrates: Double compassion?

Neal: Yes. First, because they are human and are suffering the loneliness inherent to the human condition. Second, because they are mistakenly seeking to alleviate their loneliness in ways that cannot work, and that can render them only more lonely. I suppose the situation is not much different from the case we discussed a while back. A guy has a headache, so we can feel some compassion for his pain. But he seeks to alleviate his headache by banging his head against the wall, adding considerably to his pain, and we should feel compassion for his error in thinking that he could remedy his headache in this way.

Socrates: Good. *(Mischievously)* But what if he is so thickheaded that his behavior, banging his head against the wall, is about to cause the collapse of the whole building? Should we then withdraw compassion?

Neal: *(smiling)* No, for you have taught me, against my will at times, that it is never appropriate to feel anything less than compassion for any embodied soul. It is quite possible for the bystanders to intervene, to physically prevent him from continuing to bang his head against the wall, and to lead him to a doctor who will help him with his headache. All of this can be done while feeling compassion for the poor soul, who both suffers and is deluded about the cause of his suffering. Have I passed your little test?

Socrates: *(laughing)* Good enough for now.

Plato: *(to me, with humor)* Don't look to me for sympathy. This fellow has been doing the same to me for several thousand years. But I assure you, it is much easier for we who are not embodied than it is for you to see all this clearly. You see it conceptually, or as Benedict puts it, in terms of reason and what he called the second kind of knowledge, and so there was a slight edge to your words that did not escape Socrates' notice. We see it directly in terms of eternal essences and those obscure things Benedict counts as knowledge of the third kind.

Benedict: *(with humor)* "Obscure" only to humans. What you perceive as behavior leading to the destruction of the Earth, we perceive as desperate cries for love, for a sense of lost connection with All-That-Is. Everything, as *A Course in Miracles* states, is either an expression of Love, or a cry for Love. You do understand conceptually that the obnoxious banker is really crying desperately for love. But we see his cry, or yearning of the soul, directly whereas you see only his behavior directly.

Neal: I accept what you say, and will even acknowledge that with repeated application of what reason tells me must be true, I can feel a little softening in my heart for the misery of the very wealthy.

Benedict: Good.

Neal: *(with a slight edge, and some humor)* But only a little…

Benedict: Still good. We can be compassionately playful with this, and still regard them as the "villains" and "bad guys" in this magnificent drama…

Neal: But…

Benedict: We playfully remind you of that saying that holding a grudge against someone is like drinking poison and expecting the other to die.

Neal: I understand. But could someone please tell me how we moved from our children to my ah, what shall we call it…?

Benedict: Your residual reluctance to grant full spiritual status to the impoverished wealthy?

Neal: Yeah, something like that.

Plato: Well, we told you at the beginning that the topic of our conversation has no beginning and no end, and that we would be going round and round with our various themes. You can always edit it at the end, if you feel that there are logical gaps, but for now just follow the conversation wherever it goes.

Neal: OK.

Plato: Think of it like this: we are dancing in the ballroom of linguistic expression. Sometimes we dance in place, as when we follow a train of thought in logical detail. Other times we dance wildly across the whole ballroom, unfettered with details. You are more comfortable with the former than with the latter.

Benedict: *(to Plato)* And although you've loosened me up a bit, Neal is not the only one here who is not entirely comfortable with the "wilder" aspects of this so-called dance. The "ballroom of linguistic expression" indeed. Well, whatever, I sense you will be developing this analogy a little later, and at any rate, since we have been all over the place, perhaps it is now time to dance in place a little with our children.

Plato: Agreed.

Socrates: And are we also agreed that we have caught hold of the spiritual source of ambition – the desire to do whatever it takes to gain recognition and status from others?

William: Yes, I think we are agreed that the spiritual source of ambition lies in the separation itself. Souls that previously experienced themselves as continuously connected with spiritual beings and energies are now, upon embodiment, closed off from such connectedness. In desperation they attempt to regain that lost connection by getting the attention of other embodied souls.

Benedict: And of course, getting some attention from another human being is but a poor substitute for experiencing directly "the mind's union with the whole of Nature", as I once put it.

Neal: And because this way of compensating for the loneliness inherent in the human condition does not and cannot work, they become increasingly lonely and desperate.

William: But *our* children, trained in emotional intelligence, and trained from the earliest ages in the art of giving and receiving attention, and trained to experience connection with Source through meditation, will not be subject to the particular form of madness that Benedict calls "ambition". Are we agreed on this point?

Neal: Yes, I think we are. But what about that other "species of madness" that Benedict identified? Greed. Will our children also be immune from that form of mental illness?

William: In some sense, greed and ambition are akin to one another. An ambitious person is, after all, greedy for the attention of others, and no matter how much attention he gets, it is never enough. And it is never enough because no amount of attention from humans can fill the hole caused by the separation. But a human may become greedy for things other than attention, like money and possessions. Does greed – the feeling that no matter how much material wealth one has, it is never enough – have a spiritual source, like ambition?

Neal: By the phrase "spiritual source", we do not mean to suggest that the emotion of greed might come from spirit, but rather, like ambition, arises from the separation of consciousness from its knowledge of its interconnectedness with All-That-Is.

William: Yes. So the consciousness, as it separates from the One Mind, begins to identify with some outer form, called the body.

Neal: Yes.

William: Then, finding itself in its body, it seeks to establish for its new home the same security system, so to speak, that it had in its former home.

Neal: Security system? What do you mean?

Plato: Actually, there is an interesting metaphor here.

Benedict: Just like you, Plato, unable to pass up any opportunity for a good figure of speech. But I see it too, so you might as well state what it is.

Plato: Thank you. OK, a man buys a house, but is worried about thieves, so he installs a security system. But the thieves are smart, and figure out how to override the system and break in anyway. The man then installs a more complicated security system, but the thieves figure out how to outsmart that one too. Needless to say, this is a never-ending story, and continues indefinitely, just like greed.

William: Yes, because the root of greed is the desire to ensure the permanent safety of the embodied soul's new home. So it chases after wealth and possessions, in the false belief that the more of these it accumulates for itself, the safer it will be in its material form. But at some level, the embodied soul knows that no amount of material wealth can recreate the feelings of safety it felt prior to embodiment.

Benedict: And of course, the felt sense that nothing can guarantee the safety of the body is accurate. We embrace the Buddhist teaching of the impermanence of all forms, or bodies, and our children will be taught this.

William: We might say that the greedy individual is really seeking for a security system for his body, which he mistakenly believes is his self. But, because nothing can guarantee the security of an illusion, he cannot in principle ever be satisfied by material possessions.

Socrates: *(to me, with pointed humor)* And so you see how truly spiritual they are, the greedy and the ambitious. For whereas the latter strive mightily to recapture the lost sense of interconnectedness, the former strive mightily to recapture the lost sense of safety, both of which are lost upon separation from Source, and neither of which can be regained through chasing after material forms.

Neal: I was going to say something but…

Socrates: No, no, go ahead, don't censor yourself.

Neal: Yeah, well I was going to say that, yes, they are striving mightily, but they are striving obnoxiously as well, and harm many others through their so-called striving.

Socrates: Agreed. The fact that they are so obnoxious makes it difficult for you to love them.

Neal: Yes.

Socrates: Perhaps this is the problem. Your problem.

Neal: My problem?

Socrates: *(smiling)* Why yes, here we go again. You believe, do you not, that all humans, as extensions of the Divine Being, are worthy of only lovingkindness.

Neal: Yes.

Socrates: But it is extraordinarily difficult to love that two year old throwing a temper tantrum in the supermarket, is it not.

Neal: Yes.

Socrates: Hence it is *your* responsibility to not allow the outer behavior, obnoxious though it is, to stop the flow of gentle lovingkindness within your being. Got it?

Neal: Got it. But now, tell me if I am right in thinking that one remedy for greed lies in accepting and embracing the impermanence of all forms.

Plato: Yes. Our home-owner above will keep installing ever more sophisticated and expensive security systems until it dawns on him that any security system can be circumvented by thieves who are determined to do so. The greedy individual will continue to chase after wealth and possessions until he realizes that no amount of material goods can ensure the safety of his body.

Neal: Then it seems to me that it will be important to teach this to our children, that all forms are necessarily impermanent, including their own, and that any form may come to an end any time.

Plato: Yes.

Neal: So our children will be learning about death very early in their educational process, not at the end, as I had supposed.

Plato: Well, the word "death" has such negative connotations in your culture. But it will not be unusual in our New Society for a child whose grandmother, say, has recently "transitioned" to report visits and communications from Grandma. Such communications happen all the time, but children are not allowed to talk about them in your present culture. But because our children will be encouraged to discuss such experiences, they will happen with much greater frequency, and our children will know from experience that (i) all forms are impermanent, and (ii) they are not identical with their outer form, since, obviously, they can still talk with Grandma even though she is not in her physical form.

Benedict: But of course, even accepting the impermanence of all forms, they will still strive to flourish in the particular form in which they find themselves, namely the body.

William: And we should no doubt mention that our Society, the whole world in which the child finds herself, exists for the purpose of allowing and facilitating the flourishing of all embodied souls. The physical needs and requirements of all humans – food, clothing, shelter, etc. – will be guaranteed, from conception to death. So neither children nor adults will have to give any thought to the mere survival of their body.

Neal: I think this is very important, because until now, fear and concern over bodily survival has caused many humans to abandon their ideals in order to work for the money that would allow their physical form to continue to exist. But because our New Society exists for the purpose of enabling every embodied soul, every physical form, to flourish in its own being as much as possible, no one will have to labor merely to keep alive his body, and hence there are no obstacles that stand in the way of realizing the soul's original purpose in manifesting as human. Humans will never again be compelled to compete with one another for the Earth's resources. The resources of Earth are more than sufficient to sustain all human bodies, and once the disease called "greed" – the insane desire to "have more material goods than other humans" – has been eradicated from the human species, there is nothing that could prevent a fair and equitable sharing of the planet's resources. But should we not, at this point, say something about how we shall teach our children about death? The subject is taboo enough for the adults of my present culture; it is unheard of to speak to children about it, as they are supposedly unable to handle it, conceptually or emotionally.

Plato: Well a society that is predicated on the fear of death, like yours, must never do anything that might alleviate that fear. It is your adults who fear, then impose that fear upon the children. But, as Socrates taught us at his trial, the fear of death is never rational, even if we do not know that death is just a transition from one form to another. But actually, we do know this. That is, your present scientists already know through empirical means that consciousness is not produced by the brain and, hence, cannot be destroyed by the destruction of the brain at death. Within one generation this fact will be widely known, and our children will be raised in a culture that recognizes and teaches that death is a transition, not an ending. Moreover, the terrifying stories about hell and eternal damnation, gleefully taught to many children by adults who have become insane with idiotic religion, and have nothing better to do than frighten small children, will be regarded as a form of profound child abuse.

William: And we should note that children are very malleable, and almost always absorb the beliefs, values, and habits of the culture in which they are raised. This is the "mechanism" by which insane and dysfunctional superstitions and hatreds get passed from one generation to the next. So if children can internalize false beliefs about death, or equivalently, about what life is all about, surely they can also internalize true beliefs.

Neal: Yes, and we must include among the false beliefs, not only the beliefs of most organized religions, which instill fear, but also the equally insane beliefs that revolve around greed and ambition – e.g. that the purpose of life is to amass as much wealth and status as possible, beliefs that also instill fear.

Plato: So our children will be taught the truth, and in ways appropriate to their age.

Socrates: And the Truth, lest we forget, is very simple, and can easily be expressed in a few propositions.

Neal: How would you express the Truth?

Socrates: (i) All humans are aspects of, components of, expressions of a single One Mind. (ii) All such expressions are temporary and perishable, but the Consciousness or One Mind that experiences itself now as one form and now as another form is eternal and indestructible. (iii) The purpose of what humans call "life" is (a) to grow in one's ability to give and receive Love, (b) to learn, (c) to develop and express one's talents and abilities as best one can, and (d) to have fun in so doing.

Neal: Is that it?

Socrates: You think it should be more complicated than that? What else would you add?

Neal: I can't think of anything else to add.

Socrates: *(laughing)* You're thinking, in part at least, that this is so simple that even a child could understand it? Well, but that's the point. It is that simple, and our children will be able to understand it.

Benedict: Well, I don't know if I can fully agree with that last statement.

Socrates: Oh, why not?

Benedict: Because in the case of children, belief precedes understanding. Our children will have internalized these beliefs because they are the background beliefs of the culture in which they are being raised. Children do not internalize these beliefs, or any other beliefs, because they understand them or know them to be true. It is only later, when they are able to reason that they will be able to understand conceptually why their beliefs are true.

Socrates: We do not really disagree. Of course our children can be taught (i), (ii) and (iii) above before they are able to understand all the whys and wherefores, but the beliefs of organized religion are not at all susceptible of rational understanding, neither are the beliefs that enshrine greed and ambition. The background beliefs of our New Society, which our children will internalize before understanding, are rational and true, and as our children grow in their ability to reason and understand, these beliefs will come into ever sharper focus.

William: And we should add that these beliefs resonate with the inner knowing of our children. So when our children reach the age where they are capable of reasoning, they will have no problem with the beliefs they have internalized since early childhood. They will see that the beliefs are prescribed by the "dictates of reason", as Benedict once said, and that they are in harmony with both the findings of empirical science and the child's own experience. This is in sharp contrast to the various "crisis of faith" (as we used to call it in my time) that children experienced when they reached adolescence. The so-called crisis of faith arises from the fact that children who internalize a crazy belief system undergo a crisis when they realize that their system of internalized religious beliefs (hell, sin, creationism, etc.) cannot withstand critical thinking. So either they must abandon the beliefs of their childhood or they must abandon the gift of critical thinking and reasoning. Our children will not face this dilemma.

Neal: And I suppose we should notice that the other religion of our culture, the religion of greed and ambition, also cannot survive the test of critical thinking. It is obvious to reason that a "culture" in which everyone strives to be as greedy and ambitious as possible, in which adolescents are taught that their salvation and only hope for a happy life lies in becoming as greedy and ambitious as possible, is not a culture at all. So again, reason must be abandoned in order to follow the religion of greed.

Benedict: I know we're probably a little ahead of ourselves, since reason will be discussed at length a little later, but since the subject is so dear to me…

Plato: And to me too!

Benedict: … I would like to give an example of the interplay between (1) beliefs, or habits of mind, that are internalized in early childhood, and (2) the subsequent understanding of those beliefs in adolescence.

Plato: By all means, proceed.

Benedict: We have laid down the Golden Rule, or the Moral Law, as the most fundamental belief of our New Society. Our children will learn this, not just as some empty Sunday School platitude, but as a very practical guide for living. It will be second nature for our children, before they say or do anything, to put themselves in the place of the "other" and to consider the feelings of the other. The reason for this, which they will understand much later, is that both they and the "other" are components of a single divine being, like cells in the same body, and to "harm" another is quite literally to harm oneself. Everyone who returns from an NDE emphasizes this. So our children, having internalized the Golden Rule, will, when they reach the age of reason, come to see that this Rule is among the "dictates of reason", and unlike the rules of religion and greed, is not opposed to reason, but actually is demanded by reason. Moreover, as any adolescent child can see, the Golden Rule is the only rule that, if followed by everyone, would lead to a most harmonious society. But the rules of religion and greed pit one person against another, and lead only to the chaos now evidenced in the present society. A child's reason can see this, so I suppose I must agree with Socrates after all, that it's so simple a child can see it.

Neal: But an adult, whose mind has been infected with false and inconsistent beliefs, is unable to fathom what a child can see so clearly. Perhaps we shall wait until our children are a little older, 11 or 12, before we go more deeply into the subject of reasoning?

Plato: Yes, OK, as long as we recognize that the child has reasoning capabilities almost from the very beginning, and these capabilities will be nurtured and encouraged in ways appropriate to the level of cognitive development of our children.

Benedict: And I am already thinking of interesting ways that our children can learn to reason, even at very young ages, but let's save it for a little later. I believe William has hinted at the next subject in our curriculum for the education of our children.

11) Cooperative Competition

William: I did? Oh yes, competitive games.

Neal: But I thought we were not going to teach our children to compete with one another. Why should one part of God compete with any other part of God? I thought we would be teaching our children cooperative games only, so that when they reached adulthood, they would have learned how to cooperate, and their minds would have been lifted out of the gutters of winning and losing.

Plato: I see your point, but what if we were to redefine the word "competition" so that it does not involve "winning" or "losing"?

Neal: But then how is it competition? The point of any competition is to win, is it not?

William: Historically, yes. Let's go slowly here. As you have pointed out, we have created a Society in which no one "competes" for resources, or for the means by which a given physical body may sustain and nourish itself. Because we have cured the mental aberrations called "greed" and "ambition", the earth's material resources will be shared equitably. But also, because of how we are raising our children, the psychological resources will also be shared equitably.

Neal: And by "psychological resources" you mean – ?

William: – I mean getting the attention of others. No one will be so desperate and needy for attention that he will seek fame, reputation, money, just to get attention from others, and in so seeking, become false to his soul's original purpose in manifesting as human. So competition, in the harmful sense in which it exists in the present society, in which everyone competes for morsels of food on the one hand, and morsels of attention on the other, will no longer exist.

Neal: Well that's what I thought. So why teach our children to compete through games?

William: What if what is now called "competition" will be seen as a species of cooperation?

Plato: If we were to consider the Big Picture for a minute, do we not agree that all things are a manifestation of a single One Mind?

Neal: OK.

Plato: And this One Mind is at peace within itself?

Neal: Yes.

Plato: So if we were to talk about "aspects" of this One Mind, or "components" of this One Mind… and we are not suggesting that the One Mind actually has components or aspects, but it appears that way to human language... might we not say that these various aspects or components must cooperate among themselves so as to constitute the Unity of the One Mind?

Neal: It would be ridiculous to form a concept of the Divine Being in which the various components vied with one another for dominance.

Plato: And is not what humans call "physical reality" an aspect of this Being?

Neal: Yes, of course. Oh wait. I think I see your point. So physical reality, taken in its entirety, must be a cooperative affair, not a competitive one.

William: Exactly. So when people talk about "survival of the fittest", competition for food, for territory, and for mates, they do not portray an accurate picture of how it all works. At the deepest level, what appears in the animal kingdom as competitive "survival of the fittest" behavior must, at a deeper ontological level, be cooperative in nature.

Benedict: And this follows from our general principles of Wholism, for nothing can be a Whole unless its "parts" are internally unified, rather than being at war with one another.

Neal: So we reject that view of Nature according to which all its parts are in continuous competition for survival.

Plato: Now, and this might seem like an abrupt change of subject, what is the universal behavior of the young of every species of mammals?

Neal: Huh?

Plato: Think of puppies and kittens, but all animals do this.

Neal: Well they're always playing with each other.

Plato: Yes, but what form does their play take? When we observe animals at play, what is the actual behavior to which we give the name "play".

Neal: They chase after each other, and they wrestle with one another. Perhaps all form of animal play can be described as some sort of chasing and wrestling.

Plato: Are they competing?

Neal: No, they are playing.

Plato: But take a look at their behavior. When one is chasing after another, are they not running as hard as they possibly can?

Neal: Yes.

Plato: And when two humans run as fast as they possibly can, what is that called?

Neal: A race.

Plato: And do not they both desire to win the race?

Neal: Yes, probably.

Plato: So it looks as if our puppies are competing to win a race, does it not? Now wrestling: if two humans were in such close physical contact as puppies are when they wrestle, what would you call that?

Neal: Violence? A fight? Or maybe sex?

Plato: *(smiling)* We'll be talking about sex soon enough. But you see, the puppies are not fighting or being violent when they wrestle; they are being playful. Even though it may look like they are "competing", they are enjoying the sheer exuberance of embodiment.

Socrates: And actually, the puppies are cooperating, not competing.

Neal: What do you mean?

Socrates: Neither puppy could enjoy separately the exuberance they feel while playing together. By joining with each other, chasing and wrestling together, they each experience far more joy than each is capable of separately.

Benedict: I think we will need to say more about this.

Neal: About what?

Benedict: About "joining with each other".

William: This is going to be very interesting. The puppies appear to be competing, but really they are joining together to experience joys that cannot be experienced separately. But "joining together" is necessarily a form of cooperation. So it looks as if competition is subsumed under cooperation.

Plato: Of course we emphasize that there will be no competition for material goods, attention or status, since these will be distributed equally to all. But humans will always be coming together in pairs or in small groups in order to experience joys and pleasures that cannot be experienced individually. There is of course sex and other pleasures of the senses, but there is also the development of skills and abilities, which is intrinsically joyful. Music, sports, theater, learning, and so forth are joys that require joining with others.

Socrates: We will go much further. In your present culture, the joys mentioned above, music, sports, etc., are mixed with much pain and sadness, since individuals compete for attention and status. After all, only one individual can be the "best" violinist in the orchestra, or the "best" actor in the theater, and when individuals compete for status and salary, then many will be unhappy as a result. Our new society will expunge all sadness from these activities, and introduce joy into aspects of our culture that you might think are intrinsically opposed to joy.

Neal: What do you mean?

Socrates: The corporate boardroom.

Neal: What? Are you serious?

Socrates: *(smiling)* Yes. What is the chief qualification for our leaders?

Neal: Oh yes, I see. Our leaders will be selected from among those who have gone outside the cave of corporeal existence and caught a glimpse of the Source of all there is.

Plato: And we don't need to argue this from first principles, since there is plenty of empirical evidence for the statement that those who have experienced the Being of Light or, what is the same thing, the interconnectedness of all individual beings into a single One Being are immune from the madness of greed and ambition, and are incapable of not living according to the Golden Rule. These will be our leaders, not just politically, but in all areas of public life: corporations, medicine, education, and so forth.

Socrates: And so when our leaders come together, the main task before them is to construct and sustain the kingdom of heaven on earth. Their model, of course, will be their own experience of that kingdom. And what greater joy could there be in coming together than to serve this purpose. Imagine, if you can, what corporate boardrooms will look like when no one is motivated by greed and status-seeking.

Neal: This is very difficult to imagine.

William: Yet imagine it we must, since a necessary condition of the survival of humanity depends upon, as Plato once put it, political and economic power on the one hand, and spiritual wisdom on the other, coalescing in the same individuals. We might playfully imagine the current inhabitants of our monasteries being compelled to occupy corporate boardrooms, and the current inhabitants of corporate boardrooms being compelled to join monasteries, where they might begin to recover from their addictions to wealth and status. But now, Benedict, I want to hear what you have to say about the process of "joining together".

Benedict: Well, the first thing to notice is that, according to our system of thought, everything is already "joined together". There is a single, indivisible Being, called by many names, in which we all "live and move and have our being". But from the human perspective, to which the Divine Being manifests as if it were a bunch of separate bodies, it seems that these apparently "separate bodies" can come together to form temporary wholes.

Neal: What do you mean by "temporary wholes"?

Benedict: You might call them "relationships". Of course, everything is temporary in the temporal order, including the body itself. But seen from the perspective of the body, as the body moves through time, or appears to, it forms couplings with other bodies and groups of bodies, and such couplings constitute temporary wholes that have properties over and above the sum of its parts. The whole is always more than the sum of its parts.

Neal: I notice you are using physical language, talking about bodies rather than, say, souls that have become embodied.

Benedict: Humans tend to think atomistically, and to falsely believe that they are independent beings who might "choose" to interact with others, but remain their atomistic independent "selves" even while interacting with others. When two or more puppies come together to play, the specific movements of their bodies are not under their conscious control. Agreed?

Neal: Yes. It would be absurd to think that puppies consciously plan which way to run, when to jump on the other puppy, and so forth.

Benedict: Yet the puppies are conscious of what they are experiencing?

Neal: Yes, of course. But the consciousness they experience themselves as being while they are interacting accompanies the interaction, but is not the cause of it.

Benedict: Exactly. And the consciousness that comes into being as a result of, or during the process of, the interactions of their bodies constitutes a joy that cannot be analyzed or explained in terms of their separate bodies (or minds). To see this clearly, let's try now to "explain" the behavior of the puppies' bodies using only physical concepts, since we agree that the puppies' movements are not determined by intention or planning or anything mental. We suppose that two puppies have been chasing each other and one of them, say, makes a sudden shift in the direction she is running. What, we ask, is the cause of that individual puppy's change of direction? Notice that we could ask this same question for any specific aspect of puppy play.

Neal: *(smiling)* I see why you are talking about bodies. The question cannot be answered by appealing to mental concepts. It will not do to say that the puppy changed direction because she wanted to, or because she perceived the other puppy was doing something that made her want to change directions.

William: I get it. Because our analysis of puppies will soon be applied to children at play, we want to forestall the assumption that the movements children's bodies undergo while playing and chasing after one another are caused by decisions of the child's mind.

Benedict: Yes. So let's examine this puppy's change in direction. What caused it?

Neal: That's easy. Any movement of the puppy's body is caused by muscles that contract and expand in ways appropriate to generate the given movement.

Benedict: And what causes the muscles to expand and contract in just the right way to bring about the observed change of direction?

Neal: Well, the muscles are controlled by electrical impulses generated in the brain, and sent to the muscles via nerves that attach to the muscles.

Benedict: And what causes the precise electrical impulses to be sent along the nerves that cause the muscles to move the body in the way observed?

Neal: *(Laughing)* Well at this point, our scientists would wave their hands a lot and say that it is all controlled by the brain.

William: *(also laughing)* Might as well say it's all controlled by God, as far as explaining anything goes.

Neal: Of course both are true ultimately. God is the cause of all things, and the brain is the cause of all bodily motions. But referring to the cause of all things is not of much use when trying to ascertain the cause of a specific thing, like the observed change of motion in a puppy at play.

Benedict: But we will do better. We will accept that the cause of the puppy's change of direction is his brain. The origin of the electrical impulses that cause the muscles to contract *this* way rather than *that* way is in the brain. But what causes the brain itself to send those specific electrical impulses down the neural pathways?

Socrates: It might be useful to examine the wrong answer first.

Neal: Yes, well the wrong answer is the one everybody would be tempted to give. The puppy, let's call her X, changes direction because she sees or otherwise perceives that the other puppy, Y, is about to do something. This perception somehow, a la Descartes, "causes" the brain of X to generate the appropriate signals. But this can't really explain anything, because in the first place, there is absolutely no understanding of how something mental like a perception can cause something physical, like a change in the brain…

Benedict: And no understanding of how is even possible, because the alleged interaction, between mental and physical, does not occur.

Neal: Agreed… And in the second place, the perception occurs simultaneous with, or even subsequent to, the observed changes in the brain. So the wrong answer, which assumes a causal relationship between what the puppy consciously experiences and her brain, cannot work. Whatever affects the physical brain must itself be physical, so we must speak, not of X's perceptions of Y, but rather, what is happening in X's body as she is having the visual experience that we call "seeing Y".

William: And so we must speak of the physical counterpart of the perception. What happens in X's body while she perceives Y?

Neal: And the answer to this question… perhaps I should say, the form of the answer… involves electromagnetic energy or photons reflected from the body of Y and entering the body of X through the eyes. Let's follow the causal chain a little bit: (i) the photons that have been altered by having been reflected from Y impinge on the receptors in the back of the eye (retina); (ii) chemical and electrical changes occur in the receptor cells, and these changes propagate into the brain, causing changes in various parts of the brain; (iii) the brain, thus affected by incoming signals that carry information about Y, then engages its motor system by sending electrical signals along its neurons to its muscle system. Most of the details remain unknown, but I think this is the form of an explanation of X's behavior.

William: So the upshot is that there is now something in X's brain that carries information about, or even more strongly, is actually caused by, the behavior of Y's body.

Benedict: Thus any explanation of X's behavior while interacting with Y will necessarily involve the behavior of Y, or in other words, Y's body.

Neal: Yes.

Benedict: And if we were to ask the same question about the cause of Y's behavior, our answer would be the same, would it not?

Neal: Of course. The cause of any behavior of Y's body lies in his brain, and his brain is affected by X's body in the same way that X's brain is affected by Y's body. In both cases, photons are reflected from the surface of one, and then, mediated by the body's optical systems, affect the brain of the other. So X and Y, as they interact, constitute a coupled system with holistic properties not reducible to the sum of each one considered separately.

Benedict: Ultimately of course, this analysis applies to the whole physical universe, which is a single indivisible whole, not reducible to the sum of its parts, and most certainly, not as humans conceive these "parts". But considering just humans, we may say that the brains of any two or more humans who interact with each other become linked, and hence constitute a coupled system, or, if you will, a single system whose "parts" are the individual brains of X and Y.

Plato: So is this our argument: when two puppies, or two children, chase after each other and physically interact, their brains become inextricably linked, forming what you call a coupled system. The consciousness that is experiencing all this, whether it be the minds of the puppies or the minds of the children, is able to experience joys (and sorrows too) not otherwise available to it.

Socrates: This seems to be a rather long-winded way of stating that both puppies and children chase each other and wrestle with each other not in order to "win" or "compete", but simply because it is fun to do so. They can have more fun with one another than by themselves separately. Is that it, or have I missed something?

Benedict: Yeah, well leave it to you to keep the rest of us from complicating things with too much analysis.

Socrates: And a corollary of this argument will be that neither children nor puppies could have so much fun without the other. So all games, even games that are competitive, must involve appreciation for the other.

Benedict: Yes, and it is what you have called "appreciation for the other", without whom the individual could not have nearly so much fun, that will be explicitly acknowledged and built into all games. So the games we shall teach our children, even games that are competitive, will not be about "winning" or "losing", but rather about joining in a process that (i) encourages them to try their best, and (ii) is fun. But before we move on there is something I want to say that is relevant to this "joining together" that we have been talking about.

Socrates: Go right ahead.

Benedict: I hope this won't try your patience too much. Back in my time there was an idea that gained enormous popularity regarding this "joining together" that we have been talking about. I played with it a little myself, even though it is among the more absurd ideas put forth by humans.

Neal: You mean the idea of a social contract?

William: Well, that was quite popular in my time too. Is that what you mean, Benedict?

Benedict: Yes. But I'll explain it by telling a story, the way Plato here would. Once upon a time, humans lived alone, like wild beasts in the jungle. There was no society, no laws, no rules, and anyone could do whatever he wished, just like wild animals. At some point men realized that it would be to their mutual advantage to join together, to cede their "natural right" to steal, murder, and rape at will, and instead enter into a "social contract" with other humans for mutual benefit. Now this story assumes what is an absolute fiction: that humans are born autonomous, and that they consciously relinquish some autonomy for the benefits of belonging to some social order.

Neal: I think that this story was invented by men with big egos, who were also ignorant about the so-called "wild beasts".

Benedict: What do you mean?

Neal: Well, every human being, indeed, every primate, is born into a family and every family exists within a wider social network of families. So it was never the case that humans lived alone, independently of one another. And the comparison with "wild beasts" is also silly, because the wild beasts also have families and are social animals. But philosophers and other male intellectuals have big egos that compel them to think of themselves as independent of anything outside themselves, and that is why they have been attracted to such silly ideas. Social connectivity is built into the very consciousness of each individual. The brain itself is hardwired and programmed via its interactions with other humans.

William: And while we are being a bit critical here, this (the big egos) is also the reason our colleagues in both our fields – philosophy and psychology – are more comfortable with an atomistic view of things than a wholistic view. Atomism is a "philosophy" that allows them to conceive of themselves as independent of anyone else.

Neal: And they still cling to it, even though it has been proven false by the quantum theory. But, getting back to our children, the connections between and among our children are internal, not external (as social contract theories falsely assume), and this fact can even be used to reinforce our teaching them the Golden Rule. Appreciation, mutual respect, and even love, will be built into the games we teach our children. For every child will know that without the "other" there could be no game.

Socrates: It seems to me, if I may simplify without oversimplifying, that we are concerned about two things that appear to be contradictory. (i) On the one hand we want our children to exert themselves fully, to try their best, and to play to win, whatever may be the game.

Neal: Yes.

Socrates: And (ii) on the other hand, we do not want the one or ones who "lose" to feel bad about themselves for losing, and even more important, we do not want the one or ones who "win" to feel good about themselves for winning. On the contrary, (iii) we want both "winners" and "losers" to feel good about themselves for having tried their best.

Neal: Yes. In my present culture, the desire to "win" has eclipsed everything else, even good sportsmanship and fair play. The children feel miserable unless they win.

Socrates: But perhaps this can be remedied. What do children (and adults) get when they "win"?

Neal: Everyone praises and admires the winners of any competition. Also, the players have internalized a belief system according to which it is better to win than to lose. So by "winning" they increase their self-esteem.

Socrates: So your children play to win in order to gain the attention from others, and self-esteem from themselves. But *our* children will not have internalized your belief system. They will not literally be starving for attention, for someone to notice them, for they will have received adequate attention and recognition from the very beginning of their lives. Our culture recognizes that just as no human body can flourish without adequate food, so also, no human mind can flourish without receiving attention from others. Attention, which is really consciousness itself, is the food the mind requires in order to flourish. It is the lack of such attention in the process of raising your children that causes everyone in your culture, children and adults alike, to be so desperately needy for the attention they get from "winning" something, which is why they often cheat and lie in order to win. The need for attention is that great, and when not supplied from early childhood onwards, it leads to the kind of madness so easily observed in your culture. But of course, our children will have been fed nurturing attention all their lives. They will not need to "win" at competitive games in order to feel good about themselves.

Neal: I agree. So although our children may play to win, they will not feel emotionally that "winning" means they are "better" and "losing" means they are worse. Whether an individual or team "wins" or "loses", each will feel gratitude towards the other for making the game possible, and good about themselves for having tried their best.

Socrates: So we agree that our three desires [(i), (ii), (iii) above] can be simultaneously satisfied in our society, but not in yours. Now, there is something else about games that we have not yet fully noticed, something very important that is actually the source of joy and fun in playing games.

Neal: What is it?

12) The Inherent Delight of Focused Attention

Socrates: And we can widen our net here, for if I am right it will turn out that the source of joy in playing games is the same as, or akin to, the source of joy in music and art.

Neal: Are you going to tell us what you have in mind?

Socrates: Actually, you have noticed this yourself.

Neal: Noticed what?

Socrates: You were watching a baseball game shortly after attending a concert.

Neal: Oh, I've got it! As the concert was about to begin, the conductor raised his baton, and there was this look of *total* concentration on his face. *(They had put a small balcony above the stage, and I was sitting above the trumpets, and could see the expressions on the conductor's face as clearly as anyone in the orchestra.)* Then later, watching a baseball game, I noticed the expression on the batter's face as he awaited the pitch.

Socrates: And…?

Neal: It was the same expression that I had seen on the face of the conductor.

Socrates: And what did you conclude from this?

Neal: I concluded that this is the expression on the face of any human being whose mind is one hundred percent focused in the present moment.

Socrates: *(smiling)* Exactly.

Benedict: Yes, you see, that which differentiates one human from another, aside from physical appearance, is their respective emotions and desires. Peoples' emotions – the usual suspects here, guilt, worry, anger, anxiety – shine through their faces. But when attention is focused completely in the present moment, these emotions vanish. This is what it means to say one's attention is focused in the present moment: it is not focused on the past or future. So emotions that are based in the past (guilt, anger) or future (anxiety, worry) cannot arise when attention is focused in the present moment, and to the extent that such emotions do arise, attention is not focused in the present. So both the conductor and the batter, being completely focused in the moment, are not differentiated by any emotion, and hence the expression on their faces is the same.

Plato: So one important reason we shall not banish competitive games from our New Society, as you once thought we would, or should, is that playing games is a means to focus attention. And focused attention, without emotion, is inherently delightful. After all, is what we are calling "focused attention" in a human being anything other than the presence of consciousness free from emotion?

Neal: Yes, I mean no, and the presence of consciousness free from emotions is experienced as inherently joyful and deeply satisfying.

Plato: Now, our children have already been taught basic meditative techniques, such as watching the breath, so they know how to bring their attention to the present moment. Also much of their education involves what we have called emotional intelligence, which intelligence requires some ability to detach from emotions, so that they can talk about them objectively. But playing games also brings their attention to the present moment, and this why games are both fun and important. But here's a little story.

Socrates: Oh, oh. Your stories are rarely "little". But go ahead.

Plato: Many years ago, somewhere in China I believe, an enlightened Sage was trying to teach his monks how to meditate. But the monks tended to fall asleep during the periods of meditation.

Neal: I can certainly relate to that, as I often fall asleep when I meditate. And a good sleep it is, too.

Plato: Hah! But it was not the Sage's intention to provide a good snooze for his monks, for they, like you, were already quite proficient at dozing off; rather he wanted to enlighten them, which requires one hundred percent attention on their part. So he thought about what he might do to prevent them from falling asleep. He even went so far as to whack them with a stick when he saw them begin to nod off. But nothing seemed to work. How to induce a psychological state of "being in the present moment" which means "having no thoughts that relate to the past or future", which in turn means "having no thoughts", without falling asleep?

Neal: What did he come up with?

Plato: Well, to make a long story very short...

Socrates: Thank you.

Plato: ... he came up with what is now called "Martial Arts". So instead of trying to bring the minds of his monks to the present moment through meditation, where many would fall asleep, he brought their minds into the present moment through the martial arts, where no one falls asleep.

William: *(laughing)* And if they did fall asleep, or even if their attention were to lapse slightly, they would suffer much worse than a mere whack with a stick. Actually it might not be a bad idea to teach our children some martial arts, especially when they are very young.

Neal: Why do you say that?

William: Because in many ways the martial arts are an excellent model for this "joining together" we have been talking about. The martial arts teach children (i) to honor and respect the opponent, (ii) to focus attention in the present moment, and (iii) to join with another in order to experience what cannot be experienced alone.

Benedict: And it also teaches them, as do other games, that there is something in them that is more powerful than deliberate, or calculative, thinking. If the mind is focused in the present moment, then the "part" of the mind that calculates, plans, and deliberates – in a word, the ego – must be in temporary abeyance. The experience thus transcends the ego, as the children, by joining with another, become and experience themselves as part of a larger whole. For the two combatants form and participate in a coupled system with holistic properties not reducible to each considered separately. And this is what we mean by transcendence, is it not? Athletes and musicians both report "peak experiences" in which they feel the game or music is playing them, not the other way around. They become detached from their little selves, and experience themselves as part of a larger whole, with nothing to do except observe the process. Well, perhaps

I'm getting a little ahead of our story.

Neal: What do you mean?

Benedict: Our five-year-old children can plunk at the piano and practice kicking and blocking, but they can hardly be expected to have "peak experiences". That is for adults who have mastered the game.

Neal: I understand.

Benedict: Moreover, our purpose in exposing our children to games involves a process (of joining with others), not an outcome (winning, or becoming a "master" of the game). And, for our children, a necessary component of this process will involve what your psychologists call "processing". *Our* adults will never forget, as your adults seem to have forgotten, that by far the most important thing about teaching games to our children is the children themselves. And by the phrase "the children themselves" I mean to refer to their inner lives, not to outer learning or accomplishments.

Plato: And this is an ongoing theme we shall not lose sight of. Children will be guided to discuss and express their emotions, both among themselves in small groups, and with adults. They will play their games "to win", but afterwards, "winner" and "loser" will talk about it with each other. The connection between participants in a game is far more important than the outcome of the game. And this "processing" will occur not only with respect to sports and games, but with respect to all aspects of their lives. We shall not forget, as we raise our children, that emotional intelligence is the most important component of their education, and this requires regular processing of their inner lives – emotions and desires – both with other children, as well as with adults.

William: Indeed, processing of feelings and emotions will be a regular component of everyone's lives. Any group of people who come together for a common purpose – whether a sports team, an academic department, a corporate boardroom, an office – will meet regularly, perhaps weekly, to share and express their emotions and desires. They will engage with one another first and most importantly as human beings or embodied souls, and then secondarily with respect to the task at hand. Didn't you say something at your trial, Socrates?

Socrates: *(playfully)* I said many things at my trial, William.

William: *(smiling)* Yes, but this was in regard to, oh yes, I remember. You said you were the same person in public as in private, or something to that effect.

Socrates: Ah yes, and you know that this alone is sufficient.

William: Huh? Sufficient for what?

Socrates: For our New Society. Making it a "requirement" that everyone is the same person in public as they are in private would be sufficient to generate our whole new social order.

Neal: Yes, I think I see your point. For as we have already discussed, there will be no incentive to lie, hence there will be no lying. But without lying, there can be no difference between a person's public and private persona.

Socrates: In order to be the sort of person who is the same in public as he is in private, one of two possibilities must be the case. The first possibility we are making actual through our process of child-rearing. From preschool through graduate school, our children will be participating in "group therapy" sessions. Actually, we'll have to come up with another name, since "therapy" is a process to assist with dysfunctional emotions, whereas our intent here is to prevent such emotions from arising in the first place. Maybe "group hygiene"? Anyway, our kids will be reporting and sharing how they really feel and what they really think. The adults or older children who lead such groups will be on the lookout for any tendencies of children to compare themselves with others, for almost all dysfunctional emotions (pride, arrogance, depression, envy, etc.) arise from such comparisons. It will not occur to our children to misrepresent their inner lives to others for effect.

Benedict: Through their upbringing, our children will know that their worth and value is guaranteed by the Divine Being. And our children's outer environment places no judgment whatsoever on their inner lives, so children will not be taught, as they are now, to express themselves in a manner that will gain approval from the adults. On the contrary, they will be taught, or rather, they will not be prevented from, expressing themselves outwardly in accordance with how they feel inwardly. Hence when they grow up, they will be the same person in public as they are in private.

William: Indeed, the very distinction between "public" and "private" will, to a large extent, disappear. But, Socrates, what is the second possibility you alluded to?

Socrates: *(mischievously)* Me.

William: You? Oh yes, I see what you mean.

Neal: What does he mean?

Socrates: *(smiling)* If one has had the good fortune to become what you call "enlightened", then one is incapable of lying, no matter what the outer society is like. That's what did me in, or rather, my physical form, at the trial, for as we have mentioned before, had I been able to play on the emotions of the jury, dragging my wife and children into the court and pleading for my life, the outcome would have been different. But to do so would have required that I lie, that I express emotions I was not feeling.

Neal: *(smiling)* And to this day, when they read about your trial, people still get angry at you for not doing whatever it would have taken to save your life – almost as if you would still be alive today had you bothered to save your life at the trial.

Socrates: *(laughing)* You were angry too, but I think you have finally forgiven me.

Neal: Yes. It took a while. At first I thought that your accusers were such jerks and assholes that they did not deserve being told the truth about anything. Finally I realized that you spoke the truth, not because *they* deserved it, but because *you* deserved it. You knew that to preserve the body at the expense of the soul (by misrepresenting your inner life) does some harm to the soul, or something like that.

Socrates: Yes, something like that. And those "jerks and assholes" that you less-than-lovingly referred to are still among us, waiting to learn what they were not able to learn before.

Neal: What in the world do you mean?

Socrates: Their outward form is a little different, but their essence is the same.

Neal: I still don't understand what you mean.

Plato: *(smiling, referring to Socrates)* Exasperating, isn't he?!

Socrates: Oh, don't listen to Plato. I'm not exasperating at all. Here's a little hint: consult your hatreds.

Neal: My hatreds? Now I'm really confused.

Socrates: You hated my accusers, right?

Neal: Yes, most assuredly.

Socrates: And I said (i) my accusers are still among us, and (ii) consult your hatreds. So who are you hating right now?

Neal: Oh my God, you mean the Wall Street bankers and sociopaths?

Socrates: Exactly. And I might add that you are making some progress towards relinquishing your hatreds. I was not angry with my accusers back then, and neither should you be angry with them in their present form right now. And if you like, the reason is not, as you put it, because *they* deserve it, but rather because *you* deserve it. Another reason, as you well know but routinely forget, is that this so-called "reality" of yours is merely a dream from which you will eventually wake up. So why allow your peace-of-mind to be disturbed by illusory characters in a dream?

Neal: Good question.

13) Touching One Another

Plato: And a "good question" is more important than an answer. But now, let's return to our children. The instinctual impulse of all mammals, or the young thereof, is to play, that is, to delight in the exuberance of embodiment, and the various games we have been talking about is the human form of this instinctual impulse. We've talked about wrestling and chasing one another, but there's a third kind of instinctual behavior that the young of all mammals engage in, that is important for human mammals too. Can you see it?

Neal: Yes, they love to groom each other, and to cuddle up to one another.

Plato: Exactly. Our Society will place no barriers in the way of children expressing affection to one another physically. Such expression will be encouraged, as we have been teaching them massage from the earliest ages.

Neal: But people will fear that the children might have sexual thoughts about one another, or something like that.

(Everyone laughs.)

William: Yes, yes, but the people who have those fears are people who have been raised in your current society – or even worse in my Victorian society. *(More laughter)* My goodness, what a confusing mess, where adults, horribly damaged by upbringing with respect to their own sexuality, project their repressed desires onto innocent children. But of course, we are not raising our children with a view to what may be pleasing to sexually repressed adults. There will be no such adults in our new society, and we are raising our children with a view to what is best for the children. What is natural and biological must take precedent over what is merely cultural.

Benedict: Good. And so it is Nature Herself that has determined the behaviors of the very young in all species of mammals: chasing, wrestling, and cuddling. For what we call "instinct" in the child is itself a determination of Nature. It will be a simple matter for neuroscientists to show how and in what way these instinctual behaviors stimulate the development of the brain, and whatever is good for the developing body will be encouraged.

William: And just as sports, games, and gymnastics are an outgrowth of the instinct to chase and wrestle, so massage and bodywork are the natural outgrowths of the instinct to cuddle. As they mature, all children will be taught basic techniques of massage, but some will be so good at it, and delight in it so much, that they will do it professionally. Receiving massage and body-work on a regular basis will be viewed in our culture as a necessary component of preventative health. Our neuroscientists will be able to show in great detail the many health benefits of receiving touch.

Benedict: And for the human being, the embodied soul, what is healthy for the body is also healthy for the mind associated with the body. For when the body is being touched, the mind becomes quieter, thoughts decrease as awareness is brought into the body, and the body itself becomes a portal to the "present moment", or the eternal Now. Well, perhaps we shall say more about this later.

Plato: Indeed yes, we shall have much to say about "portals" later on, but there is something that is important to say right now.

William: Yes?

Plato: When we were teaching our children competitive games, the children learned that by cooperating with one another in play they could have much more fun than by themselves.

William: Yes, they have learned that.

Plato: And when we teach them massage and basic techniques of body-work, what else will they have learned?

William: That it feels good to be touched.

Plato: And…?

William: It also feels good to touch another and give pleasure to another. So we are giving our children the direct experience of feeling good through helping another feel good.

Plato: Exactly. Now all children will be given this experience, and they will be directed to talk about it, so as to bring awareness to the simple fact that it feels good to bring joy to another human being. Of course, with respect to massage we are talking about bringing joy into the body. But many are the ways that one human can help another, and that it always feels good to help another. Now, although our children will experience the joy of helping others directly, we will remind them why this is so.

Neal: What do you mean?

Plato: We shall remind them that they are embodied souls, that the same "One Mind" that has created one soul has created all souls, and that the joy that arises through bringing joy to another is the recognition of the spiritual connection among all souls. The impulse to help another human being is rooted in a recognition of such interconnectivity.

Neal: Yes, and if I may remark in passing, altruistic behavior, which cannot be explained at all by materialist scientists, has a natural and obvious explanation in terms of our belief system.

Plato: Hold it. I get your point, but we are not here developing a "belief system"; we are developing a way of living in the world, and there will be many "systems of belief" compatible with our way of living. We have been teaching our children since before they could talk that the stories we tell them are just stories, and even the most intellectually and spiritually sophisticated system of beliefs *is only a story*. The Real can be known, but cannot be captured by words, and it makes no difference whether the "words" belong to a simple children's story or to a complex system of thought that only someone with a PhD could understand.

Socrates: *(smiling, to me)* In fact, those who hunger after "world-views" and "systems of thought" are like children nagging their parents to tell them a bedtime story.

Neal: *(whimsically)* I was once that child.

Socrates: Yes, but you have now outgrown the need for stories, or have you not noticed?

Neal: Yes, I have noticed, but it took me quite a while. When I was younger I sought sustenance in metaphysical and theological texts. Now I seek sustenance by sitting on a park bench watching the trees, the squirrels, the dogs, and the children.

(Laughter.)

Socrates: OK, but a part of you still thinks you have become mentally lazy and are unable to follow the reasonings and arguments in the texts. But the truth of the matter is that there is more Reality in the trees, squirrels, dogs, and children than in all of the texts put together, including this one, and this is why you are more attracted to park benches. Remember William's point: reading the texts are like reading menus, but the park bench is the raisin.

William: I certainly agree that beliefs *about* what is True and Real must never be confused with what *is* True and Real. But beliefs may be pragmatic and useful. All bedtime stories are just stories, but not all stories have the same effect. Some inspire sweet dreams and others inspire nightmares. In particular, the bedtime stories of theistic religions inspire waking nightmares of horrid proportions. So it won't do, I think, to summarily dismiss all belief systems as just a bunch of words. And especially *(to Plato)* your distinction between "knowledge" and "true belief" is important, and should be taught to our children.

Neal: I agree. Several years ago I read an interview with a physician who had studied the Near-Death Experience. When asked whether he believed it was real, he said in effect: "Yes, I believe it is real, but my patients *know* it is real."

Plato: Ah yes, if only our fellow namesakes (those who call themselves "philosophers") could see the point with the simple clarity of our good physician. Well, we should be gentle with them, for – and I think this is the point you were making when I interrupted our discussion on altruism – they are even unable to see that their materialist beliefs are contradicted by their own impulses towards altruistic behavior. But our children will be encouraged to take their impulses towards altruism as indicative of the Truth that all individual minds are so interconnected as to constitute a single "One Mind". And I'm comfortable retaining my distinction between true belief and knowledge. Those who have had the direct experience of themselves as a manifestation of the One Mind may be said to have knowledge; all others, like the physician above, may be said to have true belief. All our children will have this true belief, since it will constitute the major paradigm of our culture, and will be reflected through all the institutions of our culture. But the goal of our educational process is to convert true belief into the knowledge of direct experience, to whatever extent is possible.

Benedict: Our children are being raised in a culture in which the hypothesis of a "One Mind" is the dominant paradigm. It is a "hypothesis" only for individuals who lack direct experience; for those who have had direct experience – mystics, NDErs – it is not a "hypothesis", but a lived Reality. And educators will take advantage of opportunities, such as the joy one child feels while giving a massage to another, to point out to the children that, and how, their own experience is harmonious with our paradigm.

Neal: And such experiences will be further reinforced through group sharing. Children will discuss among themselves what it feels like to give and receive nurturing touch (massage). These discussions will easily be extended to many other instances of helping others. Later, when our children are a little older, we will invite our neuroscientists to explain to our children how touch affects brain development, and how lack of touch was the most important factor in causing severe mental problems and dysfunctional behaviors.

Benedict: Such as greed and ambition.

Neal: Exactly.

Benedict: And we note again that our children will be taught "good habits" (e.g. giving and receiving touch) before they are able to understand the reasons why. Actually, we should be a little careful here.

Neal: What do you mean?

Benedict: We are assuming that "the reasons why" will be in terms of what our neuroscientists say is good for the brain.

Neal: Well, what's wrong with that?

Socrates: *(laughing)* Nothing, but tell me please, when was the last time you got a massage on the advice of a neuroscientist?

Neal: *(also laughing)* Well, the last time was probably never.

Benedict: Good point, but I had in mind something a little different. Neuroscience is only one of several "systems of thought" that can give an account of the benefits of touch. The Chinese have a different system, in terms of meridians, acupressure points, and so forth; and the conceptual system of the ancient Hindus also could give an account of the benefits. And those people who can see energy patterns directly – psychics, clairvoyants, medical intuitives – can see directly what is happening in the body when it is being touched.

Socrates: So when we invite the neuroscientists to explain to our children "the reason why" massage is good for the brain, and similarly, when we invite our nutritionists to explain to our children "the reasons why" the healthy diet to which we have habituated them is good for their bodies, we will keep in mind that there is always more than one conceptual account. In terms of concepts, one can examine a thing in this way or that way. If one has vision, like a clairvoyant, one can then see these things directly, non-conceptually, yet any attempt to express what one sees will necessarily involve concepts. So we will perhaps speak of "**a** reason why" rather than "**the** reason why".

Plato: As our children mature it is to be expected that they will have many questions and will no doubt receive many answers. But no concept, or system of concepts, whether it be neuroscience or meridians or anything else, can capture the Reality of their moment-to-moment conscious experience. That alone is what is Real. So "explanations" do not really "explain". Only direct experience of the Divine answers all questions. I enjoyed, William, your analogy with a menu and a raisin.

William: Thanks. Well basically, you can eat a raisin but not a menu. A menu, although it describes a large variety of delicious foods, is not as nutritious as a single raisin. Something like that, if I recall.

Neal: Yes, concepts – and we note that all of science trades in concepts – purport to describe Reality. But a description is not the thing described. It is important that our children learn this throughout their educational process. And not just with respect to scientific or theological ideas, but more importantly, with respect to daily experience. The sentence "I feel sad (or happy)" is not the sadness (or happiness) that is felt. Our children will be taught to pay attention to the feelings themselves, and only secondarily to the words used to describe the feelings. And so a child who says those words will be immediately directed to bring conscious attention to the feeling itself.

Socrates: And this teaching will act as a powerful prophylactic against a form of mental illness that has afflicted all societies until now. Well, perhaps there remain a few tribes deep in the Amazon jungles that have remained free from this illness.

Neal: What illness? ... Other than becoming estranged from his or her own emotions, which I acknowledge is a form of insanity.

Socrates: It is a collective illness that arises when consciousness comes to believe that it is not itself, but is rather the words that others use to describe it.

Plato: Recall a while back when we said that language acquisition constitutes the second foray into the River of Forgetfulness, wherein the soul sinks more deeply into the body.

Neal: Yes, and we noted that it is traumatic for the embodied soul to learn that grown-ups lie, for hitherto the soul has no experience of deception. The embodied soul, if it is to adjust to this present society, must also learn to use words for the purpose of concealment and deception. But *our* educational process uses strong measures to prevent children from using language in this way. Through unconditional acceptance of all feelings, emotions, and behaviors, our children will not have anything to lie about, so to speak.

Plato: What you say is true. Our children will have no cause to use language to misrepresent either their inner life or outer behavior. But I wish to point out a more pervasive aspect of language.

Neal: What is it?

Plato: The overall point is not new; in fact it is well known. When a human acquires a name for a thing, or a set of concepts about the thing, he tends to experience the thing not as it is, but as it is mediated through the names and concepts. But these latter are just words and symbols, which in many humans constitute the walls that imprison consciousness, so it can no longer experience anything other than words and symbols, which it then takes for Reality itself. This mental illness is especially pronounced among your academics.

William: Hah! My colleagues would be happier with a menu than a raisin, since reading descriptions of delicious food would excite their imaginations much more than a mere raisin. But the point is that, unlike a raisin, the descriptions have no nutritional value, yet our colleagues read and read and read, and then wonder why they are still not satisfied. They are trapped, as Plato says, by their words and concepts, which they believe constitute the totality of their being, and hence believe that what cannot be said in words does not exist.

Socrates: *(with humor)* Whereas we believe the opposite.

Neal: The opposite?

Socrates: Yes, that what *can* be said in words is what does not exist.

Neal: Huh?

Plato: Well, perhaps Socrates is being a bit cryptic here. We need not divide Reality into "what does exist" and "what does not exist". But the matter is quite simple: when you awaken from a dream, you immediately conclude that what you had taken as real, the contents of the dream, does not and did not exist as part of your physical reality.

Neal: Correct.

Plato: And likewise, when you awaken from your "dream" of physical embodiment you will conclude that what you had taken as Real – physical reality – does not and did not exist.

Neal: Yes, I see. Everyone comes to this conclusion as soon as they quit the body. And since words and concepts play no role in the Real World, it follows that whatever can be captured by words belongs to the dream, not to the Real.

Socrates: Yes, but perhaps we should not be so harsh with respect to language, for it can be quite beneficial as long as its function and limitations are understood.

Plato: Good. And we can state right away that (i) language can describe the physical, (ii) language cannot describe the Real, and (iii) language can be used as a pointer, to help turn the soul around so that it faces the Real, even while still embodied.

Neal: Actually, the first point needs to be qualified somewhat.

Plato: What do you mean?

Neal: Our "best" scientific description of the physical realm is given by theoretical physics. But physics has discovered that mere words cannot even describe physical reality, and so uses mathematics.

The symbols of mathematics, although still a "language", are more powerful than words.

William: So it seems that a language of words can be used only with regard to describing, as someone once put it, a world of middle-sized dry goods. And while we are on this subject, I'd like to make a little correction to something I wrote before.

Neal: Go ahead.

William: It concerns the phrase "stream of consciousness".

Neal: What's the correction?

William: *(laughing)* Just this: Consciousness does not stream! From my present perspective, it is quite apparent that consciousness is sort of like a container – a timeless, unchanging, eternal container – in which, or through which, individual objects like perceptions, emotions, and thoughts appear to flow. But we must be careful here.

Neal: What do you mean?

William: Well, as we have said, when a child learns the word or name of some given thing, he tends to perceive the thing through its name and the name's conceptual associations.

Neal: Yes.

William: So that the perception tends to become infected with words and concepts.

Neal: Yes. And the same with respect to emotions, which is why we have been teaching our children how to experience emotion directly, without the use of words.

William: Agreed. But for those raised in the social order that produced you and me, especially for so-called "intellectuals" like us, what "flows" through the consciousness that is us are not "perceptions, emotions, and thoughts", but rather the words that would be used to describe such mental experience. The inner life has been almost entirely taken over by words and concepts.

Socrates: Ah yes, you wordaholics! Well, this is precisely the mental illness that we have taken great pains to prevent arising in our children. Our children will know from direct experience that they are not the words that stream through their consciousness. Emotional intelligence, the experience of giving and receiving pleasure, music, and games that bring intense awareness to the present moment are all experiences that do not involve words. And to further prevent words and concepts from imprisoning consciousness completely, we will call upon the semantic cops to enforce some rules of language.

Neal: What rules?

Socrates: Rules akin to the one I gave Crito when I drank the hemlock. I told him to say, not that he is burying Socrates, but that he is burying the body of Socrates.

Plato: So the use of language with respect to describing the death of any human being will connote, not an ending or finality, such as "she died", but rather a transition, such as "she has quit her body", or something like that.

William: And when children ask, "What is this?" or "Who is that?" we will not respond by saying, "This is a tree" or "That is Mary," but rather, "This is called a tree," and "That person's name is Mary."

Benedict: And with respect to emotion, children will be taught to say, not "I am sad", "I am angry", or "I am happy", which expressions identify the "I" with the emotion, but rather, "I feel sad", "I feel angry", and "I feel happy". This way of using language, if taught from the very beginning, will go a long way to prevent children from completely identifying with the emotions streaming through the consciousness. This use of language will help them to know that they are not the sadness, anger, or happiness that they are momentarily experiencing.

Neal: And I suppose we shall be telling our children the story about the difference between dogs and cats?

Socrates: Huh? What story?

Neal: I don't know for certain whether it's true, but according to the story, when you point at something with your finger, the dog will look to where you're pointing; the cat will stare dumbly at the finger itself.

Socrates: Hah! We can make a children's game out of this.

Neal: What kind of game do you mean?

Socrates: Whenever a child is caught taking a story too literally or too seriously, the other children will playfully accuse him of being a cat, and the ensuing laughter will bring the mind back to the present moment.

Plato: Words, as we have agreed, have no power to describe the Divine Being, or any being that is nonphysical. Furthermore, words have only very limited use in describing the physical. As you have pointed out, words have no power to describe the quantum processes underlying the material world, and when one attempts to use words for this purpose one necessarily becomes involved in contradictions, such as "the particle is both here and there at the same time". So our children will be taught from a very early age – a teaching that will become more sophisticated as they mature – that although words can point to something greater than themselves, they cannot describe, except in a very rudimentary way. They cannot even literally describe simple human perceptions and emotions.

Socrates: Hold on a moment. William, where did you go?

(Well, speaking of the inadequacy of words to describe anything, it seemed as if William's attention had wandered off someplace.)

William: Yes, well, as soon as you talked about dogs and cats, I was back with my colleagues at Harvard, and one by one their countenance morphed from human to cat. *(Laughing)* That was our problem, Neal, we were dogs in a world of cats, thinking at times that the cats should behave more like dogs, and becoming frustrated with them when they stubbornly remained as cats. But have you noticed that our colleagues – our former colleagues, I should say – seem to attribute magical properties to words?

Neal: Do you mean the belief that a bunch of words, suitably arranged, can have the power to describe the Real?

William: Yes, that too. No arrangement of words and symbols can capture the Real. But I had in mind something more elementary: the belief that words have meaning. Meaning pertains to consciousness, not to words. The form of consciousness called "human" experiences purpose, meaning, and intent, and sometimes uses words to express meaning to others. But words by themselves have no meaning. For example, the word "blue" has no power to convey any meaning to one who is colorblind. And whatever meaning the word "blue" conveys to one who is not colorblind originates in the collective human perceptual experiences with objects referred to by that word.

Socrates: And I might add, playfully of course, that the word "enlightenment" has no power to convey any meaning to one who is not herself enlightened.

William: *(laughing)* There are no raisins in the word "enlightenment", or in any other word for that matter. But, Neal, I wonder what you make of Socrates' remark. Since you believe you are not enlightened, does the word convey any meaning to you?

Neal: Hmm. Good question. From reading numerous accounts, I do have some vague sense of its meaning, perhaps in a way similar to how a colorblind person will have some sense of the word "blue" through experiencing the usage of that term by non-colorblind people. But for me, the word "enlightenment" does point to something. It points to an experience of consciousness insofar as consciousness is in itself, without a body. But I agree that the word by itself conveys to me no understanding of what the experience referred to by the word is, or is like.

Socrates: Actually, your last statement is not entirely true, but we shall examine it later. For now, it suffices to notice, and to teach our children, the difference between a literal use of language and a non-literal use of language.

Neal: Yes. Many years ago you said, or Plato made you say, that small children cannot distinguish between a literal and allegorical use of language, which is why it is so important to take care with respect to the stories they are told at that age. But as soon as our children are mature enough to grasp the difference, we will teach them the difference. "The book is on the table" is a literal use of language. "The book contains much wisdom" is a non-literal use of language.

William: Indeed, it is not only small children who cannot grasp the difference, but many so-called adults. Those who are "religious" for the most part take their sacred books as literal truth, and because of that, are the cause of much harm and suffering. So it will be important to teach our children the difference between a literal and non-literal use of language.

Plato: And as they mature, we can divide the "non-literal use" category finer, and teach them about allegory, metaphor, simile, and analogy. We shall do everything we can to ensure that our children, or rather, the consciousness manifesting as our children, do not become prisoners of language. Throughout their educational process, we shall teach and remind our children of both the use and limitations of language. So now, it would seem, our children are ready to mature, and we should perhaps begin to discuss the kind of education that is most appropriate for tweens and teens.

14) Appreciation Without Envy

Benedict: Tweens?

Plato: *(laughing)* Hah. You've not been keeping up on the latest use of language. The term refers to 11 and 12 year olds.

Neal: Wait a minute. We've not said anything about the particular subjects that our children should study while they are still in grade school. Is not that important?

Plato: Not nearly as important as what we have already taught them. Shall we review the matter?

Neal: Yes, please.

Plato: Alright. Let us notice, first of all, that what we have taught our children thus far is a process, not a bunch of facts or beliefs.

William: What do you mean by the term "process"?

Plato: We teach our children physical hygiene: how to wash, bathe, and clean their physical bodies. But this is not something they do just once, but rather is a process that they will do every day for as long as they are embodied.

William: Agreed.

Plato: We teach our children emotional hygiene: how to feel their emotions, how to express their emotions both verbally and nonverbally, and how to process and heal difficult emotions. Again, this is something they will do not just once, but is a process that will be with them for as long as they are embodied.

Neal: Yes.

Plato: And we have taught them how their body may flourish best through physical training, based on the instinctual impulses to chase, wrestle, and cuddle. We have also taught them nutrition, not just conceptually (although that will come later) but really, by aligning their sense of what *tastes* good with what *is* good for the body. What your culture calls "junk food" really is junk, and will play no part in our children's diet. But again, nutrition and physical training are processes that will be with them for the duration of their lives.

Neal: *(with humor)* But perhaps we will make an exception for senior citizens who, upon reaching the age of 70, may substitute sitting on a park bench for physical training.

Plato: *(laughing)* Perhaps, but don't count on it. And finally, even though we have not said very much about it, exposure to what you call the "fine arts" will be a major component of our children's early education: music, singing, painting, dance, theater are of vital importance. Children will learn that a given thought or emotion may be better expressed through a song, a drawing, or acting out, than by words. This will also reinforce what we said earlier, that meaning pertains to consciousness, not words, and can be expressed through forms other than words. And again, this is a process, since music, art, etc. will be with them throughout their lives. The specific forms of art will of course change as the child matures, and will differ from person to person, or at different times in the life of the same person.

Neal: What do you mean?

Plato: Not all forms of art resonate in the same way with all humans. Classical music resonates strongly with you, but others are just as deeply moved by other forms of music, such as jazz, folk, simple songs, etc… and even more forms will be discovered in the future. Same with painting, dance, theater, and so forth. So our children will be exposed to a large variety of various forms of art and music, and will be encouraged to pursue those with which they naturally resonate.

Neal: OK, but…

Plato: But what about the usual subjects like reading, writing, mathematics, history, geography, science, literature, and so forth. Is that what you mean?

Neal: Yes.

Plato: It goes without saying that our children will be taught whatever is necessary to function within our New Society. You should probably add using computers as a subject necessary for our children to learn. Our children will of course be taught these things in age-appropriate ways. At an early age, all children will be exposed to the same things. But as soon as a child shows natural affinity for a given subject, or a given art form, she will be encouraged to pursue that, although not to the exclusion of everything else.

Neal: Yes, because the expression "a natural affinity" indicates a talent that originates in the soul, and which constitutes a part of the soul's original purpose in manifesting as human.

Socrates: I wish to emphasize something that we have discussed before. In order for educators to discern a child's natural talents and abilities, the child must feel completely free to express those talents and abilities.

Neal: Of course. That is one reason we have given our children ample free time to play and explore; their natural talents emerge during spontaneous play.

Socrates: Yes, but we must remember well the lesson of our dysfunctional symphony orchestra, and guard against children's tendencies to imitate one another, instead of expressing their own innate impulses. This is a process, and an important component of their emotional hygiene.

Neal: Could you say more about this?

William: I think I understand Socrates' point. Our children have varying and unique talents and abilities. This is another way of stating that the souls that are now manifesting as our children have varying and unique purposes and intentions. A given soul's intent is unique to that soul, and purposes vary from soul to soul.

Neal: Although it would be fair to say that all such purposes and intentions fall under the general headings of Love and Knowledge.

William: Agreed. Now we educators know that our children have different talents and abilities, but our children also know this. We must guard against any tendency of a given child to envy, or become jealous of, another child who has a talent he lacks. If such envy is not guarded against and checked, the given child may be liable to imitate the child he envies, instead of expressing his own abilities directly.

Plato: Good. To make the issue more concrete, consider a few examples. All children, as we have said, will be exposed to the same sorts of things early on. Let's suppose that Johnny excels at gymnastics, Suzie excels at mathematics, and Peter excels at drawing and coloring. These are very distinct abilities that indicate the purposes of their respective souls in manifesting as the specific children respectively.

Neal: All well and good.

Plato: Yes, but it would not be so "well and good" if Johnny, who can draw only stick figures, admired Peter's drawings so much that he desired to imitate them. Or if Suzie, who is not physically agile, desired to imitate Johnny. Or if Peter, whose mind always wanders when it comes to numbers, becomes jealous of Suzie and tries to imitate her. These jealousies must be guarded against, as they impede to a soul's original purpose in manifesting as a specific individual with specific talents and abilities.

Neal: I understand what you mean, but I would express it differently.

Plato: Then try using some of Socrates' "other words".

Neal: Alright. We have said all along that children learn by imitation, which is why it is so important that adults and older children model and live the values and behaviors we want our children to learn. I certainly agree that Peter, whose mind we are assuming fogs up whenever numbers are mentioned, should not follow Suzie with respect to pursuing a career in mathematics, or anything that involves mathematics. But insofar as all children are initially exposed to the same subjects, Peter and Johnny will be required to learn some math, Peter and Suzie will be required to do gymnastics, and Suzie and Johnny will be required to learn some drawing and art, even if it is not among their main talents. So what better way is there to learn a subject, especially at the beginning stages, than to imitate one who is talented at the subject? If all children must learn some music, then those children who can't carry a tune should do their best to imitate those who can. But, and I believe this was your point, children who are not talented with respect to a specific skill will not be jealous of those who have the skill.

Plato: I agree. Our children will be raised to admire and even imitate a given talent or skill they do not themselves have, without being envious of the person who does have the given talent.

Socrates: And this will be the main role for the Guardians of our New Society.

Neal: Guardians?

Socrates: Yes. Since ours is a World Order, there will be no enemies from without to guard against. And of the enemies from within, none are more formidable than envy and jealousy. Our guardians will guard against the formation of such emotions in our children.

William: Then anyone who has any involvement in raising our children will be guardians in this sense. For no flower measures its self-worth by comparing itself with other flowers, and our children will be given many metaphors and analogies that make this point. Most dysfunctional emotions arise because humans attempt to find self-worth by comparing themselves with others. Such tendencies will be nipped in the bud by our guardians, and at the earliest possible age.

Benedict: And of course, if a given adult is charged with preventing the formation of envy in a child, the adult herself must be free from that emotion. For even here children learn mostly by imitation, and our guardians will "guard" by role-modeling an emotional life free from envy, with occasional interventions and reminders for the children. Whenever envy arises in the psyche of any child, this will be treated as a learning situation, and with a little assistance from a Guardian, our children's emotional intelligence will be sufficient to dispel the emotion of envy.

Neal: Wait a minute. Does this not imply that almost all adults in our New Society will function as guardians?

Plato: Yes, and the fact that this might seem a bit odd to you indicates how far your present social order has deviated from anything sane or rational.

Neal: What do you mean?

Plato: Raising children is the means by which a given culture extends itself into the next generation. By denying sufficient resources towards the education of children, your culture is actively sowing the seeds of its own destruction. By valuing "making money" and "getting status" more than you value raising children, your culture is well on its way towards becoming extinct. So yes, in our New World Order nothing will be more important than raising children, and the great majority of adults will at some point in their lives be involved with the raising and educating of our children.

Socrates: We may note again that the responsibility for raising our children lies with society as a whole, not with the biological parents or nuclear family or extended family.

Plato: Yes, and this is the reason why our children, prior to embodiment, will not need to be concerned about "choosing" the environmental conditions that maximally facilitate the development of their talents and abilities. For all our flowers, to use William's analogy, will be planted in nutritious soil, will be tended to and watered regularly, and will be admired for their inner beauty and uniqueness. But I left out something important when we were discussing this at the beginning.

Neal: I remember thinking so at the time, but have now forgotten.

Plato: We agreed then that the soul "chooses" its biological parents on the basis of the specific talents and abilities it wishes to manifest in human form. Some genetic combinations are more or less useful for specific talents and abilities. But a soul may choose its biological parents for other kinds of reasons.

Neal: Such as…

Plato: *(with some humor)* Well let's suppose that after you have transitioned and have more fully joined us here, you and William hang out a bit and decide it might be fun to reenter the physical dimension together, as siblings, say, or as mother and daughter, or…

Neal: Mother and daughter?

William: *(laughing)* Why not? After all, sex change operations are very easy over here.

Neal: Well, I understand this in theory, but balk at the details. At any rate, I get the point: two or more souls could decide to have a human experience together, and this constitutes a motivation for incarnating that is in addition to expressing particular talents and abilities.

Plato: Now, we have raised our children very well, but before rejoining our children as tweens and teens, we must bring explicit attention to a very important aspect of their playing and socializing with other children. This is something that has been bothering you.

Neal: Yes, I agree we are raising our children very well. Talking with you about the "best way" to raise children has made me painfully aware of how badly we are raising children in our, or rather my, present culture. The current process of education and socializing seems to be very painful to the majority of children, as they almost all experience teasing, taunting, and bullying. Going to school is excruciating for many children, who strive to "fit in" but feel unliked no matter what they do. They hesitate to express themselves out of fear of judgment. I could go on and on, but I want some assurance that these problems will not arise in our New Society and that our children, *all* our children, will wake up in the morning looking forward to going to school, and not have any fears with respect to fitting in and socializing with other children.

Plato: I think we can give you the assurance you seek. But first, a brief warning: you must not assume that our children will be anything like the children raised in a highly dysfunctional social order such as your own. There is no necessary connection between being a seven-, eight-, nine-, or ten-year-old child, on the one hand, and teasing, taunting, and bullying other children, on the other. The cruelty that your children manifest in their treatment of one another is *not* genetically determined, but rather is caused by how you are raising them.

Benedict: And we must remember too that our children come from a Reality in which Unconditional Love, Unconditional Acceptance, and Unconditional Belonging are the norm. As far as is possible within the constraints of physicality, we are raising our children in a way that mirrors this Truth that is inscribed in their souls. So it will be much easier for children to adapt to a social order based on Love than a social order based on an absence of Love, namely fear.

William: So you see, the "teasing, taunting, and bullying" that is a part of almost every child's experience, both in school and at home (with siblings), is unnatural. It is a visible symptom, for those that have eyes to see, that something is seriously out of whack with your current society. The present society will never be able to address the problem of bullying, for the simple reason that it is the bullies who grow up and become the corporate executives and politicians who run the society. When psychologists get serious and begin to examine the psychology of the bullies – what they think and how they feel – they will discover that it is very similar, if not the same, as the psychology of those who are driven by greed and personal ambition. They delight in hurting others because doing so enables them to feel that they are "better than" the ones they hurt. But our children have been taught from day one that their value and worth are absolute, and not contingent on any comparisons or competitions with other children. Their very bones, as we have said, have been formed around the Golden Rule.

Plato: We have also stressed that children learn mostly by imitating. So the children in your society who "tease, taunt and bully" are imitating behaviors that they have observed in their environment.

But these behaviors will be absent in our society, so our children will have no role models for these dysfunctional behaviors.

Socrates: And while we are being a bit critical of your present social order, it is worth pointing out that in your society children are abandoned by the adults and left to fend for themselves.

Neal: What do you mean?

Socrates: Look at it this way: are children expected to learn reading and writing on their own, without adult supervision?

Neal: Of course not.

Socrates: What about arithmetic? Do children learn this by osmosis, without adult instruction and supervision?

Neal: My goodness, no.

Socrates: And what about other subjects, like music, drawing, and gymnastics? Do they learn this on their own, or is adult instruction and supervision necessary?

Neal: The latter, of course.

Socrates: Then what about socializing and interacting with other children?

Neal: Oh my. Children are not born with the knowledge of how to interact with other children, so it's not innate. Therefore it must be learned. But it is not being taught in our present society.

Socrates: And so it is not learned. But consider, how important is socializing compared with other subjects that are taught?

Neal: For the child it is by far the most important subject.

Socrates: Then to teach this most important subject to our children in the right way, won't this require as much time, effort, and patience on the part of the teachers as do the more mundane subjects of reading and arithmetic?

Neal: Yes, even more time and effort.

Socrates: This is why I said earlier that adults have abandoned the children, by not teaching them the most important of all subjects.

William: There are two main reasons why this is not, and cannot be, taught in our present society. One reason is that to teach children how to socialize in the right way would require a teacher/student ratio at least ten or twenty times greater than what is now current. But the second reason is that doing so would bring about the end to a culture based on greed and personal ambition. For the principle according to which children will be taught to socialize is the Golden Rule, and capitalism will come to an end when children are socialized in this way.

Plato: And so, Neal, do you agree with us that the way we have raised our children includes socializing them according to the principle of the Golden Rule, and that the problems and suffering and misery that pervades that process in your society will be absent from the Society now under construction?

Neal: Yes, I do.

Plato: Then we are ready to rejoin our children and investigate how our New Society will deal with sexuality.

Chapter V

Sexuality

1) The Necessary Pleasures

(There was some silence, as no one seemed to know how to proceed. Finally, Socrates began the discussion.)

Socrates: Frankly, I don't care for how you have stated the question, if it is a question.

Plato: What don't you like about it?

Socrates: Your statement implies that sex is a problem that must be dealt with in some way.

Neal: So…?

Socrates: So sex is not a problem. The real "problem" is any society that makes of sex a "problem" to be dealt with. But sex is a joy and it is the right of every embodied form to experience this joy maximally. Let this be the guiding premise of our discussion.

Neal: It's hard to argue with a premise of maximal joy, yet perhaps we should address some of the concerns that have led the great majority of world cultures to adopt an opposite sort of premise.

Socrates: Well, it might be better to ignore what the "great majority of world cultures" have to say about sex, and instead proceed by developing our own account from first principles, so to speak. Nevertheless, perhaps there will be some value in putting the customary views on the table, if you can be brief.

Neal: Yes, I can be brief. I'll distill the concerns to just two: (i) many religious people say that there is something inherently sinful about sex. It is not good for humans to experience too much pleasure, so sex must be regulated and controlled. And even if it is not sinful (whatever "sinful" means), nevertheless there are profound reasons *why* those who seek spiritual enlightenment take vows of celibacy. It seems that a long and rich tradition in many cultures holds that one cannot seek for God if one is also seeking for other human bodies.

Socrates: We shall turn this concern on its head, so to speak, and argue that sex is a most glorious pathway to the Divine within. What's the other concern?

Neal: Well it is perhaps surprising to hear the atheists chime in and basically agree with the religious folks. Here's how Freud put it: (ii) sex, or the sexual energy, is Mankind's only source of energy. In order to have civilization, some of this energy must be diverted from its natural aim (orgasm) and channeled into the things that comprise a civilization, like art, business, science, architecture and so forth. If there were no restrictions on sexual behavior, then humans would be chasing after bigger and better orgasms, and there would be no energy left to construct a civilized social order.

Socrates: A "civilized social order"? Do these people, the ones who believe that sex must be regulated, do they really also believe that they are living in a "civilized social order"?

Neal: I'm afraid they do.

Socrates: So they call a society "civilized" that in the 20th century alone murdered more than 100 million members of its own species? They call a society "civilized" in which people starve to death despite the fact that the Earth produces enough food to sustain the whole population?

Neal: Yes, I'm afraid so.

Socrates: And they call a society "civilized" in which the schoolyard bullies graduate to become political leaders and corporate executives?

Neal: Again, yes.

William: *(smiling)* From my present perspective, it is all quite simple. Freud, like me, was the product of one of the most sexually repressed societies that ever existed. His belief, with which I would have agreed at the time, that sexuality must be repressed and controlled in order to have a "civilized" social order is a prime example of how a social order perpetuates itself through the thinking of its members. Freud was unable to conceive of any social order that would be better than the one in which he was raised. And of course, in order to have *that* social order – the social order that murdered over 100 million members of its own species, a social order in which people starve to death amidst abundance, and now, a social order that is destroying the planet's ability to sustain human life – in order to have the present social order then, yes, absolutely, sex must be repressed and controlled. But we are constructing a different social order altogether.

Socrates: *(playfully)* And if we are to succeed, the human race must become less like chimpanzees and more like bonobos.

William: Huh?

Plato: We will comment on Socrates' remark later. For now, let us just contrast the Freudian view with our own: the more liberated humans are with respect to their sexual energies, that is, the more they are able to fully embrace and enjoy their sexuality, the more creative and productive people will be in their lives, and the more kind and compassionate they will be in their relationships with one another. Our point of view is directly opposite to the Freudian point of view.

Benedict: It is, as I well know, a fallacy to argue from the way things are at present to the way things must be in perpetuity. Repressing sexuality is necessary only if one wants to produce a social order in which people are miserable, and because of their misery become violent and murderous. It is necessary if one wants a social order in which the worst elements (greed and ambition) of humanity rise to the top. Future psychiatrists will doubtless have a field day, turning Freud on his head, and analyzing in considerable detail how repressing natural sexual desires creates mentally unstable humans. But we shall leave that task to them. Shall we say a word or two about the other objection – the so-called religious objection to liberating sexuality?

Socrates: *(laughing)* I suppose if one believes there is something sinful about being human, or becoming embodied, then one will also think that there must be something sinful about the very force that creates new bodies. But how can there be anything sinful about the human condition?

Benedict: Since the human condition is nothing other than the Divine Being expressing Itself in a certain way, there can be nothing "sinful" or wrong about it. It is, as I once put it, according to the highest right of Nature that each should enjoy herself and seek pleasure for herself in every way consistent with our basic guiding principle.

Neal: Wait a minute. What "guiding principle" do you have in mind?

Benedict: The Golden Rule, of course.

Plato: Agreed. But while we make no concession to the Freudian concerns, we will make one concession to the so-called "spiritual" concerns.

Neal: What concession?

Plato: There is some truth to those esoteric theories that hold that the sexual energy may be turned inward and utilized for direct spiritual experience. This would be an individual decision, for advanced monks perhaps, but not for society as a whole. No one gets "brownie points" in heaven for mere sexual abstinence, contrary to what many religious people think, and our social order will not be one that encourages abstinence or in any way limits a rich, creative, and joyous expression of sexual desire.

William: I suppose we shall be dusting off the ancient manuals?

Plato: Yes, there have been occasions in human history where a more open attitude towards sexuality prevailed, or at least was not persecuted. The Kama Sutra is one example. The Gnostics also practiced sacred sexuality, as did elements in my own tradition – the so-called mystery religions – as well as the ancient Egyptians. Yes, dusting off the ancient manuals will be fine, and a lot of fun too for those involved, but our new social order will have no need of ancient texts, as we shall write our own texts. But we're getting a little ahead of ourselves, so to speak.

William: What do you mean?

Plato: Before we talk about sacred sexuality, that is, sex as a spiritual practice, as a portal to the Divine Being, we must discuss it in more mundane terms, as it applies to everyone.

Neal: OK. How shall we begin the discussion?

Plato: *(smiling)* At the beginning, of course.

Neal: What do you mean?

Plato: *(clears throat)* Ahem, once upon a time, many eons ago, one of the gods decided to amuse Herself by creating a so-called World in which She could fragment Herself into many so-called parts that would not remember their identity as Divine. Now these "parts" – little sparks of Divinity that did not know themselves – thought they were mere bodies.

Benedict: Here we go again! Well, I suppose by now there is no need to remind ourselves of the non-literal use of language, and all that.

Plato: And should I be unnecessarily sloppy in my non-literal use of language, Benedict, you are welcome to mop up after me.

Benedict: *(laughing)* I'm afraid that would be a full-time job. Proceed with your story, my friend.

Plato: Thank you. Now at first the Goddess was a bit frustrated with her plans, because the "parts" into which she splintered Herself were highly unstable, and perished after just a few days. She then realized that the "parts", in order to be stable, required constant nourishment from their environment. So She recreated the parts, this time encoding in their very being an irresistible desire for food and drink. She programmed them such that whenever the desire was satisfied, they felt pleasure; otherwise, pain. This seemed to work for a while and the Goddess was initially satisfied with Her creation. But soon enough other problems became manifest.

Neal: What do you mean?

Plato: Well, although the "parts" lasted more than a few days, they still wore out after 80 or 90 years, and so she had to keep creating the parts by Herself. And we must remember that 80 or 90 years, while it seems like a substantial length of time from the human perspective, is a mere infinitesimal flash from the perspective of the Goddess.

Well, after consulting with various other Deities, some of Whom had tried this experiment before, She realized that She could reprogram the "parts" so that they would recreate themselves in perpetuity, so as to constitute an organic species. But in order to free Herself from the task of having to create human bodies by Herself, the desire to recreate the form of the body, in a word, the human desire for sex, must be so strong, so deeply rooted that, as Benedict here would say, the human being can neither be nor be conceived without the desire for sex. So both (i) the desire to persevere and flourish in a given form (the body), and (ii) the desire that bodies perpetuate themselves in time so as to constitute a species, must be profoundly hardwired into each and every human being. These desires in human beings (for food and sex) are necessary in order that there be a human species, and the pleasures that arise from satisfying these desires we may call "necessary pleasures".

Benedict: *(teasingly)* – And is your Goddess satisfied with what She has made?

Plato: *(laughing)* Well, on the one hand, how could anyone, even anyOne, be satisfied with a species of amnesiatic beings whose forgetfulness causes them to run around like chickens without a head? On the other hand, the Goddess is in the eternal order, where everyone is always satisfied.

Benedict: OK, I propose that now we leave your Goddess to Her own Enjoyment, and take from your story the literal truth that the desires for food, drink, and sex are absolutely necessary for human beings. The satisfaction of these desires brings pleasure both to the body and the associated consciousness. The non-satisfaction of these desires brings pain both to the body and the associated consciousness or mind.

William: Putting the matter this way, it is quite obvious that to harbor any negative views towards sexual pleasure is as ridiculous as harboring negative views towards the enjoyment that comes from eating food. It is ridiculous to be "against" what is in any case necessary. But I think this analogy we are making between our two necessary pleasures will lead to a very interesting discussion.

Neal: What do you mean, Will?

William: With respect to the appetite for food, we have raised our children in such a way that their subjective sense of what tastes good and pleasurable is aligned with what is good and healthy for their bodies. And even though not all children like the same foods, there is a sufficient variety of healthy foods available so that every child and adult will find plenty of foods that are to their liking. The expression "junk food" will have disappeared from usage, since that which poisons a child's body will not be called "food". The pastry chef, although not completely banished, will be under the control of the guardians. The particular form of cultural insanity, according to which it is OK to profit by causing children to become addicted to sugar, salt, and fat, will no longer exist. A child, we maintain, can be raised to salivate at the thought of eating a green salad instead of salivating at the thought of eating candy or cake. But there is something we must add about food and the pleasures and health benefits associated with consuming it.

Neal: I think I can see where you are going.

William: Yes, it is not just the food itself that nurtures the body, but equally important is (i) the manner of preparation, and (ii) the manner of consumption.

Plato: Good. These two are involved both with respect to the nutritional value of the food, and also with respect to the pleasure derived from consuming it. The knowledge of food will not be hidden from our children, and they will all know in some detail how what is on their plate came to be on their plate.

Neal: Yes, this is important. In my present society this knowledge is hidden from children, and from adults too. Many children become vegetarians when they learn how the hamburgers they love arrive on their plate. A culture that is ignorant of the sources of what it eats – that is ignorant of what is absolutely necessary for their body's survival – is suicidally sick. So perhaps our children, at some point in their education, will be required to spend some time involved with the production of food, so they will all have firsthand experience.

William: Actually, in our New Society, many more people will work on farms and be involved with the production of food than in your present society.

Neal: Yes, in my present society, the production of food is controlled by corporate monopolies that prevent smaller, independent farms from being able to function. But in the Society under construction, there will be no such monopolies, and many more people will experience the joy that comes from working with the Earth.

William: And the manner of consumption will have to change too. It is an empirical question, is it not, if we ask: what manner of consumption is most conducive to the absorbing of nutrients by the body?

Neal: Let's consider three possible scenarios: (a) a person consumes his meal very quickly, in five minutes or less, (b) a person consumes his meal while mentally distracted by reading or watching television, (c) a person consumes his food consciously, engaging all his senses, and with gratitude for all who have been involved in the growing and preparation of the food under consumption.

William: Although we will wait for our nutritionists to objectively measure how food is absorbed under the various conditions, we suspect that (c) will be the correct answer. And we will add to (c), (d) the food is best absorbed when shared with family and/or communally.

Neal: At the risk of getting ahead of our scientists, it seems that what at first looks like a biological question – concerning the maximal absorption of nutrients by the body – turns out to have social implications.

Plato: Yes, the inner reality of the body and the outer reality of social relations mirror one another. And not only is the biological process of digestion and assimilation greatly facilitated by (c) and (d), but so is the amount of pleasure derived from eating. For under only (a) and (b) – your "American" way of eating – there is minimal attention placed on smelling and tasting the food.

Benedict: And we note that both sensory pleasure and benefit to the body is maximal when attention is focused in the present moment – on the sight of the food in front of them, on the smell and taste of the food while eating, and on the sensations in the body after food has been eaten. So mealtime can be yet another opportunity for the mind to focus in the "Now". And conversation during mealtime can be an opportunity for children to express themselves, to listen attentively to others, and in general to deepen the social bonds among the family members.

Neal: We should perhaps add that by "family members" we do not necessarily mean the biological nuclear family. We said only that each child shall belong to and be raised by a small group of adults and other children who are constantly and continuously in the child's life. The child will bond with this group and vice versa, and they all shall regard one another as "family". Families will also interact with one another so as to constitute larger communities, and this process will extend outward to include the whole world.

Socrates: And getting back to sex, if as Benedict stated, mealtime is an opportunity for the mind to focus in the Now, "sextime", if we may call it that, is an opportunity for the mind to be dragged screaming and kicking, quite literally, into the present moment.

Neal: Huh? What do you mean?

Socrates: We'll develop this theme soon enough, but I think Plato and Benedict want to offer some guidelines for our ensuing discussion.

(The two had been discussing something together.)

2) "Female" and "Male"

Benedict: Yeah, well I'll start. *(With humor)* Actually I wanted Plato to state this since they are mostly his ideas. But he thought this might be an excellent opportunity for me to do a little penance for what I had previously written about women.

William: What had you written?

Benedict: Well, having been raised in a male-dominated society, as were all of us, I asked the question whether male dominance was "by nature" or "by nurture". Every society with which I was acquainted was male-dominated, so I concluded that male dominance is "by nature", for otherwise, so I erroneously reasoned, there surely would be, or would have been, some societies that were female dominated. But Plato, considering the same question, did not just look around at the various societies he knew or had heard about. He looked at the biological natures of women and men and asked whether the present male-dominated social roles were a consequence of their biological natures. And although men and women are biologically different, in that women bear children and men do not, this difference has no bearing on the suitability of women for any and every social role. Plato concluded that his male-dominated social order was out of harmony with nature, and so are all such social orders, including yours.

William: Yes, I understand now, but at the time I certainly would have agreed with you, not Plato. For women – that would be late 19th century American women, to be specific – were physically weaker than men, and much too emotional for civic life. Besides, they were needed to raise the babies and children, which was deemed "women's work". So all the "evidence" seemed to conspire to yield the conclusion that you, Benedict, came to.

Benedict: *(laughing)* And the "evidence" was even more compelling in my time, especially considering the role for Orthodox Jewish women in that culture. It is unnatural to compel biology and spirituality to conform to some given social order.

Neal: What do you mean by "unnatural"?

Benedict: Good question. So, what is natural? The soul of course is our given, what is fundamentally real and natural. The soul, by taking on human form, agrees to limit itself to what is natural for that form. For example, unlike some other life forms, the human body cannot fly, nor can it breathe underwater. The human form also requires constant nourishment from its environment, both physical nourishment and psychological nourishment. These limitations, if one may call them that, are natural to the human form. To consider a ridiculous example, it would be unnatural for any given society to require that people stop eating, or stop having sex, or learn to breathe underwater.

Neal: Most ridiculous.

Benedict: Now consider homosexuality. It appears to be the case that approximately 10% of all mammals prefer same-sex partners. So this is what is natural for the human form too. Is it not equally ridiculous for society to pass laws against homosexual behavior, since sexual preference is determined by nature?

Neal: Yes, I agree.

Benedict: Then what about a society that passes laws forbidding women to develop their full biological and spiritual potential? *(With humor)* The only thing that could be more unnatural than that would be some philosopher who, upon noticing that women who were raised to be inferior to men were in fact inferior to men, concluded that the inferior role of women was biological, not social.

Plato: Ah, Benedict, don't be too hard on yourself. But there is a consequence, hitherto unnoticed, of any social order that limits the possible social roles of women.

Benedict: What do you have in mind?

Plato: This might be difficult for people to grasp, but I'll say it anyway. Any social order that limits the full flowering of females necessarily also limits the full flowering of males.

Neal: Explain what you mean.

Plato: Certainly. Would you prefer an "a priori" explanation or an "a posteriori" explanation?

Neal: Let's start with the latter.

Plato: We are agreed that it is unnatural for a social order to prevent women from developing their talents and abilities and participating in social roles in the same way as men do. There is nothing in a female's biological nature, as opposed to a male's biological nature, by which one could conclude that women are unfit for any given social role, be it medicine, politics, engineering, police, etc... And if it were argued, as it has been for centuries, that men are biologically taller and stronger than women, we reply that this is a statistical truth only; many women are stronger and taller than many men, and some women are stronger than most men.

Neal: Yes, we agree to all that.

Plato: But what does not get considered in these discussions is the harm done to the men. For even if we agree, say, that most women are more nurturing than most men, this is also a statistical truth only, since many men are more nurturing than many women, and some men are more nurturing than most women. Should these men be prevented from participating in the nurturing and raising of children.

Neal: Of course not, at least not in the Society under construction.

Plato: So a social order such as yours, but more so William's, Benedict's, and mine, that regards the rearing of children as "women's work", and prevents nurturing men from participating in caring for children – and no social role is more important than the nurturing and education of our children – is an unnatural social order. It is just as unnatural for a society to limit the natural talents and abilities of souls who embody as male, as it is to limit the natural talents and abilities of souls who embody as female. And you can't do one without doing the other. Shall we explore this for a while?

Neal: Yes, by all means.

Plato: Prior to taking on a body and becoming human, is the soul "male" or "female"? Do differences of gender pertain to the soul itself, or to the soul only insofar as it has become embodied? And if so, how do we define "male" and "female" in the absence of a physical body?

Neal: Before we get into this, should we not heed our previous cautions concerning the use of language to describe what is beyond the physical? And moreover, with all the gender-bending stuff going on these days, it is difficult to define "male" and "female" even with respect to a physical body.

Plato: OK, let's say then that we will use language to characterize, rather than define, the sense in which gender differences pertain to consciousness insofar as it is not embodied. And, as you probably already know, the best representation of gender from the perspective of spirit is not words, but the Taoist "yin-yang" symbol. According to this symbolic representation of gender, (i) male and female constitute a single indivisible whole, and (ii) the male resides deep within the center of the female and the female resides deep within the center of the male.

Neal: Well, this is all well and good, but how does one identify what is "male" and what is "female" when one is referring, not to bodies, but to souls or spirits? Earlier William humorously hinted that sex-change operations were quite easy in the spirit realm, but now I think we must analyze what this means. If you say that the soul is without gender or sex, then it is not difficult to comprehend that a given soul may express itself as female in one life and male in another… that is, in one life its body will have a vagina, in another it will have a penis. But what does it mean to say that the soul itself has gender, and furthermore, what does it mean to say that the soul, without a body, can change its gender?

Plato: *(laughing)* So if we cannot use penises and vaginas as markers, how will we distinguish between "male" and "female"?

Socrates: *(also laughing)* And I'm afraid your penises and vaginas will not work as markers even in the physical world, as your comment above about "gender-bending stuff" shows. For there are many bodies with penises whose inhabitants insist they are female, are there not?

Neal: Yes, and vice versa too.

Socrates: Then to get at gender differences, we must go beyond penises and vaginas.

Benedict: Agreed. So let's go back to the yin-yang symbol, and consider Plato's first point. There is a single indivisible Whole, called by many names. I used words like "God", "Nature", and "Substance"; Plato's names were "The Good" and "The One", and William, identifying the Whole from within the human perspective, called it a "Something More" (than the human perspective).

William: *(with humor)* Now I would refer to it as an "Everything

More".

Benedict: Now, when consciousness experiences itself as this Whole, it is complete and in need of nothing.

Neal: Yes.

Benedict: But as soon as consciousness experiences itself as something less than the totality of All-There-Is, duality sets in, and it then appears to that soul that there are things, like other souls, that are external to itself. The soul will experience, we might say, an environment external to itself.

Neal: Agreed.

Benedict: And do we also agree that individual souls are like individual bodies in this respect: just as every physical body is in continuous interaction with other physical bodies, or in other words, with its environment, so also individual souls – souls that experience themselves as individuated from God – are also in continuous interaction with its environment, namely, other souls or more generally, other structures within the field of God, or Consciousness considered as a Whole.

Neal: Yes, I think I can see where you're going.

Benedict: Then go there for me.

Neal: Anything that interacts with its environment – whether the thing in question be physical or spiritual – must necessarily both (i) act on its environment, and (ii) be acted on by its environment. This is the very meaning of the word "interact". Insofar as it acts on its environment, we will call it "male"; insofar as it receives from its environment, we will call it "female". But this is in the most general terms, for I fear that, as Plato might point out, to state precisely what it is for one structure within the field of Consciousness to act on or receive from another structure within Consciousness is a task beyond the ability of language.

Plato: In my time, unlike yours, it was quite usual and customary to conceive of nonphysical beings as having gender. We talked about the goddesses and the gods. We may raise the question (– but won't answer it here): are there common qualities in virtue of which one group of non-embodied entities are called "goddesses" and the other "gods". One could ask the same question of the Egyptians and the Hindus and all other cultures that differentiate between gender with respect to non-embodied beings. Why was Athena conceived as "female" and Apollo as "male"? Thinking about this might give some sense, to humans, of gender differences with respect to spiritual beings. But we need not go into this here.

Neal: Well one thing that I would like to investigate a little more, with respect to the yin-yang symbol, is the sense in which each gender contains its opposite within the heart of its very being.

Plato: *(with a little humor)* So you want to know in what sense you, who think you are male, have the female principle at the core of your being.

Neal: Yes.

Plato: And with Benedict's permission, may we use language imprecisely?

Benedict: Permission granted.

Plato: Even very imprecisely?

Benedict: *(laughing)* Don't push your luck, but go for it.

Plato: Thanks. OK, so in what sense, you ask, is the female principle contained at the core of the maleness you take yourself to be?

Neal: Yes, I ask.

Plato: Do you agree with the following statement: the soul that now appears to be expressing itself as you (but in Reality is sitting up here with us) has expressed itself as many other individual beings.

Neal: Yes, of course. This is the theme of reincarnation.

Plato: And some of these other individual beings, or past lives, are female and some are male?

Neal: Yes, I accept that the soul of which I am an expression has expressed itself both as male and as female many times.

Plato: Then where are all these past lives right now?

Neal: I don't know. In the soul somewhere? Ah, wait, Benedict and I have discussed this before. The soul is not in the temporal order, hence my so-called "past lives", if they are in the soul, cannot be in the temporal order either.

Plato: Good. We may accept reincarnational theories, but not the common implication that one's past lives are in the past and hence over with. For what humans refer to as "past" and "future" have no reality over and above the present particular thoughts and images occurring in the human mind. Only the eternal NOW exists, and thought that references past or future is occurring NOW. Well, we don't need to belabor this point. You identify as male, yet you exist within an indivisible mental structure called the soul, and the very soul that has created you also contains within itself many female elements that you sometimes refer to as "past lives". Since the soul is the center of your being, so are the female elements, which continuously affect and influence you. And this is true for everyone. Alright, Benedict, what's so funny?

(Benedict had been smiling, and seemed to be holding back some laughter. When Plato noticed, Benedict laughed out loud and said…)

Benedict: Now just look at who is trying to use language to describe what cannot be described by language.

Plato: *(also laughing)* Hah! Well I did warn you that I was going to be very imprecise in my use of language. Language, as we well know, is a temporal affair, most unsuitable for describing the eternal order.

Neal: Nevertheless, as you once said, language can perhaps be used to tell a "likely story". Our discussion of the Taoist symbol, and opposite sex "past lives", perhaps gives some sense to the notion that gender differences pertain to the nonphysical as well as to the physical.

Plato: But I think I am persuaded by Socrates that language cannot even tell a "likely story" about the eternal order.

Neal: Why, or rather, how did Socrates convince you of that?

Plato: To call a story "likely" is to suggest that it might be true. Do you agree?

Neal: Yes, of course. This is what the word "likely" means.

Plato: But can any story, told in words, about the eternal order, be literally true?

Neal: No, of course not. Oh, I see. To call a story that has no chance of being true "likely" is perhaps a misuse of language. But perhaps we can retain the term in the sense that a shadow or image has some "likeness" to that of which it is a shadow or image.

Plato: Perhaps. And so once again we reiterate the point that when we use language to say something about the nontemporal, eternal order, we are not intending to be literal or descriptive. We are using language to point to something beyond language.

Socrates: And what is it that language can point to that is beyond language?

Plato: It points to the knowledge and understanding that already exists within the soul of the time-bound human.

Socrates: OK. Now then, enough of this pointing around, and let's return to our discussion of sex. In particular, I would like to resume our discussion with the statement Benedict made a little while ago. The statement was, "It is unnatural to compel biology and spirituality to conform to some given social order." We gave a few examples. It is unnatural for a social order to forbid women from developing their skills and abilities, or in a word, from expressing their "masculine" side, and it is equally unnatural for a society to forbid men from expressing their "feminine" side. We hold the contrary, that the social order must be constructed on the basis of what is "natural" to both spirit and biology.

Plato: The mature human being, we might say, is a product of several levels of causal influence. The most important is the spiritual; that alone is Real. The soul, for reasons internal to itself, desires to manifest in human form, and agrees to allow itself to be limited by that form. However, once in human form it still needs to be raised, educated, "socialized", if you will, in order to become a mature human being. Now it is commonplace to say that there are many ways by which a newborn baby, or fertilized egg, may be raised or socialized. The particular way we are choosing to raise our children will be in harmony with the soul's original purpose and what is spiritually natural, and also in harmony with what is biologically natural.

Neal: I understand that by "biologically natural" you mean the desires for food, drink, and sex.

Plato: Yes, and also death. This is a good example of how your present social order rejects what is both spiritually and biologically natural. For it is natural for the body to die, and it is natural for the embodied soul to desire to return Home, especially if it is living a long life. A healthy social order must be in harmony with what is natural to spirit and body. In fact we may boldly state that no social order that has ever existed has been in harmony with what is natural to spirit.

Neal: I see your point. For that which is most natural to spirit is Love, Unconditional Love, and no society other than the one we are now constructing has been predicated on the Golden Rule, or Unconditional Love towards each and every member of our Society, including, especially, one's self.

Plato: And now, what about the body? What do we say is "natural" for the body?

Neal: The desires for food, drink, and sex are natural for the body. And we also stated that the desires to play, run around, and cuddle, are also natural for the body. And this is true for all mammals, not just humans.

Plato: Hence a social order that passed laws prohibiting children from running around, playing, hugging and cuddling would be an unnatural social order.

Neal: Yes, most unnatural.

Plato: And what about a society that refrained from passing such laws but nevertheless made children feel very guilty for desiring to hug one another?

Neal: A most neurotic society indeed. The impulse to hug and cuddle is not only biological, in that the body needs cuddling in order to flourish, but it is a reflection of the spiritual impulse to manifest love. A society that makes children feel guilty for harboring such impulses is a society that aims to defeat what is natural to both the spirit and the body. Inducing guilt, we may note, is a far more effective way of controlling behavior than passing laws.

Plato: Then what do you think about a social order that taught its children that sex is bad, or sinful, or even unspiritual? Or that sex, although necessary for reproduction, is otherwise ungodly, and that it is wrong to desire it, to seek it, to derive pleasure from it?

Neal: This would be a most dysfunctional social order, with most unhappy people.

William: And yet, it is our own, perhaps more so mine than yours. But the guilt people have been made to feel about their natural sexual desires, even in your present time, and even with all the acting out going on, is enormous. A society in which most people feel guilty most of the time is a recipe for much dysfunction.

Plato: May we state then, as a general principle, that any social order that induces feelings of guilt with respect to natural bodily functions is unnatural. The social order must adapt to biology, not vice versa.

William: Agreed.

3) A Social Order In Harmony With Biology

Plato: Then may I suggest, before we educate our children with respect to sexuality, that we follow the darker path of your present sex-denying society, to see in some detail how this darker path causes humans to add a layer or two to their "margins", and prevents them from a fuller expression of their essence.

Neal: We can follow the darker path for a while, but only to eventually contrast it with the lighter path of our New Society.

Plato: Fine. Until now, we observe, almost all social orders have followed the darker path, in that they attempt to force biology to conform to preconceived ideas about how people "should" relate to one another. The darkness is especially strong when religion is involved, leading to such absurdities as the belief that God does not want humans to enjoy sex, and that abstinence from sex earns one brownie points in Heaven. On one level this is an absurd and comical teaching; but on another level it has done incredible psychological and spiritual damage to individuals who have internalized this or similar belief systems. Yet people who have been raised in such a social order, which is the "norm", are not likely to fully grasp how much they have been harmed. Sexual repression constitutes the third visit to the River of Forgetfulness.

Neal: I suspected that the soul's third visit to the River would involve sex.

Plato: Let's recapitulate the River metaphor. Or was it a simile?

Benedict: Or an analogy, or allegory? *(Smiling)* You and your figures of speech.

Plato: *(also smiling)* Indeed. Well, whatever, whether simile or metaphor, the soul's descent into material form begins with its first visit to the River of Forgetfulness. The first visit causes the soul to identify with a body, and to lose the knowledge of its true identity as a holy thought in the Mind of God. It must forget that it is spirit if it is to have a human experience. The second visit involves the learning of language, which causes the soul to identify with the words floating through its mind, so that the resulting consciousness becomes focused mostly in thoughts and words, which then mediate perception and emotion. Although it is necessary to learn language, it is not necessary that language absorb the whole of a human being's consciousness. Our methods of child-rearing, emphasizing emotional intelligence, sensuous expression (massage), music, and other forms of non-linguistic conscious experience that focus the mind in the present moment, will go a long way to reduce the harmful effects of language on the mind. The third visit…

William: Wait a minute. Let's state or restate what we mean when we refer to the "harmful effects of language on the mind".

Plato: OK.

William: Thanks. I'll be brief. The first harmful effect of language on the embodied mind is the tendency of language, once learned, to absorb the whole of embodied consciousness into itself, so that the person experiences herself as merely a stream of thoughts, or worse, a stream of words. And as you mention, we strive to mitigate these tendencies through our methods of child-rearing. The other harmful effect of language is the use of language to lie, hide, and conceal. Psychologists do not yet realize how traumatizing this is to the child, whose consciousness, straight from Heaven we might say, has no model for lying and deceit. When small children first discover that their parents and other adults lie, the effect is very traumatic for the child, a trauma that remains deep within his being, even after he has "matured" and is able to use language to lie himself. For lying is always a violation of trust, and in a society of liars, there can be no trust. And by using the term "lying" I mean not only with respect to what happens in the outer world, but more importantly, using words to conceal from others one's true thoughts and emotions. But in our New World Order, which we are assuming is "in place" for our children, adults will not lie, so our children will have no role models for concealment and deceit.

Neal: So we might state, I suppose, that although our children will still have to return to the River of Forgetfulness, they will need to drink much less on their second visit. Thus our children will not be traumatized by the use of language to hide and conceal their inner lives, and when they mature, their margins will be considerably thinner. I assume, Plato, that the third visit to the River will be avoided altogether in our New Society.

Plato: *(smiling)* Yes, but first we need to go into some detail about what it is our children will be avoiding. The harm done to children by your present culture with respect to their natural sexual feelings is truly horrible, greatly thickening the margins that separate, or appear to separate, the embodied human from its Source. And not just your present culture, but just about every culture that exists and has existed has tried to impose ideological and unnatural restrictions on the expression and experience of sex. Until now, social orders have been most concerned about perpetuating themselves; they are concerned, not with what is best for the children, but rather with what is best for insuring that the children will perpetuate the beliefs and behaviors of the society, even if the latter be very harmful for the children.

William: *(sarcastically)* Well, I suppose if you want a capitalist social order that values nothing more than it values greed and personal ambition, you must alienate the children from their own inner knowing as much as possible, so that they will look only to what is outside themselves for approval and contentment.

Neal: Whereas we are raising our children so that they will look within themselves for approval and contentment. *(To William)* Since things were worse in your times than in mine, perhaps you should begin our discussion of how our culture uses sex to alienate children from their own inner knowing.

William: OK. So we imagine two-year-old little Johnny (or Suzie) exploring his body and discovering his genitals and discovering that touching them brings delightful sensations of tingling to that area of his body. He knows that touching his penis feels good. Now enter Mommy or Daddy, who themselves have been taught and believe that sex is bad or sinful. Mommy tells Johnny to stop touching himself, that it is bad, wrong and sinful to do so, and may even cause blindness. If the parents are religious – and almost all of them were religious in my time – they might say to their children that God is angry with them for touching their genitals, and if they do it again, God just might send them to hell for all eternity. And so the child, because his very survival depends upon his parents' approval, has no choice but to internalize their beliefs, and to call "bad" what both feels good and is good.

Plato: Ah…

William: Yes, I know what you're going to say. That there is a difference between what feels good and what is good, and it is quite possible for something to feel good that in fact is not healthy for the body. But that is certainly not the case with sex. Just wait. Physiologists and neuroscientists will soon enough discover and document in detail that when little Suzie is stimulating her genitals, not only do the sensations feel good, but the overall effect is very healthy for the developing brain.

Plato: *(smiling)* Good. You see, we have devoted considerable effort in raising our children to align their subjective sense of what *feels* good with objective measures of what *is* good and healthy for the body. We have aligned their sense of taste with what is healthy for the body, so that they will never desire to put in their mouths "foods" that are harmful to their body. Similarly, with respect to music, our neuroscientists will have studied in detail the effects of various sounds on the developing brain, and our children will be exposed only to music and sounds that benefit the body, and hence they will not be craving sound sensations that are harmful to the body. Much of the "noise" inherent in your current way of living will disappear, since humans are naturally attracted to harmonious sounds.

Benedict: And we must remind ourselves that we are raising our children with an eye towards what is best for the body, rather than what is best for some dysfunctional social order to perpetuate itself through infecting the minds of its children with life-denying ideologies, such as that there is something "sinful" about natural biological desires. And we are taking some of our cues from the nonhuman animal world, because animals are not conditioned to have unnatural desires, that is, desires that run contrary to their biological nature. This is what we did when we noted that the young of all mammals chase, wrestle, and cuddle. We stated that these are biologically programmed behaviors for mammals, and that our social order will encourage such behaviors, not stifle them. The first two, chasing and wrestling, lead naturally to gymnastics and sports as the children mature, and the third leads to massage, bodywork, and other forms of touching.

Socrates: Yes, now these "other forms of touching" – does that include sexual touching?

William: *(laughing)* You know it does. And your question is actually somewhat ambiguous.

Socrates: What do you mean?

William: On one reading, the phrase "sexual touching" could refer to the direct touching and stimulating of genitals. On another reading, it could refer to any sexual feelings that occur while one is being touched. One could experience sexual feelings while receiving a foot massage, for example. In fact, one can experience sexual feelings without being touched at all.

Neal: I recall that a while ago one of us (I think it was me) raised the possibility that our children might become sexually aroused during massage. But now I see that this is something to be concerned about only in a culture that practices sexual repression. Humans are sexual beings from day one, and our New Society will embrace this fact, not fear it.

William: Actually, humans are sexual beings even before day one.

Neal: Huh?

William: Sure. *(Laughing)* And don't we even have the ultrasound photos to prove it!

Neal: *(also laughing)* Yes, we have photos of little Johnny in the womb with a big erection. And although it's more difficult to observe with little Suzie, we must assume that she feels sexual stimulation in the womb too, since the male sexual apparatus develops from the female.

Plato: So we will say that sexual desires and feelings are hardwired into the body. And just as the soul, prior to incarnating, fully understands and accepts the body into which it is incarnating, so also, our New Society will be built around what is natural to the body, as well as to the spirit.

Neal: I understand that what is natural to the body includes desires for food, drink, movement, cuddling, and sex. What is natural to the spirit?

Plato: Unconditional Love. Does not the Near-Death Experience conclusively demonstrate that the natural condition of the soul – by which I mean the condition of the soul when it is not embodied – is one of Unconditional Love, and that our Social Order, through its adherence to the Golden Rule, strives to maximize this Unconditional Love through all of its institutions?

Benedict: But in order that even a pale shadow of Love manifest into the physical realm, the society into which a given soul is incarnating must fully and joyously embrace all the desires and pleasures of the body.

William: Yes, I can see it all clearly now. You see, in a social order such as mine, we were all deeply conditioned to feel guilt with respect to both sexual desire and sexual pleasure. The conditioned guilt in the first place prevented us from experiencing the full depth of joy possible, and in the second place, added a rather thick layer to the margin that separates, or appears to separate, the spiritual realm from the physical realm. Hence the Unconditional Love that is the birthright – ah, I mean "creation right", since souls are created not born – of every soul cannot easily penetrate the layers of guilt caused by social sexual repression.

Neal: And yet there is even a further thickening of the margins. In addition to being conditioned to associate the emotion of guilt with natural sexual desire, the child "learns" that she cannot trust her own inner knowing. For if touching her genitals is "bad", if what feels good really is not good, then she cannot trust her own body. And by extension, she cannot trust her own judgment about anything, since nothing is clearer to a child than the sensations of her own body. And if these sensations that feel so good are "wrong" or "bad", and cannot be trusted, then nothing else within themselves can be trusted, and the children are thus trained to always look outside of themselves for any sense of what is good or bad, right or wrong.

Plato: And this, as I remarked long ago, is the opposite of what education should achieve. Education, if it is worth anything, must constantly direct the child's attention to her own inner knowing, not to outer authority. By blocking the child's access to her body's native intelligence, which of course includes the necessary sexual desires and their consequent pleasures, your society effectively blocks the child's access to her own inner knowing. It is little wonder that after being thus alienated from their own body with respect to sexuality, they are alienated from their own body in every other way as well. The symptom of this is that adults as well as children are not able to "hear" their body's messages and promptings about what to eat or how much to eat. Neither can they hear their body's urging for movement and exercise. And my goodness, worst of all is that many people in your culture are so alienated from the natural rhythms of their body that they don't even know how to fall asleep without using drugs. One would think that such a society would have imploded long ago.

Neal: Well in a way we did implode, and are imploding. Between William's time and mine, we humans murdered well over 100 million members of our own species. Sexual abuse of children is rampant, and no social order that so abuses its own children can survive for long. And it does not take very much intelligence to see that a social order that selects for the motivations of greed and personal ambition must necessarily self-destruct, because as you have shown, once the greedy and ambitious have devoured all the resources of society, they will turn upon themselves and devour one another. We are also – how's this for imploding? – knowingly destroying the Earth's ability to sustain human life. That is, we are now in the process of collectively committing suicide.

Socrates: OK, calm down, my friend. *(Regarding me with an expression of compassion mixed with humor and a bit of mischief…)* Recall what Benedict once said, or wrote, to the effect that the part of the mind that "perishes" with the death of the body is "of no consequence" compared with the part that "remains". The part that perishes is of course the ego or personality or *(to me, with much humor)* in other words, that which you presently take yourself to be. By analogy then, should the World Soul no longer be able to manifest on Earth, the part of human collective consciousness that is destroyed with the planet will be "of no consequence" compared with the part that survives.

Benedict: *(to me, pointedly)* For never forget that the World Soul, in which you live and move and have your being, is so Magnificently Real that its Earthly manifestation is but a pale reflection. And it will indeed be of no consequence to the World Soul, nor to all the individual souls contained within the World Soul, if this human experiment were to fail.

Neal: I understand. At least I understand while I am discussing these things with you guys, but from my present embodied perspective, which I agree is quite limited, it is easy to get depressed about all this.

(Everyone laughs.)

Benedict: Well that's the point, is it not? Insofar as you communicate with us, you understand. Insofar as you understand, you cannot be depressed or otherwise unhappy.

William: *(playfully)* And communicating with us has not been smooth or easy, has it? You have had to overcome all your negative cultural conditioning about communicating with non-embodied individuals. It was quite challenging for us at times, especially initially, just getting you to sit down at your desk and listen to us. We even had to go through a medium to get your attention.

Socrates: Oh yes, but that was such fun for us, to watch your reactions to the whole process.

William: Now, unlike you, our children will have no problem communicating with non-embodied spirits, since the process will be completely normalized in our new society. Mediums and psychics will be everywhere, but more importantly, children will not be estranged from their own "inner knowing" which includes communications, verbal and visual, from beyond the margins. So because our children will be regularly communicating with spirit, they will understand, and because they understand, they will not feel depressed. But returning to the children of our dysfunctional society – yours and mine, Neal – it is clear, is it not, that the process of alienating children from their own bodies also alienates them from spirit.

Neal: Yes, for whatever prevents impulses from the body, such as sexual desire, from reaching the consciousness of the embodied mind will also prevent impulses from Spirit from reaching the level of conscious perception. But there is something else our culture does to repress sexuality that adds a bit of thickness to the margins.

William: What is it? Oh wait, I see it. It was much worse in my times than in yours, but it is still yet another unnecessary obstacle that our societies place in the path of biology.

Benedict: What are you two talking about?

William: I suppose we could say that we are talking about delayed gratification, or the time difference between (i) when the body is biologically ready for overt sexual experience, and (ii) when the social order dictates that sexual behavior is appropriate. The body is ready for sex at the age of 13 or 14. Society demands that natural sexual desires may not be acted upon until marriage, which in my time was late teens to early twenties for women, and early to mid-twenties for men.

Socrates: My goodness, this is truly horrible. What, according to your societies, are young men in the prime of sexual power supposed to do?

William: Ah, they are supposed to sublimate their sexual energies and channel them into socially productive activities.

Neal: *(sarcastically)* ... Such as greed, personal ambition, and the various competitive games men play against one another, much to the detriment of both their personal happiness and social well-being.

Socrates: Well then, shall we ask the question: how much time should elapse between when the body is biologically ready for direct sexual experience (I say "direct", because our children will be having indirect sexual experiences all their lives) and when our children will be permitted by our Social Order to have sex with one another?

Plato: We must again remind ourselves that we are constructing our Society with a view to what is best for our children. We are not seeking to preserve any aspects of your current social order. So if William here tries to come to the defense of the society in which his personality manifested, and says something like, "ten or twelve years is about right, for it takes about that long for a young man to learn a skill or profession, and to find a good wife for himself", our reply will be...

William: *(with humor)* Since you put those words in my mouth, let me at least reply to them. Ten or twelve years of enforced sexual abstinence is necessary to produce the kind of male individual (i) who happily participates in the mass murder of over 100 million human beings (between my times and Neal's), (ii) who rejoices in the suffering of those less fortunate than himself (the sociopath Wall Street bankers and corporate CEOs, and (iii) has no regard or concern for the destruction of the Earth's ability to sustain human life. This is what sexual repression has produced. Again, we repeat that the institutions of the culture under construction, including marriage, are secondary to biology.

Socrates: And Spirit as well. Unconditional Love is natural in the Spirit World, so our Society will be based upon the Golden Rule and other forms of this Love. And what Plato has called the "necessary desires" are natural to the world of physical form. The body *must* desire food, drink, and sex. Our Social Order will be predicated on what is natural to both the Spiritual and the Physical realms. And as we have said, it is the "creation right" or "existence right" of every soul, embodied or not, to feel unconditional love, and it is the birthright of every embodied soul to experience all the joys and pleasures associated with embodiment.

Neal: We agree, but let's get back to your question regarding how much time should elapse between when the child is biologically ready for sexual activity and when they shall be permitted to engage in sexual activity?

Socrates: *(mischievously)* And a most ridiculous question it is!

Neal: Huh?

Socrates: Sure. Just consider the other necessary desires. Suppose a child feels hungry and we ask, how much time should elapse between when the child feels hunger and desires food, and when he is allowed to satisfy that desire?

Neal: Why no time at all.

Socrates: What about thirst and the child's desire for drink?

Neal: That should be satisfied as soon as the desire arises.

Socrates: And what about the child's desire for warmth and shelter when the weather is cold?

Neal: Again the desire for warmth and shelter should be satisfied as soon as it arises.

Socrates: And what about the desire to pee and defecate, desires that although not usually associated with pleasure are nevertheless absolutely necessary for the body to exist. Shall our children be taught delayed gratification with regard to these desires?

Neal: Of course not. They would soon perish otherwise.

Socrates: And what about the other desires of the body – to sneeze, cough, scratch an itch – shall we teach our children that these desires may not be satisfied until they have reached some arbitrary age.

Neal: Come on now, you are being ridiculous.

Socrates: But am I being any more ridiculous than a culture that forbids its children from satisfying their sexual needs until they have reached a certain age?

Neal: Apparently not.

Plato: For if we accept (i) that sex is a natural biological need of the body, and (ii) that culture must follow biology, not the other way around, then it seems to be the case with regard to sex, as I once remarked is the case with respect to women's role in society, that the present social order is out of harmony with what is natural for human beings.

William: But what if…?

Neal: What if what?

William: Yes, well I was about to make an objection when I realized that the objection was merely my culture – the one in which I was raised – speaking through me.

Benedict: I think we might want to hear the "objection" anyway. It is very important that we avoid the error I committed shortly before quitting my body.

Plato: OK, Benedict, first you restate the error you have in mind, then William will state his "objection", or "non-objection", as the case may be.

Benedict: You want me to repeat what I just said?

Plato: Yes, for we wish to forestall any objection that would point to past and present social orders as a "reason" why humans cannot live according to the Moral Law.

Benedict: OK, well as we have discussed, when I was considering the role of women in society, I looked around and could find no social orders, past or present, in which women ruled. I erroneously concluded from this that women are "by nature" (rather than "by nurture") inferior to men and hence biologically unfit to hold positions of social and economic responsibilities. My female past lives have been teasing me about this error for centuries. But Plato, considering the same question, examined it from the perspective of biology, not from the perspective of any existing social order. He concluded correctly that there is nothing in the biological differences between the sexes that would prevent women from holding any social/professional position that men hold. He further concluded that any social order that excluded women from such roles is opposed to what is biologically natural. So even if every society that has ever existed is male-dominated, that fact is not relevant to Plato's argument with respect to the role of women in society. That "fact" merely indicates that no existing social order is in harmony with what is natural. So even if every society that has ever existed has forbidden children from having sex until they reach a certain age, or until certain social obligations (like marriage) have been met, we cannot use that "fact" to argue or justify that practice. There is no purely biological argument against children expressing themselves sexually as soon as they are able.

William: And much psychological harm is done to children by forcing them to delay gratification for so many years after sexual maturity. The objection I was going to make – and now a second objection has come to me – commits this naturalist fallacy. The "fallacy" here assumes that what is "usual and customary" for a given culture is biologically determined. So the first objection is, or rather was, that if we allow our children to run around having sex with each other, then that's all they will ever be doing, and they will neglect their studies and trainings that are necessary for them to take positions of social responsibility.

Neal: And our response here is that we are not raising our children to adapt to, or fit in with, your society or my society or any society that exists or has existed. If we were raising our children to fit in with a social order that is ruled by greedy, criminally insane sociopaths, then by all means, deny them any outlet for their natural, biologically determined sexual needs. Moreover, it does not follow that our children will neglect their studies because they are having sex. The very opposite might be the case. Their studying might come easier to them because their natural biological needs *are* being met. What's your second objection?

William: Here it is: just because children become sexually mature at 13 or 14 years of age, that doesn't mean that they are emotionally mature. Everyone knows that children are not psychologically mature until much later, 18 or 21, and so cannot handle the emotions of a sexual relationship until then. That's why our present society generally forbids sexual relations among children.

Neal: *(sarcastically)* So it is to protect the delicate emotional sensibilities of the children that our society prevents them from experiencing sex when they are ready for it. Against this we may say that our children, by the time they are 13, will be more emotionally mature than the great majority of adults either of your culture, William, or mine.

Plato: Or of any other culture that has ever existed. For unlike any culture that has ever existed, our children are able to know and express their emotions and desires, they are able to receive the emotions and desires of others, and they know that the source of their own happiness comes from within themselves, not from winning competitive games that pit children one against the other. Adults in your culture are unable to do any of these, unless they have had extensive therapy and/or a spiritually transformative experience.

Socrates: And, Neal, we want to affirm your speculation above.

Neal: What speculation?

Socrates: That it will be much easier for our children to study and train for vocations than it is for yours.

(I can feel Socrates warming up to something.)

4) Teaching Sexual Exploration To Children

Socrates: Yes, I'm warming up to the opportunity to present something in my usual manner.

Neal: What do you mean?

Socrates: Surely you know by now. Here goes: Let us imagine Johnny and Suzie, aged 13 or 14, taking algebra together. The teacher is talking about the Pythagorean theorem, and Johnny is trying to pay attention but cannot avoid noticing Suzie's developing breasts. Suzie is also trying to pay attention to the teacher, but she has a little crush on Johnny, and when she notices a certain bulge in his pants, she gets all warm and tingly inside, and loses all interest in poor Pythagoras. You will agree that this is a scenario that happens every day in every high school?

Neal: Yes, except that children are maturing earlier in these times, so we will have to include junior high school as it were, and push the age down a year or two.

Socrates: OK. Now in this situation, about which adults and teachers are in denial yet which is "usual and customary" for teens and even preteens, are our sexually aroused children able to think about algebra, or any other subject?

Neal: Not very. *(Laughing)* All their blood is going to their genitals, not to their brains.

Socrates: And do we agree that for the embodied human, bodily needs usually take precedence over mental learning? So if a child is hungry or thirsty, he will not be able to concentrate on his studies.

Neal: Yes, until his hunger and thirst are satisfied.

Socrates: And if a child's body needs to pee or poop, should he have to delay gratification for those needs?

Neal: Not at all. When the need to eliminate is strong, no one can think of anything else.

Socrates: And if we should forbid our children from scratching an itch, is this likely to help or hinder their ability to concentrate on algebra?

Neal: An unscratched itch demands 100% of one's attention.

Socrates: And now, as we are imagining, both Johnny and Suzie are itching. How likely are they to be able to pay attention to anything else?

Neal: Not very likely. But surely, Socrates, we cannot allow them to scratch each other in public, in the classroom?!

(Everyone laughs.)

Socrates: No, not likely, but neither will they eat or pee in the classroom. The question is not whether they shall be allowed to orgasm with each other then and there, but whether they shall not be allowed to orgasm together for six or seven years. The point is this: when a society prevents individuals from satisfying a natural biological need, then the minds of those individuals are unable to think of anything other than the satisfaction of those needs. So our hypothesis is, if Johnny and Suzie enjoy a little sex before algebra, or if they know that they will be enjoying one another shortly after algebra, then they will be able to focus their minds on the algebra much better than they are able to do in your present society.

Neal: Yes, so it seems that our conclusion is that children should enjoy sexual relations as soon as they are able, and that all the usual objections that come to mind are objections, one might say, that come only to minds, like mine and William's, that have been conditioned by societies that have been rendered dysfunctional and insane because of sexual repression.

William: Let us state that sexual repression is a major factor contributing towards social dysfunction, but not necessarily the only factor.

Neal: Agreed. And it is agreed that our children will be having sex as soon as they are biologically able, and hence, they will not be compelled to drink from the River of Forgetfulness a third time.

William: And by way of summary, the third visit to the River, required by our cultures, added considerable thickness to the margins that separate, or appear to separate, the embodied realm from the non-embodied realm. The added thickness is twofold: first, by conditioning the mind to associate feelings of guilt with sexual desire and sexual activity, and second, by forbidding children from expressing themselves sexually until a certain age is reached, or other social conditions are met. Indeed, in our new social order, the "social conditions" will be determined by natural biology, rather than the other way around.

Neal: So, to give an example, the present "social condition" that states that children cannot have sex until they are 18 years of age is quite unnatural, and has nothing to do with what is best for the children. The sex laws are incredibly repressive; if an 18-year-old boy or girl has sex with a 17-year-old boy or girl, the 18 year old can be prosecuted and sent to prison. This is a law meant to satisfy adults' sick religious fantasies of childhood "purity", where "purity" – whatever that means to the adults – is associated in their minds with sexual abstinence.

Benedict: There are no mental illnesses more severe than those inspired by religion. In fact, one could argue that this law, or any law that criminalizes sexual activity of teenagers, is itself criminally insane. Insane, because sexual desire is the most natural thing in the world, and it is just as crazy for a culture to forbid sexual activity as it would be to forbid satisfaction of any other bodily need. Criminally, because the psychological toll on children who have no outlet for profoundly powerful needs and desires renders many of them bitter and angry, with a need to take out their frustrations on others, and they become the greedy sociopaths now running your society.

Plato: Yes, you see, their adult personas are forming in the teen years, and in your dysfunctional society, they are forming around extreme frustration due to unmet bodily needs. This "frustration", which can take many forms, lies at the core of the developing personality, and constitutes, we might say, the additional layer of thickness to the margins. And so the adult personality is but a truncated version of what it might have been. But I think we have now sufficiently discussed the role sexual repression plays in generating the dysfunctional society of William and Neal.

William and Neal: Hey! It's not our social order.

Socrates: Oh? I suppose you were just hapless victims?

William: We were too quick to protest. It is certainly not the social order we are constructing for our children, but it is the social order into which our souls manifested and became the personas known by our names. Our personas would have been quite different if we had manifested instead into the society now under construction.

Plato: And speaking of which, there is considerably more to construct. We have discussed in some detail, although many more details could be added, how the present social conditions, in which a pubescent child first experiences the sexual needs of his/her own body, are antithetical to those sexual needs. What shall be the social conditions for our children? What social conditions will be maximally supportive of our children's discovery and exploration of the needs and desires of their bodies?

Neal: I'm not sure what you mean by "social conditions" here. The conditions will of course affirm and support their bodies' needs.

Plato: Yes, of course. But are we just going to tell our 12 and 13 year olds, "Yes, we support your sexuality, now go and play together"?

Neal: Yikes, when you put it that way, hmmm, the only guidance children receive today is wholly negative: (i) don't have sex, (ii) don't get (or get anyone) pregnant, (iii) practice safe sex. But there is absolutely no guidance for, say, experiencing sex in the most positive and joyous way possible.

Plato: Well, but you can hardly blame the so-called adults for this, since they themselves have no idea how to experience sex in the most positive and joyous way possible.

Benedict: And precisely what do you mean when you talk about "the most joyous and positive way"?

Plato: We shall be discussing that soon enough. But first I want to say a few things about how our children shall learn about sex. How shall we teach our children?

William: I'm not sure I understand what you mean by "how".

Plato: That's because you think I must mean something profound. But I mean it in the same sense we would ask concerning any other subject. What is the best way to teach children mathematics? – science? – nutrition? – music? – gymnastics?

William: Hah! In my time it was generally supposed that sex didn't need to be taught at all. It's simply a bodily function that everyone already knows how to do.

Neal: And in my time, we teach the kids a little anatomy, and if they're lucky, also a little about birth control and safe sex.

Socrates: *(mischievously)* So lectures in a classroom but no personal trainers?

Neal: What? Personal trainers?! What are you talking about?

Socrates: I'm talking about the best way to educate our children about sex. Let's go slowly here. Consider the subjects Plato mentioned above, and I will proceed in my usual manner.

William: OK.

Socrates: Suppose we want to teach music to our children. What is the best way to do so?

Neal: Well, we can teach them quite a bit in the classroom, and have them listen to a lot of music.

Socrates: Suppose several of the students wanted to learn to play an instrument, or to become a singer of songs. Would the classroom suffice?

Neal: Of course not. Learning to play an instrument requires an individual teacher, and much practice.

Socrates: And what if the instrument the student wants to learn is singing with her own voice? Would we say to the student that since her voice is a natural part of her biology, that therefore she does not need individual instruction with respect to singing?

Neal: Of course not.

Socrates: So with respect to music, children will need a personal trainer. What about gymnastics? Suppose a boy loves gymnastics and sports. Shall we tell him that, because running and jumping are natural to the body, he does not need any personalized training?

William: On the contrary. Those "natural" muscles and bones of the body need to be trained in the right way, and a personal trainer is absolutely necessary.

Socrates: And what about nutrition? Shall we be satisfied merely to lecture our children about eating a balanced diet?

Neal: No. We want our children to know about the food chain firsthand. They will all have some experience with farming and with preparing foods in ways that are both nutritious and delicious.

Socrates: Some of this can be taught in the classroom, but not everything, and certainly not the most important things. No one becomes any good at cookery by listening to lectures, but rather, much time must be spent in the kitchen under the guidance of an experienced cook.

Neal: Agreed.

Socrates: Now what about science? Can children learn science merely by sitting in their chairs and taking notes?

Neal: Of course not. They must spend considerable amounts of time in the lab, where they are personally supervised by the teacher or the teacher's assistants.

Socrates: And now mathematics. Of all the subjects, perhaps mathematics alone does not require a personal trainer?

Neal: Oh yes it does. Although the body is minimally involved in learning mathematics, the students' written work is examined and monitored individually. A student may be asked to prove a theorem on the blackboard, which she will attempt under the personal guidance of the teacher.

Socrates: Is there any subject or skill that a student can learn without personal supervision?

Neal: I can't think of any. Even games like chess require personal, that is, one on one, instructions.

Socrates: Then what about sex? Of all the subjects, is this the only one that students can master just by listening to lectures and reading books? Or do we insist that sex is like every other human activity, requiring both study and practical experience to master properly? And by the phrase "to master properly" I mean simply that we want our children, and adults too, to experience sex in a way that is maximally beneficial to both body and mind, and that is in harmony with the Golden Rule.

Neal: It is unlikely that sex is different from any other subject that requires both classroom and personal instruction.

Socrates: Remember, we are constructing our new social order with a view to assisting the soul in manifesting its intentions. For the soul, the body is a mere instrument. The instrument is not easy to manage or to keep in tune, so to speak, and requires considerable attention, lest the needs and desires of the body cause the associated consciousness to forget its original purpose in taking on a body. When a bodily need like sex is denied, or not allowed to flourish fully, the mind becomes stuck in patterns of thinking that pertain to that need. So when sexual outlets are denied to teenagers, or adults too for that matter, then the mind of the individual tends to become trapped in repetitive thinking about satisfying sexual needs, and is unable to think about anything else. So if we want to turn our children's heads around, as Plato once said, so that they face the spiritual rather than the bodily, then their bodily needs must be satisfied. Otherwise they will become obsessed with sex, that is, they will not be able to think of anything else.

William: So we are turning Freud's views, and the views of most psychiatrists, on their heads. It is *not* the case, as Freud assumed, that the sexual energy must be repressed in order to have civilization. But it *is* the case that sex must be repressed in order to have the murderous, cruel, and suicidal social order that exists at present. And it is certainly the case that sex must joyously flourish if we are to have a social order in which people are creative, attuned to spirit, and are able to live according to the Golden Rule.

Neal: But how will this work in practice? Will our 12- and 13-year-old children be assigned an individual personal sex trainer? How will the trainers be chosen? Isn't there a danger that the role of sexual trainer will attract pedophiles and other adults who prey on children?

Plato: *(laughing gently, to me)* You must remember, my dear friend, that until you quit your body and more fully join us, your mind – the consciousness that you are now experiencing yourself as being, to put it more exactly – is still under the influence of your cultural conditioning. And so your questions not unexpectedly reflect that influence, at least to some extent.

Neal: I understand the general principle, but not how you are applying it to my questions.

Plato: Let's go slowly. Consider: what does the word "pedophile" mean?

Neal: It refers to an adult who wants to have sexual relations with children.

Plato: And how does your culture define the terms "adult" and "child"?

Neal: An adult is defined as someone 18 years old or older; a child is under 18 years old.

Plato: Now, I won't comment on the fact that this definition refers only to the age of the body, and makes no mention of psychological maturity. But do you agree that many adults are psychologically less mature than many 16-year-old children?

Neal: Hah! Less mature even than temper-tantrum throwing three year olds!

Plato: So some 12- and 13-year-old children are more mature, psychologically, than some adults.

Neal: Yes, I see, so if psychological factors were taken into consideration in determining adulthood, things would be more complex than determination by mere age.

Plato: Correct. And as we have already mentioned, one ridiculous consequence of your culture's definition of sexual maturity at age 18 is that an 18-year-old boy who has sexual relations with his 17-year-old girlfriend is a pedophile, and may be prosecuted as such.

Neal: Yes, it has happened. And I agree it is ridiculous.

Plato: But maybe you think that the term "pedophile" should be reserved for cases in which there is a generation or so age difference between the two?

Neal: Yes, that is what most people think with regard to the term. It is one thing for an 18 year old to have sex with a 16 or 17 year old, but quite another thing for a 30 or 40 or 50 year old to desire sex with a child.

Plato: An older adult should not be interested in the bodies of children?

Neal: Yes, something like that.

Plato: But in your culture, is there not a whole class of older adults who are very much interested in children's bodies?

Neal: Huh?

Plato: *(laughing)* Hint: your culture refers to them as "pediatricians". Do not people who belong to this group of older adults regularly examine, probe, and inspect the bodies of our children from infancy through the teen years?

Neal: Yes, of course.

Plato: And I suppose you regard it as a good thing that there are these older adults called "pediatricians" who regularly examine the bodies of our naked children?

Neal: *(smiling)* I think I lost this argument several lines above. But I'll play my part. Yes, it is a good thing; a very good thing.

Plato: And what is the reason they are not called "pedophiles"?

Neal: Because their intent is only to help the child and monitor his or her health and growth. The pediatrician does not seek sexual relations with the child.

Plato: But when the child reaches 11, 12, and 13, it is OK for the pediatrician to be interested in the child's sexual development?

Neal: Yes, of course. It is the pediatrician's job to monitor all aspects of the child's physical development.

Plato: And so the pediatrician may inspect and examine the child's genitals, in the same way he would inspect and examine the lungs, heart, muscular development, vision, and any other part of the body?

And this is not pedophilia, you say, even though an older adult is touching the genitals of a child?

Neal: No, of course it's not pedophilia, since the doctor is interested only in the child's health and well-being, not in using the child's body for his own sexual pleasure.

Plato: And shall this be our criteria for who is and who is not a pedophile? An older adult who touches a child's genitals for the purpose of satisfying his own sexual fantasies is called a pedophile, but an older adult who touches a child's genitals for the purpose of enhancing the health and well-being of the child is called a pediatrician.

Neal: Oh my, I see something.

Plato: What do you see?

Neal: There will be no adults in the former category.

Plato: Why do you say that?

Neal: Well, we have stressed over and over again that our children's bones will form around the Golden Rule, so the social order in which our children matriculate will contain no adults who derive pleasure by harming others.

Plato: And this is a point worth stressing. We are assuming that our children are being raised in our New Social Order, which is already in place. The adults who are raising our children will themselves have been raised in our New Social Order. Many if not most of the adults in your present social order are simply unfit to raise our children, since they have been irrevocably damaged by their own upbringing. For example, the desire on the part of some of your males to have sexual relations with children who are not sexually mature is a pathology caused mostly by upbringing. The desire to rape, and the association of sex with violence is another unnatural pathology of your culture. Such unnatural desires will not exist in our New Society.

Neal: I understand. It is not easy to judge things by reason, instead of by the way one has been raised.

William: Indeed. So our "knee-jerk" objections to these ideas… a personal sex trainer for children, egads… are not the objections of reason but rather are the objections of one who has been raised in a different culture.

Benedict: And since you have just used my favorite word, I'm wondering if I could interject…

William: What favorite word?

Benedict: Why "reason", of course. We shall be discussing this topic at length soon enough, but it is important to note in passing the difference between (i) responding to something based on reason, and (ii) responding to something based on how one has been raised. The judgment, for example, that it is wrong to teach explicit sex to our children comes from how one has been raised, not from reason. But reason teaches us that the needs of the body – the "necessary desires", as Plato called them – must be addressed in order that the body become a proper tool for the soul.

Neal: Your concept of reason, and Plato's too, is poorly understood in my present culture. They confuse reason with mere cleverness, and do not see that the "man of reason" – let's change that to "person of reason" – desires, as you put it, nothing for herself that she does not desire for all other humans. They do not see that the Golden Rule is a necessary consequence of reason. But as you have said, we shall be investigating these matters soon enough. Shall we now return to our pubescent children?

Plato: By all means. I think I convinced you that an older adult who touches a child's genitals for the purpose of enhancing the health and well-being of the child is called a pediatrician, not a pedophile, and then you noticed that there would be no pedophiles in our new society.

Neal: Yes.

Plato: Now we can do one of two things: either (i) we can bring back our sex therapist from a previous conversation, or (ii) we can send our pediatrician back to school for training in child psychology and sex therapy.

Socrates: Hah!

Plato: What do you mean, "Hah!"?

Socrates: We won't need either of them. The very word "therapy" indicates some problem to be addressed, or fixed. The cultures of these two *(gesturing towards William and myself)* need a ton of sex therapists, but in our culture, sex is not a problem to be fixed; it is a joy that will be encouraged to flourish maximally.

Plato: Yes, of course. We should not speak of sex therapists. A child wanting to learn music or gymnastics, or science, or cookery would learn from individuals who are called "teachers" and "trainers" of that subject. The persons teaching these subjects are not called "therapists", and neither shall we refer to our sexual trainers as "therapists". The point is that the intent and purpose of our sex trainers is the same as the intent and purpose of trainers in every other endeavor: to encourage the flourishing of the trainees. And just like in every other endeavor, the personal trainer takes into account the specific nature and personality of the trainee. I used the term "therapist" to connote that our sex trainers will themselves have the kind of education and personality type that your successful therapists and counselors have. But Socrates is absolutely correct. Sex is not a "problem" that requires "therapy"; it is a bodily function that requires encouragement, development, and the freedom to explore in every respect. What is it, Benedict?

5) Romeo and Juliet: In Love or In Lust?

(William and Benedict had been talking quietly by themselves.)

Benedict: Well, William has been prodding me to resume my role of language police at this point, but I am hesitating because I didn't want to interrupt the discussion.

Plato: *(laughing)* No need to concern yourself about that now, since Socrates has already derailed our discussion, from talking about our children's sexual education, to talking about the words and phrases we should use when talking about that subject. So we may linger with language for a while.

William: Good. *(With humor)* Now I think the need for the language police will become evident if I am allowed to put on my costume again.

Neal: Costume? Oh, you mean that 19th Century Victorian Harvard Professor.

William: Yes, him. It's a bit tight, but I think I can still get into it. *(Aside, to me: While you're wearing the costume, it doesn't feel tight at all. It's only after you take it off that you realize how tight it was all the time, cutting off the flow of knowledge and spiritual energies.)* OK. Now, Mr. Plato, as spokesperson for my culture, I can tell you that your ideas are positively ridiculous. You talk about sex as if it were a mere "bodily function", like eating and breathing and peeing.

Plato: It's not a bodily function?

William: At the lower levels of humanity, where humans blend into the animal nature, maybe it is just a bodily function. But at the higher civilized levels of humanity, where there is an appreciation of beauty and the more noble instincts of our species, we should speak, not of mere bodily gratification, but of love, of caring, of romance, of responsibility and commitment. Is there no difference between sex with a harlot and sex with a person you love?

Socrates: And while you're at it William, you may as well add masturbation…

William: What…?

Socrates: *(laughing loudly)* Or did they not masturbate in your time, William? Perhaps your costumes were too tight?

William: *(laughing so hard that his costume bursts open)* Yeah, well the costumes did not prevent us from masturbating, but they did cause us to feel very guilty about it. And now that my costume has come apart, I can say that it is very important to keep in mind that our children have been raised in such a way that they will have no feelings of guilt around sexual pleasure, or any other pleasure.

Plato: *(smiling)* But let's look at the last thing that Victorian gentleman said, just before his costume burst open.

William: By all means. So, incorporating Socrates' suggestion, and to be very explicit, we consider three cases: (i) orgasm brought about by masturbation, (ii) orgasm with a partner towards whom one feels no emotional connection, and (iii) orgasm with a partner with whom one is "in love", and towards whom one feels caring, responsibility, commitment – the usual emotions associated with what we call a "romantic" relationship.

Socrates: And there's one more way of achieving orgasm that we should mention.

William: What's that?

Socrates: In sleep. What's your expression for that?

Neal: "Nocturnal emission" or "wet dream".

Socrates: ... Which expressions of course do not differentiate between a sexual orgasm and the occasional incontinence of a three-year-old child.

William: Yes, good, for this is a partial response to my character. For orgasms that occur in sleep show that orgasms are a natural bodily function. I believe our physiologists have shown that every human becomes sexually aroused at some point during sleep. So whatever else sex may be, it *is* a natural biological function.

Plato: So let us use the word "orgasm" to describe this natural bodily function, and separate this natural bodily function from any emotional or social attitudes. We can then explore the various possible emotional and social attitudes that enhance and cause this bodily function to flourish maximally. One such condition William refers to under (iii) above, the condition that one should be "in love" with one's sexual partner, or that one should have sex only with people one is in love with.

Benedict: And it is precisely this phrase "in love with" that is problematic, for people who use this expression typically have no idea what they mean.

Neal: So in our role as the semantic cops, the question before us is: how shall we define and use the word "love"?

Plato: We will need to examine this question in some detail.

Benedict: *(with humor)* Good. We get to dance in place for a while.

Plato: *(smiling)* ... But only for a little while. So, William, let us examine the social condition of your time, according to which one should have orgasms only with a partner one is "in love with", the latter expression being undefined.

William: Interesting. The phrases "having sex with" and "having orgasms with" refer to the same activity, but using the word "orgasm" instead of "sex" brings attention to the physiological nature of the activity. So, according to Catholics, a certain physiological function must not be performed unless one intends to have children. According to my era, that physiological function must be held in abeyance until one is "in love with" someone. But we are now constructing the social and emotional conditions based on a free and natural acceptance of human physiology, not the other way around.

Benedict: OK, now let's try to define the expression "in love with", for there is much confusion with regard to this expression.

Neal: I think that both you and Plato have given clear definitions of the term.

Benedict: But our definitions are a little different. We can discuss this later. For now, let us distinguish two possible meanings for the term, and then see which of the meanings best captures the sense of the expression "in love with" when used in a sexual context.

Neal: OK.

Benedict: So one meaning of the phrase "I love you", when used in a sexual context, is "I am sexually attracted to you and I desire to have orgasms with you."

Neal: Yes, this is Plato's sense of the term "love", as a desire for something.

Benedict: But the phrase could also mean something like "I care for you, for your well-being, and desire to help you flourish in your personal life."

Neal: Yes, and problems arise when people think they are using the phrase in the second sense, when in reality they are using it in the first sense.

Benedict: And to avoid such confusions, I wish to suggest that we refrain from using the word "love" in the first sense.

Neal: Then what word shall we use to describe the former case: X is sexually attracted to Y and desires to have orgasms together with Y?

Benedict: How about the word "lust"? We could say, in such a situation, that "X is in lust with Y", or "X is lusting after Y".

Socrates: You see, it is only because your present culture (yours and William's) has become so estranged from the natural sexual function that people have no "polite" word for sexual attraction per se. You have collectively brainwashed yourselves into believing you must be "in love" with someone to legitimize having sexual feelings towards them.

Neal: *(to William)* Yikes, this is going to let some hot air out of our cultural balloon.

William: What do you mean?

Neal: When 14-year-old Romeo says to 13-year-old Juliet, "I love you," he really means, "I am sexually attracted to you." And then all the romance novels and operas – where the hero instantly falls in love with the heroine and vice versa – these stories will have to go. One can "fall in lust" instantly, but it is sheer delusion to believe that "lust" is "love", a belief required by culture to legitimize sexual attraction.

Benedict: But this is the correct form of speaking, is it not. A 14-year-old boy is quite capable of being sexually aroused by a 13-year-old girl. But he is definitely not capable of loving her in a mature way, as she is in herself. *(Jokingly)* Or were adolescent boys exceptionally mature in your times, William?

William: *(laughing)* Adolescent boys in my time were just like adolescent boys in all times. The force of the sexual energy is so powerful that getting laid is their/our chief concern. The so-called religious and moral protestations to the contrary have done considerable harm.

Plato: So the culture now under construction will happily acknowledge the overpowering force and power of the physiological function called "sex". We will not compel our children to hide or conceal their natural sexual attractions to one another, nor shall we disrespect our biology by requiring our children to either "romanticize" or "deify" their sexual attractions. Statements like "she's the only one for me", "I can't live without her", "she is a goddess" are statements of pathology, not of love. Our children will be taught and encouraged to express and talk about their natural sexual attractions, not only with their personal trainer, but also with their peers, in small groups.

Neal: Without bravado, fear, or anxiety, our children will be encouraged to discuss their sexual feelings openly and honestly.

Socrates: Also, we should remember, they have been touching one another since they were toddlers, so sexual touching is a natural extension of what they have been learning.

William: What have they been learning?

Socrates: Yes, that giving and receiving touch both (i) *feels* good, and (ii) *is* good for the health and well-being of both body and mind.

William: Our children will be touching one another sexually?

Neal: This is almost too much even for me, but I can think of no reason why not. After all, between the ages of two and twelve, our children have been taught massage, both giving and receiving. While receiving touch, we have taught them how to focus their minds on their bodily sensations, and this focusing of the mind is a kind of meditation. While giving massage, we have taught them, in addition to various massage techniques, to try to go into the body of the recipient, to feel what the other is feeling. By consciously connecting with the other, our children have learned that it feels good to give pleasure to others. Sexual pleasure, it seems, is but a natural extension of the pleasure they have all their lives become accustomed to through touch. My goodness, our adolescents will be having orgasms all over the place.

Socrates: Imagine that!

William: *(laughing)* I'm trying, but I can't quite wrap my mind around it.

Socrates: Imagine a world in which, because the sexual needs of children are addressed when they are children, there is no such thing as sexual repression, and the multitude of illnesses that are caused by sexual repression, both physical and psychological, no longer exist.

Plato: And let us note three interrelated points: (i) the social order under construction may properly be called a "matriarchy". By the term "matriarchy", I do not mean that our social order will be ruled by women, but rather, it will be ruled by the values traditionally associated with the female side of the male/female polarity. The values, to be specific, are caring, compassion, inclusion, cooperation, and flourishing. The only purpose of our New Society is to facilitate the well-being and flourishing of each and every citizen. And these values are extended to and applied to *every* member of our New Society. Now, although there are very few role models for what such a social order might look like, I think we can state that (ii) sexual activity and pleasure will be integrated into the very fabric of our society.

Socrates: Indeed, I will venture to claim that only in a matriarchal society will males be able to experience the fullness of sexual pleasure. Maximal joy occurs when the outer Yang of the male surrenders to its inner Yin. But what is your third point?

Plato: Yes, the third point is that the problem of *male violence* will have been solved. Male violence is itself a necessary consequence of any patriarchal social order, where the males typically compete for resources, status, and females.

Socrates: And we know, or at least, we should know by now, that the problem of male violence cannot be solved in any of the ways that have been tried in the past: religious authority, laws, rules, punishments. These have all been tried and have failed. What has not been tried is a matriarchal social order in which the children are "having orgasms all over the place", as you so poetically put it. But it is not merely that children will be having too many orgasms to bother with "studying war" or plotting in other ways one against the other.

Neal: What do you mean?

6) Defining the Word "Love"

Socrates: Everyone has experienced differences in the quality, or power, of an orgasm.

Neal: Yes, everything from a little localized thing that may happen in the dream state, to what is called a mind-blowing, full-body orgasm.

Socrates: And is there any upper limit to the latter?

Neal: Huh?

Socrates: If the mind is truly blown, what is left?

Neal: Oh my, I've never thought of it like this. If by "mind" is meant the ego, or what the human being experiences as itself, then if that gets short-circuited, what remains is the Divine Being.

Socrates: Exactly. So sexual ecstasy is a path to the Divine, and it will be the main purpose of our "sex trainers" to show this path to our adolescents. *(Jokingly)* Or did you think that our trainers would merely be leading their students through the positions of the Kama Sutra?

Neal: No, I… Actually, we have not previously said what it is that our trainers will be training the adolescents to do, or to experience.

Socrates: The mechanics of sex they can easily pick up, by experimenting on their own or by discussing with other children and adults. But they need personal training (i) to breathe properly and focus the mind during sexual arousal, (ii) to be able to hold the sexual energy in the body, without needing to rush to orgasm, and (iii) to surrender psychologically to the sexual energy, which is a force greater than themselves, and ultimately, is the force that connects all human beings with one another. This, among other things, is what I learned from Diotima, my Teacher.

(In The Symposium, *Diotima is a priestess who Socrates regards as his spiritual teacher.)*

Neal: Hmm… I heard, but don't recall the details, that a small percentage of both men and women, maybe one or two percent, have reported out-of-body experiences during sex.

Plato: And nothing is more "spiritual" than finding oneself

without a body, as just spirit.

Neal: But what if such states of consciousness can be cultivated… so that what begins as sex ends up as an out-of-body experience?

Socrates: Yes, well this is what our sex trainers are for – not necessarily to induce out-of-body experiences, but to cultivate an attitude of deep surrender, surrender of the human ego to the Divine Being, from which the ego is merely a projection, or "shadow", as Plato would put it. For the first thing our adolescents will learn is that the quality or depth of their sexual pleasure is proportional to their ability to psychologically surrender to *(glancing at William)* a "Something" that is greater and more powerful than themselves.

Benedict: And something else that will be cultivated along with an "attitude of deep surrender" is a sense of deep gratitude for their body's ability to hold and experience such joy and pleasure. And we should hasten to add that one never surrenders to anything other than to deeper layers of one's own being.

William: And our neuroscientists will have much to do here, as they can measure the physiological effects of sexual arousal on the overall health and well-being of the body. I believe that they will find that the state of arousal, or rather, the various degrees of arousal are themselves beneficial for the body, and so it is advantageous to learn to be comfortable with arousal, instead of rushing to throw off the energy in an orgasm.

Plato: Yes, and this is why the males need the females to lead, if they are to experience the joys of sex deeply. The "male" principle, one might say, is to act, to rush towards the goal of orgasm; the "female" principle is to receive, to experience deeply, the sensations of the moment. Our neuroscientists, we predict, will show that maximal benefit to the body occurs when the female principle is honored. The longer our lovers – or should I say "lusters" – are sexually aroused, and the more deeply this arousal is experienced, the more endorphins flow through the body, and so forth. But I want to be clear that I was referring above to the male and female principle. Any actual case is more complicated, as some men embody the female principle more than many women, and vice versa. The female principle, the "yin", calls attention to the aspect of our being that receives from, as opposed to acts upon, its environment. To say that the male must allow the female to lead is simply to observe that to experience sexual pleasure fully one must receive it fully. Instead of rushing to orgasm, the male must learn to focus his awareness on the sensations he is receiving, and to luxuriate in those sensations. This is called "being in the present moment".

Socrates: And practices, the sexual practices, of the "mystery religions" of my time and earlier, will be investigated and revived, for here is where hedonism and spirituality join.

Neal: What do you mean?

Socrates: Consider the two questions: (i) How may sexual activity become a spiritual experience? (ii) How may the pleasures associated with sex be increased maximally? These two questions have the same answer: surrender completely to the sensations of the present moment. Of course, our children will not be able to practice this right away, and it is a practice that is not for everyone, so our children, as they explore all the pleasures of which their bodies are capable, shall be guided towards the delights of physicality, and the natural exuberance of the sexual energies flowing through their bodies. The cognitive understanding of "surrendering" to something greater than oneself will come later.

Benedict: Yet the cognitive understanding to which Socrates alludes is really quite simple. Cognitive understanding or reason comes in varying degrees, and our adolescent children are more capable of such understanding than most of the so-called "adults" in *(to me)* your society.

Neal: Well, they could understand via Plato's manner of speaking, but not your way, by deducing everything from first principles.

Benedict: *(laughing)* Granted. But let's see if we can get some cognitive handle on the term "surrender". For all the various spiritual traditions speak, in various ways, of "surrendering" to the Divine. And we have been using the term in a sexual context, as in "surrendering to the sexual energy". So what do we mean when we use this term? And I have not forgotten that we have not yet decided how we are going to use the word "love".

Plato: Yes, this has been hanging over us for a while, and it is perhaps time to discuss the meaning of that four-letter word that everyone thinks they already understand. We are not of course primarily interested in the meaning of words, especially since we believe that it is humans, not words, that have meaning. So let us discuss the kind or kinds of human experience, to which the word "love" may be properly applied.

William: Hah! Good luck with that. There is no consistency in how humans use that term. From "love of music" to "love of sex" to "love for one's children" to "love of God" to "love of sports" to "love for oneself" to "love of money" to…

Neal: Don't forget to include chocolate ice cream in your list.

William: Yeah, well that's the point. The term appears to have no consistent usage and is applied to anything and everything that humans like.

Benedict: Nevertheless, in all the ways the term is used, I think we will be able to discern several patterns, especially if we do as Plato suggests, and focus on the human experience itself, rather than the objects that may trigger the experience. Generally speaking, I believe we will find that these patterns are in accordance with various psychological scales that attempt to capture human maturity. I'll talk about you, Neal, as an example of the lowest level.

Neal: *(jokingly)* You think there is something "lowly" about loving chocolate ice cream?

Benedict: *(laughing)* Don't think we haven't heard your thinly veiled threats of never leaving your body until you receive assurance that we have chocolate ice cream over here. But yes, what I am calling the lowest level of the use of the term "love" has to do with appetite, or what is pleasurable to the body. Humans use the term "love" in connection with what they "like", with what affects the body with pleasure. Shall we call this usage of the term "appetitive love"? It covers all things that are pleasing to a given human body: food, scents and smells, pleasing colors, massage and sex, music, sports, etc... These are all things that humans enjoy, and to which they typically employ the word "love".

Neal: And this is a completely different usage than, say, the use of the term to describe (i) feelings for one's children, (ii) feelings towards Nature, (iii) feelings for Humanity as a whole.

Benedict: So when you say, for example, that you love your children and also that you love chocolate ice cream, the word "love" is being used in very different ways.

Neal: *(laughing)* To paraphrase Socrates in the first speech he gave to Phaedrus, when I'm done loving the chocolate ice cream, there's nothing left of it. But hopefully, my children fared better than the ice cream.

Benedict: So this sense of the word "love" attempts to capture the human experience of caring for someone or something that is independent of that thing's ability to give us pleasure.

Plato: And these two human experiences, (i) loving what gives one pleasure and (ii) genuinely caring for the well-being of another, are hopelessly and horribly confused in your culture's concept of "romantic love". The great majority of humans in your culture are not sufficiently mature to be able to care for the well-being of another, and mistake the "love" of sexual attraction with the ability to genuinely care for the person one is attracted to. They are very different experiences, which, unfortunately, carry the same name.

Neal: Yes, so when 14-year-old Romeo gets a hard-on while gazing at Juliet's developing body, that hard-on does not give Romeo the ability to care for Juliet's well-being. What he does care for is Juliet's ability to satisfy his lust. But because he has been raised in a culture that stipulates that one must be "in love" with whoever he is sexually attracted to, he is compelled to use the word "love" instead of the more accurate word "lust".

William: So our Romeos and Juliets will be taught to say, not "I am in love with you," but "I am in lust with you." This can happen only in our New Social Order, where sexual experience will be fully normalized and accepted by all. Romeo will use words appropriate to what he is actually experiencing. Perhaps he will say something like this: "My body gets sexually aroused when I look at you, and sometimes even when I am just thinking about you. Let's play together." And Juliet will not have to ask her parents or teachers or friends what she should do. She will simply consider whether her body is getting aroused by what Romeo has just told her.

Neal: And again, body chemistry, although delightful, is not love in the sense of "caring for the well-being of another". Our children will play together without having to fall under the delusion that they are "in love" with one another.

Benedict: So we have described two distinct, but common, human experiences to which the word "love" is applied. The most common by far is to use the term to describe what one believes is the cause of pleasure and the satisfaction of desire. But it is also the case that humans experience feelings of caring that are altruistic, that do not involve the satisfaction of desire, and use the term "love" in this regard also.

William: What would you say to people who think there is no such thing as altruism and that everyone is motivated only by egoic desires?

Benedict: I would say that such people are at a very low level of psychological development, and project their ignorance onto everyone else. Is not a person who has never experienced non-egoic caring a sociopath? Is not that the true definition of a sociopath? Someone who is psychologically incapable of caring for anything or anyone other than himself and his own desires?

Socrates: Well, if we are using terms like "psychological development", should we not state what is the highest psychological development available to a human being? We are agreed on the lowest, I believe.

William: The lowest?

Socrates: Yes, our friends the Wall Street bankers represent the lowest form of Humanity. They "love" only what aggrandizes their physical form, and would deny that any other kind of love exists.

William: Well then, what's the highest?

Socrates: Have you not heard that love pertains to the gods? Consult that passage you were so fond of.

William: Passage? Oh yes, Richard Bucke who had a mystical experience and said that "love" is the force that holds the universe together, or something like that.

Neal: Here's the passage:

> I saw that all men are immortal, that the cosmic order is such that all things work together for the good of each and all, that the foundation principle of the world, of all the worlds, is what we call love, and that the happiness of each and all in the long run is absolutely certain.

Socrates: And not just mystics, but Near-Death Experiencers also report a kind of Unconditional Love that is so powerful they are reluctant to return to their bodies. It seems to me that we should discuss the highest first. For this Love is Unconditional, and has no opposite.

Neal: Yes, and those who conceive of Earthly life as a sort of "school" tell us that this "unconditional love" is what we are here to learn. I have heard stories that in the Life Review one is immersed in Divine Love which then becomes the standard by which one "judges" the success of one's life. How much of this Unconditional Divine Love did the individual radiate into the world while embodied? Very little, for most of us humans.

Plato: Now, now, don't be too harsh on yourself and other humans. We know how difficult it is to even feel this Love while embodied, let alone radiate it into the world.

Benedict: But now, getting back to definitions, as Socrates said, God's Love has no opposite. But what humans call "love" does have an opposite, and is easily turned into its opposite.

Neal: Yes. To consider an example, the divorce rate is around 50%. When the couples were getting married, they said and felt, "I love you," to one another. Now ten years later, in divorce court, they say and feel, "I hate you," to one another.

Benedict: So in our role as the semantic cops, we need to decide whether (i) the word "love" should be used in reference to the Divine, as Unconditional, and as the force that binds all minds together into a single One Mind. Under this definition, Love has no opposite. Or perhaps (ii) we should use the word the way it is currently used, to describe whatever humans like and desire (such as your love for chocolate ice cream), and/or (iii) to describe human feelings of gratitude towards another (such as love for one's parents). Or perhaps (iv) we should continue to use the term without any formal consistency, hoping the context will render the meaning clear.

Neal: We should rule out your fourth option right away, since the lack of consistency in the use of the word is the cause of much emotional difficulties.

Benedict: You mean when humans use the term "love" in its ordinary sense, but falsely believe they are using it in the "Divine" sense?

Neal: Yes. We will bring honesty to our marriage ceremonies, assuming marriage will still exist in our New Society.

Benedict: What do you mean?

Neal: The couples pledge to love one another for the rest of their lives. They believe that when they use the word "love", they are using it in the first sense, (i) above. But actually, until they have experienced the vision of the Unity of all Beings, they are not psychologically capable of loving unconditionally. It would be helpful if humans were honest about this. Unconditional love is a worthy goal of every marriage, but it should not be assumed that the goal has been reached at the very beginning.

Socrates: We are perhaps overlooking something.

Neal: What?

Socrates: You said "unconditional love is a worthy goal of every marriage". I want to suggest two things: (i) other than growing in one's ability to love unconditionally, there is no other goal or purpose for a marriage, and (ii) marriage aside, learning unconditional love is the only truly "worthy goal" of every human endeavor.

Neal: But what are we overlooking?

Socrates: That the whole point to the human experience is for souls to deepen their experience of Divine Love. So it is not a matter of mere semantics of how we shall use the word "love". It is, rather, a matter of constructing a social order that explicitly acknowledges the very purpose and meaning of embodiment, which is to grow in our ability to receive and give Divine Love. Anything that any human does is secondary to this, the soul's goal.

Plato: Divine Love, the "foundation principle" of Creation, is necessarily the background of all things that come into being. But in our social order, it will also be the foreground. Humans will become conscious of the fact that this, the capacity for Divine Love, is what is most important about who they are.

William: Imagine that at social gatherings in our New Society, people will openly and matter-of-factly discuss unconditional love, and perhaps share the challenges they face to receiving and expressing this love in their personal lives…

Neal: … Instead of talking about the trivialities of money, sports, and politics. A New World indeed, in which people talk about what is most important… a World Order in which what is most important to humans is aligned with what is most important to the soul. As Benedict once put it, albeit indirectly, the highest thing in a human being is the capacity for Divine Love. Our Social Order will assist humans in activating this capacity.

Benedict: I don't recall saying that. But in any case, I agree.

Neal: What you wrote is:

> … reasoning is not the principal thing in us, but only like a stairway, by which we can climb up to the desired place, or like a good spirit which without any falsity or deception brings tidings

of the greatest good, to spur us thereby to seek it, and to unite with it in a union which is our greatest salvation and blessedness.

Plato: *(teasingly)* Why, Benedict, how poetic! I didn't know you had it in you.

Benedict: *(blushing slightly)* Well, I guess I got carried away.

Socrates: *(with humor)* Yes, literally "carried away". The Divine transport "carries" the human deeply into the soul, and the soul deeply into the Divine Being. And you are right to say that reasoning, although itself a gift from the gods, and hence divine, is not the principle thing in a human being. The principle thing is the capacity to experience Divine Love. And we agree, Benedict, do we not, that what we are calling the "experience of Divine Love" is the same experience that you referred to, albeit less poetically, as the experience of the union that exists between the human mind and the Mind of God.

Benedict: Yes, we agree. The different expressions refer to the same experience. It is not possible to know God without feeling this incredible Love, and vice versa.

Plato: So then, perhaps the semantic police have reached a decision. If the capacity to experience Divine Love is "the principle thing in us", then the use of the word "love" should reflect what is most fundamental in a human being. I suggest that the word "love" be used in such a way as to reflect our Divine origin. This will rule out using the term as synonymous with "desire", which is how I originally used it. Our rule of thumb will be: if what is loved today can be hated tomorrow, then it was not love to begin with. Unconditional love cannot be turned into hatred, and Divine Love is always unconditional. What do you think?

Neal: Well, I think I could get by using words like "desire" and "like very much" to characterize my relation with chocolate ice cream. So I see no need to use the word "love" to refer to what is merely desired. But I have a concern. Isn't this a bit too abstract for our children? I think maybe our teenagers could grasp the concept of a love that is unconditional, and that the purpose of human existence is to embody that unconditional love in all aspects of their lives, but whatever will we tell our five and six year olds?

William: Perhaps we won't need to tell them anything.

Neal: What do you mean?

William: The "telling" and the "grasping of concepts" comes after experience. Our children, even at five and six, will have experienced unconditional love, at least partially. Here's an analogy to what I mean: we have been feeding our children only foods that are both delicious and nutritious. Later, in their teen years, they will learn some biology and understand conceptually why nutrition is so important. They have been listening to healthy music, without understanding conceptually the effects of music on the developing brain. They have been running, jumping and chasing each other without understanding the effects of those actions on their developing muscles. And similarly, we have been raising them in an environment of non-judgmental, that is, unconditional acceptance.

Neal: Well, but as much as we may strive to provide an environment of unconditional acceptance for our children, this is not the same thing as the Divine Love reported in mystical experiences or the Near-Death Experience. That Love is visceral, much more powerful even than sexual ecstasy.

William: OK, we won't say, then, that we are giving them this experience, but we are showing them the path to this experience.

Plato: Indeed, the whole point of any educational system is to align the soul with Divine Love. Now we did not previously use that term. We constructed our educational system with a view to facilitating the soul's purpose in manifesting as human. But perhaps it will turn out, as I think, that whatever facilitates the soul's purpose in manifesting as human, also points the (embodied) soul in the direction of Divine Love. Let's briefly review two features of our educational system that makes me think this is the case.

Neal: OK.

7) Divine Love

Plato: Our children have been touching/massaging each other regularly from the very earliest ages. This will be done under adult supervision and instruction, at least in the beginning. The child receiving the massage will be taught to focus his attention on the sensations occurring within his body. Like a meditation, when stray thoughts come, he will be taught to ignore them (instead of "spacing out" following a train of thought). He will learn that it feels good to be touched, and feels best when the mind is concentrated on the sensation itself, without thinking. The child giving the massage will be taught to put his attention on the sensations she feels while touching the other. She will be taught how to place herself in the body of the other, so as to almost feel herself what the other feels. This will take some time, so initially there will be instruction about how much pressure, etc. to place on the muscles, and much feedback from the recipient. But after a while, the giver will be able to feel the body of the recipient internally, and know intuitively how to touch/massage the other. It will be a meditation for the giver too, as she will also be taught to bring her wandering mind back to the sensations in her hands as she massages the other. The giver will learn (i) that she has the ability to feel what the recipient feels, and (ii) that it feels good to give pleasure to another. Later, when they are older, they will learn some anatomy, which will explain to them why massage both *feels* good and *is* good for the body. And they will also learn about God, Divine Love, and the interconnectedness of all souls, which will explain to them why giving pleasure to another (unconditionally, I might add) both feels good and is good for the soul. Benedict, you take the other feature.

Benedict: Well I was going to say that the other feature involves the emotional intelligence our children have been learning through group therapy, but then I feared Socrates here might pounce on me.

Socrates: Quite right, Benedict. We need a term other than "therapy". We need a term that stands for "the honest expression of emotions in small group settings". I suppose "personal trainer" carries strong connotations of physical training, and the expression "emotional trainer" carries the unwanted connotation that the trainer is himself too emotional. Our basic idea is that under adult supervision, and on a daily basis, children will discuss and process the emotions experienced that day. Perhaps the best name for the adult at this point is simply "counselor", although another name might come to us later.

Benedict: OK, let's go with that term. The main task of the counselor is to provide a safe, non-judgmental environment in which the children are encouraged to express and share their real emotions with one another. Now, we have previously discussed that children, especially small children, will imitate the emotions of other children. So if one child is expressing sadness, other children will feel that sadness. The children do not have to be taught to empathize, because nothing is more natural than the ability to feel the emotions of others. But this ability must be nurtured and developed, and this is the job of our counselors. After all, it would hardly be reasonable to develop a social order around the Golden Rule if humans did not have the ability to know and feel the emotions of others. One cannot take the feelings of others into account unless one can know those feelings.

William: Yes, and sadly, this ability is shut down and atrophies in the present social order based on greed and competition. *(To me)* In our culture we teach children, especially boys, to override their natural feelings of compassion in order to "compete" against others. If, to take an obvious example, two children are competing for a "prize" that only one of them can have, then in order to win, the children must short-circuit their natural feelings of compassion for the other, so that one may rejoice when the other loses. Notice that it is not possible for children to become emotionally intelligent in any culture that stresses competition. For to compete against another, aside from trivial games, requires that both competitors repress any feelings of compassion towards the other. Following, or aspiring to follow, the Golden Rule is impossible in such a culture.

Neal: I agree. But this implies, does it not, that in the Social Order now under construction anything that involves competition will be regarded as nothing more than a trivial game. No one will hide or repress emotions in order to "win", so our counselors will guard against the tendency to repress emotions. In fact, our children will be taught that concealing emotions, consciously or subconsciously, is in the long term more consequential to them than "winning" or "losing". So as they get older, they themselves will become the guardians of their emotions, guarding against any tendency to hide their true feelings from others. To do things merely for effect, to say one thing while feeling the opposite, will not be in our children's repertoire, so to speak.

Plato: *(smiling, to me)* Well, Neal, you've just said the magic word that we have been seeking. Twice, in fact.

Neal: Huh?

Plato: Guardians! Those "counselors" that we have entrusted with encouraging our children to express emotions must also be the ones to guard against any and every tendency to conceal, hide, repress, or misrepresent their true emotions. But they are also the Guardians of our New Social Order, which is doomed to fail as soon as children are allowed to use language to conceal what they are feeling.

Neal: Yes, but at the same time, our Social Order is such that our children will have hardly any motivation to use words to misrepresent their emotions, that is, to lie.

Plato: Ah, but this perhaps depends on whether the possible motivations for lying are all external, that is, to "win" something, to avoid discipline, to gain approval, etc… these motivations will be largely absent, but remember what we said earlier – or was it in a previous conversation? – about the downward path and the upward path?

Neal: Yes, the downward path is the soul's descent into matter; the upward path is the soul's ascent back to pure Spirit, unmixed with matter.

Plato: And that both journeys are occurring simultaneously.

Neal: Yes, "simultaneously" in the eternal order, where you are. But in the temporal order where I am, or seem to be, we are constructing a Social Order that will guide Humanity along the Upward Path (the downward path having been already taken for thousands of years).

Plato: And the downward path requires or, rather, consists of hiding from the knowledge of the union that exists between the human mind and the Divine Mind, if I may paraphrase Benedict.

Neal: Yes.

Plato: And lying – using words to conceal and misrepresent one's inner life to others – is a form of hiding, and pertains to the downward path only. So it could be the case that a given soul, having followed the downward path into embodiment, desires to continue along this downward path. The way for an embodied soul to continue along the downward path is to lie, to hide and conceal his inner life from other human beings.

Socrates: Yes. So if we are now following the upward path we must tell such souls that they can follow the downward path only so far as will get them into a human form. The human form is no longer available to souls who seek to follow the downward path further than embodiment per se. After embodiment the souls must be willing to follow the upward path, and our Guardians will be on the lookout for all attempts to hide and conceal, whether internally or externally motivated.

Neal: But…

Socrates: But I see you are concerned with the plight of the downward driven soul, who is unwilling or unable to follow the upward path. Not to worry. Creation is vast, and there are plenty of arenas, or Worlds, into which such souls may incarnate and continue to hide and suffer all they want. But Earth is now off limits to such souls.

William: Yes, you see there is now a sufficient number of souls who desire the upward path. These were once referred to as the "meek", probably a bad translation, and it is now their time, or rather, our time, to inherit the Earth.

Neal: "Gentle" is probably a better fit than "meek". The Earth is now ruled by those who are aggressive and ambitious for personal power. They are, as Plato has said, then and now, unfit to rule. But souls who are gentle with themselves and with others, who upon embodiment seek the upward path, shall be the main inhabitants of our New World Order.

Benedict: Now, getting back to our emotional intelligence groups, there is one more thing, a very important thing, that our children are learning by participating in such groups.

Neal: Yes?

Benedict: One at a time, the children will be guided to share the emotions they were feeling throughout the day, as well as the emotions they are feeling while sharing. As one is sharing, the other children will be guided to express the emotions they are feeling in response to the one who is sharing. They will discover that emotions are contagious and because of that, because children (and adults) have the ability to feel what another is feeling, the possibility arises that our children can be guided towards feelings of deep empathy and compassion for one another. In any competitive social order (I'm tempted to say, in any patriarchy) such feelings of natural compassion must be repressed, otherwise the "winners" could not enjoy their "winnings". But in our new Society, such feelings will be encouraged. And this will also give our children a felt sense that they are internally connected to others.

Neal: Yes, so later, when we teach them about that interconnectedness of all beings, they will have already experienced that. Through touch, they will feel connected with the bodies of others; through emotional sharing, they will feel connected with the emotions of others. But now, are we satisfied that our semantic cops have done their job properly?

Benedict: I think we are agreed that the word "love" be used in its highest sense, not as a desire for something, but as something Divine. When the word "love" is used, it shall always carry connotations of "non-judgmental" and "unconditional". We will use, or invent, other terms that describe sexual attractions per se. Perhaps "lust" will do for now.

Neal: So our children will not be using the word "love" to mean a desire for something (Plato's sense of the word) or as a feeling of gratitude for what is believed to cause pleasure (your sense). But then, how will our children use the word "love", if they cannot use it in any of the familiar senses?

William: We can ask the same question about the word "God". The so-called "familiar" use of the term – to refer to a guy in the sky who, aside from having a bad temper and bad morals, does not even exist – will have only historic interest. We will have to come up with better, age-appropriate stories for our children – stories about the Divine Being, stories about Love as the force that connects all minds into a single "One Mind".

Socrates: But our children will have heard such stories all their lives.

William: Really?

Socrates: Yes, in fact the whole society will be permeated with such stories.

Neal: What are you talking about?

Socrates: The so-called Near-Death Experience.

Neal: Of course. I get it. Through their NDEs, many humans have already experienced Divine Love directly. As medical technology advances, many more people will be brought back from so-called death that will have had this experience of Divine Love.

William: And unlike the present society, where doctors attempt to "medicate" this experience away or send such experiencers to the psych ward of their hospitals, in our New Society the Near-Death Experience will be common knowledge, and people will be talking about it all the time. So our children will certainly have heard stories about Divine Love.

Plato: We'll do better than that. We will see to it that Near-Death Experiencers, as well as others who have experienced Divine Love in some other way, will be called upon to appear before our children in the classroom, or some other format, and talk personally about this

Love. And we will especially call upon children who have had this experience to share their experience with other children.

Benedict: And so, as you can easily see, the concept of Divine Love, or Unconditional Love will not be some mere abstraction, some high-minded concept beyond the reach of children, but a living reality. So we need not fear that our children will have any difficulties grasping this.

Neal: *(smiling)* When someone talks about their NDE or mystical experience, their sincerity and earnestness comes through strongly, and the children will get some sense of the reality and power of this Love. We may also tell them that they are closest to this love during those moments when, through emotional sharing, they feel connected with the inner being of other children. But now, Benedict…

Benedict: *(with a little humor)* I know what you're going to say. I sort of messed up when I referred to this experience as "the intellectual love of the human mind for God", as very few have any understanding of what I meant. The phrase certainly fails to convey, especially in English, what I actually experienced. But as Socrates here has taught me, an ounce of prevention is worth a pound of cure, and we are raising our children in such a way that Divine Love will often be the subject of conversation. *(Smiling)* Unlike your colleagues, and William's too, our children will have no difficulty wrapping their minds around the experience that I once called "the intellectual Love of man for God". As an aside, the Latin word "intellectus" has spiritual connotations that the English word "intellect" does not have.

Neal: Yes, I know. I once looked up the word "intellect" in Webster's Unabridged Dictionary, and one meaning of the word, listed as "archaic", is that it refers to the part of the mind that knows God.

Benedict: *(smiling)* "Archaic", eh? Well, whatever, that's the sense of the term I intended.

Plato: We are agreed, then, that the word "love" shall carry connotations of the Divine. The word "lust" may be used to describe sexual attractions per se, but that term shall not carry any negative connotations. To feel sexually attracted to someone is a positive joy, and the birthright of every child. Our use of the word love shall be guided by the maxim: "if it can turn into hate, it was not love in the first place". For Divine Love is unconditional, and has no opposite. Oh, and for you, Neal, the expressions "like" or "like very much" should suffice to describe your feelings towards chocolate ice cream. Perhaps new terms will be invented to describe the relationship between a human being and some physical object with which the human strongly identifies.

Neal: OK, I think the semantic cops have done their job, and…

William: Before we move on, there is one consequence of this usage of the word "love" that I wish to point out.

Neal: Go ahead.

William: In our culture, young people who are in lust with one another – who enjoy each other's company and enjoy having sex together and are constantly thinking about one another – perhaps like Romeo and Juliet – tend to romanticize their sexual attractions and think they are "in love". This is so typical of teens and young adults. It will be easy to teach them that their sexual attractions, although positive experiences, are not the same as love. All we have to do is ask our Romeo (a stand-in for any young male) how he would feel if Juliet (a stand-in for any young female) were to leave him for another boy. If his "love" would turn into "jealousy" or "hatred", then it was not love in the first place. These situations, which will continue to be quite common, will be discussed among our adolescents in small groups, so the difference between lust and love will become even more apparent to them.

Neal: Yes, and this teaching will be made easier by the fact that sexual attraction per se carries no negative connotations in our New Social Order, so our children will not have to use words like "love" to justify their sexual attractions to themselves and others. Now I think we need to return to a subject that we have mentioned, but not discussed.

William: Yes?

Neal: When we were talking about our children's sexual training, we said that one of the things they will learn is how to surrender to the sexual energy. We need to say what we mean by the term "surrender". What is it that is "surrendered", and to whom or what? And exactly how can this be taught?

William: The term "surrender" is perhaps a little too Christian for you, Neal?

Neal: *(laughing)* Yeah, perhaps.

William: *(also laughing)* You would never have survived reading all the material I had to read for my *Varieties* – tons more than what I put in the book. The mystical experiences I read were almost all Christian, wallowing in expressions such as "surrendering to God", feeling "wrapped in Divine Love", "surrendering my soul to Jesus" and many more such expressions of Christian linguistic excess.

Benedict: The use of language here should be regarded as poetic, not descriptive. They went over the top with respect to linguistic indulgence, but that's really because language cannot in any case capture what they experienced. So we will be gentle with them. But linguistically speaking, we will do better.

8) Surrender [Or Subduing Linguistic Consciousness]

William: I have a suggestion how to proceed.

Neal: What is it?

William: I think we should do the opposite of how we proceeded with respect to the word "love". In that case, we considered the highest usage of the term first, and argued that the meaning we attribute to the word "love" must carry connotations of its highest usage in all other usages, which are pale Earthly shadows of the Divine. But with regard to the word "surrender" I want to suggest that we begin with its Earthly usages, and then proceed to the Divine. This way of proceeding will show, I believe, that the concept of "surrender" is not just some religious idea, neither is it merely a secular term that describes a defeated army. Rather, the term marks a common psychological experience with which most humans are already familiar.

Neal: OK, William. Let's proceed as you suggest and see where it takes us.

William: Let's begin by considering how we teach children to dance.

Neal: Huh?

William: Actually, children do not need to be taught, since allowing their body to move to music is so natural that it occurs even in utero. But absorbing the restrictive influence of culture, as both you and I did, inhibits the ability of the body to move to music. You, Neal, learned to dance consciously, as an adult. In my own case, such learning was impossible – a Harvard professor dancing!? – well, I waltzed a little when I was younger, but (ahem) proper Victorian gentlemen do not give in to such vulgarities as dancing. Now notice: I used the phrase "give in to" which has the same connotations as "surrender to". After much practice, you were able to give yourself to the music, or surrender yourself to the music. What is this experience of surrendering to the music that you were able to have but I was not?

Neal: I remember, and I also remember being frightened half to death. There were special workshops back in the 80s designed to free people of inhibitions so that they could allow their body to move to the music. We would be blindfolded, to prevent us from trying to copy what anyone else was doing, then instructed to feel the music in our body and allow the body to move in response to the music.

William: And this would be called "surrendering to the music"?

Neal: Yes.

William: And how would you describe this experience psychologically? Begin with the fear.

Neal: Fear?

William: Yes, you said you were initially "frightened half to death".

Neal: Ah yes, this is interesting. The conscious part of my mind did not know what to do. It would have preferred knowing in advance what steps and motions should be taken; it would have been more comfortable imitating the motions of others. In other words, the part of the mind that likes to plan things out and be in control (or think that it's in control) was prevented from functioning in its usual way.

William: So unable to be in control, it generated the emotion called "fear"?

Neal: Yes. In order for the body to move to the music, the mind must let go of (i) any attempt to consciously direct the motions of the body, and (ii) any attempt to compare itself with others.

William: And since planning, judging, and controlling, are, one might say, the chief features of the egoic mind, it feels threatened and fearful when it is unable to do its thing.

Benedict: And we should add "incessant chatter" to the list of chief features (what we previously called the "inner dialogue"). Even when the egoic mind is not busy with planning, etc. it is incessantly talking to itself, and this talk must subside, at least somewhat, if the body is to even hear the music it is supposed to be moving to. The mind's attention must be given over to the music. We might notice here that the mental activities that must be put in abeyance – planning, judging, incessant chatter – are all linguistic forms of consciousness.

Neal: So the linguistic component to human consciousness, the ego, generates fear when it is asked to be quiet, or turn down its volume.

William: *(smiling)* Because it thinks it is the whole of consciousness, which of course it is not. Now of course, our children will not have the particular problem of dancing that we did – of surrendering the motions of their body to the sounds of the music. According to how we are raising our children, linguistic consciousness will not be as dominant a form of consciousness as it is today, especially among we so-called intellectuals, where it may rightly be called a mental illness.

Benedict: And we should also note that the psychological sense of "past" and "future" comes into being with linguistic consciousness. So when we state that linguistic consciousness – the particular form of consciousness that is infused with language – must be in abeyance if the body is to move to the music (instead of to its thoughts about how it "should" move), we are saying, in other words, that the mind must be in the present moment.

Plato: And we shall find, I suspect, that this is the general pattern that William has been looking for.

William: Well, let's put it out as a hypothesis: all cases of what is called "surrender" involve the mind's coming into the present moment, which requires that the mind let go of all thoughts that pertain to the past or the future. And empirically speaking, it seems to be the case that linguistic consciousness, as we are calling it, often generates the emotion of fear when it is not in control. We must investigate to see whether this is the case for forms of surrender other than dancing.

Neal: Yes, but first I'd like to point out two things: by defining the word "surrender" psychologically, as a reduction of linguistic consciousness, we have rendered it free from any explicit religious connotations.

William: *(jokingly)* Otherwise you and I would not be able to use the term.

Neal: Yes, so we can use the term without any Christian or religious association of surrendering to the Guy in the Sky, so to speak.

William: And your second point?

Neal: We have been teaching our children to surrender from the very beginning. Our instruction to them while receiving massage is to feel the sensations in their body. It seems trivial to say this, but to feel sensation requires being in the present moment. While receiving sensation, their minds are not thinking about past or future. Ideally, they are not thinking at all, but feeling.

William: Yes, and what you have said about the receiver is also true about the giver. Initially the giver will have to "think" and "plan" how to touch, how much pressure, and so forth. But in time, the giver will not have to think about these things, and instead will be able to intuitively sense what is needed. So the experience both of giving and receiving touch is also an experience of lessening the intensity of linguistic consciousness.

Socrates: *(to me, with humor)* And this is one reason you like massage so much. Not only does it soothe the muscles, but that overactive left brain of yours gets to take a little vacation. Now let's test William's hypothesis by examining a few other cases, or kinds of cases, where the term "surrender" is used.

Neal: Aside from dancing, which we may call the experience of the body moving to music, there is also the experience of being moved by music. In the first case, the body is moving physically. In the second case, what is being moved is not of course the body, but something within the soul.

Plato: We shall talk about this kind of experience, the aesthetic experience, a little later. It is a very important kind of human experience, as it can literally turn the soul around. But for now, let us just satisfy ourselves that this experience is a case of surrender, that is, the linguistic consciousness must be in abeyance if one is to have the experience of being moved by music. Later we will analyze the nature of the experience itself.

Neal: But it is a trivial matter to satisfy ourselves in this regard. Linguistic consciousness must be in abeyance in order that any other form of consciousness arise. For it is not possible for humans to give attention to many things at the same time, and if attention is being given to the words in one's head, then there is less attention available to give to the music.

William: So the experience of giving oneself over to the music, of feeling the music deeply, is an experience that requires a lessening of the stream of words and thoughts that flows through one's consciousness. One may then speak of "surrendering" to the music, or being transported by the music.

Neal: So our concept of "surrender" simply marks a refocusing of one's attention away from the dominant linguistic consciousness. And the various mental activities associated with linguistic consciousness, such as planning, comparing, judging, worrying… we might say that it is these activities that are surrendered when one gives oneself over to the music or whatever.

William: Yes, the "whatever" here will include all sense experiences, not just music. For example, a human can become mesmerized by a beautiful sunset, and in that moment experience a dramatic lessening of linguistic consciousness. Many ordinary visual experiences, especially in Nature, may be described as momentary "surrenders" to the beauty of the moment. And the same even with scents. When one is smelling the roses, when one's attention is immersed in the smells, in that moment there is a reduction of linguistic consciousness. And the same with taste.

Neal: I have many times surrendered to the taste of chocolate ice cream.

Socrates: Hah! Yes, you have, but not always as deeply as possible. This is because you are usually doing other things while consuming the ice cream. To fully surrender to the taste sensations you cannot be doing anything other than tasting.

Neal: Yes, I agree. I have experienced complete immersion in the taste sensation, but not usually, so I know the difference. To fully taste the food one has to almost be in a meditative state of mind. Let me put it this way: sometimes a taste sensation is so overpowering that it causes an immediate reduction in linguistic consciousness. The taste sensation has absorbed all my attention. But even if that's not the case, I can consciously direct my attention into the taste of the food.

William: So we are calling attention to the fact that "surrendering" is a psychological process that happens all the time, but people do not usually notice it unless the experience is somewhat strong. You used the expression "overpowering". People are always saying things like: "the smell of the flowers was overpowering", "the beauty of the mountains is overpowering", "that performance of Beethoven's *Ninth* was overpowering". What is it, we may ask, that is being "overpowered"?

Neal: Clearly linguistic consciousness, or the part of consciousness that involves words and thinks it is the whole of consciousness. It is this particular form of consciousness that gets "overpowered".

Plato: And I suppose that when the linguistic consciousness finds itself overpowered, it has in that moment surrendered. It's odd, is it not, that we are using military terms here, speaking of surrendering and overpowering.

Socrates: *(laughing)* Yes, the ego likes to think of itself in that way. *(Mischievously)* And maybe it should, since its existence is in any case so fragile and precarious.

Neal: What do you mean?

Socrates: *(laughing)* Have you not been paying attention to what you have yourself been saying? The ego, or linguistic consciousness, can be blown away by the smell of a flower. That's a rather precarious existence for something that thinks it is running the show. At some level it knows this, which is why it is constantly fearful. It has a military mentality, holding down the fort, always defending itself against attack, planning for its security, and so forth. And the whole thing can be wiped out by the smell of a single rose!

William: Thank you for making my point, which is that linguistic consciousness is dethroned many times every day, but it happens quickly and people usually do not notice. So at a mundane level, linguistic consciousness is "overpowered by" or "surrenders to" other forms of conscious experience, like the smell of a flower, the beauty of a sunset, the sound of a melody, or petting a dog. These common everyday experiences – and many more examples could be added – all involve a lessening of linguistic consciousness, a temporary abeyance of that ever-present "voice in the head". By calling attention to such ordinary experiences, perhaps the ego will become less fearful. I suppose the subject of non-linguistic forms of consciousness will be included in our curriculum, and our children will discuss and express their experiences of these non-linguistic forms of consciousness. But now I would like to discuss some less usual, but not uncommon, examples of surrender.

Neal: Go ahead.

William: I want to examine briefly a kind of experience reported by both athletes and musicians. In both cases, it is the same experience, but triggered in different ways. Let's begin with what's called "jogger's high".

Benedict: What in the world is that?

William: Yeah, well I suppose it started in my time, where guys would run, not to win a race, but just for the fun of it. A person who runs for the fun of it is called a "jogger". OK, so what they report is, after running at a pace for a while, they feel detached from the body, the running is effortless and happens, so it seems, by itself. Linguistic consciousness is in abeyance during such experiences. There is awareness of the body's moving, but no conscious control over the moving. It seems to the runner that the body is moving by itself, and is not under the control of the thinking mind. And at higher levels, athletes (and musicians) report "peak" experiences during which it feels, not that they are playing a game (or music), but that the game (music) is playing them. The hallmark of such experiences is complete effortlessness, heightened awareness, and of course, an absence of any thoughts that pertain to past or future. During such experiences, only the present moment exists.

Neal: So we might say that linguistic consciousness has surrendered to the game or the music. In either case, the ego, the linguistic consciousness that plans (what should I do now?) and judges (am I doing this right?) is in abeyance. In either case, what the body does from moment to moment is determined, not by the conscious mind, but by something "larger" and to which the conscious mind has "surrendered". In one case it would be the game, in the other case, the music. The athlete merges with, experiences herself as one with, the game; the musician experiences himself as one with the music. And the experience is both effortless and joyful.

William: Yes. And we should add the martial arts, as another example of "spontaneous" motion. I'm not sure if "spontaneous" is the right word...

Neal: Yes, to capture a sense of bodily motion without conscious planning on the part of the mind. It is an experience of intense alertness in the absence of linguistic consciousness. The word "spontaneous" captures this sense that it is all happening "by itself", without any contribution from the part of the mind that plans, judges, and thinks about past and future.

Plato: And this, we may remind ourselves, is the main reason we are including sports, music, dance, and martial arts in our curriculum. They give our children the direct experience of (i) mental alertness without (ii) linguistic consciousness, as we are calling the ego. By doing this, *(glancing at William and me)* we will have prevented the peculiar illness that has befallen the majority of your colleagues from afflicting our children.

William: You know, Neal, we could both have saved ourselves a lot of anguish had we thought of our colleagues as suffering from a mental illness, rather than merely being perverse, or willfully ignorant. For as we both know, among academics linguistic consciousness has usurped the throne, and likes to conceive of itself as the "highest" if not the "only" form of consciousness.

Neal: Yes, and I can see now that what was needed – what our colleagues needed – was not rational argument, to which they were impervious – but the direct experience of heightened awareness in the absence of linguistic consciousness. But all of our children will have such experiences, and talk about them, so even those who are very clever with words will have experienced consciousness without words. So we shall invite linguistic consciousness to join us at the banquet table, so to speak, but it will no longer be in charge of the menu.

William: A nice way to put it, since the human body is potential host to many forms of consciousness besides what we are calling linguistic consciousness, and there is no reason why the human being cannot enjoy the full spectrum of forms of consciousness that its body is able to host.

Neal: Linguistic consciousness, as you once said, must be made to hold its tongue. Our educational process will make our children very aware of the limitations of linguistic consciousness. When they become adults, they will not suffer from the peculiar mental illness that causes linguistic consciousness to think either that it is the whole of consciousness or that it is the highest form of consciousness.

Benedict: Ah, William, I certainly understand and agree with what you meant when you said that linguistic consciousness must be made to hold its tongue. Yet ironically, linguistic consciousness is the only form of consciousness that *has* a tongue, the other forms being nonverbal. So when our children get together to talk about their emotions, which they will do on a daily basis, it is this linguistic consciousness that will do the talking.

Socrates: And what better evidence than this for my theory that the Divine Being has a wicked sense of humor and that we are closer to the Divine when we laugh than when we lament?

Neal: Huh?

Socrates: Yeah, look, do not all spiritual teachers state that the ego or personality is the source of all problems for human beings?

Neal: Yes, this is what they say is the cause of human suffering.

Socrates: And the ego is the same structure within the field of consciousness that we are calling "linguistic consciousness"?

Neal: Yes, the ego thinks in terms of words and concepts and past and future.

Socrates: So if this form of consciousness is the problem, do you think the solution can be found by this form of consciousness?

Neal: Of course not. So this is why you think the human condition is a Divine Joke? The ego, or that which has created the problem, is the means by which humans try to solve the problem.

Benedict: The "problem" cannot be solved until egoic consciousness is removed from the throne. So, in our children's discussion groups, the leaders must be very aware of these tendencies, and care must be exerted to direct children's attention to the emotions and feelings within, and especially to prevent those who are most skilled with words from dominating the discussion and setting the menu, so to speak.

Plato: We should perhaps separate two strands of thought here: (i) we are raising our children in such a way as to avoid, if not completely then as much as possible, the "problem" Benedict refers to above – the "problem" caused by the dominance of egoic consciousness in the human condition. (ii) The second strand concerns how to help people who have not been raised in our New Society, people who are very much "stuck" in egoic consciousness. We are now concerned with the former strand, and will a little later have something to say about the latter.

William: OK, back to our children, if I may play the role of taskmaster for the moment. I believe our discussion, although rambling about, has established the psychological meaning of the word "surrender" for us, so that we may use the term without any so-called religious overtones. OK, Neal?

Neal: *(smiling)* Yes, OK.

William: Whether we call it "linguistic consciousness" or "egoic consciousness", that aspect of the mind that involves concepts and words, that plans, compares, and judges – it is this part of the mind that must surrender itself to the present moment. Or perhaps we can put it this way: we will use the term "surrender" to refer to a lessening, sometimes marked and sudden, of the intensity of the ever-constant chatter of the linguistic mind. The paradox, as Socrates humorously observed, is that the egoic mind does not know how, even if it wanted to, to lower its intensity. Now, in the kinds of cases we discussed earlier, it appears that the surrender is involuntary. The musician and athlete cannot bring about a peak experience through conscious intent; either it happens or it doesn't. But this much is universal: when it does happen, it is experienced as effortless and joyful. So now we must apply this to our children and the sexual arena.

Plato: And *this* arena, the sexual, offers some promise of a "voluntary", or semi-voluntary surrender.

Neal: Yes, but how shall we instruct our children? At 13 or 14, their bodies are ready for sexual activity, but their minds are not ready to understand all this talk of "egoic consciousness" or even the concept of "surrender", let alone the ideas involved with "sacred sex".

Plato: Well, all along we have been teaching our children "right opinion" and "right habits" long before they are able to comprehend all the "whys and wherefores". For example, all their lives we have been aligning their taste buds with what is truly nutritious for the body. Then later, as teenagers, they will learn the biology behind these "good habits" of eating that they have internalized through upbringing. Our children will be taught – "guided" is perhaps a better word – how to surrender during sex before they are able to understand the physiology, psychology, and spirituality involved in sexual joy.

9) Nonresistance To Pleasure [Or, What Diotima Taught Socrates]

Socrates: And so let's get specific. As Plato suggested, it will be useful to divide our teaching into three interrelated components: (i) physical, (ii) psychological, and (iii) spiritual. Although the third component will pervade everything we teach our children, it will be the last component to be explicitly addressed. As soon as our children are sexually mature, that is, as soon as they are physiologically able to orgasm, they shall be assigned to a trainer. The age varies of course from one child to another.

William: "A trainer"?

Socrates: Yes, we have discussed this before. We agreed to call those who assist our children with their sexual energies "trainers", or perhaps even "coaches", since they will function in that capacity. They cannot be called "therapists" because our children are in no need of any therapy. Neither can they be called "surrogates", since they are not standing in for anyone else. Now –

William: But wait a minute. You said they would be *assigned* a trainer. Who does the assigning? What if the child feels no attraction to her trainer?

Socrates: Calm down, my friend, *(glancing at me)* and you too, Neal. The challenge for you two is to rise above your cultural upbringing and consider only what is best for the child. When you were boys of

13 or 14, would it not have been most helpful to have an older girl or woman take you into the bedroom and teach you about your own body and hers too?

Plato: Indeed, is not this the fantasy of every 13-year-old boy?

Neal: Yes, at least for heterosexual boys.

Socrates: *(smiling)* The sexual proclivities of our children will be known long before they become sexually mature. Even at nine or ten, they are more aware of things than adults generally suppose, and we shall be providing them with safe environments to discuss everything that is of concern to them. Of course children who are not heterosexual will be assigned a trainer of their own sex. But we should mention that many children will identify as "bisexual"; in fact, in a generation or two most humans will identify as bisexual.

Neal: Why do you say that?

Socrates: Haven't you heard those stories according to which in this time period a lot of "old" souls are returning to Earth?

Neal: Yes, I have heard that old souls have been both male and female many times, and are impatient with any attempt to stifle a free expression of sexual feelings for whomever they choose.

Socrates: Exactly, and because human society will necessarily shift from a patriarchy to a matriarchy, from a social order modeled after chimpanzees to one modeled after bonobos, the males will become gentle within themselves, and will become gentle with one another, and heterosexual men will be able to feel affection and caring for one another, and sometimes express those feelings sexually.

Neal: OK, so let's suppose now that we have our 13-year-old child in the bedroom with his or her trainer. Now what?

Socrates: *(smiling softly)* "Now what?" you ask. Suppose a child is meeting with his piano teacher for the first time. Or basketball trainer? Or drama teacher? Or gym trainer? Or math tutor? Would you ask, "Now what?" in any of those contexts?

Neal: Well no, but these contexts are familiar.

Socrates: Yes, but just because these contexts are familiar doesn't mean that there is not some method to it. The trainer of course knows her subject matter very well, but she also knows how to teach it. That is, she knows how do adjust her teaching to the needs and abilities of the individual student. The piano teacher (i) knows about her subject matter, the piano (ii), but she is also knowledgeable about child psychology, and (iii) becomes knowledgeable about the particularities of each individual student, so that she can adjust her teaching to the needs and abilities of the individual child. Sexual training will be no different from training in other endeavors for which one-on-one instruction is required. But all right, you ask, now what?

Neal: Yes.

Socrates: I said that the training will be divided into three components: the physical, the psychological, and the spiritual. The "physical" part will be taught right away, when our children are in their early teens; the "psychological" component will be taught in their mid and later teens, and what I am calling the "spiritual" component will be an option available at any time in their adult lives. So, you ask, exactly ***what*** is the physical component?

Neal: My question exactly.

Socrates: Nonresistance to pleasure. That is the physical component.

Plato: *(laughing)* On the surface, Socrates' remark is quite ridiculous, is it not?

Neal: Yes. Who in the world would think that humans need to be "taught" not to resist pleasure?

William: Yes, but we all know from experience that whenever he *(glancing at Socrates)* says something that appears ridiculous on the surface, it is usually worthwhile to probe more deeply beneath the surface. So tell us, Socrates, exactly *how* our personal trainers will teach nonresistance to sexual pleasure to our 13-year-old children?

Socrates: *(looking at William and me, humorously)* Well, I would be happy to get into the details, but can you two prudes handle a more explicit discussion about these matters?

(At this point I do not know what to do. My little ego, or what remains of it, wants to defend itself against the charge of being prudish about sex. I can

understand and agree with the charge insofar as it applies to William, but not to myself. But that is just my ego. The rest of me is eager to hear what Socrates has to say.)

Neal: Well, I guess I'm going to go with what the rest of me wants and invite you to give an explicit blow-by-blow, or stroke-by-stroke, account.

Socrates: And when I have given my account, you will understand why I playfully called you a prude. Benedict, are you OK?

Benedict: Yes, of course. I will participate minimally in this discussion, since I did not have much experience of sex during my lifetime. But as you know, I became what you call "enlightened" in my teens, so sexual abstinence was not a problem for me.

Socrates: Isn't this interesting? I too practically came into physical form already "enlightened", but as a young man, my Teacher was a high priestess in one of the local "mystery religions". So I experienced sacred sexuality directly, and continued to enjoy sex throughout my life. So we have here two "enlightened" individuals, one forgoing sexual relations, the other embracing them. And I really mean "embracing". After all, in midlife I took a young wife and fathered children in my sixties. Even for one who is not enlightened, sex is optional for a man in his sixties, an option I chose to exercise. OK, enough of that. If you are open to it, Neal, let's examine what is behind my playfully referring to you and William as prudes.

Neal: Yes, I'm open to it.

Socrates: Good. So tell us, how did you (and William) learn about sex? And I don't mean book-learning. How did you have orgasms when you were in your early teens?

Neal: Well, we masturbated.

Socrates: *(I could tell he was warming up to a punch line that would have great effect)* And this of course is the beginning of your sexual dysfunctionality. Your very first sexual experiences were alone, by yourself, without anyone to talk to or communicate with.

Neal: Yes, that's how it is for everyone, girls too. No teen is going to discuss these things with their parents, even if their parents were open to it.

Socrates: And speaking of parents, where were your parents when you, as a young teenager, were masturbating?

Neal: *(I can't believe I'm actually writing this down; maybe I'm a prude after all)* Sleeping in their bedroom, I suppose.

Socrates: And where was their bedroom?

Neal: Across the hall from mine.

Socrates: And I suppose you did not want them to know you were masturbating?

Neal: Of course not… oh, oh my.

Socrates: You get it now, don't you?

William: Get what?

Neal: Get that our early, formative sexual experiences necessarily stifled the sexual energy itself, since we couldn't shout, moan, or scream, and we couldn't move our bodies lest the bed rock and creak and wake our parents. So instead of welcoming the sexual energy into our body, we allowed only a trickle of it to come through, just enough to orgasm genitally.

Socrates: Whereas we will be teaching our children to have full body orgasms from the very beginning. We might tell them a little story: that the Sexual Energy is the Life Force Itself, that it is the Divine glue that holds all human bodies into a single species. We will tell them that the Life Force is what has created their bodily form, and that through sex they will experience the life force directly. So they will be prepared to welcome the Life Force into their body, and allow the Life Force to take over. And by the phrase "take over", we mean *how* the body moves and the sounds the body makes will be controlled by the Life Force. So our first instruction to our children will be nonresistance to the Life Force.

Plato: Well, Socrates, perhaps you will share with us *your* first experiences with Diotima. Is this how she taught you?

Socrates: Yes, but keep in mind that the biggest difference between then and now is that the priestesses taught adult men, who, because they were not raised in the right way with respect to sex, required healing and therapy. But *our* children are being raised in the right way, and it is much easier to teach something correctly from the beginning than it is to have to undo what has been poorly learned. So I'm at the Temple and Diotima takes me into her chamber – a chamber specially designed for sexual instruction. She takes off my clothes and has me lie down on her bed. She tells me that she will be touching my body in a way designed to invite the Life Force to enter. She then instructs me as follows: "Socrates, as you feel the sexual energy arising within your body, know that this is the same Divine Energy that your parents felt, and their parents before them, know that this is the Divine Power that connects all human bodies into a single magnificent Being, of which you yourself are a part." Well, I was in my late teens, and we might have to use other words for our much younger teens. But basically, she begins with an invocation to the goddess that serves as a reminder of what the sexual energy is. She then continued: "So do not resist what is Divine. Specifically, as the energy rises in you, Socrates, you will feel tendencies and impulses to make sounds (moan, scream, cry, laugh, whatever) and also impulses for the body to move. Surrender to those impulses. Do not (as poor William and Neal were compelled to do) do anything to attempt to control those impulses." Well, as you might imagine, during the process, and with Diotima's assistance, I became aware of subtle efforts to resist the Life Force and keep some control over my body. She then said to me: "Everyone resists at first. This is because your body is about to be taken over by a Power that is greater than that of your own mind. But this is the Power that has brought your own body into existence, and when you allow it to fully enter into your being so that the motions and sounds of your body come from It, not you, you will experience Its energy as your very own, and having merged with the Life Force, you will experience the subsequent motions of your body as completely effortless." I marveled at her words, that surrendering to something actually gives more power to the one who surrenders. Yet I would still interfere with the process, and would sometimes even have thoughts that were judgmental, like, "Am I doing this right?" Noticing my concern, she said: "The reason this is a process, and that it takes more than one visit to me, is that everyone subconsciously resists. I am here to facilitate a complete letting go. I am very patient and have no expectations; every man is different. You please me simply by being here and allowing me to play with your body." At those words something in me let go, and I relaxed more deeply into the rising sexual energies. And having the mind-set that the sexual energies are sacred to the Divine greatly assisted in surrendering. She then added: "I see that for you, Socrates, allowing loud sounds to come out of your mouth is problematic, as you tend to inhibit the sounds in some way. So when you feel me touching your throat, that's a signal to turn up the volume. Or rather, get out of the way and the Life Force will Itself turn up the volume. And if I see that you are inhibiting how your body moves, I will touch you lightly on the root chakra (the perineum). When you feel my touch there, it is a signal that you are somewhere resisting a freer flow of the sexual energies." Well, there's more to tell in terms of the details of her teachings to me, but I think you get the idea; like every other skill or sport, the teachings must be individualized to the needs of the individual student.

William: My goodness, I must state that if I were not already tempted to come back to Earth as a neuroscientist, I would be even more tempted to return to experience sex like this.

Neal: And I can now understand why he referred to me as a prude, as well as you. The way we learned, or rather, mis-learned sex cannot be undone.

William: We learned it alone, stifling the energies in order to hide what we were doing from our parents, then later doing the same thing to hide what we were doing from our college roommates. Coming of age in a culture that sees a conflict between spirituality and sexual pleasure is an insufferable burden. My God, as if there is something embarrassing about a boy getting an erection in the classroom. Whereas we were taught to conceal sexual pleasure, our children will be shouting it out to the whole world. But, Socrates, how will we find

Diotima to teach our children?

Neal: And should we state that in addition to Diotima, we need to find Apollo for the girls?

Socrates: *(smiling)* Not to worry. There will be lots of trainers, male and female, and each child will receive a trainer to his or her liking. And it will not matter too much whether the trainer is the same or opposite sex as the child, in much the same way that the sex of the child's pediatrician is not very relevant. Things will be more "fluid" than they are now, and no one will attempt to constrain our children's expression of sexuality by the imposition of rigid categories.

Plato: And we should emphasize that, unlike your culture, our children will experience no guilt whatsoever with respect to their sexual desires and experiences, in the same way that no one feels guilty for being thirsty or hungry. Any social order that causes children to associate sex with guilt is necessarily dysfunctional in the extreme.

Benedict: This is important. In my time we used to refer to it as the "association of ideas", or something like that, but today we can think of it like Pavlovian conditioning. In your culture, most children have been conditioned to experience guilt in the context of their own sexual desires and behaviors. And since teenage children are almost constantly thinking about and desiring sex, they are also almost constantly feeling guilt. And this is true even for children raised in non-religious families – isn't that so, Neal?

Neal: Yes, because the guilt from Christian religion has overflowed into the whole social order. So it is not to be wondered at that the products of a guilt-inducing, joy-denying social order are not able to experience the sexual energies very deeply.

10) Befriending the Sexual Energies [Or More Teachings of Diotima]

(At this point I am feeling a deluge of thoughts that go off in different directions: Socrates has more to say about Diotima's teachings, Benedict has lots to say about conditioning, and Plato…)

Plato: ... and Plato will come to your rescue. Well, it is an unfortunate consequence of your being stuck in the temporal order that only one thought at a time can be expressed, even though the argument now before us requires several strands of thought occurring simultaneously.

Neal: *(jokingly)* Yes, I am sure it is all my fault for being stuck here in time.

Plato: *(also joking, with a little bit of seriousness)* Why yes, it is your fault. After all, if *you* were not in the temporal order, *we* would not be having this conversation, would we?

Neal: Yeah, OK, so if you guys are visiting me in this temporal order, you have to abide by its rules: one thing at a time, thank you.

Plato: We will try to refrain from sending you a zillion thoughts all at once. I'll help you organize that deluge we just dumped on you.

Neal: Thank you.

Plato: Benedict wants to point out a kind of nefarious sexual conditioning, other than guilt, that everyone in your culture experiences but no one recognizes for what it is. Socrates wants to share his experiences with Diotima that explicitly bypass this life-destroying form of conditioning. And *I* think that, under the Master's questioning, you and William should first share your own experiences with regard to this form of conditioning that is every bit as harmful as the conditioning of guilt.

Neal: My goodness, there's a form of sexual conditioning that is as harmful as the conditioning that causes guilt to be associated with sexual experience?

William: *(with a little humor)* And it is a conditioning that you and I have experienced, but do not recognize for what it really is. So, as if just guilt were not bad enough, you are saying to us, "But wait, there's more." I can't imagine what it could be, unless I were to cheat.

Neal: Cheat?

William: *(laughing)* Yeah. You see, I am no longer fully in the temporal order, although more so than these guys. So yes, I could step back from the present moment and take a little peek ahead to see where this conversation is going to end up, even though the ending has not been predetermined.

Neal: *(also laughing)* Well, all I will say now is that you are lucky I am no longer very interested in the kind of metaphysical questions that you allude to: determinism, predeterminism, free will, all that stuff. Otherwise I would compel you to stay with me in the temporal order until all such questions have been answered.

William: Which would be a very long time indeed, especially since such questions do not admit of answers in terms of words or concepts. But I suspect Socrates here is going to put us through a wringer. I'm a little more detached from my personality than you are, so feel free to lean on me for support should you need it.

Neal: Oh, come on, how bad could it be?

Plato: You'll know soon enough. But before I turn the discussion over to Socrates, I want to observe that William has just introduced an important theme that we will develop at length later.

William: I did?

Plato: Yes, you said that you were more detached from your personality than is Neal, implying that Neal is at least a little bit detached, or has begun the process of detaching. Just as the business of childhood is to *form* a personality, the business of old age is to *detach* from the personality. We shall develop this theme later.

Neal: Good. I'm getting so many thoughts about this. Just like my culture does not know how to welcome and encourage newly embodied souls, neither does it have any idea how to assist those embodied souls who are now looking the other way, eager to return Home.

Benedict: In our New Social Order, leaving the World will be seen as every bit as important as entering the world. But now, let's stay focused and invite Socrates to do his thing.

Socrates: I am certain that whatever I now say or do will fall considerably short of the expectations laid upon me by Plato and Benedict. So I have explained Diotima's teaching with respect to the body itself. The mind shall make no effort to control or inhibit the impulses to move and make sounds… impulses that come from the Sexual Energy, which we are conceiving as Divine in nature. Because the egoic mind is very clever, and does not really wish to share its body with anything else, even the Divine Being, it can resist in ways of which the person is not conscious. This is why a Trainer is necessary. The trainer can see the unconscious resistance to letting go and fully surrendering to the sexual energy, and help the person move through his own resistance. Now, before I start to talk about other aspects of her teaching, I would like to ask Neal and William a few questions pertaining to their own sexual upbringing.

Neal and William: Proceed.

Socrates: So I'd like you to go back to the enforced abstinence of your teenage years, the interval of time between when your body was physiologically capable of sexual activity to the time that you had a regular partner or outlet for your sexual desires.

William: It was a long time.

Neal: And we were at the peak of our sexual energies, with no outlet.

Socrates: But yet, you did have an outlet. You masturbated.

Neal and William: Yes.

Socrates: And neither of you went blind?

William: *(laughing)* Yes, but I can actually recall worrying about it a little. When you're just 13 or 14 years old, and hear stories that masturbating causes blindness, you really don't know what to believe.

Socrates: But you masturbated anyway?

William: The power of the Life Force, in which all bodies necessarily participate, overcomes all inhibitions.

Socrates: Then tell me, what were you thinking about while you were masturbating?

(At this question, the insight towards which Socrates is leading William and me exploded fully formed in my mind. But the only way to describe it is as if it had unfolded in a linear sequence.)

Neal: Well, there was no shortage of cute girls in my class, so I would think about "making it" with one of the girls.

Socrates: There were cute girls (and boys) in my time too, but Diotima would not allow it.

Neal: Not allow what?

Socrates: Not allow me to think about cute girls and boys while she was summoning forth the sexual energy through my body.

Neal: But how could she tell what you were thinking about?

Socrates: Diotima is a priestess. A priestess can tell. I very quickly learned that there could be no hiding from her. Once when she was arousing me and caught me thinking about some cute girl – shall we call her Suzie? – she stopped and said to me: "You are not yet the Divine Being, and have only a limited amount of conscious awareness at your disposal. Whatever awareness you are giving to the thought of Suzie now, is awareness that you are not giving to me. I want the whole of your conscious attention, not just some of it. So take your attention away from the thought of Suzie, and place it on the sensations you are now feeling in your body. Become fully aware of what is happening in the present moment."

This was initially quite difficult. Of course, when she said what she said, my awareness immediately shifted to the sensations she was giving me with her hands. But then my mind would wander back to Suzie again or to something else other than the sensations I was feeling in my body. She said: "Yes, Socrates, this is the same ever-wandering mind that you have experienced during meditation, where the ever restless, undisciplined mind wants to focus on anything and everything except the feeling of the breath as the air enters and exits the nostrils. Now at some monasteries, when the Master sees that a monk's awareness is not concentrated on the breath, he brings the disciple back to the present moment with a whack from his stick. I have no stick with which to whack you, but if I see that your mind is wandering too much away from the sensations I am giving you, I might just squeeze some delicate part of your anatomy a little bit, just to get your attention, and help you to bring your awareness from the thought of Suzie back to the sensations in your body." Well, as you might imagine, after she said that – I was still on her bed, mind you

– she had my full attention. And so *(looking mischievously at William and I)* I was saved from the unfortunate fate that has befallen you two gentlemen.

Neal: What fate are you talking about?

Socrates: When you were masturbating in your teens, you had no one to stop you from fantasizing about cute girls. A most horrible fate indeed!

Neal: But wait a minute. Why do you say it's a horrible fate? People fantasize about sex all the time. Our psychologists agree that fantasizing can be creative, stimulates the imagination, adds to the excitement, and…

Socrates: … *(laughing)* and removes the mind from the present moment, in which the sex is actually happening.

Plato: Perhaps the question we should ask is: Can fantasy, or thinking about what is not real, ever contribute to the happiness of the present moment? But I think Benedict wants to say a few things now.

Benedict: Yes, thank you. Alright, I'm going to say a few things about the process of *conditioning*, and then Socrates will no doubt want to say more about the "horrible fate" suffered by you and William through the sexual conditioning to which you were subjected.

Neal: Go ahead.

Benedict: Let's begin by considering what Plato calls the "necessary desires". The desires for food, drink, and shelter are necessary in the sense that, if a given human being did not have such desires, he or she would perish. The desire for sex is also necessary if human beings are to constitute a species. There are other kinds of desires that should also be considered as necessary, if not for the survival of the human body, then for the flourishing of the human being. The desire to connect socially with other humans is necessary in this sense.

Now, even a cursory look at the many cultures and societies that have appeared on the planet over the years shows that, although these desires are common to humans of all cultures, how they are satisfied varies from one culture to another. A child's upbringing will determine the particular foods he will think about when he feels the desire for food. A child's hunger is the same. But whether a given child, when hungry, will then think about rice, pizza, raw fish, or hamburgers is determined by his upbringing, that is, by the specific culture in which he was raised. A person's upbringing causes the desire for food to become associated, in the mind of the individual, with specific foods. The sexual appetite has been conditioned in the same way. Everyone, in all cultures, feels sexual desires. But *how* such desires may be satisfied varies from one culture to another. That is, the specific ideas and images that come to the mind of an individual in conjunction with the sexual appetite are conditioned by one's upbringing.

William: And if I may interject an example or two, young men are conditioned to respond sexually to an idealized female body. It's much more pervasive in your time, Neal, than it was in mine, but even in my time, there were plenty of images of female bodies that 13-year-old boys could attach to their natural sexual desires. But the images vary from one culture to another. The idealized female body in your culture would be rejected by my culture as too sickly and anemic. And conversely, the idealized female body of my time would be rejected as too fat by your culture. And the girls of my time were conditioned to associate their sexual desires more with the man's social status than with his physical appearance.

Benedict: And we must note well that there is no necessary connection between (i) the biological desire, for food or sex, and (ii) what the social conditioning process has caused to become associated with the original desire.

William: What do you mean? Oh, yes, like with Pavlov's dog. The dog has been conditioned to salivate at the sound of a bell. But there is no necessary connection between the sound of a bell and the arrival of food. The "connection" has been programmed into the mind of the dog.

Benedict: Yes, and there's a further point I want to make. There is no connection between (i) the specific foods and drinks that a given culture programs individuals to associate with hunger and thirst, and (ii) the nutritious value of those foods and drinks. This is especially nefarious in your culture, Neal. A child when thirsty will desire a soft drink because the culture has caused him to associate thirst with such drink. But such beverages are actually very harmful to the child's physical health and well-being. So it is quite possible, as your culture illustrates, to raise children in such a way that the necessary desires have been conditioned to attach themselves to objects that cannot satisfy the original purpose of those desires. The purpose, one might say, of thirst, the desire for drink, or hunger, the desire for food, is to supply the body with what is necessary for its proper functioning. But the particular objects that your culture has associated with the satisfaction of those desires cannot actually satisfy the purpose behind those desires. So when a child, in response to her natural desire of hunger and thirst, thinks about "fast foods" and soft drinks, as she has been programmed to think, she is thinking about things that cannot satisfy the purpose behind the necessary desires. And the same with sex.

Plato: A few examples…?

Neal: Yes, please.

Benedict: We can use the examples William alluded to. Consider a girl who has been programmed to respond sexually to males of higher social status.

Neal: OK.

Benedict: But the sexual energy is the Life Force, and has nothing to do with social status. If one is asking the question, as we are, how may one experience this Life Force in a way that is maximally beneficial to the individual, then concern with social status is irrelevant.

Neal: I see.

Benedict: But you may not see the next point, because it involves your own conditioning.

Neal: What do you mean?

Benedict: What are the specific images that boys are conditioned to associate with sexual desire in your culture?

Neal: Images of girls?

Benedict: It's much worse than that.

Neal: Oh, images of girls' body parts. Yikes, we've been conditioned to respond sexually to idealized body parts, not even to real human beings.

Benedict: And is there any connection between a body part and the Life Force, especially when *(laughing)* the body part is imagined as disconnected from the body and the person?

Plato: *(also laughing)* And lest you are tempted to defend your own sexual conditioning by protesting that some body parts, like breasts, really are intrinsically sexy, let me remind you that there are many cultures – my own for example – in which boys and men see breasts all the time and do not automatically get sexually aroused. *Our* association with breasts was that it is what you feed babies with, and I assure you the guys of ancient Greece were not walking around with erections every time we saw a nursing mother. So there is nothing intrinsically "sexy" about breasts. But more seriously, can you see how much harm has been done to both boys and girls in a society that conditions boys to associate the necessary sexual desire with breasts, especially with disembodied breasts. But now I think Socrates is ready to drive home the main point.

Socrates: Yes, so let's go back to you and William, at an age where you are just discovering the sexual energies within your own bodies. Your culture forces you to experience this energy alone, without any possibility of a human partner, for anywhere from five to ten or twelve years. When you masturbate, that is, when you summon forth the sexual energy, you do so thinking the images and fantasies programmed into your minds by the general culture. And to be specific, let's assume that in your cases, it is not a disembodied breast that excites you, but rather, a real, live cute girl who is in your algebra class. Let's call her Suzie, as before.

Neal: OK.

Socrates: So when you are experiencing the sexual energy, when you are orgasming, you are thinking about Suzie?

Neal: Yes.

Socrates: And this is a process that goes on for many years, and the formative years at that?

Neal: Yes.

Socrates: And so boys are conditioned to associate the sexual energy with the thought of Suzie, or some other girls?

Neal: Yes.

Socrates: And what is this "thought or image of Suzie" with which you have associated your sexual energies?

Neal: Huh? Oh wait…

Socrates: Yes, the thought of Suzie, or of anyone else, is a thought. This is the important thing to realize. At the deeper level, it does not matter *what* you are thinking about while masturbating. For six, seven, eight years and more, children masturbate to their *thinking*, so that the sexual energy is caused to be associated with *thinking*. Please see how harmful this is. A child raised in this way will not be able to stop *thinking* just because at some later time he now is with a real female. This is why men are constantly fantasizing; their sexual upbringing trained them to respond sexually to *thoughts* about sex, not to real female bodies. For the first six or seven years of sexual maturity, every orgasm they had was in response to *fantasizing*, which is a form of *thinking*.

Plato: Just consider the difference between your upbringing and how we are raising our children. Our 13-year-old Johnny will not have to *think* about Suzie in order to get aroused. Suzie will be in the bedroom with him. He will see her, hear her, smell her, taste her, and touch her. And *her* sexual energy will become a part of Johnny's arousal. *His* orgasms will be in response to a living human being, rather than to fantasies about human beings.

Socrates: And so what Diotima taught me was the exact opposite of what your culture taught you. The deepest sexual experiences happen when the mind is not thinking at all. When the awareness is 100% focused on the sexual sensations in one's own body, there is no room to *think* about anything. And if one is *thinking* about something during sexual arousal, then such thoughts sap one's ability to *feel* the sexual energy. Diotima taught me to feel deeply the physical sensations and to merge with the Life Force. But this cannot happen as long as one is busy fantasizing, that is, as long as what we have been calling "linguistic consciousness" is dominant.

William: I think it is important to realize that fantasizing does indeed involve linguistic consciousness, since fantasies involve words, symbols and images.

Socrates: And there is one more thing I want to mention about Diotima's teaching. Now many spiritual teachers have told us about the "here and now" as opposed to the "then and there", so this is hardly a new teaching. Linguistic consciousness, sometimes called "the ego", is almost always in the "then and there", which includes the past, the future, and all fantasies. But pleasure and joy can occur only in the "here and now". This applies to *all* pleasures, not just sex. Shall I enumerate a few, to make my meaning more clear?

Neal: We might have discussed this before.

Plato: *(smiling)* But we did warn you at the beginning that our discussion would likely be lengthy, circular, and repetitive.

Socrates: I'll try to spice up the examples, but the main point will be very obvious. Suppose a musician, let's say a pianist, is performing. While he is playing, he constantly (i) fantasizes (that is, thinks) about how someone else might play the same music, (ii) he thinks to himself that he is not playing well enough, and (iii) he wishes he had a different instrument to play on. What should we say to him?

Neal: Hah! He won't make it even halfway through the concert, with those thoughts running through his head.

Socrates: Oh?! And can you suggest better thoughts that should run through his head?

Neal: *(laughing)* Actually, no. Any other thoughts would be just as bad.

Socrates: But suppose his thoughts were about how to play and interpret the music?

Neal: Even worse. He shouldn't be *thinking* about the music at all.

As he is learning the music he will give some thought to matters of interpretation, and after his concert he may evaluate his performance, but during the performance he will be *feeling* the music, not thinking about it at all. In fact, an expression that is frequently used to describe an exceptional musician is "beyond technique". To say of a pianist that she is "beyond technique" is to say that the technical aspects of playing have been so thoroughly mastered that she does not think about them at all, and her conscious mind is fully immersed in the music and *only* the music.

Socrates: So linguistic consciousness must be in abeyance, if the pianist is to manifest the music.

Neal: And it must also be in abeyance in the audience, if they are to fully *hear* the music.

Socrates: Good. Now let's consider a different context, say a gymnastic game like basketball. Of course, as with music, linguistic consciousness is involved in preparing for the game and evaluating the performance afterwards.

Neal: Yes.

Socrates: But tell me, as the game is being played, do the players *think* about where to run, how to move their arms, when to shoot at the basket, how to prevent opposing players from shooting, etc.

Neal: Of course not. These things – the appropriate bodily movements – are automatic. The conscious mind is in abeyance.

Socrates: So it is a little bit like sex, is it not?

Neal: What? Oh yes, in the sense that the motions of the bodies are not being controlled by conscious thinking. The motions of the bodies are caused respectively by (i) the Life Force, (ii) the music, and (iii) the game. But I want to know what is this additional teaching of Diotima that you alluded to.

Socrates: Patience, my friend. But I should warn you and the others that I feel some rather bad puns are about to manifest.

William: I think we are all up to that challenge. Proceed.

Socrates: Now all three activities, sex, music, and sports, are, one might say, temporally extended objects. A sexual experience, a concert, and a basketball game have a beginning and an ending.

Neal: Yes, so?

Socrates: So a basketball player desires to win. Suppose that during the game he thinks about what he wants to happen at the end of the game. During the game he thinks about winning the game and celebrating with his teammates afterwards.

Neal: There is not likely to be much joy in the locker room after the game, if the players are thinking about this during the game.

William: The awareness of the players must be *entirely* focused in the present moment, as the game is being played.

Socrates: So even though they desire to win, they are not *thinking* about winning while playing the game. Would you agree?

Neal: Yes. And the same is true for any other sport or game.

Socrates: Now with music, every piece has an ending.

Neal: Of course.

Socrates: Let's suppose that the ending is especially beautiful, like one of those Beethoven symphonies that ends with a magnificent climax.

Neal: I detect a pun here.

Socrates: Now suppose that the conductor loves the climax of Beethoven's *Fifth* so much that he thinks about it while conducting the whole piece.

Neal: Well, if he is *thinking* about the end of the piece while the musicians are playing the beginning or middle part, then he is not actually *feeling* the music he is conducting. He is too busy *thinking* about the ending.

Socrates: But suppose the conductor would say something like this: *"The climax that comes at the end of the piece is the most important part. All the music that preceded the climax is merely a buildup to the climax itself."* What might we say to such a conductor?

Neal: Back to music school for him.

Socrates: And what would you teach him when he returns to music school?

Neal: That music isn't about the climax at the end, so he shouldn't be thinking about it at all. Every note of Beethoven's *Fifth* is just as important as the ending. He should be simply *feeling* the music as it is being played. And besides, there are many incredibly profound and beautiful pieces that end softly, not with a bang.

Socrates: So our conductor will be retrained and taught to value every instant of the music as it is being played, to be mentally present at every instant, and to have no thoughts that pertain to the future, that is, to the bang at the end, if there is one. He will not treat the beginning and middle parts of the symphony merely as stepping stones to the climax at the end, but will value and appreciate the beauty of every moment of the music.

Neal: Well, because of your little pun, the analogy with music is quite obvious. Diotima taught you to value and appreciate every stage of arousal, not because each stage is a stepping stone to orgasm, but because each stage is intrinsically valuable and interesting. If men are thinking about orgasm during the beginning or middle stages of arousal, then they are not fully present to the stages they are in fact experiencing, and hence cannot fully enjoy what they are experiencing.

Socrates: Exactly. So it is this male tendency to rush to climax that Diotima helped me bring under control, hence I was able to linger and luxuriate in each stage of the process of arousal. And, if I may mix the metaphors, just as not all beautiful music comes with a bang at the end, it is not necessary that sexual encounters end with a climax. It is very beneficial for couples to lie together in mild or moderate arousal, without orgasm. But this cannot happen until the male has befriended the sexual energy, has become gentle within, and can experience each stage of arousal, not as a means to an end, but as an end in itself. For this, he needs a Teacher.

Neal: What about the girls? I can well imagine some of my feminist friends pointing out that, here we are, five guys talking about sex, and focusing mostly on the boys' sexual education.

Plato: *(with a little humor, but only a little)* Here's what we will tell our feminist friends: the self-destructive violence that is causing the

Earth to lose its ability to support human life is caused by males, not females. We should refer to it as what it is: the problem of male violence. To protect our species we must prevent males from becoming violent. For there will be no social order at all unless the problem of male violence is addressed through upbringing. Now, in all patriarchal societies, males compete with one another for material possessions and for females. You call it "competition", but that's just another word for "violence".

The second point we will make with our feminist friends is to challenge the sense in which we are "five guys". We have explicitly stated that when we talk about the "male" and the "female", we mostly mean the values associated with the gender. All five of us are more "female" than "male" in terms of our values. While embodied, we were concerned with understanding and with helping others. The desire to understand is on the female side of the Yin/Yang division, because one must be in a receptive mode to understand anything. As William and Neal will attest, for the majority of males in academia, the desire to understand is secondary to the desires to be recognized, to win arguments, to have their own opinions acknowledged, to be respected, and so forth, desires that are very different from the desire to understand. And a further point for our feminist friends to consider is, hmm, how to put it, OK, think of it this way: the soul of which I, the Plato personality, is a part contains numerous other "lives" or "personalities", about half of which are female. For communication purposes, this soul appears as the personality Plato, with which you are somewhat familiar. *(With a lot of humor)* But I assure you, or rather, your feminist friends, should I, as the male Plato, say anything that offends my literal female soulmates, they will be sure to give me grief for it afterwards. And even you, Neal, who have no conscious memory of the many female lives within your soul, are nevertheless strongly influenced by them.

Socrates: But nevertheless, there will be training for the girls that will exactly complement the training for the boys.

Neal: Shall we say a little about it?

Socrates: Yes, and only a little needs to be said. The yin-yang symbol beautifully illustrates the point I want to make. In that symbol, the female is at the very center of the male, and the male is at the very center of the female. Our upbringing assists the male to find and make friends with the female at the center of his being. That "female" is the capacity to receive nurturing and pleasure within his own body. But what, you are wondering, is the counterpart to this in the female?

Neal: Yes.

Socrates: Simply this: the female will ***assert*** the core values of kindness, compassion, inclusion, understanding. She will **insist** that these values are not negotiable, and must **rule** over any other values, especially the values associated with male dominance. *(With humor)* And should the males falter and resist, we will resurrect *Lysistrata* to teach them aright. Ah, where is Aristophanes, now that we need him!?

William: Actually, now that you've mentioned Aristophanes, his solution to the problem of male violence makes for an interesting contrast with our own.

Neal: How so?

William: Well in his play, the women, tired of losing their husbands, lovers, fathers, brothers, and sons to stupid male violence, capture the fort and refuse to have sex until the men promise to stop with their violence against one another. So the males, forced to choose between sex and violence, give up their violent ways. Yet those tendencies towards competition and violence are still in their psyche. But because of how we are raising our children, these very tendencies will be largely absent from their psyche.

Benedict: We might say that, for males that have been raised in a patriarchy, the threat of "no sex" might very well cause the men to agree to stop fighting among themselves, at least until after they have gotten sufficiently laid. Is that the right expression?

Neal: *(smiling)* Good enough.

Benedict: But we seem to be discovering that the way to remove the tendencies toward male violence is not by depriving them of sex, but by making certain that they have an abundance of high quality sex, especially in their formative years.

Neal: They will be too busy making love to even think about making war.

Benedict: And, thanks for reminding me, our semantic cops have something to say about that phrase "making love".

Neal: Oh?

Benedict: We are agreed that the word "love" shall, for us, always carry the connotations of its highest usage: unconditional caring. But "having sex" and "unconditional caring" are very different, so that one can engage in sexual activities without much caring for the other, and of course, one can care for another without sex being involved. Since the origin of Love is the Divine Being, it is not possible for humans to actually "make" or "create" love. So we should not use expressions that suggest that humans have the power to "make" love.

Plato: Nevertheless, the sexual experience may be utilized, not to *create* love, to be sure, but as an opportunity for humans to *experience* love. For lovers, gazing into one another's eyes, may very well be led from the beauty of the lover's face, to the beauty of her soul, to the beauty of his own soul, and from thence to the beauty of All Souls in which Divine Love is embedded. So we will not say that our lovers will be "*making* love", but we will say that it is possible for our lovers to participate in Divine Love through sex.

Neal: And I suppose we will need to recruit more Teachers for that. Or is experiencing Divine Love through sex an advanced technique?

Plato: Yes and no. There are many ways, besides sex, for humans to experience Divine Love. However, at a suitable age, once the novelty of the sexual experience has worn off a bit, we can certainly give instruction to our children that will align them in this direction. When the sexual energy has been partially tamed, we will instruct our children to lie together, feel the sexual energy, and feel the joy in their body; immersed in that joy, their minds will experience thoughts that are peaceful and happy and aligned with Love. And if there is a bang at the end, they will be instructed to linger in embrace, to feel gratitude both towards one another and also to the Divine Being that has created such joy. There will of course be more advanced techniques, but these will be optional to pursue when they are adults.

Neal: What do you mean by "more advanced techniques"?

Plato: Socrates shared only the beginning stages of the "mystery religions". The more advanced stages concern using the orgasm as a portal through which one's consciousness could leave the body and actually merge with and become one with Divine Love.

Socrates: And I suppose I could share one aspect of this more advanced technique, especially since Diotima tells me she is preparing to return to Earth with an army of priestesses she has trained to heal the males. *Our* males, the ones we are raising, will not need much healing. But the males that have been raised by the current culture have been badly damaged by their upbringing, and will need much healing in order to successfully transition to our New Society.

Neal: About that army of priestesses, you're being metaphorical, are you not?

Socrates: *(smiling)* Maybe. But maybe not. You see, the priestesses were what your world today calls *trance mediums*. She could enter into a trance and allow her body to be taken over by a female spiritual energy that we may refer to as the "Goddess". When the male had been prepared, the priestess would straddle him and allow the goddess to enter and control her body. The goddess, responding to the needs of the male, would cause the female's body to orgasm at the same time as the male body. With both root chakras wide open, the goddess could send healing energies to the male. In addition to pleasure of course, the male would experience a sense of well-being, of being loved and cared for, and his mind would be calm and at peace for weeks afterwards.

Neal: And you say she's coming back with an army of priestesses?

Socrates: *(laughing)* Yes, but don't get your hopes up. It won't be in your lifetime. And besides, if you do come back, how do you know that you won't come back as one of the priestesses, instead of as a male in need of her services?

Neal: *(laughing)* Well I suppose I would be OK with that, especially since it would appear that the priestesses, in their service to the Goddess, will be enjoying themselves immensely. At any rate, I just might want to come back to investigate what is happening.

Socrates: Well I'll tell you what's happening. What do you think the expressions "as above, so below" or "on Earth, as in Heaven" or "bringing Heaven down to Earth" really mean? And before answering that, consider the Hindu terms that describe the enlightened condition.

Neal: "Sat-chit-ananda", I believe. It means infinite Being, infinite Knowledge, and infinite Bliss.

Socrates: And we have here been focusing on the "bliss" part – joy without end. So the process of bringing Heaven to Earth must necessarily involve bringing this bliss, or a portion of it, into the human experience.

Benedict: And I must confess, when I wrote about seeking for a "true good", the discovery of which would give me supreme, continuous, and eternal happiness, I was seeking, and of course, *found,* the spiritual joy that the mystics talk about. It did not occur to me then that it would ever be possible to bring such joy, or even a modicum of such joy, into the physical world. True happiness for the human soul always lies in the conscious recognition of the union that exists between the human mind and the Divine Mind. Nevertheless, the world can support much more joy than now exists. And the more joy we bring to the planet, the easier it will be for individuals to attain that supreme and eternal joy that I called "Blessedness". But we should remember that no matter how many emissaries the Goddess sends, even the most intense pleasure and joy possible for the embodied soul pales in comparison with the eternal joy of spiritual awakening.

Plato: Well, I don't think we need worry that our children will come to think that sexual pleasure is "the" ultimate joy. For the Being of Light will Itself send many emissaries back to their bodies to tell the story of Divine Love to our children. Our children will be taught that although the joys of the body are many and worth cultivating, they cannot compare to the joys that the mind feels when not embodied. Moreover, our children will certainly have heard of the more advanced sexual techniques, in which the lesser joy of sexual ecstasy becomes a portal for the greater joy of Spiritual Union with the Divine.

Socrates: And I suppose we should add that, although our children shall have individual trainers, they will also have lots of unstructured time to play together, to experiment and explore their sexuality among themselves. For the gods and goddesses that govern the Divine Force called "sex" are endlessly creative, and will seek to express themselves through the bodies of our children. So like everything else we are teaching them, sports, music, theater, and the usual academic stuff, we shall not over-structure their time, so that they may play and explore among themselves, thereby inviting the holy flower of Divine Creativity to enter into their activities.

11) The "Problem" of Sexual Jealousy

William: Well I must say, all this seems too good to be true.

Plato: And you suspect, William, that maybe it *is* too good to be true?

William: Yes, I suspect there may be problems with jealousy and envy.

Neal: And I share William's concern. The "Form of Beauty", as Plato might put it, does not bestow itself equally in all humans. Some children will be more attractive in appearance than others; some will be more popular and more sought after as sexual partners and playmates. How will our teenagers deal with the pain of rejection, since it will not infrequently happen that X wants to play with Y but Y does not want to play with X.

William: My concerns, exactly. There is perhaps no developmental stage more tender and vulnerable than the early teens. Children are eager to "fit in", to be accepted socially by their peers, and are liable to feel insecure about things…

Neal: … and their body is probably the thing they feel most insecure about. Won't children be jealous of those whose bodies are more beautiful, and because of that, get more attention?

Plato: My goodness, do you think we have been talking about *your* children? … The children raised by your dysfunctional social order do indeed have such problems. But not *our* children! Shall we review the reasons why this is so, why none of your concerns apply to *our* children?

William: Hmm, we have stated, I believe, that there are no human "problems" that cannot be solved by proper upbringing, and this *must* include the "problem" of adolescents and their negative body images, and the jealousies that ensue from that. So yes, by all means, I think a little review would be most useful. Why will our children be spared the usual emotional troubles of adolescence?

Plato: … Because "right opinion" has pervaded every aspect of their upbringing. They know that they are not their body. They know that they are aspects of a single Divine Being, and that all other such aspects are of equal importance to the Whole. They have been taught that they are like beautiful flowers that do not receive their beauty through comparison with other flowers. And because of their *emotional intelligence*, which lies at the very core of our educational process, our children know not only their own emotions but also the emotions of other children. When any group of children come together for any purpose, the first order of business for that group is the emotional well-being of each and every person in the group. We have taught them kindness and compassion, not competition, envy, and war. We have also taken great care during their upbringing that no child will ever feel "left out", that they do not belong, or that other children are better or more important than themselves. It will never occur to our children to desire a body other than the one they have.

Benedict: And here's another way to look at it. From the perspective of a doctor, all human bodies are pretty much the same. Whether a body is young or old, whether it is attractive in appearance or not, it is all the same to the doctor, who is concerned with health.

And from the perspective of Socrates, physician of the soul, the outer appearance of the body is of no importance or concern. For…

Socrates: … Yes, good, for I perceive the soul directly. The beauty of a well-ordered soul, *(laughing)* even if it is in a body uglier than my own, is infinitely more appealing to me than a beautiful body inhabited by a disordered soul. Our children will be trained to go for the soul, so to speak, to see and feel the beauty of Spirit, even as it manifests through the various bodies.

Neal: But physical beauty surely counts for something. Some bodies, if I may use Plato's terminology, embody the form of beauty more than others. Surely our children will notice this, and be naturally attracted to the bodies that radiate more beauty, even if we tell them that souls are more beautiful than the most beautiful of bodies.

Plato: But of course, we shall not merely *tell* them that the beauty of the soul far exceeds anything in the physical world, which at best merely reflects the beauty of the soul. We shall give them the actual experience, insofar as it is possible. Remember, the veil has thinned, and many children will be experiencing nonphysical beings and experiencing directly the beauty thereof. They will talk about "visiting Grandma in heaven" through meditations and dreams, and will know that the beauty of heaven far exceeds anything on earth, including the most beautiful of Earthly bodies.

Benedict: And I suppose we should point out that, because neither capitalism nor advertising will exist, our children will not have been conditioned to respond sexually to images of bodies and idealized body parts.

Neal: Nevertheless, although I agree with what you say, I want to push this point. Let's go back to high school, or perhaps junior high school, and observe the boys and girls as they talk about one another. The boys, talking among themselves, will rank the girls in terms of physical attractiveness. The girls, talking among themselves, compare the boys in their class and likewise rank the boys in terms of physical desirability. We may talk to them all we want about spiritual beauty, and that the beauty of souls far exceeds the beauty of bodies, but they will experience that they are more attracted to some bodies than to others, and there will be general agreement among them as to *which* bodies are the more attractive. Hence the more attractive bodies will be more sought after and get more attention than the others.

Benedict: But you don't know this.

Neal: What?

Benedict: You don't know whether it is true that boys and girls, raised in the way we have been raising them, will nevertheless "rank" one another in terms of physical comeliness.

Neal: I agree. I should not assume that *our* children will feel and behave as children raised in a dysfunctional culture. But still, whether they "rank" one another or not, they will not feel equally attracted sexually to other children. May we agree on that?

Benedict: Yes.

Neal: And is there such a thing as "lust on first sight"?

Benedict: Of course – especially with regard to teenagers.

Neal: Then suppose that in a group of children, all the boys are in lust with the same girl and all the girls are in lust with the same boy. Even if they understand that the inner beauty of the soul far exceeds that of the body, it is the perceived beauty of the body, not the soul, that is involved in sexual attraction.

William: We could perhaps express the point as follows: Some bodies will radiate more "sex appeal" than others. How will children with less physical beauty *feel*? Won't they be envious of those who are more "popular" and sought after because of their physical beauty?

Plato: *(smiling)* We have not guaranteed that souls manifesting in our New Society will be free from challenges. We said earlier that although the "mischief" involved in Shakespeare's tragedies would no longer be allowed, we did say that the mischief of the comedies would still be a part of the human experience. There will continue to be situations in which A is in love with – ah, no – A is in lust with B who in turn is in lust with C who in turn, etc., etc. After all, if there were no emotional issues that humans had to deal with, there would be no need for souls to incarnate. Wait, I said that backwards.

Embodiment exists, not for human reasons, but for purposes of Spirit. These "purposes" – and here I fear that language will fail us more than usual – have to do, in part, with smoothing out the rough edges in the soul. In order to do that, it selects "lives" in which the rough edges are allowed to manifest, and they typically manifest as emotional difficulties for the human. So being in lust with someone who is not also in lust with you will be a typical "arena" for such issues to manifest.

Benedict: Yes, but our children, and adults too, have the psychological tools to handle such difficulties. Let's examine the scenario you envision above, and see how our children and their teachers might handle envy as it arises in a sexual context.

Neal: Good idea. OK, let's assume we have a group of 20 children, ten girls and ten boys. One of the boys, say Peter, is handsome, smart, muscular, with a good sense of humor. All the girls prefer him to any other boy. At the same time, one of the girls, say Suzie, is beautiful, intelligent, and has the kind of figure that boys drool over. All of the boys prefer her to any of the other girls. Now this situation, or kind of situation, is the norm in my present culture, and will continue to happen in our New Society. But in my present culture, this situation, that causes so much pain to nine out of ten children, is ignored by the adults, and children are often scarred for life, as they say, because of sexual rejection in their formative years.

William: But we shall not be abandoning our children just because they reach puberty and have become sexually mature, but instead will be guiding them through it. So how shall we guide them in this situation?

Benedict: You said "nine out of ten" children feel emotional stress because of this situation. But really, it is "ten out of ten" children that will need our assistance.

Neal: What do you mean?

Benedict: In some ways, Peter and Suzie, the objects of sexual adoration by the other children, are in more need of help than the others. How do you imagine Peter and Suzie *feel*, being singled out for so much attention?

Plato: Hint: our children have been raised in such a way that the Golden Rule is at the center of their psychological being. Only in a competitive culture such as yours would people "feel good" about *having more* than others, including having more sexual appeal.

Neal: I see. So Peter and Suzie are not likely to feel entirely comfortable being sought after, as they will care about and empathize with those who are not sought after.

Benedict: And when these things are honestly shared in small groups, and the children – both those who are sought after and those who are not – express their feelings with honesty, vulnerability and compassion, as we have been training them from the beginning, what is likely to arise?

Neal: Arise?

Benedict: What have you yourself experienced under similar conditions?

Neal: When someone shares at a deep level of honesty and vulnerability, there arises in the listener profound feelings of compassion.

Benedict: What else?

Neal: I see it! Looking with compassion at the person who is honestly sharing, the physical face of the person becomes transformed, as if absorbed into a Higher Beauty.

Socrates: *(smiling)* And pay attention, Neal, to your own feelings right now as you are typing this.

(When Socrates said this, I became aware that tears were dripping from my eyes. Memories from previous experiences with groups flooded my mind. A woman who was not very attractive expressed with honesty and tenderness her feelings about that. As she shared, it seemed to me that her face became intensely beautiful and attractive through the sharing.)

Plato: So you see, it is true that beauty lies in the eyes of the beholder; quite literally, as she was sharing, the inner beauty of her soul manifested physically on her face. Do you recall a few conversations ago we asked you to consider how we, who are not embodied, experience you who are embodied?

Neal: Yes.

Plato: A good exercise to keep doing. The physical beauty that is captured by the physical eyes, mediated by light reflecting off the body, is *not* what we perceive. We perceive the embodied soul directly. And since the beauty of even the least beautiful of souls is infinitely greater than the reflected beauty of the most beautiful of bodies, mere physical beauty is of no significance to us, except to note that it is something the given soul has chosen to manifest and hence deal with. For it is not a trivial matter to choose to incarnate with bodies that get a lot of attention, like Peter and Suzie, and their spiritual lessons involve dealing wisely with the attention given to them because of their physical appearance.

Benedict: And we should note that in the group sharing with Peter, Suzie, and the other children, we are not anticipating any outcome, as if there is a problem to be solved once and for all. The process of sharing, of expressing emotion honestly and deeply, is the point. This is the process that has the power to bring the beauty of the soul into physical reality.

William: So we are not claiming to have solved the problem of envy and jealousy. Such difficulties will continue to arise. But we are claiming that our process of group sharing (i) will openly acknowledge these emotional realities, (ii) will generate feelings of understanding, compassion, and acceptance in the children, and (iii) will actually bring more Beauty into the physical, so that the beauty of the soul shall be spread upon the Earth.

Benedict: I would never have thought that the much-maligned lower emotions, like envy and jealousy, could serve as a path or portal to the higher emotions. It would appear that anything and everything can be used as an opportunity for understanding and spiritual growth.

Plato: Exactly! *(Gesturing towards William and myself)* Are you satisfied with our response to the so-called "problem" of sexual envy and jealousy?

(I was about to respond in the affirmative when Socrates jumped in…)

12) Socrates Solves the Problem [Or Socrates Sets a Trap]

Socrates: Well regardless of whether Neal and William are satisfied, I think there is a different solution altogether to the "problem" that they raised.

Plato: Oh?

Socrates: Yes, a marvelous solution whereby everyone will get what they want without all this recourse to extensive group processing.

Plato: You've found a shortcut?

Socrates: Well, I won't guarantee that my alternative solution will lead exactly to the same place, but it will be quite satisfying to all involved.

Neal: I for one am eager to hear what you have to say.

Socrates: Let's revisit your initial scenario, where one girl has the kind of body and personality that all the boys want, and one boy has the kind of body and personality that all the girls desire. Suppose that Peter and Suzie have found a way to make copies of their bodies.

Neal: OK.

Socrates: Then they could give a copy to anyone who wants one. That would solve the problem, would it not? All the children would get the body they wanted for sex, and Suzie and Peter need not be concerned about not being able to please everybody.

Neal: Well, even if I grant your premise, that it would solve the problem, how do you propose that Suzie and Peter duplicate themselves? *Cloning* would take 14 or 15 years, and our children are not going to wait that long.

Socrates: No, not cloning. What I had in mind was sex dolls or robots. They're already here – or there, or wherever it is that you are – and *(glancing at William)* peeking ahead a little bit, in a generation from now they will be indistinguishable from real human bodies, in terms of appearance and behavior.

Neal: Do we really want to go along this path? – The whole thing seems somewhat perverse to me. Sex with a robot? You've got to be joking.

Socrates: *(with humor)* And perhaps you're getting to be an old fart who is unable to wrap his mind around the possibilities afforded by robotic engineering.

Neal: Alright, explain what you see as the possibilities.

Socrates: *(mischievously)* I will, and you can hold William's hand if this gets too uncomfortable for you.

William: *(laughing, to me)* I assure you, whatever it is he has on his mind regarding sex robots, I will be considerably more uncomfortable than you.

Socrates: So in appearance the robot will look exactly like Suzie. We can program it to have her exact voice. All of Suzie's mannerisms and behaviors can be programmed into the robot. Moreover, even sexual responses and techniques can be programmed.

Neal: What do you mean?

Socrates: Suppose the girls are swooning over Peter because he has fabulous bedside techniques that drive them crazy with pleasure. Suppose Suzie, when aroused, moans and screams in ways that make the boys go nuts with passion. All such behaviors may be programmed into the robot.

Neal: And you say that in few generations from now these robot dolls will not be distinguishable from real human bodies?

Socrates: Not unless you take a knife to their skin and see the inner wiring. But wait, it gets even better.

Neal: How so.

Socrates: Let's say that one of the girls, Mary, has a "Peter" robot. She likes and is turned on by how he looks, his tone of voice, how he touches her, and so forth, but she wishes his penis were slightly thicker. No problem, because she can adjust the length and thickness of his penis to suit her desires. She can also adjust his strokes; slow, fast, rough, gentle – all these things can be programmed.

Neal: But…

Socrates: And the same for the boys. Let's say Larry has a "Suzie" doll, and is quite happy with it, except that he would prefer dark hair instead of blonde hair. You get the picture. Any physical variable can be adjusted and programmed into the robot: the words said, breast size, ways of moving when aroused, and ways of stimulating him sexually. Whether the robot is sexually passive or aggressive can also be programmed. Basically our boys and girls will be given sex robots that they can program in any way that is most pleasing to them.

Neal: I am as uncomfortable with these ideas as I am fascinated.

Socrates: Perhaps you are concerned that our robots, although they can mimic any human behavior, are not actually human, so our children will not be able to bond with them, or befriend them.

Neal: I'm not sure what I'm concerned with, but yes, this is one thing that might be troubling.

Socrates: But humans bond with inanimate objects all the time. You still remember your teddy bear, don't you?

Neal: *(laughing)* Yes, and I remember being quite upset when my mother disposed of it after the stuffings started coming out.

Socrates: So I rest my case. If you could bond with a teddy bear, then our adolescent children will have no difficulty bonding with our robots that will give them so much sexual pleasure and joy.

Neal: I believe that what you say about bonding is true. I have read stories to the effect that some men have dolls that, even with today's limited technology, they have become very attached to, and even bring to parties and social gatherings.

Socrates: I won't ask whether he shares his doll with other men, or if he has become possessive of her and keeps her only for himself. But the other men could get a doll just like his, so there could be no cause of jealousy.

William: Yes, but the bottom line is that they are just dolls or robots. They behave the way they are programmed to behave, and are incapable of spontaneous behavior.

Socrates: Ah, yet some, like Benedict here, might argue that humans too have been programmed through upbringing and culture, and are really no more spontaneous than dolls and robots. But consider the following situation: a woman is about to have sex with her robot. The robot of the future will of course be "smart", that is, capable of learning from experience. He "knows" what his woman likes, needs, desires, by way of sex. Let us suppose that he has been programmed with two or three hundred different sexual behaviors, each one of which his woman likes. We put one of those random number generators inside of him, so that his actual behavior at any given time cannot be predicted by his woman. It will then appear to her that his behavior is spontaneous, will it not?

Neal: Perhaps.

Benedict: And the implicit suggestion here is that so-called human "spontaneous behavior" might not be all that different from the robot's.

Neal: Ohhh, this is a bit too much. There is something not quite right, at least to me, with the idea of our children having sex with robots instead of with one another.

Socrates: Perhaps the words "robot" and "doll" are what bothers you. Our children will be having sex with *bodies* that in appearance and behaviors are indistinguishable from real human bodies. Moreover, they choose exactly the body and behaviors that they desire. So every child gets what he or she wants, and no one is envious, jealous or hurt in any way. And I'll bet they will be useful for our Sex Trainers, as the Trainers could program the robots to teach them specific things. A female robot could be programmed to help the boys slow down, and the male robots could be programmed to help the girls find their g-spots, or whatever. So the robots could become a very useful tool for our Trainers. So what's not to like?

William: It seems to me that there must be some difference between having sex with a robot and having sex with a real human being.

Neal: I agree with William, but cannot think of what that difference might be.

Socrates: While you are trying to think what the difference might be, if indeed there is a difference, there is even more to be said about the potential of using sex robots.

Neal: Go ahead.

Socrates: William, would you mind cheating a bit, as you put it, and take a peek behind the veil. Go a generation or two ahead, then come back and tell us what you see.

William: Oh my.

Neal: What do you see?

William: What I see is causing me to have second thoughts about coming back as a neuroscientist.

Neal: Why? What are you seeing? What are the neuroscientists doing?

William: They are programming the robots to "read" the brains of their humans, and respond accordingly.

Neal: Huh?

William: I'll describe some of the details in a moment, but you know what this reminds me of?

Neal: How could I possibly know what this – whatever "this" is – reminds you of?

William: Yeah, good question. I'll tell you. Towards the end of my life, motorized carriages started to become popular. Along with many in my generation, I could see that such vehicles would eventually replace the familiar horse-drawn carriages, and that horses would eventually disappear from human life. So I was both fascinated with the new invention but at the same time repulsed. For the loss of horses and other animals is indeed a loss.

Plato: And we shall have something to say about animals later. For a human life without animals is an impoverished life. But for now, William, could you describe the robots that your future neuroscientists are designing?

William: Yes. The first generation of robot-dolls exist right now. They can't do very much, besides vibrate here and there and talk a little. The next generation of dolls, that Socrates described, are fully programmable; that is, **any** possible human behavior, human *sexual* behavior, to be explicit, can be programmed, and they will be indistinguishable from real human bodies. They may also be programmed to interact socially (that is, non-sexually), so people could very well bring their dolls to social gatherings, where it would not be immediately obvious who is a doll and who is a "real" human. But the third generation of robots explores new territory.

Neal: I'm listening.

William: It is commonplace, even now, for people to say that the biggest sex organ is the brain. A human's sexual proclivities are determined by the brain.

Benedict: The heart too, but that won't matter for the point you are going to make.

William: So a robot that can read the brain of a human could "know" the sexual desires and needs of that human, and could respond directly to those desires. It is one thing to program a robot to respond, say, to specific sexual desires and fantasies; it is another thing for the robot to "know" one's specific desires by "reading" the brain, or the heart too, should that be involved. The robot could respond even to desires of which the individual was not fully conscious.

Socrates: How many times does it happen that, during sex, one or both of the participants find themselves wishing that their partner would do this or that. Of course, *our* children (and adults too) have not been shamed into feeling there is anything wrong about sex, so they will be able to ask for what they want. But in the heat of the moment, so to speak, humans tend to scream, moan, and thrash about and are not likely to be able to express themselves verbally. But our next-generation robots will know. Responding to signals from both the brain and the heart, the robot will know exactly what combination of sounds, strokes, pressure, etc. will take the human to the highest levels of sexual pleasure possible for a human being.

Benedict: But wait, there's more (or so I'm tempted to say)!

Socrates: What could be more than the highest pleasure possible for a human being?

Benedict: Hah! As if you didn't know. Sexual pleasure is not the highest joy possible for a human being. Just ask anyone who's had a

Near-Death Experience. Now, what if the lower joy can be utilized as a gateway to the higher joy? We have alluded to this previously.

William: Yes, *(laughing)* and now the neuroscientist in me overcomes the guy who misses the horses. We have stated as a fact that a small percentage of people have had out-of-body experiences during sexual activity. We will greatly increase that percentage, and here's how: we shall study the physiology of those who *can* leave their body during sex. The robots will examine that physiology in detail – that is, the robots will be able to know what is happening in the body, physiologically, while the individual is experiencing herself as being outside the body. The robots will then be able to induce a similar physiological state in their humans, creating a portal through which the human could exit her body, and leave the lesser joy of sexual union for the greater joy of spiritual union.

Socrates: And while there may still linger some old-timers, like (ahem) Neal and William here, who will cling to the soon-to-be old-fashioned idea that sex is something that should be between human beings, nevertheless, the handwriting is clearly on the wall. For not only will the doll be as lovely and beautiful as anything a human can imagine, and not only will the doll be able to give its human the highest possible sexual joy, it will also be able to provide a physiological portal through which the human may enter into higher dimensions with even higher joys. And I believe this will answer your previous concerns.

William: What concerns?

Socrates: About envy and jealousy arising in the context of sexual play. We give every 13 or 14 year old a doll of their choosing, and every adolescent will have a sexual playmate that is designed perfectly for their individual sexual proclivities.

William: Well, I can see how this would indeed solve the problem of envy and jealousy regarding sexual partners, but something seems not quite right to me.

Neal: I agree. I am not quite comfortable with where our argument has taken us. But if I cannot see the flaw in the reasoning that has given us this result, then perhaps I am open to the charge of just being an old fart, as Socrates has suggested. Plato, what do you think?

Plato: *(smiling)* I think you and William are wise for not falling completely into the trap that Socrates has laid for you.

13) The False Premise

Neal: Trap? What do you mean? Everything Socrates said seems reasonable.

Plato: Of course. This is what a "trap" is. Every step of the argument seems reasonable, until the whole argument ends up someplace not quite right. So even though neither you nor William can pinpoint the flaw in Socrates' chain of reasoning, you intuitively feel it is not quite right, or at least not the whole story. Your intuitions are correct.

Neal: But I still don't see what is wrong with the whole chain of reasoning.

Socrates: *(smiling)* This present situation is not unlike the situation I found myself in some 24 or 25 hundred years ago. I had given a little discourse to Phaedrus regarding sex that wasn't quite right, and my spirit guide would not allow me to leave his company until I made amends by giving a second discourse that set right the first. It's not that the first discourse was completely wrong, but it failed to tell the whole story. So now, my little discourse regarding robots is not entirely wrong, but it does not tell the whole story, and leaves out things of crucial importance. Shall we investigate?

Neal: We hardly have a choice in the matter.

Socrates: But you will have to function as my spirit guide, since I no longer have one, and make sure I stay put until we figure this out together.

Neal: You no longer have a spirit guide?

Socrates: Why would I need a spirit guide, since I am now one myself? Both a spirit and a guide. But let's not go off talking about spirit guides, and stay focused on the argument. Now I think it might be useful to recapitulate the discourse I gave to Phaedrus, and uncover the fallacious premise upon which it rests. Then we'll do the same for the argument before us, the one that concludes that sexbots will replace human partners.

Neal: OK.

Socrates: You do it, since at my present age I can hardly be expected to remember any of the details.

Neal: Very funny. But I'll do it. Consider a beautiful youth who is seeking a partner in bed, and has lots of suitors. At one extreme is a suitor who is madly, passionately in lust with her or him. At another extreme is a suitor who, although not madly in lust with her, offers her what today would be called a "friends-with-benefits" type of relationship.

Socrates: With the benefits occurring mostly in the bedroom, I suppose.

Neal: Exactly. So in pleading his case the second suitor says: *"You really should choose me. For this other guy, who is crazy about you and madly in lust with you, is by his own admission both crazy and mad. It is not to your advantage to associate with one who is crazy and mad, even if you are the object of his madness. Instead, it is to your advantage to associate with me, who will offer you a steady friendship, without trying to possess you, and without the jealousies and passions of a man who has become mad through his lust for you."*

Socrates: And we acknowledge that there is some truth to the argument, as many people do in fact become deranged through sexual obsession, and such people are wisely avoided as sex partners. But this is not the whole story. Where does the argument go wrong?

Neal: It goes wrong by assuming that all forms of madness are harmful. If the word "madness" is defined as deviations from what humans consider to be "normal", then the possibility arises that *some* deviations from the social norm might be beneficial. Some deviations from the social norm are indeed brought about by what you called "mortal maladies", whereas others are brought about through inspiration from the gods. A Divine Madness! You give three examples of divine madness: (i) the medium, such as your Delphic oracle, when possessed by the god, is taken out of her own mind, and her state of consciousness deviates greatly from the social norm. So in this sense she has become mad by being divinely possessed. Another example (ii), with which people are more familiar, is madness brought about by the Muse. Our culture has many stories of poets, composers, musicians, under possession of their Muses, becoming eccentric and deviating from social norms. Yet no one can argue with the fact that the madness of our poets and artists, brought about by divine inspiration, has resulted in much that has benefited humankind. And finally (iii), the guy who is "madly" in love with the youth, has been driven mad because he has seen reflected spiritual beauty in the body of the youth. His madness has been inspired by Divine Beauty itself, and it is to the youth's advantage then to associate with one who is under the spell of the Divine, provided that he has learned to tame the sexual energy within himself.

Well, the point is that the hidden premise, upon which the first of your discourses rests, is that all forms of madness are bad. This, it turns out, is not true. Not all forms of madness are harmful; those brought about by divine inspiration are beneficial, and presumably our youth has to learn to discern which of her suitors' madness are brought about by mortal maladies and which are brought about by divine inspiration.

Socrates: Good. And now, regarding our present argument, regarding the sex robots, can you see what the hidden premise is.

Neal: No, not really.

Socrates: Would you like a little hint?

Neal: You're such a tease, aren't you?

Socrates: I'll take that as a "yes". Consider the following two scenarios: (i) Johnny and Suzie, both humans, are going into the bedroom to play together. (ii) Johnny and Suzie go into separate bedrooms, each with their very own robots.

Neal: OK, what's the hint?

Socrates: Patience, my friend. But here's the hint: how does this situation look to us?

Neal: I don't get it.

Socrates: When humans are having sex, how does it look to us, to those who are not embodied?

Neal: Well, have we not already discussed this in a previous conversation? I mean, not sex explicitly, but rather, how you perceive human bodies.

Socrates: Yes. And what did we then conclude?

Neal: That you do not perceive bodies directly, as humans do. But you do perceive souls directly, and you can sort of access a human life through friendship with the soul that is having that life. Is that right?

Socrates: Allowing for the limits of language, that is right. Now apply this to the sexual situations envisioned above.

Neal: Yikes, I see it. Oh my, this changes everything.

Socrates: And what have you seen?

Neal: I'm not sure I can describe it.

Socrates: *(smiling)* We all labor under the limitations of language. But give it a try.

Neal: OK. Let's look at the first scenario: Suzie and Johnny are playing in the bedroom. But we need to ask, who is it that is really playing in the bedroom?

Socrates: Then I shall answer: it is Suzie and Johnny, of course.

Neal: Yes, but who are Suzie and Johnny? To what sort of being do the names "Suzie" and "Johnny" apply?

Socrates: And what possible "beings" do you have in mind?

Neal: I see three possibilities: (1) the names refer to the physical bodies that are engaging in sex, (2) the names refer to the personalities that the children experience themselves as being, or (3) the names are intended to include the (nonphysical) souls that are expressing themselves as the personalities whose bodies are engaging in sex.

Socrates: Yes, continue.

Neal: Well, based on what I have just seen, it now seems to me that we have been talking about sex mainly as if we were considering only the body's point of view.

Socrates: And there is another point of view?

Neal: Yes, it is the point of view of the soul while the bodies are engaged in sexual activity. We have not considered that perspective.

Plato: And ultimately, of course, *that* is the only perspective worthy of serious consideration.

William: Why do you say that?

Benedict: Because bodies and personalities come and go in the arena of time, but the soul is eternal. When the former perishes, the latter is what remains.

Neal: The point is, when the personalities named Johnny and Suzie are playing with each other's bodies, the souls of which they are a part are engaged. This is what I saw. Whether the sex is just casual or whether feeling and emotion are involved, there is interaction at the soul level whenever humans have sex. But there is no such "soul"-interaction when Johnny and Suzie are playing with their robots. From the perspective of non-embodied being, playing with robots is not much different from masturbating.

Plato: We have been assuming that sex is like the other necessary desires that pertain to the body, and in a sense, it is. But it is more than that. The – how do you put it – the "raison d'etre" of the sexual desire is to ensure that humans continue to exist as a species. We of course disagree with our Catholic friends who insist that one should have sex only if one is consciously motivated to have children. But nevertheless, the reason the god created humans with irresistible sexual desire is to ensure the continuation of humans as a species. So the sexual desire itself is intended to connect humans with one another.

William: And here's another way to look at it. The dolls exist for one purpose, which is to give pleasure to Suzie and Johnny, respectively. But neither Suzie nor Johnny exist for the purpose of giving pleasure to the other. So they will treat one another differently than they would treat their dolls.

Neal: Yes, and what's more – my God, how could I have missed this – you can't *give* pleasure to a robot. At least half of the fun in sex involves giving pleasure to his or her partner.

Benedict: *(smiling)* Well, that was *your* experience, but most humans are still focused primarily on their own pleasure. However, *our* children are emotionally intelligent, and through massage, have been trained to delight in giving pleasure to others.

Socrates: And this delight at giving joy to another is itself a special kind of joy that forms connections at the level of soul. There is also gratitude on the part of the one receiving pleasure that travels to the soul. The delight and gratitude, experienced at the level of the personality, travels into the soul, and there is an energy exchange at the level of soul.

Benedict: Moreover, when two humans come together, they form a coupled system with wholistic properties that are not reducible to the sum of the parts. For we agree, do we not, that the whole is greater than the sum of its parts, and this is true not only for the biggest whole – the World Soul – but even for the temporary couplings that occur within the temporal order. We discussed this previously when we were talking about our children running around and playing games or sports.

William: Yes, when humans are engaged in spontaneous play, something from the soul, or rather – yikes, language can't really describe this. OK, when two bodies are coupled in play, including sexual play, there is a kind of similar coupling that occurs at the level of soul, so that creative impulses that arise from the play of souls can penetrate even into the personalities and their bodies.

Neal: Yes, I see it. With the robots, there is no connection at the soul level. But all human creativity comes from spirit. The sexbot may be able to randomly select from among preprogrammed behaviors, and that may "appear" to be creative to the human, but there is no real creativity in merely shuffling around the robot's programmed behaviors. There is no possibility, as William might put it, of any incursion from the play of souls into the play of bodies and personalities. Technique alone cannot make for a high quality sexual experience, since "quality" comes from the soul. Our robots epitomize mastery of technique; but there is no soul, no creativity, no spontaneous play.

Plato: And as I have been saying for several thousand years now, it is in spontaneous play that impulses from the soul are able to penetrate the heaviness of physical existence, and reach the personality and body. And of course, spontaneous play is something that happens between and among human beings, not robots. Another way to put it is that we want to construct a social order that maximizes the opportunities for spirit – for non-embodied beings – to have influence. This is what creativity *means*, as all creative artists, musicians, and scientists will attest. What is called "creativity" is an incursion into the physical that originates in the nonphysical. The experience of love is such an incursion.

Neal: So the false premise that allowed Socrates to conclude that sex with robots might be better than sex with humans is the premise that *only* bodies are involved with sex. But I think I can now articulate something that has been bothering me throughout our discussion of sexuality.

Plato: What?

14) Sex and the Soul

Neal: Let's imagine we have a sex-education class, with a bunch of 14-year-old girls and boys, and their trainers. Let's suppose further that the class is being taught after the model of a massage class. The trainer demonstrates a specific massage technique and the students then go to their massage tables to practice the technique on one another. Each student will practice the technique on several other students.

Plato: Yes, and you think the sexual context might be different from the massage context.

Neal: In degree, if not in kind. Let's suppose that Johnny and Jimmy are in the class, that they are equally attractive, etc. and, one at a time, they practice the new technique on Suzie. Suppose Suzie returns to the group and reports that, although she liked how Johnny was touching her, something magical happened with Jimmy. She felt her body opening up and melting away under Jimmy's touch, but not Johnny's (nor the robot's). Something seems to have happened that cannot be explained mechanically. In such a case we would say that Suzie and Jimmy were more connected at the level of soul, and that is why she experienced his touch so differently than the touch of other boys. Influences from the interplay of their souls penetrated into Jimmy's body, and guided his hands as he touched Suzie's body. And so we speak of "chemistry", and of magical connections between bodies. And the love, the spiritual love that exists between and among souls, can be part of this magic.

Plato: And what did you mean when you said "in degree, if not in kind"?

Neal: Even with respect to ordinary nonsexual massage, people have preferences among similarly trained masseuses, preferences that cannot be entirely ascribed to technique alone. But the comparison with nonsexual massage indicates that we have missed something else of importance.

Plato: What's that?

Neal: We have been treating sexual touching after the manner of massage. Giving and receiving are separated. No one gives a massage to another while simultaneously receiving a massage. Teaching our children in this way, separating giving from receiving, accomplishes several desirable things. It allows the giver, who is herself only minimally aroused, to (i) focus on the techniques and, as a meditation, (ii) attempt to place herself in the body of the other and feel what he is feeling. The person receiving is temporarily freed from any concerns about the other, and can either (iii) allow his mind to go wherever it will while his body is being aroused, and/or (iv) as a meditation, focus his mind deeply into the sensations his body his receiving. The latter may lead to a "one-pointedness" of mental concentration that in turn may become a portal for spiritual experience.

Socrates: Well, we did say that the goddess would be necessary for the latter.

Neal: Yes, but every female is potentially the goddess, and every male potentially the god.

Socrates: Yes, good. The key word, though, is potentially. But this is not the point you wish to make.

Neal: No, but we might want to return to this later. It may be a good idea to teach our children to think of themselves as emissaries of the gods. The point I want to make, though, is that unlike massage, with sex it *is* possible to give and receive at the same time.

Benedict: I can see the situation you envisage, but am not sure that "giving" and "receiving" are the right words to use here. Actually, they are both receiving at the same time.

Neal: Yes. I am, of course, thinking of intercourse. During intercourse, there is a possibility that the sexual energies of the two become one, which wraps itself around both bodies as they move together, so that the two bodies move as one body. The union of souls that brings both bodies together can be felt by the body itself. This may become a practice of deep surrender. For only when there is little or no ego left can the conscious mind completely let go and surrender to the sexual energy that embraces both. Through the body, both may simultaneously experience the connections in their souls, as well as the love that comes through the soul.

Benedict: Both bodies, we may say, are receiving pleasure from the sexual energy that transcends either body considered individually, and their minds receive joy from the coupling in the souls.

Plato: And this raises a metaphysical issue of which we should be aware. You have heard talk about "soul-groups"?

Neal: Yes, but I take all such talk with a grain or two of salt.

Plato: What a weird expression! As if salt has anything to do with the matter. *(Laughing)* But yes, you should take all such expressions with enough salt to cause high blood pressure. And let this serve as a reminder that language cannot in principle describe what is neither physical nor temporal. So our use of language, to talk about souls or groups of souls, is always metaphorical, even when we do not use terms that explicitly indicate a figure of speech.

Benedict: Well, I'm not so sure that language is completely helpless here. Perhaps language can describe structure, but not content.

Neal: What do you mean?

Benedict: Nothing complicated; we have discussed this before. Look, between the human mind and the single "One Mind", in which the human mind is embedded, are many levels of organization. The human mind is embedded in its soul, which also contains all of its other lives or personalities. The soul itself is embedded in a higher grouping, which we may refer to as its "soul-group". This in turn is embedded in still larger structures of consciousness – in passing we may note that the "angelology" of medieval times, with which I was familiar, attempted to get at this.

Neal: What do you mean?

Benedict: You know, angels, archangels, cherubim, seraphim… these terms really designate structures within the field of consciousness.

Neal: Yes, so although language will never be able to describe the content of such structures within the field of consciousness, it can note that such structures literally exist. And I suppose that Socrates here is about to inform us that the human soul is at the lower end of these structures.

Socrates: *(laughing)* Yeah, well the thing is, when you arrive at the so-called "higher" levels, there ceases to be any such distinction. This is the difference between a theologian and a spiritual teacher, as you no doubt have noticed.

Neal: Yes, the theologian believes that distinctions are real, and that concepts and language can describe the whole thing, especially *his* concepts and language. The spiritual teacher is aware that this is impossible, and attempts only to help humans take the next step.

Socrates: And what is the "next step" for a human being, that is, for a unit of consciousness that is now experiencing itself as embodied?

Benedict: And before you reply to Socrates' question, there is one more point, or caution, I want to make regarding language.

Plato: Why, Benedict, you're sounding like me.

Benedict: Yes, I know. Language is essentially atomistic. It chops things up into names and concepts. This is why our colleagues are much more comfortable with atomistic philosophies than with wholistic philosophies. The former can be stated in language much more clearly than the latter. Christian theology, for example, is highly atomistic, in that it conceives that individual souls are intrinsically independent of one another. But souls are no more independent of one another than are cells in the same body. Indeed, just as every cell is created by the body and contains within itself, through its DNA, the knowledge of the body as a whole, so also every soul is created by the larger structure of consciousness within which it is embedded, and contains within itself the perfect knowledge of that structure. Incidentally, we must make certain that we teach our children this analogy in our biology classes.

Well, the point is that we must guard against thinking atomistically about souls because of the lure of language. The whole is always more than the sum of its parts. The soul is not merely a collection of independently existing "lives" or "personalities", but has its own autonomy, and in fact, creates the personalities that exist within it; the "soul group" is not merely a collection of independent souls, but exists as a single indivisible whole. This process that we previously referred to as "wholistic embedding" occurs through many levels until the ultimate is reached: the "One" with respect to which there is nothing else. Now, we wish to use this little bit of metaphysics to see if we can explain certain proclivities that occur at the level of personality. So where were we? Oh yes, we have Suzie reflecting on her experiences with Johnny and Jimmy. Although her experience with Johnny was satisfying, there was something magical about her experience with Jimmy. What accounts for the magic?

Plato: You know, Benedict, in spite of myself (another weird expression), I think you have convinced me of something. Formerly I would have said that *magic* cannot be accounted for in human language. That's why it's called magic. We might state in words that there is a "chemistry" that exists between Suzie and Jimmy, but not between Suzie and Johnny. *(Laughing)* But given the absence of any formulas that a chemist would recognize, the use of the word "chemistry" is hardly explanatory, but merely states that we have no explanation. Yet I now think that some account of the "chemistry" may be possible, using your distinction between structure and content.

William: And returning to structure for a moment, do we wish to state that the analogy with the body carries through to the various structures, or levels of structure, within the field of Consciousness? What I mean is that although the body is constituted by individual cells, the individual cells are themselves created by the body. So the whole creates the parts that appear to constitute it. It is most certainly not the case, as our atomist colleagues might suppose, that the cells exist as independent units that come together so as to constitute a body.

Neal: A most ridiculous picture.

William: But is it not equally ridiculous to conceive that souls exist as independent units that come together so as to form a soul group? Or should we rather conceive of the latter as a structure within the field of consciousness, with its own identity not reducible to the sum of its parts, and which, even further, creates the souls that appear to constitute it.

Neal: I agree. Our philosophy is wholistic, not atomistic, which means that at the most fundamental level, causation is top down, not bottom up. So the lower level is generated by the higher, and we may state for our purposes that the individual souls, to which the personalities Johnny, Jimmy and Suzie belong, are created or generated by a higher level of structural organization.

Benedict: So, to generate a kind of explanation for the affinity between Jimmy and Suzie, we shall introduce a few terms that will prevent our discussion from becoming too long-winded. Let's consider two different soul-groups and call them X and Y. Also, consider three distinct souls, that we shall call A, B, and C. The human personality called "Johnny" is created by and belongs to A; Jimmy and Suzie belong to souls B and C respectively. We further suppose that soul A is created by and belongs to soul-group X, and that souls B and C belong to the same soul group, Y.

Plato: And so we can say that souls B and C are familiar with one another in a way that neither is familiar with A. This explains why the personalities Jimmy and Suzie, who are really extensions within the souls B and C, experience what we have called "chemistry" between them. The chemistry originates in the close friendship between the souls of which they are a part.

William: It goes without saying, does it not, that what Suzie and Jimmy experience together cannot be replicated with any sex doll. Moreover, whereas sex is the energy that connects all human bodies into a single species, *love* is the energy that connects all individual units of consciousness into a single One Mind. Now Suzie and Jimmy cannot literally "make" love, but they *can* experience a semblance of the love that exists between their souls, especially if they take the time to gaze into one another's eyes.

Neal: Thus sex with a human, unlike sex with a robot, affords an opportunity to experience Love, insofar as there is intermingling at the level of soul.

Plato: But we must emphasize that this "opportunity" is rarely explored in your present culture, which is the deeper reason that most people are unsatisfied regarding their sex lives. Sex is not a mere bodily function – well, it *is* a bodily function but not a "mere" bodily function; it is potentially a portal through which communication with spirit, and the Love therefrom, is possible.

Neal: Sometimes I think there is analogy to be made between "fast food" and "fast sex". Fast food appears to be food, since it is put in the mouth, chewed and swallowed, usually very quickly. But it has little, or even negative, nutritional value. Compare this to a meal of healthy food, well-prepared, and consumed over a period of one or two hours, in the company of family and friends.

William: Yes, for the manner in which food is consumed has some effect on the ability of the body to absorb its nutrients.

Neal: Similarly, "fast sex" appears to be sex, in that the male puts his penis inside the body of the female; but then he ejaculates as quickly as possible, without tasting all the steps along the way, and so there is no chance to experience Divine Love. This is very unsatisfying for the female, but what has not been recognized is that it is just as unsatisfying for the male.

Plato: But our children will be different, don't you think?

Neal: Of course. They have not been conditioned to associate the emotion of guilt with sexual desire, and they have not been compelled to abstain from sex during their teen years, when the sexual energy is most powerful. This forced and unnatural abstinence causes resentment, anger, frustration, and incessant thinking, or fantasizing, about sex. And the guilt causes considerable reticence to dive more deeply into the experience. My goodness, imagine what dining would be like if humans were raised to feel guilty about enjoying the taste of food.

Plato: Yes, we take conditioned guilt and forced abstinence as constituting the third visit to the River of Forgetfulness, which the citizens of our New Social Order will no longer make. But there is something else pertaining to how we have raised our children that I think bodes well for encouraging them to explore sexuality with a view to the Divine, as well as with a view to their own pleasures.

Neal: What is that?

Plato: We have said that the very bones of our children will form around the Golden Rule. How will this affect the sexual arena, you ask?

Neal: Yes, I ask.

Plato: We have to go a little deeper here. Perhaps another little metaphysical interlude would be appropriate at this time.

Neal: I'm listening.

Plato: All along we have been teaching our children what we have called "good habits". And we are inculcating these "good habits" before our children are old enough to understand the reasons why. So, for example, we train them to wash their hands before meals *before* they are old enough to understand the germ theory of disease. We train them to brush their teeth before they understand the mechanism of tooth decay. We have aligned their taste buds with what is truly nutritious long before they study biology and nutrition in school. And we make sure they get sufficient sleep before they can understand the relevant neurology.

Neal: Yes, and these are all habits that pertain to the health and well-being of the body.

Plato: But there are also "good-habits" that pertain to the mind, or to the psychology of the individual, and we have said that our children will become habituated to the Golden Rule in the same way they are habituated to washing their hands.

Neal: Yes, and we have raised our children to be emotionally intelligent, since without such intelligence it would not be possible to follow the Golden Rule.

Plato: But now our children are somewhat grown, and at 13 and 14 years, are old enough to begin to understand the reasons behind the good habits they have learned with respect to caring for their body.

Neal: Yes, and so you are thinking that at this age they are also able to begin to understand the Reality that underlies the Golden Rule.

Plato: My thoughts, exactly. In fact, their study of biology will now enable them to grasp the analogy between (i) the body and the individual cells within it, and (ii) the World Soul and the individual minds within it. Here are three important parallels. (1) Individual cells are created by the body and have a specific function within the body; individual souls are created by the World Soul and have a specific function within the World Soul. (2) Between an individual cell and the whole body are many intermediate "levels", or systems of organization within the body, such as organs; between the individual human mind and the World Soul there are also many levels of organization, such as "soul groups", angelic beings, that some systems of thought attempt to capture. (3) But the most important parallel is this: each cell contains within itself the knowledge of the whole body in the DNA at the very center of the cell; every mind contains within itself the knowledge of the Whole Soul. More poetically, we could say that the kingdom of heaven is within. The World Soul has placed the knowledge of Itself at the very core of each and every part of Itself, just like the body, we might say, has placed the knowledge of itself in the center of every cell.

Now, you ask, how does this relate to the Golden Rule?

Neal: You're very good at asking my questions for me. But here's another one. How does this relate to our children's sex lives?

Plato: Using this analogy, we might ask our children to suppose that the cells in the body were conscious, as they are conscious, and the individual cells were contemplating that great question of ethics and moral philosophy.

Neal: What question?

Benedict: I asked it, and so did you. Think back to your late teens/ early twenties. What bothered you most?

Neal: Oh of course. It is whether to live one's life following the Golden Rule as much as possible, or whether one should live in competition with one's fellow human beings, competing for recognition, status, and approval. I thought I might be "weak" for not wanting to compete.

Plato: Which is just what those who play such games want you to think. But now, our individual cells are asking that question, and our children will answer. What will our children say?

Neal: If the cells really start competing with one another it would destroy the body and thence themselves. But cooperation among the cells is built into their very structure. If a given cell "helps" another cell perform its function, the body as a whole is strengthened, from which increased strength the well-being of the given cell is enhanced. So ultimately, an attitude of kindness and compassion towards other individual cells is in the best interest of any given cell.

William: The analogy teaches something else of importance. Just as every cell has its function within the body, so every individual mind has its function within the One Mind. Recall our dysfunctional symphony orchestra, where the musicians were all jealous of one another's parts within the orchestra. If a muscle cell tried to emulate the function of a nerve cell, or a fat cell emulate the function of a blood cell, chaos would ensue and the body itself would become a most dysfunctional orchestra. Therefore, each child, each human being, will rest content with his or her unique talents and abilities, and will not attempt to compete one against the other.

Plato: Our children have of course already internalized the Golden Rule, but now, at puberty, are beginning to understand *why* this Rule is at the center of all things. And they will begin to understand what they have already noticed: that it feels good to help another. For when one person helps another, the larger whole in which both have their being benefits, and the benefit is felt as joy by the one who helps.

William: By the time they reach puberty, our children will have had much experience that involves helping others. Aside from the joy they experience through giving pleasure to another (massage), they have been given many opportunities to assist younger children, and to contribute to the well-being of the larger social whole to which they belong.

Plato: And we will state categorically that helping others, treating others with kindness and compassion, is among the highest joys possible for a soul that is embodied.

Socrates: *(slightly mischievously)* In fact, it is a higher joy than even sexual ecstasy.

Neal: What do you mean?

Socrates: Two things: first, when given the choice, the great majority of humans would prefer to help another who is in distress than to have an orgasm. Second, other things being equal, a human who has just helped another feels much happier than the one who has just had an orgasm. These are simply facts of human experience.

William: Well, maybe, but they are "facts" that are concealed, twisted, and denied by the present culture of greed and status-seeking. This culture states that it feels best to win and gain status, which necessarily involves harming others. This is a culture that selects for the bully. But even in a culture so adverse to the Golden Rule, many people strive to enter the so-called "helping professions", simply because it feels good to help others. They recognize, subliminally perhaps, and even under adverse conditions imposed by the bullies who are running the economy and most of its institutions, that together we constitute a single whole, that we all belong to something greater than our individual selves, and that accommodation to this greater whole constitutes our highest joy and well-being.

Plato: And we shall not prevent our children from experiencing this joy, the joy of felt connectedness with others. We will encourage and reinforce such experiences. Our children will be discussing among themselves how it felt, say, to assist little brother with reading, or to sing songs at the nursing home, or to care for a pet animal. *(Smiling)* And this will occur throughout their childhood and into adulthood, not only in the lower grades.

Neal: Although I agree with what is now being said, most people raised in my culture would not agree. They would say that at best the Golden Rule is a duty, a moral burden put on people by God, who will reward them with afterlife goodies if they behave decently while embodied. Following the Golden Rule is not a joy in itself, but is a pain and hardship to be endured either for its afterlife consequences (as in religion), or because of abstract principles.

Benedict: You're thinking of Kant here.

Neal: Yes, sort of. But religion teaches the same thing. One should do one's duty, which is conceived abstractly. Kant, or the priest, might say to one of our children: "It is your duty to wash the dishes. Do your duty and don't complain." But we will say: "You have now an opportunity to contribute to the larger whole to which you belong; do the dishes, and rejoice." The idea that "doing one's duty" can be accompanied by the highest joy is foreign to the present culture.

Plato: OK, good. These are the things, or sorts of things that Glaucon and Adeimantus hurl at Socrates in my *Republic*. Today, as in my time, most people regard virtue as a burden, to be done for the sake of some reward, either in this life by acquiring more status through virtuous behavior, or in the afterlife. But we hold that virtue is its own reward, that the person who lives a virtuous life, a life of kindness and compassion towards others, is the happiest of all.

Benedict: And this is because the happiness that comes from living according to the Golden Rule involves recognizing and experiencing one's connectedness with others. This is a much "higher" joy than the pleasures of the body. "Higher" not in any moralistic sense, as religion would have you believe, but "higher" in the sense that it is directly experienced as such.

But if I may briefly speak about my own writings…

Socrates: Yes, you may.

Benedict: *(laughing)* I wasn't really asking for permission, but thanks anyway. Yeah, well I entitled my major work the *Ethics*, but no one seems to understand why. It is laughable that if you were to ask a so-called scholar of my writings to state my views about God, wholes and parts, sense experience, determinism, they will respond with something, most of it false. But if you were to ask them to state my views about the fundamental question of ethics, how a human being should live his or her life, they will stare blankly. And when I use the word "should" here, I do not mean "should" in the sense of compliance to some religious or moral duty. Rather I mean "should" in the sense of maximizing happiness. If you wish to live in such a way as to maximize your own joy and happiness, then you should live in such a way that "you do not desire for yourself anything you do not desire for your fellow human beings", if I may be excused from quoting myself. The greatest joy is the joy of conscious union with the Divine Being, or rather, to become conscious of the union that already exists. But along the way to this highest joy are numerous lesser joys that consist in uniting with structures of consciousness that are intermediate between the individual and the Whole. We experience something of this union when we help others, and when we join with others to achieve a common purpose. All such joys are experienced as greater than mere bodily pleasures, which admittedly are not inconsiderable.

William: So it seems that we are saying something that is likely to be thought ridiculous. We are saying that the joy that arises from altruistic behavior is greater than the joy of sensual pleasure, and also greater, we should note, than the joy that arises from "winning" status or wealth.

Benedict: Yes, but those who think what we are saying is ridiculous are merely parroting their own upbringing, which causes them to believe that there is nothing better than sensuous pleasure combined with wealth and status. Instead of arguing with their upbringing, we will present *our* children as the counterargument. *Our* children will not have experienced the horrible upbringing that causes them to be so needy for attention and approval, and from the earliest grades they will be discussing among themselves the joys that arise from joining with others for a common purpose, from helping one another, and from doing what they can to make their world a better place. They will know from direct experience that any doctrine that teaches that "doing good" is a burden to be done for some external reward or out of a sense of duty is absolutely false.

15) Sex and the Golden Rule

Neal: So let's bring this discussion to bear on our children's sex lives. We had asked, how will having been raised according to the Golden Rule affect their sex lives?

Socrates: The joys of the soul exceed the pleasures of the body. The joy that comes from helping another is greater than the joy inherent in any bodily pleasure. *Our* children will be vying with one another more to give pleasure to another than to receive it from another.

William: You know, Neal, boys and young men, from my time to yours, like to brag about their "conquests", or whatever they call their sexual escapades. But this will not be the fate of our young men, who will regard sex as a splendid opportunity for giving, as well as receiving, pleasure. But "giving pleasure" is not itself a pleasure of the body, but rather, a delight in the soul.

Plato: And this is the fundamental reason *why* sexbots cannot replace humans. *If* it were the case that sex is *only* a matter of the body, then the robots would win, since the robots of the future will be able to give maximal sexual pleasure to their humans. But when humans are enjoying sex together, there is the possibility for some communication within the souls. William, you once said that prayer aligns the mind with the soul and allows for incursions from the spiritual to enter into the body. Something real, you insisted, is accomplished during prayer.

William: Yes, and it would have never occurred to me that something similar is possible with regard to sex. But our children will be bringing the Golden Rule into the sexual arena, and they will consciously seek to give pleasure to the other. The Golden Rule has instructed them, one might say, to be solicitous of the other's pleasures. Under these conditions, the interactions at the level of soul may inject themselves into the bodies, in the form of creative, spontaneous play.

Neal: Or using some modern terminology, we might say that under such conditions some of the Love that is in the soul can be downloaded into the body and its personality. But, Plato, I want to point out that something William said above nicely complements something in your philosophy.

Plato: *(with humor)* Well, I still insist that my "philosophy" has not and cannot be written down. Anyone who comes to my writings must first understand what I wrote *about* my writings, but that would put out of business all your academics who fancy themselves "scholars" of my writings. But by all means, tell us what you have in mind.

Neal: We can forget about your "philosophy" if you wish, because Socrates expressed the point directly at his trial.

Plato: Alright. What is that point?

Neal: If one human harms another, she harms herself even more. For the most a human can do is harm the body of another. But doing so reflects back on the soul of the one who does harm. That's why Socrates said that although his accusers may kill him, they cannot harm him in any way. *(To Socrates)* And you even had the chutzpah to state that in defending yourself you were attempting to prevent your accusers from damaging their souls.

Socrates: *(smiling)* Well, chutzpah about such things is easy when you know, I mean really *know*, that you are not the body.

Neal: Yes, so when one human harms another, he harms not only the body of the other, but does some damage to his self. Conversely, as William said above "giving pleasure is not itself a pleasure of the body, but rather, a delight in the soul". And so those who benefit the body of another – whether it be through relieving physical suffering (feeding those who are hungry, giving shelter to those who are homeless, assisting the sick and lame), or through giving bodily pleasure to another – benefit the soul of the giver. This is the reason that altruism *feels* so good. Giving to another benefits the soul of the giver, just as harming another harms the soul of the harmer.

Socrates: *(laughing)* And so our children, in their eagerness to benefit their own souls, will be vying with each other to see who can give the most pleasure to the bodies of other children.

Plato: *(also laughing)* And certainly, by any sane standards, this will be a much healthier form of competition than the ones currently in place.

Socrates: Agreed. But I wonder, Neal, if you and William are satisfied with our somewhat lengthy response to your question.

Neal: You will have to remind me of the question.

William: I remember. It had to do with envy and jealousy. Humans are not equally bestowed with either physical beauty or sexual endowment, and those that have but a little might be envious of those who have more. The girls might prefer boys with thicker penises, and the other boys would be envious; the boys might prefer girls with larger breasts, and the other girls would become envious. Then Socrates introduced the sex dolls as a possible solution to this kind of envy.

Neal: Yes.

William: I thought at first that Socrates was being facetious, as if he were the parent of squabbling three year olds who ingeniously resolves their disputes by giving them each a teddy bear and sending them to their rooms to play with them.

Socrates: Hah! – As if the jealousies of teenagers, and adults too, are any different from the squabblings of three year olds. But what do you think now, William?

William: It now seems to me that such jealousies and envies pertain only to the body. By showing our children that we have an easy remedy for such jealousies, namely our robots, the jealousies themselves are likely to disappear. For anyone can have as a sex partner any kind of body he/she wishes. Eventually the novelty will wear off, and the robots will no longer be as satisfying as real humans. But I can see that the robots will be very useful during the transition.

Neal: Yes. For the males have been conditioned to associate sexual feelings with mere *thinking*, with their mental fantasies. The robots can satisfy all their fantasies.

Socrates: And it will do wonders for the problem of male violence to give each of the males a robot or two, and send them to their rooms along with the squabbling three year olds.

Plato: Sex with robots may not be the ultimate, but it is certainly much better than the current situation of the males taking out their frustrations by plotting war and violence against one another.

Benedict: And you are right to point out, William, that envy and jealousy pertain only to the body and its personality. We should remind ourselves that our children have been discussing such things long before they reach puberty. For we regard envy and jealousy as a kind of mental illness, and we shall do whatever we can to prevent this illness – for it is quite contagious – from arising and spreading among our children.

Neal: I think it is doubtful that we will be able to prevent envy from arising, since it appears to be closely associated with embodiment per se.

Benedict: I share your doubts, since if the soul is to have a *human* experience it must come to feel that it is its body. But by identifying with its body, it perceives that different bodies have different abilities, and can become envious of abilities that its own body does not possess. And this is why we have made it a "rule" of social organization that the first order of business of *any* group of humans of *any* age that come together for *any* purpose is the psychological well-being of every individual in the group. For if even one human in the group is infected with envy or jealousy the infection can easily spread to the rest of the group, and they will not be able to function as a unit. So even in kindergarten, our children will be talking about such feelings as they arise.

William: And we should mention that by giving our children permission and encouragement to express and explore such feelings openly, we have begun the process of healing, for dysfunctional emotions tend to dissipate in the light of conscious understanding.

Neal: This is why our "rule" is so important. Many if not most of the dysfunctional emotions involve a feeling that one is not good enough, that something is lacking within oneself. If A is envious of B, then A feels a lack of something that B has. But the process of openly sharing such feelings with others engenders empathy and compassion in the others, which compassion in turn reflects back to the person who was envious, and will often be sufficient to dispel the envy.

But I think that at this point, as our children are maturing, we should say something about the kind of Social Order into which our children are maturing.

Socrates: Yes, in a moment. I want to say one more thing about the potential use of our robots.

Neal: What is it?

Socrates: This may require considerable suspension of disbelief.

Neal: *(with humor)* Most of my beliefs have already been suspended.

Socrates: And I don't want any trouble from Benedict if I talk about a "possibility", since it has not yet been absolutely determined that this possibility will occur in your physical reality.

Benedict: *(laughing)* I assure you, I will not give you any trouble. What is this "possibility" that you are seeing?

Plato: *(with humor)* He likes to dance around his subject matter, especially when what he is about to state is outrageous.

Socrates: Now, now, the term "outrageous" can be applied only with respect to one's current beliefs. If these beliefs have been "suspended", then there will be no outrage. Besides, I was not going to state it myself, but had planned to persuade William to state it for me.

William: State what?

Socrates: OK. We're going to cheat again. I'll pull the veil back for you, and see if you can go four or five generations into the future. Here, take a look and tell us what you see.

(I could not see what William was seeing, but I could see the expression on his face change considerably. He was deeply affected by what he had seen. And through William, I was affected too.)

William: I can see it, but I'm not sure I can state it.

Neal: This body of mine is tearing up again, and I don't even know why. Will somebody explain what is happening?

William: The possible future of humankind is magnificent beyond measure, if only we do not self-destruct, which also remains a "possibility". But I don't know how to state it in words.

Plato: We agree at the outset that words cannot describe that which is beyond description. But they can serve as pointers.

Socrates: Yes, now, William, the vision you just had was of course not in the temporal order. The way to express it to those who are still in the temporal order is to state it as a story that unfolds in time. I could express the content of your vision as follows: **the gods shall once again intermingle with humans.** But such words will convey little meaning to one who has not had your vision. So tell it as a "likely story".

William: Well, unlike my brother, I'm not much of a storyteller, but here goes. Although the story has already begun, I shall begin my telling by going two or three generations ahead. The sexbots have been more or less perfected, but also, all human activity that is merely rote and mechanical has been replaced by robots. And because capitalism no longer exists, the fruits of the robots' labor are shared equitably among all humans. Now it happened that several neuroscientists who had been working on the robots died around the same time. In their immediate after-death condition, they could "see" things that they could not see while still embodied. They considered how they might reincarnate in such a way so as not to lose this newly gained knowledge when they became embodied. But they saw that the process of incarnating again is somewhat precarious, and the great majority of souls appear to lose what they know in this process. So they looked around for a safer way of imparting their knowledge to the humans, to those who were embodied.

Neal: And what did they find?

William: Yes, well the veil between the worlds was thinning, and they thought that it might be easier to give this knowledge to humans by working with accomplished mediums, rather than attempting to incarnate *without* forgetting the knowledge. And so, to make a long story short, they found a medium who had the ability to enable communication, often quite technical, between themselves and human neuroscientists. This was a very exciting time for all involved, on both sides of the veil.

Neal: OK, but what was this "knowledge" that got communicated?

William: Well, the details will have to wait for another four or five generations, but the upshot is that they were able to design a robot that could be operated by non-embodied beings. A spirit who was not embodied could put on, or "wear", a robot – like a human might wear a suit – and interact with humans.

Neal: So a deceased human could put on a robot and interact physically with its former friends and family?

Plato: Not quite. Spirits that are involved in a reincarnation cycle are not sufficiently "advanced" – and here we are using words very loosely – to know how to operate the robots. But mind you, the ratio of souls that incarnate to souls that do not incarnate is close to zero, so there will be no shortage of "advanced" souls to inhabit the robots. They will greatly facilitate rendering it "on earth, as it is in heaven". But this is for a later generation. Now, I think, we are ready to say a few things about the *kind* of social order into which our children are maturing.

Chapter VI

Reason [Or, The Flower of "Holy Curiosity"]

1) A Social Order Based On Unconditional Love

Neal: Good. We have said some general things, about the Golden Rule and our first rule of social organization. But what about things like economics and politics, and the management and distribution of wealth. Until the Earth transforms itself into pure spirit, human squabbling will still be with us, so we must have some way of resolving disputes between individuals and among groups. We said earlier that there will be no rich and no poor, but we have not said how the whole thing will be governed. If the wealth of the planet is to be distributed equitably, who will be in charge of that distribution and how will decisions be made? What will life be like, if humans are no longer allowed, or no longer desire, to compete for wealth and status?

Plato: At the risk of repeating myself…

Neal: *(smiling)* By all means, take that risk.

Plato: The question of *"how"* decisions will be made – decisions that pertain to the collective – is not as important as the question of *"who"*. I could state that the decisions will be made according to the Golden Rule, but the overwhelming majority of humans now on the planet do not have the ability to live this way, and so they cannot really understand what is meant by "living according to the Golden Rule", except perhaps in some vague way. And the details will depend on actual context that cannot be anticipated in advance. But the "who" is not difficult to understand.

Neal: *(with humor)* Except, perhaps, for those who are called "philosophers".

Plato: *(laughing)* Yes, well I'm sure we shall have some things to say about *that* sorry state of affairs soon enough. But, *(with humor)* despite the slight sarcasm in what you just said, it will serve as a reminder to me not to use my favorite expression "philosopher-king". For those who today are called "philosophers", as well as other so-called intellectuals who may have read my *Republic*, understand by the word "king" a hereditary job with dictatorial powers, and by the word "philosopher" they understand someone like themselves, with an above average ability to manipulate words and symbols. So if I were to state what I originally stated 2,400 years ago without using these terms, it would look something like this:

> ***If there is ever to be peace upon the Earth, and humanity be saved from self-destruction, then spiritual wisdom and worldly power must coalesce in the same individuals. That is, those individuals who have achieved spiritual wisdom must be the same individuals who hold temporal authority.***

And I hasten to add that the phrase "spiritual wisdom" has nothing to do with organized religion. The phrase denotes a specific state of consciousness. That person is spiritually wise who has experienced directly her identity with the World Soul, who has seen the Light of Pure Consciousness, and has experienced directly the Divine Love that holds this world and all Worlds together in a seamless Unity, or as Benedict has put it, has experienced the union that exists between her individual mind and the mind of God. This is the experience that burns away all greed and personal ambition, and enables the individual to "desire nothing for herself that she does not also desire for others", as Benedict put it.

Now until recently, such experience was quite rare, and finding such individuals was problematic. But today, many people have had spiritually transformative experiences, and like Er, have returned from physical death to tell what they have experienced. In my times Er was an exception; in fact, his was the only such case I had heard of. But today, medical technology is able to bring the body back from physical death with some regularity, and hundreds of thousands of humans have experienced the Unconditional Love that unites all individual beings into a single "One Mind". For such individuals, living according to the Golden Rule is the only way they are able to live, and it is to such individuals that we must turn for our political and economic leaders.

Neal: Yes, this was initially called "the Near-Death Experience", as it seemed to happen to people when the body was "near" physical death and in some cases the clinical conditions for "death" were actually met. But the term has led to some confusion, as people can be "near-death" without having any transcendent experience, and people can have transcendent experiences (called "spiritually transformative experiences", or STE) without being close to physical death.

William: It is perhaps pointless to attempt to enumerate the kinds and depths of such experiences. At the "high" end, the experience dispatches the ego totally, and the individual experiences herself as the World Soul experiencing Itself as the given individual.

Plato: Not a bad way to put it, William, given that we must use words. At the lower end, the individual experiences a vision, like Er, or catches a glimpse of a "Something" that transforms the personality without obliterating it. There are many varieties of such experiences, as you well know. In the deeper kind of experience, the individual effortlessly lives according to the Golden Rule. In the other experiences, it is not always effortless, but the sense of direction is clear. The main reason why people who have such experiences have so much difficulty upon returning is that the values of the present culture are inconsistent with the true values recollected in such spiritually transformative experiences. But we are constructing our social order to be in harmony with the values recollected in the Near-Death, and other spiritually transformative experiences. So we shall have plenty of individuals newly returned from Heaven, and eager to help.

William: In fact, I'll wager that if we put a dozen or so Near-Death Experiencers in a room and task them with drawing the outlines of a social order that would be in harmony with what they have experienced, that social order would be the very one presently under construction.

Benedict: *(smiling)* Truth is One; error is many. There is only one Truth, but many ways to deviate from it. This is why there will be no disagreement among those who have experienced spiritual reality; it is also why there is little agreement among those who have not experienced that reality. For without Truth, people make judgments and decisions based on what they merely imagine, and since everyone imagines differently, according to upbringing, there can be no agreement.

Plato: So our children matriculate into a world governed by individuals who have themselves experienced the Knowledge of the union that exists between their own mind and the Mind of God. Such individuals, having removed themselves from the Cave of physical embodiment and caught a vision of the sun, become like flashlights when they return to the darkness of the Cave. These flashlights will not only hold power at the highest levels of social organization, but they will also hold power at intermediate levels of temporal authority.

Neal: What do you mean by "intermediate levels"?

Plato: In terms of the present institutions of your country, it would look something like this: not only will the President be spiritually enlightened, but so will all the members of his cabinet; and so will all Senators, Congressmen, and judges. Medicine and Law will be administered by spiritually enlightened individuals, as will every business or corporation that employs more than a few thousand people.

William: And if "organized religions" continue to exist, they will be administered by the mystics among them. For *only* mystics understand the teachings of their religions in a way that does not conflict with any other religion.

Neal: *(with humor)* And if there's hope for religion, then perhaps there is hope even for academia.

William: Yes, we'll just put Plato here in charge of all those who fancy themselves philosophers, and then they will have to answer to Truth instead of to Cleverness.

Plato: Hah! Then we'll put you, William, in charge of all Psychology departments, compelling those who call themselves "psychologists" to study their real subject matter, the human psyche, rather than the behavior of rats.

William: *(laughing, to me)* I have sometimes fantasized, as I'm sure you have, what things might have been like if the chairs of our departments had been spiritually awakened individuals. But such an individual could not be very effective unless the chairs of all the other departments, and the administration as a whole, shared the values of one who is enlightened.

Plato: Yes, and this is why the changes must be top down. Spiritual values must reign supreme throughout our whole Social Order, and the only way for this to happen is for the leaders to embody spiritual maturity. Every aspect of our New Society will be governed by individuals who have personally experienced themselves as manifestations of the Divine Being, and hence are no longer able to desire for themselves anything they cannot also desire for other humans.

Neal: For those raised in the current social order, it is difficult to conceive of a world that is free from male competition. I was going to ask a question, but then it seemed to me that the question presupposed competition in some way.

William: What was the question?

Neal: About wages. Won't people who are not enlightened still compete for jobs that pay better wages? How will wages be assigned to jobs and various kinds of work?

Plato: There will be no need for wages at all.

Neal: What?

Plato: Oh come on. The very concept of "wages" is rooted in a capitalist economic system, which shall no longer exist.

Neal: Yes, but…

Plato: … but some people work harder than others, do more

important work than others, etc.?

Neal: Yeah, etcetera.

Plato: So that a person's wages should in some way be contingent upon the work he does?

Socrates: *(slightly mischievously)* Perhaps our conclusion is coming too fast for you. I'll slow it down a bit. We have stated many times that our new Social Order must be in harmony with the Divine.

Neal: Yes.

Socrates: And what is it to be in harmony with the Divine?

Neal: It is to be One with the Source of all Knowledge and Love.

Socrates: OK. Now this spiritual love, is it as the religions describe, that God metes out His Love in the manner of a boss who distributes wages to his workers, giving more to those workers who have culled his favor, and less to those who have not pleased Him?

Neal: No, not at all. The empirical data from mystics across all traditions and from those who have had spiritually transformative experiences testifies that God's Love is not conditional upon human behavior at all, but is equally available to all souls, regardless of how they have lived their lives.

Socrates: And so if we wish to model Earthly life after its Divine Source, or to use the phrase we have used before, if we really want it to be "on Earth, as it is in Heaven", then the love that our Society shows towards each and every human being within it cannot depend on the behavior of that human being.

Neal: For if it did so depend, then the love could not be called "unconditional".

Socrates: So we shall reverse what some of your religious nut-cases believe to be true. They believe that a fetus, once conceived, has a "right" to be born. By contrast, *we* believe that a baby, once born, has a right to live and to flourish, and that it is the duty of the social order to guarantee that right to every human being. And so the material wealth of the Earth will be distributed equitably among all humans. The fairness of the distribution is guaranteed by the fact that the humans in charge of distributing the wealth will all be spiritually enlightened.

Benedict: We also reject the view according to which some forms of work are more important than others, and hence "deserve" more wages. Every aspect of Creation is essential to the Whole, and those who have seen Reality through the eyes of the Divine Being know that all aspects of Creation are equally important.

Neal: So everyone receives the same wages, regardless of what they do? Then the president of a large corporation will make the same wages as the janitor who sweeps the floor?

Plato: Yes. *(To William and me, with humor)* And before you hurl your objections at us, make sure the objections come from *you*, not your upbringings.

William: *(to me, also with humor)* Hmm, well there went all my objections. How about you?

Neal: I cannot think of any objection that is not caused by having been raised in a capitalist social order. It does seem to me that the only way Earth can manifest the heavenly value of unconditional love is to guarantee that the material well-being of the body is not conditional on the behavior of that body.

Socrates: *(mischievously)* ... Even if the given body is very lazy and just lies around all day doing nothing?

Neal: Yeah, which is precisely the thing someone raised in a capitalist culture would worry about. People fantasize about lying in bed doing nothing because much, if not most work is boring and life-draining. That's because most people work for capitalists, whose only concern is their own material profit. But in *our* social order, people will work not for the benefit of a few, but for the well-being of the many. We have stated that nothing, not even sex, feels better for a human than the sense of helping another, and contributing to a larger whole. These are the values that will motivate our citizens.

Benedict: I would like to add something to your statement.

Neal: What statement?

Benedict: That nothing feels better for a human than the sense of helping another and contributing to a larger whole. There is something that feels just as good. Two things, actually.

Neal: What?

Benedict: The joys that arise through (i) understanding, and through (ii) creative self-expression.

Plato: Wait a minute. There are several interrelated themes coming together here. Our main theme for now involves, we might say, the application of sayings such as "as above, so below" and "on Earth, as in Heaven". What is it, we ask, that is true "above" and needs to be applied to "below"? What is it that is true in Heaven, but is yet lacking on Earth?

Neal: Well, in heaven all individual minds are joined so as to constitute a single One Mind. The experience of our union with this single One Mind is the highest joy possible for any individual mind. We have not only the universal testimony of mystics on this, but also the universal testimony of Near-Death Experiencers. As Benedict has written, this highest joy is the source of continuous, supreme happiness.

Benedict: And this is how it is "above" or "in Heaven". It is the natural state of the soul to feel this eternal joy continuously. The Love the soul feels and exudes while in this state is beyond description, for it is unlike anything called by that name on Earth.

Plato: And in a sense, we are asking what a reflection of Divine Love might look like, should it ever come to Earth.

Benedict: Yes, and the key to responding to this question lies in understanding what it means to say that Divine Love is Unconditional. The individual soul, in the state of union, experiences itself as Divine Love. This Love accrues to the soul because of what it *is*, a holy thought in the mind of God, and has nothing to do with how it behaves. This can be understood through realizing that *behavior* is a temporal concept – it requires time in order to do something – but the soul's *being* is eternal.

Socrates: All *behavior*, we might say, is but a dream of the soul. For the Divine Being to make its Love for a given soul dependent on the soul's dreams of embodiment is analogous to a mother making her love for her children conditional upon what the child dreamt the night before.

William: Quite ridiculous, in either case. Yet humans have been brainwashed for so many centuries into believing that God is just like them, and doles out approval and disapproval in the same way that humans conduct their affairs. So the Law of Unconditional Love that rules supreme in Heaven is not understood on Earth, except by those individuals who have had spiritually transformative experiences.

Neal: Yes, we might even say that humans have reversed our sayings, and have conceptualized God and Heaven so as to exemplify "in Heaven, as on Earth" and "as below, so above". That is, humans are much more comfortable with a concept of Heaven that exactly parallels how they are living on Earth.

Benedict: Hence our emphasis, our repeated emphasis, on the concept of Unconditional Love. We want Earth to become a reflection of Heaven, not the other way around, as your religions currently teach. If there were no obstacles to the flowering of Divine Love on Earth, what might that look like?

Neal: Every baby that is born, every soul that is newly embodied, will be welcomed and loved, after the model by which souls are welcomed back into heaven when they return. Perhaps we may conceive of the Social Order into which the baby is born as analogous to the Divine Mind in which all minds have their being. The Divine Mind extends Its Love unconditionally to all minds within Itself.

William: But of course, a Social Order cannot be said to love in anywhere near the sense of the Divine Being. Nevertheless, there is no reason why the care given to all infants and babies – care that is not conditional on how the infants *behave* – cannot be extended to humans of any and every age. This will include care for the needs of the body: food, clothing, shelter, and whatever promotes the health of the body – as well as care for the needs of the personality: inclusion, a sense of belonging, a sense of meaning and purpose, and of course, education. These are the sorts of things a social order may provide to its individuals, not because of anything the individual has *done*, but simply because, if a reason must be given, every individual human being is an embodied soul, deserving of all possible support as it courageously ventures into physicality.

Plato: And this is the only way to end slavery.

Neal: Slavery?

Plato: Yes, when one human is compelled to labor for the material gain of another human, that is slavery, no matter how your present culture tries to sugarcoat it. Capitalism is a form of slavery. It is completely foreign and counter to how it is "in heaven", where every individual soul is unconditionally loved and valued. Only when money is not attached to what humans *do* will humans be free to do what they wish, and what they *wish* to do is to fulfill the original intentions of the soul in manifesting as human.

William: Plato's point is very important. You might be tempted to think that people who play competitive games against one another, who chase after money and reputation, are doing what they wish. But this is rarely the case. We have said that no soul becomes embodied for the purpose of merely chasing after money and reputation; the real motivations of the soul pertain to (i) developing and expressing abilities and talents, (ii) understanding, and (iii) helping others. Very few individuals are able to pursue their original motivations, since under Capitalism it is usually not possible both to pursue these things and to have sufficient resources to keep the body alive. So when a young man or woman is deciding what kind of work or career to pursue, the work must carry sufficient remuneration to pay the bills. This is why the majority of individuals do not do what they truly wish to do. But the price paid for not following the soul's original purpose is the depression, frustration, anger, and misery so easily observed throughout the present culture.

Benedict: *(to me)* You had asked a little while ago that we state something about the kind of social order into which our children are maturing. Plato responded by saying something about the kind of humans who will be in charge... that they shall all have attained to what I rather dryly called "knowledge of the third kind", or in

Plato's terms, they shall have escaped from the Cave of corporeality and caught a glimpse of the Source of Consciousness. And I think this is sufficient for our purposes. There is no need for further details, since the details may be left to the future leaders, who, because of their spiritual wisdom, desire nothing for themselves that they do not desire for all humans. But you have perhaps one additional question?

Neal: Yes, but I think I know the answer. Some people reading this (not the present company, of course) will have a tough time giving up the idea that some jobs are more important to society than others. Or they will think that some jobs are so odious, that no one would want to do them unless either it paid very well or no other jobs were available.

Benedict: And what's your answer?

Neal: The answer involves an analogy we have already used. A cell is created by the body as a whole, in which it "lives and moves and has its being". This is analogous to the human mind, which is created by the One Mind, in which it lives and moves and has its being. Each cell has a function and plays a role for which it was created, within the body; indeed, it was created by the body for the purpose of playing the role that it is playing. All cells are different, but no cell is more important than any other. Each cell deserves the support of other cells simply because it exists, and by existing, it contributes to the overall strength of the body, which in turn benefits all other cells.

Benedict: And we can carry the analogy further by noticing that each cell, in its DNA, has within itself the knowledge of the body as a whole. The different cells cooperate with one another because they "know", so to speak, that they all constitute one and the same body. Analogously, each human mind carries within itself the knowledge of the Divine Being. When humans are able to access this knowledge *consciously*, then humans will experience themselves *as* the Divine Being Itself, and internal conflict among humans will no longer be possible.

William: So, Neal, are you convinced by your answer to your question?

Neal: Yes, well theoretically it certainly follows that if we are to model human life after heavenly life, then just as no soul is more important to God than any other soul, so no human role is more important to Society than any other human role. Yet something is nagging at me…

William: *(laughing)* I know; the same thing nagged at me too.

Benedict: *(amused)* Hmm. Theoretical understanding is a fine thing, but it is not complete if something still bothers you. Would you care to state it explicitly?

Neal: We have stated that no social role is more important than any other. On the other hand it seems that some individuals have greatly benefited society and humankind by how they have lived their lives; likewise, some individuals have greatly harmed humankind. Surely Shakespeare, Beethoven, Einstein, and Plato here have benefited humanity more than say Hitler, corporate executives, or some crazed mass-murderer?

Benedict: You're making an assumption. If you're going to list social roles in order of importance to Society, you must have some criteria by which you can judge which roles are the more important ones. What constitutes "benefiting humanity"? The examples you gave above reflect your personal opinions. But don't you think that only the perspective of the Divine Being is fit to "judge" what roles are important?

Neal: I suppose so.

Benedict: But the Divine Being does not judge at all. We must not presume to know how the Divine Being regards Hitlers, corporate executives, or crazed mass-murderers.

Plato: In fact, we could assume that, since they exist, they must have some importance to the Divine Being. I don't know if this is sufficient to dispel what you have called "nagging".

Neal: I think I am satisfied. *Reason* clearly states in so many ways that no social role is more important than any other. This even follows logically from the concept of Unconditional Love. For if it is the case that the Divine Being Loves all humans unconditionally, then this love can have nothing to do with how the human has lived, or is living, her life. So human social roles are not a factor with regard to the *value* of the life to God. Otherwise God's Love would be conditional on social roles. This is what *reason* tells me. So the residual *nagging* must be a remnant of my upbringing, which has caused me to value you and Beethoven more than the mass murderers and corporate executives.

2) Three Cells Walk into a Bar [Or Socrates Tells a Story]

Socrates: *(laughing)* Well said. I know of a little story that may shed some light on our discussion.

Neal: Tell it, by all means.

Socrates: I will, but first I want you to notice that you have become more relaxed and at ease.

Neal: Huh?

Socrates: For the past several pages you have been trying hard to think this through. When I said the word "story", something in you relaxed, as no effort is required to listen to a story. But much effort is required to "think through" what cannot in principle be "thought through". If you try to figure out, by *thinking,* how and in what way the life of a murderer is as worthy to the Divine Being as the life of Beethoven, *(smiling)* or even Plato here, you'll just give yourself a big headache.

Neal and William: Tell me about it.

Socrates: But if instead of trying to just think it through, you were to catch a glimpse of the Real by seeing through the eyes of the Divine Being, all residual nagging questions would come to an immediate end. When the mind becomes relaxed it is better able to get a feel for these things.

Neal: I understand. But I still want to hear the story.

Socrates: OK. Three cells walk into a bar and order a round of drinks.

Neal: What?

Socrates: Indulge me. Now the cells were from different parts of the same body. One was a muscle cell that came from the heart. Another was a nerve cell that came from the brain. The third was a fatty cell that came from a ligament somewhere. But all three cells were suffering from the same mental illness.

Neal: This better be good. What was the illness?

Socrates: Their consciousness – for all cells are conscious – was confined to the surface or cell-wall, and they had no conscious access to the interior of their own being. They believed that they were just a two-dimensional surface, unaware of the three-dimensional volume enclosed by the surface. So they did not know their own DNA, nor could they know that the other cells had the same DNA.

Neal: *(laughing)* Well they must have had a rather precarious existence, since the surface of a cell is so easily bent out of shape.

Socrates: *(laughing)* Precarious indeed, since each cell is in constant interaction with other cells and hence get bent out of shape all the time. And although the precariousness of cellular existence was often a favorite topic of discussion among the cells, especially amongst their so-called "intellectuals", our three cells decided to talk about something they regarded as nobler than mere existence. You see, since childhood they had been told that they were created by something called "The Body", and although they were all quite ignorant about The Body – because their consciousness did not extend into the DNA at the depth of their own being – they nevertheless were concerned that the role they were playing was of importance to their Creator. And so, after a few drinks, the muscle cell says, "It is obvious that I am the most important of The Body's many creations. Without my unique ability to expand and contract, the heart would not beat, nor could the body move or do anything." To which the nerve cell replies: "Hah! All you can do is expand and contract. But I'm the one who relays signals from the brain that tells you when and how to expand and contract. Without me you would not be able to do anything. Clearly, I am the brains behind this operation." Now the fatty cell had been listening to this – for the bragging of the muscle and nerve cell went on for quite a while, as each was quite possessed by her own imagined self-importance to The Body – and became very impressed with the roles of the other two cells. As a result, it came to doubt its own value, felt unworthy and unvalued by the other cells, fell into a big depression and stopped releasing lubricating oils into the ligaments.

Benedict: *(smiling)* And please excuse me for interjecting something a little more serious, but this story exemplifies that feelings both of grandiosity and of deep unworthiness have similar causes, namely ignorance.

Socrates: Why, Benedict, you think I'm not being serious? Well, no matter, for the story continues: a few more rounds of drinks and the nerve cell and muscle cell are arguing the point quite forcefully. Of course, neither cell has any clear knowledge of the organ to which it belongs, and no knowledge of The Body in which both the heart and brain live and which coordinates their activities. But as everyone knows, lack of knowledge is often the foundation for many endless discussions and arguments, and our two cells were about to come to blows when something remarkable happened.

Neal: As if the whole tale were not remarkable.

Socrates: Well it seems that just at the height of the argument they ran out of steam, and could barely speak, let alone come to blows. They felt themselves becoming weak and on the verge of passing out, when suddenly there was a commotion at the entrance to the bar. Two new cells had arrived and pushed themselves through the crowd to the bar, where the nerve cell and muscle cell were about to expire. "Thank Body we arrived in the nick of time," said one of the newly arrived cells. "You two guys have been burning energy much faster than usual; we've been looking all over for you." It then deposited one molecule of oxygen into the nerve cell, and the other new cell deposited another molecule of oxygen into the muscle cell. Both cells quickly revived, and said in unison to the stranger cells: "You have saved our lives. Surely of all the cells in The Body, you are the most important, because without you we would be dead. What is your name?" "We are called 'red blood corpuscles'," said one of the oxygen-carrying cells. "We are cells in the same Body as you, but because of our function, we get around much more than you do, and we have a much better understanding of The Body and all its parts than do you. Hence we know that all cells are equally important to The Body, and the only thing your intellectual discussions do is uselessly burn up energy, making our job a little more difficult. The energy consumed by your fruitless arguing could be much better spent penetrating the interior of your own being, wherein lies the knowledge of The Body."

Neal: But what happened to the fatty cell?

Socrates: Yes, well it was about to expire too; excessive feelings of low self-esteem caused it almost to stop breathing. Fortunately, another red blood corpuscle arrived just in time, and revived the fatty cell with a molecule of oxygen. The three cells were in awe of the red blood corpuscles and the tales they told about their adventures circulating throughout The Body. They resolved not to argue about such things anymore, and became, one might say, students of The Body.

Neal: And so our conclusion must be that all the threads in the tapestry called Creation are of equal value to the Whole, which has created each of its "parts" to be exactly what it is.

William: Thus the "Earthly reflection" of this conclusion must be a social order in which each of the "parts" – each human being – is treated exactly the same way with respect to the needs of its body.

Benedict: Yes, our conclusion seems correct: our New Social Order will unconditionally provide for the material needs of every body, and will also provide for the basic psychological needs of the personality. But I am fascinated by Socrates' tale of the cells, if we may call it that.

Socrates: What do you find fascinating, aside from enabling us to conclude that all cells are of equal importance to the body?

Benedict: I would tell you, but I am afraid you might think I am getting too metaphysical.

Socrates: *(laughing)* Well, you can get a little metaphysical, as long as you do not also try to get too literal.

Benedict: *(blushing slightly, and smiling)* Yeah. Well it would be difficult for anyone to take your tale of the cells *literally*. This is why we say it is an analogy. But the point of a good analogy – that is, the reason that a good analogy contributes to Understanding – is that there are similarities of structure between the analogy and the situation for which the analogy was introduced. The structure can be grasped easier through the analogy than through the real situation. With your indulgence, Socrates, I would like to make the analogy a bit more explicit so we can examine how it structurally depicts, or is an analogy for, the human condition.

Socrates: Go right ahead. I shall be delighted if my little tale serves a nobler purpose than the one for which the tale was told.

Benedict: And I must say at the beginning that I no longer like the term "metaphysical".

Plato: Neither do I. Aristotle coined the term to describe what he had written *after* he had written on the so-called natural world. And the word today has connotations that come from Aristotle, who had no personal experience of these things. By "these things" I refer to spirituality, to the experience of the union that exists between the One Mind and individual minds.

Benedict: Well, whether we call it "metaphysics" or "spirituality", this is what I want to talk about with reference to the tale of the cells.

Socrates: Yes, talk.

Benedict: So, to make the analogy explicit, a cell is analogous to the human mind, and The Body is analogous to what we have called the "One Mind" or the "World Soul". The relationship between a given cell and The Body is analogous to the relationship between a given human mind and the One Mind in the following respects: (i) every cell is created by the Body, in which it "lives and moves and has its being". Likewise, every human mind is created by the One Mind, in which it "lives and moves and has its being." (ii) Insofar as it is accurate to state that the knowledge of the physical body is contained in the DNA of each cell, then each cell contains within itself identical knowledge of The Body. Analogously, the knowledge of the union that exists between an individual human mind and the One Mind is contained within every human (and nonhuman) mind. This is the meaning of the phrase "the kingdom of heaven is within." (iii) In Socrates' story, we imagined that each cell was self-conscious, but its consciousness was confined to its surface and did not penetrate into the interior of its being, wherein lies its DNA, or the knowledge of its Body. Analogously, the particular form of consciousness that is the human mind does not know itself, and lies upon the surface of its own being. Because of their ignorance, the cells were insecure regarding their value to their Creator, and needed to argue about their self-importance. This argument gets resolved only by the cells "looking within" and finding the DNA that is in their interior. Then they know that the Body creates cells as needed, and all are of equal importance.

Neal: What do you mean when you say that the human mind lies upon the surface of its own being?

Benedict: *(smiling)* Good question. The statement would seem to be pure metaphor; physical objects have a surface, but what is meant by saying that the mind has a surface?

Neal: Using our analogy, I would reason as follows: a given cell is a three-dimensional physical object. All physical objects have a surface, but most of the being of the object lies in its interior, in the three-dimensional space.

Benedict: Yes, most of a cell's being lies under its surface.

Neal: So the human mind is the surface of a higher-dimensional being?

Benedict: Something like that *(laughing)*, using Plato's sense of the word "like".

Neal: With a given cell, it is quite easy to understand what is the higher three-dimensional being, of which the surface is a surface. But if we are saying that the human mind is *like* a cell in this respect, then is it not incumbent upon us to say something about the higher-dimensional being of which the human mind is its surface?

William: This will not be too difficult a task. In fact, it has already been done.

Neal: What do you mean?

William: In my lifetime I waded through what seemed like zillions of first-person reports of mystical experiences. You know my favorite cases well. Likewise, you have waded through about the same number of reports of Near-Death Experiences. What are such reports if not an attempt to depict that "higher-dimensional being" that humans experience themselves as being. And we can add to this the reports of profound experiences under entheogens. These experiences are experiences of one's own essential being, compared to which the *human* portion of their minds appears as an illusory surface phenomena.

Neal: I agree. I think reading numerous such reports is perhaps the best way for a human who lacks direct experience to get some sense of what it is like. But these reports should not be taken literally, especially since they – the writers of the reports – universally state that it cannot be put into words.

Benedict: Yes, the reports give some sense of what it, the "whole mind", is like, but not an adequate understanding of what it is in itself. Here we are content to say a little more about what it is like. Now the human, or surface, portion of the whole mind consists mostly of the memory of the body's history. Do we agree with this?

Neal: Yes. Every human, when asked who he is, will respond by naming birth, family, culture, education, social circumstances, etc., all of which pertain to the history of its body.

Benedict: And this sense of identity is what is experienced as illusory when a human experiences her mind as it really is, as in the NDE?

Neal: Yes.

Benedict: Now with Socrates' permission, I'd like to go back to the bar where we left our three cells.

Socrates: Permission granted.

Benedict: Thank you. We left our friends – a muscle cell, a nerve cell, and a fatty cell – enthralled at the tales of the red blood corpuscles. Their Creator, The Body, was much vaster than anything the cells had conceived, and they came to believe that they were aspects of a single magnificent being, who created them to serve the very purpose that they in fact were serving. But they still suffered from a kind of pervasive fear and anxiety. We are hypothesizing that the individual cells are self-conscious, but that their consciousness is still confined to the surface and does not extend into the interior of the cell. What do you suppose such a being might be fearful of?

Neal: That's easy. If I were a cell and did not know I had an inside, but thought I was only the surface, then I would worry greatly about interactions with other cells. Every such interaction changes the physical shape of the cell. If my sense of self comes from the shape of the surface, and the shape changes with every interaction, then my sense of self depends upon my interactions with other cells.

Benedict: So every cell is in continuous interaction with other cells. Each interaction affects the literal shape of the cell. Every cell, we might say, is constantly and continuously being bent out of shape. Since by hypothesis, its sense of identity is confined to the shape of its surface, its very sense of identity is constantly being bent out of shape.

Neal: A most precarious way to live.

Benedict: But if the cell could identity with its real being, its interior, then the shape of its surface from moment to moment would be "of no consequence", for the nucleus of a cell is invariant even as the surface undergoes the necessary changes.

Neal: Then in terms of this analogy, the anxiety and fear that pervade the human condition – the ego, or personality – is brought about because the human condition involves only a truncated surface of the larger mind, or soul, to which it belongs. It is constantly being "bent out of shape" by continuous interactions with other humans, and lives with a constant background fear. But as soon as an individual experiences herself as the eternal soul of which the personality is like a "surface", then all worry and anxiety drop away.

Plato: I find myself wondering whether this analogy can shed some light on what is most peculiar about the human condition.

Neal: "Most peculiar"! What do you mean by that?

Plato: Well, like our red blood corpuscles, Socrates and I travelled around a bit within this World Soul, and –

Socrates: *(laughing)* Speak for yourself, my friend, but I have preferred to stay put. After all, where is there to travel to?

Plato: *(also laughing)* I concede that when you are experiencing yourself as the eternal, infinite, omnipresent "One Mind", there is no place to travel to.

Socrates: Yes, you were speaking metaphorically. But tell us of your travels through the interior of the One Mind.

Plato: Yes, I encountered many wondrous beings, from deities to nature spirits. Infinite in both number and variety, these beings shared their stories…

Neal: *(playfully)* … While Socrates examined them for wisdom, I presume?

Socrates: *(also playfully)* Why yes, something like that.

Plato: Now the great majority of souls do not participate in the human experiment, know nothing of time, and are content to enjoy their full being as an eternal thought in the mind of the World Soul. So when I tried to share with them something of my experience as a *human* being, they had difficulty understanding it. It is impossible, they would argue, for a mind to exist that did not know it was a mind. When I would tell them that the human experiment involved creating minds that did not know they were minds, but instead thought they were bodies, they reacted in disbelief. Such a mind, they said, even if it could exist, would be utterly insane. So wherever I went and whoever I talked with in the realm of *eternal being,* there was this sense of amazement and disbelief that there could even exist a realm of *temporal becoming,* and expressed the opinion that any aspect of consciousness, any mind, that lived exclusively in the realm of becoming would be completely insane.

Neal: We have said before that many spiritual teachers regard the human condition as essentially insane. I think this analogy gives some sense in which this is true. We might say that the "normal" state of a cell is for its consciousness to extend to the whole of its being, so that it experiences itself not just as a surface, but as a full three-dimensional being. We can conceive of a body in which every cell experiences itself in this way, and hence no cell ever experiences anxiety about being bent out of shape. If this were the normal state of affairs for cells, then our three cells in the bar are relatively abnormal.

Benedict: And so compared with what is "normal" for the vast majority of souls, the human condition may rightly be called abnormal. For it is not possible to be fully sane without the knowledge of the union that exists between the human mind and the "One Mind".

Plato: Humans *have* this knowledge, of course, but they do not recollect it. And this pervasive ignorance, definitive of the so-called *human* condition, is the root cause of the pervasive fear and anxiety that distinguishes the embodied soul from all others.

Neal: *(with humor)* You guys must have forgotten how it feels to constantly worry about being bent out of shape.

William: And it is in the very nature of a surface to be constantly bent out of shape. When one's sense of self is confined to a surface, and the shape of the surface is constantly changing, then the anxiety that marks the human condition is the result.

Benedict: For the shape of the surface of any object that interacts with other objects is necessarily impermanent, whether the object in question is a cell or a human body that continuously interacts with other bodies. When consciousness associates itself with just the surface of a body, it will experience anxiety, unless it has fully embraced its own impermanence.

Plato: Yet at the deepest level, that which we call "impermanent" does not really exist. But this is the level at which the human condition is experienced as illusory; it is not the level with which we are now concerned. For only that which is impermanent can be feared; yet the sorts of things that *can* be feared – shadows and surfaces – do not really exist. In terms of our analogy, a two-dimensional object is a mere abstraction; it is not a reality in itself.

Neal: Or in terms of your allegory, we might say that the human is constantly being frightened by the shadows that appear on the wall of the Cave. But that's just because he believes that he himself is just one of the shadows. A shadow is *like* a surface in the sense that it has no reality independent of the three-dimensional object of which it is the shadow (or surface).

Plato: Yet when he beholds the Reality that is casting the very shadow he takes himself to be, he will rejoice at the unreality of what he formerly thought was real. But perhaps we have said enough for now about matters metaphysical; *(with humor)* we do not wish to try Socrates' patience more than is necessary.

Socrates: *(jokingly)* Enough jokes about my limited patience for lengthy speeches. After all, it appears that my patience is now as limitless as my being. But I wish to reemphasize the point we have often alluded to: words and concepts cannot in principle depict what transcends the merely physical. But something of "what it is like" may be conveyed through a good story; as Benedict has put it, there are structural parallels between the "story" and the "reality" we are trying to understand. Moreover, the mental effort required to grasp literal concepts that purport to depict the transcendent – that very mental effort hinders the understanding, as the mind loses itself in words and concepts. Words and concepts, we might say, are external to the Kingdom of Heaven, and the mind's efforts to understand these things through words and concepts and other symbols will not only prevent the mind from entering, but will also give it a big headache. A good story relaxes the part of the mind that thinks in terms of words and concepts, and it is more able to get some understanding than when it is focused entirely on trying to grasp at words and concepts. *(To Benedict)* As you now know, this is why the poets understood you much better than the philosophers.

William: Even in my time it was well known that insights and understandings come when the mind is relaxed, not when it has tied itself in knots with words and concepts. The temperament of a philosopher is quite different from that of a poet. The former grasps at words, concepts, and other linguistic symbols, which they take literally, as if ultimate understanding lies merely in a suitable arrangement of such words and concepts. The poets are more playful with their use of words, and are much more receptive to feeling and intuition, which goes deeper than mere words. From my present perspective I can see that great harm is done to children by a so-called educational system that relies almost exclusively on words and concepts. The full flowering of a soul into its human embodiment requires that we pay attention to *all* the modalities of conscious experience possible for a human. *Thinking* is one such modality, but so are *feeling, sensing, and intuiting*. Other modalities might be *music, theater, and art,* as well as developing *compassion* and *sensitivity* towards others. *Thinking* has usurped the throne at present, but our children will be exposed to all modalities.

3) The Stream of Thoughts

Plato: Well, this is perhaps a good segue to the next major element of our children's education.

Neal: What is it?

Plato: The flowering of *reason* in the minds of our children.

Benedict: *(to Plato)* A favorite topic of ours! Perhaps a preliminary discussion of semantics will be useful, since there seems to be no consistent usage of terms that refer to mental activity.

Plato: You have in mind, I presume, terms like "understand", "intellect", "thinking", and of course, "reason".

Benedict: ... To which we might add "awareness", "consciousness", and "idea".

William: We must remind ourselves of what we said earlier – or at least, I am reminding myself – that humans, not words, have meaning. So we are not attempting to state what these terms *mean*, but are merely attempting to state what meaning we shall give these terms for the purposes of our discussion.

Neal: And I suppose we shall be teaching our children about these things in a way that heeds Socrates' warning.

Socrates: What warning?

Neal: About the dangers of teaching *argument* – another term to define – to adolescent boys.

William: Yes, and this is why the whole field called "philosophy" – and most of what is called "psychology" – is largely irrelevant to the issues facing humanity today. For these disciplines are run mostly by males who have not outgrown their adolescent motivations. There are exceptions of course, but on the whole they want to win arguments and be thought right by others more than they wish to discern truth. They are "clever", but without depth or wisdom. OK, so we must define the difference between the words "cleverness" and "reasoning". And "intelligence", too. But how shall we begin?

Socrates: I have a suggestion.

William: Yes?

Socrates: "Consciousness" and "awareness" are the most general of our terms to be defined. Perhaps a good beginning would be for you to state your present reservations concerning your former concept of a "stream of consciousness".

William: Alright. Well, I was trying to be as empirical as possible in describing one's inner mental life. At any given moment, one is simultaneously aware of many things. To take a specific example, there is present to my awareness: (i) a tree I am looking at, (ii) a memory of climbing trees as a boy, (iii) feeling some sadness because of something at home, (iv) thinking about the lecture I'm giving this evening, etc., etc. Many items are present to my awareness simultaneously. I referred to these "many items" as a stream of consciousness. But quite clearly, it is not consciousness that "streams"; consciousness does not "go" anywhere. Consciousness is the container, or field, through which the various items – memories, perceptions, emotions, thoughts – stream.

Neal: It seems then that we have our concept of consciousness: it is the "space" or "field" in which individual thoughts, perceptions, emotions, imaginings, and everything mental arise.

Plato: Good. This is a basic distinction, between (i) consciousness as a field of awareness and (ii) the items or objects that appear to flow through, or arise within, consciousness. When consciousness identifies with the particular items that arise within it, then we shall say that "ego" or "personality" comes into being. Consciousness itself originates in the Divine Being, but becomes a "person" when it identifies with the memory of its body's history. When at death it dis-identifies from the history of its body, it knows itself as consciousness per se, as the Near-Death Experience shows.

Socrates: And when it dis-identifies from its memories *before* its body dies, we shall call that "enlightenment". We might playfully describe an enlightened human being as one whose ego has died before his body.

Plato: It is useful to have a concept of consciousness that pertains to nonhuman forms of consciousness as well as human forms. By the way, when I use the word "form" here, it is *not* in the technical philosophic sense usually attributed to me; the English word "form" was a poor translation in any case. I'm using the word in its ordinary English sense. The specifically *human* form of consciousness is one that involves identification with the various objects that appear to arise within the field of consciousness, along with a sort of amnesia with respect to its own Source.

William: This amnesia is definitive of the human condition, until now. We have stated that this amnesia is a partial cause of the madness that afflicts the human condition. But another factor that contributes strongly to human insanity is that what we have called *linguistic* consciousness has usurped almost the whole of human consciousness. For a majority of humans today, the objects that arise within their field of consciousness consist of little more than words and symbols. *Mental life* has devolved into mere words. Even perceptions and emotions are infused with the words that one would use to describe them.

Neal: Yes, but *our* children are emotionally intelligent. They know that the sentence "I feel sad" is not itself the sadness that they feel.

They know that the words "There is a tree" are not the tree that they see. *Our* children will have been taught to distinguish between their mental content and the words they would use to describe that content to another.

William: That is true, but in the present dysfunctional society, people do not generally have this ability, and so their inner mental life consists mostly of a flow of words. Shall we call this stream of words *thinking*?

Benedict: It seems mundane to use the words "thinking" and "thought" to refer to the ordinary inner life of the typical human being. But we need such a word. There is a very close connection between (i) the mental activity called *thinking*, and (ii) the words a human would use to express the content of her thinking. Is the mental activity called *thinking* anything more than the words?

Socrates: Without answering that question, we must note several distinctive features of this "stream of thinking" as it occurs within a field of consciousness. Is this manner of expression OK with you, William?

William: Yes, of course. What are the distinctive features you have in mind?

Socrates: I'll toss them into the discussion all at once. The "stream of thinking" that constitutes the inner life of the typical human is (i) automatic or involuntary, (ii) compulsory, and (iii) mostly fictional in nature.

William: Let's discuss them in the order you have mentioned them. Physiology distinguished between what is called the "voluntary" nervous system and the "involuntary" nervous system. Humans have voluntary control of some aspects of their bodies' behavior.

Benedict: ... *(smiling)* Or at least they believe they do.

William: Point noted. So humans believe they are have voluntary control over such things as what to eat, where to walk, who to associate with etc. But the body does many things automatically, or involuntarily, such as pumping blood to all the cells in the body, digesting food, and visual perception.

Neal: Visual perception?

William: *(laughing)* You and Benedict have written about this.

Neal: *(blushing slightly)* Yes, I'm now remembering. Light reflects off some object and enters the body through the eyes. The process by which those individual photons interact with the retinal cells produces signals that travel to the brain, which then decodes those signals and in some unknown way generates the visual perception – the whole process is automatic or involuntary, just like circulation and digestion. And so the "stream of thoughts" flowing through the field of awareness is like the "stream of blood" that flows through the body's veins and arteries in that neither are the result of conscious decision-making or influence.

Benedict: And this exposes Descartes' error in a novel way.

Neal: What do you mean?

Benedict: He observed that there is thinking going on in his mind, and concluded from that observation that he must exist. But this sheds no light on what it is that must exist. Is the "I" identical to the thinking – to the stream of thoughts? Or is the "I" something over and above the stream of thoughts? Descartes' conclusion seems to be towards the latter – that he is a something that thinks.

Neal: Yes, but this is fairly well known about the "cogito". What did you mean by "novel"?

Benedict: Well, maybe not too novel. If our approach is correct, then Descartes' sentence "I am a thinking thing" must be analyzed in the same way that we would analyze the sentence "I am digesting my food" or "I am circulating my blood". In the latter cases, the conscious "I" is involved neither with digestion nor with circulation because these things are involuntary. There is no agency involved. So if *thinking* is involuntary, then the "I" is not the cause or producer of the thinking any more than it is the cause of the blood circulating through the body. Now I think Socrates' second feature is a close cousin of the first: humans cannot "choose" to **not** think (aside from advanced meditators). So *thinking* is compulsory.

Neal: And I want to emphasize that in using the word "thinking", we are not using it in the sense of focused attention on a specific problem, such as "thinking about" how to solve a math problem. We are using the term to capture what goes on in a person's head when she is alone – what William called the "stream of consciousness" that we have now relabeled as the "stream of thoughts" that incessantly parade before one's consciousness. And we have noted that this stream of thoughts, if one pays attention to it, consists mostly of words – the words one would use to express the thoughts to another. But now we must say something about the *fictional* nature of this stream of thoughts that Socrates has alluded to.

Benedict: We must be a bit careful here. Thoughts in themselves are absolutely real and have real effects. So when we state that one's inner dialogue – the expression we used before – is fictional, we do not mean that thoughts are unreal, as perhaps some of your Materialists would want to believe. Rather, we mean that the content of the thought is unreal. A few examples will make clear our meaning. But first, we state or restate a most obvious truth, that consciousness never experiences anything other than "this present moment" or "now". The past no longer exists, and when it did exist it was experienced as *now*. Similarly what is called "future" also does not exist, and when it comes to exist it will be experienced as *now*. So a person who finds himself thinking about something in the past or future is thinking about something that does not exist, hence the content of his thinking is fictional. But the thoughts themselves, along with the emotions the thoughts involve, are real and have a real effect on both the body and the psyche.

William: May I interject something?

Benedict: Of course.

William: Emotions are included in the stream of thinking.

Benedict: Yes, definitely. They go together. If one feels guilty about some past behavior, then it is impossible to think about the behavior without feeling guilty. And conversely, when guilt builds up in the mind, it will generate many thoughts that trigger that emotion. But all such thoughts reference the past, which does not exist. Similarly

– and here we'll take the emotion first – if one is anxious or worried about something, the object of one's worry is always some imagined future event. Individuals who are chronically anxious are always on the lookout for things to feel anxious about. One can be anxious only about the future, which does not exist. But one's thoughts about the future do exist in the present moment, and have real (and unhealthy) effects on the body and mind. So all thoughts that pertain to either the past or the future are fictional. And I suppose for completeness we should add contrary-to-fact imaginings such as sexual fantasies, the content of which is obviously unreal.

William: And so the thoughts that comprise one's inner dialogue or stream of thinking, insofar as they reference past and future or are entirely imaginary, are fictional in nature. But to make this point as clear as possible, let's contrast *thinking* with other modalities of human conscious experience. We have exposed our children to a number of modalities of conscious experience that require focused attention, but do not involve *thinking*. In fact, the two are incompatible. Take gymnastics or sports, for example. Attention must be focused in the present moment. To the extent that an athlete has thoughts that pertain to the past or future while playing, to that extent will errors be made. The same with music. The mind of both performer and listener is focused on the sounds occurring in the present moment. To the extent the listener also entertains stray thoughts about past and future, to that extent he is not hearing the music. Moreover, our children are emotionally intelligent, which means they have the ability to feel their emotions as sensations within their own body. *Feeling* sensation is not compatible with *thinking*. To the extent that a person obsesses, that is, has thoughts about the whys and wherefores of any emotion, to that extent the person is not feeling the emotion, but is being controlled by it.

Neal: Our conclusion appears to be that of all the modalities of consciousness, only *thinking* is fictional. The others require focused attention in the present moment. My goodness, I just thought of something.

William: Hah! Careful now. Did "you" think of something or did a thought just pop into your mind.

Neal: Clearly the latter. Hmm, we humans are easily confused by language, aren't we? My experience was: a thought suddenly and effortlessly popped into my awareness. The linguistic expression "I just thought of something" falsely suggests agency, that I did something, rather than that the thought just happened.

William: OK, now what was that thought?

Neal: Yeah, well dinnertime will be very different in our New Social Order.

William: How did you get to "dinner" from our discussion of modalities of conscious experience?

Neal: The reason Americans eat so unhealthily is because they cannot taste their food. They are not able to get out of their heads and actually taste what they are eating. If they could for an instant cease their incessant *thinking* and put their conscious attention on the taste sensations while eating, they would not be able to eat the various poisons that they call "food". So dinnertime will be an opportunity to bring focused attention into the present moment, and fully experience and enjoy the sensations of taste.

William: And our physiologists, we predict, will doubtless document that consuming food in this way maximizes the nutritional value of the food for the body. But now, back to whatever we were talking about. We have made a crucial distinction between *thinking* and *focused attention*. They are mutually exclusive. This is perhaps a bit paradoxical, because the common understanding of these terms holds that *thinking* is identical to *focused attention*. To *think* about something is to focus one's attention on it. And there is no doubt that humans occasionally use thought in this way – to think through a problem that is occurring in the present moment. But the mind is constantly producing thoughts, even when there is no problem at hand. It is this constant, automatic, and involuntary mental process, by which thoughts and emotions continuously arise in the mind, to which we give the name *"thinking"* and which is incompatible with attention focused in the present moment. Well, perhaps we have said enough for now about the stream of thoughts that occur in the field of human consciousness.

4) Calculative Thinking [Or What Reason Is Not]

Plato: Yes, I agree. Our children, having made friends with the sexual energies, are now ready to learn what we shall call *reasoning*. Of course, children can and do reason at earlier ages, but *reasoning* involves an ability to see connections among ideas, an ability which arises in early teen years or a little before. But before we say what *reasoning* is, I want to say what it is not.

Neal: Go ahead.

Plato: *(mischievously)* It is *not* what is taught in your universities in courses called "Reasoning".

Neal: Perhaps that's a bit too strong, although having taught such courses myself, I'm inclined to agree. I would put it this way: what is called "reasoning" in academic circles constitute a preliminary portion of the whole of reasoning. And I suggest that we call this portion of the whole of reasoning – that which *is* taught in university courses – "calculative thinking". The "problem" is that academics believe that "calculative thinking" comprises the whole of the human ability called "reason".

Plato: Let's state Benedict's poetic characterization of *reason* again.

Neal: OK, here it is: *"... reasoning is not the principle thing in us, but only like a stairway, by which we can climb up to the desired place, or like a good spirit which without any falsity or deception brings tidings of the greatest good, to spur us thereby to seek it, and to unite with it in a union which is our greatest salvation and blessedness."*

Plato: Now, Benedict, if we were to take away your poetic license, how might you more literally state your meaning?

Benedict: *(with humor)* No one has ever accused me of having a poetic license before. But OK, here goes: (i) "the principle thing in in us" is the capacity for transcendent experience – the capacity to experience directly the union that exists between the human mind and the mind of God. (ii) This experience, this knowledge, is the "desired place", our "greatest salvation and blessedness". (iii) This quote does not define what reason *is*, but states its function, which is to motivate us to seek our "desired place", our blessedness. And finally, (iv) there is no falsity or deception associated with *reasoning*.

Socrates: But there is one more aspect of this quote that deserves comment.

Benedict: Yes?

Socrates: Your comparison of *"reason"* with a "good spirit". In my time it was a common belief that everyone was assigned a spirit guide; the function of such a guide was similar to the function you ascribe to *reason*. But for the great majority of humans, the voice of their spirit guide, or the "voice for reason", is easily drowned out by the "voice in the head" or what we have called the incessant stream of thinking.

William: Perhaps, from a pragmatic point of view, it does not matter much if we conceive the voice for reason as a spirit guide or as an inborn ability to discern Truth. The point is, the Divine Being did not just dump us on this planet without giving us the tools and resources to find our way back. The ability to reason, as Benedict characterizes it, is our main resource.

Neal: And it should be abundantly clear *why* Plato said that *reasoning* is not what is taught in universities under courses called "reasoning". It is because the concept of "salvation" or "blessedness" plays no role in contemporary universities. There is nothing, according to contemporary academics, for reason to lead us *to*. What they call "reasoning" is merely "calculative thinking" or "cleverness". Perhaps a few simple examples will make intuitively clear the difference I have in mind.

William: Yes.

Neal: OK, a woman decides to murder her husband…

William: How about a less gruesome example?

Neal: A man feels deeply that he has been wronged by another, and seeks revenge.

Plato: That's also somewhat gruesome, especially if one considers the horror that constitutes the inner mental life of the one who seeks revenge.

Neal: I can see where this is going. The general point I think we can acknowledge right away. Anytime humans deviate from what Benedict called "the dictates of reason", the results are likely to be gruesome. But gruesomeness aside, I want to use these examples to show the difference between what we are calling "reasoning" and what we are calling "calculative thinking". Given any desire, there are more or less expedient ways of realizing that desire. The woman wanting to kill her husband may consider various methods of doing so; she may make elaborate plans and devote considerable mental energy to her purpose. Academics will say she is "reasoning" to figure out the best way to accomplish her purpose. But on the contrary, we shall say that she is not reasoning at all, and that if she *were* reasoning she would not be murdering her husband in the first place. The mental activity that names what she is doing is "calculative thinking".

Similarly, the man who seeks revenge will think about the best way to achieve his goal. Academics will insist that he is reasoning; we will insist that he is not reasoning. He is calculating in his head the best way to achieve his goal, but his goal is itself unreasonable. Both murder and vengeance are desires incompatible with the "dictates of reason". And of course, the primary dictate of reason is the Golden Rule, or what Kant called the Moral Law. But we need to say more, perhaps much more, about this faculty called "reason", which the Divine Being has given to humans as a means of finding our way Home.

William: Yes, but it will be easier to define what we are calling "calculative thinking". It is the ability to manipulate words and symbols.

Neal: And we note that this is the *only* mental ability that so-called IQ tests can measure. There is no correlation whatsoever between having a high IQ and being a "reasonable" human being. If we are to associate the word "intelligence" with the ability to reason, then

IQ tests measure, not intelligence, but mere cleverness, or calculative thinking.

And here's another way to look at it: by no stretch of the imagination can one say that it is "reasonable" for humans to live in such a way as to destroy the Earth's ability to support life. No one would ever claim that it is "intelligent" to poison the water and atmosphere. Yet this is exactly what is argued by individuals with very high IQs – politicians, business leaders, corporate CEOs, and a host of academics who argue there is no other way for an economy to function. But clearly, it is not reasonable for humans to destroy that upon which their own existence depends.

Benedict: Now, there is nothing wrong with what we are calling "cleverness". It is a human ability. But what we are calling "intelligence" and "reason" pertain to the *use* of this ability. Two individuals may be equally clever, yet one uses this ability to rationalize his desires to seek wealth and reputation, the other uses this ability to seek truth and help others.

William: Indeed, we might compare *cleverness* – the ability to manipulate words and symbols – to brute strength. Physical strength is a human ability, but the proper use of strength, whether it is used for good or for bad, depends on something other than itself. We might say that the proper use of either physical strength or mental strength depends on intelligence or wisdom.

Neal: And it is a great error to equate intelligence with mere cleverness, as almost all academics do.

Benedict: We have defined the term "cleverness" explicitly; but we have not yet defined the term "intelligence". Do you have something in mind?

Neal: No, not anything explicit. But I think it will be not too difficult to give examples that characterize the difference between the two.

Benedict: Go ahead.

Neal: At the individual level, let us suppose a teenage boy kills himself "because" his girlfriend left him. I'll explain later why I put the word "because" in quotes. No one would say that suicide was an intelligent thing to do; no one would claim that the boy exhibited intelligence by committing suicide. Yet this boy might very well have had the highest IQ in his class. So, there is no connection here between intelligence and cleverness. At the collective level, the human race is in the process of committing suicide by destroying the Earth's ability to support human life. No one would say that this is an intelligent thing to do. On the contrary, it is an insanely stupid thing to do. Yet humans are led by those among them who are most clever. The leaders of business, economics, politics are all very clever; they all have high IQs and college degrees. Yet they are unable and/or unwilling to understand that their collective lust for reputation and wealth is causing the destruction of humankind. So one can have cleverness in the presence of insanity, and if *this* doesn't show the difference between "cleverness" and "intelligence", then nothing will.

Now, I want to note two things: (i) I do not claim that suicide is *never* the intelligent thing to do. In cases of painful terminal illness, suicide may very well be a better option than prolonging the process of dying. It is not intelligent, we might say, to keep a body "alive" when there is no hope of recovery. So one may easily conceive of cases where suicide is an intelligent thing to do. But teenage love-affairs (or lust-affairs) is not one of them.

And (ii) I put the word "because" above in quotes to indicate that, while the teenager sincerely believes that his girlfriend's rejection "causes" him to take his life, no practicing therapist would agree. The true causes, therapists would insist, lie in the boy's psychological makeup; it is a combination of inborn temperament and upbringing that has created a psyche, a mind-set, according to which rejection is a "reason" for suicide.

Benedict: ... Which brings us to another use, or misuse, of the term "reason". We have distinguished between reason and intelligence, on the one hand, and cleverness, on the other, by giving clear examples of unreasonable and unintelligent uses of the ability to manipulate symbols. But the word "reason" is also commonly used in a very different sense, as in giving *reasons* for one's behavior and beliefs.

Neal: Yes, giving *reasons* for one's beliefs is enshrined as an almost sacred obligation among academics.

William: How true! Whether one is a philosopher, psychologist, physicist or mathematician, one must always have *reasons* for what one believes. Whenever one asks of another: why do you believe in God? – why do you believe that F = ma? – why do you believe that the sum of the interior angles in a triangle is equal to 180 degrees? – why do you believe in the association of ideas? – the responses to such "why-questions" are called "reasons".

Socrates: *(mischievously)* This is all quite hopeless, you know.

Neal and William: What?

Socrates: *(laughing)* And you really *do* know, you two, that it is indeed very hopeless.

William: OK, what is it we both know is hopeless?

Socrates: … That there is any rhyme or reason, any intelligence, I might say, behind the academic use of the word "reason" … or the popular usage either.

Plato: Let's go slowly here. We must be careful not to throw out the baby with the bathwater (an expression no one understands today). But we may state Socrates' meaning; in the great majority of instances where people are said to offer "reasons" for either beliefs or behaviors, what they are actually offering more accurately fall under the heading of giving either "rationalizations" or "causes", the latter not at all being equivalent to one another.

Socrates: I'll suggest that first we throw out the bathwater; then what is left will be the precious baby. But we should add one more thing for which humans feel a need to give "reasons", in addition to beliefs and behaviors.

Neal: What's that?

Socrates: Emotions. If, for example, someone is feeling sad, angry, or happy, we might ask them *why* they are feeling the way they are. The response to this question is called a reason for the feeling.

Neal: I think I can now see why you called the whole thing "hopeless"?

Socrates: Yes?

Neal: Among the teachings of *A Course in Miracles* is the statement, "I am never upset for the reason I think." If one accepts this, as I do, then any and every attempt to assign a "reason" for the occurrence of any given emotion will fail. For the "reasons" one typically has for one's emotions lie in outer events. But it is never the case that outer events cause emotions.

5) On Reasons, Causes, and Rationalizations

William: But giving reasons for one's emotions is in any case an absurd thing to do. Humans certainly do not "choose" how to feel based on a consideration of possible "reasons". On the contrary, humans experience themselves as first having an emotion, then seeking a "reason", usually outside of themselves. But this use of the term "reason" is what is usually meant by "rationalize". First comes the emotion, then comes the after-the-fact pseudo-reasons for having the emotion. The mental activity called "giving reasons" for one's emotions, behaviors, and beliefs occur at a relatively superficial level of one's personality. To understand one's own emotions, behaviors, and beliefs, one must look for *causes,* rather than after-the-fact rationalizations. Any belief, etc. can be rationalized if one is sufficiently clever.

Neal: For a rationalization is merely a sequence of words that one hopes will be convincing to both oneself and to others. Perhaps a few examples would be appropriate, for our claim is a strong one. We are claiming that whenever a human gives what is called a "reason" for behavior, emotion, and belief, he is actually engaged in a sort of self-deception. What he thinks is an "objective" reason is really mere rationalization. That is to say, the mental activity called "cleverness" is engaged in finding a sequence of words that appear to "justify" or "necessitate" his behavior, etc.

William: Let's give a few examples. I'll start, and I'll use myself as an example, and I'll discuss three different beliefs that I had when I was in my physical form. Two of the beliefs were typical of males in my culture, and one was not. Like Benedict I believed, or was inclined to believe, that males were intellectually superior to females, and also that non-Caucasian races and cultures were inferior to those of European descent. These two beliefs were caused entirely by upbringing. But if I were asked to give *reasons* for those beliefs, I would never have pointed to the true cause – that I was raised that way – but would have used my cleverness to "rationalize" my beliefs by pointing to alleged facts about women and non-Caucasians. But clearly, my rationalizations and justifications would have been arising from the same conditioning process that produced those beliefs in the first place.

Neal: And the third belief?

William: It was that mediums can communicate with spirits.

Neal: Ah yes, a belief that did not arise from upbringing.

William: *(smiling)* A belief that was contrary to my upbringing, especially my medical training. And besides, Harvard University did not allow its professors to believe in such things.

Neal: *(laughing)* And to this day Harvard professors will insist that, as Plato once put it, "whatever they cannot squeeze in their hands is absolutely nothing". But then what would be the "reason" for this belief, given that it was not caused by upbringing?

William: I would have argued, or rather, I did argue, that the belief or hypothesis that mediums are for real is the belief that is most consistent with, and most supported by, a large number of empirical facts.

Plato: Let us notice that we are beginning to give a positive characterization of the mental process we shall call "reasoning". One component of this process involves examining empirical data or facts, and considering various hypotheses in the light of such data. Another component of reasoning involves moving in the opposite direction: deriving logical consequences from given premises. But let's continue with examples that illustrate the differences between reasons, causes, and rationalizations…

William: I think it is obvious that, whatever I might have given as a "reason" for my belief that males are superior to females and Caucasians are superior to Asians, those reasons would have been caused by the same forces that caused me to have those beliefs in the first place, hence they function as mere rationalizations for what I already believed. It would be sheer self-deception for me to believe that my beliefs were caused by the reasons I would have given.

Neal: Here's an example that pertains to emotions. If a person who is feeling upset is asked for the reason, she will likely point to external events. She might believe, for example, that she is upset because of what another said or did. But we know, even our therapists know, that the true cause of being emotionally distraught is that one is not aligned with the deeper levels of one's own being. As long as one believes that it is the fault of someone else, then they have given power over their well-being to factors external to themselves. So it would seem that the mental activity called "giving reasons for one's emotions" is quite futile, as it merely rationalizes whatever emotions the person is experiencing, and brings no understanding to the situation. So we shall not use the word "reason" in this way.

And I think the same is true with respect to behavior. In most situations, humans simply do not know why they behave the way they do. But we cover our ignorance through the process of "giving reasons". For example, little Johnny gets caught with his hand in the proverbial cookie jar. Mom says, "Why are you taking a cookie when I told you not to?" What's poor Johnny supposed to do? The reason he took a cookie is because he wanted to. His behavior was caused by an antecedent desire. But he knows that this explanation won't work with Mommy. So he engages his cleverness to string together some words that he hopes will placate Mommy, but which has nothing to do with "why" his hand is in the cookie jar. We may agree that all behavior is caused, but when a person is asked to give "reasons" for his behavior he will not address the causes, of which he is largely ignorant, but will instead, like Johnny, use his cleverness to come up with some words that will convince both himself and others that his behavior was justified under the circumstances. So we shall not use the term "reason" in conjunction with behavior.

Benedict: I'd like to offer my own experience again as an example. Like all 17th century males, I believed that males were superior to females. This belief was caused by my upbringing. As a schoolboy, all my teachers were male, and so were all my classmates. *This* upbringing was the cause of my belief. But as an adult, I needed to "justify" this belief by pointing to factors external to my upbringing. I explicitly considered whether the inferior social role of women was determined by "nature or nurture". All the cultures that I had any knowledge about were patriarchal, that is, male-dominated. I argued that if the inferior role of women was a matter of nurture, then surely there would be evidence of some cultures in which individuals had been nurtured differently. That is, if women were *by nature* inferior to men, then there should be no cultures in which women dominate men; but if women are *by nurture* inferior to men, then there should be at least some cultures in which women dominate. Since I did not know of any culture in which women dominated, I concluded that women are by nature inferior.

I now know that this conclusion is false, and hence, that the "reasoning" that led to this conclusion is flawed. If back in the 17th century someone had asked me *why* I believed women were by nature inferior to men, I would have pointed to the absence of matriarchal societies. But this alleged "reason" actually had nothing to do with *why* I believed in male superiority. *That* belief was caused by my upbringing. My upbringing also caused me to seek empirical support for the beliefs it engendered in my mind. So in a way, my belief – that the absence of matriarchal societies is a reason to believe that women are by nature inferior to men – was caused by the same social forces that engendered in me the original belief.

Neal: It is as if one's upbringing said: "Believe X, and also believe that Y is a reason to believe X."

Benedict: Yes. And in my case Y was false, yet even if it were true it could not function as a "reason" to believe X.

Neal: But you should not fault yourself for not knowing that matriarchal societies had in fact existed. Anthropology did not yet exist, and you had very little information available about cultures that were not a direct descendent of Greek-Roman culture.

Benedict: *(smiling)* And what little info that was available came from Christian missionaries; hardly an objective source. Yet I could have suspected that my knowledge of non-Western cultures was far from complete. It is almost as if, believing firmly in male superiority, I grasped at whatever empirical "facts" were at hand to justify or rationalize my antecedently held belief. However, even if the alleged "facts" were true, that still would not have been a sufficient reason to believe that women are by nature inferior to men. Plato here would have no difficulty exposing the error.

William: I wonder if it might be useful to go into this in a little more detail. We are using misogyny (well, not *hatred* of women, but the belief that women are by nature inferior to men), in which I too participated, as an example to show the difference, or differences, between two distinct mental processes: (i) rationalizing antecedently held beliefs, and (ii) reasoning.

Neal: Yes, and humans are deeply confused in that they believe they are reasoning when they are rationalizing. The latter involves only calculative thinking, the former something more.

William: And this "something more" is no doubt the precious baby that we shall rescue from the filthy bathwater of rationalization. But I have a suggestion as to how we might proceed.

Neal: What is it?

William: How about we ask these two *(gesturing towards Plato and Benedict)* to assume their former personalities and have a little discussion about women, nature, and nurture?

Benedict: *(laughing)* I'm going to get trounced, assuming I can even find my former persona, let alone fit into it.

Plato: Don't worry too much; I appreciate that your upbringing was considerably more misogynist than mine. But where shall we converse?

Benedict: How about I visit you in Athens? We could pretend that I'm a traveling foreigner seeking wisdom from the cities of Greece.

Plato: Alright. Let's see. I'll greet you as follows: welcome, Benedict, to the great city of Athens. I am eager to discuss philosophy with you, but first you must get out of those clothes you're wearing. They look horribly tight and uncomfortable. Try on this toga instead.

Benedict: And greetings to you also; I have heard much about you and your views, and am here to find out for myself. But why do you mention my clothes right away?

Plato: Well, they just looked uncomfortable. But I'm certain that there is an ancient saying to the effect that, if the body is buttoned up tight, then so is the mind associated with that body.

William: And excuse me for interjecting, but the future will vindicate Plato's point. All monks, in whatever tradition, wear loose fitting robes, not tights.

Benedict: Hah! As if the Divine Being cannot reach humans with tight clothes? Well OK, I'll try the robe. I suppose the saying "When in Rome…" applies to Athens as well.

Plato: Aside from feeling more comfortable, you won't look so weird, and no one will stare at you.

Socrates: And let us remember that the ensuing conversation is *not* about the role of women in society. It is about the difference between (i) using mental processes to discern truth, and (ii) using mental processes to "justify" or "rationalize" what one already believes. The former we call "reasoning", the latter "rationalizing", and it is not always easy for a human to know in any given situation whether he is reasoning or rationalizing. So, Benedict, you have been wandering around visiting the great minds of Europe and now find yourself in Plato's Athens. Mine too. We may dispense with the usual greetings and formalities, and begin the discussion right away. I will comment every now and then.

Benedict: OK. Well, Plato, I have heard much about you and your strange ideas about women. Is it really true that you believe that women should be absolutely equal to men with respect to all social roles?

Plato: Yes.

Benedict: So you think a woman can do anything a man can do?

Plato: Yes, except father children.

Benedict: So according to you, a woman could be a lawyer or a doctor?

Plato: Yes.

Benedict: What about a judge, athlete, politician, or military commander?

Plato: Yes, why not?

Benedict: Why not! I'll tell you why not. Just look around.

Plato: I'm looking.

Benedict: Do you see any of your women doing any of these things? On the contrary, your women, although dressed differently than ours, are nevertheless doing the same sorts of things as our women.

Plato: What sorts of things?

Benedict: You know. Women's work: bearing and raising children, washing clothes, preparing food, and endlessly gossiping about trivialities.

Plato: And so the question between us is whether the different social roles of men and women are due to the biological differences between the sexes, in which case we say that the roles are determined *by nature,* or whether the differences in social roles are determined by upbringing, in which case we say they are determined *by nurture.* I say the latter is true. You seem to think the former is true. Why?

(Socrates: Notice that the question, "Why?" is ambiguous between (i) what caused you, Benedict, to believe that social roles are determined by nature, and (ii) why do you think it is true that social roles are determined by nature. The first interpretation can always be addressed, since beliefs and behaviors are caused, although the cause may not be known in any particular case. The second interpretation appears to be asking for reasons, but what Benedict will give as "reasons" will be seen to be a rationalization of beliefs already held.)

Benedict: You will no doubt agree that by nature women bear children?

Plato: Yes, of course.

Benedict: And also that it is not merely a matter of upbringing that women are assigned the role of nursing babies for a year or so?

Plato: *(laughing)* I grant that the fact that men do not nurse babies is biologically determined. Although who knows whether, with all the gender-bending going on in Neal's time and later, they may find a way around this biological limitation. But for now, point granted.

Benedict: So we are in agreement that there are natural biological differences between men and women.

Plato: Yes.

Benedict: Then should we not expect that these natural biological differences manifest as natural differences in social roles?

Plato: Yes and no.

Benedict: You're going to be difficult. Look, a woman who is very pregnant, or who has to feed her baby every two or three hours, is not going to be able to function in most of the social roles taken by men. Imagine proceedings at the courthouse being held up because the female judge has to go nurse her baby. Or crucial life or death surgery has to be called off because the female surgeon just went into labor. There's no way a woman in that condition could do a man's job.

Plato: That's the "yes" part to my response.

Benedict: What's the "no" part?

Plato: Women aren't always pregnant and nursing. In fact, most of the time they're not. I certainly grant that there are social roles that are not compatible with being very pregnant or being a nursing mother. But it was not right of you to say *only* that a very pregnant woman cannot do a "man's job".

Benedict: What else should I have stated?

Plato: A pregnant woman also cannot do the job that nonpregnant *women* can do. There will of course be times in any person's life, male or female, where he or she will not be able to perform their usual social roles. Our social order will be constructed around that fact. Nothing is more important to our social order than the bearing and raising of children, for this is the means by which the society perpetuates itself. So when a woman becomes pregnant, we shall not say that she can no longer do her job, but rather, we shall say that by being pregnant she *is* doing her job, and everything else becomes secondary.

(Socrates: We have stated that all social roles are of equal importance to the "One Mind" in which every human mind has its being, so to speak. This is partly why we have separated (i) social roles from (ii) remuneration, and insist that wealth be distributed independent of social roles. But there *is* one social role that is more important than all the others put together: the bearing, nurturing, raising, and educating our children.)

Benedict: What's this? You would allow pregnant women and nursing mothers in the workplace? This just won't work.

Plato: I grant that it won't work as things stand in current social orders. But we are not discussing how women should adapt to an already existing social order, which we have shown is in any case dysfunctional and suicidal. We are talking about how to construct a social order that is maximally conducive to human happiness and well-being. Our social order is being constructed with the knowledge that women bear and nurse babies. Since it is the responsibility of the social order as a whole, not just the biological mother and/or father, to nurture and raise the child, every aspect of the social order will be friendly to infants and babies.

Benedict: But that would necessitate having nurseries everywhere there are nursing mothers?

Plato: You should make that into a statement instead of a question. Nursing mothers are in fact everywhere; why would you prefer a society that hides away nursing mothers?

(Socrates: Notice the "why" question. Will the response be a reason or a rationalization?)

Benedict: *(with wry humor)* It's becoming increasingly difficult to play this part. The "reasons" a man from my time would give...

William: ... which are the same that a man from *my* time would give...

Benedict: ... can easily be seen as rationalizations of the status quo. I could say things such as (i) men will be too distracted at the sight of women's breasts to do their work properly, (ii) work that needs to be done cannot wait for the convenience of mother and baby, (iii) we can't have crying babies or temper-tantrum throwing children in the workplace, etc. But all such objections assume what cannot be proved; in fact, they assume what is known to be false, namely that the present (dysfunctional) social order is in some sense inviolate.

Plato: Yes, in a social order that sexualizes women's breasts, so that men are programmed to get erections whenever they see a breast, then of course, in *that* social order the presence of a nursing mother would be disruptive. But we claim that the present social order is in fact an unnatural one. A more natural social order –

Benedict: And by the word "natural" I assume you mean "in harmony with human biology" or something like that.

Plato: Yes, thank you. So years back I stated that a social order that denies females equal expression as males is not natural. For there is nothing in female biology that unfits it for any social role whatsoever. The fact that nursing mothers would everywhere present a problem for today's society is sufficient evidence that today's society is out of harmony with human nature.

Benedict: So any "argument" that purports to give a *reason* for socially and economically disadvantaging the female must proceed from biology alone. Anything else is a rationalization, a rationalization that assumes the present social order to be the only one possible. And since there are no such arguments, any mental process (such as my own several centuries ago) that concludes that women are not fit for social roles is a mere rationalization of what one has been brought up to believe. The belief is caused by upbringing, not by "reasoning" or "thinking things through".

Plato: And may we generalize this conclusion?

Benedict: Yes. If one has a belief that is common to one's culture, then the cause of that belief in the mind of the given individual is his upbringing. He did not arrive at it through reasoning. If we now ask the individual, having been raised to believe X, *why* he believes X, any response to that question, other than to point to his upbringing, will be a rationalization of what he has been programmed to believe.

William: I agree. In my own case, not only did I internalize the sexism of my times, but the racism as well. I tended to believe that the Caucasian race was superior to the others. If asked *why*, I would have pointed to the way things are (or were, in my time). But "the way things were" is the result of a racist social order. The culture raises certain people to be subservient, then these people, having been raised this way, behave and feel subservient. The culture then points to their behavior as a "reason" to keep them subservient. But clearly, this has nothing to do with reason, but is merely a *rationalization* of the culture's practices. So I think we may lay it down as a rule that whenever a person utilizes his mental processes to justify what he has been raised to believe, then we shall call that mental process "rationalizing", not reasoning.

6) Discerning True Beliefs From False Beliefs

Neal: But wait. Just because one's upbringing has caused an individual to believe something, say X, doesn't mean that X is false. So if X happens to be true, then not all efforts to justify what one has been raised to believe are mere rationalizations.

Plato: OK, good. We have not yet defined *reasoning*, and we have stated that the mental process by which one attempts to justify what one has been culturally conditioned to believe should be called "rationalizing", not "reasoning". But what if the belief were true, you ask? So give some examples of true beliefs that have been inculcated into your mind by your upbringing.

Neal: Here are three such beliefs: (i) 2 + 2 = 4, (ii) moderate exercise is good for one's health, (iii) one should be kind to others. Not everyone believes (iii) of course, but I was raised to believe it.

Plato: *(smiling)* I don't know if this was your intention, but the three beliefs you mention are also three different *kinds* of beliefs.

Neal: Huh?

Plato: I guess it wasn't your intention. (i) is a belief that pertains to mathematics and logic, (ii) is a belief that pertains to science, or the empirical world, and (iii) is a statement of the Moral Law. You are right to point out that not every belief a culture inculcates in the minds of its individuals is false. How to discern, among conditioned beliefs, the true from the false? We shall have much to say regarding this question. Let us note that we have inculcated in the minds of *our* children many "true beliefs" or "right opinions". We are teaching them many good habits long before they know the reasons why. So, of course, true beliefs, as well as false beliefs, can be conditioned into the minds of individuals. The "problem" then is to figure out which is which. Are there means by which a given individual, raised in a given culture, can examine the beliefs that have been conditioned into him, and discern the true from the false?

William: We shall answer this question in the affirmative, but we note that our views are quite contrary to the "cultural relativism" that academics prefer to believe.

Neal: We'll have a good laugh over this. I swear that some of our colleagues would argue that cultural conditioning is absolute and inviolate, so that if a given culture raises people to believe that 2 + 2 = 5, then who are we to say otherwise?

William: Well, humor aside for the moment, let us define what we mean by "cultural relativism". Everyone is raised within a culture and necessarily internalizes the beliefs of that culture. *Cultural relativism* holds that there are no extra-cultural standards by which one can judge the beliefs of any given culture, including one's own. For if there were such non-cultural standards, where could they possibly come from, given that every human being is raised within some culture?

Benedict: But *we* know, of course, "where they could possibly come from". For a human being, we maintain, is an embodied soul, containing much within itself that is prior to and independent of its upbringing, or culture. Thus we can maintain that the ability to discern true from false (i) transcends culture and (ii) is innate in every human being, even though used by very few. This ability we shall call "reason" or "reasoning". Clearly, the origins of reason are beyond culture, and what I once called "the dictates of reason", such as the Golden Rule, are invariant across cultures.

Neal: So we state that human beings have the power to examine their culturally conditioned beliefs and to discern which are true and which are false. This ability to discern truth from falsity we shall call "reason".

Benedict: Yes, and this is why I compared reason with a "good spirit", because it has the power to lift the human mind above the limitations of cultural conditioning and carry it to the doors of Truth and Understanding. Well, let's now follow Plato and the three *kinds* of belief he alluded to above.

Neal: Wait a minute. I want to point out that our concept of *reason* and *reasoning* is very different from what is taught in universities under that name. For we hold that *reason* is not some neutral calculating machine in the head, but is a power that serves a spiritual purpose.

William: Yes. We have given the name "calculative thinking" to that "neutral calculating machine in the head". If one has a desire of some sort, *calculative thinking* will help satisfy the desire, without regard to whether the desire itself is reasonable, or worth satisfying. Calculative thinking will help you plan to rob a bank, develop weapons that murder humans by the millions, or make lots of money by polluting air and water. *Calculative thinking* does not concern itself with whether the desires and goals are *reasonable*, that is, worth pursuing. It is *reason* that tells us that robbing a bank, polluting the environment, and developing weapons of mass destruction are not goals worthy of a human being, and hence, any human who does have such desires is mentally sick beyond reason, if I may be permitted a little pun. That is, they are not capable of *reasoning*.

Benedict: The examples you have given illustrate the point, albeit dramatically. These examples show a divergence between calculative thinking, on the one hand, and reasoning, on the other. But I'd like to throw in some mundane examples that everyone can relate to. After all, very few individuals are presently using calculative thinking to plan a bank robbery. But most individuals *are* using calculative thinking to figure out how to make more money and gain more reputation. These goals are no more reasonable than robbing a bank, but people do not see this, because they are blinded by desires for wealth and reputation that have been programmed into them through upbringing.

Socrates: *(with ironic humor)* And one does not need to become spiritually enlightened to see the folly of pursuing such goals. They never lead to happiness, and usually to the opposite. But notice that, because of how we are raising our children, the very idea that they should accumulate more material goods than others, and/or that they should seek to acquire reputation and fame – to make a name for themselves, so to speak – these ideas will not occur to them. In fact, they will, along with our culture, regard such ideas as insane.

Neal: This present discussion will be unnecessary for *our* children, but essential for children and adults raised by my present culture and programmed to believe that their worth and value and success as human beings depends on wealth and reputation. By driving a wedge between two different mental activities that my culture conflates – *reasoning* and *calculative thinking* – we show that these conditioned desires and goals are inherently unreasonable. And, if I may vent for another paragraph, humans in my culture have accomplished an amazing feat of unconscious inconsistency.

William: I know what you mean; I'll join you in a little venting. The good Christians of my time would certainly assent verbally to the Golden Rule as the right maxim for living one's life.

Neal: Same in my time…

William: Yet at the same time they were greedy for wealth and reputation. They were unable to see that the very presence of such greed within their psyche was deeply inconsistent with the Golden

Rule they espoused on Sundays. For as Benedict has shown, and many, many others as well, if one lives according to the Golden Rule, one cannot desire for oneself anything that one does not desire for all humans. One cannot desire fame for all humans, for if everyone is famous then no one is. Similarly for wealth. So these desires are inherently unreasonable. The sorts of desires that *are* reasonable, and that *can* logically be desired for all humans, are (i) desires for what is necessary to keep the body alive and healthy, (ii) desires to develop and express one's talents and abilities as best one can, and (iii) desires to help and assist other human beings. But the desire "to be thought better than" other humans, and the desire "to have more" than other humans, are symptoms of mental illness.

Neal: And since these are the prevalent desires in today's culture, we might rightly say that our culture as a whole is insane.

Benedict: Of course any culture that is on the brink of self-destruction may rightly be called insane. But we are analyzing the insanity in terms of the desires of the individuals who constitute the culture. And we are saying that such desires are *unreasonable*. But now I think we must say more about the process of reasoning as it applies to the three kinds of beliefs Plato alluded to a little while ago.

Plato: With pleasure! "2 + 2 = 4". Now most humans would agree that if *reason* operates anywhere, it is with respect to logic and mathematics. The height of unreasonableness, everyone agrees, is to believe in a self-contradiction.

Neal: Yes, but hmm, when the human mind is occupying itself with mathematics and logic, is this the part of the mind that *reasons*, or is it the part we have called *calculative thinking*?

Plato: Good. This is an important point, for we have stated that *reason* leads to the Golden Rule and a right conduct for living, and it is difficult to see any connection between that and 2 + 2 = 4. And here is the danger to which academics have succumbed. In the absence of desire, there is no difference between *reasoning* and *calculative thinking*. So if one is engaged in a mental process of, say, deriving the theorem of Pythagoras from the axioms of Euclid, *that* mental process is calculative thinking without personal desire. And this is the hallmark of what we are calling *reasoning*. It is a mental process independent of personal beliefs and desires.

Neal: So when desires and antecedently held beliefs are present, *reason* has been contaminated, and *calculative thinking* will be used to justify and rationalize one's antecedently held beliefs and desires. Our children will be given a taste of "pure reason", by which we mean, "calculative thinking in the absence of personal desire and belief". And if I might make something you alluded to more explicit, the danger to which my, and William's, colleagues have succumbed is to believe that their inner mental process is the same when applied to logic as it is when applied to matters about which they have culturally induced opinions. They are not able to see, for example, that the mental process by which they argue and defend their beliefs in materialism, atheism, greed, ambition, and capitalism – *that* mental process is not *reasoning*, but rather, *rationalizing*. The beliefs had been "cultured" into them through upbringing, which includes education. They believe what their professors told them about these things, and use the faculty of *calculative thinking* to justify what they already believe. But when asked *why* they believe, say, that personal ambition is "good" and that it is "good" to want to make a name for oneself, they will not speak the truth, but instead will give what they take to be "reasons" for what they believe. But the simple truth is that they believe what they do because of upbringing, not "because" of the (pseudo-) "reasons" they give.

Benedict: *(smiling)* Indeed, as I wrote some time ago, the desires for wealth and reputation are kinds of madness, quite the opposite of reason. The stronger these desires are in any given individual, the less that individual is able to *reason* at all, and will invariably use her cleverness – another name for what we are calling "calculative thinking" – merely to justify what she has been caused to believe through upbringing.

Plato: Hold on a moment; I want to take note that we are subtly shifting the topic.

Neal: How so?

Plato: We had been discussing the sorts of beliefs that a given culture typically induces in its members: beliefs about women, about other races, about sex, about God and the afterlife. These are the sorts of things that differentiate one culture from another; the sorts of things anthropologists love to study. But underlying *all* these varying and diverse beliefs, there are two beliefs that *all* cultures have in common, actually just one belief.

Neal: The belief that *greed* is good, whether it is greed for wealth or greed for fame, reputation. And we are stating that this belief is the mark of mental illness, and captures a very real sense in which all cultures today are insane.

William: Not quite all.

Neal: What do you mean?

William: The few hunter-gatherer societies still in existence are not insane in this way. In fact, any individual member of such a society who showed symptoms of greed, like hoarding, would be judged as mentally ill by the society.

Plato: So the belief that greed is good is shared by all societies today except hunter-gatherer societies. Academics have been raised to believe this, just like everyone else. So in their own lives they seek to be well-regarded by others, that is, they seek to have a "reputation" or "career", and their *cleverness*, that is, the faculty of *calculative thinking*, will be in the service of these desires. And so, if an academic, even if he dares think of himself as a Philosopher, is asked *why* the pursuit of reputation is a good thing, whatever he says will be a rationalization of what he has been conditioned to believe, not a reason.

Benedict: And it is so easy to demonstrate that it is impossible in principle to give any reason for being greedy, in the same way it is impossible to give reasons for, say, disobeying the Golden Rule. Causes yes, but reasons no. It is *unreasonable*, we maintain, not to desire to live according to the Golden Rule. It is a "dictate of reason", as I put it, that one does not desire for herself anything she does not also desire for her fellow human beings. To repeat what has already been stated, one cannot logically desire that everyone be famous, for if everyone is famous then no one is. Same with wealth; it is logically impossible for everyone to have more than others. So greed and reason are absolutely incompatible with one another. And those who do dare to think of themselves as philosophers must examine whether they are following the path of greed and ambition, or the path of reason. Anyone affiliated with a university is most likely following the former path; otherwise they could not remain long at such an institution. But even so, even having been intensely indoctrinated to believe that greed is good, and that one's worth and value depends upon gathering a big reputation, even so, it is possible to *reason* one's way out of this mess, as you have done. And this is why I said that the faculty of *reason* is like a good spirit, a gift from the Divine Being with the power to lead us from confusion and despair to sanity and happiness. But now I sense we have to go back to something, but I forgot what.

Neal: There's much on the table. OK, we said that in the absence of belief and desire, *reason* and *cleverness* or *calculative thinking* amount to the same thing. We will give our children a taste of this…

Plato: … *(smiling)* More than a taste. Mathematics and logic will be an essential aspect of every child's education. Remember, *cleverness* – the ability to manipulate words and symbols – is a strength, and our children will be strong in this way. And by "mathematics and logic" I mean to include argument and Aristotle's classification of the kinds of statements there are and the syllogisms.

Benedict: So, a person may be conditioned by upbringing to believe something mathematical – the Pythagorean theorem, the sum of the interior angles of a triangle = 180 degrees, and so forth. But these mathematical beliefs may also be derived by reason, which is the same as *calculative thinking* when only mathematics is involved. *Now* we will turn our attention to the use of *calculative thinking* when more than mathematics is involved. Let's examine the second belief you listed above.

Neal: I believe that moderate exercise is good for my body. I did not myself arrive at this belief by means of any detailed study of the human body, but my doctor and everyone around me seems to believe it is true, and so do I. I present this as an example of a true belief conditioned into me by my culture. I did not arrive at this belief through *calculative thinking*, or any other mental process.

Socrates: Yes, and it is useful to note that a culture *can* condition people to have true beliefs, as well as false beliefs, as will be the case with the Social Order now under construction.

Benedict: But now, if you or someone else were to call into question whether this belief is true, how might you investigate the matter?

Neal: Well, I would talk to a biologist or a doctor, and study in some detail how exercise affects the body. I would then want to know how they define "health" with respect to a human body. If the effect of exercise on the body is in accordance with the definition of a healthy body, then the belief has been established independent of cultural conditioning. But we can also establish this empirically, by examining large numbers of humans who exercise regularly, and see if they are healthier than those who don't.

William: We believe many things by hearsay. It would be impossible not to. We assume that the experts have done their homework. The important thing to note is that their homework is accessible to all. You can take the word of your doctor that exercise is good for your health, or you can go to medical school and study the matter.

Neal: *(to Benedict)* You tried to capture this distinction with your "kinds of knowledge". The first is imaginative knowledge, what has been conditioned into you; the second is *reason*, figuring it out for oneself.

Benedict: Yes, sort of. But I want to focus now on the difference between the two *kinds* of belief: "2 + 2 = 4" is a mathematical belief, and it is arrived at by *calculative thinking*, *reasoning*, or *deduction from premises*. But your second belief, about exercising, is also arrived at through *reasoning*, but not by deduction from premises. Rather, it is an empirical belief, arrived at *inferentially* from observation and data.

Plato: You see, we are using the term "reason" perhaps a little more broadly than usual, at least, more broadly than is usual for academics. One portion of reason is *deduction from premises;* **all** of mathematics and logic is concerned with this portion of reason. A second portion of *reason* involves *inference,* that is, *arriving* at, beliefs or hypotheses on the basis of observations and data. *All* of science involves this type of reasoning. The third portion of reason involves – how to state it – the ability to apply the Golden Rule to one's personal life.

Benedict: And if I might add, the Golden Rule is itself a deductive consequence of the premises that guide our discussion.

Neal: Perhaps it will be useful to restate those premises?

Benedict: Go ahead.

Neal: (i) A human being is an embodied soul and…

Benedict: And it is not less of a soul for being embodied. While human, or embodied, the soul is still soul.

Neal: Yes. Human beings are souls, and (ii) all souls are so interconnected as to constitute a single "One Mind" or "World Soul", like cells in a given body.

Plato: And we also stated that the word "reason", like the word "love", shall be used in such a way as to serve as reminders to humans of the interconnection of all beings. So if one undergoes some mental process and concludes, say, that it is good for him to accumulate as much reputation as possible, we shall say, not that his reason has taken him to a different conclusion, but rather that he is not reasoning at all. Instead, he is using his *cleverness* to *rationalize* his antecedent desires. *Reason* always leads to what is true, and the Golden Rule expresses the highest truth about the human condition.

William: Let's emphasize this, especially because academics, from my time to Neal's, believe that "reason" is the same as "calculative thinking", and most of all, they believe that they themselves are exemplars of what it is to be "reasonable". *(With humor)* After all, you won't find any academic who believes that he himself is being unreasonable.

Neal: *(also with humor)* But of course, they will happily accuse those of their colleagues who disagree with them about any issue of being unreasonable. The sad truth is that most academics do not reason at all, but rather use the power of calculative thinking to rationalize their already held beliefs and desires. It seems to be the case that it is very difficult for humans to use calculative thinking in any way other than to *rationalize* what they already believe.

Plato: ... Which is why logic and mathematics are important. Now, you said "most academics", etc., but I think you, and William too, have in mind the kind of academics that you hung out with – psychologists and those who call themselves "philosophers". I put the latter in quotes because, as you well know, those who call themselves by that name are not practicing Philosophy at all, but have usurped the name for themselves. *(Laughing)* I suppose I still have an ax to grind around this – was that the right expression?

Neal: Well, I've never ground an ax, and have no idea where the expression came from, but yes, it is an appropriate expression.

Plato: Good. Now, getting back to your and William's experience with "unreasonable" colleagues, it is obvious that humans are most prone to having antecedent beliefs in areas of study that concern themselves, which are the Humanities and the Social Sciences. It is in these areas of endeavor that humans are most likely to project culturally induced beliefs onto and into their subject matter. And so we will turn to mathematics and science to illustrate what we take to be a fact: reason always leads to truth.

Benedict: Of course, we maintain that it is in the very nature of *reason* to lead to truth, but this can easily be established empirically. All mathematicians and logicians agree about everything that pertains to their subject matter, irrespective of their individual cultural conditioning.

Neal: That is true. There is no such thing as "Christian" mathematics or "Russian" mathematics or "atheist" mathematics. The law of non-contradiction that governs mathematics and logic is invariant under different cultural conditionings. So mathematics and logic are *the* exemplars of how, in the absence of antecedent belief and desire, *calculative thinking* invariably leads from premises to a unique conclusion. But science, which involves inferential reasoning, is not as easy to capture. There are no rules by which one can arrive at a unique conclusion from observations or data.

William: Correct, which is why something rather elusive, which we may call "intuition", often guides the scientist in forming hypotheses based on data. But notice that whereas individual scientists may disagree among themselves, yet if time be taken into consideration, the disagreements sort themselves out, and science *does* in fact lead to unique conclusions. After all, there is no such thing as "Chinese" physics or "British" biology. Science is intrinsically self-corrective, but only over generations.

Benedict: And this is what we should expect. Individual scientists are raised to believe that the current theories in their discipline are true, and these beliefs often act as barriers to new ideas. An individual scientist may very well desire that his antecedently held beliefs be validated more than he or she desires to seek the truth. This desire, of course, is not rational, and the scientist who wants what he already believes to be confirmed is using *calculative thinking*, not in the service of truth, but in the service of his beliefs and desires. That is, he is *rationalizing*, not *reasoning*. But over time, the process is self-corrective, *(smiling)* almost as if there were some benevolent spirit guiding the whole thing. What's that quip you like about death and science?

Neal: "Science advances one funeral at a time." Max Planck, one of the "founding fathers" of the quantum theory, got so upset at his colleagues' inability to wrap their collective minds around the new ideas that he remarked that the mechanism for scientific change is not new experiments and new data, but death. The older generation, stuck in patterns of conditioned thinking, eventually dies off, and younger more flexible minds come to take their place.

Benedict: *(laughing)* There's much humor in that quip, but it very accurately states that science is a temporal process. Individual scientists are human beings who come to science with antecedent beliefs and desires. In the physical sciences, unlike the social sciences, culturally induced beliefs do not play a significant role, but the beliefs they acquire through their training form the "mind-set" with which they approach their subject matter. This "mind-set" then constitutes a filter that prevents them from considering other hypotheses, and even prevents them from considering empirical data that runs contrary to what they already believe, as you and William well know.

Socrates: May I remind everyone that our theme here is the education of children, so that we don't wander too far off topic in our discussion.

William: Point well taken. We want to raise our children so that they know the difference between *reasoning* and *rationalizing*, between using calculative thinking to discern truth and using calculative thinking to "justify" what one already believes or desires.

Benedict: And whereas mathematics and logic exemplify the use of *calculative thinking* in the absence of prior belief and desire, *science* exemplifies the use of calculative thinking even in the presence of prior belief and desire. The former is understood by the individual immediately; the latter requires time, and yes, death, as many scientists have so deeply internalized what they were told in graduate school that they will never be able to wrap their minds around anything new. But we must notice that what is internalized as a graduate student is nothing compared to what is more deeply internalized through cultural conditioning in childhood, which explains why the Social Sciences and the Humanities are relatively backwards in their conceptual understandings, compared to the forward looking and, I venture to say, *spiritual* content of physics.

Socrates: So we shall be adding *the History of Science* to our curriculum.

Neal: Most definitely. For the study of the History of Science is the study of how human reason can, in time, overcome the limitations of antecedently held beliefs and desires. It is also the study of *how* such antecedently held beliefs interact with data and observation, causing the individual to use the latter to support the former.

Socrates: May I remind you, or us, that we are talking about *our* children, not the ones raised in your current social dis-order. *Our* children will not have internalized the many false and harmful beliefs with which your children are burdened. Moreover, *our* children will not be programmed to desire and want things, like wealth and reputation, that are harmful both to themselves and to society. *Your* children have been programmed to believe things that are false ("greed is good"; "unlimited growth is good"; "it is better to win than to lose", etc.). So when we discuss transitioning from the present society to *our* social order, it will be very important for everyone, but especially children and young adults, to critically examine their culturally induced beliefs and desires. But there is very little that *our* children will believe or desire that is contrary to what is in their best interests.

Plato: Yes, but it is not enough that we have raised our children to have true beliefs and life-affirming desires. They must understand the reasons why and hence become thoroughly inoculated against any and every temptation to fall into error. They will be shocked to learn that *calculative thinking* or *cleverness*, which is a mental power, has more often been used for evil than for good.

Neal: Nevertheless, science is a magnificent edifice that has transformed the planet. Without the fruits of science, our New Social Order could not come into being.

William: True. Our new social order presupposes that the Earth has the resources to feed, clothe, and shelter every human being. But this is so only because of science. It would have been impossible in your time, Plato, or even in mine. But now, with just a little more tweaking, energy from the sun will be directly convertible into forms humans can use. And because there will be no more greedy capitalists to hoard all the energy and food for themselves, no human will lack for anything. So our children must learn about science, *what* it has done and *how* it has done it. And by "how" I mean to refer to *inferential thinking*.

Neal: But unlike deductive thinking, for which there are rules, we cannot teach inferential thinking in the abstract. The only way to teach it, I believe, is through examples and experience. The former will involve case studies in the history of science, and the latter will involve, or perhaps begin with, simple science experiments and learning to observe accurately and make generalizations and hypotheses from their observations. This is already done in grade school.

But there is something else that it is important to notice. People are impressed by two stunning aspects of science: one is the astounding effect it has had on transforming the planet, and the other is the beauty and elegance of the conceptual insights offered by scientific theories. I myself was in a state of abject wonder when I first learned the equations of Maxwell, Einstein, and Schrödinger. But the most important aspect of science no one ever talks about.

7) The "Holy Curiosity of Inquiry"

Socrates: And are you going to tell us or do we have to ask?

Neal: OK, well, what is the most important thing about a human being?

Socrates: The level of consciousness that is manifested through the human form. The whole of our education is geared to maximize the "amount" (how crudely put!) of consciousness that manifests through a given human form.

Neal: So this is true of children that have grown up to become scientists?

Socrates: Yes, of course.

Neal: Then we must ask, what is the state of consciousness of scientists, from Benedict's time to mine, as they engage in the activity called "science"? For science arises from the consciousness of individual human beings.

Socrates: Ah yes, a very important and noble state of consciousness that no doubt must be inculcated in our children.

William: What are you talking about? What state of consciousness?

Neal: I'll give you a little hint: it is the state of consciousness that Einstein once referred to as a delicate holy flower, or something like that.

William: OK, got it, but it's worth getting the quote right, as it is extremely important. You know, or do you, that you don't have to go to the library to find the quote?

Neal: *(laughing)* That's still my first reflex – to go to the library and search through the card catalogues. Except libraries don't have card catalogues anymore. But here's the quote.

> *It is, in fact, nothing short of a miracle that the modern methods of instruction have not yet entirely strangled the holy curiosity of inquiry; for this delicate little plant, aside from stimulation, stands mainly in need of freedom. Without this it goes to wrack and ruin without fail.*

And by "modern methods" he is referring to education as it was in *his* time, almost a century ago. It is much worse today. So the state of consciousness of scientists, insofar as they are doing science, is ***curiosity***.

Benedict: Curiosity is the handmaiden to reason.

Neal: *(with humor)* You'll need another metaphor. No one knows what a "handmaiden" is anymore.

Benedict: *(laughing)* Kissing cousins? Peas in a pod? The point is, you can't have one without the other. *Curiosity* is the inner motivation of the individual; *reason* is the outer manifestation of curiosity. Without *curiosity, reason* has nothing to act upon, and degenerates into mere *cleverness*.

William: And this is exactly what has happened with respect to our so-called educational system. By not heeding Einstein's warning, the current educational system does everything it can to stifle children's natural curiosity, and *reason* has indeed degenerated into mere *cleverness*. Our colleagues have well-developed verbal muscles, but no idea how to use them wisely. They lost their curiosity in graduate school, and are, on the whole, more concerned with using their *cleverness* to defend what they already believe than to seek truth. But if one is not curious, there is no truth to seek, and one remains content with the beliefs instilled in him by his education and culture.

As an aside, I want to remark that a clear sign that a given social order is about to expire is when the institutions of the culture produce the opposite effect of what they were established to produce. So Education, by strangling the "holy curiosity of inquiry", destroys what it was intended to promote. Your hospitals are the third leading cause of death. Any "sane" person who spends some time in one of your mental institutions is likely to become insane as a result. Your so-called prison system is a school for criminals, and your so-called "justice system" is horribly misnamed.

Neal: What do you mean "misnamed"?

William: It is really an "injustice system", is it not? Prosecutors routinely seek convictions for people they know are innocent (because convictions look good on their record – that is, individual prosecutors are motivated more by the desire for recognition than the desire for truth). Police officers routinely lie under oath with impunity. And poor people, who are most often the victim of police and prosecutors, have no legal recourse. So your "justice" system produces not justice, but injustice.

Plato: Perhaps I'll have some things to say about justice later. But now I want to talk about reason and curiosity, and why the latter is a necessary condition for the former to function properly. But I want to borrow Benedict's poetic license, if I may.

Benedict: Huh?

Plato: You know, the license that enabled you to compare *reason* with a "good spirit" that without error leads us to the very door of the knowledge of the union between the individual mind and the Divine Mind.

Benedict: Hah! When it comes to poetic licenses, I must defer to you. Here it is.

Plato: Thank you. So when the Divine Being asked among the souls that are for volunteers to participate in his little human experiment, very few were willing to volunteer at first.

Benedict: "When"? In the eternal order there is no "when".

Plato: *(with humor)* Yes, yes, that's why I asked for your poetic license.

Benedict: OK, I'll hold my tongue, or try to.

Plato: So in order to get more volunteers, He sweetened the deal by promising that every soul that chose embodiment would receive a spirit guide whose function is to assist the embodied soul in its efforts to return Home. Now the case of Socrates here, where the Guide took the form of a direct voice, is relatively rare. More often the Guide communicates in the form of hunches and intuitions that are often ignored by the human. But most often the Guide communicates in the form called *reason*. The Moral Law, we have said, is a "dictate of reason", and it is implanted in every embodied soul and known as "conscience". *Conscience*, we might say, is a gift from the Divine Being that allows humans to steer a right path through life. But now, here's the thing: it is a Law that the gods cannot interfere with human activity unless explicitly asked to do so.

Benedict: "Law"? What law are you talking about?

Plato: *(with humor)* Now don't get literal on me. The poetic license you so kindly gave me enables me to talk this way.

Benedict: *(laughing loudly)* OK, I'll lighten up, sit back, and enjoy your story. But I do hope you indicate what it means for humans to explicitly ask for help. Most humans appear to pray and petition the gods for help all the time, but help seems rarely to be forthcoming.

Plato: Ah, yes, I was going to talk about that. You see, most humans do not know how to ask for help. They think that words like "please help me, God" are sufficient. Or they think that if they wish for a situation strongly enough, or throw a few temper tantrums, the gods will listen and make what they wish for happen…

William: *(with humor)* … specially if they are regular church-goers and give money to the church…

Plato: *(laughing)* … and in my time sacrificing an animal or two was thought to be good for getting the gods' attention. But as it turns out, there are two things about the gods that humans do not know. The first thing is that the gods cannot be bribed, neither with money nor with emotional excess.

William: What do you mean by "emotional excess"?

Plato: Many humans get very upset when their life situation causes them difficulty. They then get all emotional – depressed, angry, suicidal – and plead with the gods to rescue them from their life situation. They even attempt to bribe the gods, not with money, but with their emotions and behaviors. "Give me what I want and I will go to church, mend my ways, worship you, and be good."

William: Yes, for most humans prayer consists of little more than bargaining with God for what they want. But this is something that is known, if not to most humans, then to those who study the matter in any way. What is the second thing?

Plato: The second thing I have in mind is not known even to those who study the matter. The gods are deaf to words. Human words cannot reach the Divine Being.

William: But…

Plato: But, you say, the Divine Being is omnipotent, knows everything, hence certainly must be aware of the words that emanate from the mouths of humans.

William: Yes.

Plato: I've got a good analogy up my sleeve, or toga. Suppose a child is having a bad dream, and in his distress, dreams that he is calling out for his mother. Will his mother hear him?

William: Of course not. He is not really calling for his mother, only dreaming that he is.

Plato: And have we not said that the human condition is itself dream-like – that it is the collective dream of the World Soul?

William: Yes, I see. So language is internal to the collective dream, and whatever is expressed in language is also internal to the dream, and hence, cannot reach the gods. So neither words nor emotional tantrums reach the One Mind. Yet you said, or implied, that there *is* a way of asking for assistance.

Plato: *(smiling)* Einstein nailed it! "The holy curiosity of inquiry". *This* is the human prayer that reaches the ears of the gods. Einstein was right to call *curiosity* "holy", for the gods gave humans the gift of curiosity as a means of finding their way back to them, or *(glancing at Benedict)* to the knowledge of their union with the One Mind. And he was also right to call it a "curiosity of inquiry", rather than mere idle curiosity. The "holy curiosity of inquiry" then is the very same thing that you, Benedict, called the Intellect, which seeks only to know, to find out, to understand.

Benedict: I agree. And would you agree with me if I characterize "reasoning" as "any mental functioning that is in the service of holy curiosity." All other mental functioning we will refer to as "rationalizing" or worse.

Neal: What do you mean by "worse"?

Benedict: Yes, using mental functioning to scheme, plot, and harm others is worse than mere rationalizing, although such people will also rationalize their desires to harm others. But, Plato, continue with the story, now that you have gotten me interested.

Plato: Now, we are discussing "holy curiosity". In the psychological makeup of the majority of scientists, there are many strands that have nothing to do with the desire to know, such as the desire to win fame and recognition, and to feel comforted by already held beliefs. In many minds, these secondary desires are more forceful than curiosity or the desire to know. That is why individual scientists are not always rational or reasonable and often cling to false beliefs long after evidence against those beliefs has accumulated beyond the point where it is rational to hold them. For example, the false belief that "consciousness is produced by the brain" is still adhered to by most of your scientists, despite the overwhelming empirical evidence that has disproved those beliefs. So at the level of the individual scientist, science is not necessarily reasonable. But at the level of the collective, over generations…

Neal: *(with humor)* Thank goodness for death.

Plato: … science is self-corrective, because there is enough of the "holy curiosity of inquiry" in the minds of individual scientists to render the process self-corrective over time. But now, getting back to the gods, they cannot hear human words, but they can and do "hear" when a human is in the state of consciousness called "holy curiosity". For in that state of consciousness the mind is quiet, in honest perplexity and wonder, and desires only to discover truth.

Socrates: We might state that every scientific discovery, every new scientific understanding, is the gods' answer to the *holy curiosity* present in the minds of the individual scientists.

William: Hmm, this is the conclusion that I came to, although I would never have put it this way.

Socrates: What way?

William: That new ideas in science are the gods' response to the prayer of holy curiosity.

Socrates: And how did you put it?

William: New ideas, whether in the sciences or the arts, are incursions into human waking consciousness from the subliminal realm, or something like that. The point is that creativity does not arise from mere *cleverness*, or the mere arrangements of words and symbols, but rather, something from the nonhuman field of consciousness enters into the human realm. And for this to happen, the individual human mind that receives new ideas must be in a receptive state of mind. This state of mind, in which the human is receptive to something new, we call *"holy curiosity"*. It is akin to prayer, if the latter be conceived as non-petitional.

Neal: Needless to say, our whole educational system is designed to inculcate this state of mind in our children.

William: Or, if we take into account that this state of consciousness is innate in all humans, we might say that our whole educational system is designed to nurture and encourage, rather than to destroy, this natural state of consciousness. *This* is the state of consciousness in which the margins become thin enough for humans to receive gifts from the gods. And as Benedict indicated, when the human mind is in this state of consciousness, called *holy curiosity*, the mental activity associated with this state of consciousness is *reason*, or *reasoning*, which seeks only truth, only knowledge, only understanding.

Benedict: But please see what has happened to the world between my time and Neal's. See where the holy curiosity of individual scientists has taken the world of embodied souls.

Neal: Yes, I see. Because of science, the world is now capable of feeding, clothing and sheltering each and every human being that comes here, with much surplus left over. There is no need for anyone, ever, to worry or be anxious about the basic necessities for the preservation of the human body. The cause of this not happening right now is simply *greed*. When the motivation of greed is removed from the human psyche, as will be the case in our New Society, nothing will stand in the way of a joyous distribution of the wealth of the Earth to all humans.

William: And all this has been made possible by science, which itself is the result of *holy curiosity*. I suppose if I could get hold of that poetic license I would say that the end of material suffering of the human form is the gods' response to the *holy curiosity* of a relatively small number of individual scientists.

Plato: *(with a little humor)* I suppose I should add a little caveat here. *Holy curiosity* leads to science when directed outward, towards the world. When directed inwards, to one's own consciousness, it may very well lead one to the monasteries instead…

Benedict: Yes, but that too can be a "science", although not yet recognized as such. Science involves (i) curiosity coupled with (ii) the ability to observe without judgment. One can apply this to one's own inner states as well as to the outer world; although it must be noted that the former is considerably more difficult than the latter, perhaps *our* children will be different in that respect. But now, back to our discussion of *reason*.

8) Reason and the Three Motivations of the Soul

Plato: Yes. It has been very difficult, over the years, to get a handle on this thing called "reason". Everyone believes of himself that he or she is "reasonable", just like everyone believes of himself that he or she is capable of loving. Academics especially like to believe that they are the exemplars of *reasoning*, just like clergy and religious folk like to believe they are capable of *loving*. And we are calling both assumptions into question. We are connecting these abilities (*loving* and *reasoning*) with specific inner states of consciousness. With respect to love we have said that a person who is judgmental is not capable of *loving*, since the latter must not be conditional on anything. With respect to reason, hmm, there are really three inner states of consciousness that permit the functioning of *reason*.

Neal: OK, so one such state of consciousness would be what we are calling *holy curiosity* – the desire to know, to understand, to discover truth. It is this desire that has led to science and has transformed the world. We have also stated that in the presence of desires other than *holy curiosity*, such as the desire to win arguments, accumulate a reputation, or justify one's opinions – the sorts of desires that dominate academia today – *reason* cannot function. For in the latter cases, one's mental functioning is in the service of ego, not truth. But, Plato, what are the other two states of consciousness that allow for the functioning of *reason*?

Plato: *(smiling)* Thanks for asking, for I seem to have stumbled upon something that I did not see before.

Neal: What's that?

Plato: Back to our first principles for a moment. The human being is an embodied soul, and the process by which a soul becomes embodied is not random or haphazard. On the contrary, the soul has specific intentions in manifesting as this or that body, and that human is happiest who most fulfills the intentions of the soul that she is.

Neal: Yes, agreed.

Plato: And we said that the motivations of the soul fall under three headings: (i) to learn, to know, to understand; (ii) to help others; and (iii) to express one's innate abilities and talents as best one can.

Socrates: *(playfully)* I think we should note in passing a fourth motivation of the soul that will no longer be present in our New Social Order.

Neal: A fourth motivation? What is it?

Socrates: *Suffering.* Well, this cannot be understood through words, but for many souls, Divine Love is better appreciated when contrasted with suffering in the human form. Or, suffering in the human form may focus the mind so intently that it becomes a portal to the Divine. *(Laughing)* You, and William too, think this is kind of sick, to incarnate for the purpose of suffering, and you won't believe me when I tell you that the line of souls waiting to incarnate in order to experience the Holocaust and other cataclysmic events is wrapped around the galaxy several times over. But our New Society does not allow for suffering, except in small amounts, so those souls who are motivated by the desire to suffer will find some other realm into which to manifest.

Plato: Now most humans are a mixture of the three motivations above, with perhaps a trace of the fourth, and one will usually dominate the others. Until now, the term "reason" has been used mostly in conjunction with the first motivation of the soul, *holy curiosity*, or the desire to know. But it is clear that *reason* is also used in the service of the other two motivations. For the Moral Law is a part of *reason*. *Reason* recognizes and understands that all humans are so interconnected as to constitute a single "One Mind", and hence *altruism*, or helping others, is a "dictate of reason" as Benedict put it. As for the third motivation, developing one's talents and abilities requires intelligence sufficient for doing so. If one has a talent for music or sports or anything else, then developing that talent requires *reasoning*, or thinking in the right way appropriate for developing the talent.

So perhaps we may state that in the presence of any of the three motivations, or any combination of them, mental functioning will be called "reasoning". If other motivations dominate, such as the desire to win arguments, to be famous, to be thought smart by others, to make money, or to defend antecedently held opinions, we will say that the individual is *rationalizing*, not *reasoning*.

William: I like our result. For it depends on the inner state of consciousness of the individual whether she is said to be *reasoning* or *rationalizing*. If she is honest, seeking truth, and wanting to be helpful, then her mental faculties will be in the service of *reason*. But if she is needy for approval or greedy for reputation, then her mental abilities will be in the service of greed, and we will say that she is *rationalizing*, not *reasoning*.

Socrates: Another way to put it is to remind ourselves that the *original purpose* of the soul in manifesting as human involves only the three motivations we have discussed. As long as the embodied soul remains faithful to its original purpose(s) (developing talents, helping others, pursuing knowledge), we will say that it is *reasoning*. But when it deviates from its original purpose and becomes mired in greed and personal ambition, we will say that it has lost its way and that it is using its mental abilities to *rationalize* its desires and beliefs, rather than to seek what is true.

Benedict: I too am satisfied with our discussion. If Plato would return the poetic license he borrowed from me, I would say that our discussion renders clear the sense in which *reason* is intrinsically aligned with the motivations of the soul, and that its function is to bring the individual to the doorway of the eternal. We have separated *reasoning* from mere calculative thinking, or cleverness.

Neal: But now, how do we teach this to our children? I don't suppose they'll be given a "reason-trainer" analogous to the "sex-trainer"?

Plato: *(laughing)* I don't think that will be necessary.

Neal: But you gave rather severe warnings against teaching reasoning and argument to children until they reached the age of 40.

Plato: No, my warnings were against teaching *cleverness* in the absence of reason. Children, especially adolescent boys, love word-play, and will engage in it to win arguments, be thought smart, score points, whatever. Generally, they lack the maturity to know how to use *calculative thinking* in the service of truth. So I thought perhaps they should not be taught syllogisms and argument until they were mature enough to use those skills wisely, that is, to use them in the service of their soul's original motivations.

Neal: And the failure to heed your warning has led to the current disaster in our universities.

William: Why single out the universities? All aspects of our society suffer from the effects of *cleverness* in the absence of reason, that is, in the absence of motivations that originate in the soul. When the motivations of greed and personal ambition dominate, as they do in our whole culture, not just the universities, what arises is the present disaster.

Neal: Well, perhaps I still have some lingering expectation that universities are supposed to teach truth rather than give students the mental tools to help them pursue greed and reputation.

William: *(laughing)* Perhaps you do. But you also understand that universities are a product of the current culture, and are necessarily just as sick as the culture that created them. You thought, as did I, that they would be havens of sane, truth-seeking individuals. And we both needed to be cured of this expectation. For me personally, it was the case of Mrs. Piper that showed me that Harvard intellectuals were just as unreasonable and irrational as everyone else who had fixed opinions. It is as if my colleagues had said to me, "You have invited us to come and sit with that medium. But Professor James, since we already know that Materialism is true, all this talk of 'spirit-communication' must be a lot of bunk, and we are too busy for this kind of nonsense. Sorry that you have been taken in by it."

Benedict: And if I may point out, since your colleagues were using their mental functioning to defend what they already believed, they were *rationalizing*, not *reasoning*.

Neal: And I'm hesitating to ask, Benedict, if you would say the same thing about some your illustrious successors?

Benedict: *(with humor)* I understand your hesitation, for it would seem rather odd to conclude that Leibniz and Kant, among the more astute of human minds, were nevertheless not fully *reasoning*. Both were raised to believe in Theism, the Judeo-Christian God, or the Guy in the Sky. Their God is intrinsically separate from the world He created. They were unable to conceive of the Divine Being in any other way, and their mental functioning was used to defend and articulate this antecedently held concept of God. Because of their emotional attachment to this faulty concept of God, they were unable to *reason* about this. The "holy curiosity of inquiry" failed them in this context, because they were more concerned to defend what they already believed than to seek and discover truth.

Socrates: Yes, for the flower of holy curiosity requires what the Zen folks call "beginner's mind", and your illustrious successors, Benedict, were much too arrogant to think of themselves as mere beginners.

Neal: I know I'm digressing, but perhaps it is worth noticing how their failure to examine culturally inherited beliefs led to absurdities in their respective systems of thought.

Plato: Let's not worry now about whether we are digressing or not. Go ahead.

Neal: So Leibniz has God "choosing" which among infinitely many possible worlds He should create. The whole thing is so anthropomorphic that one would think that the co-discoverer of calculus would be embarrassed by all the mental shenanigans necessary to prop up this concept of the Divine Being. And Kant, my goodness, he just flat-out stated that the human mind cannot know Reality, as if he had never read you, Plato, or you, Benedict, or the vast literature of Christian mystics that claimed otherwise. Both of them totally disregarded a large body of philosophy that conceived of the world as included in the Being of God. Thus, insofar as they were using *calculative thinking* in support of what they already believed, they were not *reasoning*.

Plato: Good. Of course, there's a sense in which *any* concept of God is inadequate, even our own pantheistic concept. *Our* children will be taught from the very beginning that words and concepts have a literal sense only with regard to the embodied world; when applied to what is beyond the physical, words and concepts serve as pointers, not descriptors. This is the error most philosophers and theologians fall into, especially those who are completely trapped in linguistic consciousness, and have no sense that there is anything beyond the physical that words could point *to*.

William: Moreover, our children are being raised by a culture that teaches that all humans are aspects of the One Mind. Just as Leibniz and Kant and everyone else internalized the concept of the Guy in the Sky, so *our* children will have internalized the concept of a single Divine Mind in which they all "live and move and have their being".

Plato: And because of this, of how we are raising our children, I no longer have any qualms about exposing our adolescent boys and young men to *argument* and *cleverness*. They have been raised in a social order that teaches and practices the Golden Rule, so it will not occur to them to use *calculative thinking* as a weapon, to score points against one another, to win arguments, to make themselves "right" and others "wrong". After all, our children will have received a lot of *physical* training, the purpose of which is to give strength, flexibility and good health to the body. We need not worry that they, or some of them, will use their physical strength in such a way that they harm others and themselves. Similarly, they will receive a lot mental training – which will include logic (deduction from premises), inferential reasoning (from observation and data to hypotheses) – so that they will have "sound minds in sound bodies", but because of how they have been raised, it will not occur to them to misuse mental strength or *cleverness* for purposes that are harmful to themselves, to others, and to the social order as a whole.

William: And if someone, perhaps one of our colleagues, Neal, would say something like, "Well, that's all very nice but eventually human nature will prevail and at least some individuals will break through their social conditioning and use their physical and mental strengths to gain advantage over others," we will reply –

Neal: – that the person who makes this argument is *rationalizing*, not *reasoning*. For our colleagues have all been raised in a culture that believes that greed and personal ambition are necessary aspects of human nature. But this is no more true of human nature than is the belief that it is only "natural" for women to be inferior to men.

Benedict: Just as I was raised to believe in male superiority, and then used *calculative thinking* to support and defend the belief that had been programmed into me, so also, those who believe that greed and personal ambition are "natural" and necessary components of human nature have been raised to have this belief, and they then use their mental strength to support and justify the belief. Hence they are *rationalizing*, not *reasoning*. Yet it is not *merely* a matter of how one has been raised, for there is a deeper truth to the matter.

Neal: Yes, at one level, all children, however they are being raised, will internalize the beliefs and values of their culture. They have all been *cultured*, so to speak. And this is where anthropologists and sociologists stop. But we are taking it to another level and are including in our considerations the soul and the divine "social order", if I may call it that, from which all souls emerge. We are constructing a social order that mirrors the experiences of the soul as it is in itself. The soul experiences itself and all other souls as essential aspects of a single Divine Being. Cooperation rules. So does Unconditional Love. The deeper truth is that a social order based on Love and cooperation is much closer to God, to Reality, than one that is based on competition and ego games.

William: Competition is not natural to the soul, and the fact that it seems natural to some souls that have become embodied indicates how deeply those souls have lost their way and have become mired in corporeality. *Our* social order, based on Unconditional Love, or the application of unconditional love to the human condition, is much more in harmony with the Real than is the present dysfunctional order based on greed.

(To Plato and Socrates, who were whispering about something) And what, if I may ask, are you gentlemen talking about?

Socrates: Yes, glad you asked. I was trying to persuade Plato to tell a certain story, but he seems resistant.

William: What story? And why are you resisting telling it, Plato.

Socrates: Oh, he's afraid it will make people frightened and depressed to listen to it. He also thinks it might be too similar to the one he previously told.

Neal: Even so, a little repetition might be useful. Come on, Plato, what's the story?

Plato: Well, Socrates is somewhat correct. The story I have in mind is not a "feel-good" story; in fact, it is rather sad.

Neal: But you must tell it anyway. Even if it should frighten us half to death, that won't be a problem since most of us here are already dead.

Plato: It is a story about the misuse of *cleverness* on a grand scale, with disastrous results.

William: We can handle a disaster or two. Tell the story, and no more excuses.

9) A Sad and Sorry Tale

Plato: Well OK, but remember, you asked for it. I shall entitle my story: **The sad and sorry tale of the sophists.** Perhaps another title will come to me as we proceed. The sophists, as most people know, were somewhat popular in my time. They were very *clever*, that is, they had a much-better-than-average ability to manipulate words and concepts, and could captivate an audience with their verbal skills. But they had no moral compass, and used their cleverness for their own personal ambition. They thought they could teach their skills to others, and for a fee, would teach their students how to use words to get what they want. In other words, linguistic consciousness was in the service of personal ambition and desire, not Truth. This is why, to this day, the word "sophistry" has the connotation of using words and concepts deceptively, which was indeed the case. The sophists used their *cleverness* to deceive others, and to *rationalize* any and every desire and belief. Truth-seeking was not their concern at all, except the "truth" of what will make them the most money and reputation.

This much is known to all. But what is not known is the fate of the sophists after their experience in my culture.

Neal: What are you talking about? The sophists came to an end along with the rest of your culture.

Plato: Alas, would that that were true. From your studies of the NDE you well know that death is merely the separation of the consciousness from its temporary body. Most of what you think of as "personality" or "ego" does not survive the death of the body, and this is usually experienced as a joyous relief by the one who dies.

Neal: Yes.

Plato: And you also know from your studies of mediums and communications from formerly embodied spirits that the latter have usually been "debriefed" by the Light, so to speak, and no longer carry the grosser elements of their former personalities.

Neal: Again, yes.

Plato: But this is not universally true. There are souls who have become so addicted to various behaviors and emotions they experienced while embodied that they cannot shake free of it, and do not go into the Light.

Neal: I have heard of such things… "earthbound" spirits who are unable to move on, but don't really know what to make of it.

Plato: Well, there's really nothing to make of it; it's just a story. So these earthbound spirits are unable to move on, still hungering for the emotions and behaviors to which they were addicted while embodied. Now, I'm sure you have heard stories that souls who were addicted to bodily pleasures hang out in environments suitable for the satisfaction, or the attempted satisfaction, of their former Earthly addictions.

Neal: I have heard that former alcoholics like to hang out in bars, and when a human passes out from too much drink, the souls can jump into the body and enjoy the alcohol. A rather frightening story!

Plato: Indeed. But the fate of those souls who suffered from psychological addictions was much worse than those who suffered from merely physical addiction.

Neal: How so?

Plato: Now, all forms of psychological addiction fall under the general headings of greed and personal ambition. The specific form we are here investigating is that of the sophist. We may characterize the sophist as one who is trapped entirely in linguistic consciousness, who knows only *cleverness*, and whose sense of self-worth involves using words to manipulate the minds of others, either for his own advantage, or for the advantage of another who has given money to the sophist in exchange for the latter's verbal skills, which admittedly are considerable.

When the body of such a soul dies, the soul is in great distress. Unlike souls that had suffered from physical addictions, it cannot just wander into a bar to try to satisfy its craving for alcohol, or wander into a Roman orgy to satisfy cravings for sex. The particular "craving" of the soul of a sophist is to use words to manipulate the thinking of others. But alas for such souls, words have neither meaning nor influence in the after-death conditions. So they needed to incarnate again into human form where it is possible to manipulate others with words.

Now, although there are no social orders that are impervious to using words to manipulate the thinking of others, *some* are more conducive to it than others.

Neal: What do you mean?

Plato: Well, consider a religious theocracy. The poor people have been brainwashed from birth into believing what they believe, and it is unlikely that *words* would have the power to move them away from what they already believe.

Neal: Ah yes, I see. So for the sophist to ply his skills maximally, he needs a social order in which the people are not so rigidly attached to childhood beliefs that they cannot be manipulated with words… or perhaps a social order in which there are many and contrary beliefs floating around simultaneously.

Plato: And what do you think is the name of that social order that is maximally conducive to the skills of the sophist? Hint: It is something we have in common.

Neal: *(sudden flash of understanding)* Oh my, we have in common that we were both raised in democracies.

Plato: Exactly. So after they died, the sophists of my time hung around and were joined by like-minded souls from other cultures. They gathered strength, so to speak, and waited for the right time to incarnate en masse into *your* culture, where their activities now constitute the most vicious and destructive force that Humanity has ever had to face.

Neal: I think I understand your meaning. It is indeed, a "sad and sorry tale".

Plato: Yes, for the sophists of my time have become the advertising industry of yours. There is no greater evil on Earth today than the advertising industry. Their one and only purpose is to use, or misuse, their considerable verbal skills, together with their knowledge of human psychology, to manipulate the thinking and desires of other humans, so that the opinions and desires of other humans become aligned with the opinions and desires of those who paid money to the advertisers. Or do you think they serve some other purpose than this?

Neal: No, I do not.

Plato: Those who prostitute their bodies for money do no harm. But those who prostitute their minds for money do enormous harm, both to themselves and to others.

Socrates: Now it is not unlawful to influence the minds of others if the motivation is to benefit the other. The physical trainer, for example, rightfully wants to influence others to exercise properly. The music teacher wants to influence her students to practice regularly. The nutritionist influences people to eat healthy foods. So not all attempts to influence the thinking of others is evil. But the advertising agent is paid to influence people to believe and desire things without any regard for what is beneficial for the people. And this, we state, is as evil as evil gets.

Benedict: I suppose we should remind ourselves that we are using the word "evil" to mean something like a movement within the field of consciousness towards the illusion of separateness, away from the knowledge of the union that exists between the individual mind and the Divine Mind. *(Playfully)* But I'll bet there's a part of you, Neal, and maybe William too, that would like to see those advertisers occupying the lowest realm of Dante's hell.

Neal: *(laughing)* Hah! The lowest realm is not low enough for them. We'll need to resurrect Dante to invent even lower levels. But perhaps this is a good place to introduce the distinction between what you once called *conviction* persuasion and *knowledge* persuasion.

Plato: Yes, well Socrates just did. The sophists of my time were experts at *conviction* persuasion. They were prostitutes who sold their considerable verbal skills to politicians and others who wanted to impose their beliefs and desires on the city as a whole. The sophists of your time, the advertising agencies, do the same thing, except that their skill is considerably greater, and they are able to harm many more people. Their purpose is, not to teach truth, disseminate information, or inspire others to seek truth, which is the purpose of *knowledge* persuasion, but rather to implant in the minds of their victims specific beliefs and desires. The fact that the specific beliefs and desires, or *convictions*, they are paid to implant in the minds of their victims are usually harmful to their victims is not something they care about at all. This is why we say they are evil. The only thing they care about is implanting the *convictions* in the minds of their victims.

Neal: I'd like to give an example or two of the great harm that your sophists are now doing.

Plato: *(smiling)* They're *your* sophists now. But go ahead with your examples.

Neal: Actually, one of my examples is yours. You envisage a scene in which a nutritionist and pastry chef are trying to influence an audience of children about what they should eat. The nutritionist talks about the importance of a balanced diet, about fresh fruits and vegetables, and about the long-term effect of proper nutrition on the health and well-being of the body. The nutritionist is attempting to persuade the children on the basis of knowledge of the biology of the body. But the pastry chef has no concern with what is best for the children. He desires only to implant the desire for sweets in the minds of the children…

Plato: ... I must interject that at least my pastry chef used only natural ingredients. But he has now morphed into your fast-food industry, which cares only that people be brainwashed into desiring their products, overloaded with salt, fat, sugar, and many, many chemicals that are harmful to the body.

Neal: And so the fast-food industry hires the descendants of the sophists to pimp their products to children, and also, as you said, to adults who reason like children.

William: We must add "to the children of this current society". The children of our New Social Order will reason much better than the adults of the current social order.

Plato: What I called "conviction persuasion" will be unlawful in our new society. But there will be no need to pass laws against it, since it will never even occur to someone raised in our Society to use verbal skills to harm or take advantage of others, any more than it would occur to a male with exceptional physical strength to beat up and bully others who are less strong. Did you have another example, Neal.

Neal: Yes, global warming. The scientists are warning humanity that burning fossil fuels is increasing the Earth's temperature to the point that it will be difficult for the planet to sustain human life. This is an example of "knowledge persuasion". At the same time, the fossil fuel industry has hired prostitutes, the advertisers, to implant in the minds of people the conviction that the scientists are wrong. Disseminating truth is the goal of the scientists; implanting false beliefs is the goal of the advertising industry. The latter do not care if their *cleverness*, their use of verbal skills, leads even to the destruction of the human race. This example clearly shows the difference between *conviction* persuasion and *knowledge* persuasion, and why the latter is beneficial and the former is harmful. But, Plato, I think you are not quite finished with the "sad and sorry tale" of the fate of the sophists.

Plato: Yes, you see *conviction* persuasion is indeed harmful to everyone, but it is most harmful to those who engage in it. For the Universe is so structured that no one can escape the consequences of their behavior while embodied. Now it goes without saying that all souls eventually awaken from the dream of embodiment, and find their way Home to the Unconditional Love of the Divine Being. There are no exceptions to this Law, for the Divine Being needs all aspects of Itself, and is incomplete without all Its parts.

Benedict: … As if the Divine Being is composed of parts?

Plato: Yes, yes, I know. The Divine Being is indivisible and has no parts. But my poetic license permits me to talk this way. Here *(producing a scroll from his toga)* – you may inspect the license yourself.

Benedict: *(laughing)* No need to inspect the license; I believe you. I had forgotten you were just telling a story. Please continue.

Plato: Thank you. Now although all journeys lead back to the Divine Being, some journeys are more difficult than others. The after-death journey of the soul who while human followed the upward path and lived according to the Golden Rule is easy, peaceful, and joyous. The journey of those who followed the downward path of greed, subterfuge, and personal ambition involves considerable suffering and is more difficult. Shall I give a concrete example of this?

Neal: Yes, by all means.

Plato: The case I have in mind concerns a soul who, while human, worked for an advertising agency. He was very clever and exceedingly talented with words. He produced many ads that were successful, and made lots of money for his agency and the people who hired him. He was well rewarded financially, and eventually became an executive of the agency for which he worked.

William: *(sarcastically)* … A most successful life, by the standards of our present society!

Plato: That's what he thought too. Now it turned out that among his clients was the tobacco industry. They knew that the younger a person is when they begin smoking, the more addicted they will become to cigarettes, and the less likely they will be able to stop smoking when as adults they become aware of the health issues. So he hired child psychologists to figure out the best way to market cigarettes to children – and the very word "marketing" *means* "implanting convictions in the minds of others" – so they will become addicted at an early age. The ad he produced was so "successful" that hundreds of thousands of adolescent children took up the habit. So this man was part of a causal chain that resulted in the sufferings and early deaths of hundreds of thousands of humans.

While alive, it was possible for this person to conceal from himself all the pain and suffering he had caused. But when it became this poor man's time to die, he experienced all the sufferings he had caused as his own. That is the Law. But worse than that, he experienced directly the emotional sufferings of all the people who grieved the early death of the tobacco addicts. He even experienced the emotional loss of yet-to-be-born children who were deprived of having grandparents. His own suffering from what he had done was far greater than the suffering he had caused. For though he had harmed the *bodies* of hundreds of thousands of humans, he had damaged his own soul the most. The *souls* of the bodies he had harmed were not damaged in the least; but his own soul was reduced and shriveled by what it had done while human, and needed much healing before it, the soul, could move on.

This is the "sad and sorry" tale of the sophists, of the harm they have done to others, and the greater harm they have done to themselves. May it serve as a cautionary story to any embodied soul tempted to use *cleverness* in the service of conviction persuasion. But *cleverness* used in the service of knowledge persuasion is a fine thing.

Neal: What do you mean?

Plato: It is both permissible and desirable to use *cleverness* to implant in our children's minds true opinions and healthy habits. We want them to have the *conviction* that the Golden Rule is true, before they themselves have the *knowledge* that it is true. The negative psychic energy that manifested as the sophists in my time, and the considerably more harmful advertising agencies of yours, will not be allowed to manifest in our New Society. Respect for the autonomy of each and every individual will be guaranteed. And if you ask, guaranteed by whom, the answer is, guaranteed by the Guardians of our Society, all of whom have experienced the Divine directly.

Benedict: We must not forget that anyone who disrespects the autonomy of other human beings, such as the advertising industry, are now regarded as mentally ill, and will be treated that way. Our Guardians will be vigilant for signs of greed and personal ambition in our children, and…

William: … Pardon the interruption, but I want to be clear that by "personal ambition" we do **not** mean a desire to develop one's talents and abilities. It is fine to "be ambitious" with respect to developing one's "personal" talents and abilities. By "personal ambition" we mean something like a desire for reputation and influence over others, or the desire to "make a name for oneself", as it was expressed in my time.

Benedict: Good. The desire for fame and reputation is not a desire one can wish for others as well as for oneself. For as we have said, if everyone is famous then no one is; but the desire to develop one's abilities as best one can *is* the sort of desire one can wish for everyone. So our Guardians will be on the lookout for early signs of greed, status-seeking, and bullying in our children, which we will regard as a mental illness to be cured. The earlier the illness is diagnosed, the easier the cure. However, because of how we are raising our children, manifestations of this madness, as I once referred to it, will be relatively infrequent. Even so, because this form of madness is contagious, vigilance must be maintained.

Neal: Could you say a little about what you mean by calling the illness "contagious"?

Benedict: Only a little need be said. A child raised in a social order that is based on greed and personal ambition is likely to absorb those values and become greedy himself. A child raised in *our* New Social order, in which the Golden Rule is the norm, is likely to be kind, caring, and desirous of nothing that he does not also desire for everyone else. These latter desires, as we have repeatedly said, fall under three headings: (i) the desire to develop talents and abilities; (ii) the desire to help and assist others; to contribute to the happiness and well-being of others; and (iii) the desire to seek Truth and Understanding. These are the kinds of desires that one can have for oneself and also for everyone else. These desires and their consequences are what I previously called "the dictates of reason".

Neal: And we should perhaps emphasize that our concept of *reason* pertains to how one should live one's life. It is quite different from what is taught under that name in our universities, which have systematically confused *reason* with mere *calculative thinking,* or *cleverness.*

Plato: Yet we acknowledge that *cleverness,* the ability to manipulate words and symbols, is a part of *reason.* What must be added to *cleverness* in order that it becomes *reasonable* is what we may call "right motivation", as Benedict just stated.

Socrates: And perhaps we should note that it is *because* our children have befriended the sexual energy within themselves that they have become gentle, and are now quite capable of *reasoning.* It is not otherwise possible to reason, especially for the boys.

Plato: Yes, for when the sexual energy is prevented from free expression, it becomes like a wild animal, rendering the poor boys unable to think about anything else. Sex becomes associated, not with real females, but with *fantasies* and *thoughts* about females. So their whole mental life is taken over by this, to which we might add anger and frustration that arises from stifling the sexual energy. No one can *reason* or think clearly under conditions such as these. Moreover, as if more were needed, thanks to the advertising industry boys in your culture are constantly bombarded with images of females with idealized and exposed body parts. The males know that such females are forever unavailable to them – hence the need for sex robots during the transition – and their frustration turns into anger that fuels the out-of-control male violence all over the world.

Neal: On the one hand our conclusion might appear to be odd: sex before reason, to boil it down to a few words. But on the other hand, it is what should be expected. The necessary desires must be satisfied in order that reason can function. Of course *(glancing at Benedict)* there are always exceptions. But for the great majority of humans it is true. One cannot think clearly if one is starving to death from lack of food; neither can one think clearly if one is starving half to death from lack of sex. And in both cases we must add the adjective "nutritious". We know something about nutritious foods. And we have raised our children so that they experience their sexuality in a way that is maximally nutritious, nurturing, and joyous as well. So, where are we now?

Socrates: You want a map or something?

Neal: Well I suppose that by now I should know better.

William: *(gently)* I for one want to acknowledge that it takes more than a little courage to write without an outline. I doubt that I could have done it.

Socrates: *(laughing)* Either courage or foolishness. But more seriously, I would say that you now *trust* this process of writing. You show up and so do we, and you write down the words that come to you spontaneously, in the present moment. At any rate, you are hooked, are you not?

Neal: Yes, I guess so. There is nothing I would rather do than this, except perhaps sit on a park bench watching the squirrels and small children.

Socrates: But please remind yourself, or I will do it for you, that we, or you, are not writing a "Treatise" or a "Blueprint for Society". If we *were* writing a treatise, we would be anxious about covering everything and dotting all the "i's" and crossing all the "t's", as the expression goes. But anxiety rarely gives birth to anything new and vital; creativity cannot cross the barrier that anxiety produces. Rather, we are just having a little conversation together. It is sufficient that you are enjoying the process, as we are.

Neal: Actually, I must admit that this process is becoming exciting for me. I never know what's coming next. It's quite an adventure.

Plato: So we have not said everything that could be said, either about sexuality or reason, or emotional intelligence. But we have said enough to point the way. We like very much that you are totally engaged in the process, and are unconcerned with any fruits thereof.

Neal: That is true. If the Universe wants our conversation to go public, It will have to send me a publisher. I guess Socrates is correct. I am hooked by the process and give no thought to any outcome. The process is sufficient unto itself.

Plato: And there is a lesson here for our children. The process, which always happens in the Now, is always more important than any projected outcome. If the process, any process, is governed by any of the three motivations that Benedict mentioned above, or any combination of these motivations, then a beneficial outcome is assured. So our children will be guided to give their conscious attention to what they are doing and feeling in the moment, and to recognize thoughts that pertain to a future outcome as so much mental noise. Such thoughts occur in the present moment, and sap mental energy that could more happily be applied to the task now at hand.

OK, what next, you ask? Before we leave our early teens, there is one additional aspect to their education, without which they could fail to flourish maximally.

William: If I may interject something, it goes without saying that all along we have been teaching our children the usual academic subjects, as well as exposing them to various skills and techniques. Future educators will have unlimited resources to teach these things in the best possible way. And the "best possible way" always involves an increase in the child's desire to learn, and nurturing the delicate flower of holy curiosity that lives within each child.

Neal: Definitely. Our present culture does whatever it can to stifle this holy flower, so that by the time someone reaches the highest level of the present educational system, his or her natural curiosity has all but been destroyed. Because people with PhDs must scramble for jobs and reputation, they have lost their natural curiosity, and actively resist learning anything new. Sex and reason are not the usual academic subjects, but are what must be in place in order for the student to be able to learn.

Moreover, we have been observing our children while at play, for spontaneous play is the arena in which the child's natural talents and proclivities are most likely to manifest. These natural talents and abilities constitute the "original purpose" of the soul in becoming embodied, and the happiest of humans are the ones who are able to manifest that purpose. Plato, you once said that the purpose of any education worthy of the name is to "turn the soul around", from focusing its attention on the world of becoming – the temporal order – to focusing its attention on the world of being, the eternal order. It seems to me that our children will have one foot in the eternal order from the very beginning, and will have no need of being "turned around".

Plato: Yes, *(laughing)* but it is equally important that our children have the other foot in the temporal order, otherwise here will be no temporal order at all.

Chapter VII

Beauty and Inspiration

1) Sensory Beauty

William: But now, Plato, I am eager to hear what else our children need in order to flourish maximally.

Plato: I don't know what to call it. Perhaps "aesthetic sensibility", a deepening sense of the Beautiful as it manifests both in Nature and in human expression.

Neal: Perhaps you should state what you mean by "The Beautiful"?

Plato: Perhaps. But you have experienced it directly, and so has William. Why not talk a bit about your own experience, and then if necessary I will give an account in terms of our underlying premises.

William: Underlying premises?

Plato: Yes. (i) The human being is an embodied *soul,* and (ii) all souls are so interconnected as to constitute a single One Mind. The experience of Beauty is necessarily involved as the embodied soul ascends to the recognition of its union with the Divine Being.

Benedict: Actually the second premise should be reversed. The Divine Being is primary, and manifests Itself *as* individual souls.

Plato: Whatever. *(To Benedict)* We're never going to get this exactly right through words, but I find myself agreeing with you that the attempt to do so is not an unworthy exercise. In any case, the experience of Divine Beauty is the most powerful force for turning the soul around, as happened to you.

Neal: What are you talking about?

Plato: *(smiling)* Think back to when you were the same age as our children, thirteen or fourteen. What was it that turned *your* soul around, so to speak? Who was your first Teacher? (Hint: It wasn't me. I came to you when you were 16. Your first teacher came a few years before.)

Socrates: And notice the tears of recognition welling up in your eyes, as you re-cognize those profound early experiences.

Neal: Yes. My first Teacher was Beethoven, and it was his music that turned my soul around.

Socrates: And what he taught you affected you permanently. Even though later you pretended to be an atheist for a while, you knew that his music could not have affected you the way it did unless it contained, as William once put it, "ontological messages" pertaining to the nature of your own being. You spent much of your younger years trying to "validate" what you already knew through the study of science and philosophy. So it was the experience of Divine Beauty, channeled by Beethoven, that penetrated into your soul and permanently aligned it with our two premises.

Benedict: Actually, it is probably incorrect to speak of *soul* turning around, since the soul, in and of itself, is already turned around.

Plato: I'll accept that. So it is not the soul as it is in itself, but rather the soul insofar as it has become embodied, and constitutes the human being. An extension of the soul gets turned around towards its Source. How's that, Benedict?

Benedict: *(laughing)* It will do. I had forgotten you still have that poetic license, so proceed however you like.

Plato: I think you will like what I am about to say. It is a stretch of human language, even with my poetic license, to attribute any adjectives to the Divine Being. We will not say that It is wise, intelligent, beautiful, or even good. It is even a stretch to call it "One", since that might imply to someone that maybe it could have been two or some other number.

Benedict: I agree. Although I characterized the One (*Substance*, in my terminology) as indivisible and infinite, these terms are really negatives. The One is *not* finite and it is *not* divisible. So as long as we use language, it is better to try to get at the One by saying what it is not, since it is not possible to say in words what it is.

Plato: Agreed.

Benedict: So if the One Mind is not beautiful, then what is this Beauty that you are always talking about, in which humans may participate?

William: Hold on a minute. Before you two start getting theoretical on us, I want to suggest we begin with the psychological, that is, with common human experiences that fall under the general heading of "aesthetic".

Plato: I was going to reply that the "Beautiful" I am always talking about is akin to the "Reason" that you are always talking about, but perhaps we should follow William's suggestion and consider these things from the perspective of our children first.

Socrates: Most definitely. For there is a sense of beauty – an "aesthetic" – associated with each of the five senses, that our children will be guided to experience. It is only when one has a robust experience of beauty through sensory experience that one would be in any position to understand what these two *(gesturing towards Plato and Benedict)* like to talk about. *(To me)* Beethoven's music rendered you quite beside yourself, so to speak, and that made you hungry for and receptive to accounts of Beauty like Plato's. But without the power of that aesthetic experience you might not have been so receptive to Plato.

Neal: I agree. So our children will be guided to the experience of beauty in whatever they do.

William: Well yes, but let's begin with simple sense experiences, such as the sense of smell.

Neal: We have today something called "aromatherapy", which recognizes that different scents can affect the body's well-being. Even though no one talks about "olfactory beauty", it is quite clear that humans have long been guided by their noses.

William: And our physiologists will be studying in detail how molecules, emanating from substances that smell good to humans, interact with and affect the brain. Although it is unlikely that the smell of a rose or a lilac will ever be "improved upon", yet those who enjoy exploring scents and developing new scents, working together with the scientists, will no doubt discover many additional scents that are both pleasing and beneficial to the human being.

Neal: And even though Nature was not too generous with humans regarding the sense of smell, compared say with dogs, nevertheless it happens not infrequently that a given scent arrests the human mind with its beauty. Our taste buds appear to be more generously bestowed.

Socrates: But before we leave olfactory beauty, there is one thing about smells that deserves to be emphasized.

Neal: What is it?

Socrates: *(teasingly)* Well, I would say, but don't know if you prudish gentlemen could handle it.

Neal: Hah! You must be thinking about sex again.

Socrates: *(smiling)* As all dogs know, every human body emanates a distinct, unique scent. A dog could easily identity a human by scent alone. But humans have been conditioned to cover up their natural scents with perfumes and chemicals. Although humans can never become as proficient as dogs with regard to sniffing one another out, nevertheless scent could play a richer role in human relations, especially sexual relations. For human scent is stronger during sexual arousal. Indeed, sexual compatibility between two humans may be predicted based on their attraction to one another's scent, *sans* perfume.

Neal: So our children will be sniffing one another?

Socrates: ... And why not? Why shouldn't sex involve *all* the senses, instead of just seeing and touching? Is there not beauty in erotic scents?

Neal: Yes.

Benedict: Now, aside from the scent of flowers and other humans, there are many scents that are beneficial to humans, such as the scent of a forest, the ocean, and of food well prepared.

Neal: Humans will have the time and take the time to "smell the roses", and our social order will be arranged so that the natural scents of Nature are not covered up by chemicals, but available to all. I suppose for this to happen our cities will have to be redesigned so that natural beauty – parks, streams, rivers, etc. – are within walking distance for every citizen.

William: It will be a very different culture that organizes its cities to maximize the experience of natural beauty, rather than to maximize the "profits" of a small number of wealthy individuals.

Plato: Indeed. Our social order exists for the purpose of enabling all souls who come here to succeed in accomplishing their original purpose. The body has physical needs, and the personality associated with the body has psychological needs, all of which have been addressed in the raising of our children. But it is not a question of merely providing for basic physical and psychological needs. We want our children, and adults too, to *flourish* in their own being, and for *that* to happen, our social order must take aesthetics into account. The experience of beauty temporarily connects the individual mind with the Divine Mind, conveying inspiration and well-being to the individual.

Neal: I'm wondering whether we should distinguish between "what is pleasant" and "what is beautiful".

William: What do you have in mind?

Neal: Well, as you suggested, we are approaching the subject of aesthetics empirically, by considering the experiences of our children. It seems to me that there are two kinds of experiences involved. Let's say, for example, that I'm walking in the forest, alone with my thoughts.

William: OK.

Neal: I am aware of the pleasant smell of the forest, but it is in the background of my awareness. Then I come across a flower, and its scent is so strikingly beautiful that my mind comes to a full stop and my awareness is focused entirely on the scent of that flower.

William: I see. So the difference between the pleasant and the beautiful is that the latter has the power to arrest linguistic consciousness and bring the entire mind into the present moment. Many sense experiences are pleasant but some have the power to bring the mind fully into the present moment, and it is these latter experiences that we shall call "beauty".

Plato: Good, for a mind that is in the present moment, in the "now", is in the timeless eternal order, even if only for a few seconds. This is the power of Beauty, and the sense in which the Beautiful is like a good spirit that "turns around" the mind of the human and reminds it of its own connections with the eternal order. The experience of Beauty is a portal to the eternal order.

(Benedict was about to say something when Socrates said...)

Socrates: Let's first go through our children's experiences with the pleasures of the senses, and how such pleasures may sometimes become encounters with Beauty. We have already discussed the pleasures of taste, and how our culture will align such pleasures with what is healthy for the body.

Neal: Yes, all foods will be healthy, well-prepared, and taste good. Mealtime will always be pleasurable. But occasionally something will taste so good to a given individual – whether a simple fruit in season, or a meal expertly prepared with a "just right" combination of spices – that the mind will become completely absorbed in the sensations of taste. This is the experience to which we give the name "Beauty".

Plato: You used the phrase "expertly prepared". Now, all our children will be taught the basics of cookery. Like all arts, cookery involves not only learned skills, but also innate talent, or knack. Some will be so good at preparing food that the other children will prefer it to their own. *(With humor)* As everyone knows, Grandma's recipes cannot be written down. An adequate cook, one might say, can follow a recipe; but a great cook is beyond any recipe that can be written down and mechanically copied. And this pattern is generally true for all human skills and abilities.

Neal: What do you mean?

Plato: Every child is born into the world with a unique set of skills and abilities. It is the job of her teachers to identify the child's natural talents, and to assist the child in developing her talents to the best of her ability. So, turning our attention to auditory pleasures, every child will be exposed to music from an early age. Every child will be taught songs and encouraged to learn to play a musical instrument.

But some children will have so little talent for music that it will be difficult for them to carry a tune, whereas others will have so much talent that they will be inventing new tunes by themselves. *Technique* can be taught, but the creative process by which new melodies and new combinations of sounds are discovered is beyond what can be taught.

Neal: Yes, one can teach such things as harmony and counterpoint, but it is not possible to teach *how* to create a beautiful melody.

William: Creativity of any kind originates from beyond the margins. No educational system can teach creativity, but as Einstein observed, an educational system, such as the current one, may very well stifle creativity. Yet I believe we *can* investigate the conditions that best facilitate creativity. We already know a little about this – that creative ideas tend to come when the mind is relaxed and playful, rather than stressed and anxious. So we shall not overload our children with tons of "busywork", as is presently the case, but plenty of unstructured free time and playtime will be built into our education system. In this way our children's natural abilities will flower and flourish.

I also want to state that, concerning the pleasures of the senses, our neuroscientists will be quite busy detailing the physiological correlates of sensory pleasure. *How* does a combination of sounds incident upon the ear induce pleasure and joy into the mind, and sometimes the joy is so intense that it causes linguistic consciousness to come to a full stop.

Neal: Even more than pleasure and joy, music has the power to induce a kind of *knowingness* in the mind. Beethoven's music, and others' too, is not just beautiful; it is also true. I do not know if experiencing music's "ontological messages" has a physiological correlate, but it sure would be worth finding out.

Plato: *(smiling)* Well, given that you guys are talking with yours truly, it should hardly come as a surprise that our analysis points to a kind of unity between what is True and what is Beautiful. We might also add "what is Good" to the mix. Initially these three seem to be separate. But as the soul, within the human form, ascends to what is highest within itself, it discovers that what is true is also beautiful and good, what is good is both true and beautiful, and what is beautiful is true and good.

Socrates: If anyone still doubts this, they should consider descriptions of the Near-Death Experience.

Neal: Yes. Although they all say the Being of Light cannot be described, yet when they do attempt to describe it, they use expressions like "contains all knowledge", "infinitely beautiful", and "all-loving".

Benedict: Yes, and although, as Plato and I were commenting a little while ago, the Divine Being cannot be described, the individual soul, as it ascends towards the Divine Being, experiences Beauty, Goodness, and Understanding in a harmonious and blissful Unity in which itself is included. However, our children will experience these things separately at first.

But I'd like to note one difference between what we may call our two "spirit guides", Beauty and Reason. Unlike Reason, Beauty manifests directly through each of the five senses, most strongly perhaps through hearing and seeing. The embodied soul can experience manifestations of Beauty directly through the eyes. But human eyes cannot "see" Reason or Knowledge directly.

Plato: Yet the soul, when unencumbered by a body, *does* experience these things – Knowledge, Goodness, Love – directly, which makes the telling of such experience impossible.

William: OK. Now back to our children. We are guiding them as they experience Beauty as It manifests through their senses. We have discussed scent and taste, and are now considering Beauty insofar as it manifests through hearing.

Plato: And I believe that this beauty, that arises through hearing, can be divided in two: (i) the sounds of Nature (or "in" Nature), and (ii) the sounds of Music.

William: What about poetry and drama? Certainly these can induce, through hearing, the experience of Beauty.

Plato: Yes, but these are mixed forms, so to speak. The beauty of a poem or play cannot be experienced unless one knows the *language* in which it is written. So linguistic consciousness is involved to some extent, and the experience of beauty is not direct and immediate, but rather is mediated by language and culture. But (i) and (ii) above are experiences of Beauty that do not involve language; in fact, they have the power to bring linguistic consciousness to a full stop.

William: I see. And I also see some interesting work for our neuroscientists.

Plato: Yes, we have already discussed that they will be measuring the effect of Mozart's music on our children's developing brains.

William: More than that. We will take our children into natural surroundings – the sounds of the forests, seashores, rivers and streams – wire up their brains, and measure the effect such sounds have on their developing brains.

(Plato kind of stares at William for a few seconds.)

William: *(to Plato)* What's the matter?

Plato: *(laughing)* Well, I suppose you can take the scientist out of his body, but you can't take the science out of the scientist. "Wire up their brains" indeed!

William: You think it's not a good idea?

Benedict: It's a splendid idea. Look, from our present non-embodied perspective, it is unnecessary to establish physiological correlates to embodied conscious experience. Put a child or adult human next to a waterfall or ocean waves and we can "see" the effect that environment has on the human's physiology. But the "vision" that human eyes lack is circumvented by the knowledge that comes through methodological, that is, scientific investigation. It will be extremely useful for humans to arrive at the conclusion through empirical investigation that the sounds of Nature are indispensable for a full flourishing of the soul within the human form. This knowledge will be essential for architects and those who plan and design living spaces for humans. For in our new Social Order, living spaces will be designed taking into account what is best for the physical and psychological well-being of humans. It will turn out, of course, that what is aesthetically pleasing to human consciousness is also beneficial to the body.

Neal: I agree. The sounds of Nature are of course what they are, and cannot be improved upon. But what about the sounds of Music? Shall we measure, not just the effect of Mozart's music on the developing brain, but the also the effects of various combinations of sounds and rhythms?

William: Yes, of course. Not all combinations of sounds that are called "music" by your present culture are physiologically beneficial, and some are positively harmful. In the future the word "music" shall refer only to such combinations that are beneficial to physical and psychological well-being.

Plato: OK, you guys can get as physiological as you wish. What consciousness experiences as naturally pleasing, as beautiful, as uplifting, will inevitably also be uplifting and beneficial for the body. The physiological details of this latter benefit are quite worthy of being discovered. But our future composers, or sound aestheticians, will be guided by Beauty's Muse directly, and will have no need of the physiological details.

William: Agreed. But there is one more thing about music, or Beauty as it manifests through hearing, that I want to comment on.

Neal: Go ahead.

William: The experience of Beauty, through whatever sense, has the power to "turn the soul around", as Plato put it. In the presence of Beauty, the human mind comes to a stop and cannot think about anything else. But with *hearing,* it seems not only that Beauty is carried along by the sounds, but also that the sounds themselves have a certain power, a power to weaken the margins and render the soul more susceptible to the experience of Beauty itself. While watching the effects of Beethoven's music on you, in your teen years, it appeared that the sounds were thinning out the margins that separate, or seem to separate, the embodied world from the non-embodied world. And perhaps this is *why* you felt that Beethoven's music is not only beautiful, but also true.

Plato: This is a good point. We might picture the thickness of William's "margins" as something that continuously fluctuates. The margins are semi-porous to Beauty, which rides along through sensory channels. But certain sound combinations have the power to temporarily thin the margins, allowing not only Beauty, but also bits of Knowledge and Goodness to seep through.

Benedict: *(with humor)* "Bits of Knowledge"!? Let me examine that poetic license of yours again. I seriously doubt it allows you to get away with such verbal nonsense.

Plato: *(laughing)* Well, maybe you are right. But if, as some poet once said, language is a tailor shop where nothing fits, then perhaps we should not care too much about the words that we use, unless you think that some words don't fit more than other words don't fit.

Benedict: *(also laughing)* No, I don't think that. Well, maybe I do, sometimes. The point, I suppose, is that the human experience of Beauty admits of degrees, from what we may call "the pleasant" at the lower end, to what at the higher end completely arrests attention and constitutes a portal into the eternal. At this higher level, Beauty appears conjoined with Knowledge or Understanding.

Plato: ... And with Goodness and Love as well. As we have said, at the lower levels of human experience, these things – Beauty, Knowledge, and Goodness, appear separate. At the higher human levels they appear to merge. And at the level of soul, unencumbered with body, they are aspects of a single Unity, The One.

William: And at the level of our children, shall we state that for each of the senses, our children shall be guided by aesthetics, a sense of the Beautiful?

Neal: Yes, and let us briefly mention the two other senses.

William: Good. Like the Beauty that comes through hearing, the Beauty that come through *seeing* may also be divided between (i) sights of Nature – trees, rivers, mountains, galaxies, etc., and (ii) sights that originate from humans – paintings, sculpture, architecture.

Benedict: Now we have already mentioned that our neuroscientists will be quite busy mapping the physiological correlates of the experience of Beauty, for each of the senses. It will be discovered that the body functions maximally when the mind is experiencing beautiful things through its sensory channels. Our architects have been liberated from having to labor under the profit motives of wealthy individuals, so there will be nothing to prevent them from designing buildings and living spaces, and even cities, with a view to visual beauty. So our children will be growing up in an environment that engenders the experience of beauty. *(Glancing at Plato)* OK, we can capitalize that – the experience of Beauty.

Plato: *(smiling)* Thank you. I agree with you that Beauty, as well as Goodness and Knowledge, are not attributes of the Divine Being Itself. But I think you agree with me that the soul experiences these things as it ascends to the Divine Being.

Benedict: Yes, I do.

Plato: Then by capitalizing these terms, we call attention to the fact that the cause of the experience of Beauty lies in the eternal order, and only secondarily in the physical thing that is perceived as beautiful.

Benedict: Beauty, Goodness, and Knowledge are not attributes of The One; but neither are they attributes of physical things, except very indirectly. We may say in words that a certain melody is beautiful, or that a waterfall, or sunset, or human face is beautiful, but we do not mean that there is a "something" called beauty that literally resides in the waterfall, the melody, the sunset, or human face. Rather, these external objects, in interaction with a given human body, facilitate a temporary thinning out of the margins, and allow some of that Beauty to manifest into the physical dimension.

Neal: Hmm, it would seem that a consequence of this way of thinking is that, if we must look for a source for Beauty, it would have to be in the soul itself.

Socrates: Indeed, where else?

Neal: But –

Socrates: But, you say, surely Beethoven's music *is* beautiful, and so is, or was, that face that launched a thousand ships, or whatever it was that Homer said. You think it might detract something from Beethoven to say that his music is not in itself beautiful, just that it has the power to cause you to recollect the Beauty within your own soul.

Neal: Yes, maybe.

Socrates: But I say to you that it would be impossible for you or anyone else to be moved by Beethoven's music, or anyone else's music, if that beauty were not also in your own soul. The external sounds merely trigger an experience of what is already within you. Well, perhaps I should omit the word "merely", for it is no small accomplishment to produce combinations of sounds that have the power to trigger the experience of Beauty in large numbers of humans.

Benedict: *(smiling)* You do not yet know of your own inner beauty, and still believe that the beauty you experience every day is in the external object which triggers the experience, not in yourself. But tell me, when you understand something, is that understanding in yourself or in the thing you are understanding?

Neal: ... In myself, of course.

Benedict: And when you experience some outer event as morally uplifting, filling you with feelings of lovingkindness, is this lovingkindness something in you or in the external event.

Neal: – In me, of course.

Benedict: And so why are you surprised to learn – or should I say, to recollect – that outer events and objects trigger, but do not cause, the Beauty of your own soul to trickle down into the personality that you are now experiencing yourself as being? Oh wait; I see. You think it would be arrogant to believe that the beauty you experience by means of external objects is within yourself, and hence that you are yourself beautiful?

Neal: Yes, perhaps.

Socrates: *(with humor)* But you do know that you are yourself the Divine Being. I phrased that as a statement, not a question.

Neal: Yes, I noticed that. There appears to be something about this human form in which I find myself that clouds over this knowledge.

But you are right; reason has convinced me that if the One Mind is all there is, then it must be me, as well as everything else.

Socrates: OK, but I want you to have this knowledge not only as one of Benedict's "dictates of reason" but also as lived experience. Try this: next time you experience Beauty, whether in Nature, through music, or by means of chocolate ice cream for that matter, allow yourself to have the thought that the beauty you are experiencing is happening within you, and *is* you. Arrogance is involved, not in the assertion of this truth, but rather in the denial of it.

Neal: I understand. Now what about the sense of touch? Is there such a thing as tactile beauty?

Plato: Let us consider three, or possibly four, different kinds of experience that involve the sense of touch. First is the experience of touching physical objects. This sense is not very well developed in most humans, except perhaps those that are blind at birth. Their blindness compels them to rely on touch more than others, so we can examine them to find out to what extent some things are more aesthetically pleasing to touch than others. But probably nothing is more pleasing to the touch than another human body, and our children have been guided to experience this from an early age. Second is the experience of being touched by another. All children will have been given instruction in giving and receiving touch, but some will be so good at it that it will seem to those at the receiving end that something beautiful is being channeled into their bodies. So yes, there is an aesthetics – a sense of the Beautiful – involved in the giving and receiving of touch.

The third kind of experience involves kinesthetics, or the feel of the body from within.

Neal: What do you mean?

Plato: I have in mind sports, dance, martial arts, and even simple exercises. The main reason people do these things is because it feels good to do so. OK, many people exercise because of the consequences for health, but no one would throw balls at a basket for hours at a time unless he enjoyed the physical motions his body undergoes during the process. No one develops expertise at dancing or martial arts unless she enjoys the kinesthetic sensations in her body as she does these things. So an athlete, a dancer – and we should add musicians who sing or play an instrument – are attuned to inner kinesthetic sensations in their bodies, and not infrequently they feel a sense of Beauty accompanying those sensations.

Now the fourth thing I had in mind really involves visual Beauty – it is the experience of Beauty by those who watch what athletes, dancers, martial artists, and musicians, etc. are doing with their bodies. For no one would pay lots of money merely to watch others kicking balls or contorting their bodies unless the experience of watching conveyed Beauty through the eyes of the beholders.

William: And it is interesting to note that while the spectator is moved by the Beauty in what she *sees*, the athlete and dancers are guided, not by vision, but by inner kinesthetic sensation. Well, I believe we have remarked upon the various experiences of Beauty as they are conveyed through the various sensory channels. It goes without saying that our neuroscientists will be mapping the physiological correlates of the experience of Beauty, and who knows whether such mapping will enable the scientists to tweak, I mean augment, the actual experience of Beauty. *(With a little humor)* But I feel, or perhaps fear, that we are not finished talking about Beauty.

Benedict: *(smiling)* Your fear is quite justified, William, for we have not yet discussed my favorite form of Beauty. Plato's too, if I am not mistaken.

2) Conceptual Beauty

William: What is it? Oh wait, you have in mind a sort of Beauty that pertains to ideas and concepts?

Benedict: Yes, sort of. Now it goes without saying that not all forms of Beauty are equally accessible to all people. Beethoven's music, for example, does not affect everyone the way it affected Neal. And so, what I shall refer to as the experience of *conceptual* Beauty is not equally available to all humans. But it is quite obvious, is it not, that logicians and mathematicians experience Beauty all the time.

William: Yes, I would sometimes hear colleagues in the math department refer to a given "proof" as being "beautiful". I had no idea what they were talking about, but they were just as excited about it as people are after a good performance of Beethoven's *Ninth*. But actually, when as a schoolboy I learned about the Pythagorean theorem, I did think it was sort of neat.

Benedict: And aside from mathematics and logic, do you think there is Beauty involved (i) in the concepts of empirical science, and/or (ii) the concepts of philosophy?

William: A definite "yes" to your first question, and a probable "no" to the second, unless perhaps you think there might be a baby hidden in the dirty bathwater of academic philosophy.

Plato: Let's focus on the first now, and later we can investigate whether there is a baby worth saving in the concepts of philosophy – theology too.

Neal: There is a story to the effect that when some theoretical physicist was asked whether his theory is true, he replied that it is too beautiful not to be true. Many theoretical physicists have discussed how considerations of aesthetics guide them in discovering and forming their ideas and theories. There is something quite Beautiful about Maxwell's equations, the Quantum Theory, and General Relativity… but it is a Beauty that is not available to those who have not studied these concepts in some depth.

Benedict: So the deliverances of Reason are beautiful, and the process by which Reason arrives at its deliverances – epistemology – although messy in the short term, is also beautiful when time be taken into account. For the understandings given to humanity by science are the deliverances of Reason under the guidance of holy curiosity. Well actually, we've said that reason functions *only* in the presence of holy curiosity. Individual scientific theories may be quite beautiful conceptually, and also, the process by which human understanding has evolved from my time to yours is itself beautiful.

Neal: It is quite amazing to reflect upon the path that has led humans from the belief that everything is atomistic, separate, and constituted by independently existing parts, to the belief that nothing is separate and that all things are so interconnected as to constitute a single indivisible Being.

Plato: Yes, it is indeed amazing and worthy of reflection. Now mystics from all traditions and from no traditions have always believed this – that the world is an indivisible Unity, not reducible to "parts" – and their belief was based on direct experience.

William: If I may interject, I would phrase that differently. The mystics' belief in holism is not really a "belief" in the usual sense of the term; rather, it is a report of something experienced directly. There is no inference from "experience" to "belief", as is the case with the beliefs and theories of science.

Plato: I agree. But non-mystics who believed this had to base their belief on the testimony of mystics and perhaps some elusive "gut-feeling" that the mystics were right. But I did not dream, nor could I have dreamt, that there would be another way of arriving at the knowledge of Unity, or the interconnection of all things.

Benedict: Me neither. The systematic application of human reason to empirical observations has, over the centuries, arrived at this same knowledge. Now I did think that humans could just think it through, and arrive at this conclusion – shall we call it "holism"? – by logical deduction from obvious first principles. But one must have "beginner's mind" for logical deduction to work. I did not foresee that when "logical deduction from obvious first principles" reaches a conclusion that is opposite to what people believe a priori, they will prefer to stay with what they already believe. Actually, it is not a choice. When so-called scholars read my *Ethics*, I can see that their prior beliefs (in Atomism, or theism) cloud their minds so that they cannot follow my argument.

Neal: Yes, my goodness, even on page one you make it abundantly clear that you consider consciousness to be the primary existent, with everything else being defined explicitly as an appearance to consciousness. And yet they – the scholars – go on to make you into a materialist, like themselves.

Benedict: *(smiling)* Well that is not our concern. I think even then I recognized that beliefs arrived at through experience take root more firmly than beliefs arrived at through reason alone. And now, human experience over the last four hundred years has led to the conclusion that Creation is single, indivisible, and whole. And since reason applied to experience generates knowledge, we can now state that scientists, not just mystics, *know* that holism is true. However, it still remains true that the knowledge of the mystic is more firm than the knowledge of the scientist. Plato, what do you think?

Plato: We might need a stronger phrase than "more firm", but I agree with you.

Neal: This might be a good time to enumerate the points of agreement between (i) mystics and Near-Death Experiencers, and (ii) science, or the deliverances of human reason over the past 350 years.

Plato: Go ahead.

Neal: These points of agreement are items of direct experience for the former, and items of inference from empirical data for the latter:

1) All things are so interconnected as to constitute a single indivisible Whole. This is a consequence of the quantum theory.
2) Consciousness or mind is independent of the body.
3) The world of human experience – the world of objects that appear in space and time – is dependent on a higher-order reality, called the "eternal" order by mystics. This is a consequence of Relativity theory.
4) All minds are so interconnected as to constitute a single "One Mind". Each individual mind is already united with this "One Mind". Now this latter point is not as firmly established by empirical methods as the other three, but strongly suggested by parapsychological research, and of course, an item of direct experience by mystics and NDErs.

(To Benedict) Would you count these among your "dictates of reason"?

Benedict: Yes of course, although what I explicitly labeled as "dictates of reason" had more to do with applying the Golden Rule to one's personal life. But, to summarize what we have been talking about, these four "points of agreement" are really the philosophical principles that underlie our whole conversation. These principles are established in two very different ways: (i) by direct experience (mystics, NDErs), and (ii) by empirical methods over time (science). And I would add a third way, (iii) logical deduction from obvious first principles, but this way does not work if one has any preconceived ideas about these things, as people will invariably project their preconceived ideas onto whatever they read and think about.

Neal: *(with humor)* So you would not recommend this third way to people who fancy themselves philosophers or theologians?

Benedict: *(laughing)* Well there are always exceptions, such as yourself, but even you, Neal, needed the support of empirical science to corroborate your gut feelings that our principles are true. So yes, I would recommend that those who fancy themselves philosophers and theologians study the findings of science on these matters.

Socrates: Either that, or have themselves a Near-Death Experience, which would forever cure them of their cleverness with words. But now, my goodness, where have we left our children?

3) Inspiration [Or Divine Madness]

Neal: Yes, well we were teaching them about Reason, then our discussion moved on to Beauty. We followed Beauty as it moves along the sensory channels, and beyond the sensory channels to the Beauty involved in concepts and reasoning itself. The knowledge that humans have acquired through reason is itself a thing of great beauty. It seems to me that the appreciation of Beauty in any of its many forms must be taught to our children.

Plato: Do you think that aesthetic sensibility – the appreciation of Beauty – is something that *can* be taught?

Neal: Maybe not taught explicitly. But observed, pointed out, talked about, and encouraged.

William: Perhaps all teaching will be of this form. It is a bringing forth of what is within. But our educational system will encourage, not discourage, the aesthetic sensibilities of our children. There is no reason why any subject matter worthy of being taught to our children cannot be taught in a way that brings out the beauty inherent in the subject.

Neal: We may note that the appreciation of Beauty requires that the mind be in a receptive modality.

Plato: Yes, through upbringing we are transforming Humanity from human *doings* to human *beings*. This requires adding the female principle of receptivity to balance the currently out of whack male principle of "doing". And even though we have said that beauty is in the eye of the beholder, hence *in* the beholder, this is experienced as true only in the more advanced stages of development. From our children's perspective, and from the perspective of most adults, it will seem that Beauty comes from without. But you are right to state that the experience of Beauty requires that the mind be in a receptive modality, which is the main reason there are no Beethovens to be found in your music schools today.

William: Neither will you find any Tolstoys in our literature departments or Rembrandts in our art departments. That's because current universities require students to spend all of their time *doing* things, with no time left for *appreciation* or *creativity*. The professors don't know how to quantify a student's ability to appreciate and be moved by the Beauty of the music. So they pretend it does not exist, or is not important, or is a matter of mere subjectivity.

Neal: It is a major travesty of sorts that our music schools produce individuals who can "analyze" a Beethoven quartet, but cannot appreciate the Beauty of the music.

William: Yes, in the first place, the "professional" schools select for the kind of individual who is merely clever. But if a creative soul happens to get past their admissions procedure, the regiment of academic nonsense the student is required to learn will stifle any creativity. Yet the most important thing about music (or art, poetry, and literature) is its power to move the soul and turn it around towards its Source.

Plato: They, that is, your music and art schools, believe, or behave as if they believed, that music is a matter of technique alone. They do not know about inspiration, nor of Divine Madness; neither do they know that creativity originates from beyond the veil that appears to separate the eternal order from the temporal order. Now technique *can* be taught; and even if we conclude that *inspiration* and *appreciation* cannot be taught, nevertheless there are conditions that encourage creativity in our children, and conditions that discourage it. Any educational system that is designed to turn the soul around must necessarily be a system that encourages rather than destroys the student's natural ability to appreciate, to receive, and to feel moved in her soul by Beauty. Later she will be guided to understand that the Beauty that moves her is *in* her soul and *is* her soul, for the soul itself is far more Beautiful than anything accomplished by or through the soul. But that higher Beauty cannot be seen by the body's eyes, nor grasped by the human mind. Incidentally, Neal, how are you doing with that little exercise Socrates suggested for you?

Neal: *(laughing)* I'm still resisting it. The beauty I see when I look at a tree seems to be in the tree, not in myself. Yet when I perceive the tree, where can that perception possibly be but in my own mind? So the Beauty associated with that perception must also be in me.

Socrates: *(playfully)* Yes, you are having fun with this, and are making heroic efforts to resist the conclusion that the Beauty you experience through looking at a tree, or through any other external stimulus, is but the faintest glimpse into the magnificent Beauty that is your soul, or rather, the soul that is now manifesting as the human being you believe you are. But your heroic efforts are doomed for defeat.

Neal: Yes, so it would seem. But tell me, Socrates, do all external things appear Beautiful to a soul, or rather, to a human who fully experiences the magnificence of her soul? Is it only to unenlightened humans that some things seem beautiful and other things do not?

Socrates: Ah yes, what is that lovely quote from one of the gospels? "The kingdom of heaven is spread upon the earth, but people do not see it." If "the kingdom of heaven" is a thing of Divine Beauty, and if it is "spread upon the earth", then the Earth itself must be a thing of Divine Beauty. The human does not see Divine Beauty spread upon the earth, she does not see that there is nothing on the Earth that is not touched by Beauty, because she does not see the Beauty of her own Self. To a soul that fully experiences its own magnificence, there is nothing that is not bathed in its own Beauty; actually, to such a soul, there is nothing that is external to itself. But it is quite rare for such a soul to be found in a bodily form.

Neal: Actually, you have just reminded me of something I wanted to comment about pertaining to science and the beauties of Nature.

Socrates: Go ahead and comment.

Neal: Since we know that nature is a single indivisible Whole, we also know that there must be internal connections between any two or more aspects of that whole. Things that appear separate to human senses are nevertheless connected in ways that do not register to the senses, but *do* register in our scientific understanding of them. The human eye sees no connection between an orchid and a wasp, yet science understands that the two are intimate components of each other's reproductive systems. The eye sees no connection between trees and its own body's respiratory system, yet science understands that humans could not breathe at all without trees that produce oxygen. The eye sees no connection between a supernova that happened millions of years ago and its own body. Yet science tells us that without iron atoms created in that supernova, there would be no human bodies at all. So science gives us the details of the interconnectedness of all things, details that are amazingly beautiful to observe.

Socrates: Yes, that's why you're addicted to watching nature and science shows on TV; it is not just the knowledge and understanding of the details of interconnectedness, but just as importantly, the

Beauty conveyed by or through that knowledge and understanding.

William: And this will certainly be an ongoing component of our curriculum. All things are interconnected in ways not apparent to human senses. In fact, we may now define science as the study of the interconnections between and among all things. So you think our children should be watching these nature shows?

Neal: Yes, for knowledge, for beauty, and for inspiration. Aside from learning about the specific connections between specific things, like the wasp and the orchid, they will learn that most connections in Nature are hidden from human senses, but discoverable through Reason, which is the basis of all Science.

Benedict: So Reason can demonstrate things that are hidden from the senses. I agree with you that learning about these things from an early age will be inspiring for our children, but why do you think this is so? Why is learning about orchids and wasps, about supernovas and the human body, and countless other connections that are hidden from the senses but revealed by Reason – why does this inspire?

Neal: Before we can address this question, is it not incumbent upon us to define what we mean by the terms "inspire" and "inspiration"?

Benedict: Yes, I suppose you are right.

Neal: You seem somewhat reluctant?

Benedict: I fear the terms may be difficult to define, as they are used in different ways. Shall we examine several usages of the terms? Then maybe Plato here will help us find the thread that is common to all.

Plato: Or perhaps, like the term "love", we will recommend that some usages be discarded.

Neal: What do you mean?

Plato: Surely you haven't forgotten? We stated that love has a divine, not human, origin. Humans can experience this love, but they cannot create it. Hence we recommended that the word "love" not be used in connection with describing human sexual activities. We will not say, for example, that Johnny and Suzie are "making love" but rather, that they are enjoying their bodies together. It may be that a given sexual experience triggers a deeper experience of Divine Love, but that latter is something that humans do not "make". So it might very well be that some usages of the word "inspiration" will fall under a different heading.

Neal: *(smiling)* I think I see your point. On the one hand, Beethoven was inspired to write his *Ninth Symphony*. On the other hand, a few days ago I was inspired to clean up my kitchen.

William: *(laughing)* It would seem that these are quite different usages of the term, from the sublime to the mundane. Plato, you used the term "Divine Madness" to refer to poets who were overcome by the Muses, so to speak. That usage would cover Beethoven, but probably not Neal – unless you think there was some "Form" called "Cleanliness" that had infused itself into Neal's psyche at the time.

Plato: Well, you do have a saying that cleanliness is next to godliness, so maybe there was some semi-Divine Form that had momentarily overtaken him until he cleaned the kitchen, but I suspect that the source of that burst of energy that caused him to clean the kitchen had a less than divine origin. What say you, Neal?

Neal: I say that I got tired of my feet sticking to the floor and the sink full of dirty dishes.

(Laughter.)

Socrates: *(to me)* You know, it might be easier to seek for inspiration, or the definition thereof, from *our* side of the margins than from yours.

Neal: What do you mean?

Socrates: *(with humor)* I mean that in Beethoven's case there was a lot of activity on our side of the margins; in your case there was none.

Plato: OK, good, I think I can see how to begin.

Neal: How?

Plato: Did Beethoven "discover" or did he "create" that which is called "Beethoven's *Ninth*"? What do you think?

Neal: I think he discovered it.

Plato: Why?

Neal: Because the great majority of composers, artists,

mathematicians and scientists speak this way. What we call "creativity", as told by those individuals who we consider the most creative among us, appears to be a discovery of what is in some sense already there. What is called the creative process is a process that transcribes a vision into physical reality.

Plato: Could you write down that quote by Brahms that so inspired you when you first read it?

Neal: Here it is:

> Those vibrations assume the form of distinct mental images – straightaway the ideas flow in upon me – measure by measure the finished product is revealed to me when I am in those rare inspired moods...
>
> I have to be in a semi-trance condition to get such results – a condition where the conscious mind is in temporary abeyance, and the subconscious is in control, for it is through the subconscious mind, which is part of the omnipotence that the inspiration comes...
>
> ... in this exalted state I see clearly what is obscure in my ordinary moods: then I feel capable of drawing inspiration from above as Beethoven did...

William: My goodness, I'm still terribly fond of the late 19th century way of expressing these things. And Brahms must have written this before I set down my views in writing, so he couldn't have gotten it from me.

Neal: Gotten what from you?

William: That the human mind is part of the Divine Mind (referred to as the "omnipotence"), that we are connected with the Divine through what was called the "subconscious" mind – I prefer the term "subliminal" – which at the deepest levels is the same for all humans, that what is called "inspiration" involves being receptive to communication across the margins, from the eternal order into the temporal order, and that this receptivity requires that the ordinary conscious mind, what we have been calling "linguistic consciousness", be in temporary abeyance. There's a whole world-view – *our* world-view, packed into that little quote.

Neal: It appears to be the world-view of the majority of creative artists and scientists of the late 19th and early 20th century. Sometimes I feel a little sad that this world-view was abandoned in favor of behaviorist nonsense.

Socrates: Yes, but it had to be. You see, in the early 20th century, humans were not yet done with killing one another, so they needed to avoid any world-view that suggested we are all internally connected not only with a Higher Power, the omnipotence, but also with one another. Now, let's get back to Beethoven's *Ninth*. You say he discovered it, in the same sense perhaps that mathematicians say they discover their theorems and proofs. So in a sense, the music already exists. Is this what you mean?

Neal: Yes, in fact there is a quote from Mozart that makes this explicitly clear. Here, I found it:

> The whole, though it be long, stands almost complete and finished in my mind so that I can survey it at a glance. Nor do I hear in my imagination the parts successively, but I hear them, as it were, all at once. What delight this is I cannot tell!

Socrates: *(with humor)* Well, congratulations on finding it; no easy feat for you.

Neal: Thanks, and I found a few more quotes too. But this one reminds me of the "life-review" component of the Near-Death Experience. People report that however long their life was in years, they experience it all at once, and can survey the whole of it in a glance. So Mozart is stating that he "sees" (or "hears") a thirty-minute symphony "all at once", with all the parts already articulated. So clearly, he is in some sense discovering what is already "there", not inventing it.

William: Now I'm feeling a little sadness too. How different the world could have been if all the second-rate psychologists, philosophers, artists, and scientists that populate academia had listened to the recognized geniuses among them. At some point in the early 20th century, academics and artists abandoned the search for Truth and Beauty in favor of the search for reputation and career-advancement. Maybe, in addition to *The Varieties of Religious Experience,* I should have written something called *The Varieties of Aesthetic Experience*. But you say you have found some more relevant Mozart quotes.

Neal: Yes, and this one is reminiscent of that famous quote from Isaac Newton, who says that he is merely picking up pebbles on the beach, with the vast ocean of Being lying unexplored beyond. Mozart seems to be saying that there is a celestial music that not even he can grasp, but he knows it is there, and at some time will become available to humans. Here it is:

> I have never written the music that was in my heart to write; perhaps I never shall with this brain and these fingers, but I know that hereafter it will be written; when instead of these few inlets of the senses through which we now secure impressions from without, there shall be a flood of impressions from all sides; and instead of these few tones of our little octave, there shall be an infinite scale of harmonies – for I feel it – I am sure of it. This world of music, whose borders even now I have scarcely entered, is a reality, is immortal.

But wait, there's more!

> The wonders of the music of the future will be of a higher and wider scale and will introduce many sounds that the human ear is now incapable of hearing. Among these new sounds will be the glorious music of angelic chorales. As men hear these they will cease to consider Angels as figments of their imagination.

The world of music is a reality, is immortal, and is a world that even the greatest of human composers has "scarcely entered". The "glorious music of angelic chorales" exists and exists now and always. Perhaps the conditions of our New World Order will be such as to allow the "angelic chorales" to manifest in the temporal order. A number of Near-Death Experiencers report hearing celestial music, and Mozart seems to be envisioning a time when this music will become known to humans.

Plato: Well it seems that Mozart is clearly stating that his own process of composing music involves entering into the eternal order, at least partially, and copying down the music he "sees" in that order. Brahms talks about "drawing inspiration from above". But what about Beethoven? Surely, now that you have mastered the art of finding quotes on the Internet, you can find a few choice quotes from him too.

Neal: Yes, glad you asked; here are several:

> What is to reach the heart must come from above; if it does not come from thence, it will be nothing but notes, body without spirit.

> Music is the mediator between the spiritual and the sensual life.

> Music is a higher revelation than all wisdom and philosophy. Music is the electrical soil in which the spirit lives, thinks and invents.

> Music is the one incorporeal entrance into the higher world of knowledge which comprehends mankind but which mankind cannot comprehend.

> ... I hear and see the image in front of me from every angle as if it had been cast and only the labour of writing it down remains.

And, while I'm on a roll with these quotes, here are a few more by Brahms:

> Straight-away the ideas flow in upon me, directly from God, and not only do I see distinct themes in my mind's eye, but they are clothed in the right forms, harmonies, and orchestration.

And from Brahms again,

> All truly inspired ideas come from God. The powers from which all truly great composers like Mozart, Schubert, Bach and Beethoven drew their inspirations is the same power that enabled Jesus to do his miracles. No atheist has ever been or ever will be a great composer.

William: This last quote makes clear that "inspiration" – the term we are attempting to define – involves a felt connection with the Divine Being. The comparison to Jesus is instructive. The latter states, in the sexist language of his times, that by himself he can do nothing, and that his power comes from the Father. Brahms would have said that his power comes from "the omnipotence", from the eternal order. Music that is inspired connects the listener with the eternal order; music that is uninspired, that does not come from above, is "nothing but notes, body without spirit", as Beethoven put it.

Neal: Yes, and our music schools today teach only "body" because they are in collective denial about the reality of spirit.

Socrates: *(to me)* Are you done with the quotes?

Neal: Yes, although many more could be added, not only by other composers, but also by painters, poets, and scientists. Truly creative individuals throughout history are virtually unanimous in attributing the source of their creativity to inspiration from the Divine, or as William might put it, to incursions into human consciousness of energies that originate beyond the margins.

And so I think we can state definitely that Beethoven's *Ninth* was discovered, not invented. Now, Socrates, I think you should explain or elaborate upon what you meant when you said that in Beethoven's case there was a lot of activity on your side of the margins.

Socrates: I was sort of hoping you would allow that statement of mine to just slip by.

Neal: Why is that?

Socrates: If I could grab you by the soul and take you to where I am, you would see for yourself – not with the body's eyes, but with the soul's understanding – the full meaning of my statement. But if I am compelled to respond using only words, I fear my response will not adequately address the question.

Neal: Well, consider yourself compelled to respond, even under those limiting conditions.

Socrates: OK, but you must promise to keep Benedict here in check, for not even Plato's poetic license would permit me to use words in the way I shall now be using them.

Benedict: *(laughing)* Go ahead, dear friend, and I shall do my best to hold myself in check.

Socrates: Thank you. Remember a while ago we said that the rules of the theater apply to the human drama?

Neal: Yes, sort of. We said that for every individual onstage there are dozens more who are supporting that individual offstage. By analogy then, for every embodied soul there are dozens of non-embodied souls that are supporting the one who is embodied.

Socrates: Actually, the number is closer to infinity than to "dozens", but I will not even attempt to parse that with words. So all humans are supported by spirit. But what do you think catches our attention the most?

Neal: I'm tempted to say, "human suffering", but I suspect that's not the right answer.

Socrates: No, in part because human suffering is mostly self-caused, and we do not interfere with what humans want to experience. Right now, in this present moment, a memory has come to you, accompanied by strong emotions. When such things happen, you know it is not by accident, but is relevant to this writing. So share it.

Neal: I did not think much of this little story when I first heard it, but now, recollecting it is sending chills up and down my spine. I have forgotten the exact details of the story, but I think I can reconstruct it so as to preserve its meaning. Imagine a great artist, say a sculptor, who created many fine statues in a certain city, then left the city and went to live on the proverbial mountaintop. After a while, people took his statues for granted, ceased to admire them, and they became part of the ordinary background of people's daily lives. However, it happened that one young man noticed the statues, noticed their exquisite beauty, and began talking about and praising the beauty of the statues all around town. And even when the young man was not talking about the statues, he was thinking about them and their beauty almost constantly. Well, news of this young man and his appreciation of the statues' beauty reached even to the top of the mountain. The sculptor, the creator of the statues, said to himself, "Who is this young man who so deeply appreciates the beauty of what I have created? Surely I must go down to meet him, for he sees Beauty through my eyes, and we will have much in common."

Socrates: And so we might say that the Divine Being, upon receiving news that a given human is sincerely interested in Her, reaches out to the human. There are three interrelated ways in which a human shows interest in the Divine: (i) through an appreciation and love for Beauty, (ii) through a deep desire to know and understand, and (iii) through a deep desire for the well-being of all humans. Whenever a human is sincerely focused on either of these three paths, or any combination thereof – the way of Beauty, the way of Knowledge, and the way of Goodness – it catches the attention of the Creator, who reaches down and gives assistance. So when I said that there was a lot of activity on our side of the margins when Beethoven was writing the *Ninth*, I meant that his sincere and intense desire to clothe heavenly music in Earthly form, to bring Beauty itself into the temporal order as much as is possible, caught our attention and activated our support.

(With humor) But as for your "inspiration" to clean your kitchen, I regret to inform you that, alas, there was no activity on our side.

Plato: Now of course, the temporal order is not sufficient unto itself, and there is constant and continuous influence from one to the other. The stagehands on our side are always busy with day-to-day affairs. But unlike day-to-day affairs, those humans who seek the Divine through Beauty, Truth, and Goodness reach up to us in their thoughts and desires, and are constantly knocking at our door…

Socrates: … Sometimes even *banging* at our door, as was the case with Beethoven.

Plato: … so we are compelled to listen to them and give them what they want.

Socrates: And so we might state that inspiration occurs whenever humans knock at the door of Eternity.

Benedict: OK, I have held myself in check, at least until now. But as you have said, Socrates, there is always another way of looking at things.

Socrates: What I said, or what I meant to say, is, given that language cannot in principle capture the eternal order, and given that we are presently confined to using language, then it is useful to have different verbal expressions of the same thing. The "thing" here is inspiration. So I assume you have another way of describing this?

Benedict: Yeah, well this whole story is told in theistic language.

William: Theistic language?

Benedict: Yes. You knock on a door. Someone who lives inside, presumably God, opens the door, asks what you want, then gives it to you. But there is another way of describing it.

Neal: What do you mean?

Benedict: The "door" is a metaphor for the veil or margin that appears to separate our worlds. There is no one who comes to open the door. Rather, the process of knocking and banging is also the very force that causes a temporary thinning of the margins in the mind of the one who bangs. The thinning of the margins then in turn allows more Divine Light to flow from the eternal order into the temporal order, into the mind of the one who is knocking.

William: Well, however one says this in words, I think we may define inspiration as an incursion, sometimes sudden, sometimes gradual, of energies from the eternal order into the temporal order. The mechanism for *how* these energies cross the margins – whether through the grace of God or through the incessant banging of those who follow Beauty, Truth, and Goodness – probably cannot be described, except metaphorically.

Plato: I think we can accept this definition. There are two further points to discuss with regard to inspiration. We have used Beethoven as an example of one who was inspired; while he was composing his music he was receiving influences from the eternal order. But what about musicians who play his music, and audiences who listen to and are moved by his music? Shall we say that they are inspired too?

Neal: Oh, Plato, you know how I'm going to respond to this. I loved your analogy with a magnetic field.

Plato: A what?

Neal: Oh sorry, a lodestone or magnet and nails. You said the composer or poet is analogous to the magnet, the one(s) performing the music or enacting the play are analogous to the first nail attached to the magnet, and the audience listening to the music or watching the play is analogous to the second nail attached to the first. But what you could not have known back then was how good the analogy actually is. Modern physics – well, not so modern because it was known even in William's time – states that it is one and the same magnetic field that permeates both nails. The very same force that originates in the lodestone extends into both nails, although it is stronger in the first nail.

Plato: So we will state that the person who is moved by Beethoven's music, whether by performing it or listening to it, is inspired in the very same way that Beethoven was inspired when writing the music.

Neal: In fact the expressions "being moved" and "being inspired" refer to the same process, a process by which something from the eternal order makes itself felt in the temporal order.

William: It is interesting, is it not, to observe that many of our atheist friends and colleagues would attend performances of Beethoven's *Ninth* and be just as moved by the music as we were, but they would think that their experience was merely human emotion, rather than believe they were being touched by the Divine.

Plato: And this brings us to the second point we need to mention.

William: What's that?

Plato: Using the terms I originally used, I would say that humans generally cannot distinguish *divine* madness from madness brought about by mortal maladies. Beethoven was not the only creative composer, poet or scientist who was thought to be mad, and not divinely so, by his contemporaries. And many humans have been driven mad, not divinely so, by religious ideology. They falsely believe that they have become divine, or are following someone who is divine, whereas in fact their religious beliefs have rendered them criminally insane. I say "criminally" because they are quite happy to murder anyone who believes differently from themselves.

Neal: They are so insane that they believe they will get brownie points in heaven for murdering as many nonbelievers as possible. So religious ideology is a form of mortal madness that disguises itself as divine. But the poor humans who have internalized such insane beliefs actually believe that they are doing God's will, and their motivation can be very intense and their actions highly focused, just as if they were being truly inspired.

Benedict: OK, time for the semantic cops to make a brief appearance. The word "inspire", as we shall use it, carries implicit connotation of the eternal order. To be inspired *means* to be in touch with that order. The fruits of inspiration, the effects on individuals of being in touch with the eternal order, always and invariably result in an influx into the minds of said individuals of Knowledge, Goodness or Lovingkindness, and Beauty, and the associated desires to express these things in their lives. We will never say, of a person who is motivated to harm others, that he was "inspired" to do so. We will say instead that the person has become insane through identification with religious ideology; we will say that he was *motivated* by his ideology, but not that he was "inspired" by it. It is perhaps a bit arbitrary how these terms are used, but it is not a bad idea to reserve some terms, like "love" and "inspire", for use only with regard to what is divine in humans.

Socrates: You are right about the fruits, and that's one way that humans can tell the difference between those who are possessed by the gods and those who are possessed by mere ideology. The first kind of possession we call "inspiration", the second kind "madness". But from our perspective, we do not need to examine the fruits to tell the difference. We just see it directly. Shall I elaborate a little?

Neal: Please do.

Socrates: *(playfully)* A few examples will suffice: you know that every soul that takes on embodiment and comes to Earth is regarded as sort of a hero over here.

Neal: Hero? I thought that Earth was the very place that fools rushed in where angels fear to tread.

Socrates: *(laughing)* Well, perhaps there is not too great a difference between the two. At any rate, we recognize that embodied life is no easy thing for a soul, hence every soul that chooses to incarnate is provided with spirit guides and other means of support. Now I myself function as a sort of guide, and I know personally many other guides, including some of the guides that were assigned to Mozart, some that were assigned Hitler, and some that were assigned to a so-called "religious leader" somewhere in the troubled Middle East. Now in the case of Mozart, his guides once related to me something like the following: "Hey, Socrates, you know Mozart came up again for a little visit." "That's nice," I said, "What did he have to say?" "Well he really didn't want to talk much; he just sang for a while with 'the glorious music of angelic chorales', after which we gave him a few gifts, and then he hurriedly returned to his body to write down the gifts. What a joy!" But with the other two, the spirit guides were quite frustrated. One of them accosted me and said, "Socrates, I don't know if this spirit guide thing works. I'm screaming and shouting at him, but his insane beliefs are so tightly wrapped around his head that neither I nor any of the other guides can penetrate his beliefs. I feel like such a failure. He's going further and further into darkness, and bringing many others with him. Do I really have to hang around this soul for all the lifetimes it will take to repair the damage he is causing to himself? If I weren't an eternal being of some sort I would give up this spirit guide business right away."

So you can see that Mozart was *inspired*, in that he made frequent visits to our Home, which is his Home too. But the other two were not only **not** visiting Home, they were running away from it as fast as they could. So I think we are right to refrain from calling someone "inspired" who is running away from Source, rather than towards it.

Now, *we* can see the difference, but humans have much difficulty discerning who is running towards Source, and hence is inspired by a Divine madness, and who is running away from Source, and hence is motivated by merely mortal madness.

Neal: Well, we humans can tell the difference by examining the fruits, so to speak.

William: But this takes time, sometimes generations. It is especially difficult with regard to the moral dimension of human activity. But perhaps there *is* a more expedient way that might allow humans to recognize the difference between one who is moving towards Source, and hence is inspired, and one who is moving away from Source. I believe that a good medium could tell the difference just like we can. She could see us meeting up with those who are inspired, and see us desperately trying to get the attention of those who are running towards darkness.

Plato: Yes. We must remember that our New Society is very different from anything that has appeared before. Those who are "in charge" will all have had spiritually transformative experiences, either through the Near-Death Experience, through meditation, or sheer happenstance. Because of such experiences, they can "see" more clearly than other humans, and in most cases they will be able to tell whether a given human is Divinely inspired or merely suffering from mortal maladies. So humans will no longer be in danger of following after those who would lead them into darkness.

Benedict: I'd like to make a brief semantic point again: we have been using sensory language to discuss non-sensory experience. We have been saying things like: "we can see who is inspired and who is not" or "Mozart heard angelic chorales". But clearly, we do not have physical eyes, so we are not "seeing" with the body's eyes; and when Mozart was visiting us, neither was he "hearing" with his body's ears. A term like "cognize" might be more accurate than "see" and "hear", with regard to experiences in and of the eternal order.

Socrates: Good point. The case of Beethoven is instructive here, as he wrote his greatest music while completely deaf, and never heard it with his body's ears. So let's examine what he means when he states, "… I hear and see the image in front of me from every angle."

William: Yes, and applying this to a specific work, like the *Ninth*, we get, "… I hear and see the image of the whole symphony in front of me from every angle…" Clearly, when he uses the words "hear" and "see" he is not referring to physical hearing and physical seeing. He certainly knows he is deaf; hence the word "hear", as Beethoven is using it, cannot refer to physical sounds or ears at all. Rather, he is using these words, "hear" and "see", in the same sense that mystics and NDErs use these terms, when they talk about "seeing God" or "conversing with deceased relatives". It might be more accurate for Beethoven to have said, "I cognize the whole symphony from every angle," except that the word "cognize" might imply a deliberative process that takes time, whereas the words "hear" and "see" convey a sense of immediacy.

Socrates: So we shall forgive them the use of sensory language, but we ourselves shall notice when such language is meant literally, and when it is meant to refer to an immediate non-sensory cognition. But now I think it is time to address Benedict's question.

4) Why Knowledge Inspires

Neal: What question?

Socrates: The question that initiated this whole discussion about inspiration. He asked, and correct me if I'm wrong, "Why is learning about orchids and wasps, about supernovas and the human body, and countless other connections that are hidden from the senses but revealed by Reason – why does this inspire?"

Plato: Let us "deconstruct" the question by substituting, for the word "inspire", our definition of the term.

Benedict: Good. Then the question becomes, "Why does learning about connections that are hidden from the senses but revealed by reason constitute an incursion, into the mind of the learner, from the eternal order?"

Neal: I haven't thought about it like this before. But yes, I did feel moved and inspired when I studied the sciences that show deep interconnections between and among all things. Well, we have said that the eternal order, or the Divine Being, responds to three interrelated human motivations: the desires for Beauty, Knowledge, and Goodness. These three paths to the Divine Being appear separate at first, but merge into seamless Unity as the individual soul ascends to the Knowledge of the Divine, or rather, to Knowledge of its union with the Divine Being.

Benedict: OK, but if we're going to talk about "ascending", then we should state what the soul is ascending *from*, as well as what it is ascending *to*.

Neal: It is ascending from the human condition, from identification with the body.

Plato: Do you remember what we have said about the human condition, about that peculiar condition of consciousness called "human"?

Neal: Yes, I think we said that what is peculiar about the consciousness that manifests as human is that it experiences all things as separate from one another, and itself as separate from all things.

Plato: And this peculiar way of experiencing things is brought about by the soul's identification with a body, which necessarily generates what Einstein once called the "optical illusion" of separateness.

Neal: Wait a minute; I have the full quote here.

Benedict: *(jokingly)* I suppose there's no stopping you now that you've figured out how to extract quotes from the thing you call the Internet. Go ahead.

Neal: Here it is:

> A human being is a part of the whole called by us "the universe", a part limited in time and space. He experiences himself, his thoughts and feelings, as something separate from the rest – a kind of optical illusion of consciousness. This delusion is a kind of prison for us, restricting us to our personal desires and affection for a few persons nearest to us. Our task must be to free ourselves from this prison by widening the circle of understanding and compassion to embrace all living creatures and the whole of nature in its beauty.

William: I like how he conjoins the path of Knowledge ("understanding") with the path of Goodness ("compassion"). *(To Plato)* And stating that embodiment is "a kind of prison" surely must be pleasing to you.

Plato: Well of course. Where do you suppose he got that metaphor from, if not from me? At any rate, Einstein's view of the human condition is the same as ours. It is (i) a condition of consciousness in which consciousness experiences itself as separate, and (ii) this condition of consciousness is in some sense delusional; it is not an accurate depiction of the way things Really are. The world as experienced through the five senses is not the "real world".

Now here's where Benedict and I differ, not so much in our understandings, but in the way we talked about it. I would never use the term "knowledge" in conjunction with any sense-experience or any belief based on sense experience. I used the terms "belief" and "opinion" to describe whatever human consciousness gives assent to that originates in sense experience. Benedict, on the other hand, uses the rather dry expression, "knowledge of the first kind".

Benedict: *(with humor)* I suppose I should apologize for that, but what choice did I have, given that you've been hoarding that poetic license for all these centuries?

Plato: Yeah, well sorry about that. *(Laughing)*... Not that you would have known how to use such a license, even if you had it.

Benedict: I don't know. I thought I wrote a few funny jokes about Descartes, even without the license. In using that "dry" expression, I meant to refer to the "first" level of human epistemic experience, a level in which humans claim to know things. I referred to this epistemic level as "Imagination", because it is rooted in images of things provided by sense experience. Now I might change the wording, since Plato has persuaded me that it is rather strange to apply the word "knowledge" to something that is actually false. For example, an embodied consciousness experiences separateness through its senses, and based on that comes to believe that all things are separate from one another. This is a false belief, something that is imagined, but not something that is part of knowledge. So we should not use the word "knowledge" in conjunction with what is merely imagined.

Moreover, in the journey from infancy to adulthood, the human being internalizes many of the beliefs and opinions of others, either through hearing or reading about them. And so what I called "knowledge of the first kind", or the "Imagination", is an embodied consciousness that consists of sense experience, memories of previous sense experience, and internalized beliefs and opinions based on heresy.

Plato: Yes, and moving towards the further end of the human epistemic spectrum, we have what you so descriptively referred to as "knowledge of the third kind", and which I called simply "Knowledge" (with a capital K). It is the state of consciousness in which one experiences directly the union that exists between one's individual mind and the mind of God. More accurately, and more clumsily, one could say that it is the state of consciousness in which the individual experiences herself as the Divine Being manifesting as that individual.

Neal: *(to Plato)* Now in fairness to Benedict, we must mention that he did leave clues for the clueless, referring to knowledge of the third kind as our "salvation" and our "blessedness". But despite his clues, the clueless somehow managed to remain clueless. But let's keep Benedict's question in focus.

Plato: Don't worry, we're building our way to the answer. So, the human consciousness is a mode of consciousness to which things appear separate and unconnected. However, we have been teaching our children all along that this is not true. We have been nurturing them with "true opinion", so they have internalized true beliefs – that everything and everyone is interconnected so as to constitute a single One Mind, and that the Golden Rule is the right way to live one's life. As an aside, we may remark that if these things are not internalized at a young age, it is very difficult to arrive at them later in life.

Now as our children enter their teen years, and reason becomes activated within them, they learn through empirical science that what they were conditioned to believe as children is empirically true. This learning will be enormously satisfying and moving. We remind ourselves that the human experience called "being moved" is an experience that involves some influence, however slight, from the eternal order into the temporal order. It is uplifting – a lifting up of the soul – a turning around of the soul away from the temporal towards the eternal.

William: Our adolescent children will have a very different experience than the children of my time. As I've already stated, in my time we worried a lot about what we called a "crisis of faith". It was "reason vs. faith" or "science vs. religion". But this "crisis" was caused by the fact that the children had internalized false and even ridiculous beliefs about the Divine Being, beliefs that could not withstand even a little scrutiny – virgin births, the angry guy in the sky, hell, and all that nonsense. But *our* children will face no such crisis, since the beliefs they have internalized as children are in full accord with the deliverances of reason.

Neal: Yes, and I'd like to illustrate this with our most important teaching, the Golden Rule. Our children have been raised in a social order in which the Golden Rule is the norm. Everyone believes it, and the whole social order functions in accordance with it. Now that our children have become teenagers, and are able to reason, they will see quite clearly that the Golden Rule is the *only* Rule that, if everyone were to follow it, will guarantee a peaceful and harmonious world order. The "logic" will be obvious to them. They will also see, with their mind's eye, that if all minds are so interconnected as to constitute a single One Mind, then an attitude of lovingkindness is the only rational way for one mind to regard another.

Benedict: Our teenage children are now learning, or rather *(glancing at Plato)*, being reminded, that the world as seen through the body's eyes – a world in which everything appears separate – is not the Reality seen or understood through the mind's eyes, which reveals a world in which all things are interconnected. Empirical science corroborates to our children that their childhood beliefs are in fact true.

So we can now follow a given belief as it crosses three epistemic thresholds. (1) A child internalizes the belief that everything is interconnected, even though this is not what his body's eyes tell him. But the child does not *know* this; he merely believes and imagines it to be true. He has what Plato called "true opinion". (2) During adolescence he learns through science that his childhood beliefs are in fact true; he learns in some detail that all things are indeed interconnected, despite appearances to the contrary. He now knows – I would use the word "know" to refer to the deliverances of reason, although I'll spell it with a small "k". (3) Later in life, or perhaps even during adolescence, he may have what is called a mystical experience in which he experiences directly the interconnection of all things and all beings. Then he will Know (with a capital K) directly that all things are interconnected. He will even come to know, or Know, why and how his body determines its associated mind to perceive things as separate.

Plato: Good. Now in (3) the soul is completely turned around and experiences itself *as* itself, eternal, indestructible, and an intrinsic aspect of the One Mind. Under (2) it turns around only partially, but enough to realize that there is more than what is revealed by the body's eyes.

Socrates: And if I may, I would like to add that the experience of "being moved" occurs only under the second epistemic condition.

Neal: What? The experience of encountering the Divine Being directly – of seeing the sun outside the Cave – is not moving?

Socrates: Oh calm down. It's really just a little semantic point. The phrase "being moved" implies (i) there is someplace from which one is being moved, and (ii) there is someplace to which one is being moved. Do you agree?

Neal: Yes.

Socrates: The place *from which* one is being moved is what Benedict calls imaginative experience, where everything appears separate to consciousness?

Neal: Yes.

Socrates: And the place *to which* one is being moved is a state of consciousness in which one experiences the blazing sun outside Plato's cave, or less poetically, the knowledge of the union that exists between the individual mind and the One Mind?

Neal: Yes, I understand. So a soul that finds itself outside Plato's Cave and is experiencing the glory of its union with the Divine Being is no longer in the process of being moved. It has already been moved to where it always seeks to be.

Benedict: *(with humor)* And that was another clue I left for the clueless.

Neal: What?

Benedict: The word "glory". I explicitly used that word, as well as the words "salvation" and "blessedness", in conjunction with what I called Knowledge of the third kind, or the direct experience of union with the Divine. But I like Socrates' usage of the term "being moved"; it describes the journey of a soul as, with Reason as its guide, it moves away from the imaginative experience of separateness, through the knowledge given by science that all things are interconnected, and to the glorious experiential Knowing of its union with God. And I think that Plato has persuaded me to refrain from applying the word "know" or "knowledge" to any belief arrived at through sense experience and heresy, even if the belief involved is true.

Plato: So although our children *believe* that all things are interconnected, they neither know it nor Know it. The cause of their belief is upbringing. Similarly, in the moral sphere, they all believe that the Golden Rule is the right way to live. But the cause of this belief in their psyche is their upbringing. So they neither know nor Know that the Golden Rule is true. But during adolescence, their true beliefs will be converted into knowledge (with a small "k"), and this experience will be enormously *moving* to them. It will be very exciting for them, as it was for you, to learn that things that appear separate to human senses are intimately conjoined, like the orchid and the wasp, or a supernova and their own body. It is not just that what they are learning in their science courses is intrinsically interesting; it is also *inspiring* because it is moving them towards a deeper understanding of the intrinsic interconnectedness of all things.

Now, one little caveat: All children will have the same basic education, at least until the late teens, when some specialization may begin. All children will be exposed to basic science and learn something about the details of the interconnectedness, but not all children will take to it equally.

Neal: What do you mean?

Plato: The same as if I had said that all children will be exposed to gymnastics and music, but not all children will take to it.

Neal: Yes, I understand. Children, as embodied souls, have their own agendas and proclivities. An embodied soul intent upon honing bodily skills, like an athlete, or a soul who became embodied with the intent of bringing celestial music to earth, may not be as excited about learning the details of interconnectedness as a soul intent on following the path of knowledge. For them, it will be sufficient to stay with true opinion regarding the interconnectedness of all things. So with respect to the proposition that all things are interconnected, all people will have true opinion, many will have knowledge, and some will have Knowledge.

Benedict: But the conversion of true belief to knowledge is moving for all embodied souls, even if many do not take to it. I think it may be useful to examine this pattern with respect to a few other "true beliefs" that have been inculcated into our children.

Neal: Hey, I just realized something.

Benedict: What?

Neal: What you called "the dictates of reason" are the very "true beliefs" we have been inculcating into our children.

Benedict: Yes, and we may examine some in more detail later, when we discuss the Moral Law and the right conduct of life. Right now we are examining the most general beliefs, often called "metaphysical", that underlie the Moral Law. We have examined one such belief, that all things are interconnected, even though they don't seem to be interconnected to the body's eyes. Another such belief is that they, the children, are aspects of an immortal soul whose true home is the eternal order, not the temporal order in which they seem to find themselves.

Neal: Yes, this belief can be converted to knowledge through the study of science, or reason, and then converted to Knowledge through direct experience of themselves as their soul.

William: Science has discovered an eternal order underlying the temporal order? That's a question, not a statement.

Neal: Yes, quite definitely. You've heard of the Big Bang?

William: Yes, sort of. The physical universe begins with a Big Bang, or something like that.

Neal: The important point here is that according to science, space and time do not preexist, but rather come into existence with the Big Bang. So now, does the Big Bang have a Cause?

William: Benedict has persuaded me that all things have a cause.

Neal: Then the Cause of the Big Bang cannot exist in the temporal order, because the temporal order is what comes into existence with the Big Bang.

William: Hence there must be a nontemporal order of Being, an *eternal* order, in which the Cause of the Big Bang resides.

Neal: And since a Cause is always more powerful than its effects, the eternal order is greater than the temporal order. Moreover, since the eternal order is unaffected by the passage of time in the temporal order, it follows that the Cause of the Big Bang is operating *now*, and therefore we can assert that the temporal order, the whole physical universe, is continuously emanating from its eternal Source, or Cause.

William: And we will add to this, with respect to our children's upbringing, that they themselves are intrinsically connected to the eternal order through their soul.

Socrates: It goes without saying that we will teach this to our children, or rather, cause them to believe this, through age-appropriate stories. "Conviction persuasion" comes first, then "knowledge persuasion".

William: … So our children will have a sense that there are deeper levels to their own being than what they consciously experience. Then during adolescence this belief will be converted to the knowledge that they are intrinsically connected to a "Something More". I find it interesting that there is more than one path to this knowledge.

Neal: I see what you mean. One path might be through theoretical physics; another path, perhaps easier than the former for most, would involve a study of what is now called transpersonal psychology.

William: What?

Neal: You know, the subconscious or subliminal mind. A ton of studies now show beyond any reasonable doubt that the personality, or temporal mind, is deeply connected both (i) to aspects of itself that are nontemporal, and (ii) to other minds that are nontemporal. An example of the first would be a person who recollects a "past life", and an example of the second would be a person who gets a visit from their deceased grandma.

William: And because of a thinning of the margins, and even more importantly, because there will be no taboos against openly discussing such experiences, our children will be having them all the time. We can tell them that Grandma has gone Home to the eternal order, and no longer exists in the temporal order. But we shall also tell them that Home is where they came from and is the common destiny of all humans. So at a general level, they will have internalized the belief that they are "something more" than what they take themselves to be on the basis of sense experience alone.

Socrates: It is good to observe that there are several ways that this or any true belief may be converted into knowledge. But one very important way is through the testimony of those who *have* Knowledge. Mystics and NDErs have experienced the eternal order directly. They have experienced themselves *as* the magnificent eternal beings that they are, and they will share their experiences with our children.

William: We won't say that another's testimony constitutes knowledge in the mind of the hearer, but we will say that it forms an important part of the evidential basis for such knowledge, along with parapsychology and theoretical physics.

Plato: So there are many ways by which true belief may be converted to knowledge, but only one way that either true belief or knowledge may be converted to Knowledge, and that is by direct experience. But the conversion of true belief to knowledge, through reason and science, is itself an experience that *inspires*. The story of the orchid and the wasp *inspires* because it shows in detail that things that appear separate to the senses are in fact intimately connected with one another. The story of the human body and the supernova *inspires* – that is, brings about an influx of spiritual energies into the psyche of the hearer – because it shows in detail that the human body is intimately connected with events in seemingly remote parts of the universe.

Neal: We should also note that the deeper one goes into knowledge, there is an aesthetic sense of beauty. All great scientists experience this sense of beauty. And conversely, the deeper one goes into beauty, there is a noetic sensibility of truth. Beethoven's

Ninth is not just beautiful; it is also true. Great paintings are not only beautiful, but they also capture and express truth. But what about moral knowledge, or goodness?

Plato: What about it?

Neal: According to our ideas, the moral sensibility should be enlivened as one follows the paths of beauty or understanding. Conversely, as one follows the path of Goodness, both the understanding and the aesthetic sensibilities should be enlivened.

Socrates: By "the path of goodness" you mean those individuals who are led by the Form of Justice and concerned primarily with helping others and making the world a better place?

Neal: Yes.

Socrates: So you are thinking of doctors, therapists, nurses, and teachers?

Neal: Yes.

Socrates: What about police, firemen, and the men who sweep the streets and collect the garbage?

Neal: One doesn't usually think of the garbage man as being involved in a "helping profession", although what he does is indispensably helpful to society.

Socrates: How about the farmer, the plumber, carpenter, and mailman? Isn't what they do helpful and beneficial to our social order?

Neal: Yes, and I can see where you're going with this.

Socrates: Oh? Where am I going?

Neal: Here's a little analogy: every cell within the body is created by the body and serves a function that benefits the body and hence, all the cells within the body. The human soul, including its embodied aspects, is created by the World Soul and serves some function that benefits the World Soul and hence, all the other souls within the World soul. So there is no human being and no social role that is not of benefit to others.

Socrates: Good. Then one major difference between our New Social Order and your present one is that this will be common knowledge to all, and all will rejoice in the knowledge that what they are doing is in fact helping others.

William: Keep in mind that those individuals and professions in our current society that are intent on *harming* others, not helping them, will be gone. The Wall Street bankers who gamble with other people's money, the advertising industry, and those politicians and lawyers who serve them will all be gone.

Benedict: Yes, we stress again that greed and personal ambition will be regarded as forms of insanity, and there will be no social roles for such people, until they have become cured of their illness. But because of upbringing, it is unlikely that such mental illness will be anywhere nearly as widespread in our society as it is in yours.

William: So everyone will have the sense that they are contributing to the well-being of the larger whole to which they belong. This sense is a source of peace, comfort and joy.

Neal: My goodness, yes. Think about it. No one works or takes a job or goes into a profession for the sake of making money. Financial security is a given. So everyone will have a sense of belonging to and contributing to the well-being of a larger whole.

Plato: What about a person who has been inspired by the Muses and from an early age desires nothing but to follow her Muse into music, poetry, painting, dance, and has no conscious thoughts about benefiting others? Would you say that she is in a "helping profession"?

Neal: I wouldn't put it that way, but yes, many people are benefited by watching or listening to what she does.

Plato: And what about those on the path of knowledge and understanding? They are eager to understand how it all works, so to speak, and are not explicitly concerned with helping others. Shall we say that nevertheless what they do is indeed helpful to others?

Neal: Yes, definitely. To give one of many examples, James Maxwell was concerned only with understanding how electricity and magnetism works. Yet modern life would be impossible without the equations he discovered and that bear his name.

Plato: It's as if the gods wanted to give humanity the gift of electricity. In order to do that, they first had to give the understanding or knowledge of electricity to humans. This understanding can come only to minds who are actively seeking it, who are following the path of Holy Curiosity, as was the case with Maxwell. Once the understanding was in the human mind, then practical applications soon followed.

Benedict: I'd like to emphasize something in your little analogy above. Every cell in the body, merely by existing, is *useful* and *helpful* to the body as a whole, and hence also to every other cell within the body. All the cell has to do to maximize its usefulness is to be itself. The same is true for human beings. A given human who desires to be helpful and of service to others need only consult her innermost desires, for those desires were implanted into her by her Creator, the World Soul. And even if a given individual does not explicitly desire to help others, by following his own desires he will automatically be helpful to others in ways that may not be obvious. It was not obvious to Maxwell that by following his desire to understand electricity he would in fact be enormously helpful to the whole of Humanity. So one does not need to join any of the overt "helping professions" in order to be of help to others. One need only follow one's own true desires. Of course I need hardly mention that desires for fame and riches are not "true" desires, since they can form no part of the soul's original purpose for incarnating.

Plato: Yes, and this must be kept in mind. It is one thing, and an admirable thing too, for a given human to be able to hear the voice for reason in his own mind, when the whole social order is saturated with the loud and noisy voices for greed and ambition. But those noisy voices will be gone, so there will be nothing that prevents humans from following the voice for reason, which as Benedict implied earlier is a divine guide implanted in the mind of every human being.

Socrates: And now I think we must address the third and most difficult part of reason.

Neal: What do you mean?

Socrates: A little review: the first part of reason we called "deductive thinking" by which the mind deduces logical consequences from given premises and/or hypotheses. The second part of reason we called "inferential thinking", by which the mind infers hypotheses based on empirical observation. This generates the whole of what is called "science". But the third and by far most important part of reason we may call "moral thinking", as it involves applying reason to one's own personal life.

Plato: In the moral sphere, reason is the same as conscience. Whenever a human does something or is about to do something that involves harming another, she will very likely feel what you call a twinge of conscience. Something within will bother her, unless she has been so damaged by your current culture that she is completely deaf to what is within her. This is the Voice for Reason, which is a gift from the gods.

5) The Voice For Reason

Neal: I've found a relevant quote.

Plato: I see there's no stopping you now. You're becoming quite the quotaholic, so to speak. I assume the quote pertains to reason.

Neal: Yes, and it complements the earlier quote about reason by Benedict, except it is a little less poetic.

Plato: Good, *(glancing at Benedict, very mischievously)* we certainly don't need another quote that indulges in poetic excess – spirit guides and all that – when we are trying to be serious about the nature of reason. Now, let's have the quote.

Neal: There are several versions. Here is one:

> A man who wishes to lead a good and happy life must be led by reason. If his own reason is not enough to guide him, he must be led by the reason of others.

(Plato blushes slightly.)

Benedict: *(laughing, with dramatic emphasis)* Why Plato! How unpoetic! I didn't know you had it in you to be so matter of fact about a subject so dear to your heart. I commend you for *not* using your poetic license in this quote that Neal has dug up.

Neal: Not so fast, Benedict. I also dug up other translations of this same quote, some of which render the passage less unpoetic and more equivalent to your own statement.

Plato: We don't need additional translations. I'm right here and can tell you what I meant.

Benedict: *(with humor)* Nevertheless, I'm eager to hear the other translations, especially if it turns out that you were saying the very same thing about reason for which you teased me earlier.

Neal: I'm going to indulge Benedict, because I think it will be useful to show that the two of you, the historical Plato and the historical Spinoza, held identical views on the nature of reason. This is a fact of which today's scholars are completely unaware. Here are a few other translations:

> It is better for everyone to be ruled by divine reason, preferably within himself and his own, otherwise imposed from without, so that as far as possible all will be alike and friends, governed by the same thing.

> It's better for everyone to be ruled by what is divine and wise. Ideally he will have his divine and wise element within himself, but failing that, it will be imposed on him from the outside, so that as far as possible we may all be equal, and all friends, since we are all under the guidance of the same commander.

> It is better for everyone to be led by a divine and wise ruler – preferably one that is his own and that he has inside himself; otherwise imposed from outside…

> It's better for everyone to be ruled by something godlike and intelligent, best of all when he has it for his own within himself, but otherwise as something imposed from outside, so that as far

> as possible everyone may be like-minded and friends, guided by the same thing.
>
> It is better for everyone to be governed by the divine and intelligent, preferably indwelling and his own, but in default of that imposed from without…

Benedict: *(jokingly)* I rescind my previous commendation. I suppose we could digress for a while and talk about issues of translation, but isn't it interesting that the four latter translations do not even use the word "reason". Which do you prefer, Plato?

Plato: They're all OK, except for the first.

Benedict: What do you mean?

Plato: The Greek word that usually translates as "reason" has connotations of being intrinsically connected with the Divine. But the English word "reason" lacks those connotations, and so someone reading only the first translation may come to think that by "reason" I mean nothing more than what we have called "calculative thinking". Nothing could be further from the truth. Calculative thinking forms a part of reason, as we have said, but only the smallest part. The greater part of reason concerns the right conduct of life, which is why you, Benedict, entitled your book the *Ethics*. But we are completely agreed that adjectives like "divine", "godlike", "wise" and "intelligent" accurately characterize the nature of reason, for these qualities originate in the eternal order, and well-characterize the "good spirit", as you put it, that can guide a human from the illusion of separateness to the knowledge of Oneness.

Benedict: Well said. And I believe that you have succinctly stated the goal of our whole system of education.

Neal: What goal?

Benedict: It is to activate the Voice for Reason within the mind of every child.

Neal: Yes, and moreover, our children are being raised in a social order that is permeated with Reason, through and through. So if a given individual is not able to hear Reason's Voice within herself, it will be imposed from without. Maybe I should reverse this and say that reason has already been imposed on them from without, as they have been raised to believe and follow your "dictates of reason", such as the Golden Rule, before they are old enough to understand that these rules are in fact "dictates of reason".

William: And there's one more thing in that little quote that is important. When humans allow themselves to be ruled by the "voice" for greed or the "voice" for reputation and status, they are contrary to one another. True friendship is not possible in a social order that requires people to compete for such things. For if two people compete for something that only one can possess, friendship is not possible. You cannot wish another success if his success means your failure. But the Voice for Reason is the same for all humans. This Voice, originating in what is Divine and godlike, explicitly states that one should not desire anything for oneself that one does not desire for all humans. When our "commander" is reason, instead of greed and ambition, then humans will become gentle, friendly and happy, both within themselves and towards others.

Plato: Now, just before you started with the quotes, we were about to take up the third and most important part of Reason. This has to do, not with deductive or inferential thinking, but with the right conduct of life.

Socrates: I think you mean something more than just conduct.

Plato: What more do I mean?

Socrates: If by "conduct" you mean a person's behavior, then...

Neal: Yes, oh my, I see it. We are not primarily concerned with behavior, but with *feeling* and *emotion*. For how a person behaves in any situation is determined by her feelings and desires in that situation. So the Voice for Reason must concern itself primarily with emotions and desires.

Plato: Absolutely. A social order like yours may pass laws against murder, rape, and theft, but such laws will be ineffective as long as the culture, through its values, raises people to do just those things.

In a culture that lives under the guidance of reason, the desires themselves will have been eliminated, or nipped in the bud as they occur.

Socrates: Yes, and as I said before, or maybe Plato said it, it was a source of amusement for us to observe greedy legislatures trying to pass laws limiting their own greed. Greed cannot be overcome by passing laws, but it *can* be overcome first through proper upbringing, and then by awakening the Voice for Reason in the minds of our children.

Benedict: Now, although our Social Order has made heroic efforts to prevent the arising of dysfunctional emotions and desires in our children, nevertheless such emotions and desires will necessarily arise, although they will be considerably weaker in *our* children.

Neal: Why do you say that?

Benedict: Because such emotions come with the territory of embodiment. It is not possible to take on human form without experiencing the limitations of the body: indeed, that is the very point of the soul's taking on human form. These limitations – limitations that the soul imposes upon itself – include our "usual suspects" of envy, greed, jealousy, anger, and so forth. But our Social Order will be on the lookout for such emotions as they arise in our children. Just as we have "doctors of the body" who monitor and care for our children's physical health and well-being, so also we will have "doctors of the psyche" who monitor and care for our children's psychological health and well-being. When a child comes down with a physical illness, whether a fever or a broken leg, everything else comes to a halt until the illness is cured, especially if that illness is contagious. But nothing is more contagious than the emotions of greed and ambition, and the desires that spring from these emotions; so whenever a child exhibits symptoms of this illness, he or she will be receive immediate attention until the illness is cured or contained.

Neal: I'd like to give an example of this, how it might work in practice.

Benedict: Go right ahead.

Neal: OK. Eight-year-old Johnny watches his older siblings playing chess. He is fascinated by the game, the pieces, and how absorbed his siblings get while playing the game. He decides he wants to learn the game.

Benedict: Good for him. Continue.

Neal: So his mother patiently teaches him how the pieces move and some of the rules. He now thinks he knows how to play chess, and nags his big sister into playing with him. He loses of course. And loses again, and again. He feels very upset and angry with himself. He might envy his sister. He might project the anger onto his sister, or onto himself, believing that he's not smart enough to play chess. Or he might become fixated on winning.

Benedict: Yes. This is not of course just about chess, but about *any* activity or skill a child attempts to learn.

Neal: Now, we do not expect an eight-year-old child to have the skills that would enable him to cope with his emotions. In the present dysfunctional society, these emotions are not regarded as an illness, and are allowed to fester within the psyche of the child. The child's personality then develops around these sick emotions. But the Social Order in which *our* children are raised is itself under the guidance of reason, and *does* have the skills needed to assist the child. So a child who is ill in this way will be lovingly cared for by others until the illness passes. This is an example of Reason guiding the child externally.

But as Plato said, the goal of our social order is to produce adults who have the Voice for Reason within themselves, so they don't have to go running off to a therapist whenever they feel upset about something, but have the tools to handle their own emotions as they arise. In fact, this could be our definition of a mature adult: one who has the power ("virtue" was the term you used) to observe a dysfunctional emotion as it arises within herself, and to apply the remedy immediately. This is what it means to live according to the guidance of reason, or to allow reason to function as a divine guide living within one's own mind.

And I think our children will be capable of this by the time they reach the mid or late teens. I'm reminding myself that our children have been discussing these things in small groups all the time, so there will be much support and encouragement for them as they internalize the voice for reason, or equivalently, awaken what is "divine and intelligent" within themselves.

Plato: So a person is said to be a "mature adult" when he or she no longer needs to rely on the Reason that permeates Society, but has it for herself. Perhaps there should be some sort of "rite of passage" ceremony when a child has made this transition. But there is another way to describe this process, which will be useful to state.

Neal: *(glancing at Socrates)* There is always "another way" to express things in words.

Plato: Earlier we were talking about the conversion of true opinion to knowledge (with a small "k") and the subsequent conversion of knowledge to Knowledge (with a capital "K"). Actually it is not uncommon for a human to move from true opinion directly to Knowledge, bypassing the intermediate stage of reason. We took the proposition that *all things are interconnected* as an example of a true belief that is inculcated into our children at an early age. The transformation of that proposition from true belief into knowledge occurs in two ways: (i) empirically, through science, children learn something of the details of the interconnections, and (ii) logically, as Benedict did, by deriving the proposition from self-evident first principles. But now we are concerned with true opinion concerning propositions that involve the right conduct of life, such as the Golden Rule, or the dictum that "one should not desire for oneself what one does not equally desire for all human beings". The process by which these and other moral dictums transition from "true belief" to "knowledge" in the minds of our children is the very same process by which Divine Reason becomes activated in their psyches. So let's consider how the Golden Rule might transition, in the mind of an individual child, from something that is believed to something that is known.

Socrates: It goes without saying, but I'll say it anyway, that the transition to the Knowledge of direct experience may occur anytime in a person's life, or not at all. This latter transition is not governed from the human side of the margins, but whenever it occurs, the soul is completely awakened and Knows with certainty that the Golden Rule is true and is unable to live any other way. But please continue.

Plato: OK. Now we must state the Golden Rule more carefully, and especially, we must be clear about the force of the word "should". *Why* should a human being live this way?

Neal: Yes, we want to rule out "religious" reasons.

William: Wait a minute. Slow down. What do you mean by "religious" reasons.

Neal: You know, behave decently because if you don't you're going to go to Hell. Or the reason you should follow the Golden Rule is because it says so in our holy books.

William: Ah yes, I see, we shall be giving our children empirical or psychological reasons, rather than reasons based on fear or external authority. We will convince them that if they want to be happy in their personal lives, then they must strive to live according to the Golden Rule. Of course, because of how we have raised them, our children are already happy and already living according to the Golden Rule. Now they must learn the reasons why. There are already studies that show that inner happiness is correlated with an attitude of lovingkindness towards others.

Socrates: And we will tell them horror stories about past social orders that they will hardly believe.

William: Horror stories?

Socrates: Yes, we will tell them that once upon a time there were societies in which people did not live this way, and instead of following the Golden Rule, they allowed themselves to be ruled by what is worst within themselves: greed and ambition. As a consequence of this, the people lived lives of suffering and misery.

Neal: *(jokingly)* Yes, but we don't want to frighten our children too much with such horror stories.

Socrates: *(with humor)* Not to worry. We will not tell them of such things until they are old enough to handle it, say around the early teens. But you raise a more serious point, although it will not apply to our children.

Neal: What point?

Socrates: Many if not most people in your culture refrain from harming others because they fear a greater harm befalling themselves, by punishment either in this life or in the next. But *our* children will behave decently because of love, not fear.

Plato: Yes, now children will follow the Golden rule out of habit; that's how we have raised them. Those who have Knowledge – NDErs, mystics – will follow the Golden Rule automatically, because they experience, or have experienced, other human beings *as* themselves. For there is only "One Mind" in which "we live and move and have our being". But in between habitual behavior and Ultimate Knowledge is divine reason, and we want to awaken this faculty in the minds of all our citizens, or as many as possible, and this will be done in many ways, the study of History being one. So they will know what happens to people who live in social orders dominated by greed and ambition. They will see that such a social order produces little happiness, even in those who are rich and famous; they will see that such a social order produces much suffering and misery.

Benedict: They will see that this is true empirically, but they will also see – and here's where reason comes in – that this is true **necessarily**. An individual who is ruled by greed *is not* happy in fact, and *cannot* be happy in principle. A social order in which greed and ambition are the norm must necessarily produce great unhappiness among the people. So the study of history will be useful.

William: And so is the study of psychology and human emotions. Psychologists have already – well, not in my time, but in Neal's – discovered that happiness is not correlated with wealth or fame, or even the pursuit of pleasure. Well, our children won't need psychologists to tell them wherein lies their happiness because it will be obvious to them from experience, including the experience of sharing their innermost thoughts and feelings with one another. Actually the experience of honest sharing – which most people do not have in the present culture – is itself a source of considerable happiness.

Benedict: Yes, and as it turns out, not by coincidence, what we earlier called the three motivations of the soul (seeking knowledge, seeking to develop abilities and skills, helping others) are the three great sources of happiness for embodied souls. It makes sense, does it not, that fulfilling the original motivations of the soul leads to the greatest happiness possible for humans. We used the expression "helping others" but this now needs to be subsumed under the larger category of "joining with others", so as to include the ongoing sharing in small groups. For to help another is to join with them, and the mutual honest sharing of thoughts and feelings is helpful both to the one who shares and the one who listens.

Neal: I'd like to share a story that I think is relevant here.

William: Go right ahead.

Neal: A woman whose teenage son was murdered made a conscious decision to forgive the murderer. She arranged to visit the murderer in prison, after which she continued to visit him, and over a period of years they became friends. The story moved me to tears. It also convinced me of the convergence of the three paths, for I experienced great beauty in what she had done, and it also seemed to be the right thing to do, even though no one would have blamed her had she not forgiven him.

Benedict: No one would have blamed her, yet we know that holding a grudge against someone, even a murderer, constitutes an obstacle to the Knowledge of the union that exists between the individual mind and the Mind of God. For the same "One Mind" that manifests as the mother and her son also manifests as the murderer. The quickest and most direct path for the mother to heal is to join minds with the murderer, which awakens within herself a deep sense of interconnectedness not usually allowed by social custom.

William: And the experience of "being moved" is an incursion of higher energies into the temporal order. If the mother of a murdered boy can forgive and befriend the person who murdered her son, then there can be no reason why any other human cannot forgive anyone who has harmed them, so Benedict's inspiring vision is a real possibility, not some mere poetic fantasy.

Benedict: Ah, "inspiring vision"? What are you talking about? *(Jokingly)* But please tell me in a way so that Plato doesn't hear.

Neal: I doubt I can grant your wish, but here's what you wrote:

> Human beings can wish for nothing more excellent for the flourishing of their own being than that they should all be in such harmony in all respects that their minds and bodies should compose, as it were, one mind and one body, and that all together should endeavor as best they can to flourish, and that all together they should aim at the common advantage of all. From this it follows that men who are governed by reason, that is, men who aim at their own advantage under the guidance of reason, seek nothing for themselves that they would not desire for the rest of humanity; and so are just, honest, and honorable.

Plato: It is "like" Socrates' cells in a bar, who do not realize they are each ruled by the same DNA. But when they have reached deep inside themselves and discovered their genetic material, which is the same for each cell, then they are able to live in harmony with one another. So when our young adults discover the Voice of Reason within themselves – the "still small voice", as it has been called – which is the same for every human, they will collectively function as a single being, and Beethoven's vision of universal brotherhood will have been realized. It is the voice of reason that converts true opinion into knowledge.

William: So our children's own experience of actually living in a social order governed by reason, or the Golden Rule, compared with the experience of other societies that worshipped greed and self-aggrandizement, constitutes one part of the process by which true opinion is converted into knowledge. Another will be a detailed study of human psychology, with emphasis on the causes of human suffering and human joy. They will understand, as the Buddha taught, that the desire for status is itself the cause of suffering both for oneself and for others. They will also discuss among themselves that "twinge of conscience" they feel when tempted by greed, and learn to identify that twinge of conscience as the "godlike", "intelligent", "wise" and "divine" voice for reason within themselves.

Neal: And it seems to me that the conversion of true belief into knowledge will not be complete without an understanding of the logical component. If one were to ask: how may human beings live together so as to maximize happiness and well-being for all, then it follows logically that the Golden Rule is the **only** rule which, if followed by all, satisfies our criterion.

William: I have to smile a little. You know, this insight will put many of our colleagues out of business. Neither my former colleagues nor yours are able to follow the logic here, and instead invent for themselves very convoluted intellectual systems of ethics.

Benedict: Which has nothing to do with "ethics" in the sense of the term I used in titling my book…

Neal: And appears to be little more than systems of rules for greedy people so that they may appear "ethical" while preserving their greed. Academics desire status within their professions, and whatever verbiage they come up with will necessarily be one that legitimizes their desire for status and reputation. But real ethics, real morality, begins only when the very desire for status and reputation is challenged. For no one who desires status and reputation can live according to the Golden Rule. This is a point of logic, since those very desires move in a direction opposite to the Golden Rule.

William: The fact that they cannot see the simplicity of the logic behind the Golden Rule testifies to the depth with which they have internalized the values of reputation and status-seeking.

Plato: So now, let's summarize the process by which the Golden Rule gets converted from true opinion to knowledge in the minds of our children:

(i) *logical:* (a) The Golden Rule is the only rule for living that, if followed by everyone, yields maximum happiness and well-being. Also, (b) the Golden Rule is a logical consequence of the proposition that all beings are interconnected with one another so as to constitute a single "One Mind".

(ii) *empirical:* (a) The study of past social orders shows that suffering and misery always accompany deviations from the Golden Rule; (b) the study of science that shows the details of the interconnectedness of all things also supports the Golden Rule (Who would have thought that the quantum theory has moral implications?); (c) the study of parapsychology shows that there are intrinsic connections between and among humans that bypass ordinary sensory channels; and we must also include (d) the testimony of mystics and Near-Death Experiencers.

(iii) *psychological:* Our children are emotionally intelligent; they can feel their own emotions, as well as the emotions of others. The "small-group" sharings in which they have participated all their lives – and will continue to do for the remainder of their lives – has given them the direct experience of connecting with others. They have experienced the sense of well-being that arises from helping another. They have all experienced that "twinge of conscience". Discussing these things with one another will greatly reinforce the Golden Rule within themselves. They will see that they have been living according to this rule by upbringing; now they will follow the Rule by choice, for they will see that to live in any other way is to invite suffering and misery into their lives.

Benedict: When they were little, the voice for reason was imposed on them from without. We do not expect a three year old to have the maturity to refrain from throwing a temper tantrum at the local supermarket when Mommy does not buy for him whatever he wants; and neither do we expect siblings to cease and desist their infamous rivalry with one another. So their behavior will be controlled from without. But we *do* expect the mature adults in our society to be the guardians of their own inner being, to recognize their ever-fluctuating emotions, such as guilt, anxiety, anger, and especially feelings of envy and jealousy, however slight, and to be able to process such emotions by themselves. And if they are not able to process the emotions by themselves, they will seek help from others.

Neal: Perhaps an analogy with the body may be useful here. If a small child scrapes his knees or cuts himself, Mom or Dad will clean the wound and apply a bandage. A child in her teens will be able to clean the wound and apply a bandage by herself. But if the wound is severe, she will know she cannot fix it by herself, and she will seek external help. Similarly, when a small child scrapes her emotional knees, so to speak, Mom or Dad, or a teacher or older child, will be there to clean the wound and apply the bandage. But by the time they reach their mid and late teens, they will be able to clean the wound and apply the bandage by themselves. Without this ability (which the majority of adults in the present society do not have), no one will be considered fully mature. But for deeper emotional wounds, there will be plenty of healers and therapists to help; perhaps the most effective therapy will come in the form of honest sharing of emotions with others. For as we have said, the process of honest sharing with others connects one to others, and this connecting with others is always intrinsically healing.

Chapter VIII

Adults

1) What Will People Talk About?

Socrates: Well good, and here we are. We have raised our children well. In their late teens, they have not only made friends with their sexual energies – no small accomplishment – but they have also made friends with what is "godlike and intelligent" within themselves, namely, the Voice for Reason. Perhaps some sort of ceremony is in order, welcoming them as adults into our New Social Order. But we cannot leave the matter there, for life and learning, and challenges to life and learning, do not end when the child reaches adulthood. So we will follow our children as they move through the various stages of life: youth, child-bearing and parenting, midlife, old age, and death. We must give some sense of what life will be like for our citizens, not in every respect of course, since there is much we cannot now foresee.

Neal: I sometimes find myself wondering about that. For instance, what will people talk about?

William: What do you mean?

Neal: Well, most of the things people talk about now will not be relevant in our New Society. Many people enjoy gossiping, complaining about others or about their situation. Or they like to brag about their children, their income, status, who they know, etc. But money will be a thing of the past that no one will talk about, except maybe in History classes. And our children understand that their happiness lies in fulfilling their soul's original purpose in manifesting as human. Status and reputation are not part of that original purpose, so they won't be talking about that. No one will be using speech as a means to impress others.

Benedict: Well then, it seems there will be a lot less talking. Our citizens will be comfortable with silence.

Plato: And silence is a great blessing. People will be comfortable with silence because they will be comfortable and at ease with themselves.

Socrates: When humans no longer use speech to complain, brag, or deceive, then at long last humans will be able to use speech to actually communicate with one another.

Neal: I see it. People will use language to communicate their true thoughts and emotions, their conscious experiences, and what they are truly interested in. When language is used to complain, brag and deceive, there is no real connection between humans. *Real* communication occurs only when people are completely honest. So our teenagers, and hence our adults, will not be using language to compete for attention, since our Social Order has given everyone the attention and support they need. If any teenager, or adult for that matter, feels insecure or otherwise needy for attention, instead of acting out of this need they all have the emotional intelligence simply to state in words, "I'm feeling a little needy now." We shall regard statements like this as the psychological equivalent of someone saying, "I have a little headache now," or "I seem to have sprained a muscle in my leg, and am having some difficulty walking."

William: Good, for these are not really complaints, but rather honest reports about one's physical and/or psychological condition. Caring for one's emotional body is every bit as important as caring for one's physical body. In our culture today, language is often used indirectly to both express and conceal emotional discomfort. For example, one person may be angry with another, or frustrated about something, or feel sorrow about something. In today's culture, the words that are used flow out of that emotion, to justify, blame, or otherwise seek to preserve and strengthen the emotion.

Benedict: *(with a little humor)* Yes, and imagine, if you will, a person with a headache or some other physical discomfort, who uses language to talk and complain about the discomfort, but who does not seek a remedy for her discomfort.

Neal: Not a very effective way of dealing with the situation. But it is the same with those who, while experiencing emotional discomfort, use language to talk about and complain about the discomfort, but do nothing to alleviate the discomfort.

Benedict: And alleviating the discomfort involves (i) using language to report the emotional discomfort, and (ii) experiencing the discomfort as a physical sensation within her own body. Well, we have discussed these things before. But you had expressed some concern, not too seriously, regarding what people will talk about when they no longer use language to deceive, to complain, to gossip, to impress, to blame, etc. *(Laughing)* For it does indeed seem to be the case that if these subjects are taken off the table, there may be little left to talk about. We should perhaps mention that in addition to discussing thoughts and feelings, people will talk about what they are really interested in. For example, people in different trades or professions will be talking with one another about their mutual interests. Whether it's medicine, teaching, plumbing, dancing, construction, garbage disposal, or farming, there will be plenty of discussion regarding the best way to do things, and so forth. They will also talk honestly about any challenges in their lives. But overall, there will be lots more peace, quiet, and silence. Now let's return to our children, or rather young adults.

Plato: Good. And by "young adults" we may arbitrarily refer to the age group 18–28. During this time period there are two important decisions that must be made, decisions that will affect them for the remainder of their lives.

Neal: What do you have in mind?

Plato: One decision involves a choice of living situation, the other involves what is now called "career", but we won't use that word.

Neal: Why not?

Plato: Because the word has the connotation that what one does in the world, how one expresses oneself externally, is a mere accretion to the ego, something one "has" or "possesses". You, I mean your culture, speaks in terms of a "successful" career, or what will be "good" or "bad" for one's career. The phrase "choosing a profession" is also problematic, unless everything anyone does is considered a "profession". Let's try using the phrase "expresses oneself in the world", and see how that feels.

Neal: OK. The phrases may be problematic, but we all know what you mean. Perhaps the phrase "social role" will work too. In the absence of any need to "compete" for material necessities (food, shelter, etc.) and in the absence of any need to compete for psychological necessities (a sense of belonging, inclusion), every individual will be completely free to do whatever she likes, or in the terminology you suggest, everyone will be free to express themselves in the world in a manner that is most congruent with their talents and abilities, and that gives them the most joy. And we have stated that maximum joy and happiness arise when an individual is living in such a way as to express and fulfill the original purposes of her soul in manifesting as human.

William: Our young adults should not have much difficulty discovering which social role is best for them. My goodness, we have been observing them at play throughout their whole childhood, and their talents, abilities and proclivities are known to everyone, including themselves. Certainly anyone who is destined to express herself as an artist, musician, or athlete will know this by the time she is eighteen.

Plato: Yes, but we don't wish to encourage specialization too soon, although every child is unique, and our education system is flexible enough to respond to the uniqueness of every child. But roughly speaking, we might say that until the age of 18 (give or take a year or two), the subjects students study are more or less determined by the teachers, who always take into account the child's interests. But after 18, it is the child, I mean young adult, who decides what subjects to study, and may choose then to specialize or to continue sampling different subjects. Of course some subjects require longer training than others. A concert pianist might very well be expressing herself in the world at the age of 21 or even younger; but someone who wants to be a brain surgeon would have to wait another ten years before she could acquire the necessary skills to slice open the brain of another human being.

William: And I suppose that in cases where the young adult is unsure of what her true interests are, or is interested in several things that cannot be pursued simultaneously, we will have counselors available to assist them.

Plato: And if that doesn't work, there will be plenty of mediums and psychics around who can connect the individual with its soul directly, and ascertain the "original purpose" of that soul.

Socrates: Good. So it seems that everyone will find their unique calling in life, some very easily, others with a little guidance. But I want to comment on the little semantic quibble Plato raised. We won't use terms like "career" or "profession". The expression "social role" is also somewhat problematic.

Neal: How so?

Socrates: Recall what I said at my trial.

Neal: You said many things at your trial.

Socrates: You liked it very much.

Neal: I liked many things you said then very much.

Socrates: *(smiling)* You're being difficult. *Big Hint*: you remarked that the phrase I used contained the recipe for our whole New Social Order.

Neal: "I am the same person in public as I am in private."

Socrates: Finally! This statement will be true for all our citizens. So whatever our citizens do "in public" will be an authentic expression of who they are "in private". They will not be playing "roles", if that word carries connotations of being artificial or inauthentic. They will be expressing who they are.

Plato: Indeed, if we had asked at the very beginning of our conversation, what kind of social order allows for humans to be "the same person in public as in private", the answer would generate the very same social order that we have here constructed. This is clearly not possible under capitalism, or any kind of social order in which humans are made to compete for material resources or for status and recognition. What a person does in public will be an authentic expression of his or her inner being.

William: And if I may, I'd like to comment on something I believe we mentioned earlier.

Plato: Go right ahead.

William: It is the idea of an "invisible hand", so popular among economists in my time, and even in yours, Neal. In my time everyone believed it, because the material fruits of capitalism were everywhere. We believed that everyone should be as greedy and ambitious as possible, and that one person's greed would limit another person's greed, and everything will work out for the greater good. However, as Plato long ago demonstrated, the motivations of greed and ambition lead only to strife and destruction, and there is no "invisible hand" or anything else that guides and unifies a social order generated by greed and ambition. But *our* social order will indeed have an "Invisible Hand" that guides and connects the apparently separate "parts" – individual human beings – into a single being, as Benedict indicated.

Benedict: Yes, for the Voice for Reason is the same in all humans, and is the "invisible hand" that guides and connects all human and social activities. It is like the DNA which structures all cells so as to seamlessly constitute one and the same body. But the Voice for Reason can operate *only* in a social order that has eliminated greed and ambition from the domain of human motivations. Only in a social order based on the Voice for Reason is it possible for a human to be the same person in public as in private. For if we were to investigate why it is that in the present society people are not able to be the same person in public as in private, the culprits would be our usual suspects: greed and ambition. People *lie* in order to impress others and achieve status, or to cheat on contracts, or because they fear some harm if they tell the truth. Under the present economic system, it is impossible for a human to be the same person in public as in private. But our New Social Order removes greed and ambition as motivators, and offers no barriers to authentic self-expression.

William: And we might even state that under such conditions

our "Invisible Hand" will guide and structure individual talents and desires so as to harmonize with the needs of the whole Society, in much the same way that DNA, which is the same for all cells, creates and structures cells so as to harmonize with the needs of the body as a whole. Only then will Benedict's vision be realized.

Neal: Let's play it again:

> [Humans] can wish for nothing more excellent for preserving their own being than that they should all be in such harmony in all respects that their minds and bodies should compose, as it were, one mind and one body; that all should strive together, as far as they can, to flourish in their being; and that all, together, should seek for themselves the common advantage of all. From this it follows that humans who are governed by reason, that is, humans who seek their own advantage under the guidance of reason, seek nothing for themselves that they would not desire for the rest of Humanity; and so are just, honest, and honorable.

Benedict: *(slight smile)* Yeah, well thanks for cleaning up the sexist language, replacing "Man" with "Humans". But it doesn't work with *all* such expressions.

Neal: What do you mean?

Benedict: Let's see you clean up the language of Schiller's poem in Beethoven's *Ninth*. You know, "all men are brothers".

Neal: *(laughing)* I could clean it up, but the poetry would be lost. "All humans are brothers and sisters." "All men and women are brothers and sisters." I would go for the poetry of such phrases – "The Brotherhood of Man" – and hope that our sisters will make allowances for the cultural sexism of the past. But I'm sure that our New Society will come up with its own expressions of Unity and Oneness, especially since such Unity will pervade the whole culture. The "Force" will be everywhere. But now I think we need to discuss the second of the two decisions our young adults need to make, that pertaining to living arrangements.

Plato: Yes, well here we might have to be deliberately vague.

Neal: What do you mean?

Plato: It is not possible for us now to foresee in any detail the kind of living arrangements that our young adults, having been raised differently than children in any past culture, will choose for themselves. Also, we shall want to balance flexibility with stability. And before you ask again what I mean, let me state that by "flexibility" I mean that a young adult will have maximum choice with regard to where, how, and with whom, she will live. At the same time, we don't want people to be moving around all over the place, because under such circumstances it will not be possible to form stable neighborhoods and communities. And we regard stable communities as absolutely essential when it comes to raising babies and children. In fact, the primary responsibility for raising our children lies in the community as a whole, which of course will include the birth parents. But I'll venture a few suggestions of a general nature.

Neal: I'm listening.

Plato: OK. We are considering young adults, the age group from 17 or 18 to mid-late twenties. Of course, the actual biological ages are not the important thing; but rather the level of maturity that usually, but not in every case, accompanies the given age. Some mature earlier, others later. But in general terms, this stage of life involves separating from the living arrangements of their childhood and teen years. This separation is an important rite of passage for our young adults, and our Society will recognize this, and it will be discussed and acknowledged by all parties involved (e.g. parents and siblings).

William: Yes, but at 18 the children are ready to move out, but they are not yet ready to move into stable living arrangements on their own.

Plato: I agree. For what we are calling a "stable living arrangement" requires that the person know (i) how they will express themselves in the public arena (what used to be called "career", "vocation", "job"), and also know (ii) the social role they will play with regard to raising and caring for children. They won't know this until their mid or late twenties. But this is "in general". Some will know much sooner. So we need to put them someplace in the interim, between the time they leave their former stable living situation and the time they are ready to form or join their adult stable living situation.

William: And of course, we will not be putting them into any old place, but rather into an environment which allows them to receive as much education and training as they wish, as well as opportunities to explore their inner consciousness so as to arrive at a happy resolution of (i) and (ii) above. They need flexibility, exposure to many different things, opportunities for socialization and experimentation, and privacy.

Neal: Well then, it seems that we shall be placing our young adults in dormitories, with maximum opportunities to travel and study abroad. They will have the privacy of their own rooms, socialization whenever they step into the common areas, exposure to many different things by means of education programs and interactions with other young adults, and the flexibility to come and go as they please.

William: *(smiling)* And we should recollect to ourselves that *our* young adults, especially the males, will be different from anything that has yet arisen on our planet.

Neal: You mean they will be emotionally intelligent?

William: … And everything that entails. Wealth and status-seeking are no longer topics of conversation. And because the young men have befriended their sexual energies, they will not be bragging to one another about how many sexual partners they have had. They will not be competing with one another at all, except playfully, with one dormitory "competing" with another in sports, chess, music, dance, whatever. And no one, absolutely no one, will be so psychologically weak-minded that they feel a need to "bully" or gossip negatively about other people.

Neal: *(laughing)* It would seem that our young men will have nothing left to talk about.

William: Nothing except how they are truly feeling, what they are truly thinking about, and how they wish to express themselves in the world.

Plato: In other words, they will have nothing to talk about except what is real to them in the moment. They will also, as we have said, be comfortable with silence. It will not be uncommon, say, for two 21-year-old friends to take a walk in the woods together without uttering a single word. They will experience that nonverbal communication can be very profound.

Benedict: So far so good. But now, as our young adults approach their mid-twenties, they must decide upon a more stable living situation, one that is conducive to the bearing and raising of children.

Plato: Yes, and although not everyone will be involved in caring for and raising children, most will be. For the desire to have children is not merely the desire for sex. It is psychological as well. There is something deep within the soul of a human that craves the company of children, babies, and yes, even screaming infants. So most people, those who desire to be involved with children, will lose the flexibility to come and go as they please. But even so, there will be a variety of living situations compatible with our criterion for bearing and raising children.

William: What criterion?

Plato: In order to bond, babies and children must have a small group of adults and other children with whom they are in constant and continuous interaction, and a larger group with whom they are in occasional interaction. Sort of like the traditional nuclear family and extended family, except we do not insist that the connections be biological. By "extended family" I have in mind not just the usual uncles and aunts and cousins, but more importantly, the immediate local environment, the neighborhood. But I think it will become difficult to explain what I have in mind for the "nuclear family".

Socrates: *(laughing)* That's because you don't have anything definite in mind yet.

Plato: *(also laughing)* You continue to see right through me. Well, we have two things that must be satisfied simultaneously. The most important thing is a stable environment for our children. The other thing, also important, is the choice of living arrangements for our young adults, now in their mid-twenties. Obviously, those who wish to participate in the process of child-rearing – and most adults will desire to so participate – are more restricted in their choice of living arrangements than those who do not wish to raise children.

Neal: So our red blood corpuscles will be prohibited from caring for children?

Plato: Huh? Oh, I get it. Yes, our New Social Order will have its "red blood corpuscles", individuals who travel all over the world and do not stay in any one place for very long. Such a lifestyle does not provide a stable environment for raising children. But let us notice right away that what we are calling a "choice of living arrangement" is very different from "choice of a lifelong sexual partner" which is what your so-called traditional monogamous marriages are. Our young adults, because they have befriended the sexual energies, will be able to distinguish between the question, "Who to have sex with?" and the question, "Who to live with?" It goes without saying that sexual attraction will figure in the latter decision, but it will not be the deciding factor.

Socrates: And is this the time to announce what is already widely known but never discussed?

Plato: What do you mean?

2) Living Arrangements [Or Learning from the Bonobos]

Socrates: Human beings are not by nature monogamous creatures. And our new social order will honor our biological nature, rather than try to deny that nature by restricting sexual curiosity in ways that are harmful both to the individuals and to society as a whole. As I said before, we shall be studying the bonobos, and learning from them. And if you ask, "Learning what?" my reply would be, "Learning how to have a social order that is stable and conducive to rearing babies while at the same time not restricting in any way the natural sexual expressions of the individuals."

Plato: So, my thoughts seem to be getting a bit more definite, and I can conceive of three kinds of living arrangements that will be sufficiently stable for child-rearing.

Neal: What are they?

Plato: Before I state what I think they are, let me first state that we cannot predetermine these things in advance, and when the time comes, it will certainly be possible that living arrangements that cannot now be foreseen will come to pass.

Neal: I agree. When our children reach maturity, as is now the case, they will have a very different perspective on things, a perspective that we cannot claim to know in advance. But because we have raised them to be friends, not only with their sexual energies, but also with the Voice for Reason within themselves, their vision and judgment will be beyond what we can now only see dimly.

Plato: So with this in mind, here are three kinds of living arrangements that seem to appear through the dimness of my vision: (i) the traditional couple, expanded to include couples that are male/male and female/female. (ii) A slightly larger group, say three or four people. There is no reason why three or more people cannot live together, have sexual relations with one another, and raise children together. Perhaps the only consideration is that we want our children to be exposed to both male and female adults, so four gay men, or four gay women, who wanted to live together and raise children, would have to find some way of including opposite sex adults in the raising of their children.

Neal: And this should not be too difficult. We must remind ourselves that our whole social order is constructed around what is best for babies and children. For as we have said, the problem is not that pregnant women or nursing mothers or fathers with two year olds are "inconvenient" for the workplace, as is the case in my present society, but rather, that the workplace is not designed to accommodate parents of babies and young children.

William: Also, we think that the neighborhood, not the immediate family, is the proper unit for raising children. So our family of four gay males might live next door to a family of four gay females, and their children will be running around freely through both households. Problem solved. But, Plato, what is your third possible kind of living arrangement?

Plato: Oh, just a little experiment I have in mind.

Socrates: Hah! You've had that "little experiment" in mind for several thousand years. There's no point trying to conceal your eagerness to try out your grand social experiment, so let's hear it.

Plato: Alright. My thoughts about this have changed over the centuries. Originally I thought that if things could be arranged such that the biological parents did not know who their children were, and the children did not know who their biological parents were, then in such a community all adults would regard all children as their own and extend lovingkindness to all children equally, not just their biological offspring; that, I thought, would eliminate all the social hanky-panky that is caused by parents favoring their biological children and seeking special social advantage for them. Also, I thought that the children would feel loved and cared for by all the adults around them, not just their biological parents.

Neal: And you also had in mind some genetic engineering, whereby those who were physically and mentally strong would be encouraged to mate often…

Plato: Yes, but that has all changed now. For the purpose of genetic engineering is to improve the species. But the human species *has* been improved by how we have raised our children.

Benedict: Good. For the human form, body and mind are deeply interconnected, so much so that we have already altered the genetic makeup of humans through upbringing. So, Plato, what do you have in mind now?

Plato: I have in mind a group of young adults of child-bearing age, say 25–30 years old, deciding to live together, having sexual relations with one another, and raising their children in common.

Neal: Well option (ii) covers this, does it not?

Plato: Option (ii) refers to very small groups, say three to six individuals. The third option envisions a larger group, say 12–15 men and women each, perhaps even larger. Although parents will know the identity of their biological children, and vice versa, all the parents will raise all the children together, and the children will regard all the adults as parents, and one another as brothers and sisters.

Neal: How will they live? The adults can't all sleep in one big bed. Or do you envision them living in houses with thirty bedrooms?

Plato: *(smiling)* We can leave such details to them. There is no reason why our architects cannot design living spaces for 30 to 50 people (+ children) to occupy together, living spaces that creatively balance the need for privacy with the need for social interaction. We must remind ourselves that the so-called "profit motive" will be a thing of the past. Architects will no longer be required to design buildings that bring monetary profit to their employers. So they are now free to design buildings for the benefit of those who will live in them, and hence will be able to design living spaces of great beauty.

Neal: But don't you think that such a living situation could generate feelings of jealousy? Who will sleep with who on any given night? Some individuals will be more desired as sex partners than others.

Plato: There is no conceivable living situation that is free from problems and challenges. Did we not state that the "mischief" of Shakespeare's comedies would still occur (but not the mischief of his tragedies). And what a perfect living situation to explore such mischief! On some given evening, John wants to sleep with Suzie, Suzie wants to sleep with Bill, and Bill wants to sleep alone. Don't you think our emotionally intelligent adults will be able to resolve this situation by themselves, to the mutual satisfaction of the parties involved?

Benedict: I'll answer that question. Yes of course, and here's why. Our young adults are emotionally intelligent, which means they know their own emotions and the emotions of others. Most will have internalized the Voice for Reason, which means that they do not desire for themselves anything they do not desire for their fellow human beings, especially the ones they are cohabiting with. So whenever conflict or challenges arise, as will necessarily be the case, they put the Golden Rule first, and considering their own desires on a par with the desires of others, and vice versa, arrive at a resolution that is satisfactory to all concerned.

We might mention that this applies not only to resolving issues that arise from sleeping arrangements on any given night, but for conflicts and differences of opinion that arise anywhere in the social order. For we insist, at least Plato and I insist, that the Voice of Reason is the same in all, as mathematics and science demonstrate.

Plato: Yes. As we have said, there is not "my" geometry and "your" geometry and "their" geometry. Neither is there Chinese geometry, American geometry, or Catholic geometry. There is simply, geometry. The same is true for Reason. There is not John's reason and Suzie's reason and Bill's reason. There is just Human Reason, flowing equally through the minds of John, Suzie, and Bill. They will figure it out to the satisfaction of all parties. If someone scrapes his or her emotional knees on this or any other issue, he or she will know how to clean the wound, or if not, get assistance from others who will be ready at hand. For in our New Social Order, there is nothing more important than the consciousness of the individuals who comprise that Order.

William: *(with a little humor)* Well I must remark that the distinguished Victorian gentleman that once was me cannot easily wrap his Victorian mind around all this business.

Neal: What business?

William: Young people living together and having sex together. I suppose you can even envision threesomes and foursomes –

Plato: And even manysomes. Why not? Remember that our adults have been raised to feel the emotions of others and to rejoice within themselves while giving pleasure to the body of others through massage. Giving sexual pleasure to another will be experienced as a great happiness by the one or ones who give. Also a group setting affords an opportunity to experiment with ritualized sex, as was not uncommon in the Temples of my time and before, as well as among the Gnostic Christians. And there will be opportunities to invite the sex Trainers and Teachers into their community to talk about latest techniques while giving live demonstrations thereof. But, William, if your Victorian gentleman has some objections to make, give him a voice and we'll all listen.

William: *(laughing)* Hah! It didn't work out so well the last time I tried it. Yes, I can hear him screaming and kicking a little, but now that I've become emotionally intelligent myself, I know how to soothe his ruffled feathers. But I do have something to say, not insofar as I carry the Victorian gentleman within me, but rather insofar as I am a psychologist.

Plato: I'm listening.

William: The time for explicit sexual exploration is roughly from the early teens until the mid-twenties. When they reach their mid-twenties, our young adults are ready to decide whether they wish to participate in the process of bearing and raising children. We expect that the majority of young adults will choose to so participate. Those who choose not to participate are free to live however they choose, but those who do participate must live in such a way as to be maximally conducive to the well-being and flourishing of our children. I think we are all in agreement about this.

Plato: Yes, continue.

William: And we said that the most important thing for the first years of life is that the child bond with adults and other children.

Plato: Yes, this bonding is necessary for psychological health and well-being.

William: But the human form is limited, and a baby cannot bond with an indefinite number of other humans, any more than an adult can be intimate friends with an unlimited number of other adults.

Plato: True.

William: Now I agree that a baby can bond with more than one or two adults, but I doubt it could bond with as many as 30 adults who have agreed to raise their children in common. We have also stated that the biological mother's milk is the most nutritious food for the baby, and the deepest bonding occurs through nursing, both ways.

Plato: Yes, both ways. For nursing will be a deep meditative experience for the mother, during which time she may even feel in communication with the soul of the child she is nursing. This connection constitutes a permanent bond between her and the child. The child and mother have also been bonding during gestation.

William: And so, if our babies are to develop in the best possible way, the bond between mother and baby is sacred, and living situations must be designed with this in mind. I do not know, but I question whether 30 people living together would be the best possible arrangement for healthy mother/child bonding. At any rate, when we are considering possible living situations for our young adults of child-rearing age, we must consider foremost the emotional needs of pregnant women and nursing mothers. I am comfortable leaving the matter as an empirical question to be determined by future psychologists.

Plato: I'm OK with that too. But there is another issue that we should mention regarding bonding and the limitations of the human form. For in any living situation it is not only the mother and child that bond, but everyone else as well. You rightly stated that adults cannot be intimate friends with, that is, bond with an unlimited number of other adults. A man or woman may have sex with an unlimited number of other people, but he or she cannot psychologically bond with all of them. One must spend considerable amounts of time with another for bonding and friendship to occur, and alas, only a finite amount of time is allotted to humans.

Socrates: *We* of course are not limited by such a gross restraint as time. *(To me)* But you humans *are* so limited. That's part of what you sign up for when you agree to become human.

William: Perhaps the issue may be framed as "breadth vs. depth". In educating our children, we strive to obtain some balance between the two. We want them to have a broad education, where they know basic things about a wide variety of subjects, but mastery of a "wide variety of subjects" is impossible for a time-limited human being, so they will have to make choices about which subject to pursue in depth, choices that will exclude other possibilities. And the same is true with respect to living arrangements. We want our young adults, including our nursing mothers, to have a wide variety of friends and acquaintances, but depth is possible only with a small number of others.

Socrates: And depth is the same thing as what we are calling bonding, don't you agree?

William: Yes.

Socrates: Now any group of two or more humans that come together for a common purpose will bond with one another.

William: Yes.

Socrates: And is there any human purpose that goes deeper, that is more important, that is more sacred, than the purpose of being the vehicle through which souls may become embodied?

William: No, there is no greater purpose, and hence no greater bonding.

Socrates: And so it seems that the greatest depth of bonding will occur between two or more adults who decide to live together for the purpose of bearing and raising children.

Benedict: When two humans, each of whom are governed by Reason, come together, they form a "being" with holistic properties that are greater than the sum of the individuals considered separately. If they are not governed by Reason, but instead by individual desires, they do not constitute a single being, but rather squabbling individuals that are typical of the marriages in the present culture. But we are envisioning a social order that is governed entirely by reason. Now, I did envisage extending this outwards so as to consider the whole of Mankind, er, I mean Humanity, as a single individual. From our present non-embodied perspective, Humankind **is** a single individual, and that individual **is** what Plato has referred to as the World Soul, or something like that. But from the limited human perspective, well, you humans can gaze into only one pair of eyes at a time, hence it is not possible for a human to bond with more than a few other individuals, never mind the whole of Humanity. I fear that a living situation like Plato's experiment with 30 or so adults might be too diffuse to allow for depth of bonding.

Neal: So are we back to the nuclear family? Mom, Dad, and the kids?

Plato: Not quite. The word "nuclear" is quite telling here, for it suggests that the family is like an atomic, independent unit of social organization. First you have the family, then families come together to form communities, which in turn come together to form cities, and so forth. But this is a false picture, even in your present social order. Families are not "independent units" but are organically interconnected with the larger community. The primary responsibility for raising children lies in the larger community, not the nuclear family. The expression "it takes a village" to raise children is literally true. The reason that children are not being raised properly in your culture is because this truth is not heeded in the present social structure. Unlike the present situation, the communities of our New Society will be very involved in raising their children, and parents will feel supported and assisted in every way.

Socrates: *(with humor)* And we shall most certainly do away with that ridiculous saying of your culture, that Johnny and Suzie got married and *lived happily ever after*. As if stagnating into fixed roles of "Mom", "Dad", "husband" and "wife" were the recipe for happiness. For the individuals involved, even though they have merged so as to form a larger system called "a couple" *(glancing at Benedict)*, are nevertheless still individual expressions of their own unique soul. So learning, growth, expression at the individual level does not come to an end when the children arrive. Nor shall we insist upon sexual fidelity.

Plato: Now before that Victorian gentleman comes up with the usual objections, we must stress that choice of a life partner is very different for us than it was for him. For us, it is not a choice of who to have sexual relations with. They have been befriending their sexual energies since their early teens, and because of that, sex is not a problem at all. It will be common knowledge that a given human being will be sexually attracted to far many more humans than she could possibly sleep with in a lifetime. The choice of a life partner, a partner to have and raise children with, is too important to be based on bodily chemistry alone.

Neal: OK, but how will this choice be made? Let's say I am now a 26-year-old male. I am emotionally intelligent. And having been sexually active under guidance since my early teens, I am sexually intelligent as well. I have found my calling in life – it used to be called a "job" or "profession" or "career", but now we are thinking of it as an "outer expression of my inner nature", or something like that. Now I feel ready to participate in the raising of children. How do I go about finding a suitable partner?

Socrates: *(laughing)* Why not take out an ad or join some dating service? Something like: "wanted: attractive, intelligent woman who wants to bear children". That should do it.

Neal: *(with humor)* A wonderful, but generic, description of our young women, and young men too, all of whom are attractive and intelligent, and of whom the great majority desire children. But it doesn't help me selecting a life partner.

William: It is interesting to note that the kinds of considerations that went into choosing a life partner in past societies will not be relevant in our present culture. No one will choose a mate for financial security, social status, or sexual attractiveness.

Neal: OK. So I know how the choice will not be made. But here I am, a mid-twenties male, wanting to have children. *(Playfully)* Won't anyone help me find my partner?

Socrates: Help is on the way, and you will have it as soon as you can see where it is coming from.

Neal: Huh? Stop speaking in riddles.

Plato: *(laughing, to me)* I'm afraid that if we restrict him from speaking in riddles, he won't be speaking very much at all. But shall I give you a little hint?

Neal: Please do.

Plato: OK. We are agreed that the choice of partner will not be made on the basis of physical appearance or sexual attractiveness. This will in any case be impossible, since almost all our women, and men too, will be sexually attractive.

Neal: Actually I agree with that statement, since what makes a woman sexually attractive is her command of the sexual energies within her. Because of upbringing, the majority of our women, and men too, will have that command.

Socrates: And moreover, if physical appearance is what a man is looking for, we will have plenty of sex robots to give him, and we shall regard him as not yet mature enough to participate in child-rearing until he has outgrown the robots, at least to some extent.

Plato: So physical appearance is not a deciding factor. Neither is status or financial security, since all citizens have equal social status and financial security.

Neal: Wait a minute, are you guys saying that nothing in the physical world or in the society at large is a factor in the choice of life partner?

Plato: It's not just "us guys" who are saying this, but you yourself are saying this.

Neal: I am?

Plato: Can you think of any physical or social factor that should be taken into account in selecting a life partner?

Neal: No, which is why I asked for your help.

Socrates: In *my* time, when we had some problem that couldn't be resolved by ordinary physical or social methods, we consulted the oracle.

Neal: *(flash of understanding)* Oh. The help is coming from your side of the veil.

Plato: Exactly. You see, the problem facing the 26-year-old young man you introduced us to, is *not* a lack of women with whom he is sexually and psychologically compatible. His problem is that he knows *many* women who fit that description. And the same is true for the women. Winnowing down to a single person will require a more than human perspective. Potential partners will meditate, go on spiritual retreats, and consult with mediums and psychics. What is desired by the souls of the individuals involved? And we of course mean to include the souls of future children. And if we were to take… ah, pardon the expression, a *platonic* view of things, we might say that all such choices have already been made in the eternal order, so our 26-year-old young man is not really making a choice, but rather discerning the choice that has already been made in the eternal order.

Benedict: But in many cases there will be no need of mediums or oracles, because our young men and young women are so emotionally intelligent and spiritually attuned, that the very cells in their bodies will "know" when they are in the presence of their life partner.

Neal: It would seem then, that the choice of a life partner, or finding one's life partner, is a serious and sacred enterprise, very different from what is called "marriage" today.

3) Partnering

Benedict: Yes, but we must be careful about that word "sacred".

Neal: What do you mean?

Benedict: Recall what I once said about the word "miracle". If by the word "miracle" we mean "caused by God", then everything is a miracle since everything that is, is caused by and is an expression of God. So if by "sacred" you mean "connected to God" or "involving the Divine", then there is nothing that is not sacred.

Neal: I see your point, but nevertheless, to we ordinary human beings, some things seem closer to the Divine than others.

Socrates: *(with a hint of mischief in his eyes)* Well then, since you are the "ordinary human being" in our midst, perhaps you will tell us what kinds of human activities are closer to the Divine and hence more sacred than others. And also which are further from the Divine and hence less sacred.

Neal: *(I'm having that funny feeling again that this is an argument I have already lost)* It seems obvious that helping a child in distress, or helping an elderly person die, touches the Divine in a way that washing the dishes does not.

Socrates: So helping another human being is spiritual, but washing the dishes is not? Is that what you think?

Neal: Yes, sort of.

Socrates: *(laughing)* Sometimes a little equivocation is a good thing. But let's move on from the dishes to dirty laundry. I suppose you find nothing spiritual about doing the laundry?

Neal: No.

Socrates: And what about organizing your books and papers, and clearing up the general messiness in your living place? I presume that such activity is not very high on your list of things that are sacred and spiritual.

Neal: (*laughing a little; I'm beginning to see where this is headed)* Hah! This is one activity that never even made it to my list of what is sacred. To misquote George Bernard Shaw, whenever I get the impulse to organize my apartment, I lie down until it passes.

(Everyone laughs.)

Socrates: But aside from the three specific items I mentioned that are distasteful to you, perhaps you feel that helping another is more spiritual than anything one does alone? After all, as Benedict puts it, when you assist another, you become part of a coupled system that is greater than the sum of its parts. So perhaps it seems that any joining with another is more "spiritual" than whatever one does alone. What do you think?

Neal: No, I don't think that. Monks who pray and meditate alone in their cells are very spiritual, and their solitary activities affect the well-being of the whole planet.

Socrates: So it would seem that you have no criterion for "what is sacred" and "what is not sacred", other than your own likes and dislikes.

William: Keep in mind that there are people for whom the saying "cleanliness is next to godliness" is literally true. For them, cleaning their living space is indeed a spiritual activity, bringing them psychologically closer to what is Divine in themselves. And also don't forget the feng shui folks, for whom organizing one's living space is about as sacred an activity as there is.

Socrates: You *do* understand that from *our* perspective everything is sacred because we experience the Divine Being directly. We experience ourselves as the Divine Being manifesting as us. We do not experience some things as more or less spiritual and sacred than other things. But humans *do* make a distinction between what they do and do not regard as spiritual or sacred, although not all in the same way. It is a false dichotomy with consequences. For what is believed to be not sacred will be experienced that way. *(Smiling)* I assure you, my friend, that if you fully believed that washing the dishes was a sacred activity, you would experience it as such.

William: And it will be good to consider the consciousness of the human mind when it is in the presence of what it regards as sacred. Such a mind will be more focused, more alert, and more aware than otherwise.

Socrates: So you think the distinction should be, not between what is sacred and what is not sacred, but rather, between what is believed to be sacred and what is not believed to be sacred?

William: I agree with Benedict. I do not believe it is possible to define the word "sacred" in such a way as to single out a class of behaviors, objects, beliefs, whatever, for inclusion under the definition, and another class of behaviors, etc. that are excluded. But if we define "sacred" as whatever a given individual *believes* is closer to the Divine, or enables a heightened sense of the Divine, then I think we may continue to use the word.

Benedict: I'll agree with that, even though a given individual's beliefs are actually false.

William: What do you mean?

Benedict: A person may falsely believe that some objects are "holier" than others, such as a cross or a star; a person may falsely believe that some books were even written by God; a person may falsely believe that *some* behaviors, like ritual and prayer, will bring them closer to the Divine. All this is nonsense, which will be largely absent from our Social Order. But individuals who have such beliefs will experience things accordingly, and will experience a settling down of their thoughts in the presence of that symbol, book or ritual. So in the presence of what is believed to be sacred, the minds of individuals become more focused and attentive.

Plato: And what is it to be more focused and attentive other than to be fully aware in the present moment, and the mind's irresistible tendency to wander into past, future, and fantasy is in temporary abeyance. It follows, then, that if humans regarded all things as sacred, then they would enjoy this heightened state of consciousness all the time. What is truly sacred is not any outer event, object, or behavior, but rather, consciousness itself.

Socrates: *(smiling, to me)* And so, my friend, you who believe that listening to Beethoven's *Ninth* is a spiritual experience but washing the dishes is not, it is quite possible to bring the same sense of the sacred to the latter experience as you do to the former. It requires only that your consciousness be entirely focused in the present moment.

Plato: In a social order based on greed and ambition, the "present moment" is never sufficient unto itself. It is always only a stepping-stone to *more*, and *more* is always in the projected future. So the mind of such an individual is never content with "what is" in the present moment. Hence it is always restless, unsettled. For such a mind, certain objects and behaviors may cause it to settle down a little, and then those objects are called "sacred". But the minds of *our* citizens will have made friends with "what is", and will not be seeking escapes from the present moment, in which all happiness truly lies. Now, shall we get back to our young adults?

Neal: Yes of course. Well, we don't need to use the word "sacred", but choice of a life partner, like the choice of "career" (the phrase "outer expression of one's inner nature" is surely too long to use), is very important.

Benedict: Let's try using platonic language here. It might be insightful.

Plato: Hmm, I wonder. I see where you want to go with this suggestion. OK, it might be useful. Let's see where it takes us.

Neal: What are you two talking about?

Socrates: A choice that is not a choice is determined by that which is not determined.

Neal: *(slight sarcasm)* Well that clears everything up nicely.

Socrates: Sorry, I couldn't resist a little playing with words. I think Plato and Benedict want to examine the consequences of regarding the "choice" of life partner similarly to how we regard the choice of parents.

Neal: Huh? What do you mean by that? No one chooses her or his parents.

Socrates: Oh? Is that really so?

Neal: The human being is a consequence of a choice that has been made at the level of soul.

Socrates: But is not the human being an expression of the soul, and is not the mind of the human fully contained within the consciousness of the soul?

Neal: Yes, of course.

Socrates: So ultimately, you the human are not other than That, the soul, is not that so?

Neal: Yes.

Socrates: And the soul chooses its parents?

Neal: Yes.

Socrates: And this is true even if some aspect of the soul suffers from temporary amnesia and does not recollect the decision-making process. An actor on a stage playing some role is still the very same person he was prior to deciding what role to play?

Neal: Yes. So the actor has determined his role, but the character the actor has become has not; the character is not really real, but is only a consequence of the prior choice.

Socrates: Now, please don't just believe me when I tell you this, but consult with what Near-Death Experiencers are saying: *you*, the individual that you think you *are*, are not "really real", but are – I won't say "only" – a consequence of choices made in the eternal order, which alone is real.

Neal: The "I" that I am now experiencing myself as being is a consequence of the choice of parents made by the "I" of the soul of which I am a part, and in fact, is the real agent who is experiencing itself as "me".

William: *(laughing)* We need that Rumi quote right now, before language befuddles us all.

Neal: *(also laughing)* Here it is: "language is a tailor shop where nothing fits".

Socrates: And with that in mind, it is difficult to take seriously anything that can be written down, is it not?

Neal: OK, so there is a sense in which it is true to state that I choose my parents.

Plato: And we want to play with the idea that in that very same sense it is true to state that an individual chooses his or her life partner. That is to say, the "choice" has already been made in the eternal order, and the personality in the temporal order merely needs to discern the choice that has already been made. In many cases, the humans will simply recognize one another.

Now, I must emphasize that we are not talking about traditional "marriage", where two people "fall in love", marry, and live happily ever after.

Neal: Perhaps it will be useful to state the difference.

Plato: The very phrase "fall in love" should raise suspicions. It indicates that one has fallen in some way. What has one fallen away from, or fallen into, when one has "fallen in love"? Does not the phrase indicate that one's rational abilities, one's reasoning, has been overcome? So one has become helpless to resist something, similar to the helplessness one feels when, after stumbling, the body falls helplessly to the ground. So the word "fall" is very problematic in the phrase "fall in love". But so is the word "love". We have said that love pertains to the Divine, and that humans can participate in that love to the extent that they are aligned with what is Divine within themselves. But humans cannot generate this love, nor can they feel it by "falling". On the contrary, they feel it by rising or growing in their ability to align with the Divine within. So in our social order, people will choose partners that afford maximum growth in their ability to align with the Divine within, and we may refer to this process as "rising in love", not falling in it.

Neal: And by the time they have reached their mid-twenties, our young adults will have had enough sexual experience to discern the difference between sexual attractions and life partnering, or with our new terminology, the difference between falling in lust, and rising or growing in love.

Benedict: Actually the phrase "growing in love" describes the life purpose of every human life on the planet, whether partnered or not. Our young adults will not think that they need to find a life partner in order to grow in love. For one can grow in this way through whatever one does, once the phrase is understood as meaning alignment with the Divine within. So the main purpose of partnering is really the bearing and raising of children.

Neal: I agree, but we need to say more about the differences between marriage as it exists in my present culture, and partnering as it will exist in our new society. The divorce rate is over 50%, which causes much distress for the children as well as the parents.

Plato: Good. I mean, good to raise this point. We anticipate a much lower divorce rate, close to zero actually.

Neal: How is that possible?

Plato: Your current divorce rate is caused by a combination of three factors, factors that will be entirely absent in our New Society. Can you see them?

Neal: I see one very clearly. Emotional intelligence. This is a rarity in my present culture. People generally lack the emotional intelligence necessary for honest communication, and no relationship can long survive a lack of honest emotional communication.

William: Yes, people generally act out of emotion, rather than try to feel their emotions and understand them. *(Smiling)* It really isn't possible for two people to "live happily ever after" when they don't know how to communicate with each other.

Neal: But what are the other two factors, oh wait, I can see one of them now.

William: What do you see?

Neal: Sexual curiosity. Since humans are not by nature monogamous, the requirement of sexual monogamy on marriages is a burden too great to bear for most people. In our social order, partnering will be in harmony with natural sexual curiosity, not opposed to it. Also, aside from sexual curiosity in itself, people who have partnered will not be prevented from forming close friendships and affections with others of both sexes, and it will be not uncommon to express such affection sexually. So sexual curiosity is one cause of divorce.

William: And what would you say if a certain Victorian gentleman were to object and state that it is only natural to be angry and jealous and sue for divorce upon learning that his partner has had sex with her handsome coworker.

Neal: Well I would quote Benedict here, if I could find the passage.

Benedict: *(chuckling)* Let me help you. I can't find the passage either, but the gist of it is that whether a person repents of a deed or exults in it depends entirely on upbringing. So I would tell that Victorian gentleman that the anger and jealousy that *he* would feel if *his* wife had a good time in bed with the handsome butler, or whoever, is caused by *his* upbringing, and that his emotions are triggered by his wife's dalliance, but not caused by it.

Neal: And the upbringing of *our* children has been quite different, so they will respond differently to this kind of situation.

Plato: *(with humor)* Let's make this a little more concrete by imagining the following scenario between John and Susan over dinner.

Susan: I had lunch with Bill today and we enjoyed a little sex afterwards.

John: Oh that's nice. I'm so glad you enjoyed it, but then, I would not have predicted that you wouldn't. How is Bill doing?

Susan: He's fine, and his oldest child is recovering nicely from a bout with the flu.

John: Glad to hear it. (Smiling) *By the way, did you perchance learn any new bedroom techniques that I might benefi t from?*

Susan: (laughing) *Oh c'mon, honey, it was just a litt le quickie, what could I have possibly learned?*

Plato: Does anyone see any reason why the above scenario could not be the norm in our culture? Instead of reacting with anger and jealousy and running off to the nearest divorce lawyer, he reacts as if this is the most normal and natural thing in the world. And don't you think that the bond between John and Susan has become stronger because they interact in this way?

Neal: Yes. For the little dialogue indicates several things: (i) there are no secrets between John and Susan; John knows about Bill and his family. (ii) John's first concern was his partner's enjoyment of the process. (iii) And his second concern – not a concern really – was to playfully wonder whether he might personally benefit in the bedroom from his wife's encounter with Bill.

Socrates: *(with humor)* And this makes Benedict's point beautifully, for the same behavior that in your present culture is regarded as a cause of the marriage falling apart, will in our culture be regarded as a cause of the partnership enduring. For *our* culture fully honors the fact that humans are hardwired biologically to be sexually curious, and the pain and suffering caused by trying to force biology to "adapt" to perverse religious nonsense that denies natural human sexuality has been enormous. Couples will no longer be compelled to engage in the mandatory big lie – the lie that they are *not* sexually attracted to anyone but their partner. People will partner with one another with the expectation that each will at times be attracted to others. They will look upon your current system of serial monogamy as unnatural.

Neal: So, two of the three factors that will prevent divorce are

(i) emotional intelligence, and (ii) honoring natural sexual curiosity. What is the third factor, Plato?

Plato: The responsibility for raising children will lie not with the so-called nuclear family, but with the community as a whole. We shall not abandon our parents or parents-to-be as soon as they have found one another. The awesome responsibility of raising children is too great to place on the biological parents alone. We cannot now specify any details, but we want an outcome where parents and children feel deeply connected to their neighborhoods and communities. We want the children to feel a sense of belonging to the community. *How* this will be accomplished we must leave to them. And there is no reason we, or rather, they, cannot experiment with this, and form different kinds of communities.

Neal: I suppose that thirty people living under one roof and raising their children in common would be a "community" of sorts.

Plato: Yes, but it's not for everyone. The point is that partners raising children will not feel that the responsibility for raising the children lies entirely with them. The children will feel cared for, not just by their biological parents, but by the community as a whole. Neighbors will know one another. And because of the cushion of a neighborhood, parents will be able to do what is so essential for themselves and their partnership.

Neal: What do you have in mind?

Plato: They will regularly take time off from parenting. They will be able to, say, leave their children with friends and go off for a weekend by themselves. Or they can go to workshops and meditation retreats, separately or together. For the growth and flourishing of our adults does not stop when the children arrive; in fact, it never stops. We shall make certain that no one stagnates because they feel overwhelmed with the burden of caring for children.

William: *(smiling)* Well now, isn't this interesting. We seem to be reverting back to the good old days, when marriages were "made in heaven" and were expected to last "until death do they part". Of course in the past, marriages lasted because of religious, economic and social pressure. *Now* those pressures are relaxed and people are free to come and go, and many choose to go. But in *our* social order, you think people will choose to stay with their partners?

Plato: Yes, I do. Couples split up for three basic reasons, none of which apply to us: (i) they lack the emotional intelligence to communicate with one another, (ii) they are sexually curious and fantasize about sex with others, and (iii) the responsibility for raising children without community support is overwhelmingly stressful, and they lack the emotional intelligence necessary for dealing with stress.

Now I want to say something about the religious belief that marriages are "made in heaven". There is a sense in which this is trivially true. For every Earthly event is a downward projection, a "moving image" of events in the eternal order.

Neal: *(with humor)* I suppose we could even go so far as to say that Earthly events are mere "shadows" of the Real.

Plato: Yes, thank you, we could even go that far. So even in William's "good old days", the Earthly event of John and Susan getting married was connected with the two souls, in heaven of course, of which the humans "John" and "Susan" are temporal extensions. But such unions will be quite different in our New Social Order.

William: How so?

Plato: Well for one thing, from the Earthly perspective, family, social status, and sexual attraction will not be factors at all. Rather, John and Susan will find each other by connecting consciously with the intent of their own souls. They will discover for themselves what has been "ordained in Heaven". As we suggested before, if they have been raised according to our suggestions, the very cells within their bodies will resonate when they come into one another's presence. *(Laughing)* And I know what you're now thinking, Neal.

Neal: *(also laughing)* Yes, when I was a young man, "the very cells" in my body would resonate whenever I saw a shapely female. But we are speaking about a deeper kind of resonance than mere sexual attraction.

Plato: Much deeper. Now of course there is such a thing as sexual resonance or "chemistry", which is all fine and good. But spiritual resonance is much deeper. *You* experienced that resonance when I first came to you in the library. You felt me viscerally, even though at the time you had no idea what was happening.

Neal: Yes, chills up and down my spine, shaking and trembling, tears. And although sixty years have passed, the memory of the event can still bring tears to my eyes.

Plato: And do not mediums also talk about getting the chills when the spirits are near, or however they refer to it?

Neal: Yes.

Plato: So there are physical signs and symptoms by which a human may recognize the presence of spirit. Now you know what is called the "déjà vu" experience?

Neal: Yes, of course. So the "déjà vu" experience is also a sign that the eternal is near.

Plato: Yes. Now we must keep Rumi in mind here It is very misleading to speak of "John's soul" or "the soul of Susan". For it invites one to think that the bodies/personalities called "John" and "Susan" possess something called "souls", in the same way that they may accurately be said to possess arms and legs. But the soul is the greater reality. The soul may be said to "possess" a body and personality, but not the other way around. What is called "Susan" is a temporal projection, or a dream or shadow that is contained within the being of the soul. But human language has names only for bodies, not for souls. So when we use locutions like "the soul of John" we mean to refer to the real being in the eternal order of which "John" is a projection or "shadow".

That said, we may state that John and Susan, like all our humans, will feel much closer to and more connected with their souls than humans do at present.

William: – A direct consequence of a thinning out of the margins between our worlds.

Plato: And so they will be much better able to feel communications from their souls. Then it is quite possible, even likely, that the souls will be able to send the chills or some other sign to their extensions in the temporal order, when the latter are in one another's presence. And if internal signs prove not sufficient in any individual case, external signs, like consulting with a medium, are always available.

4) A Possible Portal

(Benedict and Socrates seemed to be whispering about something for the last several pages. With Plato's last remark, their whispering ceased and I asked:)

Neal: What have you two been talking about?

Socrates: Neither of us is partial to idle speculation, but we seem to have caught a glimpse of a remarkable possibility.

Benedict: But we are not certain whether to mention it now, since anything that is a "possibility" invites speculation, and we do not see it with sufficient clarity to state anything definite. But the possibility is quite profound, and perhaps worth mentioning.

Neal: Please do. What is this "possibility" that you are seeing?

Socrates: The possibility that through their union, John and Susan become portals for one another.

Benedict: And by "portal" we of course mean an opening into the eternal order. They will feel the eternal within themselves whenever they gaze into one another's eyes. And by the way, we prefer the word "union" to the words "marriage" or "partner", since the very souls are "in union" with each other, and their Earthly extensions may aspire to and *feel* the union that exists within their souls. It is this "feeling" of the union that exists at the level of soul that we are referring to as a portal. We are thinking this "feeling" can be projected into the temporal order, so that the souls' extensions in time, which we are calling "John" and "Susan", will themselves feel this union between themselves.

Socrates: And this may very well be the means by which Benedict's vision will be realized.

Neal: You mean the vision of the whole of Humanity, guided by Reason, acting as one Mind and one Body.

Socrates: Yes. It goes without saying that in order to act as "one mind and one body" each human must feel this from within. For if everyone were what you call "enlightened" then everyone would feel themselves as part of the Divine Mind. There would then be no need for portals. But the way to this "New Earth" may very well be facilitated through the union of humans two at a time.

Neal: So perhaps the union of two individuals, ostensibly for the purpose of raising children, is also a stepping stone to achieving the vision of the "Brotherhood of Man", where every human consciously *feels* herself as an essential part of the Whole, instead of as a skin-encapsulated ego.

Plato: From the collective perspective of our Social Order, the most important event in the life of any individual is the process by which two individuals come together for the purpose of bearing and raising children. For this is the means by which the Society perpetuates itself and exists as a temporally extended entity. Hence the full resources of our social order will be available to assist individuals who wish to serve in this most profound way, by becoming parents. And the main form of assistance will be to help the individuals recognize and *feel* the connection between them that already exists within their souls. Secondary help will be available from mediums. But what we are calling a "portal" is the *feeling*, in the temporal order, of the connection that exists in the eternal order. So each individual partner will *feel* himself or herself as part of the other, who then ceases to be "other".

Socrates: I think we should now heed Rumi's warning, as we have been saying all along, and not try too hard to capture these things with language. But I'll say this much: when I was wandering around the streets of Athens, my subjective experience was that everyone I saw or spoke with seemed to be a version of myself. I felt myself united with the whole city, even my accusers, which is why I couldn't be angry with them. But short of enlightenment, it seems quite possible that individuals might feel this union two at a time.

Benedict: Here's an analogy. When an individual dreams, she

falsely believes that what she is experiencing is real. In lucid dreaming, which is analogous to enlightenment, the individual realizes that she is the person who is asleep and dreaming, not the person she seems to be in the dream. Everyone she encounters is encountered as herself, as created by the mind of the dreamer. The kind of situation that Socrates and I were playfully exploring would be analogous to a person who, while dreaming, *recollected* that she was dreaming only in the presence of one other individual in the dream. I fear I'm not stating this in the right way.

Plato: As if there **is** a "right way" in which any of this could be stated. So we must become content with the intrinsic limitations of language. Rumi's statement is not so much a complaint as it is a simple statement of fact. And we honor that fact by not trying too hard to "get it right" with regard to our locutions. It is sufficient to give some sense of what it might be like, and be content.

William: I'm content, but there's something I can't let pass.

Plato: What?

William: You stated: "From the collective perspective of our Social Order, the most important event in the life of any individual is the process by which two individuals come together for the purpose of bearing and raising children." Your statement implies that might be another perspective, from which vantage point another event in a person's life might be more important.

Do you have in mind another perspective?

Plato: Yes, there is another perspective besides that of the Social Order.

William: Well, what is it?

Plato: *(playfully)* The only reason you don't see it right now is because you are too close to it.

William: What do you mean?

Socrates: *(laughing)* He means that you're so close to it that you *are* it.

(Much laughter, as William [and I] finally get the point.)

Neal: I suppose there is no getting around the fact that the individual human perspective is the most important one for individual human beings.

Benedict: Yes. Even though there are many and diverse kinds of unitary couplings.

Neal: What do you mean by "unitary couplings"?

Benedict: Two things come together and form a third thing with wholistic properties not reducible to the sum of the parts. For example, a molecule is a unitary coupling of two or more atoms.

Neal: OK, but we are talking about consciousness, not atoms and molecules.

Benedict: I know, but I wanted to make an analogy.

Neal: Oh, you mean that individuality is preserved. So if we take the atom to be the basic unit of matter, it can couple with other atoms to form molecules, which themselves can comprise other material systems, which are also individuals in their own right. The atom retains its individuality and has its own perspective even though it constitutes other systems that also have their individuality and perspective. Is this what you meant?

Benedict: Something like that; we shall not try too hard to be exact. But we must understand that atoms are not the basic unit of matter; in fact, there are no basic units of matter.

Neal: Yes.

Benedict: Similarly, the human being is not a basic unit of consciousness; neither is the soul. In fact, there is only One Consciousness, and no "basic units" thereof.

William: Well, we can leave out the word "basic". We are here considering the human perspective, not all the infinitely many perspectives, many of which are themselves infinite, that constitute the being of Consciousness.

Plato: No need to get into this. We are considering the human being: a rather unique and peculiar perspective within the field of consciousness. The human has the ability to form couplings with other such beings. These couplings – partner, children, community – will of course be "unitary" in the sense that they will have wholistic features not reducible to the perspectives individually considered. Benedict and Socrates explore the possibility that humans may partner in such a way that each becomes a portal to the eternal for the other. But even if this were to become possible, each would retain his or her individuality. So yes, there will be such a thing as the "collective perspective of the whole social order" and at the same time there will still be the perspective of the individual human being. From the former perspective, the most important event in the life of any individual is as we have stated: coupling with another human for the purpose of raising children. Now can you tell me what is the most important event for latter perspective?

William: Yes, death. Or if Socrates thinks the word "death" is too negative, we can call it "The Grand Homecoming" or "The Return".

Socrates: Well, we shall be discussing this at greater length soon enough.

Plato: Yes, and "old age" too. But now I want to consider a question Neal previously raised, perhaps only playfully, yet there is also a serious side to the question.

Neal: What question?

Plato: It was, "What will our young adults talk about?" – or something like that. The question really asks for some insight into what the social life of our young adults will be like.

Neal: Yes.

Socrates: And I think perhaps the best way to approach this question is to remove the qualifier "social" from Plato's sentence above.

Plato: Good. I see your point, and agree.

Neal: What point?

Socrates: *(with a little humor)* The point that your present social order is schizophrenic; in fact, it is doubly schizophrenic.

Plato: OK, I'll explain before you complain that you're not following this. Let's begin with the phrase "social life" and ask what work is done by the adjective "social".

Neal: The adjective is meant to focus on just one aspect of a person's life – how she connects with other people – and exclude other aspects of a person's life, such as their work or job.

Plato: And what are the other aspects to a person's life? Let's list them all.

Neal: OK. I can think of four aspects to life in my culture: (i) *personal* life – this would include whatever a person does when alone, such as reading, meditation, walks, writing, and so forth. Then there is (ii) *family* life, which includes time spent with children, parents, siblings, extended family, etc. There is (iii) *work* life – job, career, profession – what one does to pay the rent, and finally, (iv) *social* life, or what one does with others for fun, dinner parties, friends, etc. But I can see that this fourfold division of a person's "life" will not work so well in our new social order. Oh *(glancing at Socrates)* is this why you referred to it as double schizophrenia?

Socrates: *(smiling)* Yes. The basic distinction is between one's private life and one's public life, the former of which is further divided between personal and family, and the latter of which is divided between what you call "work" and what you call "socializing".

Plato: Let's examine (iii) first. We have stated that no one will have to "work" for a living, because food, clothing, and shelter are unconditionally guaranteed. People will do whatever they wish. The phrase "outer expression of one's inner nature" is too cumbersome to use, but it accurately states how people will feel about what they do. Slavery will finally come to an end.

Neal: Slavery?

Plato: Whenever one person is compelled to labor for the material benefit of another, that is slavery. Under capitalism, a person is technically "free" to change jobs, but then he is merely exchanging one master for another. There is no getting around the fact that capitalism is a form of slavery, especially when one can see where it has led. A few people own everything, and control the lives of many.

Let me develop this theme a little bit. In my time, slavery was acknowledged for what it is, the "ownership" of one human being by another. In your time it has become more insidious. For what is "owned" is not the physical body, but the mind itself. The wealthy do not control the body of their slaves, but rather, the actual thinking of their slaves, so that the thinking of the people is aligned with the interests of the rich.

William: Yes, there are two ways to control the behavior of another: (i) through force or threat of force or (ii) by conditioning and causing their minds to believe what the wealthy want them to believe. The second alternative is a much more effective form of slavery, since the "slaves" will deny that they are in fact slaves, and in your so-called "democracy", the slaves will happily vote for the candidates approved by their masters. But in our new social order the advertising industry will no longer exist, hence our citizens will be truly free.

Neal: The advertising industry is perhaps the most evil element in our present culture, as its sole purpose is to influence the desires and thinking of people, without any regard for what is best for the people.

Plato: Yes, and as we have said, *my* sophists have devolved into *your* advertising agency executives. Now it goes without saying that any society *must* inculcate certain beliefs, desires, and behaviors into its citizens. This is what we call "upbringing". But *our* social order is the first to come into being that will align the inner life of the human with what is truly best for him or her. So as we have said, children will be conditioned to desire only foods that are healthy for the body. Children will be conditioned to believe and follow the Golden Rule. They will be conditioned to believe and feel that greed and status-seeking are forms of mental illness to be cured rather than followed. And most importantly, they will *not* be conditioned to feel guilt with respect to natural sexual desire. In *our* society, children will have no role models for lying or for inauthentic behaviors of any kind. Because of this, there will be no need for a schizophrenic distinction between public life and private life. Everything our citizens *do*, whether at home or in public, will feel to them as an outer expression of their authentic inner being.

William: In fact, many neuroses and other forms of mental

dysfunction in the present culture are directly caused by the induced schizophrenia that arises when people are not allowed to be authentic. The inauthenticity required in order for people to adapt to the present culture causes enormous amounts of stress on the individual. Therapists can't see this because they themselves participate in it, and have been raised to believe that it is "normal".

Neal: Benedict, you wrote somewhere that that society is best in which people were free to think what they want, and say what they think.

Benedict: Yes, something like that. But I was thinking of "political" freedom, not metaphysical freedom. People do not first "want" to think something and then "decide" to think it. So I might rephrase that as "that society is best in which people feel free to experience, and express without inhibition, the flow of thoughts passing through their minds." I suppose I should include emotions too.

Neal: Yes. May we state then that mental illness necessarily arises when one's inner life is externally controlled?

William: I think I see what you mean. But elaborate a little.

Neal: Let's say that a person's mind – her inner life – contains the belief that seeking for money and status will bring happiness. We know that this is a false belief, both empirically and from first principles. Now babies are not born with this belief, and we regard it as unnatural for a human being. Cooperation is natural, but competition is not. The belief that competition is necessary and natural is externally caused by culture, especially the advertising industry. The person who has internalized this belief is mentally ill, by our standards of sanity. This belief, widely shared in the present culture, is the soil in which schizophrenia takes root, since seeking for wealth and status requires one to conceal and hide one's thoughts and feelings from others, in order to gain material advantage over others. Hence the split between private life and personal life, a split that psychiatrists would easily recognize as classic schizophrenia were it not for the fact that they too have been raised to believe it is "normal".

William: When you say that "cooperation is natural but competition is not", you are referring to that which is deepest in a human being, the soul.

Neal: There is no competition in Heaven, so to speak. Let's see if I can find that favorite quote of yours… ah, here it is:

> I saw that all men are immortal; that the cosmic order is such that without any peradventure all things work together for the good of each and all; that the foundation principle of the world, of all the worlds, is what we call love, and that the happiness of each and all is in the long run absolutely certain.

William: Yes, you are right, I love that passage. Richard Bucke succinctly expresses the content of his mystical vision, the same content that all mystics and NDErs report. He does not use the word "cooperation" in that passage, but states its meaning when he says that "all things work for the good of each and all". Perhaps it's not a bad idea to have our children memorize this passage and many other such passages that emphasize cooperation, love, happiness and immortality. Our new social order will incorporate these principles into its very structure. But now I'm wondering if you think our young man seeking a partner has been adequately helped in finding one.

Neal: *(smiling)* Yes, for he understands that the choice is not really a choice, but a recognition of what has been determined by the eternal order that is itself undetermined. So he rests assured, confident that he will recognize his partner when the time comes.

But now, may we address the question of what people will talk about? I agree that our citizens will no longer be required to become schizophrenic, and to separate their "work" life from their "social" life, or their "personal" life from their "public" life. These distinctions will be gone –

Plato: – except perhaps as temporal markers.

Neal: What do you mean?

Plato: *Now* Susan is performing heart surgery; *now* she is having a glass of wine with a friend; *now* she is changing diapers; *now* she is discussing the latest surgical techniques with a colleague; *now* she is exercising her body; *now* she is on a meditation retreat; *now* she is enjoying sex. We could categorize these various activities as "work", "play", "parenting", "work", "physical training", "spirituality", and "play", but Susan is not defined by these activities or categories. What she talks about will be germane to what she is doing and/or how she is feeling.

(With humor) But I think that perhaps you are more concerned with what she will **not** be talking about.

Neal: *(laughing)* I suppose you are right. It seems that most of what people talk about in our present society will not be relevant to anything in our new social order.

Plato: Yes. Well, let's list some of the topics that will no longer be relevant to our New Society.

Neal: OK. Here are some: (i) money, (ii) status, (iii) complaining and gossip, (iv) politics, and (v) religion.

Plato: Good. Let's say a little about each.

Neal: The first one is easy, since money will no longer exist. So no one can talk about how much money they are making, or wish they were making.

William: The second is easy too, since what is called "status" is equally distributed across the whole population. Because of upbringing, no one will feel more, or less, valuable to the social order, or any component thereof, than anyone else.

Benedict: And gossip will have become a thing of the past, especially when one considers the causes. Let us define gossip as talking negatively about people who are not present. People indulge in gossip as a way of feeling better about themselves by comparison. But our citizens will feel intrinsic self-worth, and will not be comparing themselves to others. Neither will they be whining and complaining about their external circumstances.

Plato: But *politics*, perhaps unlike the others, may still be the subject of conversations, although much differently than at present.

Neal: How so?

Plato: May I first define the word again, as I originally did?

Neal: Of course.

Plato: *Politics*, then, is the art and science of caring for the well-being of the people as a whole.

Neal: Yes, I seem to recall you wrote something like that, and then added that Socrates was the only politician in Athens.

Plato: Yes, for those called by that name in my time, and yours too, are seeking financial gain and status more than they are seeking the well-being of the people. They are not seeking the well-being of the people as a whole. Hence they are not really politicians. Indeed, they do not have the slightest idea *how* to care for the people as a whole, even if they wanted to.

Neal: I agree. For the only way that one can truly care for the well-being of the people as a whole is to first have a vision of "the people as a whole", that is, a vision of the World Soul or of the deep interconnectivity of all things. That is why only those who have had a spiritually transformative experience will be allowed to become politicians.

Plato: Yes, and our analogy with a symphony orchestra – a properly functioning symphony orchestra – is quite appropriate. The conductor must have an inner sense of the music as a whole, and it is this inner sense that guides how she conducts the orchestra. She may not herself play any of the instruments, but she knows the function or part that each instrument plays in generating the whole symphony. Similarly, the conductors of our social order – we should use the plural, "conductors", as there will be many – will have had the required vision described by Bucke and many others, and will have a sense of the deep inner harmony and interconnectedness of all humans as outer manifestations of the single Divine Being. It is only such people who, as Benedict put it, cannot desire for themselves anything they do not also desire for all humans, and hence, it is only such people that can be entrusted to guide and lead our Social Order.

Benedict: I want to add that Reason can and does lead to the same conclusion, and perhaps an individual who lacks direct experience but in whom the Voice for Reason is very strong might still be suitable for politics. But I want to hear from you, Plato, how politics might still be the subject of conversations.

Plato: Well, anything may be the subject of conversation without at the same time being the object of decision-making.

Benedict: Oh, of course. People who are not musicians may nevertheless talk about music; people who are not athletes may still talk about sports; and people who are not doctors may still talk about health. But we are agreed that decision-making in these endeavors shall be left to those who have expertise, training, and knowledge relevant to these subjects.

Neal: It would seem that democracy and knowledge are incompatible. For in every human endeavor that involves skills and knowledge, such as the ones mentioned by Benedict, no one would think that those who lack the relevant skills and knowledge should be involved in decision-making with respect to those subjects. No one would think that those who lack relevant musical knowledge and skills should be allowed to vote about how a piece of music should be interpreted, or that those ignorant of medicine should vote about whether brain surgery is necessary in a given case. Everyone agrees that such decision-making must be left to those with the relevant training and knowledge.

William: And to add a little to the list, no one would suggest that non-carpenters should vote on how a carpenter should do his work, nor that non-firefighters should vote on how fires should best be put out, nor that non-farmers should vote on when to plant crops.

Plato: But somehow a certain whacky idea has infected the human mind, going back to my time. It is called "democracy" – the idea that people with absolutely no knowledge about how to govern a city, or anything else, should nevertheless be able to vote on who should lead and how to govern. This idea is just as ridiculous, and in some ways even more so, than allowing people who are ignorant of medicine to vote on medical decisions.

Neal: What do you mean by "more so"?

Plato: Medicine involves caring for the health and well-being of the body. Politics involves caring for the health and well-being of the embodied soul's form of outer expression.

Neal: Huh?

Plato: Hmm, this sounds more complicated than it is. The soul is greater than the body, and that's all I meant by the phrase "more so". But let's consult our metaphysics for a moment. The soul itself is a focal point, an expression of the World Soul, which contains within itself an infinitude of such expressions. The soul, upon embodiment, requires care and nurturing – I speak now of the soul itself, not the body, which is duly cared for by the art and science of medicine. Now I could perhaps define *Philosophy* as the art and science of caring for the soul insofar as it is itself, and *Politics* as the art and science of caring for the soul insofar as it is compelled to live in community with other embodied souls while it is embodied.

Socrates: It would seem then that the same knowledge is required for both politics and philosophy. For well-ordered communities cannot arise in any way other than from well-ordered individual souls.

Neal: And for a soul to become "well-ordered" within itself, it must have had a vision of the interconnectedness of all things, or of the One Mind of which all minds are expressions.

Plato: But now we must add some qualifications to what we have been saying.

Neal: What do you mean?

Plato: We have been saying all along that the guardians and rulers of our social order – those entrusted with governing and decision-making – must have had a vision of the Divine Being or what is the same thing, of the interconnection of all things.

Neal: Yes, that is what we have been saying.

Plato: But do you think this vision is sufficient for producing our leaders and politicians, or is something needed in addition to the vision?

Socrates: *(mischievously)* Perhaps the vision removes more than it gives.

Neal: Well it removes all desires for "status", all desires to gain material advantage over other embodied souls. And it leaves behind Unconditional Love for all humans. So I suppose in some weird way you could say that many more desires are removed than are left behind.

Socrates: Yes, well I was just joking in my weird way, as you point out. But if we look at enlightenment from a Buddhist perspective it becomes clear that nothing is added to the soul, but rather, clouds that blocked clear perception were removed.

Neal: So then the ability to govern, the ability to make wise decisions with respect to communities and large numbers of people – this ability is not automatically given in the experience of the knowledge of the mind's union with God. Rather, the vision removes the obstacles to the proper functioning of this ability.

Socrates: Yes, something like that. Besides, many people who have the vision are driven mad because of it, and should no more be trusted to make communal decisions and judgments than a four-year-old child.

Neal: What are you saying, Socrates? Surely they are driven sane, not mad.

Socrates: Oh, lighten up. Surely there is a sense in which "sane" by Divine Standards is "mad" by human standards.

Neal: OK, I get the point. Actually, it's quite obvious. Just examining the after-effects of the Near-Death Experience, it is obvious that the experience does not automatically give one the ability to govern at all, let alone wisely. And many find themselves so possessed by the Muse that they are unable to think about anything besides poetry or music. So we are saying that the vision of Unity is necessary for our rulers and guardians, but not sufficient. So how will we find our politicians?

Plato: That's easy. We have been "finding" them all along.

Neal: Really? And how have we been doing that?

Plato: By observing our children at play.

Neal: Oh.

Plato: Shall we return briefly to the playground, and take another look at our children while they are at play?

5) Identifying Leadership Qualities

Neal: Yes. And I suppose that we shall be looking for leadership qualities that emerge in their spontaneous play, and then encourage those qualities and those children?

William: OK, but we must be clear about what we mean by "leadership qualities". For the world is deeply confused about this.

Socrates: *(playfully)* We must go easy on what you have called "the world", for it is being compelled to undergo a transformation of major proportions, and a major component of this transformation involves a conscious shift of the psychological qualities deemed necessary for a leader. Within a single generation "the world" will come to understand that the psychological qualities it previously thought were necessary for good leadership were more like the qualities of our four-year old little boy throwing a temper tantrum in the local supermarket than like the qualities necessary for real leadership.

Plato: Actually, as the social and political outer forms of human life shift over the centuries, so do the qualities for leadership under the given social forms. In my time, for example, *war* was an essential component of human life, so any "leader" had to know about war and military strategy, and had to be OK with regard to killing human beings. But the psychological qualities needed to lead a city or state into battle are very different from the qualities needed to sustain a World at peace. Now, we have stated that outer peace – a peaceful world – can come into existence only under the leadership of those who are at peace within their very souls. And only the Vision of Unity brings about such a permanent peace, which is why we are requiring this vision for our leaders.

Neal: But we have also said that the Vision, while necessary for our leaders, is not sufficient.

Plato: – Which is why we are back at the playground, observing our children at play. For children are not born all alike.

Neal: Yes, I agree, but what are the specific qualities we are looking for?

Socrates: We are looking for qualities that are the opposite of what has been considered leadership qualities up until now. And lest you accuse me of being cryptic, a child might be thought to have leadership potential if he can "take charge" and impose his will upon the group, either by physical strength or psychological manipulation.

William: I can see why you said we must go easy on the world. For these very psychological qualities that have been historically the case, involving stereotypical "male" strength, are now utterly useless if the world is to survive. Well, we know what we are *not* looking for: the child who brags and bullies, who enjoys imposing his ideas upon others and is easily upset when things don't go his way, who is concerned about "winning" games and arguments, who needs and seeks recognition from others, and is limited with respect to the ability to feel compassion for others.

Socrates: *(laughing)* And we shall devise a new kind of grease for our squeaky wheels.

Neal: Huh?

Plato: Let's stay with this. What is the opposite of a squeaky wheel?

Neal: A wheel that doesn't squeak.

Plato: Which is exactly why it is more difficult to observe. Everyone notices a wheel that squeaks, for it stands out and threatens to damage the smooth functioning of the machinery taken as a whole. But a wheel that not only (i) does not squeak but also (ii) runs even more smoothly than the other ones that do not squeak is more difficult to spot.

William: *(with humor)* I can imagine a large piece of machinery, whirring along doing its thing, until one component begins to malfunction and makes various sounds. Everyone pays attention to the malfunctioning part. But no one notices the component that functions exceptionally smoothly, and that greatly assists the other parts in performing their functions.

Socrates: Now the olde-tyme grease of which I previously spoke consisted of placating the squeaky wheel, of acceding to its imagined needs, and even conceding political power to those least capable of wielding it. Anything to keep that wheel from squeaking.

Neal: Then the new grease of which you spoke consists of therapy.

William: It is a bit ironic, is it not, that the very qualities that were considered indicative of leadership ability are the qualities that in our New Social Order will be considered indicative of mental illness.

Benedict: Which is yet another way to see that the world is presently insane.

Socrates: *(laughing)* Well, we have said before that the lunatics are now running the asylum. However, it must be said that because of how we are raising our children, we expect much fewer cases of such madness.

Benedict: Yes, but we cannot eliminate them entirely, for as long as the knowledge of the union that exists between the human mind and the mind of God is lacking in any individual human being, that individual will be susceptible to the dis-ease of becoming a squeaky wheel. So our guardians will be on the lookout both (i) for behaviors and qualities that might require some correction, as well as (ii) for qualities and behaviors that might be indicative of leadership abilities.

Plato: We can now be a bit more specific about the second set of qualities. We have defined *politics* as the art and science of caring for the citizens considered as a whole. Some of the qualities of our future politicians, insofar as they might manifest on the playground, are (i) a concern for the emotional well-being of the other children, (ii) inventing games that generate happiness in other children, (iii) an ability to resolve conflicts that might arise among children. Our future leaders are happiest when they have engendered and inspired happiness in others. They shall exhibit exceptional emotional intelligence, and as Socrates might put it, they shall have an inborn talent for greasing the wheels of those around them so as to prevent squeaks from even arising. We shall observe them as they mature, and those who all their lives show a consistent pattern of caring for the well-being of the citizens and their communities shall in midlife be groomed for positions of leadership.

We must remind ourselves that the usual "rewards" that until now have accompanied positions of leadership shall be entirely absent in our New Society.

Neal: You mean the rewards of status, wealth, control over others…

Plato: Yes. The rewards for leadership are the same as the rewards for anything else. That is, there are no rewards other than the joy intrinsic to performing one's function in this life.

Neal: You also stated that midlife is the time to identify those who will be chosen for leadership. Shall we be more specific?

Plato: By all means. Let us state, somewhat arbitrarily, that midlife begins approximately when the children have left home and are on their own. At this age, around 50, our citizens have fulfilled their child-raising responsibilities, and it is an appropriate time to take stock of one's life, so to speak.

Now, what I refer to as "taking stock of one's life" is really an ongoing process, as our citizens are sharing thoughts and feelings regularly in small groups as part of their lives. But there will be times when it will be useful for an individual to step back from what he/she has been doing, and with guidance, consider what she wants to do next.

William: But wait a minute. Were we not just looking for qualities in our children that would be indicative of leadership ability? And now suddenly we are at midlife, without yet having a firm grasp of the qualities we were seeking in our children, and how to encourage those qualities throughout their lives.

Benedict: *(with humor)* Don't worry, William. Plato is just dancing all over the place again. Eventually we shall rein him in.

Plato: *(jokingly)* Hah! Don't count on it. But I think I can see an analogy that might illustrate what I wish to state, and also unify our diverse themes.

Neal: Are you thinking of our symphony orchestra?

Plato: Why yes, how did you know?

Neal: Orchestras are very good at unifying diverse themes, literally.

Plato: Ah yes, but actually I shall be using the orchestra metaphorically, not literally. Well anyway, let's suppose that John, when he was a child, showed great interest in music, and that when a variety of musical instruments were placed before him, he became completely fascinated by the flute. Johnny never needed to be reminded to practice, since it was a passion for him. In fact, he needed to be reminded to stop practicing the flute, so he could do other things and become more well-rounded. His parents and teachers spotted his talent early, and saw to it that his environment was populated with flutes, flutists, flute teachers, and everything needed to develop and encourage his inborn talents.

Now as we have said, all children will be exposed to music, and most will take up a musical instrument. But for most children, interest in the instrument will wane as the child matures. The same with most other things. For example, all children will take up sports and gymnastics, but few will have the talent to continue into adulthood. And the same for all professions and vocations. For example, Johnny's friend Suzie starts playing the violin at the same age that Johnny starts with the flute. Suzie has some talent for it, and after a few years enjoys playing her instrument very much. She even sits in the same school ensemble as Johnny. But when she is 12 years old she takes a biology course and is fascinated by the human body and how it works. Her interest in the workings of the human body soon eclipses her interest in playing the violin, and she goes on to become a brain surgeon. Johnny is fascinated by many things, but his interest in the flute continues unabated. He joins a major symphony orchestra in his mid-twenties, where he has been honing his skills and perfecting his craft until we find him now, at age 50, with his children all grown-up. It seems that there are several different directions his life could take at this point. Shall we explore them?

Neal: Yes of course.

Plato: (i) He could continue playing the flute in the orchestra. (ii) He could do something with his craft besides playing in an orchestra, such as teaching and inspiring children. (iii) He could abandon his craft altogether, and explore paths not taken.

Neal: What do you mean?

Plato: Most of our children will be interested in more things than can be pursued in a given lifetime. Some of these things *must* be pursued in youth, but others may be pursued later on in life. For example, we may suppose that in high school and college John had some athletic talent and loved playing basketball. He had to relinquish sports to study the flute, and now at age 50, it is too late to become an athlete. But if he were interested in massage and bodywork, it would not be too late to take up these skills, especially since everyone is exposed to them from early childhood. So this would be an example of exploring a "path not taken".

William: And we must remind ourselves that explorations undertaken at this time, or at any time, are not hostage to financial necessities, so that people are really free to explore their interests. But I don't see how this midlife exploration helps us identify our leaders.

Plato: You will, for there is a fourth possibility, as fine as it is subtle. It happens when our flute player, proficient in his part, begins to notice the other musicians in his orchestra, and the sounds coming out of their instruments.

Neal: Wait a minute. Surely John has been noticing these sounds all along.

William: He could hardly avoid hearing the loud sounds coming from the trumpets and trombones, to say nothing of the percussion.

Socrates: Ah, but there's hearing on the one hand, and *hearing* on the other.

Neal and William: Huh?

Plato: Well, maybe "noticing" is a better word than *hearing*. Consider an orchestra – a fully functional orchestra, I might add, under the baton of a great conductor. Does the audience hear the same thing as the conductor?

Benedict: I can see the point you are heading towards. So that we do not get bogged down with semantics, let us agree that the sound waves that emanate from the orchestra and impinge on the respective ears of the conductor and audience are the same. So in this very ordinary sense of the word "hear", they are hearing the same thing. But the conductor will notice, or *hear*, details that escape the audience. The conductor will *hear* how the parts are internally organized so as to constitute a coherent whole, whereas the audience hears the coherent whole.

Neal: And the conductor also hears parts that the audience does not hear at all, yet which are essential for providing the texture of the overall effect. When the music is loud, no one in the audience can hear the violas or the bassoons, even though the sounds that they produce are essential for the overall effect.

William: So we might say that the conductor *hears* or *notices* how all the various and diverse parts fit together so as to produce a most glorious overall effect, whereas the audience hears mostly just the overall effect.

Benedict: I like this analogy. It is a good model for the "part-whole" relationships that will permeate our Social Order. It also gives a hint about *why* the whole is always greater than the sum of its parts, and in what that "greater than" consists.

William: What do you mean?

Benedict: The sounds emanating from our symphony orchestra are the "whole", the "parts" of which are the sounds emanating from the instruments considered separately. It would seem obvious that the whole is "nothing but" the sum of the parts, don't you think?

William: *(smiling)* No, I don't think.

Benedict: Oh, c'mon, play along with me here.

William: OK, happy to oblige. Well, it is obvious that the overall sound produced by the orchestra consists of the sum of all the individual sounds made by all the different instruments. So how, and in what way, could the overall effect, the whole, be greater than, or more than, the sum of its parts. And in what does this "more than" consist?

Benedict: Thanks for asking. We assume that each musician in the orchestra has perfect knowledge of his or her own part. But we do not assume that she has the knowledge of how the parts fit together so as to constitute an organic whole. And actually, the symphony is not composed one part at a time, but rather, the composer has a coherent vision that is realized through the various parts. The conductor has a knowledge of this vision, which he then imposes upon the musicians, so that the individual parts are woven into an organic whole.

Neal: So it is *intelligence* that organizes the parts into a coherent whole.

Benedict: Yes, so if one is to ask what it is that makes the whole greater than the sum of parts, the answer is, it is the knowledge of how the parts are organized into a coherent whole. In our example, this knowledge is contained in the mind of the conductor.

Neal: Plato, what did you mean by calling this knowledge "fine and subtle"?

Plato: No conductor could state in words what it is that she does. Rather, there exists something within her that we might call "a feeling for the music as a whole". This "feeling for the music as a whole" is not analyzable. It is experienced as a unified whole, which the conductor then projects onto the orchestra, so that the musicians are individually guided by the conductor's vision of the music, and collectively project the conductor's vision of the whole into the audience. We could state that it is the knowledge, or intelligence, of the conductor that organizes the various "parts" into a single unified whole.

So getting back to John, our flutist, and what I referred to as the fourth possibility for midlife change. He begins to notice *how* the sounds that emanate from the various instruments constitute a single whole. This noticing is "fine and subtle", as I said, and reflects an inborn talent that perhaps is not teachable. But once this feeling for the part-whole relationship takes hold of a person, the skills of a conductor can then be honed and practiced.

Benedict: I think that the symphony orchestra – the fully functional orchestra in which everyone is content to play their own part – is a good model for the "part-whole" relationship insofar as it pertains to humans and the social groupings to which humans necessarily belong.

William: A sports team might be another model for what we have in mind. Each member of the team plays his or her part, but the coach or manager has an internal sense of how all the parts cohere together, so as to constitute a "team" rather than just a bunch of individuals. Some, but by no means all, players develop an internal sense of this coherence and when they retire from playing, go on to become coaches and managers, or as Plato here might put it, guardians of the game.

Socrates: Ah, but we are after bigger game than a sports team or a symphony orchestra, useful as these are as analogies, no actually, as *instances* of what we are after.

William: What do you mean? What "bigger game" do you have in mind?

Socrates: The Game of Embodiment. But before we get to that, or rather, on our way to getting to that, we must (i) identify a very important talent our leaders must have, and (ii) say something about the intelligence that binds the individual parts together, something that does not show up in our two examples.

Neal: We're listening.

Socrates: The first point may be illustrated in terms of our examples. In addition to having a feeling for the part-whole relationship, our conductors and coaches must also have the ability to *inspire* their musicians and athletes to play their best. It is because of their ability to inspire that the best conductors and coaches are so loved and admired by those they lead.

Neal: It would seem that this ability to inspire is among the "fine and subtle" talents that have been alluded to before.

Plato: "Fine and subtle", but not uncommon, as every good teacher must also have this ability to bring out the best in her students. By calling it "fine and subtle", we are merely stating that this ability cannot be analyzed in words; nor, in all probability, can it be taught explicitly. So in this sense, it is like the ability to recognize the part-whole relationship in particular social contexts.

William: I think this is correct. "Fine and subtle" though it is, everyone knows who are the good teachers, coaches and conductors. They inspire those they lead to do their best, even though no one can state what it is they do that inspires. But we should now say something about how this applies to social contexts other than sports teams or symphony orchestras.

Neal: OK, but I also want to hear what Socrates has in mind regarding the intelligence that binds the individual parts together, and that does not show up in our examples.

Benedict: Let's follow William's suggestion first, unless Socrates objects.

Socrates: No objection.

Benedict: Very few humans belong to sports teams or symphony orchestras…

Neal: Wait a minute. It is true that very few humans will, as adults, be athletes or musicians, but all will be exposed to both sports and music as children. So everyone will have had the experience of being in groups where their own talents for music and sports, minimal though they may be, are encouraged and inspired.

Plato: Yes, and this is a good way to restate our present task. Everyone in our social order has experienced inspiration, for our teachers must have this ability. Our task now is to identity this ability in others, and as Benedict was about to say, apply it to other social contexts.

Benedict: Good. I'll identify several social contexts to which humans necessarily belong. Now, we should first note that many of the traditional social contexts shall no longer exist in our New Social Order. I have in mind things such as race, religion, class, economic status, and so forth.

Neal: And we should also note that some social roles will no longer exist, especially that of the gambler. So there will be no insurance companies, no advertising agencies, no bankers, no financial advisors.

Benedict: Agreed. Let's now consider a few social roles other than musician and athlete, so that it will be clear that our analysis is universally applicable. We must remember that prestige and status are no longer attached to social roles, so John the flute player has the same status as the conductor of the orchestra. And Fred, the waiter at the local restaurant that John goes to for a snack after the concert, has the same social status as John. For although it is important to select our leaders for appropriate skills and abilities, those leaders once selected will have no more status than those they lead. We wish now to get a sense of how John and Fred are alike, both with respect to the various social contexts to which they belong, and with respect to identifying innate leadership qualities.

Neal: Well one obvious social context in which they are alike is biological: they are both born into families, so that would be one social context. Another context is given through their work situation, or rather, through the external context in which they express their inner natures, or something like that. So John belongs to an orchestra, Fred belongs to a restaurant.

Benedict: And since neither orchestra nor restaurant exist in a social vacuum, but rather are connected with a larger community, John and Fred also belong to that larger community.

Neal: Yes.

Benedict: Let us further suppose that John and Fred have children who attend the same school. Fred and John, then, also belong to the community of parents who have children attending that school. So this is another social context to which they both belong. We may also suppose that they have hobbies and interests that connect them with others who have similar hobbies and interests. They also have to eat, so they are connected to the farmers who produce the foods they eat. They also need clothes and shelter, and so are connected…

Neal: Yes, but wait a minute. It is obvious that every individual is thus connected to the Social Order as a Whole, which one quickly gets to after biology and the immediate work context. And our social order is constituted by wholes within wholes within wholes. But there's something I'm not understanding very well.

Benedict: What?

Neal: What is the immediate social whole to which Fred belongs, after family?

Benedict: You yourself have said that, as John belongs to the orchestra, so Fred belongs to the restaurant in which he works.

Neal: That's not what I mean. The orchestra, under the guidance of a conductor, produces music to which John contributes. Who is the "conductor" of the restaurant, and what is the "music" it produces?

Benedict: Ah, I see the question, the answer to which will shed a little light on the difference between your present society and the one now under construction. When you go to a concert, you enjoy the overall effect of music, produced by a conductor who (i) understands the whole/part relationship with respect to the music being played – or in other words, has internalized the vision of the composer, and (ii) has the ability to inspire his musicians to play their best. So now you are asking, with respect to the restaurant, (a) what is the overall effect, (b) what is the whole/part relationship, and (c) what or who is the analogue of the conductor?

Neal: Yes, that's what I am asking.

William: The answer might involve Plato's "fine and subtle". I suppose that the various "parts" to any restaurant include designing menus, ordering supplies, preparing the food, serving it to the customers, and cleaning up. These parts must be properly integrated to produce an overall effect, which we may call a fine dining experience for the customer.

Plato: And aside from the food itself, is there not something called the ambience of the place?

William: Yes, of course. Here comes the "fine and subtle".

Plato: Indeed. For everyone recognizes and appreciates a

restaurant with good ambience, although it is difficult to state in words what this ambience consists of.

Benedict: But we *can* state that it involves harmonious relationships among all the "parts" of the restaurant, just like an orchestra, in which the overall effect depends upon harmonious relationships among the musicians that comprise the orchestra. When everyone who works at the restaurant thoroughly enjoys what he or she is doing, this enjoyment is projected outwards to the customers.

Neal: In the orchestra, it is the role of the conductor to ensure and engender such harmonious relationships. Shall we state that, in the case of our restaurant, it is the role of the manager to engender the harmony among the various parts?

Plato: Yes. Our manager must have knowledge of the part-whole relationship with respect to the restaurant, she must have an overall vision of a well-functioning restaurant that she can project onto the "parts" – the people who work there, and most important, she must have the ability to inspire others to do their best. Like our conductor, she must have the ability to convey to the "parts" her sense of the whole, so that all who work in her restaurant feel that they belong to and are contributing to something greater than themselves.

William: And from a psychological perspective, the most basic need for a human being is to *feel* that she belongs to, and contributes to, something larger than herself. So one of the responsibilities of our conductors and managers is to inculcate this feeling in those they manage. We have stated that the first order of business of any group that comes together for any purpose – making music, running a restaurant, whatever – is the consciousness, the inner life so to speak, of each and every human involved.

Neal: This is a *very* different conception of the role of a "manager" from that of the present society. But before we say more about the role of the manager, I'm wondering if the pattern we have described – that of the conductor and the restaurant manager – is generalizable to all work situations. I'm using the term "work" instead of our more cumbersome expression "outer expression of one's inner nature", or something like that.

Benedict: Yes, the pattern of our two examples applies to most, if not all, work situations. Every unit in the public domain – symphony orchestra, restaurant, factory, hospital, school system, farm – requires coherent behavior on the part of the humans who work there. We may continue to use the word "work", although our citizens will feel that they are at play. It is the function of the manager to engender and inspire this coherence. For coherence among those who work, or "play", in a factory is just as important to the overall functioning of the factory as it is to the overall functioning of a symphony orchestra.

Neal: *(with humor)* Except that the discordant sounds that emanate from a dysfunctional orchestra are immediately obvious to everyone, whereas the "sounds" that emanate from a dysfunctional factory are perhaps a little less obvious.

William: "Less obvious" only to those who have been raised in the present social order. In the present order, in almost every workplace the workers and managers, and even those who manage the managers, suffer from all kinds of unhappiness: they are upset, angry, depressed, and frustrated much of the time. By contrast, *our* citizens are emotionally intelligent. To one who is emotionally intelligent, this psychological distress will be as obvious and discordant as the cacophony of noise emanating from our dysfunctional orchestra.

Neal: I'd like to contrast, just for a moment, the role of a manager in the present social order with that of our new social order. In the present social order, the main order of business for the manager is to make a financial profit for his boss. To this end, he squeezes his employees as much as possible, arranging their schedules for his benefit not theirs, paying them as little as possible, etc. That is, the well-being of the individuals he is "managing" is not part of his concern. But in our new social order, the well-being of the individuals being "managed" is the major concern of our managers, for being emotionally intelligent themselves, they understand that the output, or rather, the quality of the output of the factory or group they are managing depends crucially on the well-being of those who are doing the work.

And we may remind ourselves that, with the profit motive now a thing of the past, our managers are no longer constrained to purchase monetary gain at the expense of the workers' happiness. Hence they are free to manage in a way that maximizes both the quality of what is being produced and the happiness of those who are doing the producing.

Plato: And so, as we select our managers, we are looking for two qualities: (i) leadership ability, and (ii) knowledge of the functioning of the "unit" to be managed. The second we have sufficiently discussed, through the examples of John and Fred. I'll add only this to what we have said: perhaps the best way to get a feeling for the functioning of the whole is the way John did, to play his part in the orchestra under a conductor, then gradually become interested in the other "parts" and how it all coheres to produce a wondrous overall effect. But this is not the only path to becoming a conductor, as many great conductors never themselves sat in an orchestra. So we shall not insist that all our "managers" themselves have experienced being managed in the same unit that they wish to manage, although it is difficult to conceive how anyone could properly manage anything, a hospital, factory, school, etc., in which they have had no personal experience.

William: Let us state explicitly what we mean by the phrase "leadership ability", since it appears that what *we* mean by the phrase is the exact opposite of what the present culture thinks it is.

Neal: Yes, the present culture confuses leadership with bullying. A "leader" is thought to be one who imposes his will upon others, gets others to do his bidding, and so forth.

Plato: *(with a little humor)* … A confusion which is causing your present culture to self-destruct. For no culture can long survive without the ability to identify and select suitable leaders. Ultimately, as I have said, leadership ability is identical to spiritual wisdom, which latter is the same thing that Benedict called "the knowledge of the union that exists between the individual mind and the mind of

God". This is the knowledge of mystics and Near-Death Experiencers, and it is only this knowledge – I think we used a capital "K" before – that renders the individual human incapable of desiring for herself what she does not also desire for all humans.

Neal: But surely we do not insist that the conductor of a symphony orchestra or the manager of a restaurant be spiritually wise or enlightened?

Plato: *(laughing)* You are concerned that, with such a requirement, our New Society would experience a shortage of restaurants and orchestras? No, not to worry, the highest levels of spiritual attainment are required only for the highest levels of governing and leadership.

Neal: Good. I am relieved.

William: Nevertheless, all of our leaders, from the lowest level of social organization (like an orchestra, restaurant, school, etc.) to the highest, are cut from the same psychological cloth. This cloth, we maintain, is identifiable in early childhood, and I think we should say something about *how* we can recognize this cloth as it appears in the behavior of our children.

Neal: Shall we compare and contrast the cloth of our future leader with that of the current bully? Do we maintain that both cloths are identifiable in early childhood: one to be encouraged, the other to be corrected?

Plato: We've said enough about the latter. In any case, the "bully" will have become a thing of the past, since such behavior is caused mostly by bad upbringing. We must remember that young children will have no role models for the bully, the one who gets his way by imposing his will on others and who rejoices internally when he causes other children to suffer physically and psychologically. The Golden Rule, or "right opinion", has been etched deeply into the minds of all our citizens. But what we are calling "leadership qualities", or the psychological cloth that William referred to, are more difficult to identify in our children.

Neal: What you say seems to be so, especially since only one of the two cloths, the bully, is singled out for attention in the present culture.

William: Yes, and aside from the fact that the bully is likely to do better under a capitalist economic system than someone with the opposite personality, the bully seeks attention whereas the leaders we are seeking avoid attention. It is more difficult to notice a child who does not seek attention than one who constantly seeks attention.

Plato: So let's state it: the first quality we seek in our future leaders is a lack of concern for receiving attention or status from others. Anyone who seeks attention from others is, by his very seeking, unfit for leadership in our New Social Order.

William: Yes, because the seekers of attention are the neediest among us, insecure in their own being, needing continuous affirmation from those around them.

Neal: OK, but this is a negative requirement. What are the positive qualities and behaviors of our future leaders as children? I agree that as children they do not seek to stand out, to be praised for whatever they do, and so forth.

Plato: Ah, but what you bemoan as a negative requirement reflects a positive strength. Recollect for a moment one major difference between our two perspectives. You, representing the perspective of the embodied soul, perceive mostly the outer behavior of other humans. But we who are not embodied perceive the inner structure of the soul directly. Between the two – inner structure and outer behavior – are the emotions, or the emotional body. Although we believe that humans can become emotionally intelligent through proper upbringing – which means they can perceive the emotions of others directly, not just the outer behavior – still, it is only with great difficulty that the inner state of the embodied soul can be perceived by other embodied souls. So, from the non-embodied perspective, the soul of the bully "looks" as different from the soul of the leader as do their respective behaviors look different to the embodied perspective.

Benedict: In particular, there is an underlying fear in the soul of the bully that is absent in that of the leader. We perceive that fear directly. In the current social order, this underlying fear is allowed to fester and even flourish; fear and neediness motivate the bully to gain the social and economic status that he believes he needs in order to feel safe. In the social order under construction, the fear that motivates the bully will be identified in early childhood, and treated with compassionate therapy. It is doubtful that the fear will survive our process of upbringing, and we expect that there will be no adult "bullies" in our new social order. That is, there will be no individuals whose sense of self and self-worth depends on harming other individuals physically and psychologically.

Plato: And, also from *our* perspective, the lovingkindness in the soul of the future leader is directly perceived. But actually, and this is difficult to state in words…

Socrates: I beg to differ, and here are the words: when there are clouds in the sky, humans perceive the clouds; when there are no clouds in the sky, what do humans perceive?

William: I think I understand your meaning. Fear and neediness are clouds that obstruct the light of understanding, a light that is the same for all souls, human and otherwise, and always accompanied by feelings of gentle lovingkindness.

Neal: We could express this by saying that the absence of fear allows Divine Love to permeate the soul of the individual, whereas the presence of fear blocks the flow of the Love, and the individual possessed by fear becomes unable to receive what he most needs, which is Love, either from God directly, or from other humans.

Socrates: *(to me)* Please accept this slight correction: *all* Love comes from God, or the One. It may manifest through the human form, if the form is sufficiently clear, or uncloudy. It may also come through other forms, such as pets, Nature, and harmonious music. After all, do you not believe that when the Divine Being took the form of Mozart, She was expressing Her Love for humans?

Neal: Yes, I suppose so.

Socrates: Good. But of course I agree with Benedict that the most direct experience of Love – or what is the same thing, the *complete* absence of fear in the soul of a human – is the experiential knowledge of the union that exists between the individual mind and the One Mind.

William: OK, I agree too. But we should note that most humans will still experience some fear in varying degrees.

Neal: Why do you say that? Oh wait, I think I understand. The complete absence of fear would render physical embodiment unnecessary. Fear is the result of embodiment per se. We are calling for a thinning out of the margins, not a complete eradication.

William: Yes, that's what I was thinking. And to use Socrates' rather unoriginal analogy of a cloudy sky, cloudy days are not all alike.

Neal: What do you mean?

William: With respect to the analogy, a completely sunny day with no clouds whatsoever corresponds to the so-called "enlightened" human being, quite literally filled with Divine Light. By contrast, a completely overcast day corresponds to a fear-filled human, completely driven by ego-based needs. But there are also days that are partially cloudy, where sometimes the sun can be clearly seen, other time completely obscured. There are also hazy and foggy days, where the light of the sun, although visible, is severely diminished when it arrives at the Earth's surface. I assume Plato would agree that there are personality types associated with each of these elements from our analogy.

Plato: Yes, but we shall leave that for our future psychologists. We have our two extremes: (i) complete transparency to Divine Love, and (ii) complete obstruction of Divine Love, and many in-between possibilities of partial blockage. Now, we shall not expect to observe complete transparency among our children, since enlightenment, if it happens at all, usually happens later in life. But we do expect to observe children (a) who rejoice at the happiness of other children, (b) who invent games in which there are no losers, (c) who are quick to offer assistance to younger children, (d) who have a reputation among other children for breaking up fights and resolving arguments. These are behaviors that are impossible for one who is completely clouded over with fear. Complete spiritual enlightenment is required only for leaders at the highest level of social organization. At lower levels of organization, say a school, a hospital, a factory, or even a city, partial sunlight will be sufficient, especially since the values and behaviors that derive from complete enlightenment will pervade the whole Social Order.

Thus, I believe we have adequately described the character traits in our children that are auspicious for future leaders. But we shall be keeping an eye on them as they live their lives, and if they manifest these qualities consistently throughout their lives, then in midlife they shall be chosen for leadership roles. For their character renders them natural guardians and conductors, as we have been calling them. We of course also insist that they are knowledgeable about what they are conducting – knowledge about the inner workings, say, of a factory, an orchestra, a university, a city. Spiritual enlightenment, although certainly desirable wherever it occurs, is a requirement only at the higher levels of management, and an absolute requirement for the highest leadership roles – the Council for Planetary Government, or whatever we shall call it.

6) Of Wholes and Parts

Socrates: There is one slight difficulty that we should perhaps mention.

Plato: Go ahead and mention it.

Socrates: In the present social order, the desire to rule seems to be inversely proportional to the desire for spiritual experience. So perhaps the last thing a spiritually enlightened human being desires is to rule.

Neal: But did we not state, perhaps humorously, that monks and spiritual teachers will be compelled to change places with the present politicians and corporate leaders?

Plato: Yes, somewhat humorously. But it will not be a problem. For all enlightened individuals understand that they are merely forms through which Divine Love may be channeled to the Earth. They also know that their Earthly forms are in any case very temporary, and that they will soon enough quit their forms and return Home. So it will not be much of a burden for them if we require them to do what their physical form was created to do.

(To Socrates, with much humor) And *you*, my friend, will no longer be allowed to hang out in the marketplace, but rather we shall drag you, screaming and kicking if need be, into the highest levels of governing, and compel you to take your seat at the aforementioned Council.

Socrates: *(laughing)* Well I suppose I must suffer my fate with dignity, although it will not be unpleasant to sit around the table with other enlightened individuals. But even so, I assure you I will find some way to escape my confinement on the Council and pursue my first love, which is to wander around the marketplaces and hang out in cafes.

Neal: Yes, and it is a good thing to have leaders who enjoy hanging out with those they lead, instead of closeting themselves and feeling superior. But, Socrates, were you not about to say something about the intelligence that binds the parts together into an organic whole?

Socrates: Yes, but I was sort of hoping that you had forgotten about that.

Neal: Why is that? Is the subject too "fine and subtle" to put into words?

William: Even so, we are already agreed on the limitations of words, and have said much to that effect. We know not to regard the words as literal descriptions of anything.

Socrates: Well, I don't want to be accused of getting metaphysical here.

Neal: What do you mean?

Socrates: You asked me to say something about "the intelligence that binds the parts together into an organic whole."

Neal: Yes.

Socrates: Well consider this statement, and then tell me if you think it is "metaphysical".

Neal: What statement?

Socrates: The intelligence that binds the parts together into an organic whole is the same intelligence that expresses itself as the parts themselves.

Neal: *(smiling)* Well, I suppose your statement qualifies as "metaphysical", depending on what we mean by that term. But at the highest levels of creation it appears to be trivially true. At lower levels I'm not so sure.

Socrates: All great truths have an air of triviality about them, don't you think. But let's investigate. What do you mean by the phrase "highest levels"? I think I know, but it will good to state it.

Neal: There is a single Intelligence, a "One Mind", that expresses itself as the many minds, together with what the "many minds" observe as occurring external to themselves. So since there is only one intelligence, it is that intelligence that creates a realm of "Many". And since the "One" intelligence is a unified whole, even as it expresses itself as Many, the many "parts" are intrinsically bound up into that organic Whole.

Socrates: *(smiling)* Well, I suppose that would satisfy anyone's definition of the term metaphysical.

Benedict: Yes, but, Socrates, your original statement is not quite correct.

Socrates: Indeed, I would be surprised if *any* of my statements are "quite correct". But what are you finding problematic?

Benedict: You talk about "the intelligence that binds the parts together into an organic whole." Yet we must resist thinking of the "parts" as somehow preexisting, and then needing to be externally "bound" into an organic whole.

William: Although this is how it does appear to humans.

Socrates: Good. Let us investigate the whole-part relationship, not abstractly, but as it shows itself in three examples we have already discussed. We'll begin with the restaurant example, which I believe illustrates the whole-part relationship as it commonly occurs in human relations. What are the various "parts" that require an intelligence to organize them into a single whole?

William: OK, well the "parts" are both human and nonhuman. The former include cooks, waiters, managers, people who farm the food for the restaurant, and people who deliver the food to the restaurant. The nonhuman "parts" are the food, the tables, dishes, stoves, and all the equipment necessary for a restaurant. The various activities of all the humans need to be externally coordinated so as to create the overall effect of a restaurant. So it looks like, in this case, the various "parts" – the cooks, waiters, tables and chairs – do preexist, and need to be externally organized into an organic whole by the intelligence of the manager. This is how it appears to humans, not only for restaurants, but also for all other forms of social organization.

Plato: A human being will belong to many "wholes" during the course of a lifetime. The cook, we say, is a "part" of our restaurant. But he is also "part" of his family, his neighborhood, and many other groups that come together for a common purpose. But we are discussing the cook, not insofar as he is an individual human being, but only insofar as he is part of our restaurant. As such, he is tasked by the manager to perform a specific function within the larger whole that is our restaurant. As a "part" of this larger whole, the function of the cook is structured by the vision, or intelligence, of the manager. The manager of the restaurant, before she opens the doors to the public, *must* have a coherent vision of the functioning of the restaurant as a whole, with all the parts functioning coherently as a single unit, making a "unity" out of a "many".

Benedict: Interesting. I suppose we might state *(glancing at Socrates)* that the real function of a manager is to make a "one" out of a "many", if that's not too metaphysical a thing to say.

Neal: So the managers of our factories, offices, schools, whatever, will function after the model of coaches and conductors. The coach projects his vision of how the game is to be played into the minds of the individual players. It is his vision that constitutes the intelligence that binds the individual players into a single organic unity. And the conductor projects her vision of how the music is to be played into the minds of the individual players, so that a coherent unity is generated through the actions of the individual musicians taken together. But now, Socrates, what are the other examples, and how is the whole/part relationship different in them?

Socrates: The example I'm thinking about is more akin to the "big picture" than the one we have just discussed, and my third example will be intermediate between the two.

Neal: The "big picture"? Oh, you mean like the Divine Being manifests both as the "many" individual beings *and* as the intelligence, or force, that binds the individuals into a single organic Whole?

Socrates: Yes.

Neal: But what could possibly be a model for that, short of the Whole thing Itself?

Socrates: You.

Neal: Me?

Socrates: *(laughing)* Well, actually, not really *you*. By "you", I meant to refer to the human body, which as you well know is not the real *you*.

Neal: Yeah, I know, but it seems real to me now.

Socrates: ... And isn't this the definition of a perfect illusion? It *seems* so real, although the seeming is beginning to lose its grip on you, and we will discuss this soon enough when we talk about the latter stages of human life. For now let's examine the whole/part relation as it pertains to (i) the body as a whole, and (ii) the cells that constitute it. But wait, I think Benedict is eager to say something.

Benedict: Yes I am. Now, before you take us back to your three cells in a bar, or something equally ridiculous, I want to add a few words about this "illusion" you just referred to.

Socrates: *(with humor)* "Ridiculous", you say? Have you no pity for those unfortunate cells, who were about to expire because they burned up their energy arguing and doing other useless things, instead of directing their energies towards the source at the center of their beings? Oh well, I suppose you're going to compel me to get serious.

Benedict: God forbid. I just wanted to point out that separateness is part of the illusion of embodiment. It *seems* to embodied souls that wholes are "nothing but" the sum of their parts, and that the parts have an existence independent of the whole. But science has now shown that this atomistic appearance of things, as if they existed separate from and independent of one another, is as Einstein said an illusion generated by the structure of the human senses.

So, if we state that one thing, call it X, is made up of other things, call them Y, this statement could have two very different meanings: (i) Y exists independently of X, and when lots of Ys are put together and arranged in a certain way, one gets X. I suppose a house and the materials that make up the house would be an example of the "parts" existing prior to the whole. But in the case of any living organism this is not the case, since the cells that constitute the body are created by the body they constitute. So in this kind of case (ii) X, the whole, is primary, and creates the parts Y that appear to constitute it. Now Creation is analogous to (ii), not (i).

Plato: And even in the case of a house, which appears to be made up of parts, those "parts" don't just spontaneously assemble themselves into a house. In this case, the intelligence that organizes the parts into a building is the plan of the architect. And in the case of any workplace, restaurant, factory, office, university, etc., it is the intelligence of the manager that organizes the various "parts" into a harmonious whole.

William: Hmm, interesting, so it is quite misleading to state that the building is made up of its parts, since without intelligence, without the architect's plan, those "parts" would never arrange themselves into the form of a building. So intelligence, the plan or design, must be included in our account of the whole/part relationship, even for a building.

Neal: Yes, but for the body, it is obvious that it is not constructed in the manner of Frankenstein, from preexisting body parts or cells. So when we say the body is "made up of" cells, we must not treat this atomistically, as if the cells preexist the body and require some external intelligence to arrange them all into the form of the body. For every cell in the body is created by the body.

Plato: Just like every soul there is is created by the World Soul or the One Mind. Ultimately, causation is top down. But now, you say that the cells do not require an external intelligence to organize them into the whole that they constitute.

Neal: Yes, of course.

Plato: But they are so organized?

Neal: Again, yes of course.

Plato: So where is the intelligence that organizes them into a coherent whole?

Neal: I believe biologists would say it is located in the DNA that lies at the center of every cell. After all, from a single cell it is possible to clone the whole organism. So the knowledge of the whole must be contained in the DNA at the center of every cell in the body.

Plato: So the knowledge of the whole body is contained in the center of every cell in the body. The intelligence that coordinates the activities of all the cells into a single whole is internal to the cells themselves. And so the cells perform their various functions not directed from without, but spontaneously, according to their individual natures, as determined by the Body that created them.

Neal: This is perhaps a good analogy for understanding the meaning of expressions such as "the kingdom of heaven is within".

Socrates: Yes, and it's also a good analogy for understanding the illusion of separateness that pervades the human condition.

Neal: What do you mean?

Socrates: Recall our three cells in a bar. They were suffering from a rather peculiar condition, if I recollect correctly.

William: Peculiar indeed! Although the cells were conscious through and through, it seems that some sort of barrier or margin had formed between the outermost layer of each cell – its surface, so to speak – and the rest of the cell. Because of this margin, the surface thought that it was an independent unit, unconnected with its own depth.

Socrates: And this was a most dreadful state of affairs for the cells involved, for believing they were only the surface, they were always worrying about being bent out of shape, which quite literally happened every time they interacted with another cell. They could not understand that it is in the very nature of cell walls to be bent out of shape, as the cells are necessarily in continuous interactions with other cells.

Benedict: But the intelligence that guides and structures the whole process is contained within each cell. So instead of identifying with their external shape, the cells could instead identify with the "God" within – the DNA, in our analogy – and consciously participate in the union that exists between its own mind and intelligence according to which all cells come into being, perform their functions, and die. It participates in this union by overcoming the barrier of separation and reaching deep into the interior of its own being to access the knowledge contained within its DNA.

William: OK, we have discussed two examples, one in which the "parts" required an external intelligence to make them into a "whole", and one in which the "parts" are created by the very "whole" that they constitute. Shall we now discuss the example to which you have alluded that is intermediate between the two?

Socrates: Thanks for asking. Now the main difference between the two examples we have discussed is that in one case, the restaurant, the "parts" – waiters, cooks, tables, chairs, suppliers – appear to exist independently of one another, and require an external intelligence, that of the manager, to organize them into a harmonious whole. In the other case – cells and body – the knowledge of the whole is internal to each of the parts, so no external intelligence is required. In the case of an orchestra, the individual musicians have some awareness of the music as a whole, not only of their individual parts, but they still require an external intelligence, that of the conductor, to make a "one" out of "many". But in smaller musical groups, such as a trio or quartet, no external intelligence is needed, as each of the musicians have internalized their own parts together with a shared vision, or interpretation, of how the music is to be played. Their shared vision is the intelligence that organizes the parts into an organic whole.

And the answer to your question is, "Probably not, but worth thinking about."

Neal: What? Oh yes, the question flashed through my mind while you were talking. And I think I can see why it wouldn't work.

William: I can't quite anticipate your thoughts the way he can *(gesturing towards Socrates)*. What's the question?

Neal: Is it possible that every member of a large orchestra internalizes the music-as-a-whole the way the members of a quartet do, so that they wouldn't need an external intelligence to shape the music? Actually there have been a few such cases, of an orchestra playing without a conductor.

William: Well this is interesting; maybe I do have some modest psychic abilities after all, as I seem to have caught a glimpse of the lovely thought behind that question. But I think I agree with Socrates, that it won't work.

Neal: Lovely thought? What do you mean?

Plato: Wait a minute, everyone is getting ahead of themselves here. We'll discuss the lovely thought when Neal becomes conscious of it. It is indeed worth talking about. But for now, let us state the reasons why we think a small group of three or four *can* internalize a single vision of how the music is to be played, and so not require the guidance of an external intelligence, but not a large symphony orchestra.

Socrates: *(jokingly)* You can make a "one" out of a "many", but you cannot make a "one" out of a "too many".

Benedict: *(laughing)* Not quite right, old man. The correct statement should be something like: the "many" can make a "one" out of themselves, but a "too many" will require an external intelligence.

Neal: Yes. Three or four musicians can agree among themselves how the music should be interpreted. But the likelihood of such agreement must necessarily decrease as the number of humans involved increases. It is doubtful that 80 or 90 musicians would ever agree among themselves about how to interpret any given piece of music.

Plato: And if they were to agree, it would close the door to spontaneity, and hence, to the Muse.

Socrates: A bit like Heraclitus, don't you think?

Plato: Yes, but we will have to explain it. Heraclitus, you see, could not step into the same river twice. The river was always changing, so the waters into which he stepped the second time were not the same waters he stepped into the first time. The "waters" here are analogous to the inspiration that flows from the Muse into the conductor and the individual musicians. These waters are always in flux and never the same, and that is why no great musician ever plays the same piece the same way twice. The only way a musician or an orchestra can play the same piece the same way twice is if she has learned it mechanically and plays by technique alone. An orchestra whose musicians have learned a piece of music mechanically might be able to perform without a conductor, but the performance would be devoid of inspiration. On the other hand, a smaller group of three or four is not "too many" to be open to spontaneous inspiration. During a performance, say, one of the musicians gets a sudden inspiration to play a certain passage louder or softer or a little faster or slower. The other musicians, well-attuned to one another through years of association and practice, immediately and spontaneously adjust their playing to what the other is doing. But a large symphony orchestra could not function in this way. Too many cooks in the kitchen, or something like that.

Neal: So our conductor, like an individual soloist or small group of musicians, must be both technically fluent and receptive to spontaneous incursions from the Muse during a performance. For no two conductors interpret the same piece in the same way, and no conductor conducts the same piece in exactly the same way on different occasions. The Muse may equally inspire two conductors, but she inspires them in different ways. In a very small group, the respective inspirations may be brought under one heading; but this cannot happen with a "too many" group such as a large orchestra.

Plato: Now about your little vision, fleeting though it was…

Neal: Yes, I've got it. Every cell in the body knows its own function, what it was created to do. A given cell does not need to be told what to do, nor "managed" into performing its function. It spontaneously does what it was created to do. By analogy, could it ever be the case that humans are so attuned to their function, what they were created to do, that they will not require to be externally "managed"? In any context, people will naturally desire to do what is required by their function.

William: And this is a goal worth thinking about, even if unrealizable in the physical world. Any group of humans that come together for a common purpose – to build a bridge, run a museum, organize a university – must be structured by intelligence. In your vision, you ask whether this intelligence might perhaps be equally distributed in the minds of each of the individuals. But this "intelligence", since it originates from our side, does not follow any kind of blueprint, but allows for spontaneous creativity that is different in different humans. So it will express itself differently in different minds, and people will have difficulty agreeing to which and whose inspirations to follow. There is more than one way of doing things. So it is likely that managers will always be needed.

Plato: But we must remark that, hmm, although we are regarding managers as providing the external intelligence necessary to organize a "many" into a "one", it will *feel* to those being organized that they are expressing themselves naturally and spontaneously. For aside from being knowledgeable about what it is they are organizing, our managers have the ability to inspire others. But when a human feels inspired, she feels that she is doing what she wants to do. That is, the inspiration she feels is an internalization of the "external" intelligence of the manager.

Benedict: But now, here is a vision that *is* possible.

Plato: What do you have in mind?

Benedict: Our musicians, under the inspiration of a conductor, both know and feel that every note they play contributes to the greater whole, the overall effect. I have a vision in which everyone who works at our restaurant has the same experience as do the members of our symphony orchestra: under the inspiration of a manager they know and feel that everything they do contributes to the greater whole of a well-functioning restaurant. And this will be the case for every work situation.

William: And from the point of view of psychological well-being, this cannot be stressed enough. For we regard the *feeling* of belonging to a larger whole as a psychological need, satisfied by our new social order but ignored in the present one. This need cannot in principle be satisfied under a capitalist economic system, or any system based on greed and personal status-seeking. Such a system *must* have "winners" and "losers", with many more of the latter than the former. The suffering and psychological pain that arises from the failure to address this human need has led to neuroses, great unhappiness, and *(glancing at Plato)* a "mortal madness" not required by embodiment per se.

Plato: I'd like to comment on this. It is a psychological need for humans to feel a sense of belonging to something larger than themselves. Ultimately, the source of this need is the apparent separation of the human mind from, as Benedict puts it, the experience of the union that exists between itself and the Divine Mind. So humans are always seeking for this sense of belonging, but until now, have sought it in ways that cause unhappiness and strife.

William: Why do you say that? Certainly, the most immediate group to which humans feel a sense of belonging is their immediate family. How could that be a cause of strife and unhappiness?

Plato: Ego.

Neal: I think you need to give more than a one-word answer to William's question.

Plato: *(smiling)* Very well. I believe we have established that humans are happiest when they live according to the Golden Rule, and that social order is best that abides by that Rule in all its institutions, and inculcates that Rule into the minds of all its citizens.

Neal: Yes, we have said that the very bones of our children will form around the Golden Rule.

Plato: So in *our* society, humans will be able to satisfy the longing to belong without causing harm or conflict. In a social order not constructed around the Golden Rule, but instead constructed around the values of greed and personal ambition, it is not possible to satisfy this longing without harming others. But, William, you are thinking perhaps that even in such a social order people could still feel a sense of belonging to their families?

William: *(with humor)* Well yes, but now I can see your point. When ego is involved, then *my* sense of belonging to any group, whether family, city, or religion, occurs at the expense of *your* sense of belonging. I will favor *my* family, *my* city, *my* religion over yours, hence conflict will necessarily arise. So the need to belong to something larger than oneself, in a social order that is not in harmony with the Golden Rule, will invariably lead to conflict among the various groups to which humans belong and with which humans identify.

Neal: So the trick here is for humans to belong to various social groupings, and to rejoice in so belonging, but without any sense of ego identification with the groups to which they belong.

Plato: Indeed, for human beings are sons and daughters of the gods. This is their true identity, and will be common knowledge in our society. It is only their bodies that may be said to be the sons and daughters of their parents and the social order into which they are born. The greatest happiness, and ultimate satisfaction of the need to belong is given by the direct experience of their spiritual parentage, to know and become the gods that created them.

Benedict: And with this Knowledge, conflict among humans is impossible. As Socrates might say, two cells with identical DNA cannot be in conflict with one another. In Divine Knowledge, the human has connected with the spiritual DNA that binds all humans into a single "One Mind", hence conflict, either between humans, or between the various social groups to which humans belong, is not possible.

Socrates: *(smiling)* Well I'm glad you're finally warming up to my cells-in-a-bar.

Benedict: *(laughing)* Actually, the example is better than I first thought, and quite accurately mirrors something about the human condition. A cell whose consciousness has gotten truncated on the cell wall and has no access to the depths of its insides is like the human whose consciousness is truncated at the interface between its body and the external world. Both cell and human, ignorant of who and what they really are, live anxious about their external shape. But the cell whose consciousness permeates the whole of its being is analogous to the human who, fully conscious of the eternal union that exists between her own mind and the "One Mind", lives at ease, and rejoices in the eternal necessity by which she "lives and moves and has her being", and is not anxious about the body and its personality. The cells that can access their DNA know that they belong to one and the same body. Similarly, humans who can access the Divine within know that all humans belong to the same Divine Being. Such humans do not desire for themselves anything they do not also desire for others, so conflict cannot arise.

Plato: Very well. There are a few more things still to be discussed, but I believe we now have our New Social Order in hand. Not in every detail of course, which would be impossible, but in broad outline. Shall we now turn our attention to the Grand Homecoming, or as your present culture morosely puts it, death and dying?

William: Wait a minute. We have perhaps omitted something important.

Plato: What do you have in mind?

William: We have talked about *managers*, and stated that their role is to make a "one" out of the "many" that are involved in whatever they manage.

Neal: Perhaps "inspire" is a better term than "make". I seem to recall a verse from the *Tao Te Ching* that states that a great leader inspires those she leads such that they feel they are doing it by themselves, rather than feeling compelled or "made" to do anything.

William: Yes, I'll accept that correction. But my point is, between a restaurant manager and a World Manager there are numerous intermediary levels.

Socrates: World Manager?

William: *(laughing)* Yes, that Council for World Government, or whatever we called it, on which you shall be compelled to serve. Now I think it likely that the present form of political structures – mayor of a city, governor of a region, president of a country – may not survive intact, but something *like* it will.

Neal: And we insist that the higher the political structure the deeper the spiritual realization of those individuals who are to govern. For we all agree with Plato that temporal power and spiritual wisdom be must be unified in the same individuals, if the human race is to survive. So ascendency in temporal authority – manager, mayor, governor, president, World Council – must be matched by depth of spiritual realization.

William: So how will we guarantee that such conditions will be met, and only fully enlightened individuals will serve on the Council with Socrates?

Socrates: *(with humor)* What's this? You want a guarantee?

William: *(smiling)* OK, I suppose I should know better than to think that anything about this Grand Illusion of Physicality can be guaranteed. But still…

Plato: But still, I think we can do better than just shrug our shoulders. For our whole World Order depends on this: that only spiritually enlightened individuals are allowed to rule at the highest levels of social organization. If I may, William, I'd like to reformulate your question.

William: Go right ahead.

Plato: We envisage a highest governing body for the Earth, that we called the World Council, all of whose members are spiritually enlightened. How will we ensure that *only* enlightened individuals are allowed on the Council? What will prevent some ambitious fool, eager for the prestige and power of Council Members, from manipulating his way onto the Council, thus derailing our whole social order?

William: Yes, that is my question. After all, there is no higher governing body than the Council itself to oversee the proper choice of new members to the Council.

Plato: I have several responses to your concerns. First of all, an enlightened human being Knows, with a capital K, who is enlightened and who isn't. So our ambitious fool will not be able to fool the members of our Council. Second *(with humor)*, because of how we have raised our citizens, there will be a great lack of such ambitious fools. For our citizens have been imbued with the wisdom to know when they do not know, and the arrogance of *your* culture's fools will be a thing of the past. Third, everyone in *our* culture will have what I have called "true opinion". The spiritual world-view we have here developed will be common knowledge to all. Because of this, the spiritual cream will be allowed and encouraged to rise to the top of our social order.

William: Which is the exact opposite of the current culture, in which the worst elements of Humanity rise to the top of the social order.

Plato: And, just to be clear, by "worst elements" you mean those who have drunk heavily from the River of Forgetfulness, and are hence fearful, competitive, and greedy.

William: Yes, whereas those who bring into embodiment some distant memory of the unity of all things are unable to participate in competitive games that damage the souls of those who play them, and are forced to live a more private life *(glancing at Socrates)* if they are not to be killed by the others.

Plato: But in *our* culture, the "unity of all things", in particular, "the unity of all human beings" will not be a mere distant memory, but a living reality. There will be plenty of exemplars, that is, fully enlightened individuals bringing Divine Light into human affairs.

Such humans have Knowledge. In addition, there will be many more individuals who, although lacking direct experience, are nevertheless fully convinced by reason of the correctness of our world-view, and have aligned their thoughts and emotions accordingly. Such humans have knowledge given by reason. And everyone else, through upbringing, has been indoctrinated with "right opinion". Thus in *our* social order the spiritual cream of Humanity will indeed rise to the top. But, as if this were not sufficient to address William's concern, there is one more check on the purity of the Council.

William: What is it?

Plato: Well, in my time, if a city had to make a very important decision, do you know what its leaders would do?

William: No, oh wait, yes, they would consult with the oracle.

Plato: Exactly. And like in my times, the Social Order we have constructed will make full use of mediums and oracles, especially for important decisions. And no decision is more important for our Society than membership on the World Council. And so, new members for our Council will be chosen by the members of the Council, all of whom are spiritually enlightened, with the blessings of the gods conveyed through the mediums.

Neal: I don't suppose the average citizen gets to vote on who should be on the Council.

(Much laughter, especially from Plato.)

Plato: *(jokingly)* Well yes, maybe we should allow our citizens to vote on this. And while we're at it, we should also let them vote on how Susan should perform brain surgery, how John should play the flute and Fred serve his restaurant. What a fine mess that would be!

Neal: Not "would be", but "is". It is because people are allowed to vote on things about which they are totally ignorant that the Earth is losing its ability to support human life.

Plato: Well, we won't say that Democracy per se is the cause of the Earth's demise, but rather, Democracy in the hands of people who are fearful, greedy, and ambitious. For such individuals, who are the majority at present, will invariably vote for those whose personality is most like their own. But in our Society, the guardians will be on the lookout for symptoms of such mental illness early in childhood, and such children will be treated and cured of the madness of greed and ambition. So I think, when all we have said is taken into account, there is no need to worry that our Council will be infiltrated by those who are the "worst" among us, those with the thickest margins and hence the greatest fear and ignorance. Are you satisfied, William?

William: Yes, I am.

Plato: Then it seems we must complete our circle by discussing the final stage of life: old age, dying, and death.

Chapter IX

Old Age, Dying, and Death

1) Preparing For the Return Home

Socrates: As we have already stated, the words "old age", "dying", and "death" are burdened with such negative connotations. Yet as I implied at my trial, death is indeed the greatest of blessings for a human being.

William: *(with humor)* And you may add the expression "grim reaper", "croaked", "kicked the bucket", and "deceased" to your list of words that depict the holy and sacred process of returning Home.

Socrates: *(also with humor)* It's quite amazing, when one thinks about it, that the most joyful experience available to a human being – the return Home, the merging of the self with its Soul – is referenced only by words that have negative connotations.

Neal: Well, that's beginning to change, at least a little. Although no one is yet using the expression "Grand Homecoming", some people are now using the term "transition" instead of "death".

Benedict: Perhaps we may continue to use these terms, but give them new meanings. From the perspective of the body and its personality, death is indeed an ending. But from the point of view of the experiencing consciousness, what is called "death" is a transition from one form of consciousness to another, like waking up from a dream.

Plato: Yes, and your last phrase is important. The transition from the dreaming state of consciousness to the waking state of consciousness is indeed the death of the dream. But prior to waking, the dreaming consciousness did not know it was dreaming, and that its experiences were unreal. But in the act of waking, the dream consciousness merges seamlessly with the waking consciousness that is then experienced as the greater reality.

Benedict: In fact, upon waking, both the dream and the

consciousness that thought the dream was real disappear and are of little or no consequence to the waking consciousness. Similarly, upon dying, the consciousness that believed that physical embodiment was absolutely real will disappear, along with the so-called physical world itself, but this is in no way experienced as a loss, since the experiencing consciousness merges seamlessly with, or "wakes up" to, a higher version of itself, which is experienced as infinitely more real than what it had thought it was while embodied.

William: We should note that the present culture's view of death and dying is now being transformed by the so-called "Near-Death Experience". Empirically, this is the best source of knowledge about what happens at death. This is why many physicians and nurses who attend to the dying now use the term "transition" instead of "death".

Neal: Yes, and as medical technology improves, more and more individuals will be brought back from death's door, through which they might have taken a little peek. Many more people will have experienced the beginning stages of the transition and will tell their stories to a culture that is receptive to them, reinforcing in themselves and others the true values of Unconditional Love and the Golden Rule. For the difficulties that NDEers now have in returning to their bodies is due to the fact that the present culture is not aligned with the Truth of Love – nor, for that matter, with the Love of Truth – which they now know are the only real values.

Plato: What you say is partly true. Yet even in a culture that is based on the Golden Rule, NDEers might still experience some difficulty returning to their bodies. Even though embodiment will be a much happier dream in our New Social Order, it is still a dream-like experience to the soul, lacking in the Beauty, Aliveness, Goodness, Knowledge and Bliss that the soul experiences in its natural habitat.

Neal: *(with humor)* Well, thank you, Plato, for reminding me of how miserable I must be in my present embodied state.

Plato: *(laughing)* You're most welcome. Nevertheless, people do not want to return from the NDE not only because the present culture's values are the opposite of what is revealed in the NDE, but also because they do not wish to leave a Real World for one that is illusory and dream-like. Even if we have here given the recipe for a happy dream, it is still a dream, and the soul who visits Home would usually prefer to stay at Home than venture forth into illusion again.

Benedict: Perhaps we should not be too careless with the word "illusion". Embodiment may very well be an illusion, but if so, it is an illusion that serves a purpose. For it is not at random that souls make their entrances and exits onto the stage of embodied life.

Plato: Good, for this brings us back full circle to our concept of "original purpose". Now Socrates here might object to our using terms such as "old age", or even the usual euphemisms like "the golden years" or "senior citizens", but we have to have some way of referring to the closing years of embodied life, so we may as well retain those terms. Or *(glancing at Socrates)* do you have a better suggestion?

Socrates: Yes, as a matter of fact, I do. The term "old age" refers only to the body, since the soul is eternal. Let's retain the term for now, as you suggested, but be open to new terminology as we discuss the purpose and function of the body's final years.

Neal: I assume that the "purpose and function" of the soul's hanging out in an old body is more than just to burden relatives and society with caring for an individual who can no longer work or procreate.

Socrates: Much more. In *our* social order, but not in your present one, old age will have a purpose – a Divine purpose – for the individual, and a most important function for the social order as a whole.

Neal: I assume that the purpose, as far as the individual is concerned, has to do with preparing for the journey Home.

Socrates: Yes, although unlike every journey undertaken while embodied, for *this* journey the individual will be busy **un**packing his bags, rather than packing them. For as wise men and women have always stated, one should leave embodied life the same way one entered it: simple, childlike, and without psychological attachment to one's personality or anything from one's so-called "past". It is good to die before one dies, as some spiritual teachers have put it. I like how you put it, Benedict.

Benedict: Me? Oh I think remember. If a person is to enter into conscious union with the Divine Being, then everything that pertains to the body's history and its personality must become of "no consequence".

Plato: Because the body's history and its personality ***is*** of "no consequence", compared with the eternal Reality of the soul. One might say that when the body dies the soul awakens, not really of course, since the soul does not sleep. I once defined "death" as the separation of the body from its soul, but from the perspective of the human who dies, the process of dying is experienced as the merging of the personality into the soul, so that the former is totally absorbed into the latter… sort of like waking from a dream, where the "dream consciousness" experiences a seamless merging with the waking consciousness, which it immediately recognizes as its own identity.

Now, the first stages of human life are preparatory for forming one's social identity. And the latter stages of human life, what is called "old age", is preparatory for one's return Home. This is not recognized in the present culture simply because nothing that the present culture *values* – money, status, etc. – plays any role during this final stage of life.

Neal: So instead of helping old people to prepare for the journey Home, we medicate them and put them in front of the television.

William: Well, to do anything different would require that our culture be cognizant of the things that really matter, like spirit, love, meaning, and knowledge. But these topics will be the norm in our New Social Order, and because people will be discussing these things throughout their lives, they will not be at a loss to discuss them with one who is old and/or dying.

Neal: We have talked a lot about educating our children as they develop and find their way in the world. Do we have a curriculum for our senior citizens to help them find their way out of the world?

(Everyone laughs.)

Socrates: *(smiling)* We have a definite goal, but probably no fixed curriculum, as there are many ways to reach the goal.

Neal: Goal? What do you mean?

Socrates: When *your* time comes, how would you want to feel, assuming you can decide?

Neal: Oh that's easy. I would want to feel at peace with myself and with how I've lived, I want to feel only love and gratitude towards those with whom I have interacted throughout life, and I want to feel joy as I leave the body. No regrets, no resentments, no anger.

Socrates: Good. So this is the goal, to die in peace. *How* this goal will be achieved may vary from one person to the next.

Plato: Now of course, Death can come to anyone at any stage of life. There will always be illness and "accidents", but –

Neal: Wait a minute. Why did you put quotes around the word "accident"?

Plato: Ah, Divine Determination!

Neal: Huh? Oh, I think I understand.

Plato: What do you understand?

Neal: A man is crossing the street and gets hit by a truck and dies. Everyone would say that this was an accident.

Plato: *(smiling)* Yes, that's what everyone would say, except for…

Neal: *(smiling)* … except for the man who got hit by the truck. After going through his after-death debriefing, as we might call it, he understands that the time and manner of his death was not a fortuitous "accident", but was a part of what you called a "Divine Determination" and hence, absolutely necessary.

William: And actually, we have some splendid empirical evidence for this claim. Many Near-Death Experiencers are sent back to their bodies against their conscious will, strongly protesting what they experience as getting kicked out of heaven.

Socrates: And there is a perspective from which this is quite comical, as they are dragged from the higher regions back to their bodies, screaming and kicking the whole time.

Neal: *(with humor)* That would be *your* perspective, I presume.

Socrates: And yours too, soon enough. But the point is that NDErs are all given the reason *why* they cannot stay and are being sent back.

William: And the *reason* is the same for all. They are all told, simply and emphatically: "You have to go back because it's not your time to quit the body." This is the "empirical evidence" I referred to. This logically implies that the time for departure has already been set, and humans may not leave until their timing is right.

Neal: Yes, I agree. But then *why* are some people given a taste of heaven only to be kicked out against their will? It is so very difficult for NDErs to find themselves once again a prisoner in their own bodies.

Socrates: *(laughing)* Exactly, this is why it's so comical. You see, every NDEer, without exception, agreed prior to incarnating that they would undergo this experience. Being sent back was what they had agreed to prior to birth. In fact, most had not only agreed to being sent back but enthusiastically volunteered for the assignment. Yet when what they themselves had planned actually happens in the temporal order, we get the observed screaming and kicking.

And in case you are asking *why* anyone would volunteer for such a frustrating experience – the NDE is of course not in itself a frustrating experience, just the part about being sent back – is the answer not obvious, and not at all comical? Or should we prevail on Plato here to tell us a little story about it?

Neal: The question of "why" did cross my mind, but the answer quickly followed.

Socrates: Then perhaps *you* will tell us the story?

Neal: I'll try, although I'm not as long-winded as your friend, so it will be a rather short story.

Plato: I'll ignore that last remark.

Neal: But to keep it short I might risk offending Benedict by using an anthropocentric conception of the Divine Being.

Benedict: Here's your poetic license. I will not take offense if you use it.

Neal: Alright. Now, we know there is no such thing as an absentee

Creator, according to which God creates the World, winds it up, then leaves it alone to its own devices. For the world, including human bodies, continuously emanates from the Divine Being. The physical world is just one of infinitely many such emanations. But it is a special emanation, because consciousness can hide from itself within it. Then, when consciousness returns Home after experiencing a great lack of Unconditional Love, its joy is immeasurable upon realizing that it is not the body it had thought it was. But it happened that when God withdrew some of His attention from the Earth – after all, the poor Guy-in-the-sky has infinitely many such worlds to look after – something unexpected happened. Now it goes without saying that a split-second of Divine time could amount to many centuries of Earthly time. So when God refocused his attention on his Earth experiment he was dismayed to realize that it had gone awry, and that humans, instead of returning to Him in joy and glory, were quite busy planning the destruction of the whole planet.

How do you like the story so far?

Benedict: *(with humor)* I must say that your phrase "Guy-in-the-sky" should prevent anyone from taking it seriously. Please continue.

Neal: So the Divine Being was somewhat at a loss for what to do. He thought maybe he should terminate the experiment. After all, it would not take much effort for Him to nudge a comet slightly out of its orbit so that it would crash into the earth, and end the suffering and misery of all the embodied souls down there. For he felt much compassion for the poor souls trapped in their bodies, who were completely clueless about finding their way Home, and were in fact collectively heading in the wrong direction, towards ever increasing suffering and misery. For misery and suffering are the inevitable consequences of worshipping the gods of greed and ambition. Although out of compassion He thought he should put humans out of their misery, He also was reluctant to terminate His experiment. He would have consulted with other Intelligences, if there were any, but then realized that He is Himself the One, and that all Intelligences are contained within His One Mind. It was at this point in His, ah *(glancing at Benedict)* deliberations that the most brilliant and satisfactory Plan for the salvation of the human experiment came to Him.

Benedict: *(laughing)* As long as you have firm hold of the poetic license, you may continue to refer to God as "deliberating". I will strive to not roll my eyes at that ridiculous idea. So what was the "Plan"?

Neal: Thank you. Now, God saw immediately that the insanity among humans was caused by their inability to perceive the Divine Love "in which they lived and moved and have their being", for what Paul had said is true even when humans are not aware of it. So He decided that all he had to do was to increase the awareness of Divine Love among humans. But this was a bit tricky.

Benedict: What do you mean?

Neal: Well, sending the comet crashing into the Earth would certainly make all humans aware of Divine Love, as they all exited their bodies at the same time. So the trick was to increase awareness of Love without ending the experiment.

William: Well it seems that God Himself struggled with the same problem we have already discussed: how to reduce the thickness of the margins without destroying them altogether.

Plato: ... Or how to allow a little more light into the Cave of human existence without destroying the Cave.

Neal: Exactly. So God did some statistical analyses on the problem, and concluded that if He showed Himself and His Love to a small percentage of humans while they were still embodied, these humans would become His messengers and spread His Word to the whole of humanity. So, well you know the rest of the story. He asked for volunteer souls who would be willing to be yanked out of their body in the midst of their incarnation, return Home briefly to recollect Divine Love, and then return to their bodies to share what they had experienced. The souls who volunteered knew in advance that they would not be able to stay, for the very Plan for which they had volunteered required that they return. But quite obviously, when the time came to execute the Plan, they forgot what they had previously agreed to, hence all the screaming and kicking that Socrates finds amusing.

Socrates: But humor aside, I acknowledge the difficulties involved. It's like waking up from a nightmare, feeling great relief from realizing it was only a dream, but then being compelled to reenter the nightmare again.

Neal: But even if in a particular case the dream is relatively pleasant and not a nightmare, it still involves an absence of the experience of Divine Love. No soul easily chooses to leave its immersion in this Love; no soul easily choses to reside where Love seems not to be. I have heard of a case where a woman with three small children and a happy marriage and career did not talk about her NDE for over ten years. She did not want to return and argued with the Being of Light about being sent back. She was at a loss to explain to her children why their mom would have preferred to stay dead. There's really no way to explain this to anyone, so she kept quiet until her children were grown-up.

Incidentally, this little tale explains why it is that not everyone whose body dies and is resuscitated experiences the NDE. For these experiences are not determined by physiological conditions, but only by prior agreement with the Divine Being.

Plato: Yes, for we are agreed that all entrances and exits from the Earthly theater are determined in and by the eternal order, not from within the play itself. And this includes the temporary exits and re-entrances involved with the NDE. So humans will be at ease with regard to the impermanence of their physical form. The man who gets hit by a truck realizes afterwards that it was indeed his time to depart, and is content. But from the *human* perspective it seems like a purposeless accident. At any rate, what I wanted to say is that although death can befall anyone at any stage of life, we will here consider it as if it were something that could be planned for in advance. If I may, I would like to set up a somewhat arbitrary model, and examine what such planning might look like in terms of our model.

Neal: This seems like a reasonable way to proceed.

2) The Spiritual Delights of Old Age

Plato: Let us state, then, that because our social order is internally harmonious, not competitive or contentious, the human body will also be internally harmonious and will hence enjoy a longer life span, say 100 years. The first 20 years involves acquiring an ego, or a social identity. The final 10–20 years will involve a loosening and weakening of the ego, or social identity. The latter years of one's life will be a wondrous opportunity for spiritual growth. But we will *not* be isolating our seniors, putting them in nursing homes, or in any way removing them from society. They will be *seen*, so that the process in which they are engaged, the sacred process of returning Home, will be visible and known to all. Their collective wisdom will be sought, not avoided, and their honored presence within the social order will serve as a constant reminder of the impermanence of all things, and will greatly assist in preventing younger humans from taking themselves and their social roles too seriously.

William: I agree that our senior citizens or our *very* senior citizens should not be shunted off to "retirement communities" but should live among people of all ages. For we especially desire that our children be exposed to all stages of life, so as…

Neal: *(with a little humor)* So as to spare them the shock that awaited the Buddha when he first saw a very old person in the streets.

William: *(smiling)* Yes, we could put it that way. The full spectrum of human life will be visible to those entering it and adjusting to it, and also to those in the process of leaving.

Benedict: OK, semantic police here. We are giving the word "dying" a new meaning, a psychological meaning. Until now, the term "dying" has been used to refer to a body that is facing a terminal illness of some sort. So-and-so is dying of cancer, so-and-so is dying of injuries sustained when he was hit by a truck, and so forth. But now we are talking about transcendence of ego and social identity, which is a process of *dying* to what the person thought she was. And this is a much more profound kind of *dying* than the death of the body.

Socrates: Yes, and because our seniors will be studying death and dying, they will not be shocking our children the way Gautama was shocked.

Neal: Why do you say that?

Socrates: Because many of our very old citizens will have successfully cast off their personalities and hence the Light of the Divine Being will shine through them into the world. *Our* children will rejoice in the presence of the very old. For they – the children – are newly emerged from the Light, and recognize it and are drawn to it when they see it shining through their grandparents or great-grandparents.

William: Now of course, because of a general thinning of the margins that appears to separate our worlds, if I may put it that way, more humans will become enlightened at all ages than is the case in the present culture, but during old age, there really is nothing else for the human to accomplish, other than to die to their social identities, or egos, before their body gives out. This is the task facing our seniors…

Socrates: And a most joyful task it will be. For if I may state categorically what I hinted at during my trial, *death is indeed the greatest of blessings for a human being,* and to die with the full support of the social order in which one has lived, is an even greater blessing, if such a thing were possible.

Plato: Agreed. But let's examine for a little while the reasons why old age presents the greatest opportunity for spiritual growth.

Neal: I think I can see some of the reasons.

Socrates: Actually, you mean *feel,* since you yourself are approaching old age.

Neal: Yes, and here are some things I am noticing: I really don't think about the future very much, except for practical things, like planning a trip. Young people are always thinking about the future, but I already know what the future holds for me. This body is going to perish, and I shall soon enough be with you guys.

Socrates: You already *are* with us guys. But your point is that you do not think about career, partners, children, parents, and all the usual things that younger people think about and worry about, so there is more room in your mind than before.

Neal: Yes. And also I do not think about the past, except fleetingly, as memories arise here and there. And, thank God, I am no longer tormented by constant thoughts about sex.

Socrates: So if you are not living in the past or the future, and not thinking about sex, then there is more room in your head to live in the present moment, which is another way of referring to the spiritual life.

Neal: Of course, I realize that not everyone who reaches my age feels this way. Many suffer from anxiety about their body and its imminent decline, as well as guilt pertaining to past actions or inactions. So one purpose of old age is to provide our seniors with all the assistance they need to remove all guilt and anxiety about their lives, so that they can be fully present in the moment, and enjoy the depths of the consciousness that they are.

Socrates: Ah, but we must be careful not to confuse *our* seniors with yours.

Neal: What do you mean?

Socrates: The majority of seniors in your present culture carry lots of guilt and anxiety. Do you think the same will be true for the seniors of *our* culture?

Neal: *(flash of understanding)* Oh, no. *Our* citizens of every age will carry much less guilt. But we need to understand *why* more clearly.

Benedict: I agree, even if it means repeating some things said earlier.

Plato: But we did state at the beginning that our unfolding conversation would be circular and repetitive, like a symphony, with various themes appearing in various combinations. So we won't be concerned with that. Now we want to compare and contrast our two cultures, and show *why* guilt is necessarily much stronger in one than the other.

Benedict: We need a definition of the term "guilt".

Plato: *(with humor)* Oh, you and your definitions. But go ahead and define away.

Benedict: *(smiling)* Thank you. Let's distinguish personal, or psychological guilt, from impersonal, or metaphysical guilt. The latter is the basis for the former. Impersonal guilt is a consequence of *hiding*. The Earth experiment is a domain in which consciousness *hides* from the knowledge of what it is. It *pretends* to be ignorant of its union with Source, or God. The purpose of the *margins* that William describes is to keep the full Light of Source from reaching into the Cave of human embodiment. Now one main consequence of all this *hiding* is the persistent, low-level feeling of unease and restlessness – a feeling that something is not quite right – that characterizes the human condition. It is like the background radiation left over from the Big Bang. This is what I am calling "metaphysical guilt" or "original guilt". What I shall call "personal guilt" is the activation of original guilt in an individual's mind through actions or inactions together with memories of past actions and inactions.

William: And, as you once put it, the specific behaviors that trigger guilt in any given individual depend entirely upon *how* that individual was raised.

Socrates: Mostly, but not entirely.

William: *(smiling)* Let me state the "mostly" part, then you will state the "not entirely" part.

Socrates: OK.

William: Some obvious examples: a person raised in a culture that believes sex is sinful will feel guilty whenever he thinks about sex. And since he cannot *not* think about sex – unless of course he's over 70, like Neal – he will feel guilty all of his life. Or in other words, his original guilt will become activated whenever he perceives a female form. But obviously, *our* children will experience no guilt in connection with sexual thoughts or behaviors. Similarly, a person raised in a culture that values money and status, and who fails to achieve either, will feel guilty for being a failure. Examples could be multiplied without limit; the specific behaviors that trigger the emotion of guilt vary from one culture to the next. But I intuit the "not entirely" part will be more interesting.

Socrates: There is something here that is invariant to cultural differences and how one has been raised. The origin of guilt is impersonal – the separation of consciousness from God – and has nothing to do with culture. The various triggers for this guilt depend mostly, as William said, on culture and upbringing. But there is also an objective standard, independent of culture, which comes into play especially in old age.

Neal: What is this objective standard?

Socrates: But you already know it. What's that little quip about people on their deathbeds?

Neal: *(laughing)* No one on his deathbed has ever expressed regret for not having spent more time at the office. But it's more than a quip; it's literally true.

William: Well, I suppose we could find a few sociopaths who did regret not having made more money or achieved more status, but on the whole, the regrets of the dying are mostly concerned with their personal behaviors towards others.

Socrates: And tell me then, what is the universal standard that dying people automatically use, according to which they feel regret and judge themselves guilty?

William: Yes, I see it. The standard is the Golden Rule, or the Moral Law. Hence a culture that values money and status is completely out of alignment with the Moral Law, and individuals who are raised to pursue such false values will necessarily violate the Moral Law in almost everything they do. For it is not possible to worship the gods of greed and ambition without harming others.

Plato: But as they age, you see, the values of Home begin to seep through the cracks of their cultural conditioning, and their guilts and regrets tend to become aligned with the true values of the Golden Rule. But *our* culture *is* aligned with the Moral Law, and hence *our* seniors will feel very little guilt or regret.

Benedict: And we should remind ourselves again that our citizens are emotionally intelligent, which means they have been discussing and processing emotions as they occur all their lives. They have been discussing the Moral Law and the Life Review since childhood. So it is unlikely they will have hidden very much deep within their psyche that could snap back at them with guilt and remorse when they reach old age.

Plato: So we have every reason to believe that the process of aging and dying is inherently joyful.

Neal: What? I think you had better bring forth some of those reasons you have in mind. Aging has always been associated with pain, suffering, and loss.

Plato: I'll list some reasons in a moment. But first we must be absolutely firm in our belief that death is experienced as a loss only to embodied humans left behind, but never to the person who dies. When heaven is gained, the human life that is lost is experienced as being "of no consequence", as Benedict put it.

Neal: Yes, of course I believe this. Almost all the stories about death and dying are told from within the human perspective…

William: … which is why they are so morose. But here's the good news: as the body weakens in old age, it is very natural for one's social identity or ego to also weaken, and so the perspective of the *aging* human begins to shift from that of the *human* to that of the *soul* itself.

Socrates: So we could say that in old age, the individual is neither here nor there, or just as accurately, the individual is both here and there.

Plato: And do we not agree that this condition of consciousness – a mix we might say of the embodied with the non-embodied – is inherently delightful? Is it not joyful when rays from the Light of pure consciousness penetrate through the opening cracks of the ego-identity the human thought she was?

Neal: *(jokingly)* It would seem that there is no greater joy for the human being than the ending of being human.

Plato: And to use an analogy that's not quite right, is it not joyful for humans to think about and look forward to a magnificent adventure?

Neal: Yes, so just thinking about dying and returning Home is naturally joyful for humans about to undertake the adventure. But nevertheless, you cannot deny that unless someone dies in her sleep, old age does bring infirmity and pain.

Plato: Old age brings a loss of full usage of the body. Is that your point?

Neal: Yes.

Plato: Do you think that lack of full usage of the body is necessarily a cause of suffering and sorrow?

Neal: No, of course not. Babies and toddlers do not have full use of their bodies, and there is no suffering or sorrow involved. More to the point, perhaps, is that many cripples and invalids, that is, many people who formerly had full use of the body but now do not, have accepted the limitations of their bodies and hence do not suffer.

Plato: Then is it not likely that in *our* Social Order, people will be guided and assisted to accept whatever physical limitations may arise?

Neal: Not "likely", but "certainly".

Socrates: *(with a little humor)* Besides, they well know that whatever condition may arise – whether arthritis prevents them from playing a musical instrument, or their fragile bones give way and they can no longer walk, or *(glancing at me)* God forbid, their body can no longer digest chocolate ice cream – they will soon be altogether free from any limiting condition. Any discomfort is more easily endured if it is known that it is only for a little while.

William: And we should add that the physical pain associated with aging and dying, much feared and much experienced in my time, will not be a problem. For all pain can be alleviated with medication, and in the near future there will be available medication for pain that allows the consciousness to remain clear. In fact, pain will be treated without medication, by using biofeedback and/or sound vibrations to stimulate the brain directly.

Plato: Good. So physical pain will no longer be a problem. But there may be some psychological pain associated with separating from one's social role. Who is Susan, if her hands tremble and she can no longer do surgery? Who is Fred, or was it John, if he no longer has the breath to play the flute? Their former social identity is gone.

Socrates: *(laughing)* Social identity is the first bag to *un*pack as our seniors prepare for the journey Home. But there are other bags too.

Neal: Such as?

Socrates: *(mischievously)* Consult your fears.

Neal: What?

Socrates: You heard me. OK, I see your resistance, so we'll slow down a bit. As you yourself begin to enter what is called "old age", you have comparatively little fear.

Neal: Thank you.

Socrates: I said "comparatively little". But you still have enough to deal with, and to make the process of old age an interesting challenge for you.

Neal: I thought I was done with "interesting challenges".

Socrates: *(laughing)* You well know the old joke –

Neal: *(also laughing)* As long as you're breathing, you aren't done with your Earthly challenges, or something to that effect.

Socrates: Then if you think about what you most fear, as you enter the senior years, you will get some inkling of challenges that still remain for you.

Neal: Well, I'm not afraid of pain, because I know that can be controlled. I'm also not afraid of losing my social identity, since I've already more or less lost it and feel no attachment.

William: But wait a minute and reflect. This is no mean accomplishment. I myself retained my social identity, the Harvard Professor, until the very end. That's who I thought I was. But you have already relinquished that role.

Neal: Well, perhaps it was easier for me than for you, since I was not successful in that role, whereas you were.

William: If "success" is defined in terms of writing books and articles, and acquiring a reputation, then you are right. But if "success" is defined in terms of influencing students in ways that add meaning to their lives, then you are mistaken. Also, one downside of "success" is a greater tendency to identify with the social role that has brought one "success". At any rate, *(laughing)* there was a time when we both knew lots of stuff and thought we were very smart. I had to die before I could realize that I didn't really know anything. But you know that now.

Neal: Yes, it's true that I used to know lots of stuff, or thought I did, but now I have nothing to profess.

Socrates: So you have achieved the highest point of human wisdom, which is to know that you do not know, and to be content. For human knowledge is insignificant compared with Divine Wisdom, and the human who knows this is already on his way Home. But the loss of social identity is not a problem for you, since *(laughing)* as you pointed out to William, you did not have much of an identity to begin with. So what is left to fear?

Neal: I'm not sure…

Socrates: Oh yes you are! What do you sometimes say to friends and families about growing old?

Neal: I don't care how long I live, but I want to have full use of my body for the duration.

Socrates: So you are saying, are you not, that you fear living past the point where you have full use of your body.

Neal: Well…

Socrates: OK, maybe you want to call it "dread" instead of "fear". But it is the same thing, is it not?

Neal: Yes.

Socrates: So let's go there in thought. Let's assume that it has been ordained that during the last two years of your life you will be in a wheelchair with very limited use of your body. You cannot walk, you cannot dress or bathe yourself, and you cannot use the bathroom without assistance.

Neal: I don't want that. I would rather die and be done with the whole thing and join you, rather than be stuck in a body that no longer works.

Socrates: Yes, this is your preference, and it's based on fear. What are you afraid of, should these conditions come to pass?

Neal: I, or this body, will require assistance from others.

Socrates: And why do you fear this possibility? I'll tell you the answer in a moment, but first, please tell me if you see any connection, necessary or otherwise, between (i) receiving assistance from another, and (ii) feeling fear.

Neal: Well, no…

Benedict: But in *your* mind, Neal, there is a connection between them. Two connections, actually. One psychological connection has to do with the usual male tendency to feel he is not a "man" if he is dependent on others. So you fear a loss of identity as an "independent" male. But the second connection in your mind generates more fear, and is the more important one to examine. Socrates is about to state it.

3) Fear of Love

Socrates: You are afraid of receiving Love.

Neal: What's this you are saying? I should stay around in a dysfunctional body just to experience caring from other humans? My goodness, I could be dead instead, and bathing in Divine Love directly, instead of being a burden to whoever ends up caring for this body. Plato, help me out here. I thought we have similar views about souls who hang out in sick bodies, so that all their efforts go into taking care of the body, and they perform no useful social functions but are a burden to everyone.

(Everyone laughs, for quite a long time.)

Plato: I'll help you out by bringing to your awareness that you have difficulty even acknowledging that you have difficulty receiving Love. As far as my former opinions go, a philosopher may change his mind over the centuries. Also, what was fitting for a city-state may not be fitting for the world-society we are now constructing. We will see soon enough that our senior citizens perform a most useful social function.

But the topic now is fear of Love. You suffer from this fear, as do all humans. The "problem" of receiving Love is not personal. It is not "your" personal problem, but rather structural to the human condition in which you are now participating. Shall we investigate?

Neal: Yes.

Plato: Good. Let's begin by contrasting the two scenarios you envision above.

Neal: What two scenarios?

Plato: I'll flesh them out for you: you are now 95 years old, confined to a wheelchair, and reside in a nursing home. It goes without saying that such facilities in *our* Social Order will be vastly different, more humane, more spiritual, than what exists at present. But even so, the basics are the same. You're stuck in a wheelchair for however many years you have left. That's one scenario. But then you protest, "I could be dead instead, bathing in Divine Love directly." That's the other scenario. What is the point, you ask, in staying with a body that requires care from others when you could be free from the whole thing?

Neal: Yes, I'm asking.

Socrates: *(with a little humor)* But wait; let's put some more flesh into our scenarios.

Neal: What do you have in mind?

Socrates: OK. You're 95 years old, stuck in a wheelchair, when suddenly you have a heart attack.

Neal: *(playfully)* Ah, my exit from the first scenario.

Socrates: *(laughing)* Not so fast, for you are now having a full-blown Near-Death Experience and are experiencing Divine Love directly. In fact, you are experiencing that you *are* that Divine Love.

Neal: Your whetting my appetite.

Socrates: But let us suppose that the Divine Being informs you that you now have a choice: either you can return to your body or you can stay in Heaven. The Divine Being also informs you that should you choose to return, there will be no miraculous healing for the body, as sometimes happens, but your body will continue to require care from others.

Neal: Well, this is a no-brainer, if ever there was such a thing.

Socrates: Or so you think. But *our* task *(glancing at everyone else)* will be to convince Neal to return to his body and live out the remaining years in a wheelchair, receiving care and nurturing from others. What do you think? Are we up for the challenge?

Neal: Hah! Good luck. You'll need it. There's no way I would choose to remain stuck in the mud of embodiment when given a choice to become free from it all. After all, in the scenario you envision for me, I have no social responsibilities that require my care, and the care of my body is a burden to others, so I am free to leave. Why in the world would I choose to stay?

Socrates: ... To increase the amount of Divine Love that penetrates into the world through the human form.

Neal: You're being inscrutable again.

Benedict: No, he's being obvious, not inscrutable. But let's go back to our scenario: a heart attack has kicked you out of the body, you've had the classic NDE and now have to decide whether to return to your body. You wish to stay, but we are making the opposite argument. We wish to convince you of two things: (i) it is to your advantage to return, and (ii) it is also to the advantage of the nurses and those caring for your body that you return.

Plato: Now, without getting too metaphysical, we note that every soul, prior to incarnating, has the same choice: to remain immersed in Divine Love or to leave Heaven in order to have a human experience.

Benedict: Of course, from the soul's perspective, there is no such thing as "prior", since the soul is in the eternal order where concepts such as "before" and "after" have no meaning. But metaphysical niceties aside, it is clear the human embodiment would never have occurred...

Socrates: *(playfully)* ... If indeed it has occurred at all.

Benedict: ... unless some souls chose to leave Divine Love and enter a realm where Love seems not to be. All souls have this choice prior to incarnating, and some have it again during their incarnation.

William: So you see, there is such a thing as choosing to become, or remain, embodied, even when one does not have to. The "choice" then is profound, and hardly the "no-brainer" you perhaps thought it was. Now let's examine your concerns, or fears, about returning to your body. You said you do not want to be a burden to others.

Neal: I don't.

William: Do you recall our list of activities that bring joy and happiness to humans?

Neal: Yes. Sensuous pleasures, developing talents and abilities, following one's natural curiosity, and assisting others are all activities that bring joy without harming others. We contrasted this list with pursuing wealth and status, which always brings suffering.

William: So when one human helps or assists another, this brings happiness to the one who assists.

Neal: Yes, and this will be especially so in our culture, in which the so-called helping professions will be honored.

William: And does this include the particular individuals who will assist in caring for your invalid body?

Neal: Oh. So one reason, you seem to be saying, for me to return to a decrepit body is to afford my future caretakers with the opportunity to feel some happiness by caring for it?

Socrates: The reason is for *you,* while still in physical form, to feel some happiness by allowing that form to be completely cared for by others. William was convincing you that your "burden-to-others" argument is not a legitimate concern. After all, if no one is ever willing to be a burden to others, then no one would experience the happiness intrinsic to helping another. So those who require care from others are indeed performing a useful social function. Moreover, those who return from a Near-Death Experience are also performing a most useful social function.

Benedict: And I think we could convince you that being in a decrepit body, as you put it, would offer you wonderful opportunities for experiencing the vulnerability or impermanence of the human form.

Plato: Surrendering care of the body to other humans in old age might be a good way to prepare for surrendering the soul to the Divine Being at death. So we might say to you: the main reason for you to return to your body is the opportunity to practice surrender, and also to recognize that the hands that care for your invalid body are really inspired by Divine Love. The very structure of the ego itself requires some barriers to this Divine Love, so this recognition assists with the dissolution of the ego. So you see, there is much opportunity for spiritual practice in one's final years.

Neal: Yes, I see. I also believe that it is better to face one's fears in the present life than to postpone them for the next. So the mere fact that I have some fear around this indicates it would be an opportunity for growth.

Plato: *(smiling)* Every life situation is an opportunity for growth, especially old age, which affords the wonderful opportunity to observe the decay of one's body together with the decay of one's social identity. But also, do you not believe what *A Course in Miracles* states about fear, you know, "Nothing real can be threatened, nothing unreal exists"?

Neal: Yes.

Plato: So the presence of fear in you, at the thought of requiring care from others, indicates something is being threatened?

Neal: Yes.

Plato: But this "something that is being threatened" is not real and does not exist?

Neal: So it would seem.

Socrates: Notice: we are shifting our attention from *what* threatens you, or elicits fear in you, to the "you" who is feeling threatened. The statement, "Nothing real can be threatened," is easily misinterpreted to mean that outer events that seem to be threatening are not real; but what it is really saying is more profound: any structure within the field of Consciousness that experiences itself as being threatened, or in other words, that experiences fear, is itself unreal.

Neal: *(with humor)* Well then, that would be me.

Socrates: *(also with humor)* Well then, that would be a specific structure, called "the ego", within the real field of consciousness that is You. And so you see, at last, that any fear or resistance you feel pertaining to the vulnerability and helplessness of an old body and the care it requires indicates the illusory nature of that which is experiencing the fear, namely the ego. But to see this even more clearly, how do you think you would feel if you were enlightened?

Neal: Huh?

Socrates: You're 95, in a wheelchair, and your body requires round-the-clock care. But you've become "enlightened" and are no longer dragged around by its fears. A nurse or nurse's aide is now bathing your body. How are you feeling?

Neal: Um… good, I suppose.

Socrates: How do you think *I* felt when the women were washing my body just before it became a corpse?

Neal: I think you enjoyed every minute of it.

Socrates: You bet I did. And the only thing that would prevent you from enjoying every minute of your bath is the clutter in your mind. Hence, what a wonderful opportunity to observe and remove the clutter! But now, on the supposition that your ego has dissolved like mine, how do you experience the hands that are touching your body.

William: Hint: Walt Whitman.

Neal: Got it, thanks. The *Song of Myself*. There is but one "Divine Being", and Whitman experienced himself and all others as aspects of the Divine Being. So if I were enlightened, then I would experience the hands that are bathing me as my own?

Socrates: Good enough. Because the words "me" and "my" in your last sentence refer, not to the *person* you think you are, but to the Divine Being Itself. But we're not going to get hung up on verbal niceties. So, enlightened or not, have we convinced you to stay with your decrepit body for a little while longer?

Neal: Perhaps. I suppose that if I really were enlightened I would experience some bodhisattva-like duty to return and use my physical form, falling apart though it might be, to radiate Divine Love into the world. And if not enlightened, returning to a decaying physical form might afford me the opportunity to unpack any remaining psychological baggage, and to practice surrender, so that I am fully ready for the journey Home. However, I make no promises.

William: Good. For any promise you make now would limit the freedom of the person you will be twenty years from now. But I think we have convinced you that the latter years of human life (i) offer enormous opportunity for spiritual growth for the individual, and (ii) contribute enormously to the spiritual and psychological well-being of our whole social order.

Plato: And I would like to comment a bit more on the second point. I sort of missed it when I was alive, that is, I did not fully see the use to society of seniors and invalids who not only could not function well, but also required assistance from others in order to keep the body alive.

Neal: Yes, I want to hear what you have to say about this now, since I seem to recall that you made fun of a certain man who was seriously ill, but managed to keep his body going by seeing doctors, herbalists, and nutritionists. His whole life was spent just keeping his body alive. That was his function, and you didn't think much of it at the time.

Plato: *(smiling)* Well, I still don't think much of it. What is the point of a soul choosing to become embodied if it can't do anything with its body, if it has to spend all its energies and resources just to keep the body alive. However, this is not the kind of case we are now considering. For our seniors, we are supposing, have in fact led the lives that were appropriate to them, and are now hanging out in their bodies after having led a productive life.

Moreover, in my times, in fact until very recently, material resources were very limited, and resources that went to keep a sick body alive could instead have been used to keep children healthy. But at this present moment in history, the Earth has the ability to feed, house, and shelter every human being now on the planet. This will be the case in our New Society. It is only greed and ambition – the disease that is destroying the planet – that prevents this from being the case at present.

So, one of the most important lessons we want our children to grasp is the impermanence of all forms. We will not hide the fact of death from them, as your present culture does. Neither will we hide from our children the fact of aging, illness, and dying. They will see and interact with fragile seniors who manage their bodies with difficulty. They will know that old age will happen to their own body. Learning the impermanence of form at an early age is a wonderful prophylactic against greed and ambition.

Benedict: And what we have called the "ego", or "social consciousness", is the psychological form that accompanies the physical form of the body. As the latter weakens, so does the former, hence more Divine Light and Love shine through the physical form. Our children will see this, and the younger ones will recognize the Light as the same Light from which they themselves have emanated.

Socrates: *(holding back laughter)* Ah yes, but the doctor's orders are different for the two parallel cases.

Benedict: *(with humor)* Dr. Socrates, Physician to the Soul, you've thought of something funny? But what do you mean?

Socrates: *(laughing)* As the physical form weakens, deteriorates, and decays, the doctor will order that everything possible be done to keep the form functioning as well as possible. But as the psychological form begins to weaken and crumble, the doctor will order that everything be done to hasten the decay of the personality, or ego. Also, in the case of the body, the doctor will order whatever medication necessary to control for physical pain. But in the case of the ego, there will be no medication to ease psychological pain that may arise from a clinging ego, an ego unable to surrender to the fact of its imminent demise.

Neal: *(also laughing)* What's this you're saying. No tranquilizers or antidepressants to keep our seniors happy?

William: *(more seriously)* The meds are really used to keep seniors from getting depressed over being senior, that is, over facing death and the end of their egos. It keeps them dull, not happy.

Socrates: Ah, but for psychological pain, the doctor has something much better than drugs.

William: What's that, I hesitate to ask?

Socrates: Travel agencies.

William: *(laughing)* I knew it was a mistake to ask. But before we let you tell some joke, there is a serious side to the psychological pain that seniors may feel as they lose their former social identity. Susan, now 80 years old, can no longer do brain surgery; John has a touch of arthritis and his fingers can no longer find their way on his flute; and Fred, the waiter, has become a danger to himself and others in the kitchen. Their social roles afforded them with an "identity" through which they did something well, and enjoyed the companionship of others in the process. You may talk about your "travel agencies" or whatever, but you must show *how* it, or they, will assist our seniors in overcoming all sense of loss from losing their former social identity.

Socrates: Not to worry, William. For the travel agencies I have in mind are those that assist and escort the individual from Earth to the underworld – er, ah, sorry for that. There's no underworld any more. Well, at any rate, these aren't geographical places we're talking about, but levels of consciousness.

Benedict: *(with a little humor)* You know, I think I have given up trying for verbal exactitude.

Plato: Congratulations. What has prompted you to make that statement?

Benedict: Humans have always conceived of an afterlife as some sort of "place" to which they or their soul will travel after the body dies. But as Socrates said, there are no such "places", just shifts in the nature of one's consciousness. But I suspect that language will always compel humans to think of the afterlife as a geographical "place" – underworld, heaven, whatever – to which one goes.

Neal: And this is just as ridiculous as if a person, while dreaming, hears about something called "waking up", and conceives of it as a "place" that exists within his dream. But now, Socrates, I want to hear about the travel agencies you have in mind. Obviously they are not in the business of selling tickets to anything, since everyone gets their ticket Home as soon as they are born, if not sooner.

Socrates: Quite right. When I used the term "travel agencies" I had in mind the colorful brochures, video clips, and testimonies from other travelers that such agencies use to advertise their destinations. But no sales pitch, of course, since everyone already has their ticket.

Neal: OK, but now, as William urged, you must tell us how your travel agencies are the antidote to depression and any feelings of loss and discomfort our seniors will feel about losing their social identities. We also desire that our seniors have no anxiety regarding the process of dying itself.

Socrates: Actually, the travel agencies of *our* culture permeate the whole culture, so our citizens are exposed to them their whole lives. But the exposure becomes more intense as they approach the time of their own departure. OK, you want some specifics about what will be in their brochures?

William: Yes, something like that…

Socrates: I'll enumerate: (i) Stories of Near-Death Experiencers will abound, and everyone will be exposed to them, beginning with small children. But now, in old age, our seniors will be more attentive to such stories about what it is like to die, and what one experiences during and after the process. (ii) Mediums will abound, and many seniors will be able to have conversations with deceased individuals they knew and loved, conversations that will greatly reduce fear and anxiety. (iii) Because of a general thinning out of the margins, more humans will experience After-Death Communications directly, without the need for a medium. (iv) There will be significantly more "enlightened" humans in our culture, whose very presence induces calmness and peace of mind in others. (v) And if you recall our earlier experiments with sound vibrations, where we talked about the effect of Mozart's music on the body, it will turn out that certain sounds and combinations of sounds have the ability to reduce anxiety and induce calm and peace. Finally, (vi) our travel agencies will have plenty of expert therapists on hand, just in case anyone has special difficulty unpacking their baggage and clings to who they thought they were. For as Benedict put it, their social identity, everything they thought they were, is "of no consequence" compared with Who they really are, which is nothing less than the Divine Being Itself.

Neal: My goodness, what a sales pitch! You've certainly whetted my appetite. I am unpacking my baggage even now!

Plato: *(laughing)* You've read too many NDE stories. But we're keeping you on your side of the veil for a little longer.

Neal: *(jokingly)* I thought maybe I could get some time off for good behavior?

Plato: No such luck for you, my friend. There are still some things for you to do and to learn from within your current form of consciousness. But as you have doubtless noticed, you *are* becoming lighter.

Benedict: Yes, because you are already unpacking your bags, detaching from social roles, and relinquishing any sense that you know who or what you are. You have no plans for the future, your past is evaporating before your very eyes, and you no longer argue with "what is"; so there is very little to prevent your consciousness from being fully present in the moment, wherein lies happiness and true peace of mind.

Socrates: And if I may appear inscrutable again, insofar as you, or some part of you, prefers to be done with embodiment, then you still have some things to learn by being embodied.

Neal: I think I understand your meaning, inscrutable though it is. Hmm, as long as I object to, or complain about, "what is", then I am not accepting *how* the Divine Being is manifesting in the present moment. For "what is" or alternatively, "what happens", is the face of the Divine Being as it presents itself to human consciousness. To the extent I resist still being embodied, I am arguing with "what is".

Socrates: *(with humor)* … An argument you are certain to lose.

Neal: *(laughing)* Actually, this is an argument I have lost so many times that I've given up on it.

Benedict: *(smiling)* Good. And if I may add to what you just stated, it is certainly true that "what happens in the present moment" is the face of the Divine Being as it presents itself to human consciousness. But it is equally true that the very human consciousness to whom the Divine Being presents itself through "what happens" is none other than the Divine Being Itself.

Socrates: ... And so, should any infirmities come your way in advanced old age, such that your body requires care from others, you will not complain about the situation by saying or even thinking such things as, "I could be dead instead." But you will welcome whatever challenges Life presents to you. These challenges, you know, do not come at random.

William: And you see, just on this one point alone, the enormous value to our social order in having our seniors well-integrated with the whole order. For young people argue against and bemoan "what is" all the time. It will be greatly to their advantage to be around seniors who have successfully worked this through.

But I'm curious now to explore the meaning of Socrates' last statement.

Socrates: I shall defer to Benedict here.

4) Divine Determination

Benedict: Oh, I don't know if we should go into this now. I certainly agree with Socrates that nothing happens "at random", but...

William: ... but (sorry to interrupt) maybe, without going into metaphysical niceties, we can contrast the psychological effects on an individual who believes (i) that challenges that arise in her personal life are random with one who believes (ii) that such challenges are not random, but purposeful.

Plato: OK, but let us state at the outset that even in our utopian social order, there will never be a human life free from challenges and obstacles.

Benedict: When you put it that way, William, it seems that the second option leads to greater happiness. It is more difficult to argue with "what is" – and by "what is" we mean "what is presented to the consciousness of the individual in the moment" – if one believes that it is purposeful rather than random.

Neal: I know of a spiritual teacher who says we should regard every life situation, everything that seems merely to happen to us, ***as if*** we had chosen it freely.

Benedict: *(smiling)* A most brilliant teaching…

Socrates: *(laughing)* … even though slightly deceptive. He, the teacher, says this with a straight face, without laughing?

William: Before you two unpack the joke here, if there is one, may we state that for practical purposes it is better to believe that the challenges one faces in one's life are purposeful, rather than random or arbitrary?

Plato: Yes of course. It is important that our Social Order has something to say about the challenges, the disappointments, and the frustrations that are built into the human condition. It is much healthier, psychologically, to believe that such things are purposeful opportunities for growth, rather than that they are random events, or just bad luck, that get in the way.

Neal: I certainly agree that if something challenging presents itself to a person, it is better to ask, "What am I supposed to be learning from this?" (assuming purposefulness), than to wail against fate and fortune (assuming randomness). But tell me, Plato, do you regard this belief as a "true opinion" or as a "noble lie"?

Plato: It is a true belief to state that all personal challenges that come to any and every individual are purposeful, not random, and moreover, the purpose of such challenges in to induce spiritual growth. An attitude of acceptance towards "what is" facilitates such growth.

Benedict: And what we are calling an attitude of acceptance towards whatever happens is exactly the result aimed at by the aforementioned spiritual teacher. For if people could get into the psychological state of mind of believing that whatever challenges they are now facing in their lives were freely chosen by them, then clearly they would be more inclined to face such challenges head on, and to take responsibility for them, instead of resorting to blame or feeling a victim of circumstances. But of course, the "as if" is a clever ploy.

William: What do you mean?

Benedict: The "as if" is literally the case.

Socrates: ... Hence the brilliance of this teaching. If he were to say to someone, "You freely choose your life situation," very few would believe it. They would protest most strongly: why in the world would I, or anyone, freely choose to have cancer, to have an alcoholic mother, or to lose a child in an automobile accident. So to avoid such protests, he used the phrase "as if".

Benedict: Now there are many ways in which this particular teaching can be expressed. My favorite way is to reflect on the truth that nothing could be other than what it in fact is. This way of putting it easily eliminates all the "would haves", "could haves", and "should haves", that drain so much energy from the human mind. But this way of putting it does not make immediately clear the sense in which the "as if" is literally true. Yet I hesitate to talk about choice and so-called free will.

William: I think you wish to avoid getting into a more metaphysical discussion. Perhaps things will become clearer if we discuss this in terms of a common concrete example.

Benedict: Go ahead.

William: Most humans have problems and difficulties with their parents at some point in their lives. It is obvious that the human who believes she has chosen her parents will deal with her issues much more effectively than one who believes that her parents "just happened" to her randomly, or by chance. But of course, no human will easily believe that she has chosen her parents. That is not her conscious experience. From within the human perspective, her "free will", if there is such a thing, does not extend retroactively before her birth. So she is told to pretend, to make believe that she *has* chosen her parents.

But then, when she transcends her personality, either by death or some other spiritually transformative experience, her perspective – her subjective sense of who she is – merges seamlessly with the perspective of the eternal soul, or who she really is. But from this latter perspective, she sees that she did in fact "choose" her parents, and all the other determining circumstances of her embodied life.

Socrates: So the "as if" is literally true, but does not become known to the individual until enlightenment or death. The literal truth cannot be seen from within the human perspective. That's what tickled me. Tell them the literal truth, but don't tell them it's literally the truth. Brilliant! ... And funny, too. That's why I asked if he said it with a straight face. You see, a good spiritual teacher must be a pragmatist too. What is the best psychological attitude for humans to have towards the various challenges and difficulties that Life places before them? The answer to this question is: believe that the challenges were freely chosen. Actually, they *were* freely chosen. But humans are unlikely to believe that they did freely choose their parents. So the "as if" works more effectively than trying to convince people that they did, in fact, choose their parents.

William: It is "as if" a man freely chooses to climb a steep mountain. Halfway up he forgets his former choice, and experiences many challenges that seem merely to happen to him. But actually, all challenges come to him because of his prior choice to climb the mountain. He'd be much better off facing each challenge directly, without complaining or whining about his life situation. In this sense, every challenge any human faces is the result of a prior choice to incarnate.

Benedict: And not only to incarnate per se, but to incarnate as the particular individual he now experiences himself as being. However, the phrase "prior choice" needs to be qualified somewhat. The human being is a consequence of, or is determined by, what we may call a "choice" on the part of the soul. Strictly speaking, the human does not "choose" its parents, but rather, comes into being as a result of a choice made at a higher level, the soul. Yet the human, also strictly speaking, is not other than the soul in which it "lives and breathes and has its being" – (I love that phrase). So with that in mind, it is not incorrect to state that one chooses one's parents.

William: *(smiling)* Well, one good quote deserves another, even if it has already been stated. Pragmatically speaking, we want our social order to be permeated with beliefs and attitudes that are maximally conducive to the well-being of people, beliefs that help and assist the human to flourish in her being, as Benedict might put it. Obviously, cultural beliefs, such as sex is sinful, things happen for no reason, humans are competitive by nature, and greed is good, are very harmful both to individuals and to society as a whole. The general belief that one's immediate familial circumstances are *purposeful* rather than *accidental* is greatly beneficial to both individual and society.

Benedict: Yes, but what's your quote?

William: OK, I'm getting to it. But I wanted to preface the quote by stating that although on the one hand it seems to be poetic and inspirational, yet on the other hand it is deeply pragmatic – by which I mean humans should regard it *as if* it were true, even though it actually *is* true. Here's my favorite quote once again:

> I saw that the Universe is not composed of dead matter, but is, on the contrary, a living Presence. I became conscious in myself of eternal life. It was not a conviction that I would have eternal life, but a consciousness that I possessed eternal life then; I saw that all men are immortal; and that the cosmic order is such that without any peradventure all things work together for the good of each and all: that the foundation principle of the world, of all the worlds, is what we call love, and that the happiness of each and all is in the long run absolutely certain.

It seems to me that these principles should form part of the background beliefs, or common notions, of our New Social Order.

Socrates: *(smiling)* And I think it tickles *you*, William, that pragmatism and spiritual metaphysics converge into the same teaching. Pragmatically, what Bucke states are the most useful things for people to believe, if they are to flourish and be happy. Yet at the same time, they are literally true.

Plato: Good. Let's list these as "true beliefs" that we will inculcate into the minds of our children.

1) The Universe is a Living Presence.
2) Humans possess eternal life.
3) The Universe is a cooperative affair. Without any effort, all things work together for the good of each and all.
4) Love, Divine Love, is the foundation principle of all Creation.
5) The happiness of every human being is, in the long run, absolutely certain.

To these five principles, we add what we have already discussed, namely,

6) Within the Universe, there are no accidents or random events, but rather, everything that happens has purpose and meaning.

Benedict: So these principles will constitute the "common notions" of our social order, and our children will be raised in a society that embraces these truths. We could quibble with the precise wording, and perhaps some things could be added. But there is no doubt that adults who have been raised in such a society, and who have internalized these beliefs, will constitute a very different kind of "human being" than the kind now at large on the Earth.

Neal: I don't want to quibble with the wording, but another way to state the third principle is that Creation is a cooperative affair, not a competitive one. We could state, we have stated, that there is a single Divine Being who has created "all things" – or more accurately, has manifested as "all things" such that they cooperate one with another so as to constitute the Whole.

Benedict: These principles may of course be arrived at through holy reason, as you have done. But Bucke *experienced* them directly, as do all mystics and NDErs.

William: Yes, and we must not forget that because of advancing medical technology, many more humans will be resurrected from what formerly would have killed them, so lots of humans will have experienced directly what Bucke experienced, and they will be talking about it with others, so there is every reason to believe our whole social order will be permeated by stories that illustrate the above principles. Thus it will be ingrained in humans that outer events that they experience as difficult and challenging have come their way neither at random nor by accident, but rather have been sent to them by their Creator for the benign purpose of assisting the soul to grow and to flourish.

5) Healing Emotional Residues

Neal: But you know, if I may play devil's advocate, there are those who say that the purpose of embodiment is not to make people happy, but to make people wake up spiritually. One is more likely to wake up from a dream that has become a nightmare than from a dream that is pleasant. So a social order that is completely out of harmony with spiritual principles, such as the social order presently on the planet, will create such a nightmare for humans that they will become motivated to wake up.

William: You mean "has created" rather than "will create".

Neal: Yes.

Plato: Well then, the nightmare is already upon the Earth, and our whole conversation has been about how humans may awaken from their collective nightmare. It is certainly true that great suffering can and has caused many to wake up from the dream of embodiment. But it is equally true that humans *can* wake up without suffering.

Neal: Yes, yes, I agree. As one spiritual teacher has put it, humans need to suffer until they realize they don't. But we seem to be talking about a social order in which no one needs to suffer, in which…

Socrates: … in which "suffering is optional". Remember that the

Buddha preached "the end of suffering". If that can happen to an individual, why not also to a large group of individuals, that is, to a society as a whole? But I think you have a slightly different concern?

Neal: If everyone were to become enlightened, which I grant is possible, then there would be no further need for embodiment, and hence, no further need for any social order. The Earth experiment, in that case, comes to a successful end.

Plato: You're making an assumption that may not be true.

Neal: What?

Plato: You are assuming that souls that are enlightened, that don't "have to" become embodied, would never choose to become embodied.

Socrates: Ah, I see your concern now.

Neal: Then tell me what it is.

Socrates: Yes, the view that many people have had is that the Earth-plane is a sort of cosmic hellhole, the main purpose of which is for embodied souls to escape from.

Neal: The Earth is that very place into which fools have rushed where angels fear to tread. We humans are those fools.

Socrates: And yet we are talking about transforming this hellhole into a paradise for which even the Angels will be standing in line in order to incarnate. Is this not the purpose of the human experiment? … To transform human consciousness so that it *is* "on Earth as it is in Heaven"? … To transform human consciousness so that embodied life becomes a Garden of Earthly delights into which even the gods and angels will happily manifest?

Plato: So the success of the human experiment does not necessarily imply the end of embodiment per se, just the end of human suffering.

Socrates: *(to me, with penetrating eyes)* I'm reading you now, and I can see the sorrow that has been creeping up on you throughout our conversations. The same sorrow doubtless has infected many others too. May I reflect it back to you, so that we can quickly excavate the sorrow, not only from you, but from others as well?

Neal: Yes, of course.

Socrates: *(playfully)* But first you must acknowledge that you have a tendency to be nostalgic.

Neal: What do you mean?

Socrates: For example, when you visit the city of your birth, you like to walk around in your old neighborhood. You enjoy seeing the very same buildings that were there when you were a boy, and are grateful they are still standing. You would feel, or think you would feel, a loss were your old neighborhood to disappear, and you could no longer revisit it. That's nostalgia.

Neal: Guilty as charged.

Socrates: And when you watch old movies, do you not sometimes pause the movie in order to get a closer look at the streetcars and trolleys that you so loved when you were a boy?

Neal: *(blushing slightly)* Guilty as charged.

Socrates: So now, as we have been discussing these things for months and years, it has become increasingly clear to you that there are only two possible outcomes for the human experiment. In one outcome humans successfully manage to destroy themselves. The collective pain brought about by worshipping the gods of greed and status-seeking will cause humans to commit suicide collectively. Global nuclear war is one such way to commit suicide, but more likely is the poisoning of the planet, so that Earth can no longer sustain human life. In this scenario, the old neighborhood will no longer exist, so to speak, and souls will no longer be able to incarnate on Earth.

The other outcome, the one we are hoping for, is that our New Social Order will come into being. We do not insist that the New Society be exactly as we have described it, but we do insist that **only** a social order that is thoroughly permeated by the Golden Rule – so that there is no aspect of the society that is not governed by this Rule – can save the Earth from what humans have become through worshipping idols and false gods.

Neal: Yes, these seem to be the only two possibilities.

Socrates: *(with humor)* But it has occurred to you that the second possible outcome will also be the end of the old neighborhood.

Neal: Yes, for I can see now that eventually there will be no stopping the thinning of the margins. More and more humans will become spiritually enlightened. When all humans have become enlightened, or rather, when all souls that are now participating in the human experiment have become enlightened, we will say that the experiment is successful, but having succeeded, there is no further need to continue with it. Enlightened souls have no need for embodiment, and hence, after a number of generations during which humans live according to the Golden Rule, the Earth itself will have outlived its usefulness.

Socrates: So whether ultimately successful or unsuccessful, you have concluded that either way the human experiment will have come to an end. In the first scenario it comes to an end within a few generations; in the second scenario, humans get their prophesized thousand years of peace, after which it also comes to an end. *(With humor)* Not a happy choice for someone as nostalgic as yourself.

Neal: Hah! It *is* a happy choice. I can deal with what you call my nostalgia. But you are right to call it to my attention. *(To William)* My goodness, every time I walk through the Harvard Yards I get nostalgic for the old pump that was there when I was a boy.

William: Well, and how do you think I felt when they started digging that tunnel under Harvard Square? All the noise and cacophony. I was both fascinated by the technology, and saw that motorized coaches would soon replace the horse and buggy. The thought of a world without horses saddened me very much. So I was nostalgic too. But you know what? Once you quit the body, nostalgia drops away.

Neal: Yes, this seems to be the case empirically. The great majority of NDErs are not at all nostalgic to return to their body in order to experience things from that perspective.

William: And so when all humans become enlightened there will be no feelings of nostalgia for the vanished Earth.

Socrates: *(with humor)* So if you wish to feel nostalgia, *now* is your opportunity, while you are still embodied.

Plato: Ah, but what vanishes is only the Earth as it exists for human consciousness. When human consciousness is transformed, so that it is no longer *human,* then the Earth itself is likewise transformed. And we should keep in mind that the Earth is not some external "place" to which souls go to become embodied. For the Earth has been created by the same "World Soul" or "One Mind" that has created all humans, and both the human and the Earth have their very being within the single Divine Mind. We cannot say much about what a transformed Earth will look like, but it will be a place into which angels will no longer fear to manifest.

Socrates: And if I may wax prophetic, after ten generations or so during which humans live in a manner we have here prescribed, or similar to what we have laid down, the Earth itself will become a "New Earth". No longer necessary for spiritual growth, the New Earth is a "Garden of Earthly Delights", into which beings higher than heretofore will manifest. And if you were to ask, why would they manifest when there is no need to…

Neal: Yes, that question has crossed my mind.

Socrates: I'll answer in terms of an analogy. Imagine a theater that was technologically equipped so as to give people the feeling of utmost reality. They have special goggles and headphones that make images and sounds appear real; they wear special suits that give them the same tactile sensations that the protagonist in the movie is experiencing. Even sensations of smell and taste can be duplicated. Now, no one is compelled to attend this theater, but…

Neal: The line to get in would wrap around the block several times over.

Socrates: And the reason would be…?

Neal: To experience sensory delights.

Socrates: Good. And so, we might envision that when the Earth is transformed, the line to get in will wrap around the galaxy, or at least, around the solar system.

Plato: So the Earth itself need not come to an end after it has served its purpose. It could instead become transformed: from a realm of tears and suffering to a Garden of Earthly Delights! A New Earth!

Socrates: *(to me, with humor)* So how's your nostalgia doing?

Neal: Well who could be nostalgic for a realm of tears and suffering? *(Laughing)* But I'll keep a little nostalgia for the old streetcars.

Socrates: Good enough. After all, nostalgia is really just a memory around which a little sweetness has been attached. But I assure you, once you get here you can join with William and many others and recreate all the streetcars your hearts desire.

William: *(laughing)* No, no, we're from different generations. I'll be busy recreating the horse and buggy. *(More seriously)* But not really.

Neal: What do you mean?

William: There's a difference between *nostalgia* and *longing*. The former, as Socrates has put it, is a memory around which some sweetness has been attached. The latter is a desire to make the conditions of the memory actual again. For example, I might be nostalgic for the horse and buggy, but I have no desire to incarnate into a context where horse and buggies are real. And the same for you. You are nostalgic for the water pump you drank from when you were a boy. But you do not seriously desire that they replace modern sanitary plumbing with a rusty old pump.

Neal: No, not really. Well, at any rate, I suspect that desire and longing are quite different from your perspective than mine.

William: Yes, and there is no point trying to describe it in any detail, since language is inadequate. Suffice to say, from the human perspective, desire and longing involve time, since the things desired and longed for are projected into the future; from my current perspective there is no time.

Benedict: So, whereas longing and desire appear to involve future time, nostalgia appears to involve past time, since it involves events that have happened in the so-called "past". But actually both desire and nostalgia occur in the present moment. A memory of something past is a thought-form occurring *now*. A desire for something future is a thought-form occurring *now*. It is tempting for humans to regard "past" and "future" as real existents, which such thoughts are "about". But what are called "past" and "future" are merely thought-forms that always occur in the present moment.

Now, our seniors know that they have no future, or rather, that the next "future" event that awaits them is the death of their body. So they will not have many thoughts or desires that pertain to the future. But they will have their memories, that is, thought-forms that arise in the present moment that appear to reference a non-existing "something" called "the past". Their main task, at this final stage of life, is to remove any emotional residue associated with such thought-forms.

Socrates: And what a noble task it is! *(Smiling)* Everyone knows I said the unexamined life is not worth living, or something to that effect, but everyone seems to be clueless about what it is that must be examined, if life is to be worth living. So let me state explicitly that among the more important things that must be examined, if life is to be worth living, are the emotions that are attached to thought-forms.

William: It is interesting to note that had we used the phrase "emotions that are attached to memories", that wording would invite people to think that we are talking about emotions related to "the past". But actually, we are discussing thought-forms that occur *now*, and the emotions involved have nothing to do with a fictional "past", but rather are occurring in the present moment.

Plato: Our seniors of course are emotionally intelligent, and have been examining their lives the way Socrates recommends since they were small children. But everything comes to fruition in the final years. Let's say a little more about this sacred "main task", as our seniors unpack their bags in preparation for their final journey. For brevity, I suggest we retain the word "memory" as a shorthand way of referring to the expression, "a thought-form that references a non-existing past", or something like that. As long as we are clear that when we are talking about memories we are talking about what exists in the present moment, then we may continue to use that term.

Benedict: OK. To examine one's life is to examine one's memories.

In this process of self-examination, what is one looking for?

Neal: We are looking for emotions that may be attached to various memories.

Benedict: And would you agree that the majority of those thought-forms called "memories" are neutral with respect to emotion?

Neal: Yes, the memory of what I ate for breakfast is not associated with any emotion.

Benedict: And *some* memories are associated with emotions that are benign and cause no difficulties.

Neal: Yes, the memory of riding streetcars through the streets of Boston. Although we did warn that *nostalgia* not be allowed to develop into *longing*.

Benedict: And again, *some* memories are associated with emotions that are challenging to the person who suffers from them. Of these, there are two fundamental kinds.

Neal: Yes, one kind we called an "emotional residue". Here are some examples: a man's wife has left him. He feels hurt and angry. Twenty years later, as he recalls or narrates the event, he feels the same hurt and anger, as if the event had happened yesterday. In a sports event, a referee misses a call and the athlete involved is upset. Twenty years later, the now former athlete gets upset whenever he thinks of that event. Or a woman narrowly avoids getting killed by a truck; years later when she remembers this event she feels the same fear that was appropriate when the event took place. These individuals have not processed the emotions that occurred when the events happened, so they have been carrying them around with them, and they (the emotions) present themselves to the individual whenever he recalls the original event. This is what we mean by the phrase "emotional residue".

Benedict: Good. And we may predict that *our* seniors, because they have been raised to be emotionally intelligent, will have a lot less difficulty with emotional residues than is currently the case. But there is another kind of emotional challenge with respect to memory that our seniors will face. *These* emotions are caused by mental attitudes that are associated with memories. I'm sure you could give us a few such examples, since you are still suffering from this a little bit.

Neal: Me?

(Everyone laughs, including me.)

Socrates: *(teasingly)* Do we need to call up that memory of yours regarding a seven-year-old boy stealing penny candy from a store? Or have you forgiven him yet?

Neal: *(laughing)* I'm still working on it.

Benedict: So this memory involves a slight feeling of guilt, which involves the belief, the false belief, that you, or rather, the seven-year-old boy who was you, should have known better. This false belief is what I meant by a "mental attitude" associated with memories. The same mental attitude is involved when a memory is associated with blame. "She should not have done that to me" implies that she *could* have not done that. But nothing could be other than what it in fact is. So emotions of guilt and blame involve a nonacceptance of "what is", and a belief that "what is" could be, or could have been, other than what it in fact is.

William: Yet not everyone is philosophically inclined by temperament, so not everyone will be able to work through these things by referring to philosophical first principles (e.g. that nothing could be other than what it in fact is). But everyone is capable of applying to themselves Benedict's technique of detaching the emotion from specific thoughts about its cause, and feeling the emotion in the body directly.

Benedict: Actually, both approaches together are the most effective. So, if I may use you as an example, when the memory of that seven-year-old candy-stealer comes to mind, notice any feelings of guilt, shame, or embarrassment that are attached to this memory. Then (i) reflect on the fact that the feeling of guilt presupposes that the little boy "could have" and "should have" behaved differently. This in turn involves the false belief that "what is" – stealing the candy – could have been other than what it was. All human emotions of guilt and blame involve this false belief. But in addition to philosophical reflection, our seniors will be able to (ii) detach the feeling of guilt, which is occurring *now,* from thoughts about its cause, which in this case are memories of past behaviors. We would say to our seniors (and to *you*), remove your attention from the memory – from thoughts about past behavior – and instead place it on the feelings and sensations occurring *in* your body *now*.

Plato: And we must state that we are by no means encouraging our seniors to live in the past. For the memories that come to them come in the present moment. Any emotions that accompany specific memories are also happening in the present moment. The memories simply trigger emotions that already exist within the psyche of the individual, and our task has been to assist seniors in dealing with, in healing, emotions that were not fully processed when they first occurred. So the process we are describing is really a process for connecting more deeply with the present moment. This is the process of unpacking one's baggage in preparation for the journey Home. When the unpacking is complete, the individual will be able to recollect any past event without emotion.

Socrates: Now, my friends, something more must be said, for we must not leave the impression that we are removing the richness of human emotions from the psyche of our seniors.

Benedict: On the contrary, when the usual emotions that characterize the human experience are deeply penetrated and removed, what remains is an inner peace and happiness that has no opposite. We desire for our seniors a taste of that eternal joy before their body dies. Removing the emotions called "guilt" and "blame" are the prerequisites for this taste of heaven.

However, in addition to removing dysfunctional emotions from the minds of our seniors, we wish to inculcate something positive, that we may call "an attitude of gratitude".

William: Of course, our citizens have been expressing gratitude towards one another all their lives. Since childhood, they have been expressing feelings of appreciation to family, friends, and many others who have assisted them and who have challenged them. But now we want them to feel thankful, not only for the specific individuals in their lives, but for the very life they have just lived. They will reflect on what they have experienced, on what they have learned, and on what they can take with them when they return Home.

Neal: We talked earlier about "original purpose". Like cells in the body, each human is created in order to serve a specific purpose, or fulfill a certain function. The "purpose", since it is Divine in origin, always involves Love and Understanding, which are the only things that may be taken Home. Ultimately, feelings of gratitude towards the life one has lived involve understanding and appreciating that one's original purpose has been fulfilled. One has learned what one came here to learn; one has expressed what one came here to express. There is nothing that remains to *do*, and the mind reposes in *being*.

Socrates: *(to me, with humor)* ... Even if the body associated with that mind is stuck in a wheelchair?

Neal: *(laughing)* Yes, even so. But there's one more thing related to this that should be mentioned.

Socrates: What do you have in mind?

Neal: While one is going through it, the events in one's life appear to be random and accidental. We even speak of "accidents of birth" which we know are not accidents at all. It seems to be mere coincidence and sheer happenstance that we meet the specific individuals who become the central characters in our lives. Yet when one gets older and reflects back, it almost seems...

William: *(smiling)* ... that there was a plan or plot to the whole thing.

Plato: We probably should not say too much about such things, since they cannot be fully understood by *human* intelligence. But we can state this much now: in the immediate after-death state of consciousness, the consciousness that was formerly *human* comes to understand that there was indeed a "plan" to its previous life. We want our seniors to catch a glimpse of the plan for their lives before they quit the body. And so they exit the theater of Earthly life rejoicing, with waves of gratitude carrying them up to the highest levels of consciousness.

Socrates: And the gratitude they feel is not only their own, but also the gratitude felt by every human who knew them, and whose lives were enriched by theirs. We must reverse that old joke.

Neal: What old joke.

Socrates: I've forgotten whether we have already told it. But it goes something like this. When a baby is born, everyone is happy except the one who is born; when a human dies, everyone is sad except the one who dies. There is something not quite right with this picture, don't you agree?

Neal: Yes, but, Socrates, we cannot forbid humans from crying when someone they have cherished leaves them.

Socrates: Yes, but the tears can be coated with a, ah…

Neal: … a layer of sweetness…? You know, I have heard it said that excessive wailing and grieving hinders the soul's upward journey and keeps them earthbound.

Socrates: You heard that from me, remember? The wailing does no good for anyone. But tears are OK, especially when accompanied with understanding.

William: Here's a little analogy: when parents send their kids off to college, they may shed some tears, for something has come to an end. But the tears are accompanied by the understanding that this event – leaving home – is in the natural order of things, and is absolutely the right thing to happen. The parents also know it is not an absolute ending and that they will of course see and relate to their children again, but not as the children they were. *(To me)* Speaking of nostalgia, eh? And so it will be with death in *our* social order. It will be common knowledge that death does not end a relationship, and so tears will be tempered with the knowledge that they will meet and interact again, although in a different form.

Benedict: But there is yet another kind of tear that may flow in the presence of death.

Neal: What do you mean?

Benedict: These are the tears that flow from your eyes when you listen to Beethoven's *Ninth*; you call them "tears of recognition". I suppose we could also call them "tears of gratitude".

Plato: Actually both are involved. What is being recognized, of course, are the deeper layers of one's own soul, as the force of the music temporarily thins out the margins and one is literally "moved" towards realms of deepening understanding, which movement is always accompanied by deepening joy. With this experience of "being moved" comes gratitude towards that which has triggered the understanding. And so the death of someone may trigger in another such tears of gratitude, behind which is profound peace and joy. Thus the one who dies rides the waves of gratitude that emanate from everyone with whom he has interacted during his life. The gratitude deepens the one who emanates it, and lifts up the one who receives it. But I think, Neal, you will be sharing a personal story about this soon.

Neal: What story?

Plato: *(smiling)* It will come to you soon enough. But to come full circle, let's say a few words about the other side to that joke, if it is a joke. For the trauma called "birth" can affect the individual for the whole of her life. Everything must be done to reduce this trauma, and we shall take an experimental approach to the specifics. No doubt William here will be measuring the physiology of our infants to ascertain what is best for them.

William: *(laughing)* I doubt that would be sufficient to motivate me to return. But one thing we can state, or restate, is that physical contact between the infant and the mother is absolutely essential. The body of the newly born infant is immediately traumatized when it no longer hears and feels its mother's heartbeat. The physiology of a newborn who is birthed underwater at body temperature and then immediately placed on its mother's chest is different from the physiology of an infant birthed in a temperature 25 degrees lower than what it was used to, and removed from its mother's body.

Socrates: And it will be fine for humans to welcome and celebrate the birth of a baby, but the profound and challenging nature of birth – that is, of a soul voluntarily limiting itself for a Divine purpose – will also be acknowledged. In particular, it will be recognized that babies always cry for a reason, and that reason involves, over and above physical discomfort, the loss of connection with Source. So we shall be gentle with our newly born humans, and give them every possible Earthly comfort. But now let us return to our newly departed, riding the waves gratitude that emanate from family and friends. *(To me)* So has the relevant story come to mind, about what we referred to as "waves of gratitude"?

Neal: I think so, but I'm not sure I can tell it.

6) Waves of Gratitude

Plato: I think I see your difficulty. Perhaps it will be useful to distinguish between two very different kinds of events that humans call "memories". Ordinary memories refer to time, or duration. They are images of events that happened to the body. But another kind of event that is also called "memory" is actually an incursion into the personality of knowledge that originates in the soul, that is, in the eternal order. For example, the Near-Death Experience has nothing to do with the body. It is an incursion, into the personality, of Truths that emanate from beyond the veil, from the eternal order. I'll suggest that we use the word "recollection" to describe such experiences, and retain the expression "ordinary memory" to refer to the body's experiences in time. So with this usage of terms, we may say that a person *remembers* what they had for breakfast, but *recollects* what they experienced in their NDE.

And we may state that, for reasons already discussed, language is quite adequate for describing *ordinary memories*, but woefully inadequate for describing *recollections*. This is why NDErs insist that what they experienced cannot be put into words. But the NDE is by no means the only kind of incursion from the eternal order into the personality. "After-Death Communications", "past-life memories", and powerful aesthetic experiences – or in my former terminology, encounters with the Form of Beauty – are *recollections*, not *ordinary memories*.

Now, as you have no doubt heard, the human mind can occasionally receive communications from the eternal order while sleeping. The ego – that is, that structure in the field of consciousness that functions as a barrier to such communication – weakens during sleep, and hence it is easier for non-embodied spirits to reach the personality under the conditions of sleep.

Neal: Yes, such experiences are not uncommon, and people often report them as "an extraordinary vivid dream", or as "a dream that was more than a dream" or "a dream that seemed so real".

Plato: Yes. The point is that through the dream state of consciousness, humans may receive communications from our side of the margins, and even cross the margins and visit with us for a little while. People conflate such transcendent experiences with ordinary dreams. So we may state that language is adequate to describe ordinary dreams, but is not adequate to describe *recollections* that occur through the dream state.

Neal: I agree.

Plato: *(smiling)* So you see, when we asked you to describe your experience with "waves of gratitude", a *recollection* that came to you through the dream state, you hesitated to state it because…

Neal: … language is inadequate.

William: Your hesitation may also be generalized as follows: whenever a human feels that something they have experienced cannot be described in words, that is a sure sign that the experience involves something more than just what is happening to their body in the temporal order, but rather, involves an incursion of information from our side of the margins. Actually humans have many such experiences that are not recognized as such.

Socrates: Yes, and, Neal, you have experienced several such *recollections* that came through the dream state of consciousness. Would you care to share?

Neal: …

Socrates: Well share anyway. This is not about you, the personality. It is about structures within the field of consciousness and hence common to all humans. We use you merely as an example, not as a special case, if that's what you're concerned about.

William: And we will preface your account with the caveat that these experiences or *recollections* are ineffable, so no one is expecting your words to be adequate to what you experienced.

Benedict: *(laughing)* And if you need further encouragement, here is that poetic license, which allows its possessor to use language in any way they wish, even as excessive as our friend Plato here.

Neal: OK, OK. I'll mention three *recollections* briefly, then talk about the "waves of gratitude" *recollection.* (i) I *recollect* visiting with and conversing with my deceased maternal grandparents. The first such after-death communication occurred when I was 17 years old, yet when I *recollect* it, it is as fresh as if it had happened last night.

Plato: That very "freshness" indicates a *recollection* rather than a mere *memory*. For, as NDErs know, experiences in the eternal order do not fade with time, as do ordinary dreams. You have no memory of what you dreamed last night, yet what you experienced almost 60 years ago is fresh.

Neal: Yes.

Plato: What else?

Neal: (ii) Again through the dream state, I seemed to hear a loud click or something, then found myself in a "magic garden" where everything was alive and conscious. It was "realer than real", as they say. I *recollect* wondering how I could ever have forgotten about this garden, since I knew I had visited it many times before. This experience, and the one to follow, happened about thirty years ago. A similar experience involved (iii) hearing celestial music, as Mozart tried to describe. I felt myself becoming absorbed into the music, which like the garden was alive and conscious. With both these experiences, I was upset when I woke up and found myself still embodied. If I had had a choice I would have remained in the garden, and in the music, forever.

Benedict: *(laughing)* ... Which is precisely why you did not have a choice.

Socrates: *(also laughing)* Yes, if you give these humans too much of a taste of heaven, they'll never want to come back to their bodies.

William: Now, (i), (ii), and (iii) are *kinds* of experiences that many humans have had. The NDE literature is filled with many accounts of such experiences, or rather, attempts to describe such experiences in words. So we will not discuss them any further. But your "waves of gratitude" experience is less common than the other kinds of experiences that are accessed through the dream state of consciousness, although not uncommon among Near-Death Experiences.

Plato: So with the poetic license firmly in hand, give it a try.

Neal: OK. I think the *recollection* occurred at a time when I was studying the Near-Death Experience, especially the "Life-Review" aspect of the experience. It seemed like, through the dream state, I was offered the opportunity to experience the Life Review. I was eager to know what NDErs were talking about, so I embraced the opportunity to find out.

Socrates: *(laughing)* ... Speaking of fools rushing in...

Neal: Yes, indeed, as I soon learned. Well, it was not at all what I had expected.

Socrates: Humans, when they first hear about a Life Review, immediately bring to mind everything for which they feel guilt – that is, they remember every time their behavior deviated from the Golden Rule. So you no doubt were expecting to see that notorious candy-stealer compelled to give an account of his dastardly deeds?

Neal: *(laughing)* You've gotten me to lighten up a little. But yes, I was expecting to experience all the pain and suffering I had brought to others through my past unconscious behaviors. So with some trepidation, I braced myself for what was to come. But as it turned out, there is no "bracing" for what I did experience.

Benedict: Continue.

Neal: Yes, I was in the classroom. It was a large lecture class with over a hundred students. Something I had just said had triggered an understanding in the mind of a student who sat in the back of the classroom. This particular student I did not know and had no contact with. The understanding that got triggered was something very relevant to the student's personal life. Simultaneous with that understanding, a wave of gratitude emanated from him to me.

William: Can you describe this wave?

Neal: *(smiling)*… No, of course not.

William: Ah, but you've got the poetic license.

Neal: OK. I saw and felt the wave as it approached me. As it came closer, I "saw" that the wave was constituted by Unconditional Love. The closer it came the more I was awed by what was happening. There is no way to prepare for this. It was visceral. I felt, or feared, that the wave would consume me. And even if I could withstand *this* wave – from someone I didn't even know I had helped – I could not have withstood the waves of gratitude from those I knew I had helped. So I stopped the process, and forced myself to wake up.

William: *(smiling)* From the human side of the margins, this Unconditional Love is definitely not for the faint of heart. But don't feel bad because you forced yourself to wake up…

Socrates: *(laughing)* … almost as if you didn't know the difference between Divine Love and a nightmare.

Plato: You joke, Socrates, but perhaps there really is not that much difference. After all, I think a little analysis might reveal that what is frightening about a nightmare is the same thing that is frightening to humans about Unconditional Love. *(To me)* You said you could not have withstood the waves of gratitude, had you allowed the experience to continue. Who is it that could not have withstood God's Love?

Neal: Yes, I see it. It was the ego that feared its own dissolution in the onslaught of waves of Unconditional Love.

Plato: And in some previous conversation, we described the human condition as a sort of *hiding* from the Divine Being. The physical world is a "place" where God seems not to be. But is there any difference between hiding from God and hiding from Unconditional Love?

Neal: No.

Plato: *(with humor)* So in your experience, you were not done with your hiding, so you resisted the dissolution of what you thought was your self. For the ego or personality cannot sustain its form, or structure, in the presence of Divine Love. And the same with a nightmare, for what is frightening about a nightmare is not what appears to happen externally, but rather, the dissolution of the ego. One's very sense of self is what is threatened. But do we not know from *A Course in Miracles* that that which feels threatened is fundamentally unreal?

Benedict: The situation here is very much the same as in that old Zen joke that has recently come to mind.

Plato: What joke?

Neal: I'll try to tell it. A certain monk was eager to become enlightened, and traveled from one monastery to another in the hope of finding a Master who could enlighten him. He hears about a certain Zen Master who had better than average luck in enlightening his monks, so he travels to the monastery, and says to the Teacher: "Master, *I* want to be enlightened. Will you please enlighten *me*?" The Master replies: "*You* cannot be enlightened. *You* are the problem. When *you* dissolve, what remains will be enlightenment."

Benedict: So, using our poetic license, we may replace the term "enlightenment" with the term "Unconditional Love". *You*, Neal, the separate personality that you are experiencing yourself as being, cannot experience Divine Love. *You* must dissolve, and then what remains is Divine Love. And each wave of gratitude that comes your way contributes to the dissolution of the ego. For what we are calling a "wave of gratitude" is really a morsel of Divine Unconditional Love manifesting through the individual who emanates it to the individual who feels it.

Plato: Remember, the student in question was not, at the conscious level, doing anything. He was not consciously sending out gratitude. Rather, the feeling of gratitude is internal to his feeling that he has been helped in some way. The same analysis holds more generally.

Benedict: Yes. Let's extend our analysis to several other areas of human experience. (i) The perception of beauty triggers a wave of gratitude towards what is perceived as beautiful and its cause. (ii) The feeling that one has been assisted by another triggers such waves, as does (iii) the sense that one has understood something. So, for example, internal to the listening of Beethoven's *Ninth* are feelings of gratitude toward both the music and to the one through whom the music was brought to Earth.

Neal: My goodness, then all the waves of gratitude from all the humans who have been moved by that music must have lifted Beethoven clear out of the whole Universe. No human personality could possibly survive such an onslaught of Divine Love, channeled through all the humans he has helped.

Plato: Exactly. Even the flower is aware when a human appreciates its beauty. But now we must return to our seniors, for we must do our best to prepare them for the Divine Love that awaits them, preferably a little before they quit the body, but certainly afterwards.
William: Yes, and when we spoke of inculcating an "attitude of gratitude" in our seniors, we now recognize from Neal's experience, that this "attitude" must go both ways, both giving and receiving.

Neal: And I will testify that receiving gratitude is more difficult than expressing it, much more.

Socrates: That is certainly the case for you. But I wonder whether you think the difficulty in receiving gratitude is intrinsic to giving and receiving, or whether the difficulty is caused by culture.

Neal: A "nature or nurture" question?

Socrates: Yes. After all, you, the personality, are a product of a culture that is completely out of balance with respect to the mutual flow of yin-yang energies. The "male" principle of *doing/acting* excessively dominates the "female" principle of *being/receiving*. Do you think *our* seniors will experience the same difficulties as *yours*?

Neal: I think I've come to the conclusion that the only thing humans are "by nature" is mortal. Everything else pertains to upbringing. Oh wait, your question is more complicated than I had thought.

Socrates: What do you mean?

Neal: At first I thought that *our* seniors, raised in a culture that is balanced between giving and receiving, will have no more difficulty receiving gratitude than giving it. After all, they have been practicing receiving all their lives. For we have made birthdays an opportunity for receiving gratitude from others, not in a perfunctory way, but as spiritual ritual, in which the individual is guided in quieting her mind and opening her heart to fully receive affection, appreciation, and love from others in her life. But then I realized that the ego naturally fears its own dissolution. The fear will be *less* in our social order, but it will still be present.

Now, an expression of gratitude from one human to another is really nothing other than a morsel of Unconditional Love, originating in the Divine Being, and channeled through the human who expresses it. For when one feels gratitude towards another, there is no expectation of getting anything back, hence the love is truly unconditional. And every morsel of Divine Love, properly received, chips away at the boundaries of the ego, so that the individual receiving the Love recognizes that she is more than a separate, skin-enclosed being.

Socrates: *(smiling)* By Zeus, you are making the Divine Being seem like a Boogey-Man of some sort. Watch out, or He'll Love you to death.

Neal: *(laughing)* Which is exactly why we humans have been hiding from Him for so long. It is not his wrath that we fear, but his Love. For the ego, that which we humans think we are, cannot sustain its structure in the presence of Divine Love. So I guess my response to your question is that it is both nature and nurture. It is in the nature of things for the ego to experience some fear and trepidation at the prospect of its own demise, as I did, and also, our seniors have been *nurtured* and prepared through upbringing to face this fear directly. And if I may add, this "being Loved to death" refers not to the death of the body, which is a relatively small thing compared with the dissolution of the ego.

Plato: And so it seems that Divine Love will be the main subject of conversation for our seniors in their final years. Any residual thoughts and feelings of unworthiness will be expunged from their minds. Perhaps the best way to practice nonresistance to God's Love is to surrender deeply to smaller morsels of Love that come through receiving gratitude from others.

William: We should also note that our citizens have been practicing surrender in other ways, not just on birthdays. They practice surrender through receiving massage, through sex, and through the perception of Divine Beauty in whatever Earthly form it takes.

Benedict: You know, I think maybe we could use one more visit from the semantic cops.

William: Why do you say that?

Benedict: The word "surrender" has connotations of passivity; one just gives up resisting something or other. But there is also a very active sense of the term that is important to emphasize. I think I can explain what I have in mind with a simple example, if Neal doesn't mind.

Neal: We're listening.

Benedict: OK. Now, when you receive a massage, you surrender to the sensations of touch.

Neal: Of course.

Benedict: But do you really?

Neal: Huh?

Benedict: Consider two extremes: (i) while receiving touch, your mind wanders all over the place; perhaps you even fall asleep; (ii) while receiving touch, your mind is singularly focused on the sensations in your body. Both cases are conceived as instances of "surrender", but in the former case, only the body is surrendered, and in the latter case the mind has surrendered to the sensations of touch.

Neal: Oh my, that's why I love the deep-tissue stuff so much; it focuses my mind directly on the sensations occurring in the moment. So surrender, *active* surrender, brings the mind fully into the present moment and involves a heightening of consciousness.

William: Yes, so when athletes talk about *surrendering* to the game, or musicians speak of *surrendering* to the music, they are referring to a state of consciousness that involves a heightened awareness. *What* they are surrendering are all thoughts and emotions that reference a "past" or "future". Their consciousness is entirely focused in the here and now.

Benedict: In the state of surrender, there are no "could have beens" or "should have beens". Indeed, any event that a given human experiences as external to herself is the "face" that the Universe, or the Divine Being, presents to the individual in that moment. So "surrender", or acceptance of *what is,* is much more than a passive nonresistance to something external to oneself, but rather involves a conscious embracing.

Neal: And if I may use myself as an example again, when another person speaks to me the psychological dynamics are similar to receiving a massage. On the one hand, sometimes when a person is talking to me, my body is there but my mind is not. Either I'm daydreaming while the other is speaking, or I'm rehearsing what I'm going to say next. But on the other hand, sometimes my mind is fully attentive and focused on what the other is saying. In this case, I hear not only every word that is said, but am also aware of any emotions and feelings behind the words. Therapists call that "active listening".

William: Yes, isn't this interesting? In the present dysfunctional culture, it seems that this skill called "active listening" is largely absent. That is a main reason why people feel so lonely; they talk a lot, but nobody is really listening, so they are unable to feel connected with psychological structures beyond themselves. *Active listening* requires being present in the here and now; it requires the ability to suspend one's own thoughts and emotions in the moment.

Neal: The inability of humans to listen to and receive the "other" without judgment, is, I believe, a major factor in the coming demise of the present culture. But in our New Social Order, our citizens are taught communication skills from the very beginning. They have much practice accepting without judgment the thoughts and emotions of other human beings. This is what is involved in producing humans who are emotionally intelligent.

Plato: So following Benedict, when we use the term "surrender" we intend its active sense. When we tell our seniors to accept that their body is ill or frail we are not telling them to stop complaining and passively accept their life situation.

Neal: Although at a minimum they should do that.

Socrates: But ours is not a minimal social order. You have heard it said that "whatever form the Divine Being desires, that form the Divine Being becomes".

Neal: Yes.

Socrates: And do you also believe the inverse of that expression? – That "whatever form exists, exists because it is desired by the Divine Being".

Neal: Yes.

Socrates: And is this true in advanced old age? Is the physical form of an old man, frail, ill, unable to care for itself – *(glancing at me)* perhaps even stuck in a wheelchair – is this form also desired by the Divine Being?

Neal: Yes, that follows. As Benedict would put it, nothing can be nor be conceived without the Divine Being.

Socrates: Is it not pointless and futile to resist what has been determined by the Divine Being?

Neal: Yes, very futile.

Socrates: And is not the expression "determined by the Divine Being" the same as "what is"?

Neal: Yes.

Socrates: So acceptance of "what is" is the same as "acceptance of what is determined by the Divine Being". But now tell me, what is it that the Divine Being determines?

Neal: Well, since there is nothing other than the Divine Being, the only thing the Divine Being *can* determine is Itself.

Socrates: So "surrender to what is" is the same as "surrender to the Divine Being". Then in these terms, tell me who is it that is doing the surrendering?

Neal: It would have to be none other than the Divine Being Itself, or the form the Divine Being assumes in becoming an individual unit of consciousness.

Socrates: And so to live surrendered to "what is" is to live with heightened consciousness, fully present to what is Divine in all things and oneself, untroubled by imaginary thoughts that pertain to a non-existing "past" or "future". But I think Benedict put it most succinctly.

Benedict: I did?

Neal: Yes, you did. Here's the passage I think Socrates has in mind:

> We are a part of the Whole of Nature, whose order we follow. If we clearly and distinctly understand this, that part of us that is defined by the understanding, that is, the better part of us, will be fully resigned and will endeavor to persevere in that resignation. For insofar as we understand we can desire nothing but that which must be, nor, in an absolute sense, can we find contentment in anything but truth.

Benedict: Hmm… The English word "resigned" is not quite right, as it implies passivity, which is the exact opposite of the meaning I had intended.

Neal: Yes, different translators use different terms, such as "content" and "satisfied". Perhaps the best term to use is the term "surrender", in the *active* sense we have described.

Benedict: OK, that works. And of course, the expression "that which must be" is identical to the expression "what is".

Socrates: Now, what is it that humans desire when they desire something other than "what is" or "what must be"?

Neal: *(laughing)* When you put it that way, it's very funny. There is nothing other than "what is". So the desire for something other than "what is" is a desire that what an individual merely imagines becomes actual. People imagine what "could have, would have, should have been", and spend a lot of mental time immersed in such imaginings. They really seem to believe that the Divine Being could be, or could have been, other than what it in fact is. And so they live unconscious, in a world of their own imaginings.

Benedict: Yes, and we summarize two points: in the first place, "what is", or the face that the Divine Being presents as external to a given individual, is determined by the Divine Being, and could not be other than what it in fact is. Second, the very individual to whom the Divine Being is appearing in the form of "what is" is itself nothing other than a form assumed by the Divine Being. For the true Home of the wise man is in the eternal order; yet insofar as he partakes of the temporal order, he is still, by virtue of a certain eternal necessity, conscious of himself, of God, and of things.

William: Thus we desire that our seniors begin their journey Home before they quit the body. We want them to have a little taste of that "eternal necessity" according to which all things come into and pass out of existence. In particular, we want them to experience their lives and their very selves as aspects of Divine eternal necessity.

Benedict: And the more they have surrendered to Divine Necessity, the more at peace they will be, and when they quit the body, will have little or no difficulty ah – *(with humor)* crossing the various rivers and obstacles that lurk in Plato's imagination.

Plato: *(laughing)* I'll let that pass. But more seriously, the obstacles are not lurking in *my* imagination, but rather in the imaginations of those who quit the body while firmly believing that they *are* the persons or roles they have just played. They are like actors who stay firmly in character after the play is over.

Socrates: *(also laughing)* And that's why we need so many therapists over here.

Neal: What do you mean?

Socrates: Imagine this scene: a play has come to an end, but all the actors suffer from amnesia, and do not recollect (I use that term in our technical sense) that they are actors playing a part, but rather think they are the characters they have just portrayed. Now they are wandering around off stage, outside the theater, quite confused, as the world does not respond to their costumes or who they think they are.

William: *(smiling)* But the world *will* respond to them, just not in the way our actors think they should. For, if our amnesiac actors wander around town in full costume after the play, believing they *are* the characters just portrayed, they would soon be tended to by therapists who would use whatever means possible to restore them to the full recollection of who they really are. In cases where role-identification is especially strong, and the person is carrying guilt, pride, anger, or any other emotional residue from her role, she will be taken to a sanatorium, or place of rest and healing, until she has completely recovered.

(With humor) In my own case it was quite amusing, even to me at the time. No one responded to "Professor James", and the authority of Harvard University held no sway whatsoever. Perhaps I appeared confused to these guys *(gesturing towards Plato, Socrates, and Benedict)* but I thoroughly enjoyed it and lingered with the process.

Neal: What process?

William: The process of removing my "William James" costume. I think some other beings were assisting me, but I'll tell you this, as the layers of the costume were being peeled away, I felt a joy, a mental clarity, and a Love that is both beyond words *and* exactly as Bucke described it.

Socrates: Yes, but you were a relatively easy case, as will be Neal here. But you'd be surprised, or maybe not, at the number of poor souls that have to be dragged off stage, screaming and kicking, and desiring nothing other than to stay stuck in their costumes. But not to worry, we have an abundance of such sanatoriums and therapists on our side of the margins. However, we are hoping that, with our new Social Order in place, the need for such sanatoriums will greatly diminish, as everyone, not just mystics and saints, will be prepared to go when the play is over.

Plato: Good. We might state that we are moving the sanatoriums from the eternal order into the temporal order.

Benedict: *(laughing)* I see your point. The latter years of our seniors' lives will be spent in sanatorium-like conditions. They will reflect on their lives, and process residual emotions while still embodied, instead of dragging them, or trying to drag them, into the eternal order. We believe that many, if not most, of our seniors will have been doing this all their lives, so they will already be emotionally clear as they enter advanced old age. And the phrase "emotionally clear", let us remind ourselves, means no anger towards anyone, no guilt with regard to how they have lived their lives, and no desire that anything be other than what it in fact is.

William: We should add that it is not only our departing seniors who will be processing residual emotions, but also their family and friends, who will discuss any emotional residues they may have towards those about to leave, preferably prior to death, but certainly afterwards. I like the idea of a "living funeral". It is a blessing to depart the world without leaving any emotional residues, either in oneself or in others.

Plato: Yes, for such emotional residues are a drag on the soul, and tend to keep it earthbound. We desire that the souls of our seniors ascend to the highest levels possible for them, and that's why we shall assist them in unpacking their emotional baggage, or as much of it as is possible, before they leave. No doubt we could mention various rituals that might be useful both for end-of-life processing, and for after-death processing on the part of those left behind. But we will leave these and other details to the citizens of our New Social Order.

So what do you think, my friends? Are we complete?

7) Justice

Neal: *(smiling)* You have taught me well that nothing in the temporal order is "complete". So the question should be, "Are we complete for now?"

Plato: Good. I'll accept your emendation. So…?

Neal: Perhaps we are complete for now. Yet…

Plato: Out with it, my friend.

Neal: Well, I was going to say, we have been constructing our

New Society for quite a while, yet we have said nothing about your favorite topic.

Plato: *(laughing)* You mean like *justice*.

Neal: Yes.

Plato: There is no need for explicit discussion about this, since *divine justice* pervades every nook and cranny of our social order. But perhaps we could say a little bit about how a truly *just* social order handles such things as disputes among citizens or wrong-doings of any kind.

Neal: Yes, I would welcome that.

Plato: First let us note that your present legal system is not a system of justice, but rather, is intrinsically unjust.

Neal: What do you mean?

Plato: In both your civil and criminal cases, both sides aim to win in court?

Neal: Yes, of course.

Plato: And is truth a factor in their desire to win?

Neal: No. But they will say that it is the jury's job to discover what is true.

Plato: And can juries be manipulated by the cleverness of the lawyers and prosecutors, whose goal is only to win, not to discern truth?

Neal: Of course. Just ask Socrates here.

Plato: So juries cannot in fact be relied upon to discern the truth. The fact that so many innocent men are convicted of crimes they did not commit shows this quite clearly. Only a system of social justice that is thoroughly motivated by truth on all sides will be fair.

Neal: So no more lawyers? What do you suggest?

Plato: Here's an analogy to show what I have in mind: two six-year-old children are squabbling about something. Their parents hire lawyers to advocate for their children. The lawyers argue before a jury of children, each claiming that their client was right and the other was wrong. Does this seem to you like a good way to resolve disputes among children?

Neal: Quite laughable. The dispute should be handled by adults who are wiser than children, and who are motivated by the desire to discern what is true, not by any desire that one child should prevail over another.

Plato: And when adults squabble with one another over this or that, are they behaving any differently than emotionally immature children?

Neal: No.

Plato: Then disputes among adults should be handled by those who are wiser than the ones who are quarreling. Perhaps a team of therapists, or a council of elders. But everyone involved will be concerned, not with "winning", but with finding truth. For without truth, there is no justice. Yet we have reason to hope that such disputes will be very minimal in our society. *Our* citizens have been raised to be emotionally intelligent; hence they will for the most part have the maturity to resolve any disputes that might arise among them. But have you noticed that in our social order there is no motivation for crime?

Neal: I think so. As we have been saying all along, our social order recognizes, and fosters, three motivational forces in human beings: (i) curiosity, or the desire to know; (ii) compassion, or the desire to assist others; and (iii) self-expression, or the desire to develop and express inborn talents and abilities. The various motivations that the current dysfunctional social order recognizes and fosters are the desires for wealth and status. But these latter desires receive no encouragement or support in our new social order, so they will in time atrophy and eventually disappear from human consciousness. The Earth's material resources are shared equitably among all citizens, so no one can covet what another has. And the psychological need of citizens to feel that they belong to something larger than themselves will also be fully satisfied, so no citizen feels alone or uncared for. Moreover, *greed* and *ambition*, the source of all crime, are now regarded as forms of insanity that threaten our social order if not guarded against. So yes, I agree there is little or no motivation for crime in our new society.

Plato: So it is a not unremarkable achievement to have constructed a social order that is fair and just with respect to both civil and criminal disputes. *Justice*, we have said, requires truth-seeking and *only* truth-seeking on the part of everyone involved. But it is even more remarkable if our New Society is such that civil and criminal disputes do not even arise; for if everyone is internally just within themselves, then there is no need for an external "system of justice".

But *our* citizens have indeed been raised to have self-control and to be internally *just*. For they are all ruled by reason, preferably their own, but in any case by the reason that permeates the whole of our social order.

Benedict: And the ultimate "dictate of reason" is of course the Golden Rule. The justice of the Moral Law will permeate every fiber of our Society, and hence, will permeate the very bones of every human being born into our social order.

William: Recall that passage in Bucke's description of his experience where he states that he saw in the spiritual dimension everything, without effort, automatically works for the benefit of itself, of others, and the Whole. I remember thinking at the time that that might work out in heaven for a society of angels, but could never work out for a society of squabbling human beings. Now I see that squabbling is not intrinsic to human nature per se, but only to a human nature that has been raised and structured in a social order that teaches greed, ambition, and competition. However, in a social order governed by Divine Reason and hence permeated by the Golden Rule, it becomes possible to render Bucke's vision "on Earth, as it is in Heaven". In *our* social order, every human being, by following her innate and natural desires, automatically contributes to her own well-being, the well-being of others, and the well-being of society as a whole.

Neal: A rather inspiring thought for the future of humanity.

William: *(with humor)* Either that, or there is no future at all.

Plato: Yes, and this should be emphasized. For someone reading this, if not persuaded by our arguments, might be skeptical of what we are saying, and continue to believe that humans are "by nature" greedy, squabbling, and competitive. To harbor such thoughts is to doom the human race to extinction. Our skeptical friends must see, through their own reason if possible, that their very skepticism is caused by their own upbringing. But if their reason is not sufficiently developed to see this, they at least should be able to understand that the present social order is on the verge of self-destruction, so they should be willing to examine anything that is offered as a remedy.

William: I agree, although we should note that many individuals are so attached to what they already believe that they are quite happy to die rather than to relinquish their beliefs.

Plato: And die they will, if there are too many of them. For one thing that could prevent our Social Order from coming into existence is the belief, popular among academics, that such a social order is contrary to what they suppose human nature consists of: namely, greed, status-seeking, and competition that forever pits one human being against the other. This belief alone could doom the human race.

William: So for those who fancy themselves as "thinkers" and "intellectuals", this is a time to think clearly, boldly, and in consultation with the better angels of our nature. The belief that our human nature has "no better angels", so popular among our former colleagues, must be exposed for what it is: a false belief conditioned into their minds through upbringing by a dysfunctional social order based on greed and competition.

Socrates: Yes, for the *examined life* requires, not only a conscious awareness of one's own emotions, but also a conscious examination of one's culturally conditioned beliefs and motivations. And is it not ironic, if not comical, that your professors who make their students read what I said about the unexamined life being unworthy for a human being are nevertheless unable to examine their own lives, but instead are motivated by culturally conditioned desires to gain status and reputation for being a so-called "scholar" of me?

Benedict: *(laughing)* Tell me about it. But perhaps this is not the time to lament about those who have eyes and can read what we wrote, but do not see the meaning. Having been raised and conditioned to believe that competition is both necessary and good, they are completely clueless when it comes to understanding passages where I state that a person who *reasons* does not desire for himself anything he does not also desire for others. They are unable to understand that the Golden Rule is what I called a "dictate of reason". Yet they believe about themselves that they are reasoning, when they are merely, but cleverly, defending the beliefs that have been programmed into them. Well, perhaps we shall get together again to discuss these things in more detail.

Plato: Yes, and perhaps I shall have some more things to say about art and aesthetics. And I might want to write that treatise I had in mind before I quit my body.

William: What treatise?

Plato: "The Philosopher". Now of course I understand why I couldn't write it while embodied, despite feeling it would be important to do so. It needed to wait until the right time, which perhaps is now.

8) The Transition

Neal: Somewhere at the beginning of our conversation we said we would be making some remarks regarding the transition from the present society to our new social order. Do we wish to do that?

Plato: Actually, we do not know *how* the transition will occur. We know that either it *will* occur or humans will destroy themselves. The question is: how much suffering do humans wish to create for themselves during the transition? It is highly unlikely to occur in an orderly manner. It is highly unlikely that the leaders and institutions of the present social order will come together and state that our individual and collective greed is destroying the planet and so we have to create a new social order based on love and cooperation. The present leaders, just like religious fundamentalists, would rather die than abandon the beliefs that support their own greed and ambition. I believe that many of the current social structures will need to collapse, and cause much suffering, before humans will be sufficiently motivated to examine their collective beliefs. Nevertheless, I could be wrong about this, and hope that I am.

Now that said, there are certainly some factors that could greatly ease the upheaval involved in transitioning from a "me-based" social order to a "we-based" social order. By far the easiest way to transition is to place spiritually realized women and men in charge of all the institutions of the present culture. Heads of State and heads of corporations shall all be spiritually enlightened. But this would require that those presently in charge come to know that they do not know how to govern, so that they graciously relinquish power and control.

More promising is the use of media to spread the "good word". People will share their Near-Death and other spiritually transformative experiences, and they will talk about communicating with deceased loved ones, either directly or through a medium. They will talk about their experiences of Divine Love, and what happens in the Life Review. The latter is important; as more and more people experience and tell their stories about the Life Review, people will come to know that there is no hiding from the harm and suffering they have caused through their greed and ambition.

Benedict: *(with humor)* Are you going to frighten us again with stories of naughty souls being punished in pits of fire and spat out of volcanoes until they receive forgiveness from those they have harmed while alive?

Plato: *(laughing)* Well I suppose I did get a bit carried away back then. However, there is no such thing as "punishment" in the eternal order, nor will there be in *our* Social Order. There is such a thing as consequences, but that is very different from punishment.

Benedict: Yes. A child who eats too much candy will experience a stomachache as a consequence. The stomachache is not an external punishment for what he has done, but merely a natural consequence of it, determined by the laws of biology. Similarly, those greedy corporate executives and their politicians, who while embodied violated the Moral Law and caused much suffering and pain to others, will necessarily experience that suffering and pain as happening to themselves. Embodiment allows for the illusion that each human being is a separate individual, unconnected to one another, and hence, it seems that one person may inflict suffering on another without himself experiencing that suffering. But in the after-death circumstances it is seen that separateness was an illusion, that all souls are so connected and interconnected as to constitute a single "One Mind". And so the harm they did to others was done to themselves. This is what is experienced in the Life Review. There is no escape from the Moral Law, any more than a child can escape from the laws of digestion, so to speak.

Plato: *(smiling)* So there will be no need to frighten people with stories of fire pits. Stories from Near-Death Experiencers about the Life Review, when they permeate the present social order, might be sufficient to scare our sociopathic politicians and corporate executives into behaving more decently, since in the final analysis, it is only themselves who they harm. As more and more individuals talk about their own spiritual experiences, the cultural taboo against spirituality will gradually wither away, and the concept of Unconditional Love will begin to permeate the society and become normalized. But Unconditional Love is incompatible with greed-based capitalism, so as the former becomes normalized, the latter will inevitably fade away. The harbingers of our New Society are the people who have had spiritually transformative experiences and have the courage to talk about them.

Socrates: And don't forget the robots, or sex dolls.

Neal: Huh! What does that have to do with the transition?

Socrates: Well, quite a bit actually. The males already raised in the current social order have been raised to be greedy and competitive, and to derive their sense of self-worth from their status within some hierarchy. These males, as I said at my trial, are "ambitious, violent, and numerous". The same is true now.

Neal: And if I may, I want to take some liberties with what you said right after the above words in quotes. You stated that these men "are continually and convincingly talking about me; they have been filling your ears for a long time with vehement slanders against me."

Socrates: And what liberties do you wish to take with this passage?

Neal: I want to replace the word "me" with the phrase "my teachings" or "Divine Love". For these individuals have a quarrel not with you personally, but with you insofar as you teach the possibility of a life based on reason and a social order that is intrinsically harmonious and fair and just for all.

William: Yes, students at our universities hear many vehement slanders against the possibility of a social order based on Unconditional Love.

Socrates: So they are still slandering me, even while supposedly teaching "my" or Plato's philosophy. But don't worry, I know what will quiet them down, and make them gentle inside.

Neal: The sex robots?

Socrates: Why yes. After all, they are much less likely to be violent and ambitious if they are busy satisfying all their sexual desires and fantasies. They might not be so opposed to the idea of Divine Love if they receive a little physical loving through their bodies. The robots could be programmed to keep the men sexually aroused most of the time, and *(laughing)* sexually drained the rest of the time, so they will have no energy left for creating social mischief and havoc.

William: We could even program the robots to emit sound vibrations that could deprogram the male brain from its tendencies toward violence and ambition, so that in time they become more gentle with themselves and "friends of the Forms", as Plato once put it.

Neal: Well, this seems to be a win-win solution to the problem of male violence. The social order "wins" because the most violent, ambitious, and ruthless males, being otherwise occupied, will no longer seek to rule or govern, and the men themselves "win", since their violent nature is itself caused by a dysfunctional social order that failed to satisfy their natural sexual needs and desires.

Plato: So men who through poor upbringing and sexual frustration have become hardened, cynical, and violent in their thinking, who have become ambitious and vengeful, and who think that gentleness in a man is a sign of weakness, not strength – these men, and women too, shall be given two or three sex dolls each to keep them from meddling in the affairs of our New Social order. For our whole edifice will surely crumble if those who are very ignorant but believe that they know anything are allowed to participate in the management of our Social Order. But there is something else we must invoke with respect to such ambitious people, who desire only to "win" and to be thought better than others.

Neal: What do you have in mind?

Plato: First answer this question: Should parents who have a communicable illness be allowed to raise their children while they are ill, if it is virtually certain that they will communicate their illness to their children? Or should the children be separated from such parents, and placed in a healthy environment, until their parents recover?

Neal: Children are not their parents' property, and it is the responsibility of our Social Order as a whole to raise and care for the physical and psychological well-being of our children. So of course, if the parents have a contagious disease, the children should be removed for as long as their parents' illness is contagious. The parents themselves should want this, if they care for their children.

Socrates: But in actuality, most parents care more for their illness than for their children's well-being.

Neal: My goodness, Socrates, how can you say such a thing? *(One might think that by now I would be used to his sometimes cryptic remarks.)*

Socrates: Hey I heard that. There is nothing at all "cryptic", whatever that means, about what I just said. We are talking about what we called "the transition". This necessarily involves parents who were raised by the present dysfunctional social order, yet who are raising children who will adapt to our New Social Order. The parents, because of how they were raised, have necessarily internalized the dysfunction of the present social order. *(Smiling)* Now, when I used the expression "communicable illness", you probably thought I meant *physical* communicable illness, like the flu or something.

Neal: Yes, that's what I thought.

Socrates: But you did state "it is the responsibility of our Social Order as a whole to raise and care for the physical and *psychological* well-being of our children". You are right, of course, that parents with a communicable physical disease would desire that they be removed until they are no longer a threat to the physical health of their children. But I am talking about a kind of illness, a psychological illness, that is far more contagious than any physical illness, and far more harmful too, not only to those who are so infected, but also to everyone who comes into contact with them.

Benedict: Yes, and, Neal, remember when we discussed that just as the human body can be invaded by organisms (viruses, bacteria) whose own self-interest (their DNA) is incompatible with that of the human organism they have invaded, so also the human mind can be invaded by thought-forms whose own self-interest is incompatible with the natural flourishing of the human mind. These harmful thought-forms get communicated from parent to child, because the child, although by no means a "blank slate", is nevertheless infected or conditioned, through his parents, by the same dysfunctional patterns that have infected the minds of his parents.

William: Perhaps a few examples will suffice to clarify our meaning.

Benedict: By all means.

William: But first I want to expand upon what you just said. The analogy with the body is instructive. Not everything that is "in" a person's body is "of" it. An individual cell is both "in" the body and "of" the body, but a given bacteria is "in" the body but not "of" the body. Of those things that are "in" the body but not "of" the body, some are beneficial to the body and some are harmful to the body. Some bacteria, by pursuing their own self-interest, aid the body with digestion. Other bacteria are incompatible with a healthy body, and will destroy any body they have invaded. So it is important to know, as any physician will testify, which external things assist the body in its efforts to flourish, and which will impede that effort.

Similarly, the adult mind has been infected with, or has internalized, many beliefs, ideas, and various thought-forms, some of which assist the mind in its efforts to flourish, others of which impede the mind. And it will be very important for our psychologists to know which is which, so that all harmful thought-forms that through upbringing have been conditioned into the mind may be rooted out. And if parents do not wish to examine their beliefs and remove dysfunctional thought-forms, then at the very least they must be prevented from infecting their children with them.

Benedict: Well said. And if I may do a little more penance, among the more harmful of the thought-forms by which the human psyche has become infected is the belief that males are superior to females. Most cultures suffer from this infection, some extremely so. This is a communicable mental illness, for any mind that at a young age is exposed to parents who are thus infected will itself come down with the disease.

Plato: Yes. And it seems that there are several possible choices for people who, through no fault of their own, have been psychically damaged through having internalized this false belief. (i) They may come to realize that they are mentally ill, and voluntarily submit to a process of gentle reconditioning to expunge from their minds the mental virus that females are inferior to males; (ii) if they are unable to recognize their own illness and have instead been completely taken over by it then they shall not be allowed to raise or otherwise influence our children; and (iii) if such sick individuals already have children and yet are unwilling or unable to seek a cure for their illness, then our Society's obligation to our children requires that we separate them from their parents, so that their minds do not become damaged by what has infected and damaged the minds of their parents. For parents must not be allowed to transmit their own mental illnesses to their children. Let's examine a few more of the social viruses that have infected the minds of humans raised in the present social order.

Neal: It seems to me that religious beliefs must be examined too, and perhaps discarded. Now of course, *some* beliefs that are called "religious" are also beneficial to the human mind, such as the belief in an all-loving deity, the belief that *all* humans are created by a benevolent power, and so forth. But other beliefs that are called "religious" are quite harmful to a full flourishing of human nature.

William: Yes, and certainly the aforementioned mental illness, the belief that men are superior to women, has been a major portion of the insanity promulgated through organized religions. Aside from that, we have the belief that humans are sinners even before they are born, that God punishes souls for wrongdoing, and that God is opposed to human pleasure.

Neal: Perhaps the most serious mental illness caused by religion is the belief, or meta-belief, that it matters to God what people believe.

William: Yes, they tend to take themselves so seriously, deadly seriously, that they believe that whoever does not believe what they believe is an outcast from heaven.

Neal: *Deadly* serious indeed, for people infected with this particular virus will happily kill anyone who has different beliefs. But spirituality has nothing to do with what people *believe,* and everything to do with how people *feel,* on the one hand, and *behave,* on the other hand. So any religion that teaches "it's our way or the highway" will have to go, and any humans in whom such an infection has taken hold must not be allowed to infect children, their own or anyone else's, with such criminally insane beliefs.

Benedict: *(smiling)* Certainly *any* religion that believes of itself that it has captured the Divine Being with its words and concepts must not be allowed to function, and anyone who has been raised to believe otherwise has become insane, and must not be allowed near our children. The Divine Being is well beyond all human words and concepts, and one who has been conditioned to believe otherwise is quite mad. Yet words and concepts are necessary to represent the Divine Being to human consciousness. The question I want to raise is: how shall the Divine Being be represented to human imagination?

Plato: Good. We should say something about this. Now, with respect to *human* knowledge of the Divine, there are three possibilities.

Benedict: What possibilities are you talking about?

Plato: The very ones you wrote about. One such possibility – *(with humor)* the one that you so poetically called "knowledge of the third kind" – is that the human has direct experience of the eternal order, either through a Near-Death Experience, through deep meditation, or some other way. For such humans, there is no need to represent the Divine Being by words or concepts at all, since they Know, and know that what they Know cannot be captured by words or concepts. Another possibility is that a human can work it out through reason, beginning as you did, with the concept of "Substance" or "Independent Being", and working out the consequences. In the present culture, very few individuals are capable of reasoning, as you yourself discovered. We hope that in our New Social Order, many more individuals will be capable of reasoning than at present, and many more will have direct experience.

Neal: And if I may briefly interject, to be capable of reasoning is to understand, among other things, that the Golden Rule is what Benedict called a "dictate of reason".

Benedict: Yes, those who do not see this, or cannot see this, have confused reasoning with calculative thinking, or mere cleverness.

Plato: So they are among those who think they know but do not. Yet, even though many people from our social order will be able to follow your reasoning, there will still be many more who cannot. For *these* people we must have a way to *represent* the Divine Being in their imaginations. And they must be told that whatever representation takes hold in their imaginations, it is not literally true, but merely something that at best points to truth, and can be used as a guide to action. So our social order will be permeated with metaphors and analogies that attempt to characterize, not "what it is", but rather, "what it is like". Without waxing theological, I think we may safely state that any representation of the Divine Being in *our* Social Order must also represent human beings as included in, as internal to, the Divine Being. All souls, including their human expressions, are part of the Divine Being itself.

Socrates: So instead of representing God as external to humans, we shall represent humans as internal to God. The analogy of cells in a body is something that can easily be imagined by the human mind, and captures something of the relationship between God and humans. From this little analogy, Paul's dictum immediately follows, as does the Golden Rule.

Benedict: I agree. There is no reason why the human imagination cannot be filled with true opinions through upbringing, and hence be aligned with what is true. For as Plato said, right opinion is no less a guide to action than knowledge.

William: OK, but we are talking about the transition, and about parents who have internalized false concepts of the Divine, and believe that God is that "Guy in the Sky" with a chip on his shoulder who rewards his friends and happily punishes those who believe otherwise with everlasting torture.

Benedict: *(to Plato, with humor)* See? You and your pits of fire! Half the people have made a religion out of imagining that those they dislike will suffer excruciating pain for all eternity; the other half have made a religion out of imagining that their own "sins" have doomed them to endless suffering. No sane social order can tolerate such beliefs.

William: So parents whose minds have become infected with such beliefs will not be allowed to promulgate their beliefs into the minds of our children.

Neal: I like how you phrased that. For we regard the children as *ours* – as belonging to our Social Order, which alone bears the responsibility for raising them. If their biological parents have been infected with such dysfunctional beliefs, and are unwilling to seek a remedy for their illness, then they are mentally incompetent and cannot be entrusted with the sacred duty of raising our children.

Plato: We have discussed beliefs pertaining to male and female, and beliefs pertaining to the Divine Being, and beliefs pertaining to the relationship between humans and the Divine. In addition to these false beliefs, or perhaps as a consequence of them, we must now discuss what I regard as the most harmful of all such dysfunctional beliefs.

Neal: Yes?

Plato: It is the belief that greed and ambition are necessary and good, and that such motivations must be fostered in the psyches of children. Children, especially males, are told to "get ahead", to "make something of themselves", to achieve wealth and status. Children are taught that what's important is not to *do* their best, but to *be* the best. They are taught that what matters is the outcome – winning – not the process. This is a disastrous teaching insofar as social harmony is concerned, and parents whose minds have been infected with such insanity must not be allowed anywhere near our children until they heal themselves and become sane. For when children's minds are infected with the thought-form that *winning* is what matters, not the integrity of the process, then these children will grow up to become the adults of the present culture, who lie, deceive, cheat, and steal in order to get the outcome they want, that is, to win.

William: Indeed, the present social order is so dysfunctional *because* it is being managed or ruled by those who have only the gambler's talent: the ability to lie with a straight face.

Neal: Yes. Those who hold economic and political power today are a bunch of criminals who can think of no purpose for embodied life other than to amass as much wealth and power as possible. So they happily steal from their brothers and sisters, and purchase politicians who pass laws to legitimize their criminal activity.

Benedict: And they have even hijacked religion in order to frighten and brainwash people into voting against their own economic interests. They perpetuate harmful ideologies according to which they deserve to have more than others and that it is God's will that there be rich and poor.

Plato: But actually, when they return Home, they have less than others, much less. For those who while alive seek only for wealth and status must necessarily neglect their original purpose in manifesting, which always falls under our three headings: curiosity, compassion, and self-expression. And so after their body dies, they have nothing to show for having been embodied, and their life review is necessarily painful, since it is not possible to spend a life seeking fame and fortune without harming many in the process.

Neal: And as you have always said, one who harms another harms himself much more.

Socrates: The Moral Law works both ways.

Neal: What do you mean?

Plato: Recollect your experience with waves of gratitude coming to you from a student who felt benefited by something you had said.

Neal: OK.

Plato: The student was not consciously sending waves of gratitude. Rather, the waves of gratitude emanated from him simultaneous with his feeling that he had been benefited. In the state of heightened consciousness that you had entered through the dream state, it was as if everything about that interaction had been stripped away and only waves of gratitude remained.

Neal: Yes.

Plato: Because in that heightened state of awareness, *how* humans have treated one another is the *only* thing that matters; everything else fades away. There is no external judgment, of course, but in this heightened state of awareness humans judge themselves, and the basis for self-judgment is always with respect to how much Divine Love they had radiated into the corporeal dimension. Now, *(with humor)* I don't wish to frighten Benedict here with tales of fire pits and volcanoes, but when one human harms another, the same Law applies as it did for you, when you had benefited another. In the after-death state of consciousness, any and every pain and sorrow that one human inflicts on another comes back to the one who inflicted it, greatly magnified in the hyper-real state of consciousness of the after-death conditions.

Benedict: *(with humor)* Well I suppose I should thank you for not frightening me, but actually, I did believe that most humans needed to be frightened in order to behave decently.

Neal: Yes, you wrote that if humans have nothing to fear then they themselves become something to be feared, or something like that.

Benedict: Yes, and until now it has been true. Many humans over the years have been restrained from even worse behavior out of fear of after-death consequences. Plato's tales of fire pits…

Plato: *(laughing)* … which the good Christians elevated to a level of gruesomeness far beyond anything I could conceive at the time…

Benedict: … had a moderating influence of some sort on some people. But that was for a social order that lived only on the basis of what humans could *imagine*. *Our* social order is based on *reason*. We have, one might say, created a new species, such that people will express lovingkindness, not because they fear a greater harm coming to them if they don't, but rather because they *understand* that lovingkindness is a dictate of reason, and expressing lovingkindness brings them joy.

Plato: … Joy while embodied, and something even deeper afterwards.

9) "I Forgot We Were Only Playing"

Socrates: Ah, my friends. We are perhaps forgetting something.

Neal: What are we forgetting?

Socrates: Remember when Plato had me discussing these things with his brothers?

Neal: Yes, in *The Republic*.

Socrates: There was a line in there that caught your attention.

Neal: Many passages in *The Republic* caught my attention.

Socrates: Yes, I know, but this was a comment *about* our whole discussion, and the comment is as relevant to this present discussion as it was to the previous one.

Neal: Oh, I remember it now. You had been discussing something rather intensely when you stopped yourself and said, or Plato had you say, "I forgot we were only playing," or something to that effect.

Socrates: Exactly. And we are playing here too. It is perhaps not unimportant to keep the *playful* nature of our conversations in mind. For we have been playing with words, hopefully words that offer some guidance, but words nevertheless. *(Smiling)* A ruthless corporate executive, the kind you so love to hate, could read what we have discussed and not be swayed to change his behavior. But if he were to have a full-blown Near-Death Experience, then his behavior would instantly change. This shows the superiority of direct experience over mere words. Direct experience *must* be taken seriously. So we will take a playful attitude to the words and concepts we have here been using.

William: Furthermore, empirical investigations clearly show that creative ideas, original ideas, and novel ways of looking at things are much more likely to come to a person who has a playful attitude towards what she is doing. Without an attitude of playfulness, people will not be able to think outside the box, and will keep reinventing the by-now-very-squeaky-wheel of competition and capitalism.

Socrates: And may I remind you, Neal, to continue to strive to regard the corporate executives – those lying, cheating, murdering band of criminals – from *our* non-embodied perspective rather than from your present embodied perspective.

Neal: *(with humor)* OK, but it will take some serious striving on my part.

Socrates: From *your* perspective, you see them in fancy Italian suits, squandering the stolen wealth of the planet on useless toys, like yachts and private jets. You also see all the misery and suffering caused by their uncontrollable greed.

Neal: Yes, I see all that.

Socrates: But from *our* perspective, which is always experienced as infinitely more real than yours, what do you see? Or rather, since you are not currently *in* our perspective, what does your reason see?

Neal: My reason "sees" that in their Life Review they are experiencing all the suffering they have brought to others.

Socrates: And which is greater? – Suffering they brought to others while embodied or suffering they are now experiencing in a greatly enhanced state of awareness?

Neal: The latter. For in the *loving* presence of the Divine Being, they judge their life to have been a failure. Yes, I see that I tend to get a bit overheated with anger at them.

Socrates: Never forget that they are like four-year-old children throwing a continuous temper tantrum. They are acting out their inner pain and torment, so it is not your anger they need, but your compassion and lovingkindness.

Neal: *(smiling)* I guess I still have a little work to do with this lovingkindness business.

Socrates: Do not judge against yourself, but instead develop a playful attitude towards your own such judgments. Yes, it is very difficult for a human to feel or express lovingkindness towards a kid who is throwing a temper tantrum so obnoxiously. But you'll see, once you shift to *our* perspective, the lovingkindness will flow naturally. A soul who while embodied got mired deeply in identification with its body and personality did so out of ignorance, and when they arrive here they are helped and assisted, and yes, loved, until they can regain their bearings, so to speak.

Plato: Yet, even with our playful attitude made explicit, we shall still protect our children from contagious mental illness. Adults who through poor upbringing have become infected with beliefs about wealth and status must not be allowed to pass on their disease to our children. We do not need to be angry with these adults, but we do need to protect our children from them.

William: We have been discussing ways to *ease* the transition from a *me-based* to a *we-based* social order. It is also imperative that technology survives the transition. For one possible outcome is that the world's major institutions collapse overnight, and some humans survive, but without electricity, clean water, or a reliable source of food. Then we're back to hunter-gatherer units, and the whole process starts again. We have mentioned three things that, if adopted, could greatly facilitate the transition. I'll list them, and then suggest a fourth.

(i) Spiritual wisdom and temporal authority must reside in the same individuals. As much as possible, the institutions of our New Society will all be headed by individuals who have had spiritually transformative experiences, and are hence unable to desire for themselves anything they do not also desire for everyone else.

(ii) People who have had such experiences will share them with others, so that using social media, the nature of these experiences, by which I mean descriptions of the experience of Unity, of Universal Brotherhood, and Unconditional Love, will permeate the whole social order.

(iii) Adults who are mentally ill must not be allowed to pass on their illness to the next generation. Psychologists and psychiatrists will "officially" recognize that *some* beliefs are both insane and highly contagious. They – the psychologists – are beginning to recognize that religious fundamentalism is a form of insanity. But they do not yet recognize that greed and ambition are also "species of madness", as Benedict put it. The transition will be greatly assisted if people who have such insane beliefs, sometimes criminally insane, were prevented from passing on their insanity to children.

Neal: OK, what's the fourth?

William: This is an idea you have played with some years ago. We may have mentioned it when we were talking about *lying*.

Neal: Oh yes, how could I have forgotten? The present social order, based as it is on greed and ambition, essentially involves deception, concealing, scheming, conniving and every other form of lying. But there is no lying in Heaven; one cannot hide from the Divine Being. So if it is ever to become "on Earth as it is in Heaven", then lying and deception must be excluded from all human relations. But this is a very tall order. A generation that has been raised to believe there is nothing wrong with little "white" lies is unlikely to raise their children to be truth-tellers.

William: But you yourself conceived of a way to eliminate lying in a single generation. You called it "the Pinocchio effect", or something like that.

Neal: Yes, I was just playing with ideas a little.

Plato: Well…?

Neal: Suppose the lie detector were perfected. Scientists discover a physiological correlate to lying, and are able to magnify that correlate so that it is visible to everyone else. Parents might, for example, plant a chip in their children's brain that will cause the nose to turn bright red whenever the child lies or deceives. Very quickly the children would learn that lying is impossible, and so the impulse to lie would atrophy. This is one way that parents, who themselves were raised to be liars, could raise children that were truth-tellers. But capitalism would collapse overnight if there were no liars left to promulgate greed and ambition.

William: But now it appears that our neuroscientists have in fact discovered such a physiological correlate, and there will be no need to implant chips into the heads of our children.

Neal: I heard about it too. *(Laughing)* The discovery was presented as a way for young women to tell whether their boyfriends had been cheating on them. But I saw that this little device would change everything, and in fact, induce the very transition we are hoping for.

Plato: What have the neuroscientists discovered?

Neal: When a person lies, or contemplates lying, the part of the brain that correlates with what we have been calling "cleverness" is more active than usual.

Plato: Because the liar has to keep track of many more things than the truth-teller.

Neal: This increased brain activity causes the pupils of the eyes to involuntarily contract, slightly but measurably. It can easily be measured by an ordinary cell phone. So if everyone knows and realizes that any lie they tell, or think about telling, will immediately be detectable by anyone and everyone, then lying and deception become in principle impossible. In this way, lying could be wiped off the planet in a single generation, and the whole edifice of me-based capitalism comes to an end.

Socrates: *(playfully)* Hush, my friends, lest you give away our little plan.

William: What little plan?

Socrates: Capitalism, the present greed-based social order, is already about to collapse. Our little plan will not only hasten the collapse, but do so in a way that minimizes the amount of turmoil involved with the transition.

(With humor) Here's how it will happen. Our lie-detecting device will first be marketed to parents. No parent could possibly refuse a little gadget that told them when their children were lying. Very quickly children would learn that it is not possible to conceal the truth from their parents, and so they would stop trying to deceive. The children then demand such devices for themselves, so they could know for certain when their friends were distorting the truth. Very quickly, the children would stop lying to one another. Then some of the children would turn the tables on their parents, and catch their parents using language to conceal the truth. Parents who are caught lying by their own children will naturally stop lying themselves. One day a judge who had used the gadget successfully with her own children brings it with her to court, and uses it on the lawyers who are arguing their cases before her.

Neal: *(with humor)* Oh my, that would be the end of our legal system as we know it.

Socrates: Exactly. And it is a very short step from there to a scenario where everyone in the corporate boardrooms has our lie-detecting device, which is used on all executives and politicians.

Neal: And that's the end of capitalism. Well, I see your concern about hushing it up. If the present bunch of politicians and corporate executives got word of our plan, they would certainly take measures to ban our device.

Socrates: Well, we need not worry too much, because they are all so caught up in their wheeling and dealing that they have no time for our playful musings. By the time they are aware of what is happening, it will be too late, and the transition will have taken root.

Neal: And then, when lying is no longer possible, humans will no longer be constrained to live in schizophrenic insanity, but will be able to live as you did: the same person in public as in private.

Socrates: *(smiling)* I was able to live *honestly*, not because of any special talent or virtue, but only because I was fortunate enough to have had one foot firmly planted in the eternal order during my Earthly journey. But in our New Society, based on reason, in which no one lies or deceives, everyone will be able to live an honest life.

Plato: And it will be good to notice that we have in fact created a new species upon the planet. For the transition involves not only a change from one social order to another; more importantly, it involves a change from one *kind* of human being to another. A human being who *cannot* lie is a different species than one whose whole life – personal, professional, and social – is based on lying, that is, on using language to hide, conceal, distort, exaggerate, etc. the truth. A Social Order in which humans do not practice deception – and all deception is, in the final analysis, self-deception – is the next step in the human evolutionary process.

William: I would not be surprised if, after a generation or two of being raised in our New Society, scientists observe a change in the genetic structure of our new species of humans. In order to adapt to a social order based on deception, certain structures in the brain need to be activated. These structures are the physiological correlates to what we have called "cleverness". But without external reinforcement, these structures will no longer dominate the brain, and other structures – those that correlate with creativity and compassion, for example – will be allowed to develop and come into play. So I predict that there will be striking physiological differences between those individuals raised in a social order that values greed and competition, and those individuals who are raised in *our* social order, based on inclusion, honesty, and cooperation.

Plato: Yes, for the outer social order and the inner human psyche and physiology are mirrors of one another. To the extent we have described a New Social Order we have also described a New Human Being.

(A silence descended upon me, and for a while there were no words in my head. I noticed Socrates looking at me quizzically, with raised eyebrows.)

Socrates: *(smiling)* Well, my friend, it seems that you have the same problem now that you had just before we began this conversation.

Neal: What do you mean?

Socrates: You were at a loss for how to begin, and now *(laughing)* it appears that you are at a loss for how to bring our conversation to a close for now.

Neal: Yes.

Socrates: For we have stated our main themes, have varied and developed them, and have clothed them with rich harmonies and counterpoint. Moreover, we have constructed a fully functional orchestra in which each and every member rejoices in her own unique contribution to the harmony of the whole. Perhaps, you are thinking, we need to have some sort of "grand finale", and end our symphony with a Bang, rather than just fade away?

Neal: *(laughing)* Yes, sort of.

Socrates: And at the same time you realize that *ours* is a never-ending story. As you yourself said, any ending is just "for now".

Neal: Yes.

Socrates: So perhaps we could close with a little flourish rather than a Big Bang. Besides, *(with humor)* it would probably be difficult to find an appropriate Bang. But you have some ideas?

Neal: Well, I thought I might ask each of you to briefly summarize what you take to be most important in what we have been discussing. That's my idea for a Big Bang at the end.

Socrates: Yikes! You would impose a most difficult, if not impossible, burden on us.

Plato: You see, the *process* of discussion is at least as important as the content we have been discussing. But a *process* cannot be summarized in a few paragraphs; it must be experienced.

Socrates: So we'll dispense with the Bang, and settle for a little flourish. What do you have in mind?

Neal: I thought I might cite from your writings a specific passage that has influenced and inspired me.

Socrates: Good, *(with humor)* although you might have some difficulty finding anything that I wrote.

Neal: Not at all, for what you said at your trial, although not written down by you, was nevertheless faithfully captured by Plato.

Socrates: OK, I accept that. However, make sure you don't get lost trying to do what we said was too burdensome for *us* to do.

Neal: *(laughing)* Don't worry. I won't attempt a grand summary of your philosophies, just a little tidbit from them. So, William, I'll start with you, if I may.

William: Go ahead.

Neal: I can't find the exact passage, but what stuck in my mind was a little quip – I may have referred to it before – to the effect that there can be no theory of ethics until the last human being has lived his or her life.

William: Oh yes, that was a talk I gave to some Ethics Society at Harvard.

Neal: I came across the passage at a time in my life when I was seeking after grand theories. So I did not like being told that there can be no theory until *(laughing)* the human race had become extinct. But it stayed with me, and together with what Plato said about words and writing, caused me to give up looking for theories. For theories must be expressed in terms of words and concepts, and no words or concepts can capture the fullness of what it is to be human. The human being necessarily transcends any concepts that humans come up with. And so I went more deeply into my own consciousness. And your little raisin/menu metaphor also impacted me. A single raisin is more nutritious than a detailed menu. You can't eat a menu. And so a single human being is infinitely richer than all the theories about humans put together. Indeed, I came to realize that by ignoring spirituality, academics are only chasing after bigger and better menus, oblivious to the spiritual nourishment that surrounds them.

William: One might say that *theories* are created by the human mind, but the human mind is itself created by – which inadequate words shall we use? – the Divine Being, the One Mind, Consciousness, God.

Socrates: And if I may point out, the oracle's injunction to "know thyself" does not in any way involve theories or concepts. Rather, self-knowledge begins with the experiential knowledge of one's emotions, in the manner described by Benedict and many other therapists, and ends with the knowledge of the union that exists between one's own mind and the mind of God, also described by Benedict.

Neal: Well, as you may imagine, it came as quite a shock to me to realize that theories and concepts had little to do with the experience of Truth.

William: Well, wait a minute. Theories and concepts may point to Truth, even though they must not be mistaken for "the" Truth.

Neal: I agree. After all, the philosophies of Benedict and Plato, expressed through words and concepts, inspired me greatly. I now understand that the very inspiration I felt and feel is the pointer that flowed through their words.

William: Yes, and what humans call "inspiration" is simply an incursion into the human mind of energies from our side of the margins, the eternal order.

Plato: These "energies" are of course native to the soul, which is why what is called "inspiration" feels right and natural.

Neal: Let me pursue this theme of inspiration. When I was a young man, nothing inspired me more than the concept of the Brotherhood of Man – the idea that humans taken together constitute a single Being. Nothing has inspired me more than what you wrote, Benedict, when you said:

> humans can wish for nothing more useful for the preservation and flourishing of their being than they should all be in such harmony

in all respects that their minds and bodies should compose, as it were, one mind and one body, and that all should strive together as best they can to flourish in their own being, and that all, together, should seek for themselves the common advantage of all. From this it follows that humans who are governed by reason, that is, humans who aim at their own advantage under the guidance of reason, seek nothing for themselves that they would not desire for the rest of humanity.

Benedict: Well, that's quite lovely, even if I do say so myself. Yet it is not quite true that "nothing has inspired you more" than those words.

Neal: What do you mean?

Benedict: My words, let us say, point to something – a social order that is so harmonious that humans experience themselves as constituting a single "One Mind" and "One Body". But many poets and musicians, through their poetry and music, also point to the same vision. In actuality, Beethoven's music pointed you towards that vision much more powerfully than my words.

Neal: Yes, you are right.

Benedict: So after Beethoven had already oriented you towards this vision, reading my words merely confirmed that what you already knew in your heart was true.

Neal: OK, I agree. It was music, and not only Beethoven's, that gave me a sense of spiritual direction in my teen years. As William wrote, "music gives us ontological messages", and I heard those messages loud and clear. But your words are inspiring nevertheless.

William: And the message, to be clear, was the inspiration felt in your soul. Inspiration, we should note, if we haven't already, is immediate and non-discursive.

Neal: Yes, and you also convinced me that Divine Knowledge cannot be conceptual. "God's knowledge cannot be discursive but must be intuitive." And so, with your guidance I eventually stopped seeking after theories and concepts, and began looking more directly within my self. But now I want to look at something Plato wrote, and although at first it seems different from Benedict's inspiring words above, leads to the same thing.

Plato: What do you have in mind?

Neal: I'll cite the passage in a moment, but the basic idea is that the best form of social organization for humans is one where the citizens use the words "me" and "mine" to refer to the same things, as much as possible.

> Is there any greater evil we can mention for a city than that which tears it apart and makes it many instead of one? Or any greater good than that which binds it together and makes it one?
>
> There isn't.
>
> Well, doesn't sharing pleasure and pain bind it together – when, as far as possible, all the citizens feel more or less the same joy or sorrow at the same gains or losses?
>
> It most certainly does.
>
> On the other hand, doesn't the privatization of these things dissolve the city – when some are overwhelmed with distress and some are overjoyed by the same things happening to the city or some of its inhabitants?
>
> Of course.
>
> And isn't this what happens whenever such words as "mine" and "not mine" aren't used in unison? And similarly with "someone else's"?
>
> Precisely.
>
> Then is the best-governed city the one in which most people apply the words "mine" and "not mine" about the same things on the basis of the same principle? – Then, whenever anything good or bad happens to a single one of its citizens, such a city will say that the affected part is its own and will share in the pleasure and pain as a whole.

Now of course, you were thinking in terms of a city, and we are thinking in terms of a world order. But nevertheless, since we humans exist in the temporal order, it is not possible for us to relate individually to a very large number of people, let alone a world order; rather, humans can relate personally only to a relatively small number of individuals that constitute a community, a neighborhood, or a city. And so we have a social order in which the joys and sorrows of the individual are the joys and sorrows of the community, and everyone feels cared for.

But as soon as joys and sorrows are privatized, as is necessarily the case in any social order that allows for greed and status-seeking, then the harmony of the whole disintegrates. For if two or more individuals compete for something that only one can have, the inevitable outcome is that one feels joy and the other feels sadness, which leads not to social *order*, but rather, to social *dis-order*. In our social order, the concept of ownership, either of persons (as in *my* husband, *my* children) or property (*my* house, *my* toys), will atrophy.

William: *(with humor)* Although I suppose people may be said to own their toothbrushes.

(Laughter.)

William: Well, perhaps there is no reason an individual may have unlimited use of something – clothes, a vehicle, a house – without needing to "own" it.

Neal: We have stated that our designers of homes and buildings will design buildings and public spaces for the benefit of all citizens. In every community there will be numerous public buildings, parks, and places that our citizens will individually refer to as "my" and "mine" and collectively refer to as "ours". Citizens will of course have use of private space, but the concept of "ownership" will disappear. When an individual dies, the material circumstances of his life – living space and so forth – reverts back to the community, not to his biological descendants.

Plato: Identification with private property is a poor substitute for identification with other human beings and community, and as we have said so many times and in so many ways, the soul is always worse-off by such identification. But it is a short step from here to Benedict's exalted vision. A community in which individuals use the words "mine" and "my" to refer to the same things – toothbrushes excepted, of course – in which the joys and sorrows of each individual are shared by the whole is a community that functions as an organism, as a single being in which "all together seek the common advantage of all", as Benedict put it.

Benedict: And if I may make something explicit here, the *way* a given individual seeks the "common advantage of all" is not discursively, through thinking about it, but merely by examining and following her own natural desires. Once the insanity of greed and status has been removed from the human psyche, the only kinds of desires left are the ones that automatically satisfy the Moral Law. These desires, which a person may consistently desire both for himself and for others, fall under our headings of (i) assisting others, (ii) developing talents and abilities, and (iii) following holy curiosity wherever it may lead.

Neal: I suppose we may add desires for bodily pleasure, especially the necessary pleasures of food and sex.

Benedict: Yes, for although Plato has shown that what *feels* good to the body and what *is* good for the body are not necessarily the same, yet through upbringing we have aligned the two as much as possible, and hence our citizens will delight in sensuous pleasure without causing harm to their bodies.

Neal: And may we state that we have done the same thing with the psyche as with the body?

Benedict: What do you mean?

Neal: For individuals who are greedy and ambitious, it *feels* good to them when they have more money, status, and reputation than others. But this "good feeling" is harmful to their soul, since it requires that others suffer from having less money and status. So for greedy status-seekers, what *feels* good and what *is* good are quite different. But when humans become cured of the madness that is called "greed and ambition", they will be able to do whatever they wish without harm to themselves or to others, either in mind or in body.

Socrates: And of course, what people wish is to be happy, but until now have been terribly mistaken in their beliefs about where happiness is to be found. *Our* citizens will not be like that poor man in the Sufi joke. Hey, did we ever tell that joke?

Neal: We alluded to it, but I don't remember if we actually stated it.

Plato: It's worth stating.

Neal: OK.

A man is strolling down a street and he notices another man frantically searching for something in front of his house. The ensuing conversation goes something like this:

1st man: What are you looking for?

2nd man: My wedding ring. I can't find it, and my wife will kill me if she finds out I've lost it.

1st man: I understand. Let me help you.

(Together they comb the bushes in front of the house, inspect the sidewalk and surrounding area, but don't find the ring.)

2nd man: Do you recall exactly where you lost it.

1st man: Oh yes. In the bedroom closet.

2nd man: What? You lost it in your bedroom closet?! Then why are you looking here in front of the house?

1st man: Because there is more light out here.

Plato: And so the poor man is searching for his ring where it cannot be found. This has been the tragedy of the human race until now – actually, it's as much a comedy as it is a tragedy. But it accurately mirrors the human condition. Humans have been programmed to seek for happiness where it cannot in principle be found, by following the gods of greed and ambition. The result has been suffering at the individual level and disaster at the collective level.

Benedict: But once the madness of greed and ambition are removed from the human psyche, every remaining desire automatically leads to happiness, both individually and collectively. For the "remaining" desires are the ones that spring from reason, and are necessarily harmonious.

William: Yes, and even now psychologists have a ton of data that shows that happiness never comes to greedy status-seekers, but does come to those whose desires fall under our three headings: (i) developing talents, (ii) helping others, and (iii) seeking knowledge and understanding. These are the kinds of desires that remain when humans are cured of the madness called "greed" and "ambition".

Neal: And these are the kinds of desires that obey the Moral Law – desires that one may have both for oneself and for all other human beings. They are also the very desires the pursuit of which *does* bring happiness and joy. Well we have stated and restated this theme many times.

Socrates: Yes we have.

Neal: But now I wish to state something that perhaps has not been stated before, at least, not with the emphasis I wish to give it now.

Socrates: What do you have in mind?

Neal: It is something you said at your trial.

Socrates: *(with humor)* I said many things at my trial.

Neal: It has to do with ignorance, death, and fear of death. Here's what you said:

> *To fear death, gentlemen, is no other than to think oneself wise when one is not, to think one knows what one does not know. No one knows whether death may not be the greatest of all blessings for a man, yet men fear it as if they knew that it is the greatest of evils. And surely it is the most blameworthy ignorance to believe that one knows what one does not know.*

William: Of course, to update the passage a bit, we *do* know that death is the greatest of all blessings for a human being. We know this empirically, from Near-Death Experiencers, who are often very upset about having to return to their bodies.

Benedict: And I like how you connect the emotion of *fear* with beliefs about its cause. Every instance of fear involves fear of death, but the latter fear involves a false belief. One cannot fear death when one knows that it is the most joyous experience in a person's life. So the presence of fear involves the false belief that death is something bad.

Neal: But then, Socrates, you go over the top when you state that death, *your* death, cannot harm you in any way. For humans believe the exact opposite... that to be killed is the ultimate harm one can experience.

Socrates: I suppose anyone who believes that she *is* the very body that she merely inhabits is necessarily subject to such fear.

Neal: Yes, and our psychologists would have much to say about the importance of self-preservation, and how just about any behavior is permissible if it leads to the avoidance of death. But here is what you said at your trial:

> *Be sure that if you kill the sort of man I say I am, you will not harm me more than yourselves. Neither Meletus nor Anytus (my accusers) can harm me in any way... certainly he might kill me, or perhaps banish or disenfranchise me, which he and maybe others think to be a great harm, but I do not think so. I think he is doing himself much greater harm doing what he is doing now, attempting to have a man executed unjustly. (30d)*

I understand your meaning now, but when I first encountered the passage it seemed sort of ridiculous. Socrates cannot be harmed by being killed?!! What a weird thing to state.

Socrates: *(playfully)* Yes, well I put it that way because I actually agree with your psychologists when they talk about the importance of self-preservation. At my trial I did everything possible to preserve my self. Although *(laughing)* the self that I was concerned to preserve during my trial had nothing to do with the body and its personality, and this is what confuses your psychologists. Needless to say, when my accusers experienced their life reviews, they understood the harm they had done to themselves.

Plato: The great majority of humans, psychologists included, confuse the real "self", which is the soul, with the body and its personality, which latter are merely temporary expressions of the soul. To violate the Moral Law by harming another is detrimental to the soul of the one who harms, but in no way affects the soul of the one whose body is killed or otherwise harmed.

Socrates: To speak plainly, my subjective sense of self was the soul, not its temporary expression as body and personality. The demise of the latter was "of no consequence" to me *(to quote Benedict)*; during my trial, I preserved my self – what I experienced as my identity – by guarding against any feelings of anger towards my accusers, who like me, were also temporary expressions of the Divine Being. The difference was that I knew it and they didn't.

Neal: And then you add, "death is something I couldn't care less about – my whole concern is not to do anything unjust or impious." (32d)

William: This is wonderful advice for all our citizens. One of the things I observed in my immediate after-death condition – it seemed to me that I was watching the theater of life from a balcony – was that every soul becomes embodied and then un-embodied exactly on cue. All entrances and exits from the theater of embodiment happen on schedule, and there are no accidents. So humans should follow the advice Plato gives somewhere, to assume that the time and manner of their body's death has been set in advance, and that no amount of worrying will have any effect, except on the mental health of the one who worries.

Plato: And so, although one should care for the body as long as one has it, one should not waste time obsessing about the body's survival, and in particular, one must never violate the Moral Law, even if by so doing one could prolong the life of one's body.

Neal: *(smiling)* You know, Socrates, sometimes my students would get very upset with you for *not* doing whatever you could to save your life, or I should say, to allow your embodied form to live a little longer. They say that the jury did not deserve your high-minded affinity for truth telling.

Socrates: *(laughing)* As if had I begged for mercy, or brought my small children into court, or otherwise manipulated the emotions of the jury, I would still be alive today. Yet even if my accusers and the jury did not deserve my "high-minded affinity for truth", *I* deserved it – the self that I wanted to preserve, deserved to speak only the truth. *(Smiling)* So you see, I was very much acting in my own self-interest.

Benedict: And in our New Social Order, everyone will identify her true self-interest in the same way that Socrates has. Those who have wisdom will know this directly. Those who have understanding will know it by deducing it from first principles. Everyone else, because of proper upbringing, will have true opinion. So our citizens will learn from Socrates, and not be anxious about the body's demise.

Plato: *(with humor)* I notice that you are not using your more poetic terminology.

Benedict: What do you mean?

Plato: You know: Knowledge of the first kind, knowledge of the second kind, and knowledge of the third kind.

Benedict: *(laughing)* Yes, well I thought I would defer to you regarding matters of poetic excess.

Neal: Actually, I am somewhat delighted by how well you two have gotten along.

Socrates: Actually, you should have expected them to get along.

Neal: I sort of did, but why do you say that?

Socrates: Because at some point you "saw", with your mind's eyes, what very few so-called "philosophers" are able to see: that Benedict and Plato express through their writings one and the same *philosophy*. The only differences are the words and concepts they use, and the way they use them. But words and concepts are pointers at best. Unlike your colleagues, who get hung up on words and concepts, *you* could see what they were pointing to.

Plato: But now, Neal, I would like to close our playful conversation by quoting something from myself, *(laughing)* if I can sneak it past you.

Neal: What do you have in mind?

Plato: Although written many years ago, the passage I will cite expresses my thoughts both about our writing and about you, and also segues nicely to our next possible topic of conversation. I might alter or comment on the passage as I quote from it.

Neal: OK, I'm listening.

Plato: "If someone has written a political or philosophical or theological document which he, the writer, believes embodies clear knowledge of lasting importance, then this writer deserves reproach." And this is because the writer does not know the difference between a menu and a raisin, to use William's analogy. Suppose a person seeking Divine knowledge reads a thousand-page treatise about God (the menu), and has some ideas and concepts in his mind. A second person has a Near-Death Experience (the raisin) and has the Knowledge of God engraved in his soul. As I wrote:

> … to be unaware of the difference between a dream image [menu] and the reality [raisin] of what is just and unjust, good and bad, must truly be grounds for reproach.
>
> On the other hand, consider a man who thinks that a written discourse on any subject can only be a great amusement and that no discourse worth serious attention has ever been written in verse or prose. He believes that at the very best, these writings can serve only as reminders to those who already know. And he also thinks that only what is said for the sake of understanding, what is truly written in the soul concerning what is just, noble, and good can be clear, perfect, and worth serious attention.

Socrates: "And what name would you give to such a man, who when he writes, himself makes the argument that his writing is of little worth?"

Plato: *(smiling)* Thanks for asking. "To call him wise, Socrates, seems to me too much, and proper only for a god. So instead we shall call him 'wisdom's lover and seeker' – a philosopher."

ACADEMIC AND SPECIALIST

Iff Books publishes non-fiction. It aims to work with authors and titles that augment our understanding of the human condition, society and civilisation, and the world or universe in which we live.

If you have enjoyed this book, why not tell other readers by posting a review on your preferred book site.

Recent bestsellers from Iff Books are

The Fall

Steve Taylor

The Fall discusses human achievement versus the issues of war, patriarchy and social inequality.

Paperback: 978-1-90504-720-8 ebook: 978-184694-633-2

Brief Peeks Beyond

Critical Essays on Metaphysics, Neuroscience, Free Will, Skepticism and Culture

Bernardo Kastrup

An incisive, original, compelling alternative to current mainstream cultural views and assumptions.

Paperback: 978-1-78535-018-4 ebook: 978-1-78535-019-1

Framespotting

Changing How You Look at Things Changes How You See Them

Laurence & Alison Matthews

A punchy, upbeat guide to framespotting. Spot deceptions and hidden assumptions; swap growth for growing up. See and be free.

Paperback: 978-1-78279-689-3 ebook: 978-1-78279-822-4

Is There an Afterlife?

David Fontana

Is there an Afterlife? If so what is it like? How do Western ideas of the afterlife compare with Eastern? David Fontana presents the historical and contemporary evidence for survival of physical death.

Paperback: 978-1-90381-690-5

Nothing Matters

A Book About Nothing

Ronald Green

Thinking about Nothing opens the world to everything by illuminating new angles to old problems and stimulating new ways of thinking.

Paperback: 978-1-84694-707-0 ebook: 978-1-78099-016-3

Panpsychism

The Philosophy of the Sensuous Cosmos

Peter Ells

Are free will and mind chimeras? This book, anti-materialistic but respecting science, answers: No! Mind is foundational to all existence.

Paperback: 978-1-84694-505-2 ebook: 978-1-78099-018-7

Punk Science

Inside the Mind of God

Manjir Samanta-Laughton

Many have experienced unexplainable phenomena; God, psychic abilities, extraordinary healing and angelic encounters. Can cutting-edge science actually explain phenomena previously thought of as 'paranormal'?

Paperback: 978-1-90504-793-2

Vagabond Spirit of Poetry

Edward Clarke

Spend time with the wisest poets of the modern age and of the past, and let Edward Clarke remind you of the importance of poetry in our industrialized world.

Paperback: 978-1-78279-370-0 ebook: 978-1-78279-369-4

Readers of ebooks can buy or view any of these bestsellers by clicking on the live link in the title. Most titles are published in paperback and as an ebook. Paperbacks are available in traditional bookshops. Both print and ebook formats are available online.

Find more titles and sign up to our readers' newsletter at http://www.johnhuntpublishing.com/non-fiction

Follow us on Facebook at https://www.facebook.com/JHPNonFiction and Twitter at https://twitter.com/JHPNonFiction